D0238704

An Introduction to Law

THE L'?

Since the publication of its first edition, this textbook has become the definitive student introduction to the subject. As with earlier editions, the seventh edition gives a clear understanding of fundamental legal concepts and their importance within society. In addition, this book addresses the ways in which rules and the structures of law respond to and impact upon changes in economic and political life. The title has been extensively updated and explores recent high profile developments such as the Civil Partnership Act 2005 and the Racial and Religious Hatred Bill. This introductory text covers a wide range of topics in a clear, sensible fashion giving full context to each. For this reason, *An Introduction to Law* is ideal for all students of law, be they undergraduate law students, those studying law as part of a mixed degree, or students on social sciences courses which offer law options.

PHIL HARRIS is Professor of Legal Education at Sheffield Hallam University.

WITHDRAWN FROM THE LIBRARY OF UNIVERSITY OF ULSTER

100509209

The Law in Context Series

Editors: William Twining (University College London) and
Christopher McCrudden (Lincoln College, Oxford)

Since 1970 the Law in Context series has been in the forefront of the movement to broaden
the study of law. It has been a vehicle for the publication of innovative scholarly books that
treat law and legal phenomena critically in their social, political and economic contexts
from a variety of perspectives. The series particularly aims to publish scholarly legal
writing that brings fresh perspectives to bear on new and existing areas of law taught in
universities. A contextual approach involves treating legal subjects broadly, using materials from other social sciences, and from any other discipline that helps to explain the operation in practice of the subject under discussion. It is hoped that this orientation is at once
more stimulating and more realistic than the bare exposition of legal rules. The series
includes original books that have a different emphasis from traditional legal textbooks,
while maintaining the same high standards of scholarship. They are written primarily for
undergraduate and graduate students of law and of other disciplines, but most also appeal
to a wider readership. In the past, most books in the series have focused on English law,
but recent publications include books on European law, globalisation, transnational legal
processes, and comparative law.

Books in the Series

Likosky: *Law, Infrastructure and Human Rights*
Likosky: *Transnational Legal Processes*
Maughan & Webb: *Lawyering Skills and the Legal Process*
McGlynn: *Families and the European Union: Law, Politics and Pluralism*
Moffat: *Trusts Law: Text and Materials*
Norrie: *Crime, Reason and History*
O'Dair: *Legal Ethics*
Oliver: *Common Values and the Public-Private Divide*
Oliver & Drewry: *The Law and Parliament*
Picciotto: *International Business Taxation*
Reed: *Internet Law: Text and Materials*
Richardson: *Law, Process and Custody*
Roberts & Palmer: *Dispute Processes: ADR and the Primary Forms of Decision-Making*
Scott & Black: *Cranston's Consumers and the Law*
Seneviratne: *Ombudsmen: Public Services and Administrative Justice*
Stapleton: *Product Liability*
Tamanaha: *The Struggle for Law as a Means to an End*
Turpin: *British Government and the Constitution: Text, Cases and Materials*
Twining: *Globalisation and Legal Theory*
Twining: *Rethinking Evidence*
Twining & Miers: *How to Do Things with Rules*
Ward: *A Critical Introduction to European Law*
Ward: *Shakespeare and Legal Imagination*
Zander: *Cases and Materials on the English Legal System*
Zander: *The Law-Making Process*

An Introduction to Law

Seventh Edition

Phil Harris

Professor of Legal Education at Sheffield Hallam University

CAMBRIDGE
UNIVERSITY PRESS

100509 209

349.42
HAR

CAMBRIDGE UNIVERSITY PRESS
Cambridge, New York, Melbourne, Madrid, Cape Town, Singapore, São Paulo

Cambridge University Press
The Edinburgh Building, Cambridge CB2 2RU, UK

Published in the United States of America by Cambridge University Press, New York

www.cambridge.org
Information on this title: www.cambridge.org/9780521697965

© Phil Harris 2007

This publication is in copyright. Subject to statutory exception
and to the provisions of relevant collective licensing agreements,
no reproduction of any part may take place without
the written permission of Cambridge University Press.

First published by Weidenfeld and Nicholson, 1980
Sixth edition published by Butterworths, a division of Reed Elsevier Group plc, 2002
Reprinted by Cambridge University Press, 2005

Printed in the United Kingdom at the University Press, Cambridge

A catalogue record for this publication is available from the British Library

ISBN -13 978-0-521-69796-5 (paperback)
ISBN -10 0-521-69796-4 (paperback)

Cambridge University Press has no responsibility for
the persistence or accuracy of URLs for external or
third-party internet websites referred to in this publication,
and does not guarantee that any content on such
websites is, or will remain, accurate or appropriate.

Contents

Preface

This book is written for students who are studying law on courses ranging from 'A' and 'AS' level and BTEC through to a wide range of undergraduate degree courses. Students studying for law degrees will find much material which introduces them to most of the foundation subjects, as well as familiarising them with legal concepts, legal method, and many aspects of the English legal system.

Apart from students enrolled on academic courses, it is hoped that this book will also be of interest to others who are fascinated by English law and the legal system. We live in a society in which everyday life is touched by legal regulation more than at any other period in history. Laws themselves are the result of intricate historical processes and of contemporary policies; those processes and policies are often controversial, and are themselves interesting and rewarding areas of study, helping us understand why our law takes the form that it does.

For if we are to have law at all (and every known social group has had codes approximating to what we would recognise as law) then it must be responsive to the needs of society. If the law, or any part of the legal system, fails to respond to those needs, then it clearly becomes open to criticism. I see neither use nor virtue in presenting or studying law as if it were merely a package of rules; or in a way which suggests that there is nothing wrong with it. And if criticisms of the law lead to criticisms of the society whose law it is, then so be it. If the critical comments in this book have the effect of stimulating further thought and discussion on the part of the reader, then one objective, at least, will have been achieved. This, indeed, is one of the approaches taken in this book, the other being that law cannot properly be understood, and certainly ought not to be studied, in a way which fails to take account of the social, economic and political contexts out of which the law arises and in which it operates.

Consequently, the reader will find that this book differs from most other law texts. I have tried to locate legal rules and institutions within the context of their historical background, taking into account the economic and political forces which have shaped – some might even say distorted – English law. To do this, I have incorporated, where appropriate, materials from disciplines other than that which is conventionally regarded as law. This approach, together with the inevitable constraints of space and time, has necessitated a considerable degree of selection as to the topics covered. Within these constraints, I have concentrated on those areas of law – contract, tort, property, crime, the European Community, administration and aspects of the legal system – which are the main concerns of students taking the kind of courses indicated above.

It is worth repeating that this is an introductory text. The reader is warned that he or she will search in vain for the outcome of painstaking research, new theoretical formulations or even original insight. Rather, I have tried to draw together various strands of development, debate and controversy, and to present them within a framework of 'law in context'. Naturally, the contents have been updated throughout.

Once again, thanks are due to a large number of colleagues and friends who have helped in various ways in the preparation of this book. Among the contributors to this edition are Jim Hanlon, Nigel Johnson, Lesley Lomax, Cathy Morse, Andrea Nollent, Peter McGregor, Mark O'Brien, Andy Selman, Colleen Smith, Doug Smith, Rob Sykes and Adam Wilson. As always, special thanks go to Sue and Dominic, without whom this book would probably have been written, but it wouldn't have been half as much fun.

Although, like all authors, I wish I could blame someone else, errors which remain are of course my own responsibility.

Phil Harris
August 2006

Table of statutes

Table of cases

1

Law and society

One of the many ways in which human societies can be distinguished from animal groups is by reference to social *rules*. We eat and sleep at certain intervals; we work on certain days for certain periods; our behaviour towards others is controlled, directly and indirectly, through moral standards, religious doctrines, social traditions and legal rules. To take one specific example: we may be born with a 'mating instinct', but it is through social rules that the attempt is made to channel this 'instinct' into the most common socially-sanctioned form of relationship – heterosexual marriage.

Marriage is a good example of the way in which social rules govern our lives. Not only is the monogamous (one man/one woman) marriage supported by the predominant religion in British history – Christianity; it is also maintained through *moral* rules (hence the traditional idea of unmarried couples living together being 'wrong') and by the operation of rules of *law* which define and control the formalities of the marriage ceremony, lay down who can and who cannot legally marry, specify the circumstances whereby divorce may be obtained, define the rights to matrimonial property upon marital breakdown, and so on.

Marriage is only one example of social behaviour being governed through rules. Legal rules are especially significant in the world of business, with matters such as banking, money, credit and employment all regulated to some extent through law. Indeed, in a complex society like our own, it is hard to find any area of activity which is completely free from legal control. Driving, working, being a parent, handling property – all these are touched in some way by law. Even a basic activity like eating is indirectly affected by law, in that the food we eat is required by legal rules to meet rigorous standards of purity, hygiene and even description.

In this introductory chapter, attempts by various writers to analyse and explain law will be examined. We shall also consider some important social, economic and political developments over the past century or so which have profoundly affected the nature and extent of the regulation of social life by means of legal rules and procedures. In addition, some of the important themes running through this book will be introduced, such as the proposition that the law is never static; it is always changing, being reinterpreted or redefined, as legislators and judges strive, with varying degrees of success, to ensure that the law constantly reflects changes in society itself.

This, in turn, leads to a second important theme: that law can be properly understood only by examining the ways in which it actually operates in society, and by studying the often extremely complex relationship between a social group and its legal code.

Analysing law

Most of us, if asked to define law, would probably do so in terms of rules: for instance, we understand criminal law, forbidding certain activities, as a set of rules defining the types of behaviour which, if indulged in, result in some form of official 'retaliation' through police intervention, the courts, and some form of criminal *sanction* such as imprisonment, or a fine. Criminal law and the notion of legal sanctions will be examined in a later chapter. For the moment, the fundamental notion for us is that of a 'rule'.

In their work on the subject, Twining and Miers offer a wide definition of a rule as 'a general norm mandating or guiding conduct or action in a given type of situation'.[1] A rule prescribes what activity may, should or should not be carried out, or refers to activities which should be carried out in a specified way. Rules of law may forbid certain activity – murder and theft are prohibited through rules of criminal law – or they may impose certain conditions under which activity may be carried out (car drivers and television set users must, for example, have valid licences for those items before they can legally drive or use them). Again the law contains some rules which we might call 'power-conferring' rules: rules which enable certain activities to be carried out with some form of legal backing and protection, the best example of which is perhaps the law of contract, which provides rules which, among other things, guide us in the manner in which to act if we wish to make a valid contract.[2]

Because a rule guides us in what we may, ought or ought not to do, it is said to be *normative*. We can best grasp the meaning of this term if we contrast a normative statement, telling us what *ought* to happen, with a *factual* statement, which tells us what *does* happen. For instance, the statement 'cars must not be driven except on roads' is a normative, 'ought'-type statement, whereas 'cars are driven on roads' is a factual, 'is'-type statement. All rules, whether legal, moral or just customary, are normative, laying down standards of behaviour to which we *ought* to conform if the rule affects us.

Although the notion of a 'system of rules' probably corresponds closely to most people's idea of law, we can soon see that this is not sufficient by itself to be an accurate or adequate account of law, because there are, in any social group, various 'systems of rules' apart from law. How do we distinguish, for example, between a *legal* rule and a *moral* rule? In our society, though we consider it immoral to tell lies,

1 W. Twining and D. Miers, *How to Do Things with Rules* (4th edn., 1999, Butterworths), p 123.
2 See chapter 11.

it is not generally against the law to do so.[3] Of course, some moral rules are also embodied in the law, such as the legal rule prohibiting murder. This does not mean, however, as we shall see in chapter 2, that law and morality *always* correspond. It would take a very wide definition of 'morality', for instance, for the idea to be accepted that a driver who exceeds the speed limit by only two miles per hour (a criminal offence) would thereby be acting *immorally*!

Again, how do we distinguish between a legal rule and a rule of custom or etiquette? What is the difference between a judge's ordering a convicted person to pay a fine for breaking a criminal-law rule and a father's ordering his son to forfeit his pocket-money for disobeying him? Clearly, there *are* differences between these types of rule, and perhaps the only feature which they all have in common is their normativeness. But where do these differences lie?

The analysis of law, and the specification of the distinctions between law and other rules, have proved surprisingly difficult to articulate. Writers have, over the years, adopted various perspectives on legal analysis, sometimes concentrating on law as a system of rules of an official nature (as in the work of H L A Hart), sometimes focusing upon individual legal rules, their origin and their operation as part of an overall system (as can be seen in works within the sociology of law).[4] Some writers have analysed law as if it were a 'closed' system, operating within its own logical framework, and divorced in important ways from the wider social context. John Austin, writing in the nineteenth century, is an example of such writers.[5] Others have insisted that law and the legal system can only be analysed by considering them in relation to the other processes and institutions within the society in which they operate – as stated above, such is the perspective within this book.

Still other legal writers have provided accounts of law which take as their central issue the various *functions* which law is supposed to perform in a society. Two examples of this approach are worthy of note. First, the American writer Karl Llewellyn expounded his 'Law-Jobs Theory',[6] which is a general account of the functions of legal institutions in social groups of all kinds. Llewellyn argued that every social group has certain basic needs, which are catered for by the social institution of law by helping ensure that the group survives as such, and by providing for the prevention of disruptive disputes within the group. Should any disputes

3 There are various exceptions to this general statement, of which the best known are perhaps the offence of perjury (lying in the witness box), the making of a false statement in order to induce someone to buy something, which may fall foul of the Trade Descriptions Act 1968 (creating criminal offences for false or misleading trade descriptions, discussed in chapter 11), the law relating to misrepresentation, or lying on an official document (such as an income tax return or claim for income support benefit) which may lead to prosecution.
4 For a useful discussion of some important contributions in this area, see B. Roshier and H. Teff, *Law and Society in England* (1980, Tavistock), chapter 2; R. Cotterrell, *The Sociology of Law: An Introduction* (2nd edn., 1992, Oxford University Press).
5 See the discussion of the work of John Austin in R. Cotterrell, *The Politics of Jurisprudence* (2nd edn., 2003, LexisNexis Butterworths) chapter 3.
6 K. Llewellyn, 'The Normative, the Legal, and the Law-Jobs: The Problem of Juristic Method' (1940) *Yale LJ*; and see also K. Llewellyn and E. A. Hoebel, *The Cheyenne Way* (1941, University of Oklahoma Press).

arise between members, the law must provide the means of resolving them. The law must also provide the means whereby the authority structure of the group is constituted and recognised (such as a constitution) and, finally, the law must provide for the manner and procedures in which the above 'law-jobs' are carried out.

A second example of this approach is that of Robert Summers.[7] He identified five techniques of law, which may be used to implement social policies. These are, first, the use of law to remedy grievances among members of a society; second, the use of law as a penal instrument, with which to prohibit and prosecute forbidden behaviour; third, law as an instrument with which to promote certain defined activities; fourth, the use of law for managing various governmental public benefits, such as education and welfare policies; and fifth, the use of law to give effect to certain private arrangements between members of a society, such as the provisions of the law of contract in our own legal system.

We can contrast the analyses of Llewellyn and Summers with those of writers such as Austin, in that their accounts relate the law to its social context, whereas Austin treats rules, including legal rules, as though they were amenable to analysis 'in a vacuum', so to speak, or, put another way, in a manner divorced from social contexts or settings. For Austin, the hallmark of a legal rule (which he terms 'positive', or man-made, law) lies in the manner of its creation. He defined law as the *command of the sovereign body* in a society (which may be a person, such as a king or queen, or a body of elected officials, such as our own law-making body which we refer to formally as 'the Queen in Parliament'), and these commands were backed up by threats of sanctions, to be applied in the event of disobedience.

A major problem with Austin's analysis concerns his use of the idea of the 'command'. Although the rules of criminal law, mentioned above, may perhaps approximate to the idea of our being 'commanded' by the law-makers not to engage in prohibited conduct, on pain of some criminal sanction, there are very many rules of law which do not 'command' us to do things at all. The law concerning marriage, for example, never commands us to marry, but merely sets out the conditions under which people may marry, and the procedure which they must follow if their marriage is to be valid in law. Similarly, the law does not command us to make contracts, but rather lays down the conditions under which an agreement will have the force of a legally binding contract. This type of rule may be termed a '*power-giving*' rule, and may be contrasted with the *duty-imposing* rules which characterise criminal law. As Hart, among others, has pointed out, there are many other instances in law where the legal rule in question cannot sensibly be described as a form of 'command': 'Is it not misleading so to classify laws which confer powers on private individuals to make wills, contracts, or marriages, and laws which give powers to officials, eg to a judge, to try cases, to a minister to make rules, or a county council to make by-laws?'[8] The law, then, is far too complex, and contains far too great a

---

7 R. Summers, 'The Technique Element in Law' (1971) 59 *Calif LR*.
8 H. L. A. Hart, *The Concept of Law* (2nd edn., 1994, Oxford University Press), p 26.

variety of *kinds* of legal rules, for it to be reduced to the simple proposition that 'laws are commands'.

What other formulations and classifications of law may be offered by legal writers? One significant attempt in recent years has been Hart's own theory, contained in his book *The Concept of Law*, in which he sets out, first, the basic legal requirements, as he sees them, of any social group which is to be more than a 'suicide club'. Every such social group, Hart suggests, must have certain rules which impose duties upon the members of the group concerning standards of behaviour. These 'primary' rules, which might contain rules approximating to basic criminal-law rules but which might also impose what we would call civil-law duties (akin to duties contained in the law of tort – see chapter 9), could conceivably comprise the *only* rules within a social group; but, Hart argues, in a developed and complex society, these 'primary' rules will give rise to certain problems which will have to be dealt with by means of additional, 'secondary' rules. The first problem with such a simple code is that there will be no settled procedure for resolving doubts as to the nature and authority of an apparently 'legal' rule. To remedy this, the introduction of 'rules of recognition' is needed: these rules will constitute the hallmark of what is truly a *law*, and may do so by reference to a set of other rules or institutions, such as a constitution, a monarch or a representative body, such as Parliament.

A second problem will be that the primary rules will be static: there will be no means of changing the rules in accordance with changes in the circumstances of the social group. The remedy for this defect, says Hart, is a set of 'rules of change', enabling specified bodies to introduce new rules or to alter existing ones. Third, the primary rules will be inefficiently administered, because their enforcement will be through diffuse social pressures within the group. The remedy for this, says Hart, is the introduction of 'rules of adjudication', which provide for officials (judges) to decide disputes authoritatively. It will be appreciated that these secondary rules are really 'rules about rules', and Hart argues that the characteristic feature of a modern legal system is this *union* of primary and secondary rules.

Interesting though this approach is, it has suffered at the hands of critics. To begin with, some commentators have argued that Hart's reduction of all duty-imposing rules to a category which he calls 'primary' rules is far too great a simplification. Can this category really usefully embrace areas of law, all of which impose duties of various kinds and with various consequences, as diverse in content and objectives as contract law, private property law, family law, criminal law, tort law and labour relations law? It may be argued that a much more complex classificatory scheme is required in order for such differences adequately to be analysed and understood.

Another criticism is that Hart's treatment of a legal system as a 'system of rules' fails to take into account the various other normative prescriptions contained within a legal system which affect the course, development and application of the law, but which are not 'rules'. In particular, Dworkin has argued[9] that Hart fails to take

9 R. M. Dworkin, *Taking Rights Seriously* (1977, Duckworth), chapter 2.

account of the role of *principles* in the operation of the law. Principles, he maintains, differ from rules in that whilst the latter are applicable in an all-or-nothing manner, the former are guidelines, stating 'a reason that argues in one direction, but [does] not necessitate a particular decision'.[10] Thus, suppose that a man murders his father in order to benefit from the father's will which, as he knows, provides that all the father's property will come to him upon the father's death. Irrespective of the liability of the man for murder, the question will fall to be considered whether he will ultimately acquire that property. Normally, the law attempts to give effect to the wishes of the maker of a will, but here the outcome may well be affected by the *principle* that 'no man should profit by his own wrong' and the result may well be that, through the operation of this principle, and *despite the existence of legal rules* which would otherwise have operated in the son's favour, the murderer does not receive the inheritance.[11] Whether or not this type of principle is *part* of the fabric of legal rules, as Dworkin argues, is a difficult question: all parts of the law contain principles as well as 'hard rules' – an example might be principles of public policy which affect judicial deliberations concerning the law of negligence, which we shall consider in chapter 9 – but for the moment, it can be appreciated from the above discussion that there is much more to law than merely legal rules.

A more general point which must be made here is that, although the 'law as rules' approach has, through the work of writers such as Austin and Hart, greatly influenced patterns of legal thought in this country and elsewhere, it is by no means the only approach which may be taken in legal study. Already we have mentioned the approach which looks at law in terms of its functions within society. Other writers have taken the view that law is best understood by examining the actual *operation* of the legal system in practice, and by comparing the 'letter of the law' with the way it actually operates. Such an approach is taken by those writers whose work is usually categorised as 'Legal Realism' – principally, Karl Llewellyn, Jerome Frank and Oliver Wendell Holmes. Other writers, at various times, have analysed law in terms of a society's cultural and/or historical background, whilst still others, adopting an anthropological approach, have argued that the idea of a legal system may be illuminated by considering and comparing modern legal systems with the systems of small, technologically less developed, societies.

Authority and obedience to law

Another important aspect of rules in general, and legal rules in particular, is the phenomenon of obedience to those rules, and the acceptance that those rules are both legitimate and authoritative. Again, there are many analyses of these issues, one or two of which may be briefly considered here.

10 Ibid., p 26.
11 These were the facts in the American case of *Riggs v Palmer*, 115 N.Y. 506, 22 N.E. 188 (1889), discussed by Dworkin, ibid., at pp 23–24. For Hart's response to Dworkin's criticisms, see *The Concept of Law* (op. cit.), esp. pp 259–268.

For example, Austin's idea of why we obey law is found in his notion of the 'habit of obedience' to the sovereign body in a society, which, together with the ever-present threat of sanctions, explains obedience to law. Few, however, would accept this idea as an adequate explanation. It is a questionable assumption that we obey law out of habit or for fear of official reprisals. Do we really go through our daily law-abiding lives with such things kept in mind? Surely not. Rather, as Hart[12] argues, most of us conform to law because of more complex social and psychological processes. Hart's own explanation of obedience to law lies in the idea of some inner psychological inclination whereby we accept the *legitimacy* or *authority* of the source of the law; we obey because we consider it 'right and proper' to do so. Hart calls this acceptance the 'internal' aspect of obedience to law, and argues that people usually obey because of such acceptance.

Of course, as Hart acknowledges, there are exceptions. Some might obey out of a genuine worry about the consequences of disobedience; others might disagree with the entirety of the legal and social arrangements in our society, but obey the law out of sheer convenience. Everything depends, of course, upon the kind of society and legal system in question, for an extreme and oppressive regime might deliberately obtain obedience to its dictates by instilling terror into the population. In our own society, however, few of us would seriously dispute the idea that most people accept the legitimacy of existing legal, social and political authority, as defined through constitutional doctrines and principles, and our everyday 'common-sense' notions of legal authority.

This question of the idea of authority in society is worthy of closer attention, however. One sociologist who wrote extensively about law, Max Weber, identified three *types of authority* in social groups.[13] First, he argued, the authority of a leader or ruler may be the result of the personal, individual characteristics of that leader – his or her *charisma* – which sets that person apart from the rest. Examples might be Jesus, Napoleon, or Hitler in Nazi Germany, Eva Peron in Argentina, or Winston Churchill in Britain, all of whom, it might be said, to some extent and to varying degrees, rose to their exalted positions and maintained those positions as leaders through their extraordinarily strong personalities.

A second type of authority, according to Weber, is *traditional* authority, where obedience to the leader or regime is sustained because it is traditional: 'it has always been so.' Third, Weber identifies in modern Western societies a form of authority which he calls *rational-legal* or *bureaucratic*, where the authority of the regime is legitimised not through personal charismatic leadership, nor through pure tradition, but through rules and procedures. Although such a type may correspond roughly to authority in our own society, where the system of government and law-making depends upon a constitution providing formal procedures for law-creation and the business of government by Parliament, Weber's three types of authority

12 H. L. A. Hart, *The Concept of Law*, op. cit.
13 M. Weber, *Law in Economy and Society*, ed. M. Rheinstein (1969, Harvard University Press), esp. chapter 12.

have rarely, if ever, existed in reality in their *pure* form. Most societies have elements of more than one type. Our own society has elements of all three – the traditional (as seen in the ceremonies surrounding, say, the formal opening of Parliament), the charismatic (such as the leadership of Churchill during the Second World War) and the rational-legal (as in bureaucratic political and legal institutions such as the civil service). The issues raised by notions such as 'obedience to law' and 'sources of authority', then, are clearly much more complex than Austin's simple idea of a 'sovereign' might suggest.

Law and society

We have seen that there is no one way of undertaking legal study: whilst all the various approaches may well have something useful to offer, none has yet managed to produce an analysis of law and legal systems which answers all the many and varied questions which students and researchers might want to ask about this complicated and fascinating subject. The perspective taken in this present book is that an understanding of law cannot be acquired unless the subject matter is examined in close relationship to the social, economic and political contexts in which it is created, maintained and implemented. To equip us for the task of understanding something of the *society* in which the law operates, as well the law itself, we must turn our attention to some analyses which take law as but a part (albeit an important part) of the wider social arrangements.

When a lawyer uses terms such as 'society', the picture often conjured up is of a rather loose collection of people, institutions and other social phenomena in the midst of which law occupies a central place, holding these social arrangements together in an orderly fashion. But if law were suddenly relaxed, would society immediately plunge into chaos and disorder? Most of us doubt that this would happen. One reason why it would not happen is that society is not just a loose group of independent units, but rather exhibits certain regular patterns of behaviour, relationships and beliefs. What gives a particular society its uniqueness is the way in which these patterns interrelate at any given time in history. Law, far from being a kind of social glue holding us all inside a boundary of legality and punishing those who try to extricate themselves, is but one component of the overall *social structure*, having links and dependencies with other social elements and forces. We can identify various social phenomena which constitute parts of the overall structure of a society, including, in addition to law, political institutions (Parliament, political parties), economic and commercial institutions (trade unions, manufacturers' associations, patterns of production and trade, and so on), religious institutions, institutions concerned with the teaching of social rules and standards (such as schools and the family) and cultural institutions (such as literature and the arts, the press, television and radio). We shall, at various points in our examination of the place of law in society, refer to these other facets of the social structure.

If we imagine a society as a complex network of the kinds of institutions and social forces mentioned above, we could map out the ways in which they relate to each other without too much difficulty. But some institutions and social groups are more important than others; some groups have more political power, or more economic influence, than others. Some groups may enjoy considerable prestige, whereas others may be thought of as less worthy. Within a society, therefore, groups and individuals may be differentiated, or *ranked*, by their place on a 'ladder of influence', with some ranking higher in terms of power, prestige, wealth, or some other criterion, than others. Sociologists use the term *social stratification* to express this idea, and there are many ways in which social stratification may be analysed. If we are interested in prestige groups in India, for instance, we may look at the stratification of groups in terms of the caste system, in which some groups, or 'castes', are regarded as higher in status than others. In a simple tribal society, stratification may occur through a ranking system descending from king, or chief, at the top, through, perhaps, village elders and religious officials, down to the ordinary family unit, which may itself be stratified in terms of power (male elders frequently being the heads of households). Or, taking our own society, we may classify people in terms of social class – a very important aspect of our society, particularly when we come to consider political and economic power and position.[14]

Some sociologists would go on to analyse social institutions and processes in terms of their *function* in society; we noted above how such an approach might be applied to an analysis of law. Put simply, the 'function' of a social institution or process is the contribution it makes to the overall social structure and its maintenance. We may say, for example, that the function of the family unit in our society is to ensure continued procreation, to ensure socialisation, and to bolster the economic base of the society through its activities as a consumer unit.

Armed with these concepts of social structure, social stratification and social function (none of which, for reasons of space, we are able to explore further here), we can begin to examine some approaches to law in society taken by sociologists. One of the most influential writers in this field was the French sociologist Emile Durkheim, whose major works appeared at the end of the nineteenth century. One of Durkheim's main concerns was the problem of social cohesion: what is it that keeps a society together? We noted above the fact that societies exhibit regularities, and patterns of behaviour and attitudes. What provides this cohesion?

Durkheim, in trying to resolve this problem, presented two contrasting 'types' of society[15] – an analytical device frequently used by social scientists to enable us to draw contrasts. The first type discussed by Durkheim is a relatively simple, technologically undeveloped, society; the other type being 'advanced' in terms of

---

14 Students might follow up discussion of these concepts in any textbook on sociology: for example A. Giddens, *Sociology* (4th edn., 2001, Polity Press); T. Bilton et al, *Introductory Sociology* (4th edn., 2002, Palgrave); M. Haralambos and M. Holborn, *Sociology: Themes and Perspectives* (6th edn., 2004, Collins).

15 E. Durkheim, *The Division of Labour in Society* (1964, Free Press, New York; Macmillan, London).

technology and social structure. He argued that the primary characteristic of the first type will be that the whole group exists and acts collectively towards common aims, the moral and legal code (the 'collective conscience') being acknowledged and accepted by the whole group and keeping the group together. This is called 'mechanical solidarity'. In the event of any deviance from these collectively held norms of the group, sanctions are brought to bear on the offender through *repressive* (criminal, or penal) law, which expresses the community's anger and avenges the offence against the collective moral sentiments of the group. Not only does this repressive law serve to identify and punish the deviant, however; it also fulfils the function of maintaining the boundaries between acceptable and unacceptable behaviour, thus helping maintain the collective conscience, and hence the cohesion of the group. Central to Durkheim's thesis is the proposition that the interests of any one individual in such a group are identical to those of the group as a whole; there is no room for the expression of individual creativity or dissent from group norms.

As the social group becomes more complex (larger, with increasing economic and other ties between social units and with other social groups) there occurs, argues Durkheim, increasing *occupational specialisation*, or *division of labour*, where no single individual occupies a self-sufficient position as both producer and consumer of his or her everyday needs. Instead, tasks become divided among members of the society. The making of bread, for example, becomes no longer a task undertaken by each family for its own needs, but is rather a series of tasks, divided between farmer, flour mills and bakeries. Each, therefore, is occupationally specialised. But more than this: in the complete bread-production process, the bakery is dependent on obtaining supplies of flour from the mill, and the mill is in turn dependent upon the farmer for the supply of corn. The farmer is dependent on the flour mill for payment for the corn; and the flour mill is similarly dependent upon income from sales of flour. Each of these units, then, is not only occupationally specialised, but *economically dependent* upon the others involved in the process.

It is precisely this interdependence, argues Durkheim, that is the keynote of social solidarity in advanced industrial society. There is a radical change in the nature and range of the collective conscience, in that the individual takes on a new social importance in his or her own right, rather than occupying a social position simply as one member of a collective. The individual, encouraged socially to develop and realise talents, skills and potentialities, is elevated to quite a different status.

These changes are accompanied by a corresponding change in the type of law present in the society. Whereas law in the 'simple' type of society is, according to Durkheim, repressive, or penal, law in the 'advanced' type of society takes on the form of *compensatory* rules, where the object is not to punish, but to solve grievances by trying to restore the aggrieved person to the position he or she was in prior to the dispute. The disputes dealt with through the law in such a situation are not those between, so to speak, the group and the individual deviant, but rather those which occur between individuals or between groups, within the society.

Durkheim's analysis has been very influential; nevertheless many have found problems with his work. He greatly overestimated the extent to which repressive law would decline and give way to compensatory law in an industrialised society. He himself explained the continued existence of repressive, criminal-type rules in modern society as being due to the incomplete, defective or 'pathological' forms of the division of labour to be found in existing industrial societies, and put forward suggestions as to how these 'pathological' forms of the division of labour might be remedied to facilitate the development of a pure or 'spontaneous' form of division of labour where repressive law would decline much further. Yet today we have as many criminal-law rules as ever.

Also, it is clear from later research that Durkheim underestimated the degree to which compensatory, or *civil*, law already exists in 'simple' societies. Many tribal groups, for instance, have firm relationships within and between families and other groups, giving rise to patterns of mutual dependency ties having the force of legal obligation; many have clearly discernible political and legal structures, and property relationships involving obligations and rights similar to those existing in our own law. Whilst there may well be certain differences in the manner in which disputes are solved (we shall come to this issue later), it is clear that Durkheim's twofold classification of types of society, though containing useful insights, will not do the analytical job for which he fashioned it.

The researches of social anthropologists, studying simple societies, have also provided us with useful information concerning law in society, although we must always be careful not to assume that what may hold for a technologically undeveloped group will necessarily be applicable to a complex and advanced society. We referred above to the American writer Llewellyn: with an anthropologist, Hoebel, Llewellyn studied American Indian groups and based his ideas as to the social functions of law on their researches. It is interesting that similar conclusions as to the functions of law have been reached by Hart (a lawyer and philosopher), by Talcott Parsons (a sociologist)[16] and by Hoebel in his own work *The Law of Primitive Man*.[17] As Schur points out:

> However their terminology may differ, anthropologists, legal philosophers, and sociologists are in general agreement that a legal order must, at the very least, provide for the authorisation and recognition of legitimate authority, provide means of resolving disputes, and provide mechanisms for facilitating interpersonal relationships, including adaptation to change.[18]

To what extent, then, can such functions be identified in our own society?

Law plays an important part in the definition and regulation of all kinds of social relationships, between individuals and between groups. Thus, for example, the basic social unit in our society, the family, is defined and protected through legal rules and institutions. The marriage bond is created partly through deference to

16 See in particular T. Parsons, 'Law and Social Control' in W. M. Evan (ed.), *Law and Sociology* (1962, Free Press).
17 E. A. Hoebel, *The Law of Primitive Man* (1954, Harvard University Press).
18 E. Schur, *Law and Society* (1968, Random House), pp 79–80.

religion, partly through the necessity for legal formalities. Divorce, too, can only be obtained through legal channels, and of course the law prohibits multiple (polygamous) marital relationships through the law on bigamy. The rights and obligations of members of the family, as spouses and parents, are defined through law, and there is provision, through the Children Act 1989, for removing children from unsuitable homes with their natural parents and placing them in the care of local authorities or with foster parents. In the business world, too, the law regulates the activities of the limited company, the partnership and the trade union. Financial deals between people in business are subject, normally, to the law of contract, at least in theory,[19] and there are many obligations contained in Acts of Parliament such as the Companies Acts, with whose regulations all companies must comply.

Regarding the identification and allocation of official authority, it is through legal rules that specific powers are vested in Parliament to enact new laws, and in the courts to administer the law and to mete out sanctions and remedies in criminal and civil cases. This body of law, known as *public law*, deals with constitutional rules, the authority of elected representatives such as councillors, or members of Parliament, and the powers of bodies such as the civil service, the courts, tribunals, the police, local authorities and bodies such as the Post Office and the National Health Service. We shall examine various aspects of all these matters later, and we shall look in particular at the relationship between law and public administration in chapter 12.

It is by means of such constitutional rules that social changes may become reflected in, or in some cases encouraged by, changes in the law. One of the most important facets of law, as we noted earlier, is its *dynamic* character; social conditions, and hence law, change all the time. Some changes are little more than passing fads, and make little impact upon the legal structure. But others bring with them permanent and far-reaching effects, and such developments usually result, sooner or later, in changes in the fabric of legal rules. The development and increased use of the motor car in the twentieth century is a good example. Given the proliferation of cheaper, faster and more reliable cars, it is not altogether surprising that the legal code responded by the enactment of numerous rules designed to protect both car-drivers and others, through the regulation of car safety, speed and driving skills – a far cry from the somewhat crude device of having someone carrying a red flag walk in front of the slow-moving early mechanical vehicles! This example illustrates not only the reflection in the law of these developments, but also the way law may be, at least partially, used as an *educative* instrument. Road safety and motor-vehicle law may be viewed as a means of inculcating public awareness of the dangers of modern road conditions, thus encouraging the development of attitudes of safety-consciousness. Other similar instances are the use of law in race relations and equal opportunities (currently through the Race Relations Act 1976, as amended by the Race Relations (Amendment) Act 2000, the Sex Discrimination Act 1975 and the Disability Discrimination Act 1995) not only to

---

19 See chapter 11.

outlaw discrimination on the grounds of race, sex or disability in the workplace, in the provision of goods and services, and elsewhere, but also to play a part in changing people's attitudes and, arguably, to help to create a social environment in which prejudice diminishes and, hopefully, disappears.

The changing nature of law is seen in all aspects of the legal system, not least in those areas concerned with one more 'function' of law: dispute-settlement. Now, whilst most studies of law in various types of society have revealed the existence of more or less formal mechanisms of dispute-settlement, it is possible to see, as Chambliss and Seidman argue, certain differences between advanced and undeveloped societies in the way that the legal system goes about this task: 'The dispute-settlement systems of simple societies tend toward compromise, or "give-a-little, get-a-little"; the official dispute-settlement systems of most complex societies tend toward "winner-takes-all".'[20] This distinction, say Chambliss and Seidman, is connected with certain factors about the types of society in question. Simple societies, as we noted above when discussing Durkheim's work, tend to be community-based, relatively self-sufficient, and with low degrees of technology and division of labour. It is this type of society which some writers have called *Gemeinschaft*, or 'community', as distinct from *Gesellschaft*, referring to a more complex, differentiated society.[21] In societies approximating to the community-type (these terms referring, like Durkheim's types, to hypothetical models, or 'ideal types' which never actually occur in reality in their 'pure' form), social relations tend to be fairly permanent; indeed the continued existence of the community group depends upon the continued existence of social ties, and consequently in such groups the type of dispute-settlement is often *compromise*.

In a modern, differentiated society, on the other hand, there are many disputes involving no desire or need by the parties to continue their relationship; the example given by Chambliss and Seidman is a typical personal injury claim: 'When a person gets injured in an automobile accident, usually he had no prior relationship with the other party and anticipates no future relationship. In such cases, the parties typically expect in the end that if necessary they will settle their dispute in court on a "winner-takes-all" basis.'[22] Nevertheless, in such situations negotiations and compromise may well take place. As we shall see in a later chapter, bargaining and negotiations through insurance companies, and between the parties' lawyers, will more often than not result in the settlement of disputes outside courts of law. But, as Chambliss and Seidman point out, such negotiation is mainly to save time, trouble and, in particular, expense: 'They bargain, not in an effort to make possible a future relationship, but in light of their estimates of the probabilities of a favourable outcome of the potential "winner-takes-all" litigation.'[23] Only in cases where the parties *do* anticipate future relations is there any genuine attempt to 'give a little, take a little'. Such cases would include those discussed by

---

20 W. Chambliss and R. Seidman, *Law, Order and Power* (2nd edn., 1982, Addison-Wesley), p 38.
21 See, esp., F. Tönnies, *Community and Association* (1887).
22 Chambliss and Seidman, op. cit., p 40.   23 Ibid.

Macaulay,[24] where business firms negotiate with a view to *avoiding* disputes, or, where disputes arise, to *compromise* rather than take the dispute to court, because good business relations are essential if a business is to continue to flourish.

From the foregoing discussion, certain additional features of law, particularly that of modern Western societies, may be identified. Whereas, for instance, law may be used to provide an institutional setting for the resolution of disputes between private individuals, as discussed in the last paragraph, the use of law to achieve certain *positive objectives of social or economic policy* may be, by contrast, a somewhat different function for the law to perform. State intervention in the sphere of motor-vehicle use, or in the field of race relations, expresses such general policies, which are of clear benefit to the community. Other examples of state intervention brought about through the use of law would include the development of the welfare state, the post-Second World War nationalisation of various industries, such as the railways and coal-mining; the health service, and the provisions and regulations constituting town and country planning.

Such intervention by the state, usually presented by governments and by politicians as being 'in the interests of the community as a whole', is often the expression and attempted realisation of the political convictions of those governments and politicians. In Britain in the years following the Second World War, a number of industries and activities (such as coal-mining and the provision of health care services) were nationalised (that is, owned and run by the state) and were for many years part of a range of nationalised industries that included most energy and public utility organisations. In the 1980s and early 1990s, however, the Conservative government pursued policies of placing many nationalised industries into the hands of private organisations. Thus we saw the privatisation of the telecommunications, water, rail transport, electricity and gas industries in line with the government's commitment to a return to a national economy based substantially upon free private enterprise. Since the election of the first New Labour government in 1997, there has been a continuation of such policies, such as a proposal to extend privatisation to the air traffic control service. It is not altogether surprising that state intervention along these lines is often highly controversial. Since the twentieth century there has, none the less, been continuing interventionist regulation, often expressed through legal rules and procedures. Such regulation, affecting many of the areas discussed in this book, raises important questions about the relationship between the state and private individuals and groups, and about the appropriateness or otherwise of using *legal* mechanisms for the realisation of political policies and objectives. It is vital, therefore, to appreciate the historical,

---

24 S. Macaulay, 'Non-Contractual Relations in Business' in V. Aubert (ed.), *Sociology of Law* (1972, Penguin). See also H. Genn, *Hard Bargaining: Out of Court Settlement in Personal Injury Actions* (1987, Clarendon); M. Palmer and S. Roberts, *Dispute Processes: ADR and the Primary Forms of Decision-making,* (1998, *Law in Context* series, Butterworths); C. Menkel-Meadow, 'Lawyer Negotiations: Theories and Realities – What we Learn from Mediation' (1993) 56 *MLR* 361. And see below, chapters 6 and 11.

social and political context of these developments – a context which requires exam-ination of the far-reaching changes which were subsequent upon rapid industrial advances taking place within an economy based upon capitalism. Some aspects of these developments – affecting, for instance, the world of commerce – are discussed in later chapters. For the moment, it is useful to examine briefly the ways in which developing industrialisation brought changes in employment relationships, and in more general *social* relationships within the developing economy.

Industrialisation and the role of law

Although the eighteenth and nineteenth centuries are usually regarded as the most important period for the growth of industry and commerce, the period does not mark the *origin* of industrial or commercial development: Britain's economy had long been tied to trading at home and abroad. What the period does signify is a change in the *scale* and *nature* of industry and trade – the emergence and consoli-dation of *capitalism* as the basis for the economic system. By 'capitalism' we refer to the mode of production which is geared to the making of private profit, and it is no accident that this mode of production flourished in Britain during the period of the eighteenth and nineteenth centuries.

Many factors contributed to the expansion of manufacturing industries, among them the availability of natural resources (notably coal) and the suitability of certain areas for the use of water- and steam-powered machines. More important, the acquisition by Britain of overseas colonies not only yielded an abundance of raw materials but also provided a market for goods manufactured in Britain.[25]

Another supremely important factor was the existence of a *free market in labour*. This refers to a situation in which workers 'sell' their labour in exchange for wages, as opposed to being 'tied' to farms, estates and small, family-run manufacturing concerns. Prior to the industrial revolution, when the economy was primarily, though not exclusively, dependent upon agriculture, the dominant mode of pro-duction was feudalism. This gave rise to social relations in which agricultural labourers or peasants were tied to, and economically dependent on, the land-owning gentry and nobility (their lords and masters); for upon the feudal relation-ship between lord and servants depended the latter's livelihoods and homes. From the mid-1700s, however, the enclosure movement, whereby land – including land previously regarded as 'common' land – was parcelled up and acquired by landlords, had the effect of forcing many farm labourers, many of whom had depended for their survival upon the old traditional rights to the common land, out of their agri-cultural settings and, for many, into the expanding new towns to become workers in the developing factory industries.

These factories were owned and run by those 'captains of industry' who had invested their capital in the new machines, many powered by the recently invented

---

25 For an excellent discussion on this, see E. J. Hobsbawm, *Industry and Empire* (1969, Penguin).

steam-engine (another factor contributing to the rapid industrial development of the period), which required industrial workers to operate them. The factory system thus helped crystallise the new formations of social class. No longer could the population be divided only into agricultural peasants and powerful landowners, with a sprinkling of tradesmen and artisans, for now the industrial revolution had brought two new classes: the industrial working class and the industrialists who employed them, paid their wages and frequently provided them with housing. Together with the commercial entrepreneurs who traded in the manufactured goods and brought raw materials to be worked in the factories, these constituted the rising new 'middle classes', the 'bourgeoisie', a social class distinct from the landowners who had traditionally possessed the wealth and political power and who had until then been the sole 'ruling class' in England.

Such class formations brought tensions. Not only did the middle classes make demands for a greater political voice in Parliament (something they felt was their due, given their developing key role in the country's economic affairs),[26] bringing them at times into conflict with the established landowning class, but also many of the working classes, conscious of the iniquities of the factory system (low wages, appalling working conditions, long hours, bad housing and the systematic exploitation of women and children), were beginning to make demands for improvements in their working conditions, and for a political voice. Hence, we see many cases of attempts by workers to form themselves into associations – what we would now recognise as trade unions – in order to press collectively for better pay and conditions. And there were movements, such as Chartism in the 1840s (a working-class campaign for more political involvement), which involved demands for universal male suffrage, removal of the property qualification for members of Parliament and the holding of annual general elections.

It is easy to see in these latter developments the basis of what we would today call industrial relations problems, but the period was not, in fact, the beginning of such potential or actual conflicts. Legal controls of employment relations date back to periods long before the industrial revolution, and one or two brief instances reveal the repressive attitude of law-makers and judges to any attempt by working people to improve their lot by collective action. In 1563, the Statute of Artificers gave power to justices of the peace to fix wages; in 1698 a body of journeymen were successfully prosecuted for having 'combined' to negotiate with their employers over wages; the Master and Servant laws of 1823 provided for the imprisonment of any workers who 'broke their contracts of employment' by going on strike; and various statutes outlawed 'combinations of workers' – the forerunners of trade unions – throughout the eighteenth century.[27]

---

26 See chapter 5.
27 K. W. Wedderburn, *The Worker and the Law* (3rd edn., 1986, Penguin), p 76; and see generally S. Deakin and G. S. Morris, *Labour Law* (4th edn., 2005, Hart Publishing); H. Pelling, *A History of British Trade Unionism* (1973, Penguin); A. Harding, *A Social History of English Law* (1966, Penguin); E. P. Thompson, *The Making of the English Working Class* (1975, Penguin).

These early laws regulating wages and prohibiting 'combinations' are, of course, examples of direct state intervention which, though no doubt legitimated as being in the interests of the national economy, nevertheless clearly operated to the advantage of employers and to the detriment of employees. The effect of these restrictions was, moreover, to enhance the conflicts inherent in the employment relationship – conflicts which become clearer when we examine the relative positions of *power* between them.

Then, as now, recurrent unemployment was a problem for many, and if people wished to work for an employer, they had little choice but to accept employment on the terms dictated by that employer. Workers were in no position to argue or negotiate, for they had little or no bargaining power. The strike (that is, *collective withdrawal of labour*) was one of the few means of bringing any kind of pressure to bear on employers for improvements in pay and conditions, and it is not altogether surprising that the law was one of the principal weapons used to try to prevent any such disruptions which might damage employers' business, and perhaps ultimately the whole fabric of trade and industry upon which the national economy had come to depend. Even when these Combination Acts were repealed, the judges were still able to interpret strikes as 'conspiracies to injure' the employers' interests. The turbulent events of the French Revolution at the end of the eighteenth century caused many members of the English ruling classes to fear lest similar troubles should occur on this side of the Channel; indeed, the period saw frequent uprisings by ordinary working people: food riots, and of course the machine-breaking riots and the Luddite movement in the early nineteenth century, directed against the use of machines which threatened the jobs of skilled workers in some parts of the country.[28] These were reasons why every sign of workers' resistance to the existing and developing economic and political order was severely repressed. It was not until well into the second half of the nineteenth century that the beginnings of trade union activity, especially free collective bargaining over terms and conditions of employment between workers and employers, began on a legal, organised basis. Even then (some would argue, even now) the attitude of the judges, when disputed cases came before them, was typically one of conservatism and anti-trade unionism. The landmark cases are recounted in all the major works on labour law,[29] especially those cases dating from the turn of the last century to the present day, in which the judges have consistently interpreted the law in a manner against the interests and activities of the unions.

The relationship between employer and employee is, in law, one of *contract*; that is, a legally binding agreement made by two parties, containing the agreed rights and obligations of each party, any breach of which entitles the aggrieved party to a legal remedy for *breach of contract*. This idea of the contract, discussed here in the context of the employment contract, applies to many other situations, notably, as

28 See in particular, Thompson, op. cit.
29 For example, Deakin and Morris, op. cit; Wedderburn, op. cit.

we shall see in chapter 11, to the buying and selling of goods and services. Ideas of social relations based on the contract were particularly prevalent during the nineteenth century, when the dominant social and economic philosophies were those of 'freedom of contract' and *laisser-faire* individualism. By this was meant that each individual in society should be left free to regulate his[30] own affairs with as little interference as possible by the state. Relationships between people in business and employment were regarded as best left to the parties concerned, to drive as good a bargain as they could get for their goods or services. Consequently, in line with this dominant ideology, there was relatively little state intervention through legal controls over, or restrictions upon, business, industry or employment, although piecemeal legislation in the nineteenth century did begin to lay down minimum standards of working conditions; for example, by means of the Factory Acts.

Laisser-faire involved the assumption, then, that all members of society were free and able to regulate and arrange their affairs with others (including their employers), and that all were equal in terms of their bargaining positions. If people were to be left free and equal then, according to dominant social and economic philosophies, competitive trade and industry would flourish, and the nation would thrive. In fact, as we have noted, there was, and still is, a fundamental *in*equality in terms of wealth, social position and bargaining power between people of different positions within the social structure. Two business representatives, negotiating over, say, the sale of goods, might have been in more or less equal bargaining positions; but the same was certainly not true of the relationship between most employers and employees. Nevertheless, the employment contract (supposedly freely made between employer and employee) was deemed to be made between people of equal standing, and even today the expressions 'freedom' and 'equality of contract' remain the basis for many areas of law involving contractual agreement. Given the predominance of these ideas about freedom and equality of contract, what particular problems confronted the parties to an employment contract in the nineteenth century, and to what extent has subsequent state intervention successfully tackled them through legislation?

To begin with, the fact that the terms of an employment contract might be oral, coupled with the frequently vague and complex nature of the terms of such a contract, led to the law being called upon to settle the many and varied disputes arising from employment situations. For example, an employee who was injured at work might claim compensation (see chapter 9); or an employee who was dismissed might bring a claim against the ex-employer alleging that the dismissal was unlawful. The difficulty is that many legal rules and remedies are only applicable if there is a proper 'employment contract' as opposed to other situations where one person

---

30 The omission of the feminine adjective is deliberate: the position of women in nineteenth-century society was such that they were thought not to have any affairs to regulate; the struggle for equality for women has continued throughout the twentieth century. Today, we have legislation dealing with equal pay and sex discrimination, but apart from legal enactments, the social and economic struggle for women's rights continues.

does work for another: if I call a taxi which carries me to my destination, the driver may be said to be doing work for me, but is hardly to be called my 'employee'.

The old legal test for ascertaining whether an employment relationship existed was the 'control' test, expounded in the case of *Yewens v Noakes*[31] in 1880, and formulated in terms of the extent to which the employer exercised effective control over the workers. However, the growth of specialised and highly skilled occupations led to many cases where the employer could not sensibly be said to be 'in control' of the activities of the employee, and this test has been discarded. Unfortunately, no acceptable substitute test has yet found full favour with the judges. In *Short v Henderson*[32] in 1946, one judge referred to the need to take into account a multiplicity of factors in deciding the issue, and in 1953 Denning LJ observed that 'the test of being a servant does not rest nowadays on submission to orders. It depends on whether the person is part and parcel of the organisation.'[33]

This 'organisation' test, like all other tests resting upon single factors, has been found unworkable in practice. The modern approach to the problem has been to consider many factors, notably the power to appoint and dismiss, the mode of payment and the making of deductions for National Insurance and income tax, the organisation of the workplace, and the issue of who provides the tools for the job.[34] This is the 'multiple' or 'mixed' test – still of practical importance since in English law the status of the worker is still the basis of most employment protection rights.[35]

It is noteworthy, however, that today many employers are using labour much more flexibly than in the past: more use is being made, for example, of part-time workers and short-term contract workers, and the European Union is seeking to protect the rights of such workers. Interestingly, although the British government is attempting to resist such moves, recent legislation has tended to blur the old distinction between a contract of employment and other types of working relationships. The Wages Act 1986, s 8,[36] for example, extended employment rights somewhat by providing a rather broader definition of 'worker' than simply one who is in a contract of employment.

Of course, once the relationship has been established as one of employment, there will remain the substantive issue of the case, which may be over a dismissal, a redundancy or some alleged breach of the contract by either employer or employee. The infinite variability of terms of employment contracts, coupled with the fact that in many cases employees suffered the double disadvantage of inability

---

31 (1880) 6 QBD 530.   32 (1946) 115 LJPC 41.

33 *Bank voor Handel en Scheepvaart NV v Slatford* [1953] 1 QB 248 at p 295.

34 See *Ready Mixed Concrete Ltd v Minister of Pensions and National Insurance* [1968] 1 All ER 433; I. T. Smith and G. Thomas, *Smith and Wood's Industrial Law* (8th edn., 2003, Butterworths); H. Collins, K. Ewing and A. McColgan, *Labour Law: Text and Materials* (2nd edn., 2005, Hart); M. Sargeant and D. Lewis, *Employment Law* (3rd edn., 2005, Pearson).

35 See *O'Kelly v Trusthouse Forte* [1984] QB 90; *Hall v Lorimer* [1994] 1 All ER 250.

36 Now consolidated into the Employment Rights Act 1996 (Pt II) which is the statute containing individual employment rights.

both to negotiate those terms and readily to ascertain the terms as dictated by the employer, has led, over the years, to a large number of instances of state intervention, through a series of statutes, in the field of employment. Changed philosophies about 'state interference', the reforming zeal of individual politicians and campaigners and, most important of all, the gradual absorption of working-class interests into the political process – through the widening of the franchise, the emergence of the trade union movement as a vociferous pressure-group, and the development and electoral success of the Labour Party – have all played their part, at different times, in furthering such legislative intervention. Work conditions, the existence of hazards, hidden and apparent, and insecurity of employment have long been regarded as worthy of legal intervention. A number of separate Acts of Parliament have provided, for example, for the physical protection of workers. Today the Health and Safety at Work etc Act 1974 lays legal duties upon employers, employees, sub-contractors, manufacturers and others to observe due care in installing, using and maintaining equipment and premises; the Act provides various administrative sanctions for the enforcement of its provisions, and contains a legal framework for worker-participation in safety at work.

With regard to terms and conditions of employment, the Employment Rights Act 1996, now substantially amended by the Employment Relations Act 1999, provides that the employee must be given notice of the main terms of the contract of employment. The law also provides for increased protection for employees in most industries by providing for redundancy payments (paid out when there is no longer any work for an employee to do, and first introduced in 1965); and for unfair dismissal (first introduced in 1971), whereby an employee who successfully alleges, before an Employment Tribunal, that he or she was unfairly dismissed may be offered reinstatement (the same job with the same employer), re-engagement (a different job with the same employer) or compensation (the remedy which is most frequently sought). The Employment Relations Act 1999 also extended maternity rights and introduced a new right to three months' paternity leave; and a new 'national minimum wage' was introduced the previous year by the National Minimum Wage Act 1998.

Protective legislation affecting work and working conditions is only one important area in which state intervention has taken place – often on the grounds of benefit to the community. The nineteenth century saw the beginnings of local government services, in fields such as public health, urban amenities and improvement, and, later, slum-clearance programmes which would, in time, sweep away the foul and inadequate housing stock which had characterised many industrial towns. These beginnings prefaced the acceleration of central and local government intervention in areas of social life which had previously been private, not public, domains; and the twentieth-century 'welfare state ethic' of state intervention (ostensibly) for the benefit of the community stands in direct contrast to the nineteenth-century individualist *laisser-faire* ideal of leaving people alone to manage their own affairs as best they could, without state help or 'interference'.

During the twentieth century, the state has played a significant role in all aspects of everyday life, especially in the context of various schemes which we associate with the term 'welfare state' – income support, job-seekers allowance, incapacity benefits, old-age pensions, social services and so on. Other aspects of the welfare state are the state-run education system, the health service, and local authority services ranging from refuse disposal to the provision of housing, and from street lighting to the maintenance of highways. These examples are clear cases where the state has accepted a large measure of social responsibility for providing for the *whole* community in key areas.

It should not be assumed from this, however, that interventionist policies are invariably seen as operating for the benefit of all, or that 'welfare statism' has met with support from all government administrations. The Conservative administrations under Margaret Thatcher during the 1980s, and the ideas of 'Thatcherism', were highly critical of what became derided as the 'nanny state', with a large measure of approval of old ideas of self-determinism for the individual. And apart from the fact, noted above, that party-politically inspired measures will attract party-political opposition both inside and outside Parliament, there are other levels at which doubts, fears or anger may result from policies introduced by particular governments, which may be seen as operating *against* the interests of certain sections of the community. Private landlords, for example, may oppose the legal protection of tenants against eviction; property developers may resist the introduction of legal requirements for satisfying conditions imposed by planning or building regulations; employers may oppose legislation which they see as tending, directly or indirectly, to impose new financial burdens upon them (such as the introduction of the minimum wage); and so on.

In assessing the strengths and weaknesses of arguments for or against such measures, and indeed any legal rule, procedure or institution, we need, at a more general level, to be able to make analytical and theoretical connections between law and the various aspects and components of modern social structure. By what means can such an analysis be carried out?

Law and society: consensus or conflict?

Law may be regarded as a benign facilitating mechanism, making transactions possible between men and solving awkward problems as they arise; it may, alternatively, be seen as a mechanism of social control, regulating activities and interests in the name of either the community, a ruling class or the state. The state itself may be defined as either 'neutral arbiter' or 'interested party' in the solution of disputes and the balancing of interests. Again, law may be seen as an institution for the furtherance and protection of the welfare of everyone, or it may be seen, crudely, as an instrument of repression wielded by the dominant groups in society.[37]

---

37 P. J. Harris and J. D. Buckle, 'Philosophies of Law and the Law Teacher' (1976) *The Law Teacher*, p 6.

The above alternative standpoints are simplified statements of what are usually extremely complicated political views and positions, but the point is that people do have very different views as to what law, in general or with regard to specific rules, is for.

Within the field of legal and social study, there may be discerned a whole range of alternative or competing viewpoints about law and society, which at its simplest may be presented as debates as to whether our society and its legal system are representations or reflections of social *consensus* or social *conflict*. The former position perceives law as protecting social values to which everyone subscribes; the latter holds that there is no such single, universally agreed set of social values, but rather a whole variety of different social values, certain of which are protected by a less-than-neutral legal system in order to protect some interests as against others.

One important sociologist adhering to the 'consensus' view of society was Talcott Parsons. His view of society as a 'system' comprising actions and institutions, each functioning to maintain social stability and order, has been frequently criticised, not least because of its assumption that society is indeed characterised by a shared consensual value-system. Some critics have pointed out,[38] for example, that Parsons' analysis concentrates on examining those elements within society which tend towards the maintenance of order and equilibrium, at the expense of considering those elements which tend towards social conflict and instability – elements which must be accounted for in any theory of social order.

Another basic criticism of the Parsonian functionalist position is that there is very little evidence of a monolithic, universally shared value-system within society. We shall see many examples of this assertion in due course, especially in chapter 2, but drawing on material presented so far in this chapter, the existence of disputes and the necessity of providing, through law, the means of dealing with them, indicates the presence of conflict between individuals and groups within society. The very creation of a legal rule implies that some people may well be inclined to engage in the behaviour it prohibits, suggesting that those persons may well disagree with the content of the rule. Conflicts are resolved through law; as White has put it: 'The consensus model views society as basically unitary. Parliament represents us all; the executive acts in the common interest . . . the law is equal and just to all and is administered without fear or favour for the common good . . . Conflicts that there are will be on a personal level.'[39]

Opposing ideas about the nature of society may be classified as falling into some form of 'conflict' or 'pluralist' theories of society and the social and legal order. Both types of theory take for granted the fact that there is no 'shared value-system' in our society. The pluralist view, in its 'pure' form, accepts the existence of conflicting groups and interests, but maintains that the constant interaction and negotiation between conflicting groups, all of which are assumed to have more or less equal

38 For example, D. Lockwood, 'Some Remarks on "The Social System"' (1956) 7 *BJS*.
39 R. White, in P. Morris, R. White and P. Lewis, *Social Needs and Legal Action* (1973, Martin Robertson), p 15.

bargaining-power, helps maintain social stability and equilibrium. The role of the law and the state is portrayed as 'neutral arbiter', or 'honest broker' – taking no sides in these conflict situations, but providing the machinery of conflict-settlement either through law or through political debate and policy-making by government.

The trouble with such a view is that the multitude of interest-groups in society do not possess equal power, in either political, legal or economic terms. Some groups have the power to influence law-making and the implementation of those laws; others do not. In general, the stance taken in this book accepts as accurate the proposition that those interest-groups possessing political and economic power and control of key institutions in society will be found to exert the most profound influence over the making and the implementation of law.

Given that this is the case, does this imply some sort of political conspiracy, in which the powerful groups in society impose their policies, and laws for the protection of their interests, upon the less powerful groups and social classes? Most people would find such a sinister notion rather extreme and lacking in credibility when applied to our own liberal-democratic society. How, then, do the less powerful come to accept the views and policies of the ruling groups? How do we identify those ruling groups, and what are the relationships between these various groups and between law, state and society?

There have been many answers put forward to questions such as these. Some writers have questioned the extent to which social conflict pervades society, and have argued that propositions as to degrees of social consensus have been too easily dismissed by writers taking a 'conflict' perspective. Some of these writers have presented analyses which are highly complex, whilst others have taken a stance which may be termed a basic 'liberal-democratic' viewpoint, involving the acceptance of social conflict whose manifestations are played out within boundaries of socially accepted norms in terms of the legitimacy of official legal and governmental authority whose concerns are the resolution of such conflicts. White, for example, discusses not only the basic 'consensus' and 'conflict' theories, but also presents a third model of society, which he calls an 'open' model, where:

> Conflict is expected to continue in different forms between interest groups but it is assumed that these conflicts can be resolved through a legitimate process. There will be basic agreement that conflict-resolution can be achieved within a framework of negotiation, arbitration, judicial decision and electoral battle, backed up by strike or rent strike but without resort to revolution.[40]

Before drawing our own conclusions as to the appropriateness or otherwise of such a model of society, it is pertinent here to consider, albeit in very simplified form, the work of the nineteenth-century German philosopher and social scientist Karl Marx, whose work has been very influential both in terms of political developments in various parts of the world, and in terms of later academic debates.

40 Ibid., p 17.

Marx was concerned with the analysis of capitalist societies, though he wrote at a time when capitalism in Europe was less developed than it is today. Capitalism, according to Marx, involves the exploitation of the working classes by the capitalist class. The exploitation springs from the fact that, in order for an employer (capitalist) to make profit, the workers must be paid less, in wages, than the value of the goods they produce, hence producing 'surplus value', or profit. Marx distinguished between the working class ('proletariat') who possess the labour power; the capitalists ('bourgeoisie') who own the capital and means of production (factories, business concerns and so on) and the landowners, who derive their income from the rent of their land. The latter two classes occupy the powerful economic and political positions in society through the exploitation of the working class, and the relationship between the classes clearly cannot be one of equality, since exploitation necessarily involves the subjugation of one class to the interests of another.

How, then, did Marx explain the continued exploitation by one social class of another? Marx recognised that exploitation could continue only as long as bitter revolutionary confrontation could be avoided, and the most effective way of avoiding this was, according to Marx, for the capitalist classes to maintain control of the official state institutions. For Marx, the state was 'the form in which the individuals of a ruling class assert their common interests';[41] by control of state apparatus (government, law, police and so on), the interests of the dominant classes could be protected and perpetuated through the continued oppression of the working class.

But how is it that so many 'exploited' people in a capitalist society accept the fact of political and economic domination? One reason, according to Marx and other Marxist writers, is that the ruling classes have control of those state institutions which give expression, when the need arises, to *forceful* repression: the army, the police and the law. But apart from these 'repressive state apparatuses',[42] the ruling classes also control, through various public and private institutions, the dominant ideas, opinions and attitudes about how society operates: 'the ideas of the ruling class are in every epoch the ruling ideas: ie the class which is the ruling *material* force of society is at the same time its ruling *intellectual* force.'[43] This collection of ideas, values, standards and beliefs – this *ideology* – finds expression, according to later Marxist writers such as Gramsci[44] and Althusser[45] through social institutions such as the school, the family, political (including trade union) organisations and, importantly, *law*. The Marxist views law as an important means whereby the interests and values of capitalism are protected and maintained, and sees the legal system as part of what Althusser termed both *repressive* and *ideological* state apparatuses. In terms of capitalist ideology as expressed through law, private property is regarded as fundamental to social and economic stability; the values of justice

---

41 K. Marx, 'The German Ideology' in T. Bottomore and M. Rubel (eds), *Karl Marx: Selected Writings in Sociology and Social Philosophy* (1961, Pelican), p 228.

42 L. Althusser, 'Ideology and Ideological State Apparatuses' in B. R. Cosin (ed.), *Education: Structure and Society* (1972, Penguin/Open University).   43 Bottomore and Rubel, op. cit., p 93.

44 A. Gramsci, *Prison Notebooks* (1971, Lawrence and Wishart).   45 Op. cit.

and legal neutrality are presented as endemic in our legal system (obscuring the 'reality' that law is in fact operated for the protection of the interests of powerful capitalism), and the legal system is presented by lawyers and politicians as providing justice for all.

Now, whilst it is vital to recognise that this brief and simplified sketch of the implications of Marxist writers cannot possibly reflect the richness and complexities of the analyses of both Marx himself and later writers who have developed Marx's ideas,[46] it is believed that enough has been said to indicate that the liberal-democratic, 'neo-consensus' theories about the legal and social order can themselves be accommodated within Marxist analysis. Beliefs concerning the 'agreed' values as to the legitimacy, equality and justice of law and government may *themselves* be ideological constructs serving to bolster and justify capitalist institutions and processes. The question then becomes not whether there *is* any basic consensus within society on any given issue, but rather why, how and when such consensus occurs, how it is maintained, and how deeply any such consensual ideas are held by the members of the society in question. Some areas of apparent consensus may, in fact, hide the process whereby sectional interests, inherently oppositional to other groups' interests, become defined and presented as 'basic' interests, or interests which are 'in the national interest' or 'for the common good'. Examples of such processes will be discussed presently. Other areas of apparent consensus may be the result of complex historical processes whereby certain interests come to be embodied in legal and other social institutions because of their fundamental importance to the economic or political structure. The outstanding example of such a process is the development of the social value attached to private property, as reflected in both law and everyday social practice. In chapter 5, we will see how the *particular* institutions of private property in our society have their roots in the economic and political changes which took place hundreds of years ago.

The theme to be developed in this book, therefore, is not that of a simple denial or assertion of consensus or conflict, but rather the exploration of basic questions regarding the roots of such consensus or conflict, the ways in which social conflicts are manifested and controlled by law and other agencies, and the manner in which areas of apparent consensus are maintained through legal and other social institutions and processes. In particular, a sense of history is vital for the understanding of these questions, for, as we shall see time and again in the course of this book, legal rules and institutions can only be fully understood by perceiving them in the context of the social structural formations and arrangements, at any given historical period, in which they arose.

---

46 See in particular, A. Giddens, *Sociology: A Brief but Critical Introduction* (2nd edn.,1986, Macmillan); and for more detailed discussion see R. Miliband, *The State in Capitalist Society* (1973, Quartet Books); N. Poulantzas, *State, Power, Socialism* (1978, New Left Books); L. Althusser, *For Marx* (1977, New Left Books); Gramsci, op. cit.

2

Law and morality

In this chapter we examine the relationships between law, society and morality. A society's 'code of morality' may be defined as a set of beliefs, values, principles and standards of behaviour, and such codes are found in all social groups. We noted in chapter 1 how the sociologist Emile Durkheim presented a theory of social cohesion, part of which rested on the notion that in technologically undeveloped societies, such as small tribal groups, there tends to be a single, consensually held moral code (the 'collective conscience') to which all members of the group subscribe. In a technologically advanced society such as our own, however, with immense differentiation in terms of social status, income, occupation, ethnic background and so on, it is unlikely that we will find such a monolithic moral code. Rather, as will be argued later in this chapter, there is diversity of moral attitudes on all kinds of social and personal issues.

Most of us, if asked to give an example of an area of moral rules in our society, would probably think of sexual morality, or perhaps acts of violence against the person. It is important to emphasise, however, that morality embraces much more than sex and violence; it is part of dominant ideological currents,[1] whereby dominant beliefs and attitudes conducive to the maintenance of the overall status quo are 'translated' into a positive general code involving social attitudes to property, politics and social relationships in general. And, as we shall see, a moral code may not be wholly without its inconsistencies and contradictions: established institutions such as the Church, for example, may condemn apartheid, or racial segregation, on moral grounds, but other established institutions, notably at government level, may nevertheless maintain commercial and political relations with states which are structured around policies of apartheid, as was seen for many years in the attitudes of various Western countries, including Britain, towards South Africa during the years that that country operated a social, economic and political system based on apartheid and systematic racial oppression.

And in the years following South Africa's removal of its apartheid regime and its replacement by one based upon democratic government, concerns about human rights have been increasingly discussed at national and international levels, with

---

1 Chapter 1.

criticisms being levelled at many nations – including Afghanistan during the period of the Taliban regime, China, and Turkey, among many others – over their failure to recognise and protect the human rights of their citizens. In Britain, following the general election of 1997, the New Labour government vowed to support the cause of human rights, and apart from the passage of the Human Rights Act 1998 (which in effect incorporated most of the European Convention on Human Rights into English law), announced that its foreign policy would be based on sound moral principles linked to human rights. The moral soundness of pursuing a foreign policy grounded in promoting support for the sanctity and quality of human life has been contrasted by critics with the government's support for various arms and other military equipment deals with foreign powers having dubious human rights records.

We noted in chapter 1 some general features of law and morality: we saw that, though having much in common, law and morality have important points of divergence. Legal rules, for instance, are backed by official state sanctions and procedures, whereas moral rules, if they involve any sanctions at all, rest upon more diffuse and generalised *informal* sanctions – we might call this 'social disapproval' – as where, for example, neighbours may shun a person whom they have discovered to be engaging in prostitution. In some instances, particular behaviour may offend both legal and moral codes, such as the commission of murder, but in other cases behaviour may be defined by some people as immoral, though that behaviour is not unlawful. Examples are telling lies or committing adultery. In yet other cases, social behaviour may be unlawful even though no moral disapproval attaches to the action in question – the example used in chapter 1 was the criminal offence of exceeding the speed limit by only two miles per hour.

Morality is connected with the law in many ways. To begin with, the conditions under which a person may be held liable in law may be seen as based on the moral idea of 'blame' or 'fault'. Although liability in law is examined in more detail in later chapters, it is useful at this point to outline some general considerations.

'Conditions of liability' may conveniently be divided into 'general' and 'specific' conditions. Specific conditions of liability will depend upon the precise scope of a given legal rule or set of legal rules, each of which will be different according to the context of the rules, their history and their objectives. For example, in criminal law (see chapter 10) the definition of 'theft' is the dishonest appropriation of property belonging to another with the intention of depriving the other of it (Theft Act 1968, s 1(1)), whilst the definition of murder is accepted as 'when a man of sound memory, and of the age of discretion, unlawfully killeth within any county of the realm any reasonable creature . . . under the king's peace, with malice aforethought . . . '.[2] These two legal rules clearly lay down different conditions which must be proved by the prosecution before liability can follow. The same variety will

---

2 Under the old common law, the death had to occur within 'a year and a day' after the attack by the accused. Recognising the fact that modern medical techniques can often prolong life for substantial periods after an initial criminal assault, the 'year and a day' rule was abolished by the Law Reform (Year and a Day Rule) Act 1996.

be found in the body of law we know as the law of *torts*, or civil wrongs (see chapter 9) which includes rules specifying the conditions under which a defendant will be liable to a plaintiff[3] for wrongs such as assault and battery, trespass to land, nuisance, defamation, negligence and various others; and yet other conditions of liability are found within the law of contract (see chapter 11).

Apart from the specific conditions of liability contained within individual rules, however, there are, underlying the idea of liability in law, certain general principles perceived by judges and legislators alike as being fundamental to liability in any branch of the law. These principles are rooted in conceptions of morality (of which the notion of justice is one of the most important), and the way in which these moral principles are incorporated into the law may best be appreciated by means of the criminal law examples cited above. It will be noted that before a person can be convicted of theft, it must be established not only that the accused person 'appropriated property belonging to another', but also that this appropriation took place 'with the intention of depriving the other of it'. Again, a conviction for murder can occur only if it is established not simply that the accused brought about the death of another, but also that this was done 'with malice aforethought'.

It follows that if someone takes another's property in the belief that it is his or her own, or that if someone causes another's death by accident, then convictions for theft or murder cannot follow. In general, then, it is not considered acceptable in English law to subject a person to legal sanctions unless it can be shown that that person did the act in a 'blameworthy' manner, since we do not normally attribute blame in situations where injury occurs accidentally, or by reason of an honest mistake, or where the person concerned cannot be said to have been responsible for his or her actions. This means, then, that 'blameworthiness' – a moral principle – is normally required before we consider it acceptable to subject a person to legal sanctions. By way of illustration of this point: it is a defence in criminal law to show that the accused was, at the time of the commission of the alleged offence, suffering from some mental illness, or was for some other reason not in control of his or her actions. If X is hammering a nail, and D comes along, seizes X's wrist, and uses it to strike P with the hammer which X is holding, it will be D, not X, who will be liable for that injury.

Similarly, in the law of contract, special legal rules apply regarding the capacity to make contracts of minors (persons under 18 years of age), mentally disordered persons and drunken persons. Where contracts are made by minors, the law presumes insufficient maturity to appreciate fully the contractual bond, although there are exceptions to this: it has long been held that minors may be held bound by the terms of contracts for 'necessaries' (food, clothing and other items deemed essential). With regard to the other exceptional cases, their state of mind is likely to

---

3 The word 'plaintiff', referring to the person bringing a civil legal action, has now been replaced by the term 'claimant' (Civil Procedure Rules 1998, SI 1998/3132 made following the Civil Procedure Act 1997). Students of English law need, however, to be aware of the meaning of the older word: throughout this book, both terms are used as appropriate to the context.

be such as to affect their capacity to understand what they are doing and the contractual obligations which they are taking on.

These general principles may be summed up in two propositions: first, the law holds liable, as a general rule, only the actual wrongdoer; and second, the law insists, as a general rule, that a person's liability will depend on whether that person may be said to be morally blameworthy. These underlying general principles, referred to by such phrases as 'individual responsibility' and 'no liability without fault', have long been at the root of liability in English law, and are, despite certain exceptional situations discussed in later chapters, still regarded as fundamentally important.

In examining more closely the relationship between law and morality, we begin by discussing some philosophical ideas about this relationship and the ways in which such ideas have found their way into the law; we then discuss the social basis and definition of moral ideas and how the social and economic structure of a given period can generate moral, as well as legal, attitudes and norms which may not necessarily be accepted by all sections of a society. It will be argued that morality, and especially specific ideas within a moral code (such as definitions of what constitutes 'deviant' behaviour), are *relative* concepts. By this we mean to emphasise not only that different individuals and groups often have different ideas about the rightness or wrongness of particular forms of behaviour, but also that moral climates shift over periods of time, and that these changes have corresponding shifts in the nature and extent of formal regulation through legal rules.

An illustration of the first of these propositions is the furore which followed the publication in early 2006, first in Denmark and then in some other European countries, of cartoons depicting the Islamic prophet Muhammed. The pictorial depiction of images of the prophet is considered by many Muslims to be offensive and even blasphemous, and the world-wide protests by Muslims which followed these publications resulted in strained relations between Denmark and predominantly Muslim countries, death threats being made against those responsible for the drawings, and protests by Muslims in many countries, which ultimately involved fatalities and damage to property. The responses by many European politicians and newspapers focused on the central issue of freedom of speech – considered in most of Europe to be a fundamental human right, and one which is protected by Article 10 of the European Convention on Human Rights. The responses from many European politicians, in summary, argued that, whilst freedom of speech remains a central moral value, it ought to be tempered by sensitivity to the feelings of other sections of the community. Not all sections of society agree on the morality of unrestrained freedom of speech.

The second proposition may be illustrated by the example of the changing legal position regarding homosexuality. As we will see later in this chapter, the complete legal prohibition on male homosexual activity, backed by criminal sanctions, has gradually given way, along with shifts in cultural and social attitudes, to a milieu in which, in 2006, it became possible for gay couples to register their relationship, and for that relationship to enjoy legally protected rights, by means of a new civil ceremony.

We shall consider presently how moral standards, values and rules are created, and frequently embodied within the law; but first we must consider how very closely law and morals have been connected throughout history, principally because of the historically important and close relationship between religious doctrine and political structures in the Western world. In particular, we must consider the impact on law and state of the long-established philosophies of *natural law*.

The early natural-law philosophers enquired into the 'essential nature' of human beings and their relationship with other phenomena occurring in the natural world. For the Greek philosopher Aristotle, writing in the fourth century BC, people were as much a part of nature as trees, rocks and birds, the only differentiating feature being the human capacity to *reason*, through which people formulate their will and direct their activities towards the attainment of their desires. Moreover, men and women are, according to Aristotle, *political* beings, in that they live, by nature, in social groups. The laws of nature thus create the community, or state, the laws regulating people's behaviour being made by men and women through the exercise of reason. Just as the trees are there 'because nature decrees it', so the 'state' (which at various periods in the history of many societies has involved institutions for which we could today find no moral justification, such as slavery) is there because nature has decreed that it 'ought to be there'.

This connection between fact and value, between what 'is' and what 'ought to be', can be traced through all natural-law ideas, and in its later formulations the philosophy is accompanied by strong theological connotations. The history of natural law is long and complex, with various schools of thought emerging at different periods in different parts of the world. Over the centuries, and certainly by the Middle Ages, the notion of the 'law of God' came to replace the Aristotelian conception of the 'law of nature' as the *ultimate criterion* whereby society, law and human existence might be evaluated. One reason for this link between religion and philosophies of law and state was that, as European societies developed and the struggle between the traditional power of the Church and the new and increasing political power of emerging nation-states and rulers became more pronounced, natural-law philosophy, which could be seen as often, though not invariably, having conservative overtones ('what is, ought to be, because nature has decreed it'), came to be a useful weapon for the justification of the existing political and social institutions and the resistance of radical change. In the course of this historical process, over many centuries, natural-law philosophies became closely and inextricably tied to morality and to religious doctrine.

This connection between natural law, human law and society was crystallised into the classical formulation of natural-law theory as we know it today (despite the many guises it may take) through the writings of St Thomas Aquinas in the Middle Ages. Aquinas related 'Divine' law to human or 'positive' law, and acknowledged the role of the latter in social and political affairs:

It was not the least of Aquinas' contributions that, in his synthesis of Aristotelian philosophy and Catholic faith in a universal divine law, he rejected the idea that civil government was necessarily tainted with original sin and argued for the existence of a hierarchy of law derived ultimately from God, and in which human or positive law had a rightful though lowly place and was worthy for its own sake.[4]

Human law derived ultimately from God's law. Since it was perceived as obvious that God's law constituted the ultimate and absolute criterion of good and evil, right and wrong, human law, in general, was such that it was beyond criticism. The conformist and conservative uses to which this doctrine could be put are clear, as is the foundation for the notion of morality, being derived from religious principles of right and wrong, as an all-embracing, universally applicable set of values and rules.

But natural-law arguments were by no means always limited to attempted justifications for the social or political *status quo*. The idea that there existed a body of values higher than those contained in the practical social arrangements of a society contained the potentialities for *revolutionary* arguments, used to justify radical change in social and political structures, through the notion of universal and inalienable *human rights*. Here the argument is, at its simplest, that everyone has, or should have, certain basic human rights which civil government should respect. In the event of particular social and political arrangements which do not respect and guarantee these 'human rights', people are justified in struggling against such regimes in order that their human rights may be recognised.

History has seen many examples and many variants of this basic argument. The French Revolution, for instance, was influenced to an extent by the arguments of philosophers who argued for the liberty of the individual, such as Montesquieu and Rousseau; the United States Constitution, providing and guaranteeing certain rights and freedoms for every American citizen, is regarded by many as embodying natural-law principles; and similar rights are embedded in the constitutions of, for example, Germany and Canada. Following the Second World War, the European Convention on Human Rights was signed in 1950 by the Council of Europe, with the intention of promoting the protection of human rights. Most of the Convention rights are now incorporated into English law by means of the Human Rights Act 1998.[5]

Apart from individual states' constitutional guarantees, innumerable campaigning groups have, nationally and internationally, sought more protection for human rights (including individuals' civil rights usually associated with democratic government), and have demonstrated their opposition to groups and political regimes thought to be guilty of infringements of 'basic human rights'. Examples include the mass demonstrations during the 1960s in the United States against racial discrimination and segregation; the workers' struggle, through the trade union 'Solidarity' in Poland in the early 1980s, for the rights of the individual

4 Lloyd's *Introduction to Jurisprudence* (7th edn. by M. D. A. Freeman, 2001, Sweet and Maxwell), p 105.
5 See chapter 4.

against an oppressive state; the condemnation and economic sanctions from many Western countries over the South African policy of apartheid; the energetic efforts in the 1980s by campaigners against nuclear arms, notably, in England, the Campaign for Nuclear Disarmament and the active opposition by many thousands of women to the installation of American nuclear missiles on British soil; the student-led demonstrations in 1989 against the Chinese government in Beijing's Tiananmen Square; and, more recently, the anti-capitalist demonstrations (notably in Genoa in the summer of 2001) protesting against the increasing domination in the Western world of the interests of global capitalism, which many view as influencing the policies of elected governments to an unacceptable degree. In all these and many other campaigns and incidents, it is possible to discern strong natural-law themes invoking respect for human life and liberty.

On the international stage, there have been, especially since the end of the Second World War, concerted actions to deal with atrocities committed by individual states against certain classes or groups of their citizens, though the aims of such actions may not *necessarily* be based on idealistic conceptions of human rights. On occasion, such actions may be motivated by politics or by pragmatism, though motivations frequently merge so that political action can be obscured by idealist rhetoric. After the Second World War, for example, there took place at Nuremberg the 'war crimes trials', where the victorious allied forces took on the task of trying individuals who had been responsible for the perpetration of various atrocities, especially against the Jews, under the Nazi regime in Germany, using charges such as 'crimes against humanity'. Critics have suggested that, although these trials may have been perceived as necessary in order to avoid unofficial reprisals against the perpetrators of the horrors of the Nazi regime, to dress up what was essentially a political act by the victors as 'law' obscures the true nature of that act by introducing legal form and terminology into a setting where no precedent for such trials, or for such charges, had previously existed.

Nevertheless, the notion that states – or their political leaders- may be guilty of 'crimes against humanity' has persisted, with arguments based on such notions being used, for example, against the United States over its involvement in South-East Asia (the Vietnam war) in the 1960s, and against Israel over its treatment – political and military – of the Palestinian people. And by the end of 2005, two important trials were in progress at which charges of, or relating to, crimes against humanity were brought against ex-heads of state. One was the trial before the International War Crimes Tribunal of Slobodan Milosevic, ex-president of the former Yugoslavia, facing charges relating to atrocities carried out in Kosovo in 1999, to crimes against humanity committed in Croatia in 1991 and 1992, and to alleged genocide in Bosnia-Hercegovina between 1992 and 1995.[6] The second was

6 Milosevic died in prison in March 2006, before the conclusion of his trial. In August 2001 the International War Crimes Tribunal in the Hague convicted Bosnian Serb General Radislav Krstic to 46 years in prison for the crime of genocide. Krstic had overseen the massacre of over 7,000 Muslim men and boys at Srebrenica in 1995.

the trial of Saddam Hussein, ex-President of Iraq, before an Iraqi court, on charges of ordering the killing of Iraqi citizens.

The importance of bringing the formalities of legal procedure, and of the central legal value of the 'rule of law' has recently been emphasised through the establishment, in July 2002, of the new International Criminal Court, based at The Hague in the Netherlands. The ICC had been proposed in 1998 at an international conference in Rome, and the 'Rome Statute', which set out the proposal in detail, specified that the Court would come into existence once 60 states had ratified the Statute. This level of ratification was achieved in April 2002, although a number of major countries had at that time either failed to sign up to the original treaty (including China, India and Pakistan) or failed to ratify despite being a signatory (including Israel and Russia). The position of the United States is that, although it signed the 1998 treaty during the Clinton administration, the George W. Bush administration is wholly opposed to the Court, partly on the ground that an international court would undermine America's own sovereignty over judicial matters potentially affecting its subjects, and partly on the basis of apprehension that US soldiers might potentially be brought before the court as a result of US military action.[7]

The jurisdiction of the ICC, according to the Rome Statute, is 'limited to the most serious crimes of concern to the international community as a whole' and in particular is concerned with genocide, crimes against humanity, war crimes, and the crime of aggression (Article 5). Each of these crimes is explained in detail in Articles 6–8, and it is made clear that the criminal activities in question will be unlawful acts affecting either a national, ethnic, racial or religious group (in the case of genocide) or acts committed as part of a widespread or systematic attack directed against any civilian population (crimes against humanity). The International Criminal Court complements, but does not replace, the national legal systems of signatory states, and will hear cases only when individual states cannot or are unwilling to prosecute through national court systems.

It is too early to evaluate the work of the International Criminal Court, though it is certainly true to say that its reception by and integration within the international legal community would be made easier if major states who have so far failed to ratify the Rome Statute did so. The United States, in particular, is undoubtedly the leading nation in the condemnation through political rhetoric and through military action of all forms of terrorist activity and abuse of human rights, and yet refuses to support an international legal development which has, in effect, the very same objectives. And given current world conditions in which oppression and terrorism occur all too frequently, it is perhaps easy to appreciate that notions of 'freedom', 'legality' and 'justice' may continue to be merged with, or even possibly used as a mask for, political or even military action.

7 Article 28 of the Rome Statute specifically provides that a military commander may be liable in certain defined circumstances in respect of criminal actions committed by forces under his or her effective control.

Whatever the political uses to which natural-law doctrines may still be put, however, the combination of law and morality within those doctrines is an invariable feature. The 'higher truth' or 'ideal' is presented as the highest moral authority for all human actions: as the ultimate criterion whereby we identify the good and the evil, and as the yardstick whereby we assess the morality or otherwise of human laws and human political actions. And, according to the classic formulation of the doctrine as propounded by Aquinas, if human law is found not to coincide with the principles of the 'ultimate' (in Aquinas's terms, 'Divine') law, then *it is not to be accorded the status of 'law' at all.* Such an analysis of law, which stresses the importance of the substance of law, and insists on the connection between law and morality, may be contrasted with some of the theories of law discussed in chapter 1, which concentrate upon the *formal* aspects of legal rules, paying much less attention to their *content.*

In this classical form, natural law is no longer given much credence by legal philosophers or political theorists, at least in most of the English-speaking world. The hold which the Church once had over political life has long ceased to grip very strongly: the age of religious supremacy gave way in the period of the industrial revolution to an era of scientific rationality, in which the dominant philosophers of the eighteenth and nineteenth centuries, such as Jeremy Bentham, scorned natural law for its metaphysical, unprovable principles. In today's secular, technologically advanced society where the role of the Church has decreased considerably in the lives of many people, natural law and its premises appear to many to be strangely irrelevant and too far distanced from the material and political claims and needs of the majority of the population. In short, too many criticisms have been levelled at the classical natural-law position for it to remain unscathed, although the equation of law with morality, and occasionally with religious notions, is still discernible in many modern ideas about law. And to be sure, some modern writers have presented newer variants of natural law, among them Lon Fuller and John Finnis.

Fuller was far less concerned with 'absolute values' than with the *procedural* aspects to a legal system. Referring to what he termed the 'inner morality of law',[8] Fuller argued that in order to create and maintain a system which can properly be called a 'legal system', certain procedural requirements should be satisfied. These are (i) that there should be rules in the first place, as opposed to a series of *ad hoc* judgments; (ii) those rules must be made known to all those affected by them; (iii) rules should not have retrospective effect; (iv) the rules should be understandable and (v) consistent; and (vi) should not require the impossible of people; (vii) the rules should not be changed so frequently that people cannot orient their actions by them; and (viii) the rules as announced should coincide with the actual administration of those rules.

Fuller claims that 'a total failure in any one of these eight directions does not simply result in a bad system of law; it results in something that is not properly called a legal system at all'.[9] The 'natural law' element in Fuller's writings tends to

---

8 L. L. Fuller, *The Morality of Law* (1964, Yale University Press).   9 Ibid., p 39.

be reflected in this concern with *legality*, or due process, rather than in a concern with the substance, or content, of laws; this 'internal morality' of law – a set of criteria whereby a legal order may be evaluated – constitutes a series of guidelines, or ideals, to which a legal system should *aspire*.

This modern variant of natural law has met with various criticisms. Why, it has been asked, should a legal system that adopts Fuller's eight procedural requirements necessarily be a 'good' legal system? As Lloyd has said, 'the Nazi legal system was faithful, with one possible exception,[10] to Fuller's standards, yet it was able to promulgate laws contrary to the most fundamental principles of humanitarian morality'.[11] Finnis has countered this objection with the observation that a tyrannous regime is usually founded upon either the rulers' self-interest or a fanatical pursuit of some ideological goal which they consider good for the community; either way, tyranny is inconsistent with the values of reciprocity, fairness and respect for persons which Fuller's criteria rest upon. Moreover, 'Adherence to the Rule of Law . . . is always liable to reduce the efficiency for evil of an evil-government, since it systematically restricts the government's freedom of manoeuvre.'[12]

Finnis himself develops[13] a theory of natural law which rests upon the idea of a set of basic principles of human existence which are *good in themselves*: that is to say, they are not 'good' because they are thought 'morally good'. Rather, they are 'good' because they constitute the 'basic values' of all human existence which in turn underlie both human activity and, indeed, subsequent moral judgments. In other words, these 'basic values' are 'obvious' and 'even unquestionable'.[14] The point about these values is, argues Finnis, that *no one can deny them*: every social group accepts and adopts them.

What, then, are these 'basic values'? Finnis argues that there are seven;[15] life, knowledge, play, aesthetic experience, sociability, practical reasonableness and 'religion' ('questions of the origins of cosmic order and of human freedom and reason'[16]). They relate to the concept of law and legal systems in so far as human beings live in social groups, and only in this context can these basic goods be pursued; a legal system is required to achieve these ends, and so law should strive to maximise the achievement, or satisfaction, of these basic goods for the benefit of the community.

Now, it must be admitted that at the end of the day Finnis' conclusions may seem rather vague: it may be thought that his list of seven basic goods is highly subjective, in that other thinkers might offer a longer, a shorter or a quite different list; and as Lloyd says, 'as with much natural law theorising, we are left . . . not with a

---

10 This exception being that of requirement 2.   11 Lloyd, op. cit., p 127.
12 J. Finnis, *Natural Law and Natural Rights* (1980, Oxford University Press), p 274.   13 Ibid.
14 Ibid., p 59.
15 To the objection, 'why not more? Or less?', Finnis asserts that 'other objectives and forms of good will be found, on analysis, to be ways or combinations of ways of pursuing (not always sensibly) and realising (not always successfully) one of the seven basic forms of good, or some combination of them' (p 90).   16 Ibid., p 89.

blueprint for legal and political action, . . . but with hints, no more, of how to better ourselves and the communities within which we live'.[17]

Although natural-law theories are open to the criticisms of vagueness and inconclusiveness, there is no doubt that many still insist on a connection between law and morality. In particular, many judges still hold that the foundations on which law (especially criminal law) is based are those of religious morality. To take one example, Lord Devlin has written: '[I feel] that a complete separation of crime from sin . . . would not be good for the moral law and might be disastrous for the criminal.'[18]

Lord Devlin argued that there are ultimate moral principles and criteria whereby social behaviour must be judged, though he acknowledged that the principles of Christianity upon which these principles are based no longer constitute the foundation of moral attitudes in our secular society. Nevertheless, Lord Devlin held that ultimate standards of right and wrong *do* exist, and based this notion upon the necessity for a binding moral code – a 'public morality' – which serves to hold a society together; without such consensual moral beliefs, he said, 'the society will disintegrate. For society is not something that is kept together physically; it is held by the invisible bonds of common thought. If the bonds were too far relaxed the members would drift apart.'[19] This argument is another modern version of natural-law theory, and as such is vulnerable to the criticisms which have been mentioned above. The idea of 'invisible bonds of common thought' is not susceptible to any empirical or rational analysis of morality and law: *which* bonds of thought? *How* 'common' must they be? Exactly how would this 'drifting apart' take place? Some other implications of Lord Devlin's attitude (which is not uncommon among members of the judiciary) are discussed in chapter 14, but at this point we must ask some important questions about law, society and morality which are raised by natural-law philosophy in general, and by the views of writers such as Lord Devlin in particular.

The social definition of law and morality

To begin with, both 'classical' natural-law ideas, based upon religious doctrine, and modern variants (such as those of Finnis or Devlin) based upon more 'secularised' criteria, suffer from the fact that it is not possible to demonstrate empirically and scientifically the existence of such values. More than this, there is little agreement among natural-law scholars about the precise *content* of any absolute moral code. It was argued in chapter 1 that, contrary to the premises of natural-law philosophy, societies, especially modern industrialised societies, show far more divergence than convergence where moral values are concerned. To take the example of the controversy surrounding abortion: the attitudes towards this subject range from the strong

17 Lloyd's *Introduction to Jurisprudence*, op. cit., p 138.
18 Lord Devlin, *The Enforcement of Morals* (1959, Oxford University Press), p 4.   19 Ibid., p 10.

anti-abortion stance based on the view that all taking of life is wrong, through the 'medical stance', whose adherents argue that abortion is justified if the medical condition of the mother or the foetus warrants it, to the view taken by many feminists that abortion should be available 'on demand' – a view based on the idea of 'a woman's right to choose'. Can any of these be shown to be the 'right' view?

The Abortion Act 1967 provides that abortion may be lawful if it is certified by two medical practitioners that to continue the pregnancy would involve risk to the life of, or injury to, the pregnant woman or her existing children, and that that risk is greater than if the pregnancy were terminated; or that there is a substantial risk that if the child were born it would suffer serious physical or mental handicap. In considering the matter, it is permissible for the doctors to take into account the pregnant woman's 'actual or reasonably foreseeable environment' (the 'social clause'). It should be noted that this Act does not affect the provisions of the Infant Life (Preservation) Act 1929, which makes it a criminal offence to terminate a pregnancy when the child is 'capable of being born alive' (s 1(1)) – normally after 28 weeks or more of the pregnancy. In fact it has been held that abortions carried out before that time may be unlawful.[20]

Over the years, a number of attempts have been made by means of Private Members' Bills to amend the Act and to restrict the availability of abortions. So far these bills have not been successful. The most recent was a bill introduced in 1988 which sought to limit the period within which abortions could lawfully be carried out to 18 weeks. Opponents of this bill argued that this would mean that babies might be born with handicaps which could not be detected until after 18 weeks of pregnancy, and that the time-limit in the 1967 Act enabled pregnancies involving serious deficiencies or handicaps to be aborted. Supporters of the bill argued that the reduced time-limit would result in fewer abortions which they felt had been too easily available under the 1967 Act.

The current statutory provision in this controversial area is s 37 of the Human Fertilisation and Embryology Act 1990, which provides, among other things, that a pregnancy which has not gone beyond 24 weeks may be terminated if its continuance would involve risk, greater than if the pregnancy were terminated, of injury to the physical or mental health of the pregnant woman or any existing children of her family, but no time-limits are imposed in cases where termination may be necessary to prevent 'grave permanent injury to the physical or mental health' of the pregnant woman, or risk to her life, or 'if there is a substantial risk that if the child were born it would suffer from such physical or mental abnormalities as to be seriously handicapped'. Department of Health figures reveal that in the first year after the implementation of these provisions, the number of late (that is, after 24 weeks

20 See *Rance v Mid-Downs Health Authority* [1991] 1 QB 587. It was held in this case that, had an abortion been carried out on a 27-week-old foetus, it would have been unlawful, since the judge was satisfied on the evidence that the baby had been capable of being born alive, in that the child could breathe and exist independently of its mother, if only for a short time, at that date. See now s 37 of the Human Fertilisation and Embryology Act 1990.

or more of pregnancy) abortions rose considerably from around 22 to 60, although all these cases involved diagnosis of severe abnormalities such as spina bifida, genetic abnormality and renal and heart conditions.

Despite these legal developments,[21] many people still feel that the Abortion Act 1967 should be repealed altogether, and that *all* abortion should be unlawful;[22] others feel that the present law does not go far enough. The point is that none of these views can be justified by means of any *uncontested* moral principles. The anti-abortion lobby may introduce moral arguments based on religion, or the 'rights of the unborn', but the pro-choice lobby may produce equally strongly held arguments based on conceptions of women's rights, and the importance of recognising a woman's personal integrity and independence in treating her own body as she wishes. The debates over embryo experimentation,[23] surrogate motherhood and the sterilisation of the mentally handicapped, raise difficult and sensitive issues of law, morals, and medical and scientific ethics.

In 1986 the question as to whether contraception advice and facilities should be available to girls under 16 without parental consent was brought into public debate by the *Gillick* case,[24] where the plaintiff sought a declaration from the court that guidance from the Department of Health and Social Security to area health authorities, which contained advice as to the provision of advice on contraception to young people under the age of 16 without parental consent, was unlawful and wrong in that it undermined parental rights and duties. The House of Lords held that the guidelines concerned essentially medical matters, and that in such matters girls under 16 had the legal capacity to consent to medical examination and treatment, including contraceptive treatment, as long as they were sufficiently mature and intelligent to understand the nature and implications of the proposed treatment. Consent to the medical treatment of people aged between 16 and 18 may be given by the patients themselves: the Family Law Reform Act 1969 provides that such young people may give their consent 'as if they were of full age'.[25]

The controversial relationship between law and morality became the centre of debate once again in 2000, over the impossibly difficult case of the conjoined (or 'Siamese') twins – referred to as 'Jodie' and 'Mary' during the legal proceedings in

---

21 See, for a recent discussion, E. Lee, 'Tensions in the Regulation of Abortion in Britain' (2003) *Journal of Law and Society* vol. 30 no. 4.

22 The Pro-Life Alliance, for example, reiterated its commitment to repeal of the 1967 Act in its 'Manifesto' of 2001. In the same document the Alliance condemned, among other things, embryo experimentation, surrogate parenting and the decision in the *Conjoined Twins* case discussed below.

23 See the commentary on the Human Fertilisation and Embryology Act 1990 (Current Law Statutes Annotated, vol. 4, 1994). This Act created the Human Fertilisation and Embryology Authority, among whose functions are the monitoring of developments in the field of embryology and the provision of advice to the Secretary of State on such matters.

24 *Gillick v West Norfolk and Wisbech Area Health Authority and Department of Health and Social Security* [1986] AC 112.

25 For a full discussion of the difficulties which may arise in this area, see J. Fortin, *Children's Rights and the Developing Law* (1998, Butterworths), chapter 11.

order to protect the identity of the babies and their parents.[26] The situation, as described in summary by Ward LJ in the Court of Appeal, was as follows:

> In a nutshell the problem is this. Jodie and Mary are conjoined twins. They each have their own brain, heart, lungs and other vital organs and they each have arms and legs. They are joined at the lower abdomen. Whilst not underplaying the surgical complexities, they can be successfully separated. But the operation will kill the weaker twin, Mary. That is because her lungs and heart are too deficient to oxygenate and pump blood through her body. Had she been born a singleton, she would not have been viable and resuscitation would have been abandoned. She would have died shortly after her birth. She is alive only because a common artery enables her sister, who is stronger, to circulate life sustaining oxygenated blood for both of them. Separation would require the clamping and then the severing of that common artery. Within minutes of doing so Mary will die. Yet if the operation does not take place, both will die within three to six months, or perhaps a little longer, because Jodie's heart will eventually fail. The parents cannot bring themselves to consent to the operation. The twins are equal in their eyes and they cannot agree to kill one even to save the other. As devout Roman Catholics they sincerely believe that it is God's will that their children are afflicted as they are and they must be left in God's hands. The doctors are convinced they can carry out the operation so as to give Jodie a life which will be worthwhile. So the hospital sought a declaration that the operation may be lawfully carried out. [This] was granted on 25 August 2000. The parents applied to us for permission to appeal against [the] order.[27]

Many difficult issues arose in this case. Apart from the moral dilemma posed by the fact that the doctors' opinion in favour of surgical separation was fundamentally at odds with the wishes of the parents, there were problematic issues raised by principles of both family law and criminal law. It is a basic proposition deriving from family law, now enshrined in s 1(1) of the Children Act 1989 that 'the child's welfare shall be the court's paramount consideration'. Although surgical separation might well be in the best interests of Jodie, the stronger twin, how could the operation possibly be in the best interests of the weaker twin's welfare when it would certainly result in her death?

> That Mary's welfare is paramount is trite observation for family lawyers. Welfare dictates the outcome of the question relating to her upbringing which is before the court. It means no more and no less than that the court must decide what is best for her, taking all her interests and needs into account, weighing and then bringing into balance the advantages against disadvantages, the risks of harm against the hopes of benefit which flow from the course of action under consideration.[28]

Ward LJ recognised that as far as Mary's health interests were concerned, there were none to be gained by the operation, during which she would inevitably die; and furthermore, 'if one looks to the operation as a means of meeting any other needs,

26 *Re A (children) (conjoined twins: surgical separation)* [2000] 4 All ER 961. For critical discussions of this case, see esp. the articles in (2001) *Medical Law Review*, vol. 9 no. 3.
27 Ibid., at 969.   28 Ibid., at 997.

social, emotional, psychological or whatever, one again searches in vain. One cannot blind oneself to the fact that death for Mary is the certain consequence of the carrying out of this operation.'[29] Moreover – and here we raise criminal-law issues to which we return later – it was acknowledged on all sides that any intentional act whereby the death of a human being is caused is undoubtedly unlawful, and yet this was precisely the scenario under consideration. Morally, the judge felt compelled to accept that 'each life has inherent value in itself and the right to life, being universal, is equal for all of us[30]. . . I am satisfied that Mary's life, desperate as it is, still has its own ineliminable value and dignity.'[31] The judge's conclusion on this point was, therefore, that:

> the question is whether this proposed operation is in Mary's best interests. It cannot be. It will bring her life to an end before it has run its natural span. It denies her inherent right to life. There is no countervailing advantage for her at all. It is contrary to her best interests. Looking at her position in isolation and ignoring, therefore, the benefit to Jodie, the court should not sanction the operation on her.[32]

However, it was equally clear that the operation, which would – according to the medical evidence – give Jodie a good chance of living a reasonably normal life, was very much in Jodie's best interests, and obviously Jodie's welfare was just as 'paramount' as was that of her weaker twin sister: 'because it is the right to life of each child that is in issue, the conflict between the children could not be more acute . . . Given the conflict of duty, I can see no other way of dealing with it than by choosing the lesser of the two evils and so finding the least detrimental alternative. A balance has to be struck and I cannot flinch from undertaking that evaluation, horrendously difficult though it is.'[33]

Although the moral right to life of both twins was equal, the balance was unequal when it came to considering the worthwhileness of the proposed treatment. Taking into account the condition of each child, the advantages and disadvantages of the proposed operation for each, the quality of life which each child enjoyed and might enjoy in the future,

> the balance is heavily in Jodie's favour . . . Mary may have a right to live, but she has little right to be alive. She is alive because and only because, to put it bluntly, but none the less accurately, she sucks the lifeblood of Jodie and she sucks the lifeblood out of Jodie. She will survive only as long as Jodie survives. Jodie will not survive long because constitutionally she will not be able to cope . . . Into my scales of fairness and justice between the children goes the fact that nobody but the doctors can help Jodie. Mary is beyond help.[34]

But apart from these important considerations of 'best interests' and 'welfare', there remained the question – arising from criminal law rules and principles – as to whether the proposed operation would be lawful. The court considered carefully

29 Ibid., at 998.   30 Ibid., at 1000.   31 Ibid., at 1002.   32 Ibid., at 1004.
33 Ibid., at 1006.   34 Ibid., at 1009.

the law relating to homicide, and had little difficulty in concluding that, at first sight, the operation to separate the twins, which would inevitably result in Mary's death, would satisfy the requirements for liability in the law relating to intentional homicide: in other words, the surgeons might be guilty of murdering the weaker baby.[35] On the other hand, the law of homicide might be equally applicable if the surgeons were under a duty to save Jodie, and, by not carrying out the operation, failed to do so.

In confronting this dilemma, Ward LJ expressed, in several passages in his judgment, the view that the surgeons were under a 'duty to Jodie' to save her by means of the operation, though it is not easy to discern from where, in law, this duty arose. The dilemma – and hence the question as to the lawfulness of the proposed operation – was resolved by means of recognising a conflict of legal duties: the duty to respect Mary's right to life, and the duty to save Jodie. After some consideration (and rejection) of the proposition that the termination of human life by omitting to act is distinct from termination of life by some positive action,[36] and examination of the problematic place in criminal law of the doctrine of necessity, together with the judicial statements in previous cases that necessity could never justify the taking of one life in order to save another,[37] in this unique situation, according to Ward LJ,

> faced as they are with an apparently irreconcilable conflict, the doctors should be in no different position from that in which the court itself was placed in the performance of its duty to give paramount consideration to the welfare of each child. The doctors must be given the same freedom of choice as the court has given itself and the doctors must make that choice along the same lines as the court has done, giving the sanctity of life principle its place in the balancing exercise that has to be undertaken . . . For the same reasons that led to my concluding that consent should be given to operate so the conclusion has to be that the carrying out of the operation will be justified as the lesser evil and no unlawful act would be committed.[38]

It has been argued that the decision is open to serious criticism on a number of grounds. To begin with, had the twins not been conjoined, no court would have contemplated the removal of a healthy organ from one twin, causing the death of that twin, in order to transplant that organ into, and thus save the life of, the other twin. Is there a difference – morally and legally – between that situation and the case of Jodie and Mary? Second, it is difficult to reconcile the judge's reasoning with regard to the moral value of the sanctity of life – in which he recognised that each

---

35 See the judgments of Ward LJ and Brooke LJ. For more detailed discussion on some difficult aspects of this area of criminal law, see chapter 10.
36 Ibid., at 1015. See also *Airedale National Health Service Trust v Bland* [1993] 1 All ER 821, discussed in chapter 4.
37 Ibid., at 1013–1014; 1032–1050. See also the leading case of *R v Dudley and Stevens* (1884) 14 QBD 273, in which sailors, cast adrift in a small boat and facing death, killed and ate a young cabin-boy, and unsuccessfully pleaded necessity. For an excellent account of the case, its background and the legal issues discussed at the trial, see A. W. B. Simpson, *Cannibalism and the Common Law* (1986, Penguin Books).   38 Ibid., at 1016.

twin's right to life was equal – with the conclusion in the case that the operation would be lawful. The distinction between on the one hand the evaluation of the twins' lives, and on the other the evaluation, in terms of each twin's 'best interests', of the proposed operation, might be considered to be a false distinction: evaluating the 'best interests' with regard to proposed treatment might be thought in fact to be indistinguishable from an evaluation of their lives.

Third, it is not readily apparent from which legal source the judge derived the notion of the 'duty to save Jodie'. In the law of torts (see chapter 9) which governs civil liability in such cases, there is no legal duty to rescue a person in peril, regardless of any moral imperative which may exist; and generally speaking there is no duty to act positively for the benefit of another. In the case of medical practitioners, there is no doubt that doctors, surgeons and others are under a legal duty to take reasonable care to patients in respect of treatment which is already undertaken, and this would certainly include the post-natal treatment which both Jodie and Mary had been receiving in hospital. But it is surely a substantial step to move from that post-natal treatment to a highly invasive separation operation, especially one which will have the effect of causing the death of the other twin. Indeed, in a statement which might be thought difficult to square with the notion of a 'duty to save Jodie', Ward LJ suggested that 'it would . . . have been a perfectly acceptable response for the hospital to bow to the weight of the parental wish however fundamentally the medical team disagreed with it . . . there could not have been the slightest criticism [of the medical team] for letting nature take its course in accordance with the parents' wishes'.[39] Why would this not have been a breach of the 'legal duty to Jodie'? And if, moreover, the legal basis for that duty is indeed uncertain, what, then, were the *legal* reasons – regardless of the *moral* aspects of the case – why the court could not resolve the dilemma by acknowledging that the parents' wishes should be respected and allowing nature to take its course?

There can be few recent cases in which the affinities and the tensions between law and morality have been so dramatically presented. The moral issues surrounding the question of the intentional taking of human life, the relationship between the deliberations of the court and the position taken by the parents, the dilemma faced by the medical practitioners – all these factors and many more remind us that the substantive content of a moral code is rarely uncontentious and straightforward: the decision in the *Conjoined Twins* case has been strongly criticised.

But it is worth remembering that moral arguments in areas such as this – as well as those surrounding issues such as cloning, embryological research, and in-vitro fertilisation – follow inexorably from advances in scientific knowledge and techniques. Not too many years ago, the limitations of medical knowledge and surgical techniques might well have prevented such a tragic dilemma as the one discussed above facing the parents or confronting the court: it would seem that the more medical science progresses, the more controversial the issues of ethics and law become.

39 Ibid., at 987.

The examples discussed here illustrate graphically the basic point that, despite what Lord Devlin would like to believe, there is very little consensus in our society over particular moral issues, or over the extent to which law should be used to enforce moral principles other than the basic prohibitions on violence which are clearly necessary for any social group to survive.

The argument which is put forward here is that both law and morality, far from having their origins in mysterious revelations through religious visionaries or other mystical sources, are firmly rooted in social conditions and practices. Law and morality are human constructs, having their foundations in scriptures as written and interpreted at various times, in traditions or cultural patterns, or in the conditions of social life prevailing at different periods, which are informed and underpinned by historically specific economic and political formations. The diversity of moral values which we observe in discussions of law and morality is therefore to be seen as a reflection of the diversity of economic and political interests existing in a society at any given time. In matters in which the state intervenes to prohibit or control moral behaviour through law, we find, as we shall see, that such intervention is usually the outcome of the workings of an intricate complex of pressure-groups, political parties and other interested individuals and groups who possess the *power* to influence the creation of legal rules.

Rules, both moral and legal, arise as responses to social or political problems and crises. Even our most basic rules forbidding the taking of human life extend far back into early history, for such rules are clearly a fundamental prerequisite for the continued existence of any stable social group. Again, rules and values which uphold the family unit – whichever form it may take[40] – are found in most societies at most periods, because of the importance of ensuring reproduction and survival of the social group, as well as of the economic importance as a productive and consumer unit which the family has in a social structure.

Another example of the social origin of moral and legal values and rules is the position in Western societies of the social institution of *property*. Private property is so basic to our society that we readily condemn any infringement of our rights – legal and moral – to acquire, possess and enjoy our personal property. But in a society where property is held *communally*, such a value as the 'sanctity of private property' can have little or no meaning.[41] In such a social setting, any attempt by one individual in the group to treat property as his or her own 'private' possession would be regarded as an affront to the entire community. The value we place upon private property in our own society must therefore have its origins in the social and economic structure, at various periods in history, whereby the development of an economy dependent upon the acquisition, accumulation and transfer of property

---

40 We find considerable variation in the particular structure of the family unit in different societies at different periods; for example, the Israeli *kibbutz*, and polygamous forms of marriage giving rise to extensive and complex family structures.

41 And even in post-revolutionary Soviet Russia, contrary to popular Western beliefs, the Constitution provided for the private ownership of certain amounts and types of property.

from one private individual or group to another (that is, trade and commercial dealing) was taking place.

Thus, the development of the modern law of theft can be seen as a response to the growing needs of commercial interests, from about the fifteenth century onwards, which demanded adequate legal protection from unauthorised incursions upon property belonging to others.[42] Hay, writing about the criminal code of the eighteenth century, notes:

> As the decades passed, the maturing trade, commerce and industry of England spawned more laws to protect particular kinds of property. Perhaps the most dramatic change in the organisational structure of British capital was the growth of promissory notes on banks as a medium of exchange, and the increase in negotiable paper of all kinds. This new creation was exposed to fraud in many ways never foreseen by the ancient criminal law. The result was a rash of capital statutes against forgeries and frauds of all kinds, laws which multiplied towards the end of the century.[43]

And Hay notes also how the 'sanctification' of property was almost complete by the eighteenth century, citing Blackstone, a well-known legal writer of that time, who wrote that 'there is nothing which so generally strikes the imagination, and engages the affections of mankind, as the right of property'.[44]

Property, then, and the moral and legal codes which justify and protect it, must be seen as developments arising from economic bases; we shall see the connection between *landed* property and capitalism in chapter 5. In the above-mentioned context of the growth of movable and negotiable property in the period of developing capitalism, the 'rash of capital statutes' can be seen as a consequence of the needs of the propertied classes to protect their wealth against the frauds and other encroachments of the property-less. The elevation of property and wealth to one of the highest social and moral values belongs only in a society based on material gain; it certainly has little place in the more traditional and orthodox sources of our moral code: 'It is easier for a camel to go through the eye of a needle, than for a rich man to enter the kingdom of God' (Matthew 19:24).

These connections between law, morality and the social and economic structure are intricate and complex. The ideological function of the socially defined codes of law and morality is the underpinning of particular social structural processes, relations and institutions (law, state, capital, the social order and so on) by means of providing 'master definitions' of beliefs and ideas, inculcated through various socialisation processes (family, school, the mass media) and the legitimised sanctions of the law. Because of the divided and diverse nature of our society, however, it is inevitable that clashes will occur, at various levels and in various institutions, between the adherents of *differing* moral values and views. Returning to the earlier example of the abortion controversy, we have seen several such clashes between,

42 J. Hall, *Theft, Law and Society* (1952, Bobbs Merill).
43 D. Hay, 'Property, Authority and the Criminal Law' in D. Hay et al., *Albion's Fatal Tree* (1977, Peregrine), p 21.   44 Ibid.

specifically, those wishing to repeal the existing law and tho
that law to permit abortions in more, or even all, cases where
desires it. It would be easy to catalogue many other such
however, is not simply that such pluralities of moral value
stated already – but rather how we analyse and unders
complex moral stances on these and many more issues; th
giances and opposition to proposals for change; the ways in which ѕѡ...
other, interest-groups succeed in getting *their* definitions of morality accepted,
enacted and enforced through the legal process; and the ways in which moral viewpoints, state responses through law, and the wider processes and institutions of the
social structure are interrelated.

Morality and the law

'Social groups create deviance by making the rules whose infraction constitutes
deviance, and by applying those rules to particular people and labelling them as
outsiders.'[45] This well-known and often-cited statement by Becker highlights the
crux of our concern with law and morality. Given that rules are social constructs,
it is vital to appreciate the social context in which particular rules are created, especially when we are faced with situations where persons falling foul of such rules are
being processed through official machinery such as the legal system and courts of
law. At the same time, we must keep in mind the *reality* of moral codes. Moral codes
exist, for whatever reasons, and the object of discussion here is not the denial of this
fact: indeed, some have argued that the creation of deviance as such through the
making of rules fulfils an important social function. As Durkheim wrote, the social
condemnation of the deviant by other members of a community serves to maintain and reinforce the values against which the deviant has offended, and so plays
an important part in the maintenance of the social order. Moral and legal codes
mark the boundaries of the acceptable and the unacceptable. But given that conflicting moralities may surround a given social activity, we are concerned to
examine by what processes and with what consequences a particular moral attitude
may become embodied in law, to the exclusion of any other competing or clashing
moral stance.

It is instructive to examine such processes in the context of particular legislative activity, and in England perhaps the best examples of moral reformism
through legal change were the reforms of the 1960s. Thought by many critics to
symbolise the high-water mark of the 'permissive society', the 1960s saw a
number of Acts of Parliament whose effect was to relax, in many areas of social
life, the rigidity of what many regarded as an outmoded moral code, much of it
embodied within the law. Let us examine briefly some of the more striking
reforms of that period.

45 H. Becker, *Outsiders* (1963, Free Press of Glencoe), p 9.

mes without victims'

Schur[46] used the term 'crimes without victims' to refer to certain activities which were all, at the time of his writing, criminal offences. The examples he discussed were drug use, homosexuality and abortion. The common characteristics of these crimes, argued Schur, are that, first, they are activities which involve no harm to anyone except the participants; second, they occur through the willing participation of those involved, with the result that, third, there is no 'victim' of the crime to register complaints to the law enforcement agencies, and so (fourth) the law is very difficult to enforce. Schur argued that given the existence of a social demand for consensual (as between the participants) activities such as these – a demand, moreover, which continues to be met, despite prohibition, in the form of back-street abortions, clandestine drug supply and use, and so on – and in the absence of any demonstration that prohibition brings greater social benefit than decriminalisation, such prohibitions as existed should be abolished.

It is possible, of course, to take issue with Schur on a number of points. Is it true that drug-use and abortion only harm the participants, and no one else? What of the argument that some may be 'corrupted' into using illicit drugs? Or that the social cost of drug addiction (medical care, rehabilitation programmes) is such as to affect the community as a whole? What of young people, who may not appreciate the dangers of drug-use? And what difference to Schur's arguments is made by the fact that illicit intravenous drug-use carries the serious risk of HIV infection and potential full-blown AIDS?

And is there really no 'victim' of an abortion? What are we to make of the argument presented by anti-abortion organisations that abortion is equivalent to murder of the unborn human being? And how much force is there in the point that laws against 'victimless crimes' are difficult to enforce? Some other offences, notably burglary, involve extreme difficulty in enforcement and apprehension of offenders: few would argue that burglary should, therefore, cease to be an offence.

We shall return to some of these problems presently. For the moment, however, let us note that reforming legislation on two of these areas – homosexuality and abortion – was passed during the 1960s. In 1967, the Sexual Offences Act provided that homosexual acts between two consenting male adults[47] in private should no longer be criminal offences (there remains a number of offences concerning

---

46 E. Schur, *Crimes Without Victims* (1965, Prentice Hall). For a more extended debate on this issue, see also E. Schur and H. Bedau, *Victimless Crimes* (1974, Prentice Hall).

47 'Adult' in this context means 'person aged 16 or over' (Sexual Offences (Amendment) Act 2000). The 1967 Act, which had provided that male homosexual activity was legal only between men aged 21 or over, was amended by the Criminal Justice and Public Order Act 1994 with the effect that the age of consent was lowered to 18. There was considerable public and parliamentary debate over this issue: many – including a number of MPs as well as gay and lesbian activist groups – had argued strongly for the age of consent to be lowered to 16 (the same age as for heterosexual relations). The New Labour government which came to power in 1997 supported the reduction in the age of consent to 16, which was effected in the Act of 2000.

homosexuality, notably those prohibiting acts done in public, or when more than two are involved, or acts involving persons under the legal age of consent). In the same year, the Abortion Act 1967, discussed above, was passed as a Private Member's Bill (see chapter 7) introduced by David Steel MP.

It has been suggested that the starting point for the process of moral reformism during the 1960s was the *Report of the Committee on Homosexual Offences and Prostitution* (the Wolfenden Committee) in 1957. This report, and the philosophical/ ideological moral stance running through it, arguably 'articulate[d] the field of moral ideology and practice which defines the dominant tendency in the "legisla- tion of consent" '.[48] Two passages from the Wolfenden Report indicate the line of thought adopted by the Committee. Referring to prostitution and homosexuality, the report states:

> In this field [the function of the criminal law] as we see it, is to preserve public order and decency, to protect the citizen from what is offensive or injurious, and to provide sufficient safeguards against exploitation and corruption of others, particularly those who are specially vulnerable because they are young, weak in body or mind, inexperi- enced, or in a state of special physical, official or economic dependence. It is not, in our view, the function of the law to intervene in the private lives of citizens, or to seek to enforce any particular pattern of behaviour, further than is necessary to carry out the purposes we have outlined.[49]

The proper role of the law in preventing the public expression of private morality is stressed; in relation to prostitution, says the report, the law should confine itself to:

> Those activities which offend against public order and decency or expose the ordinary citizen to what is offensive and injurious; and the simple fact is that prostitutes do parade themselves more habitually and openly than their prospective customers, and do by their continual presence affront the sense of decency of the ordinary citizen. In doing so they create a nuisance which, in our view, the law is entitled to recognise and deal with.[50]

The Wolfenden recommendations on homosexuality were incorporated, ten years after the report, in the Sexual Offences Act 1967 noted above. On prostitution, the report felt that though prostitution itself should not be made a criminal offence, public manifestations of prostitution (street-walking and brothel-keeping) should remain criminal offences. Though much of the law relating to prostitution and related offences is contained in the pre-Wolfenden Sexual Offences Act 1956, the 'public nuisance' aspects were embodied in the Street Offences Act 1959, designed to 'clean up the streets' by prohibiting 'common prostitutes' from loitering or solic- iting in a street or public place for the purposes of prostitution.[51]

48 S. Hall, 'Reformism and the Legislation of Consent' in National Deviancy Conference (ed.), *Permissiveness and Control* (1980, Macmillan), p 9.
49 Cmnd 247 (1957, HMSO), para 13.   50 Ibid., para 257.
51 These provisions were extended by the Sexual Offences Act 1985. Another 'nuisance' aspect of prostitution was dealt with by s 46 of the Criminal Justice and Police Act 2001 which makes it an offence to place advertisements for prostitution in or in the vicinity of public telephone boxes.

The Wolfenden recommendations met with a considerable degree of opposition, of which the best known is perhaps the argument presented by Lord Devlin, writing extra-judicially in 1959 about the enforcement of morality through the law. Criticising the Wolfenden Report, Lord Devlin had this to say:

> Societies disintegrate from within more frequently than they are broken up by external pressures. There is disintegration when no common morality is observed and history shows that the loosening of moral bonds is often the first stage of disintegration, so that society is justified in taking the same steps to preserve its moral code as it does to preserve its government . . . the suppression of vice is as much the law's business as the suppression of subversive activities.[52]

Devlin's views were, in turn, responded to by Hart,[53] who relied heavily upon the writings of the nineteenth-century philosopher John Stuart Mill who, in his essay *On Liberty*, made his position on such issues perfectly clear: 'The only part of the conduct of anyone, for which he is amenable to society, is that which concerns others. In the part which merely concerns himself, his independence is, of right, absolute. Over himself, over his own body and mind, the individual is sovereign.'[54]

Lord Devlin's views, although out of step with Parliamentary reforms, might be thought of as fairly typical of those charged with the administration of the law – the police, and more especially the judges – who from time to time have found themselves confronted with behaviour which calls into question the enforcement of morality through law.[55] Such cases continue to appear before the courts from time to time despite the undoubted changes over the years in social attitudes towards various forms of sexual expression.

For example, the question as to whether the law should interfere in the private affairs of adults who consent to certain sexual practices was considered once again by the House of Lords in 1993 in the extraordinary case of *R v Brown and others*.[56] Although the facts of the case raise, albeit rather indirectly, issues which go further than that of sexual practices between consenting adults,[57] our discussion will concentrate on this aspect of the facts. The six appellants were convicted of a number of offences under the Offences Against the Person Act 1861. They had belonged to a group of homosexual men who had willingly participated in the commission of acts of sado-masochistic violence against each other involving the use of, among other things, heated wires, map-pins, stinging nettles, nails, sandpaper and safety-pins. The evidence showed that the various activities had been videotaped by the

---

52 Devlin, op. cit., pp 13–14.
53 H. L. A. Hart, *Law, Liberty and Morality* (1962, Oxford University Press).
54 J. S. Mill, *On Liberty* (Everyman edn., 1962, Fontana), p 135.
55 *Shaw v DPP* [1962] AC 220; *Knuller v DPP* [1973] AC 435.   56 [1993] 2 All ER 75.
57 One defendant had been charged and convicted of taking, and a second defendant of possessing, indecent photographs of children – a much more worrying matter than that of the private activities of consenting adults. These defendants had pleaded guilty to the various charges, and now appealed against their sentence, not their convictions.

participants, though not for any profit or gain; that the injuries inflicted were not permanent; that no medical attention had been sought; and that none of the 'victims' had complained to the police. It was clear that this was a group of individuals who had all consented to a series of bizarre sexual practices, carried out in private, over a substantial period of time.

The men were charged with the offences of assault occasioning actual bodily harm contrary to s 47 of the Offences Against the Person Act 1861, and unlawful wounding, contrary to s 20 of the same Act. The crux of the matter was whether the victims' consent to these activities negatived the charge of assault, given that assault may be defined as 'the unlawful touching of another without that other's consent'.[58] The court discussed several cases where the issue of consent had arisen, including *R v Donovan*[59] in 1934 in which the court stated that:

> 'bodily harm' has its ordinary meaning and includes any hurt or injury calculated to interfere with the health or comfort of the prosecutor. Such hurt or injury need not be permanent, but must, no doubt, be more than merely transient and trifling;[60]

and *A-G's Reference (No 6 of 1980)*[61] in which the Court of Appeal had stated that 'it is not in the public interest that people should try to cause or should cause each other bodily harm for no good reason'.[62]

Ultimately, however, the House of Lords recognised, as had Lord Lane in the Court of Appeal, that:

> [T]he question whether the defence of consent should be extended to the consequences of sado-masochistic encounters can only be decided by consideration of policy and public interest.[63]

In Lord Templeman's view,

> The violence of sado-masochistic encounters involves the indulgence of cruelty by sadists and the degradation of victims. Such violence is injurious to the participants and unpredictably dangerous. I am not prepared to invent a defence of consent for sado-masochistic encounters which breed and glorify cruelty . . .[64]

And his Lordship concluded that

> [S]ociety is entitled and bound to protect itself against a cult of violence. Pleasure derived from the infliction of pain is an evil thing. Cruelty is uncivilised. I would . . . dismiss the appeals of the appellants against conviction.[65]

The appeals were dismissed, by a majority. In one of the two dissenting judgments in the case, however, Lord Mustill reviewed the relevance or otherwise of consent in many other contexts in which varying degrees of harm might be caused by one

---

58 [1992] 2 All ER 552 at 558.   59 [1934] All ER Rep 207.
60 [1934] All ER Rep 207 at 212 per Swift J.   61 [1981] 2 All ER 1057.
62 [1981] 2 All ER 1057 at 1059 per Lord Lane.
63 [1993] 2 All ER 75 at 82 per Lord Templeman.   64 Ibid., at 83.   65 Ibid., at 84.

person to another, and concluded that the law recognises that there are a number of individual 'special situations' in which consent is recognised as a valid defence. After discussing the guidance which might be obtained from the European Convention on Human Rights, his Lordship argued that this was an area of private morality, into which the criminal law should not venture:

> I do not invite your Lordships' House to endorse [the appellants' conduct] as morally acceptable. Nor do I pronounce in favour of a libertarian doctrine specifically related to sexual matters. Nor in the least do I suggest that ethical pronouncements are meaningless, that there is no difference between right and wrong, that sadism is praiseworthy, or that new opinions on sexual morality are necessarily superior to the old, or anything else of the same kind. What I do say is that these are questions of private morality; that the standard by which they fall to be judged are not those of the criminal law; and that if these standards are to be upheld the individual must enforce them upon himself according to his own moral standards, or have them enforced against him by moral pressures exerted by whatever religious or other community to whose ethical ideals he responds . . . the state should interfere with the rights of an individual to live his or her life as he or she may choose no more than is necessary to ensure a proper balance between the special interests of the individual and the general interests of the individuals who together comprise the populace at large. Thus, whilst acknowledging that very many people, if asked whether the appellants' conduct was wrong, would reply 'Yes, repulsively wrong', I would . . . assert that this does not in itself mean that the prosecution of the appellants under ss 20 and 47 of the Offences Against the Person Act 1861 is well founded.[66]

It is questionable whether such a prosecution could take place today, in an era in which both hetero- and homosexual relationships can be openly sought through 'dating' websites on the internet or through the 'contacts' columns of any newspaper or magazine, and gay and lesbian relationships may, by virtue of the Civil Partnership Act 2004, be recognised in law. As Devlin acknowledged, the 'limits of tolerance' (or rather the boundaries of what comprises socially acceptable behaviour) change.

But from the point of view of our discussion as to whether, and in what circumstances, the law *should* intervene to control such sexual behaviour, the *Brown* case raises interesting questions. Bearing in mind that none of the injuries sustained by the 'victims' in *R v Brown* was serious or of a lasting nature, on what grounds should the law now *not* declare the 'sport' of boxing to be unlawful, especially when we take into account the recent cases where death has resulted from injuries sustained in the boxing ring, and the medical evidence that boxing, even if it may not usually result in fatal injury, can lead to serious and permanent physical damage? If consent cannot make lawful a fight in the street, why should it make any difference to a fight in the boxing-ring, which is, moreover, undertaken with a view to financial gain? And, as the Law Commission pointed out in its consultation

66 [1993] 2 All ER 75 at 115–116.

paper in 1994,[67] 'the intentional infliction of serious injury (is) not only something that is permitted within the rules, but in reality the essence of the sport'.[68]

Again, leaving aside any revulsion that the particular activities involved in *Brown* might cause us to feel, what implications does the decision have for other, perhaps less bizarre, consensual acts carried out in private in the course of sexual relationships? Counsel for one of the defendants in the case had asserted that 'a youth who gave a girlfriend a love bite would fit exactly'[69] into the definition of unlawful assault given by the judge at the original trial of the men, and that 'love bites caused longer lasting bruises than the cuts and bruises the men in the group had received'.[70] Presumably such an act would be 'for no good reason'?[71]

And what of the freedom of the individual? Although there are situations, easily imaginable, where the state, through the law, ought properly to put individual health or well-being or public safety before the untrammelled freedom of the individual, it is arguable that cases such as *Brown*, involving consensual if distasteful activity, are at least borderline. Article 8 of the European Convention on Human Rights[72] states that everyone has the right to respect for his private life, and that there should be no interference with the exercise of this right except where it is necessary in the interests of national security, public safety or the economic well-being of the country, for the prevention of disorder or crime, for the protection of health and morals, or for the protection of the rights of others. Does *Brown* fall within any of these exceptional cases, or was this prosecution an unjustifiable breach of Article 8?

Certainly, in *Dudgeon v United Kingdom*,[73] in 1981, the European Court of Human Rights held that the prohibition in Northern Ireland of homosexual acts between consenting males was a breach of Article 8, in response to which the law was changed. The court recognised that some degree of regulation of sexual activity – whether homosexual or heterosexual – through the criminal law was justified, but denied that any perceived social need to criminalise consensual homosexual activity in private outweighed the detrimental effects which prohibition had on the life of the individual. Could similar arguments not be made out in respect of situations like that in *Brown*? In 1995, the European Commission of Human Rights ruled that applications by three of the defendants in the *Brown* case, that their convictions were in breach of the European Convention's provisions on the right to privacy, were admissible before that court. The court's decision, however, delivered in February 1997, was that the United Kingdom government, through its laws, *did*

67 The Law Commission, *Consultation Paper No 134: Consent and Offences Against the Person* (HMSO, 1994).
68 Para 101.19, p 27. See also M. Gunn and D. Ormerod, 'The Legality of Boxing' (1995) 15 *Legal Studies* 2; and the judgment of Lord Mustill in *R v Brown*, op. cit., at 108–109.
69 Reported in the *Independent*, 5 February 1992.   70 Ibid.
71 To appreciate fully the complex and confused nature of this area of law, see especially the Law Commission's *Consultation Paper No 134*, op. cit., particularly Part 2.   72 See chapter 4.
73 (1981) 4 EHHR 149. See D. J. Harris, M. O'Boyle and C. Warbrick, *Law of the European Convention on Human Rights* (2nd edn., 2002, Butterworths).

University of Ulster LIBRARY

have the right to interfere in people's private lives in order to protect the morals and the health of the public. The applicants' claims were therefore unsuccessful.

Finally: who benefits from such prosecutions? Was the prosecution in *Brown* justified on grounds of public safety, health or morals? Who was being protected by means of this prosecution? Surely no one could seriously argue that the public might be tempted to indulge in gay sado-masochistic activities were the accused in *Brown* to go unpunished?

Censorship

Some of the cases considered above lead us to consider a rather different aspect of the relationship between law and morals. It is one thing for the law to withdraw from control over various activities done consensually in private; it is quite another when such activities are brought into the public view by means of the written word, photographs and films, and theatrical and television productions. Various organisations (such as Mediawatch UK – successor to the National Viewers and Listeners' Association) and individuals have sought support for their concern about what they feel is an overly 'permissive' society. One individual campaigner initiated the successful prosecution, for the little-used offence of blasphemous libel, of the editor of the newspaper *Gay News* in 1978, for the alleged blasphemous content of a poem published in the paper;[74] and was also responsible for starting proceedings (subsequently dropped) against the play *The Romans in Britain* in 1981, again invoking what many thought to be an inappropriate offence: that of procuring others (in this case, actors) to commit homosexual acts (though in this case, simulated). The view of such campaigners is that the existing law relating to obscenity and pornography is too weak, and is in need of strengthening.

Ranged against such positions, of course, are the arguments of writers, journalists, producers and many others who argue the case for less, not more, censorship on the grounds of freedom of expression and freedom on the part of citizens to choose whether to read books or view films or television for themselves. And another dimension to debates about pornography has come from the feminist movement, arguing against pornography not on the ground of 'excess permissiveness', but rather on the ground that pornography exploits, and thereby oppresses, women depicted within it, and women in general. The feminist criticism extends beyond the explicit portrayal of sex, and covers, for example, feature films on general release which show, and in the feminist view glorify, male violence against women.[75]

74 *R v Lemon* [1979] 1 All ER 898.
75 See, for example, A. Dworkin, *Pornography* (1981, Women's Press); C. McKinnon, *Feminism Unmodified* (1987, Harvard University Press) and *Only Words* (1994, Harper Collins); for articles containing useful discussions of these writers' arguments, see the *Guardian*, 6 December 1993 and 28 May 1994.

Blasphemous libel, the common law offence which was successfully charged against *Gay News* in 1978, reappeared in 1991 in an attempt to convict the writer Salman Rushdie, author of the book *The Satanic Verses*, and his publishers, of the offence. The furore triggered by the publication of this book, which Muslims in many countries regard as deeply offensive to the religion of Islam, reached its climax when Iran placed Rushdie under what was literally a sentence of death for having written and published the book. The author spent some years in hiding, and diplomatic relations between Britain and Iran remained somewhat difficult. Against this background, consider *R v Chief Metropolitan Stipendiary Magistrate, ex p Choudhury*[76] in which the applicant sought summonses against Rushdie and his publishers accusing them of blasphemous libel. The Queen's Bench Division of the High Court, after carefully reviewing the history of this offence, concluded that the common law offence of blasphemous libel was confined to protecting only the Christian religion; the court would not extend the law to cover other religions:

> The mere fact that the law is anomalous or even unjust does not, in our view, justify the court in changing it, if it is clear. If the law is uncertain, in interpreting and declaring the law the judges will do so in accordance with justice and to avoid anomaly or discrimination against certain classes of citizens; but taking that course is not open to us, even though we may think justice demands it, for the law is not, we think, uncertain.[77]

Furthermore, the court pointed out that, even had it been open to the court to extend the law, it would not have done so, since, among other problems, the boundaries would be too difficult to draw as to what might constitute a religion.[78] The court asserted that such a change in the law was properly a matter for Parliament. It is difficult not to be sympathetic to the court's stance in this matter, since religious affairs may be a matter of much deeply felt sensitivity to many people: but none the less it may be thought disturbing to note that the review of the history of the offence of blasphemous libel in the judgment of Watkins LJ reveals not only that this offence fails to protect the religion of the many British people of the Muslim faith, but also, apparently, any religion other than that of the established Church of England. The government introduced in the summer of 2005 a Bill which might go some way towards addressing what may be seen as an anomaly in the law: the Racial and Religious Hatred Act 2006 creates the offence of incitement to religious hatred, building on the existing criminal offence of incitement to racial hatred. The Act, which covers all religious groups, was strongly criticised on the basis that criticism of a religion or of religious beliefs, whether through humour or through serious commentary, would be criminalised, though government supporters argued that the legislation would outlaw incitement to religious hatred, and not criticisms or mere statements of disapproval of religions or beliefs.

76 [1991] 1 All ER 306.   77 [1991] 1 All ER 306 at 318.
78 See, for example, the debate as to whether Scientology should be recognised as a religious organisation: see G. Robertson, *Freedom, the Individual and the Law* (6th edn., 1991, Penguin), pp 383–386.

Turning to consideration in more detail of the law relating to obscenity and pornography, we find that the relevant statutes stem from 1959 to 1968. In 1959, the law relating to obscene publications, until then confusing and unsatisfactory to libertarians and would-be censors alike,[79] was reformed in the Obscene Publications Act. This Act was amended in 1964 by the Obscene Publications Act. In 1968, the Theatres Act ended the system whereby *any* play could be banned by the Lord Chamberlain, one of whose functions was to censor theatrical productions prior to their public performance. Theatrical productions, with the curious exception of strip-tease shows and the like, are now subject to the Obscene Publications Act 1959. Strip-shows are dealt with, where appropriate, by the common law offence of conspiracy to corrupt public morals.

The Obscene Publications Act 1959 recognised that there was a difference between sheer pornographic representation and works of art, literature or learning which may necessarily contain material which some people do not consider to their taste. Section 1 of the Act provides that an article is obscene if, *taken as a whole*, 'its effect is to tend to deprave and corrupt persons who are likely, having regard to all relevant circumstances, to read, see or hear the matter contained or embodied in it'. It is clear from this section that it is no longer possible for prosecuting counsel simply to select for the jury those portions of a work which might be deemed obscene; rather, such passages must be presented in the overall context of the entire work. Section 4 embodies the distinction referred to above. It provides that no offence under the Act is committed if 'it is proved that publication of the article in question is justified as being for the public good on the grounds that it is in the interests of science, literature, art or learning, or of other objects of general concern', and the section further provides that expert opinion as to the scientific, literary or other merit of the work is admissible in evidence. It is *not*, however, permissible to introduce expert evidence as to the issue of obscenity – that is for the 'ordinary men and women' of the jury to decide for themselves. The Obscene Publications (Amendment) Act 1964, which was introduced in the attempt to control what was regarded as a worrying increase in the importation of pornographic literature from other countries, created a new offence of being in possession of an obscene article for publication for gain – an offence which may be committed before there is any actual publication of the material.

What the 1959 and 1964 Acts failed to do, however, was to throw any light on the precise meaning of the word 'obscene'. They maintained the pre-existing definition – 'that which tends to deprave and corrupt' – without any further help for judges or juries as to what these words entail.[80] It is clear that 'obscene' refers to

---

79 See Robertson, ibid., chapter 5; and G. Robertson, *Obscenity* (1979, Weidenfeld and Nicolson), esp. chapter 3.

80 See Robertson, *Freedom, the Individual and the Law*, op. cit.; and Robertson, *Obscenity*, op. cit., where several examples of judicial attempts to clarify the meaning of the term, with varying degrees of success, are given. See also relevant chapters on the law of obscenity in standard texts on criminal law.

material of a higher degree of unacceptability than does the word 'indecent' (a term used in legal provisions relating, for example, to the sending of obscene *or* indecent matter through the post),[81] which has been held to mean material 'which an ordinary decent man or woman would find to be shocking, disgusting or revolting'.[82] The law relating to indecency, rather like that relating to street offences, discussed above, is concerned to prevent the 'nuisance aspect' of material which might otherwise come before an unwitting public gaze. The law relating to 'obscenity', on the other hand, would seem to refer to the need to control material of a much more positively dangerous nature – that which 'tends to deprave and corrupt'. The difficulty lies in explaining exactly what it is to be 'depraved and corrupted', how these states identify and manifest themselves, and how to assess the vulnerability of those who might come into contact with such material.

In practice, much material suspected by the police as being obscene, and kept in any premises for publication for gain, is dealt with by means of a procedure laid down in s 3 of the 1959 Act, whereby such material may be brought before any magistrate; if the magistrate decides that the material is obscene, and kept for publication for gain, then the material must be forfeited: the 'public good' defence is available, but the significance of this procedure is that the defendant is deprived of a jury trial: the decision as to whether or not the material is obscene is in the hands of magistrates. Not surprisingly perhaps, many have criticised this procedure for this very reason.

The Home Office Committee on Obscenity and Film Censorship, which reported in 1979,[83] realistically confronted these and many other problems, remarking laconically that the law was 'in a mess'. Their report proposed the abolition of all the existing law in this area, replacing it with a single statute in which prohibition would depend on the likelihood that the material in question would harm someone. Such harm would include the fact that children had been exploited for sexual purposes, or that physical violence appeared to have been perpetrated and recorded on film or photograph. Pornography would be available only in shops specialising in such material, where people under 18 would be denied access, and whose contents were made the subject of a warning notice. To date, no legislative activity has been directed towards reforming the obscenity laws themselves, though several recent statutes in this area should be noted. The first is the Indecent Displays (Control) Act 1981, which originated as a Private Member's Bill, and which prohibits the display of indecent material in public places. Second, local authorities may now, by virtue of the Local Government (Miscellaneous Provisions) Act 1982, require sex shops and cinemas to operate only with a licence from the local authority, and may refuse such a licence. An applicant who has been refused such a licence may, however, appeal against such a refusal to the magistrates' court.

Concerning videotapes, the Video Recordings Act 1984[84] (once again, a measure which began as a Private Member's Bill) introduced a system of censorship covering

---

81 Post Office Act 1953, s 11.   82 *Knuller v DPP* [1973] AC 435 per Lord Reid at 458.

83 Departmental Committee on Obscenity and Film Censorship, Report (1979, Cmnd 7772, HMSO).

84 Now amended by the Criminal Justice and Public Order Act 1994, Pt VII.

videotapes (and now DVDs). Ostensibly designed to control and curb the supply to the public of videotaped films portraying explicit sex and violence, the Act requires *all* videotaped films and other programmes to be 'classified' (that is, censored) before being supplied to the public in shops or video libraries. Certain types of programme are exempted from the Act (works designed to provide information, education or instruction, or concerned with sport, religion or music) although even these exempted materials must be submitted for classification if 'to any extent' they portray any of the prohibited acts or images, which include human sexual activity, mutilation, torture or acts of force or restraint associated with sexual activity. The censoring authority has the responsibility of classifying videotapes as suitable (or not) for home viewing, and if the authority considers the material unsuitable for viewing, no classification certificate will be granted. In such cases, the video will be prohibited from supply, or may be limited for supply by licensed sex shops only. Any person supplying or offering to supply an unclassified videotape to the public (and not fulfilling the sex-shop condition, if it applies) may be fined up to £10,000. Critics of this wide-ranging Act argued that the provisions would not only apply to the 'video nasties' which the Act ostensibly controls, but also 'news contained on videos of war . . . videos of childbirth . . . videos dealing with serious subjects . . . would similarly be open to censorship . . . [and] even films that have been shown already in cinemas or on television must be resubmitted for classification and possible censorship before they may be distributed in video form'.[85]

It seems certain that the controversies over obscenity and censorship will continue, with fears of corruption and decline of moral standards expressed by one lobby being met with equal and opposite indignation from the other, claiming the paramount freedom of the individual, both of expression and of choice in what and what not to read, see or hear. The type of concerns expressed in cases such as the *Gay News* case in 1978 and the *Romans in Britain* case in 1981 found recent expression in the (unsuccessful) attempt by a religious group to take legal action in the High Court against the BBC in 2005 over the television broadcast of the musical play *Jerry Springer: The Opera*.[86] Majority views may change dramatically over time – it would have been unthinkable for such a production to have been broadcast during the 1970s, or even, in the 1960s, to have been presented on a theatrical stage – but this recent attempt at legal action (and indeed the 47,000 complaints received by the BBC prior to the broadcast)[87] remind us once again that we do not live in a society characterised by consensus on moral values.

As regards the portrayal of violence on television or in films and videotapes, does exposure to such material in some way lead to violent behaviour on the part of certain individuals? Extensive research carried out over the years has failed to establish any such causative link, but the suspicion remains firm in many people's minds that such a connection must exist. Clearly, if such a link *were* to be established, the issue could no longer be expressed solely through arguments about

---

85 (1984) *NLJ*, 16 March, pp 245–246.   86 The *Guardian*, 16 June 2005.   87 Ibid.

individual freedom; clearly, there are aspects of the debate about pornography which go well beyond the issue of personal freedom. There would seem to be little doubt, for example, that strenuous efforts should continue to be made to prevent the availability of child-pornography: recent developments in this area include s 84 of the Criminal Justice and Public Order Act 1994, which extended the existing prohibition on the possession and distribution of such photographic material to 'pseudo-photographs' – images created (usually by means of computer graphics) which appear to be photographs.

As hinted in the last paragraph, the availability of unacceptable material is, moreover, no longer confined to the printed word, photographs, films, mainstream television or videotape. New technological developments are causing severe problems for control organisations such as the police and customs and excise. The development of digital images stored on electronic storage media and accessible by means of a computer, together with the possibility of sending and obtaining pornographic images to and from anywhere in the world by computer through the Internet, has caused worries about the widespread availability of this technology, and the inherent difficulty of policing it. The Crown Prosecution Service reported in 1994 that of the 976 obscenity cases dealt with between 1991 and 1993, only 11 cases concerned computer pornography; in 1992–93, customs and excise seized a total of 44,767 indecent and obscene materials, of which only 144, or 0.3%, were computer items.[88] However, in a written answer to a parliamentary question in 1998 concerning prosecutions for offences relating to photographic and computer material comprising child-pornography, the Home Office provided figures indicating that prosecutions for such offences had risen from 90 in 1994 to over 200 in 1996.[89] And the number of people cautioned or charged for internet-linked child pornography offences quadrupled between 2001 and 2003, to 2,234 cases.[90] Clearly, many more police resources – both nationally and internationally – have been invested in the fight to track down and prosecute offenders for these offences in particular; but it remains impossible to ascertain the amount of pornographic material being accessed through the Internet – something which, police acknowledge, it is at present almost impossible to control. Satellite television, too, has brought similar problems. In 1993 and again in 1995, 'erotic' television channels, beamed via satellite from other European countries, were banned in the United Kingdom, though, again, existing policing arrangements may not be adequate to prevent reception of these broadcasts, especially if, as has been reported in the press, the 'smart cards' necessary for decoding the broadcast signals become available on the black market.[91]

From time to time, controversy over censorship moves into the realm of *political* censorship. Examples in recent years include the injunctions obtained by the government in 1987 to prevent the broadcast of a series of television programmes

---

88 The *Guardian*, 23 June 1994.   89 *Hansard*, 15 July 1998.
90 Recorded Crime Statistics, 2003.   91 See the *Guardian*, 13 March 2002.

called *The Secret Society*, and a three-part radio series, *My Country: Right or Wrong*, which examined the role of the security services. In 1988, the broadcasting authorities were ordered by the Home Secretary not to broadcast anything spoken by any representative of Sinn Fein, Republican Sinn Fein and the Ulster Defence Organisation, despite the fact that none of these organisations are illegal bodies. An action challenging the validity of this directive[92] was unsuccessful, the Court of Appeal being of the opinion that it was not open to the court to intervene in the Home Secretary's decision: the court's view was confirmed in the House of Lords in 1991.

In 1986, when *Spycatcher*, the memoirs of an ex-security services official, was pending publication in Australia, the British government attempted unsuccessfully to prevent its publication in that country by legal action. That failure, and the book's subsequent appearance, did not prevent the government from taking legal action in other countries to prevent its publication in those countries, nor from taking steps to persuade the British courts to prevent British newspapers from publishing extracts from the book. The House of Lords, to the astonishment of many observers, the sharp criticism of ex-judges such as Lord Scarman and Lord Devlin, and the distaste of dissenting judges in the case, upheld the government's attempt to suppress publication of these extracts on the ground that the importance of state security outweighed that of the freedom of the press – despite the fact that the book could readily be imported into Britain and its contents perused by any individual choosing to track it down.

Although more recently there have been signs that what some critics have referred to as an almost obsessive concern with state security[93] has softened somewhat (with the publication, for example, of the memoirs of Stella Rimington, ex-head of MI5), it is clear from the David Shayler case that the state's determination to prevent the publication of material it considers 'sensitive' remains as strong as ever. Shayler had been a member of MI5 between 1991 and 1996, and had resigned after becoming disillusioned with what he felt was incompetence within the service. He disclosed information to a Sunday newspaper about a number of matters relating to MI5 activity (in particular, that MI5 was incompetent, and that the agency kept files on Labour ministers including Jack Straw and Peter Mandelson), and in 1997 various articles duly appeared in the press. After a failed attempt by the British authorities to have Shayler extradited from France where he was living in 1998, Shayler returned to Britain in 2000, and was arrested and charged with offences under s 1 of the Official Secrets Act 1989 (disclosing information without lawful authority). In May 2001, in a pre-trial hearing in the High Court, Shayler argued that there was available to him a defence that the disclosures (which he admitted) were made in the public interest – specifically, to expose serious illegality by the security services and to avert threats to life or limb or serious damage to property.

---

92 *R v Secretary of State for the Home Department, ex p Brind* [1991] 1 AC 696.
93 See N. Whitty, T. Muphy and S. Livingstone, *Civil Liberties Law: The Human Rights Act Era* (2001, Butterworths), chapter 7.

Shayler also argued that if such a defence was ruled out, then this would be incompatible with the 'freedom of expression' provisions in the Human Rights Act 1998.[94] It was held, however, that the Official Secrets Act 1989 itself contained provision, in effect, as to 'proper channels' through which concerns such as those felt by Shayler could be dealt with, and that there was ample justification for preventing disclosure to anyone else without lawful authority. The 'public interest' defence was therefore not available to these charges. Furthermore, it was held that the interests of national security was sufficient to render the 1989 Act compatible with Article 10 of the European Convention on Human Rights (dealing with freedom of expression and permissible restrictions on such freedom), and hence with the Human Rights Act 1998.

On appeal, the Court of Appeal considered that, in principle, the defence of necessity *was* available for charges under the Official Secrets Act 1989, but only in situations where the defendant's act was carried out to avoid an imminent danger to life or serious injury: even then, however, the defendant's act must be no more than was reasonable to prevent the harm. In this case, there were no such circumstances, and the defence could not therefore apply. As to the argument about freedom of expression, the court held that the prohibitions in the Official Secrets Act 1989 had to be balanced against the fact that the Act was designed to protect national security; in the circumstances (and taking into account the point made by the High Court concerning the provision within the Act for 'proper channel' reporting), the Court considered that the restriction on freedom of expression was justified.

In March 2002, it was confirmed by the House of Lords, after considering Shayler's appeal to that court, that the relevant sections of the Official Secrets Act 1989 afforded no possibility of a 'public interest' defence: this was made clear by the wording of the sections themselves, and was also clear from the wording of the 1988 White Paper[95] which preceded the Act. It was clear, in the court's view, that the Act indeed restricted freedom of expression, but that these restrictions did not amount to an absolute ban: the 1989 Act allowed disclosure of information as long as lawful authority had been obtained for the disclosure, and these provisions were consistent with the requirements of the Article 10 of the European Convention. The appeal was dismissed.

What David Shayler had done was, in essence, to 'whistleblow' the deficiencies, as he saw them, of MI5. It is interesting to note that the Public Interest Disclosure Act 1998 was passed in the attempt to provide legal protection for 'whistleblowers' – that is, employees of organisations who become aware of wrongful or untoward activity on the part of those organisations and who reveal those malpractices in the attempt to ensure that the organisation is accountable for their actions. It has been argued that in many reported cases of whistleblowing by employees, the consequences have been largely negative – ostracism by colleagues, veiled threats by the

94 See chapter 4.   95 See chapter 7.

employer, difficulty in obtaining other employment and problems of physical and mental health.[96] Whatever the intentions of the whistleblower – greater accountability and transparency, personal revenge, attempting to impose higher standards on the employing organisation, or whatever – it appears that when it comes to alleged incompetence or malpractice by agencies concerned with state security, 'the security services can take comfort from the fact that they are immune from whistleblowing'.[97]

The legislation of morality

Above, we looked at the issues of 'victimless crimes' and censorship in the light of law reforms occurring during one period of 'reformism', the 1960s. During that period, however, various other reforms in areas pertaining to law and morality were enacted. Capital punishment was suspended in 1965, and abolished altogether in 1969;[98] the law relating to young offenders was changed in 1969 in the attempt, among other things, to 'decriminalise' juvenile court proceedings in such cases and thus try to reduce what many felt was the harmful stigmatising effect upon a juvenile of appearing before a criminal court.[99] In 1969, too, the Divorce Reform Act was passed, which, when implemented in 1971, led to the easier availability of divorce following marital breakdown. In other related fields, however, despite attempts by pressure-groups to change the law, proposals for reform on moral issues failed – examples are proposals to permit euthanasia[100] and proposals to relax the penalties for certain offences connected with cannabis use, the latter being noteworthy for their embodiment in an official report of a committee chaired by Lady Wootton.[101]

On all these issues, there was considerable public debate during the 1960s. Regarding capital punishment, the debates generally comprised abolitionist arguments questioning the morality of 'a life for a life', and denying the effectiveness of the death penalty as a deterrent, backing up the latter arguments with evidence and experiences from other countries. Those wishing to retain the death penalty were 'disposed to rely more on psychological arguments (based presumably on introspection) as to how a criminal would be likely to react to abolition'.[102] The debates as to the effectiveness and appropriateness of the juvenile court system, during a period in which juvenile crime was seen by many as an increasingly serious social

---

96 J. Gobert and M. Punch, 'Whistleblowers, the Public Interest, and the Public Interest Disclosure Act 1998' (2000) 63 *MLR*.

97 David Shayler, after the High Court decision (as reported in the *Guardian*, 17 May 2001).

98 The Murder (Abolition of Death Penalty) Act 1965 was extended indefinitely by parliamentary resolution in December 1969.

99 Children and Young Persons Act 1969. See also the White Paper which preceded this Act, *Children in Trouble* (1968, Cmnd 3601, HMSO), for a full statement of the philosophies underlying the Act.   100 See R. Leng, 'Mercy Killing and the CLRC' (1982) *NLJ*, 28 January.

101 *Report of the Advisory Committee on Drug Dependence* (Wootton Report) (1968, HMSO).

102 B. Wootton, *Crime and Penal Policy* (1978, Allen and Unwin), p 144.

problem, drew on a number of crucial matters, including the problem of stigmatising juveniles and branding them as 'criminals'; the question as to whether juveniles are best dealt with by punishment or treatment, given that in many cases young offenders come from similar home backgrounds of deprivation and inadequacy as do children who commit no offences, but who are taken into local authority care by reason of neglect, deprivation or parental cruelty; and whether a court of law having criminal jurisdiction is the best forum for dealing with juvenile offenders.[103] The culmination of a decade of public debate on these matters was the Children and Young Persons Act 1969.

With regard to marriage and divorce, the factors informing the controversies over proposed divorce law reform were many and varied. The very nature of the basic social institution of the family was thought by many to be endangered by such trends as increasing numbers of illegitimate births and of one-parent families, and the growing numbers of women who, especially since 1945, choose to earn an independent income through paid employment, usually as well as fulfilling the 'traditional' woman's role of wife, housekeeper and mother.[104] More specifically, reformists based their arguments upon the proposition that the existing law relating to divorce was out of step with social trends and changed attitudes towards divorce, and that the number of marriages ending in divorce under the old law did not reflect the actual number of marriages which had broken down.[105]

Such observations and events lead us to ask a number of difficult questions about reformism, and about the relationship between legislation and morality. To what extent did the legislative changes in the 1960s *reflect* general social attitudes (if such can be measured), as opposed to *generating* changes in attitude? Were the reforms the outcome of diffuse social pressures, or were they the result of proposals by specific organisations and groups, possessing different degrees of political influence? To what extent do the mass media, especially the less responsible daily newspapers but also the reporting practices of the 'respectable' press, play a part in *creating* public attitudes and *generating* public reactions towards these issues? Can it be said that any perceptible shift towards a more rigid moral code constitutes a reaction against the 'permissiveness' of the 1960s and, as claimed by some critics mentioned above, the consequent 'decline in standards' of morality in Britain? How do we explain the success of some reform campaigns, and the failure of others? On a somewhat different level, we might ask how appropriate are *legal* controls in areas of morality; and is it possible to 'legislate morality'?

103 See A. Morris, H. Giller et al., *Justice for Children* (1980, Macmillan); D. Thorpe et al., *Out of Care* (1980, Allen and Unwin).

104 For an excellent discussion on these issues, see A. Morris and S. Nott, *Working Women and the Law: Equality and Discrimination in Theory and Practice* (1991, Routledge and Kegan Paul); M. Barrett and M. McIntosh, *The Anti-Social Family* (1983, Verso).

105 See Law Commission, *Reform of the Grounds of Divorce: The Field of Choice* (1967, Cmnd 3123, HMSO); Church of England, *Putting Asunder: A Divorce Law for Contemporary Society* (1966, Church of England).

With regard to the influence of individual campaigning pressure-groups, the intricate relationship between these and the eventual creation or repeal of legal rules has been studied in detail by Pym.[106] Such groups were actively campaigning (particularly during the 1950s and 1960s) for changes in the law relating to abortion, divorce, homosexuality, capital punishment and euthanasia, and worked to acquire public support for their causes together with parliamentary support which would result in new legislation. Pym found that analysing the intricacies of the various relationships between the campaigning bodies, parliamentary and other institutions, and the eventual outcome of the campaigns was extremely complex: 'Intuitively, we would recognise as a successful group, one which emerges from nowhere, produces a Bill, persuades everyone to vote for it and generally carries through the whole campaign. This vision of "Do-it-Yourself democracy" is far from reality.'[107] Pym found that the groups themselves played a relatively minor role in the production of each bill that came before Parliament on these various issues; the precise content of each bill was determined far more by behind-the-scenes discussion and compromise between parliamentary draftsmen, political figures (such as the Lord Chancellor) and official bodies (such as the Church of England and the Law Reform Commission) than by active and influential participation by the members of the pressure-groups under examination.

Apart from Pym's work, there have been many studies of the origins of legislation in the field of morality, and of the activities of what have been called 'moral crusaders', where the protagonists of legal and moral reform:

> typically want those beneath them to achieve a better status. That those beneath them do not always like the means proposed for their salvation is another matter. But this fact – that moral crusades are typically dominated by those in the upper levels of the social structure – means that they add to the power they derive from the legitimacy of their moral position, the power they derive from their superior position in society.[108]

Thus, one study discusses the creation of the laws outlawing alcohol in the United States ('Prohibition') in the 1920s.[109] This study of Prohibition illustrates some of the points raised earlier: that consensus about the 'wrongness' of a given activity often does not exist, and that support for particular causes from influential political and legal institutions must often be fought for through publicity campaigns and intensive lobbying. The acknowledged failure of the American Prohibition laws, and the fact that a large number of American citizens managed to obtain unlawful liquor during the Prohibition era, illustrate the former point, whilst the latter proposition is illustrated by the existence of the different kinds of groups who argued in favour of Prohibition. We see that it is not always only the centrally committed members of pressure-groups who campaign for change, for the Prohibition campaign was supported not only by temperance and religious groups, and others

---

106 B. Pym, 'The Making of a Successful Pressure Group' (1973) *British Journal of Sociology* 4.
107 Ibid., p 451.   108 Becker, op. cit., p 149.
109 J. Gusfield, *Symbolic Crusade* (1963, University of Illinois Press).

concerned with what has been termed the 'legislation of morality',[110] but also by industrialists and employers, who favoured the movement in the belief that sober workers would be more manageable and productive.

The diversity of groups and individuals prepared to campaign for legal change is shown also by studies which have pointed out that, once *some* legal regulation exists in a given area, it can occur that the agencies entrusted with enforcing that legal regulation can themselves engage in subsequent campaigns as supporters of *further* legal intervention. Thus, Becker's study of the Marijuana Tax Act in 1937 in the United States reveals how the Bureau of Narcotics was instrumental in extending its control over drug-use;[111] Paulus's account of the development of laws controlling the purity of food and drugs[112] includes the point that the inspectors and analysts involved in the enforcement of existing laws constituted substantial opposition to later attempts by manufacturers to avoid the law; and Gunningham makes a similar point with regard to the development of anti-pollution legislation[113] – that once created, the bureaucratic agencies of control comprise in themselves an interest-group who attempt to *increase* that control.

Several other aspects of the 'legislation of morality' emerge from the considerable number of studies of drug-use – one of the 'victimless crimes' which, despite pressure-group and other efforts, has consistently failed to attract relaxation of legal controls in Britain.[114] One writer has explained that this area is significant because 'more than any other form of deviance, the history of drug-use contains an abundance of material on both questions of legislation and morality, and of the relationship between them'.[115] Duster traces the history of drug-use and its legal control in the United States around the turn of the last century. In 1900, most drug-addicts in the United States were from the middle and upper classes, who had become addicted to morphine through the use of lawful 'patent medicines', many of which contained this drug. The shift in the pattern of the social status of the addict came to the fore when the Harrison Act of 1914, prohibiting 'dangerous drugs', opened up the way for the black market, operating from the 'criminal underworld'. It tended to be the lower classes who had the most contact, relatively speaking, with the underworld, and this meant that drug-addiction came rapidly to carry the same moral stigma as crime, which had certainly not been the case prior to the legislation when addiction carried little or no moral stigma. Thenceforward, the equation of drug-addiction with criminality, explicit in the 1914 Act, came to dominate thinking in this field. It is not, therefore, surprising that by the 1960s, when prohibited non-addictive drugs (notably cannabis) were becoming increasingly used, in the main by young people, this development easily

110 T. Duster, *The Legislation of Morality* (1970, Free Press, New York).
111 Becker, op. cit., pp 135–146.
112 I. Paulus, *The Search for Pure Food: A Sociology of Legislation in Britain* (1974, Martin Robertson).
113 N. Gunningham, *Pollution, Social Interest and the Law* (1974, Martin Robertson).
114 Some other European countries, and some American states, have, however, relaxed somewhat the laws concerning possession of small amounts of cannabis.   115 Duster, op. cit., p 6.

inherited the moral stigma which had, arguably, been at least partly created by the introduction of legal controls 50 years earlier.

Addressing the British situation regarding the control of drug-use, Young[116] has pointed out that much depends on the standpoint of the observer: from the point of view of those who believe in a 'moral consensus' view of society, the drug-taker operates outside that moral consensus, and is therefore 'maladjusted' and 'sick'. To those who consider that 'one can only judge the normality or deviancy of a particular item of behaviour *relatively* against the standards of the particular group you choose as your moral yard-stick',[117] however, 'Drugtaking . . . is not necessarily deviant nor essentially a social problem; it is deviant to groups who condemn it and a problem to those who wish to eliminate it.'[118]

According to Young, it is the former view which dominates everyday definitions of the nature of drug-taking, represented by politicians, medical practitioners and, in particular, the media and the police. It is this clash of values, epitomised in encounters with the police but generally dominating the attitude towards drug-users held by many others in society, which enhances the strong *moral* connotations of the issue. In other words, it is not simply the condemnation of drug-use because it is *medically* harmful; the issue is infused with value-judgments about drug-use so that the user is seen as socially, or morally, 'sick'.

Acknowledging the fact that certain aspects of these studies (such as the role of the official agencies of enforcement) may be applicable *generally* in any discussion of the legislation of morality, certain questions remain about the wider social and political contexts in which state intervention through law takes place. To restate some of our earlier problems: how do we explain the general shifts in social climate between periods of liberalism, toleration and reform, and periods of rigid moral codes and authoritarianism? Does the legal control of morality *reflect* or *generate* changes in attitude within the various communities in society?

Hall, in an interesting analysis of periods of reform,[119] points out that during the two 'reformist' periods under discussion (1957–61 and 1965–68) the emergence of reforms in the law cannot be explained by any party-political commitment, as 'the reformist impulse . . . cut across formal party alignments';[120] neither can they be explained by the existence of any general social agitation around the relevant issues, for although there were, as we have seen, a number of active pressure-groups at work, these groups were not the outcome of any manifestation of popular concern, and therefore 'cannot explain why these issues became socially pertinent in the first place'.[121] On the other hand, Hall finds that the influence of religious bodies cannot be discounted, for religious sentiments, or echoes thereof, can be seen in many of the campaigns of the periods, and indeed may be discerned in various aspects of the reformist legislation which emerged. More perplexing, perhaps, is the fact that,

116 J. Young, *The Drugtakers: The Social Meaning of Drug Use* (1971, Paladin).
117 Ibid., p 50.   118 Ibid., p 51.
119 'Reformism and the Legislation of Consent', op. cit. See also, in the same volume, V. Greenwood and J. Young, 'Ghettos of Freedom'.   120 Hall, op. cit., p 3.   121 Ibid., p 4.

according to Hall, the period which saw the publication of the Wolfenden report, discussed above, also saw widespread public 'moral panic' about the supposed increasing extent of such 'problems' as prostitution and homosexuality, which, of course, makes subsequent relaxation of legal controls even more difficult to explain.

Noting that each of the particular areas of reform arose from different causes and origins, Hall perceives a unifying thread which permeates the major legal reforms in the field of morality during the period we have been discussing. This unity, apparently at odds with the more usual ideas of the 'permissive sixties', is constituted by the tendency, in all the legislative reforms affecting prostitution, homosexuality, abortion, divorce, and others, to *strengthen* state control whilst *at the same time* placing certain aspects of the 'problem' outside legal controls. Thus, prostitution itself remained lawful, being a matter left to 'private morality', but at the same time Wolfenden recommended increases in legal penalties for public manifestations of prostitution, street-walking and living on the earnings of prostitution. Homosexuality between adults in private was rendered legal, but again, penalties for soliciting and male importuning were increased. The changed law on divorce nevertheless 'did not shift an inch from the orthodox defence of the institutional basis of marriage and the regulation of sexuality by marriage'.[122] And Hall maintains that the 'social clause' in the Abortion Act 1967 allowed personal criteria to be used in some cases whilst the general tenor of the Act was to *tighten up* the availability of abortion by laying down strict medical criteria and placing it in the hands of the medical profession. Thus, Hall argues,

> in each domain there is an increased regulation by the state, a greater intervention in the field of moral conduct – sometimes making more refined distinctions, and often taking a more punitive and repressive form than previously existing mechanisms of regulation and control. At the same time, other areas of conduct are exempted from legal regulation – and, so to speak, from the gaze of public morality, the yardstick of respectable, 'right-thinking' man – and shifted to a different domain, to be regulated by a different modality of control: that of freely contracting private individuals. This is the core of the tendency: increased regulation coupled with selective privatisation through contract or consent . . .[123]

What part did the main political parties play in the reformist era? Hall doubts that Labour was the 'party of moral reform', or that the Conservative Party was necessarily against such reform. Rather, he argues, the period of moral reform was characterised by divisions *within* each of the two major parties. In the Conservative Party, the division was between the older, traditional social and political values, and a newer, more adaptive wing, which, in a period in which inflation and other economic forces were threatening the status of the middle classes, recognised the need for a progressive reformist outlook. Within the Labour Party, the reformist current

122 Ibid., p 16.   123 Ibid., pp 17–18.

also broke away from the traditional party outlook and, according to Hall, took its cue from the view that the basic economic problems of post-war capitalism had been essentially solved: 'its aim was nothing short of bringing into line and formalising social, moral and ethical trends already set in motion by the reformation of classical capitalism. And the motive and mechanism of this reformism was to "deregulate" moral conduct, to "liberate" it from the compulsions of legal and state regulation . . .'[124] And, in turn, the presence of countervailing forces within the major parties facilitated a reaction against moral reformism and 'permissiveness' when, by the 1970s, the economic crises – manifested in rising inflation, problems of industrial relations and other factors, indicated that the economic and moral 'boom' of the 1960s was over. Thus, says Hall, 'If . . . the emergent state capitalism of the "boom" period seemed to find a sort of expression in a more fluid and "liberalised" personal and moral regime, this same capitalism, under conditions of world recession, seemed to require a return to moral and ideological orthodoxy and authority.'[125] Arguably, it is this same 'moral orthodoxy and authority' which, on one view, characterised the Conservative government elected in 1979, which encouraged the 'traditional' moral virtues of discipline, work and respect for established institutions (law and order, the family), and which thus may represent a continuing reaction against liberalism and moral reformism which marked the 1960s.

Hall's account, drawing upon the analytical tools of Marxism (the centrality of economic forces, the changing nature of the social class structure and so on), is of course only one of a number of possible explanations for the shifts in moral climate in Britain, frequently accompanied, as we have seen, by changes in the law. But our discussion of Hall's study serves to highlight a number of important aspects of the relationship between law and morality. First, phrases like 'changes in public opinion' can mask the extremely complex and subtle social, economic and political forces which, taken together at any historical moment, form the moral and ideological framework within which legal change may take place. Second, far from resting upon the kind of absolute and ultimate moral values presented, in particular, by natural-law philosophy and its variants, it seems that moral values and codes must be characterised by a dynamism and relativity which reflect the fact that such codes, and indeed the legal rules embodying them, are subject to different perceptions and definitions, and that often it is the possession of effective political *power* which finally determines which and whose definition of morality is reflected within the law. Thus, in conclusion, the complex and dynamic interplay of party politics, pressure-group activity, religious and philosophical debates, and judicial interpretation of thorny problems of law and morality: all these factors will, in various ways, affect the legal system, its rules and procedures. We might go further and assert that, far from being restricted to rules about individual 'immorality' of the kind noted above, there is very little about our legal system which is not coloured by the moral and ideological overtones and assumptions of powerful social and

124 Ibid., p 33.   125 Ibid., p 38.

political groups throughout the long period of development of English law. Moral climates change over time: some observers perceived a significant shift away from the social and political milieu of reformism in the 1960s, to a much more rigid and authoritarian atmosphere in the 1980s. Several examples have been discussed above which suggest that, at the end of the twentieth and the beginning of the twenty-first century, a degree of liberalism has returned: apart from these instances, we might observe that in 2001, the British Board of Film Censors passed, for general release, a film explicitly depicting sexual activity. In 2003, the Home Secretary, through statutory instrument,[126] re-classified the drug cannabis as a 'Category C' drug,[127] which means that offences connected with cannabis attract lesser sentences, though it was specifically enacted in s 105 of the Criminal Justice Act 2003 that possession of cannabis remains an offence for which the police can arrest without warrant.[128] Though these changes do not amount to decriminalisation of the drug – as was stressed by the Home Secretary[129] – the measure will reduce the number of prosecutions for possession of cannabis. It remains true, however, that the Home Secretary's essentially *political* action in 're-legislating' the law relating to drugs could only be carried out with the active support of the police, Home Office civil servants, and other organisations with a direct interest in the matter, and in the belief that such an action would not produce antagonism on the part of the voting public.[130]

At various points in our discussion so far, we have noted the often close connections between law and the economic environment which, according to some commentators and critics, characterise many legal rules, institutions and procedures. In the next chapter, we turn our attention to these complex and often difficult questions surrounding law and economic activity.

126 The Misuse of Drugs Act 1971 (Modification) (No. 2) Order 2003
127 Schedule 2 to the Misuse of Drugs Act 1971 classified 'controlled drugs' as Category A (the most addictive or dangerous, including heroin, cocaine, LSD, ecstasy and opium), Category B (amphetamines and cannabis) and Category C (containing drugs such as steroids and tranquillisers which, though prohibited, were thought least dangerous).
128 The penalties for dealing in prohibited drugs, however, remain high, and the energies devoted by the police and customs and excise to prevent their importation and sale remain substantial.
129 The intention was to release police time spent dealing with what many police officers saw as 'trivial' offences relating to cannabis possession, in order that police resources could be concentrated on more serious crime.
130 Such a belief appears to have been justified: the *Guardian* reported, at the end of October 2001, the results of a survey which revealed that 54% of the sample of the public supported his decision to relax the law on cannabis. Support rose to 65% among the 25–34 age group in the sample.

3

Law and the regulation of economic activity

It is a commonplace assertion that the last hundred years have witnessed state intervention, especially in affairs involving economic activity, on a scale greater than at any other period in history. In chapter 1 we noted some examples of this phenomenon and discussed some of its basic aspects. But if we now pursue the matter, and ask exactly what is meant by the term 'state intervention', we find that this expansion of intervention has not come about in a straightforward fashion but has occurred through complex changes in the structure of society and the economy, and in the very nature and role of the state itself. As we shall see presently, the notion of 'the state' is itself surrounded by problems of definition, and by controversy both as to the precise nature of the modern state and as to what the most appropriate role for the state should be in advanced capitalist society. Of course, state intervention is by no means confined to the economic sphere: the state has taken on a more active role with respect to many other areas of social life, such as public administration and the growth of what is usually termed the 'welfare state'. We shall discuss these developments presently, but for the moment we examine some of the main issues concerning state regulation of economic activity – a sphere of social life which is central to the existence of any social group.

What do we mean by 'the state'? Many writers and theorists have expounded theories and critical accounts of the state, and we invariably find that the approach taken to this difficult topic reflects, or is closely bound up with, their general perspectives on and theories of society.[1]

From the various propositions argued, however, we can identify several persistent issues relating to analyses of the modern state. Does the state act in the interest of the whole population, or does it act principally in the interests of certain sections of the population? Does the state play an active, directive part in the social and economic affairs of a society, or does it take a more passive, supportive role, in particular in relation to economic life? To what extent is the notion of the state bound up with the monopoly of legitimate recourse to force, and in what circumstances should such force be utilised?

1 See A. Heywood, *Politics* (2nd edn., 2002, Palgrave Macmillan), ch.3; B. Jones, D. Kavanagh, M. Moran and P. Norton, *Politics UK* (5th edn., 2004, Longman), and for more detailed discussion see C. Hay, M. Lister and D. Marsh, *The State: Theories and Issues* (2005, Palgrave Macmillan).

The traditional legal approach to the analysis of state activity, especially when that activity takes place by means of the use of law as an instrument of control or regulation, tends to ignore these basic questions. Most texts on public or constitutional law concentrate on issues such as the nature of the constitution, analyses of various organs of public administration and government, and descriptions of the various legal and conventional practices, powers and duties of the different components and agencies of the state. Unfortunately, such analyses tend, on the whole, to adopt a traditional constitutional perspective on the composition of the state, informing us that the three 'arms of the state' are the executive (the government), the legislature (Parliament) and the judiciary. The constitutional doctrine of the 'separation of powers' (see chapter 6) tells us that these three 'arms of the state' each exercise different functions, and are possessed of powers and duties whereby each 'arm' effectively serves to 'check and balance' the powers of the other two, thus ensuring that no single state institution accedes to a position of exclusive or arbitrary political power. As we shall see later, this notion of the 'separation of powers', at least as applied to modern Britain, is largely fallacious, in that there is considerable overlap between the functions of these three institutions. The doctrine of the 'separation of powers' is, moreover, bound up with the principle of the 'rule of law'. This idea was discussed and defended at length by the influential English constitutional lawyer A V Dicey, towards the end of the nineteenth century,[2] who argued that in Britain we live under a government of laws, and not of the arbitrary whim of individual rulers. The principle of the 'rule of law' requires that every governmental action must be justified by legal authority, and that the operation of government itself is carried out within a framework of legal rules and principles.

We shall discuss these issues in more detail later, but for the moment we can see, after some reflection, that the composition of what we ordinarily understand as the state is rather more complex, and its definition rather more elusive, than these conventional constitutional-law propositions would lead us to believe. We would probably include as part of the category of 'state agencies' such institutions as the police, the judges, the prisons, the apparatus of the political establishment (government, Parliament, the monarchy), the armed forces and perhaps the established Church. But some would go further and include as part of state 'apparatuses' the media, business and trade, the trade union movement and the various educational and cultural institutions in our society, operating, to be sure, predominantly through the dissemination of 'dominant ideology' rather than through any overt coercive measures.[3] Others view 'the state' not as a series of institutions, nor as an apparatus, but as a form of *activity* – in other words, they define the state not in terms of what it *is* but rather in terms of what it *does*.[4]

---

2 A. V. Dicey, *The Law of the Constitution* (first published 1885, 10th edn., 1959, Macmillan).

3 See L. Althusser, 'Ideology and Ideological State Apparatuses' in L. Althusser (ed.), *Lenin and Philosophy and Other Essays* (1971, New Left Books).

4 For other perspectives on the state, see R. Miliband, *The State in Capitalist Society* (1973, Quartet Books); N. Poulantzas, *Political Power and Social Classes* (1973, New Left Books); R. Quinney,

Some advocate what might be termed a minimal role for the state: that the state in any society should carry out certain basic functions to ensure the stability of that society. Through the state, it is often said, social order and national security are maintained, as is the system of defence against aggression from foreign powers; domestic stability is assured through the balancing of interests of competing groups within society. Though there are problems in analysing even these basic functions, the difficulties of analysis are compounded when we consider other, additional functions taken on by the state in the social, political or economic sphere. Again, it may be generally agreed that one characteristic attribute of the state is its monopoly of the legitimate use of coercive power, through agencies such as the police, the courts and the prisons. Whilst recourse to such physical coercion may be rare, as we have suggested, the fact remains that coercive power by the state is unhesitatingly used where circumstances are deemed to warrant it. A recent example is the Prevention of Terrorism Act 2005, which empowers the Home Secretary to issue a 'control order' imposing, without trial, certain restrictive obligations on any individual if he has (s 2) 'reasonable grounds for suspecting that the individual is or has been involved in terrorism-related activity' and also 'considers that it is necessary, for purposes connected with protecting members of the public from a risk of terrorism'. The Act provides that the issue of such an order must be with the permission of a court of law, though the court's function here is simply to ensure that the Minister's decisions on the matter are not 'flawed' (s 3(12)). The obligations which a control order may impose include, among other things, restrictions on the individual's business or other activities, restrictions on association or communication with other people (either specific people or people in general), and restrictions on movements to, from, or within the United Kingdom.

Not surprisingly, these measures, which potentially deprive affected individuals of some or most of their freedoms without trial, were fiercely debated both within and outside Parliament. Clearly, such highly controversial measures did not have the full support of many within the population at large, though to say this is, of course, simply to reiterate the point made in chapters 1 and 2: that in a society such as ours, relatively few social, political or economic activities or attitudes can be regarded as reflecting any kind of universal social consensus as to their rightness or otherwise.

For the time being, let us adopt a fairly uncontentious working definition of 'the state'. We will proceed on the basis that the state comprises *those elements in a society which, taken together, represent the central source of legal, political, military and economic power.* This definition will hold for all periods in British history although, as we shall see in exploring more rigorously the relationships between law, state and economic activity, the precise form, or guise, which the state adopts will depend upon the historical period under examination. To begin an

Critique of Legal Order, (1974, Little, Brown); J. Holloway and S. Picciotto, *State and Capital* (1978, Edward Arnold); and see works cited at footnote 1, above.

investigation of the legal regulation of economic activity, we will return to a distinction made earlier between, on the one hand, a *passive, supportive* role for the state and, on the other hand, an *active, directive* role. The argument will be presented that, over the last century or so, the state in Britain – which could once be fairly accurately characterised as having a passive role – has moved towards the adoption of a much more active role.

Our starting-point once again is the period we have already identified as the great period of increased commercial and industrial activity, and *laisser-faire* attitudes held by the middle classes towards official regulative activity: the eighteenth and nineteenth centuries. As we saw in chapter 1, this period can be regarded as the high-water mark of economic *laisser-faire* philosophy. The dominant ideas of 'free trade' and freedom of competition in the marketplace carried with them the corollary that the economy was best left to regulate itself, unimpeded by any form of directive regulation by the state. This is not to say, however, that *no* regulatory measures were taken. If the role of the non-interventionist state in this period was to adopt a non-directive position with regard to the economy, it certainly had a part to play in supporting that economy. This supportive role can be seen both in the creation, often through law, of an economic environment conducive to trade and industry in a capitalist economy, and in the various measures which were taken to protect the economic interests of the business community. Generally, such measures were responses to the calls of private business interests, and it has been noted that, far from being an absolute and unshakeable creed, *laisser-faire* had its limitations as well as its uses:

> Most businessmen . . . feared radical and socialist reformers who wanted to use the government as a means of achieving greater equality and they welcomed any theory that concluded that the government should not intervene in the economic process. Even though they themselves used the government extensively to promote their own interests (through special tariffs, tax concessions, land grants, and a host of other special privileges), they relied on *laisser-faire* arguments when threatened with any social reform that might erode their status, wealth or income.[5]

Government policy regarding foreign affairs also supported the growth and consolidation of the industrial and commercial economy, particularly during the eighteenth-century period of rapid economic expansion. As Hobsbawm points out:

> British policy in the eighteenth century was one of systematic aggressiveness . . . Of the five great wars of the period, Britain was clearly on the defensive in only one. The result of this century of intermittent warfare was the greatest triumph ever achieved by any state: the virtual monopoly among European powers of overseas colonies, and the virtual monopoly of world-wide naval power. Moreover, war itself – by crippling Britain's major competitors in Europe – tended to boost exports . . .[6]

5 E. K. Hunt and H. J. Sherman, *Economics: An Introduction to Traditional and Radical Views* (6th edn., 1990, Harper and Row), p 80.
6 E. Hobsbawm, *Industry and Empire* (1969, Penguin), pp 47–48.

Support for free, competitive trading also came from the judiciary, engaged, particularly during the nineteenth century, in constructing the legal framework within which business affairs could operate smoothly and predictably. The legal notion of the *contract* (see chapter 11) was, and still is, the essence of the relationship between buyers and sellers of goods and services, and the basic legal rules concerning contract and remedies for breach of contract spring almost wholly from cases decided by the superior courts during the nineteenth century.

The insistence by nineteenth-century judges on deciding cases and creating legal contractual rules on the basis of the juristic equivalent of *laisser-faire* economics – the notions of freedom and equality of contract – led eventually to legislative intervention during the course of the twentieth century, especially in the area of consumer protection. The common-law rules of contract (that is, rules developed by the judges – see chapter 7) afforded no special protection to the ordinary consumer: the maxim *caveat emptor* – 'let the buyer beware' – applied, so that the consumer was expected to look out for his or her own affairs as a 'free agent' in the marketplace, and presumed to operate on an equal footing with traders and substantial businesses (see chapter 11). The same notions were applied to the contractual relationships between employers and employees, as noted in chapter 1, and this particular area is perhaps especially significant as one in which direct state regulation, in the form, originally, of prohibitions upon workers' combinations, was regarded by business interests (though not by groups of workers) as legitimate for the protection of the best interests of trade and industry. Less obviously, but equally importantly, the nineteenth century also saw the development of legal rules pertaining to the *form* which business enterprises might take, and to the legal protection which particular types of enterprises enjoyed.

The form of the business enterprise

The most common forms of business enterprise were, and still are, the *limited company* and the *partnership*. Taking the limited company first, if we examine the history of the company, we see that ventures in the form of 'joint stock' companies, where several members put their individual resources together for the running of a single enterprise, can be traced back many hundreds of years, though the 'limited liability company' was expanded and consolidated in business practice and the law during the eighteenth and nineteenth centuries.

The advantages of forming a business into a limited liability company are, first, that by dividing the business into shares, which are then sold to persons wishing to purchase a stake in the enterprise, it is possible to secure the release of large amounts of capital finance from shareholders, which enables the business to proceed on a more ambitious footing than it could if the available capital were restricted to, say, that of one man and his immediate associate who together run the business. Second, the term 'limited liability' means that the liability, in law, of each shareholder to the company's creditors is limited to the amount which the shareholder has agreed to invest in the company, that is, to the value of the shares held. This provides protection for the shareholder, and also constitutes a clear incentive for potential shareholders to invest money in the business. The company, like the contract, is the creation of law and, as Hadden has put it: 'Company law is about capitalism. It provides the formal legal structure necessary to the operation of the capitalist system.'[7]

As can be appreciated, the above advantages make the limited liability company an attractive form of business enterprise. We shall see in more detail later some of the ways in which the law regulates the company and its affairs, but we may note at this point one striking feature of the legal attitude towards the company: once it has been properly formed, the company is regarded in law as if it were a *person*. Even though the company has no 'real' physical existence apart from the personnel who run it and own it (directors and shareholders), it is, in law, a *corporate body*, an entity quite separate from these persons, and can therefore be said to be an 'artificial legal person'. The company can thus enjoy various rights, and can labour under various legal duties: it can own and transfer property, it can enter into contracts, it can sue and be sued in court, and can be prosecuted for criminal offences, though in the last case the only penalty normally used is the fine, paid from the company's assets.[8]

This legal device clearly forms an important component of the regulatory framework of state support for certain forms of economic activity. By treating the company as a person, having ownership of corporate assets, the law not only allows the relatively free use of those assets in the running and expansion of the business, but also provides significant protection for individual shareholders. The regulatory framework of company law amounts, in effect, not to the proposition 'you must not do this', but rather to the proposition 'if you wish to do this and to enjoy the protection of the law, then this is the way in which you must do it'. The mechanism of the limited company has had, at times, somewhat startling consequences. In the case of *Lee v Lee's Air Farming Ltd* in 1961,[9] for example, Mr Lee, who had formed, and who was the majority shareholder in, Lee's Air Farming Ltd, was killed in an air crash whilst working. His wife claimed compensation from the company in respect of his death, and the court decided in favour of her claim on the basis that at the time of the accident Mr Lee was working for the company as its employee – even though in every sense except the legal, Mr Lee and Lee's Air Farming Ltd were one and the same physical entity.[10]

---

7 T. Hadden, *Company Law and Capitalism* (2nd edn., 1977, Weidenfeld and Nicolson), p 3. See S. Mayson, D. French and C. Ryan, *Company Law* (22nd edn., 2005, Oxford University Press).

8 Individual directors can, of course, be personally liable for such offences as fraud and some offences in the area of environmental protection. In such cases, the complete range of sentences is available upon conviction. It is also worth noting that during the 2005–6 Parliamentary session, a new Corporate Manslaughter Bill was introduced and discussed widely within and outside Parliament. If passed, this would create a new offence of corporate manslaughter, providing sanctions if companies and other organisations are found to have been grossly negligent in their senior management, leading to fatal consequences.   9 [1961] AC 12.

10 The decision follows the earlier case of *Salomon v Salomon* [1897] AC 22.

Apart from enjoying legal powers to enter into contracts and so on, the company also labours under special legal *duties*. It is obviously reasonable, given that a company invites others to invest in it, to try to guard against fraud, misuse of company funds, or misrepresentation as to what the enterprise is worth or what its business activities are. The law therefore requires, through a series of Companies Acts (the main one now being the Companies Act 1985, as amended by the Companies Act 1989) that certain formalities be observed by those intending to bring the company into being. All companies must register a Memorandum of Association with the Registrar of Companies, which contains information regarding the company's intended activities. The 'objects clause' of this Memorandum must state the purposes for which the company has been formed. This represents, in theory, an important mode of regulation of a company's activities for, given that the company is able to enter into legally binding contracts in its own name, those contracts (or any other activities) must pertain only to the purposes set out in the objects clause. If the company purports to act in a way inconsistent with these stated objects, the position prior to 1972 was, again in theory, that the company could not be bound to fulfil any contractual obligations so made, as they would be *ultra vires*, or *beyond the powers of* the company. The doctrine of *ultra vires* is found in other areas of law, but in this context the leading case is *Ashbury Railway Carriage and Iron Co v Riche*[11] in 1875. In this case, the company's stated objects were the manufacture and sale of railway plant, machinery and rolling stock; the business of mechanical engineering; and the purchase and sale of mines, minerals, land, buildings, timber, coal, metals and other materials. The company entered into a contract to finance the construction of a railway in Belgium, and later, when the agreement was repudiated by the company, the other party sued for breach of contract. The House of Lords held that the agreement did not fall within the stated objects of the company, was *ultra vires*, and that therefore the company could not be held liable for breach of contract since there was no legally valid contract to be breached.

Such a doctrine restricting the legal rights and duties of the company may seem hard on the party with whom the company is purporting to do business, as it would seem unable to recover compensation for such an alleged breach of contractual agreement. To a large extent, however, this result has in practice long been avoided by the use of very wide objects clauses in Memoranda of Association. Such a wide clause was approved by the Court of Appeal in *Bell Houses Ltd v City Wall Properties Ltd*,[12] and the Companies Act 1985, as amended by the Companies Act 1989, provides in s 35 that the validity of an act of the company shall not be called into question by reason only of anything in the company's memorandum. This provides protection for persons dealing with the company, and to the company itself, even though technically the act in question may be *ultra vires*. Further, the 1985 Act also provides that a company's objects clause may specify that the company is a 'general commercial company', which effectively means that the company can engage in any (legal) business or trade.

11 (1875) LR 7 HL 653.   12 [1966] 2 All ER 674.

Connected with this issue is the situation where a person acting as agent[13] of an *as yet unformed* company enters into contracts with others on behalf of the unformed company. Legally, until the company has full legal existence, it cannot make contracts or ratify those made in its name prior to that existence. On this point, s36C of the Companies Act 1985 gives statutory force to the pre-existing common-law position, which was that in such a case, the purported agent, and not the company, is personally liable for any breaches of contracts thus made. The changed position with respect to the *ultra vires* rule in the 1985 Act improves the legal position, both with regard to creditors who might otherwise lose out by a strict application of the rule and by giving legal effect to the economic reality of business transactions as opposed to an over-insistence upon legal formality at the expense of the true business intentions of the directors of the company.

In addition to the 'objects clause', the Memorandum of Association must also contain details of the company's name (which, if a private company, must end with the word 'limited' and if a public company, must end with the words 'public limited company': the distinction between private and public companies is explained below), and information as to whether the company's registered office is in England and Wales or in Scotland, and as to whether the liability of members is limited by shares or by guarantee. A company limited by guarantee is one in which the members guarantee to contribute specific amounts to the company's assets in the event of the company being 'wound up', that is, terminating its existence as a corporate body by reason of its insolvency or by reason of a desire on the part of its members that it should cease to operate; this form of organisation is often used by charitable companies or co-operatives (see below).

The distinction between a public and a private company was first introduced into the law in 1907. A private company was defined as a one in which there were at least two,[14] but not more than 50, members; in which the transfer of shares was limited (perhaps in order to keep the control of the company within a family or some other such exclusive group); and which could not offer its shares to the public. The position is now governed by the Companies Act 1985, a private company being defined as one which does not meet the legal requirements of a public company. The 1985 Act provides that, in order to be a public company, the enterprise must use the words 'public limited company' (or the letters PLC) after its name; it must comprise at least two members; it must have a minimum share capital of £50,000, of which at least one-quarter of the nominal value of each share has been received by the company; it must state in its Memorandum of Association that it is a public

13 In the law of agency, an agent is one who brings about a contract with one person on behalf of another. Thus if an estate agent sells a house on behalf of the seller A to the purchaser B, then the contract is between A and B. A is said to be the agent's principal. Note that the relationship between the agent and the principal, usually said to be a 'consensual' one, may well be contractual.

14 The effect of the Companies (Single Member Private Limited Companies) Regulations 1992, SI 1992/1699 was to insert into the Companies Act 1985 a provision that a private company may, after July 1992, be formed by a single person.

limited company; and finally it must be registered under the provisions of the Act. Any company which does not meet these requirements is a private company.

Apart from the Memorandum of Association, the company must also lodge with the Registrar of Companies a document called the Articles of Association. This contains details of the company's rules and structure, and also constitutes a contract between the shareholders and the company. The Articles may be individually drawn up by the company, or the specimen Articles now contained in the Companies (Tables A–F) Regulations 1985, SI 1985/805 may be adopted. Once the Memorandum and Articles of Association, along with various other documents and items of information, have been deposited, and the Registrar of Companies is satisfied that all the statutory requirements have been met, a Certificate of Incorporation is issued and the company can begin its activity. It should be noted that in the case of a public company, a second certificate must be issued, this being evidence that the statutory requirements as to nominal capital, nominal value of shares and so on have been complied with (Companies Act 1985, s 117). Until this is issued the directors must not commence trading on behalf of the company; should they do so, they will incur personal liability.

The main impetus for the most recent companies legislation was the need to harmonise the relevant companies legislation of the European Community member states, and the Companies Acts of 1980 and 1981 were in fact implementations of Community Directives.[15] The objectives of these Acts (now consolidated by the Companies Act 1985) were to ensure uniformity among public companies in terms of share capital; to deal with certain malpractices among company directors, such as 'insider dealing',[16] whereby a director makes use of inside knowledge of the company to make personal profit or gain; to deal with matters pertaining to the publication of companies' accounts and the disclosure and display of the full name of the company and the address of the registered office on all business documents and in places where the business is carried on. The 1981 Act also provided that the name of the company need no longer meet with the approval of the Registrar of Companies, although new companies must not take the same name as any existing company, and must not adopt names which are offensive or which suggest government approval.

Apart from the provisions already noted, the law also contains a host of other regulatory provisions. Types and transfer of shares, company borrowing, the frequency, composition and procedure of meetings, the procedure and consequences of winding-up, and the rights and duties of directors: all are within the ambit of legal regulation. Space does not allow further detailed consideration of all these rules[17] but enough has been said to show how, as long as the various legal

15 See chapter 8.   16 Now dealt with by the Criminal Justice Act 1993.
17 See any standard text on company law, for example, R. Pennington, *Company Law* (8th edn., 2001, Butterworths); Mayson, French and Ryan, op. cit. The Company Law Reform Bill, discussed by Parliament during 2005-6, aims to simplify the legal administrative burden on smaller private companies, and to update and clarify the law relating to most aspects of the regulation of companies.

formalities are complied with (and so long as no other legal rules are breached), a company can continue its affairs in its own name in whichever way it pleases.

A business enterprise does not have to be formed into a limited company in order to engage in group activity in the business world. The major alternative to the company is the *partnership*, which is an *un*incorporated association (that is, it is not treated in law as a 'person') and which is defined by the Partnership Act 1890 as a relationship between persons 'carrying on business in common with a view to profit'. Usually, partnerships come into existence by explicit agreement between the partners in the *firm*, and because the firm is not a corporate entity in law, the partners themselves act in the furtherance of the business as *agents* of the other partners. This means that if one partner enters into a business transaction relating to the firm's business with X, then that transaction (or contract) is regarded as made with *all* the other partners; in the event of the firm being in breach of that contract, then all the partners will be equally liable. The only exceptions to this will be in cases where X does not know that the contract was with a partnership, or where X knows that the partner who made the contract had no authority to do so. Note that the transaction must concern the firm's normal business: if it does not, then only the contracting partner will be liable unless the other partners agreed to the particular transaction.

Other important differences between partnerships and limited companies include the fact that, unlike that of shareholders in a company, the liability of the partners for the firm's debts is generally unlimited; there is however provision in the Limited Partnership Act 1907 for partnerships registered under the Act to comprise two types of partner: *general* partners, who are fully liable for debts of the firm, and *limited* partners, who contribute a specified amount to the firm and who are liable only for debts up to that amount. Limited, or 'sleeping', partners must not, however, participate in the running of the firm, otherwise they will become fully liable for the firm's debts just like the general partners.

A new form of business organisation was introduced by means of the Limited Liability Partnerships Act 2000. A limited liability partnership resembles a general partnership – every member of the partnership is, in law, an agent of the firm – but if registered with the registrar of companies, the limited liability partnership becomes a corporate body, and has separate legal personality from that of its members. In such a case, the Act provides that the general law relating to partnerships will not apply, and the members of the limited liability partnership will not be responsible for the debts of the enterprise. So far, this new form of business has had a modest impact: by June 2004, there had been between 8,000 – 9,000 registrations with Companies House.[18]

Of course, in order to set up in business it is not essential to form the enterprise into either a limited company or a partnership. It is true that, as can be seen, there will be certain advantages in many cases in doing so, but it may well be that for

18 Companies House journal *Register*, issue 59, June 2004. This figure may be compared to almost 2 million limited companies, and just over half a million partnerships, currently registered.

many enterprises neither form of business is appropriate. Many small businesses, for instance, operate as *sole traders*. This simply refers to a business which is run by a person in his or her private capacity, such as a small corner shop or a building or plumbing business. No special rules apply to such cases: liability is unlimited, the enterprise has no corporate status, and there are no special devices for raising money with which to operate the business.

A final alternative method of forming a business enterprise is to structure the business as a *co-operative*, though this form of business is not as widespread in Britain as in certain other European countries. Some co-operatives, or management buy-outs, have been formed by groups of employees effectively taking over a non-viable business for which they had previously worked and running it themselves, often by modifying or diversifying the business operation. This has frequently meant, however, that they were also taking over the ailing business's problems, and many such co-operatives have failed. The essence of a co-operative is that the management of the enterprise is in the hands of the workers themselves, who make decisions as to the operation of the business, make appointments to managerial posts, and control the finances of the business; and, most important, all profits made are retained within the business, rather than being distributed as dividends to members. Furthermore, if the co-operative registers under the Industrial and Provident Societies Act 1965,[19] the enterprise can enjoy the benefits of corporate status and limited liability, as long as the basic requirements for a co-operative (especially with regard to profits and to control of the enterprise) are satisfied.

Given this range of forms of business enterprise, it will be appreciated that it is very important for any business to adopt the form which will be most appropriate in the circumstances, and which will provide optimum benefits and flexibility (especially with regard to the possibilities of expanding the business, raising capital or protecting individuals' financial interests) for the personnel involved.

If we now turn to other aspects of the business environment, we can identify a number of ways in which the state, through law, helps provide a supportive, and in many ways protective, milieu within which economic activity can be profitably pursued. To begin with, the law of contract itself (discussed fully in chapter 11) can be seen as a framework within which businesses can conduct their affairs on a stable and predictable footing, although there is evidence that, in practice, people in business tend to avoid close entanglement with the law and with legal actions, preferring to settle their disputes in other ways such as arbitration (see chapter 6). And the law relating to cheques and other negotiable instruments (discussed in chapter 5) provides an important framework for the execution of convenient, flexible and legally protected business transactions.

Another important aspect of law which has special relevance for economic activity is that relating to *insurance* (see chapter 9). Whilst every business venture clearly involves a degree of risk (for example, as to whether there is a viable market for the

19 As amended by the Co-operatives and Community Benefit Societies Act 2003.

goods which a company produces, or whether the goods produced are priced in a way which reflects customer demand), there are some eventualities which can be anticipated, and their effects offset or mitigated. Suppose that a factory is burned down, a shop is ransacked by burglars, an employee is injured at work and sues for compensation, or goods are destroyed or lost in transit by road, air or sea. It is clearly wise to try to guard against the losses thus incurred by taking out insurance policies to cover these and similar risks.

The law relating to insurance is governed partly by common law and partly by statute. An insurance agreement is a contract, and as such is subject to the ordinary legal rules relating to contracts. In addition, however, it is firmly established at common law that insurance contracts are contracts *uberrimae fidei* ('of the utmost good faith'), which means that the person wishing to take out the insurance policy (the proposer) is under a strict legal duty to disclose, truthfully and accurately, all material facts to the insurance company. Failure to do this will enable the insurer to avoid all liability under the insurance contract. This rule applies to all insurance contracts, though what constitutes a 'material fact' in any given case will, of course, depend upon the circumstances: in essence, the insurer will want to know of any fact which might affect the decision to take on the risk, and invariably will require answers to questions put to the proposer which the insurer considers significant in assessing that risk. This information is vital, because of the very nature of an insurance contract, which is basically an agreement whereby the insurer undertakes to indemnify or compensate the proposer for any loss sustained by the latter which is covered by the terms of the agreement. Usually, business enterprises insure against the kind of losses mentioned above. We might also note that car-drivers *must* insure against (at the very least) injury to third parties[20] and passengers, this being required by statute,[21] and prudent householders will normally insure against damage both to the house itself and to the contents of the house.

It is important to appreciate that the insured person or business will only be covered for risks specified in the insurance policy, and there will invariably be certain specified eventualities which are *excluded* from the cover. For example, a typical motor insurance policy will exclude any claim arising from accidents whilst the car is being used for racing or other sporting purposes. In exchange for the insurance cover, the proposer pays a *premium*, usually annually, which is payment for that cover. The amount of the premium will depend upon the nature of the insurance taken out, and on the extent of the risk being undertaken by the insurer. For instance, if a racing-driver wishes to insure against injury arising from racing, then, given the very high risks involved in that activity, the driver must expect insurance premiums to be extremely high – if, indeed, an insurance company can be found which is prepared to take on so great a risk.

20 In an insurance contract, the first two parties are the insurance company and the insured person. The 'third party' is then the person who is not a party to the contract, but to whom insurance money may be payable in the event of liability on the part of the insured person to that third party where such liability is insured against.   21 Road Traffic Act 1988, s 143(1), as amended.

The attractiveness of insurance to business enterprises is clear. It is a means of protection against losses arising from certain kinds of risk, and thus provides a degree of security for the enterprise. In addition, however, there are certain statutory requirements relating to insurance in business, notably the requirement contained in the Employers' Liability (Compulsory Insurance) Act 1969[22] that employers take out insurance to cover themselves against claims by their employees who suffer illness or injury arising out of the course of their employment. This requirement not only protects the business enterprise, but also clearly offers protection to the employee who, in the absence of such insurance, may find that the employer (especially if the business is a small one) is unable to meet the compensation claim.

The last-mentioned statute is a good example of the state's intervention, through the use of law, in a situation where the common law is held to be inadequate to deal with a particular matter, or where law-makers take the view that public policy requires that a particular risk (in this case, to employees) is too important to be left to the individual concerned (in this case, the employer's choice as to whether or not to insure against liability to employees). It is thus one instance of the state, acting through law, stepping into a situation with a *positive direction* to the person or group affected: here, the law does not say 'do this if you wish, but follow this procedure if you wish to enjoy the protection of the law', but rather, simply, 'you *must* do this'.

The state has increasingly intervened, often through the use of law, in many areas affecting economic activity, and has done so, moreover, in ways which can be described as *directing* economic behaviour. This intervention can operate on a number of levels. At one level, the state may impose a duty on employers to insure, as in the example just noted. At a more general level, the state may involve individual enterprises in national economic planning, with a view either to combating particular problems, such as inflation, or to directing the economy towards an improved 'state of health', such as through the encouragement of enhanced levels of export of goods. In considering such developments, we must now address ourselves once more to an earlier theme – that of the changing role of the state – and try to identify those areas of legal regulation which may be said to have a much more positive and directive thrust than the nineteenth-century pattern of relatively passive support for economic activity.

The changing functions of state and law

During the last few centuries the modern national state has had an increasing tendency to become the Leviathan of which Hobbes wrote, not only the repository of physical and legal restraining power and the protector of the nation against an external enemy, but also the main directive force in the shaping of the economic and social life of the nation.[23]

---

22 And see Employers' Liability (Compulsory Insurance) Regulations 1998, SI 1998/2573 and Employers' Liability (Compulsory Insurance) (Amendment) Regulations 2004, SI 2004/2882.
23 W. Friedmann, *Law in a Changing Society* (1972, Penguin), p 321.

In order to understand something of the changing function of the state with regard to the regulation of economic activity, we must examine two closely related problems of analysis. The first concerns the nature of a country's economy, and the second concerns the nature and function of the state and its relationship to that particular economic structure.[24]

Capitalism in its 'purest' form involves, among other things, an economic structure which is responsive only to the forces of free competition in the marketplace. The ideas of free trade and competition, the economic idea of the 'law of supply and demand', the absence of state interference or guidance, and the uncontrolled accumulation of private property and of profit would characterise an economic system which we would term a *private enterprise economy*. Britain in the nineteenth century and the United States in the twentieth are probably the instances which come closest to this 'pure' model, although in both cases the uncontrolled forces of the free competitive market have been subject to some state regulation through law. In the twentieth century in particular, the purity of the private enterprise economy, though still regarded by many as the ideal economic system in a 'free world', was diluted by the perceived necessity by governments throughout the Western world to intervene more and more in order to try to offset some of the economically damaging consequences of unbridled freedom of competition.[25]

At the other end of the spectrum, there emerged during the twentieth century national economies based on the ideals of socialism, in which private enterprise is replaced by *public* ownership and control, through the state, of the national economy. By means of the nationalisation of industries, central economic planning and rigorous regulation of nearly all aspects of economic activity, the state endeavours to maximise economic efficiency in the interests not of private companies and individuals, but of the whole community. It is this type of economy, whose principles were so deeply embedded in the political systems and ideologies of the 'communist bloc' (or 'Soviet bloc') countries of eastern Europe, which collapsed in the massive political and economic upheavals in those countries during the late 1980s.

In practical terms, most Western countries, including Britain, operate with economic systems which fall between these two 'pure' types – systems which we usually call *mixed economies*. Here, private enterprise operates side by side with some degree of public ownership and control, and though the precise 'mix' will vary from country to country, the general tendency has been for public utility industries

---

24 See generally W. Hutton, *The State We're In* (1996, Vintage).

25 In the United States, often thought of as the epitome of free-market competition, we find, paradoxically, a far more extensive system of state regulation of business and industry than in the United Kingdom. This regulation is largely carried out by a myriad of specialist Federal agencies, the best-known of which is probably the Federal Trade Commission; among the many legislative provisions regulating the American business world is the 'anti-trust' legislation, the equivalent of European competition law, which is designed to combat, among other things, monopolisation of sections of business and industry through mergers, take-overs, and restrictive practices which might well result through the unrestricted freedom of large and powerful business enterprises to dominate the market, and thus reduce competition, by such means.

(power, communications and transport), coal and steel to be taken over by public corporations. This is partly because of the central importance of these industries to the national economy, and partly because they involve matters of national rather than local or sectional development and policy. Of course, the divergent economic philosophies of successive governments within any particular country can mean that the 'mix' of public and private sectors will change over time. In Britain the Conservative administrations of the 1980s and early 1990s, wedded to ideals of free private enterprise and hence denationalisation, returned certain industries, at least partially, to private hands. British Telecommunications, the gas and electricity industries, the water authorities, British Airways and, most controversially, British Rail have been subject to legislation bringing about a considerable degree of privatisation, and the post-1997 New Labour administrations have proposed to extend privatisation to other industries such as air traffic control, the health service and the London Underground. In contrast, twentieth-century Labour governments tended to be more or less committed to programmes of nationalisation and *public* ownership and control, although it seems doubtful that in the twenty-first century New Labour will place re-nationalisation of these industries on its political agenda. In making these observations, we are, of course, referring to the relationship between state and economy, and this brings us to our second problem: the changing nature and function of the state itself in modern Western society.

As we have seen, there are various perspectives which can be taken on the 'state', especially when we begin to delve more deeply into the issues which our simple working definition raises. Broadly speaking, however, the most widely held view of the modern British state is that which we would term 'pluralist'. There are many definitions of this term, but the following are offered as principal defining characteristics of the 'pluralist' perspective.

First of all, pluralism assumes that the role of the state is *supportive*, and not *directive*, of social and economic affairs. Its functions as regards the economy are therefore akin to those discussed earlier – the maintenance of a social, political and economic environment which is conducive to the smooth running of society's affairs, the provision of machinery for the resolution of disputes and conflict, and the provision of protection – legal and otherwise – for legitimate economic interests. Second, the pluralist view, whilst recognising the existence of diverse and often conflicting interest-groups in society, holds that despite the differential possession of political and economic power among such groups, a kind of equilibrium is none the less maintained through the democratic political process, so that no single interest-group can dominate politically or economically. Third, the state has, as a major function, an important part to play as *mediator* between competing groups, favouring no particular group but negotiating compromises as solutions to conflicts of interest between them. Fourth, this political and economic edifice stands on a bedrock of *value-consensus*: the assumption that agreement exists, broadly speaking, within society as to its political, social and economic institutions and policies, and also as to the legitimacy of those institutions and policies – a legitimacy which in turn springs from the democratic right of all individuals and groups to involve themselves and have their say in the political processes of society (see chapter 1).

Standing in direct opposition to the pluralist perspective is the Marxist model of capitalist society. This view holds that the state acts in the interest of capital (that is, of powerful economic interests) which it strives to maintain and protect against the opposing interests of the working class; far from being democratic, the capitalist political structure reflects, and is responsive to, the needs and dictates of capital. In reality, according to Marxism, the 'democratic' nature of that political structure is an ideological construct serving both to obscure the 'real' social relations of capitalist production and to maintain an essentially exploitative economic system. Marxist views, whilst differing from the pluralist perspective in crucial respects, may none the less acknowledge a relatively passive, supportive role for the capitalist state – indeed, the state in Britain maintained this role during the very period of which Marx was writing. Such views may be contrasted with those perspectives on the state which are usually termed *corporatist*, and which present a radically different function for the state in this particular respect.

Although there have been many contributions to the analytical literature on the growth of the corporate state, there would seem to be considerable diversity of views as to the precise definition and delineation of the term.[26] Essentially, corporatism refers to a *mode of participation* by the state, and to the proposition that the state takes on a high degree of centralised, *direct control* of national economic affairs. Some writers contrast 'liberal' with 'state' or 'authoritarian' corporatism: the former arising within liberal-democratic societies, and usually co-existing with the social and political mores of liberal democracy, whilst the latter tends to be associated with totalitarian regimes of, say, Hitler's Germany or the old Soviet Russia. Liberal corporatism, growing as it does out of systems of mixed economy, thus 'combines *private ownership* and *State control*. It contrasts with capitalism's private ownership and private control and with State socialism's State ownership and State control.'[27] The liberal corporatist state, then, reaches into private enterprise in an active, positive way, involving it in exercises of economic policy and planning and in the regulation of industrial relations through negotiations between trade unions and employers, requiring it to conform to state-defined economic guidelines, and generally adopting a much more directive role in economic activity at a number of levels.

In Britain, it is true that at a number of levels, and in a variety of ways, positive and directive state intervention in economic activity has occurred, and interventionist policies have frequently, though not invariably, been implemented through law. The last 40 years or so have seen many examples, such as the attempts by the 1970–74 Conservative government to impose curbs on rising wage and price levels

---

26 See R. M. Martin, 'Pluralism and the New Corporatism' (1983) *Political Studies*.
27 J. T. Winkler, 'Law, State and Economy: The Industry Act 1975 in Context' (1975) *British Journal of Law and Society* 103 at 106.

in the effort to control rising inflation and other economic problems; the creation in 1975 of the National Enterprise Board, set up to further the development of the United Kingdom economy; and the control of anti-competitive business activity through the Competition Acts 1980 and 1998.[28]

New institutions have been created through statutes, charged with the regulation of various sectors of the economy. The regulation of financial services, through the Financial Services Act 1986 and the Financial Services and Markets Act 2000 is a good example. The legislation includes powers to license and monitor financial organisations and creates new criminal offences (notably carrying on an investment business without authorisation). The Act of 2000 set up the Financial Services Authority, covering the regulation of all financial services, and Government involvement is written into the Act by means of the participation of the Secretary of State for Trade and Industry. Similarly, regulatory systems are in place regarding the privatised telecommunications, gas, water and other industries. Although most commentators acknowledge that modern Britain cannot be described as a corporate state,[29] it would seem that one of the essential characteristics of corporatism – state involvement in the management of industry, commerce and business in general – remains a feature of government in Britain.

One feature of liberal corporatism, however – the involvement of the trade unions in the management of the economy – has virtually disappeared, largely, it cannot be doubted, because of the decline in the influence of trade unions brought about by a series of statutes passed during the 1980s. Attempts to control the activities of trade unions, as we have already seen, are by no means new. The long struggle by unions to achieve legal recognition, and the various devices by which the courts, in particular, tried to curb industrial action, taught the trade union movement long ago to regard the law with some suspicion.

None the less, both Labour and Conservative governments in post-war Britain perceived trade union activity as potentially and actually disruptive of the smooth running of the economy, and in their different ways sought to regulate trade union activity more closely. The Labour government during the 1960s introduced plans to legislate to control trade unions, though it was the Conservative government which came to power in 1970 which finally introduced legislation, in the form of the controversial and short-lived Industrial Relations Act 1971, in response to what many saw as a continuing crisis in industrial relations manifested by a series of strikes in a number of industries. This Act dealt with the regulation of various aspects of union activity, and was highly unpopular with trade unionists and also with many employers. Critics regarded the Act as a clumsy and inappropriate means of dealing with situations which often needed a more delicate touch, especially over collective bargaining between unions and management.

The 1971 Act was repealed in 1974, when Labour was again returned to power, and there followed a period during which the government tried to base its

---

28 As amended in 2004.   29 See, for example, Hutton, op. cit., esp. chapter 4.

dealings with the trade union movement on a more informal *voluntary* basis through, first, the 'social contract' and then the 'social compact'. These were agreements between government and the Trades Union Congress (TUC) which promised closer involvement for the latter in matters of economic policy, in exchange for the TUC's undertaking that matters such as bargaining over wage increases would be handled in a voluntary though 'responsible' way. In addition, the Labour government undertook in 1974 to investigate ways in which employees, through their trade unions, might play a more active role in negotiation and company planning through representation on company boards. This proposal (which some would regard as a typical corporatist-state development) led to the establishment of the Committee of Inquiry on Industrial Democracy (the Bullock Committee) which reported in 1977.[30] The report contained recommendations that union representation should be introduced as an extension of collective bargaining, though the government's White Paper which followed the report fell short of the full Bullock proposals, and, of course, the Labour government itself was defeated in the general election of 1979.

The Conservative governments of the 1980s and 1990s, not surprisingly, showed rather different attitudes to industrial relations, and a series of statutes concerning trade unions was enacted between 1980 and 1990. These statutes were ostensibly inspired largely by the government's conviction that the rights of the individual worker – whether a member of a trade union or not – needed strengthening, not in relation to the power of employers, but rather in relation to the collective power of the trade unions themselves. The Employment Acts of 1980, 1982, 1988 and 1990, and the Trade Union Act 1984, provided, among other things, for the holding of secret ballots prior to industrial action, the removal of legal protection for closed-shop agreements and, to a large extent, picketing during industrial action; 'secondary' industrial action (that is, the extension of industrial action against one employer to another employer not primarily involved in the original dispute)[31] has virtually become unlawful, as is industrial action inspired by alleged 'political' motivations as opposed to a genuine dispute with an employer. The individual worker's right *not* to join a union without incurring the risk of dismissal – a risk which is clearly present in the case of a closed-shop agreement – is now protected in a number of ways, though of course this particular development runs against the ideological commitment of many trade unionists to the proposition that only by uniting and acting collectively can parity with management in terms of bargaining power be achieved; the closed-shop agreement, it may be argued, is a logical consequence of this view.

Taken as a whole, there can be no doubt whatever that this series of statutes seriously weakened trade unions legal powers and protections, and this systematic undermining of unions' previous legal position was accompanied in the 1980s and

---

30 (1977) Cmnd 6706.
31 Such a dispute lay at the root of, for example, *Express Newspapers Ltd v McShane* [1980] 2 WLR 89; and *Duport Steel and others v Sirs and others* [1980] 1 All ER 529.

1990s by an almost complete refusal to include trade unions in discussions on the national economy at government level.

> By 1993 nine major pieces of legislation had been enacted, all but one under Mrs. Thatcher's leadership, which transformed British industrial relations. In 1979 there were 5 million members of closed shops; by 1993 the closed shop had been outlawed. Union membership in 1979 stood at 13.3 million; by 1993 it had shrunk to under 9 million, with only 31 per cent of employed workers belonging to a union – the lowest level since 1946. Close to three-quarters of the workforce were paid under collective bargaining arrangements in 1979 but by 1993 these applied to well under half of it and pay was now linked to profits in nearly 50 per cent of all companies.[32]

Shortly after New Labour was returned to power in 1997, the new government published a White Paper, *Fairness at Work*,[33] which made it clear that although there was no intention to return to the era of widespread industrial action, there was government support for trade union recognition by employers (thus encouraging collective bargaining, but also encouraging employers and unions to work together harmoniously, rather than each representing oppositional interests, to raise productivity) and for enhancing basic standards at work. The legislation which followed, the Employment Relations Act 1999 (which contains the current law), provides for statutory recognition of unions by employers[34] if voluntary recognition agreements fail. In addition, the Act extends remedies for unfair dismissal by providing that employees may claim unfair dismissal before an Employment (previously 'Industrial')[35] Tribunal after one year's employment instead of two. The maximum amount of compensation payable for successful claims is currently around £60,000, though the majority of awards are for far smaller sums.

Also in 1998, the government introduced the 'minimum wage' (National Minimum Wage Act 1998). In October 2005, this was, for workers aged 22 or over, £5.05 per hour, though lower rates apply for those below this age.

Following the general election of 2001, the New Labour administration introduced the Employment Act 2002 which, among other things, increased the maximum period of maternity leave, and introduced a two-week paid period of paternity leave, the intention being to make this available to fathers following the birth of a child (or the placement of a child for adoption). Further changes to the law relating to trade union rights were introduced in the Employment Relations Act 2004: this Act, among other things, amended the law on trade union recognition by employers, and made changes to various procedural issues concerning the management of trade unions.

In a wholly different context, there has been a gradual development of direct regulation of business enterprises in a number of ways. The general picture of industrial and commercial activity in the private sector in Britain has changed radically

---

32 Hutton, op. cit., p 92.   33 Cmnd 3968 (1998).
34 As long as certain conditions are satisfied: see the Trade Union and Labour Relations (Consolidation) Act 1992, Sch A1.   35 Employment Rights (Dispute Resolution) Act 1998.

over the years. Today, Britain's major industries revolve not so much around large numbers of small concerns, as was the pattern in the nineteenth century, but rather around huge multinational organisations which dominate the economic scene and exercise considerable economic and even political power.

The growth of near-monopoly trading and certain other practices which have the effect of restricting freedom of competition is clearly antagonistic to any economic system based upon free private enterprise. In the United States, anti-monopoly ('anti-trust') legislation was first introduced at the beginning of the twentieth century, though the first British statutory controls on company takeovers and mergers were not introduced until 1965. The present system of control in this area is partly statutory and partly self-regulatory, in that there is some provision in the Companies Act 1985 and the Insolvency Act 1986 affecting certain aspects of takeovers, but in the main this area is regulated by the City Code on Takeovers and Mergers. The Code is produced by the Panel on Takeovers and Mergers, whose chair and deputy chair are appointed by the Bank of England, and whose membership is constituted by representatives of City of London financial institutions, including the Stock Exchange. The Code applies to offers to take over all public companies and those private companies whose shares are bought and sold publicly, and affects all those, including directors of companies and professional advisers, seeking to gain control of companies through takeovers or mergers. The Code seeks to provide for fair dealing in the area of takeovers and mergers, and for the provision of full information for shareholders of companies affected. Breaches of the Code are dealt with by the Panel by means of a hearing, followed, if appropriate, by sanctions, which may include public censure or reporting the offender's behaviour to another institution, such as the Stock Exchange, for additional action to be taken against the person offending against the Code. It is possible to appeal against a Panel decision to the Appeal Committee of the Panel, and decisions of the Panel are subject to the process of judicial review (see chapter 12). This self-regulatory system seems to work effectively, and the United Kingdom system was adopted as the model for harmonisation of European law on takeover bids in the proposed 13th Company Law Directive proposed by the European Commission, which although initially rejected by the European Parliament in 2001, is now the subject of a European Directive issued in 2004 (see chapter 8).

Apart from mergers and take-overs, it may happen that two or more enterprises, engaged in the same type of business, join together to agree between themselves on matters such as the price of the goods or services they produce, or the terms and conditions on which, or the people to whom, or the areas where, such goods and services are sold. Such agreements may be regarded in law as 'restrictive trade practices', tending to reduce freedom of competition, and may be prohibited either at common law or by virtue of the Competition Act 1998. This area of law is complex and, in the opinion of one commentator at least, 'competition and consumer law are new and growing subjects, each taking up ground previously occupied by contract law, whilst growing away from it as successive statutory measures seek to serve the public interest better than was the case under the old regime'.[36] It is an area, too, where the complexities are multiplied by the impact of Britain's membership of the European Union, whose competition rules apply to all member states (see chapter 8). Although it is not the purpose here to expand on the detail of this area of law, it must clearly be recognised as another sphere of economic activity in which the state has intervened directly, providing for restrictions and controls 'in the public interest'[37] and in the interests of maintaining a competitive economic system.

In periods of recession, with problems over the balance of payments, falling rates of profit and high levels of unemployment, companies both large and small experience serious financial problems. Some larger companies may be able to put pressure on banks and other sources of borrowing (including the government) for aid, whilst many others, especially small businesses, have simply gone into liquidation. High rates of inflation, fluctuations in the price of oil on the international market and pressure from international bodies such as the International Monetary Fund in the 1970s gave way to a period of growth in the 1980s, which were indeed boom years for some, though the end of that decade and the early 1990s saw the onset of a deep recession, with the usual accompaniments of high rates of unemployment, fluctuations in interest rates and lower consumer spending power.

It is not only economic cycles of growth and recession that may affect industry and even national economic policies, and state intervention in economic matters may not always be the result of government policies. Events beyond the control of commercial organisations or of governments occur which have the gravest impact on private industry and on national economies. Poorer countries, already labouring under the burden of indebtedness to richer countries, periodically face natural disasters such as flood, drought or famine; nearer to home, the British farming industry was seriously affected by the twin scourges of the BSE crisis in the 1990s, and the foot-and-mouth disease epidemic of 2001. Most dramatically and tragically, the terrible events of 11 September 2001 in New York and Washington, and their aftermath, had a powerful and global impact on the economic well-being of many industries, particularly the airline industry and those industries associated with it, such as international tourism. In such situations, those affected – organisations, individuals and communities – will actively seek government 'intervention' in the form of compensation, subsidisation or other forms of support.

Although the main theme of this chapter has been the examination of the expansion of direct state regulation of economic activity, it must not be forgotten that economic policies have repercussions on other spheres of social life. Indeed, it is with respect to the *social* consequences of national economic policy that many are deeply critical of government. Every administration since 1979 – both Conservative and New Labour – has emphasised the need for careful and controlled public expenditure, as well as the need to seek *private* investment, in the provision of

36 J. Tillotson, *Contract Law in Perspective* (3rd edn., 1995, Cavendish), p 206.
37 See chapter 14.

public services. Restrictions on public expenditure have inevitable implications for the provision of services such as health, welfare benefits, education, public transport and social services. Since the New Labour administration first came to power in 1997, all these areas have been the subject of government promises and agendas for improvement. The continuing government commitment, however, to the notion of 'public/private partnerships' in the provision of many of these services has resulted both in uncertainty as to how *real* benefits will be achieved (for example, in the health service), and in scepticism as to the *real* extent of government spending commitments – for example, on improving safety in the railway industry. It seems certain, however, that for the foreseeable future the state will retain its hold on the active direction of the economy, whichever political party may be returned to power in the years to come.

Summary

In this chapter we have explored some aspects of the transitions through which our society has gone over the years with regard to the relationship between law, state and economy. In particular, we have seen how the nineteenth-century emphasis on *laisser-faire* ideas, carrying the implications of freedom from state intervention and control in economic life, has given way to a context in which the state, through various government policies, enters into the economic life of the country in a much more active and directive way. These changes have not been without their accompanying problems and tensions, many of which have yet to be resolved. Many of the changes are the outcomes of political programmes pursued by successive governments, against a background of many different groups competing for a voice in the economic affairs of the country. Often, such groups call upon the use of the law and the legal system, either as a force for change, in their attempts at reform, or as a force for conservatism, in their attempts to resist further change which, in their view, might be to their disadvantage. It is hard to resist the conclusion that, contrary to the pluralist view of the state, it is the demands of the powerful that are most readily heard, but we shall examine the strength of such a conclusion in more detail as we explore other contexts involving legal regulation in later chapters.

4

Some important legal concepts

The importance of legal concepts will already be appreciated from the preceding discussions, in which we mentioned such notions as 'freedom' and 'justice' and their role within the legal system. Apart from these concepts, however, which play a part in influencing the content and operation of the legal system, there are other fundamental concepts within the law itself, whose significance must be understood. Such concepts as 'ownership' and 'possession', for example, referring to what may be quite complex relationships between individuals and concrete things, are basic to the notions about property embodied in law, and these particular ideas are dealt with in chapter 5. At a rather more fundamental level are concepts of 'rights', 'duties' and 'persons', which are so basic to the operation and implementation of rules of law that we can think of them as the 'units of legal currency' whereby rules become 'translated' and applied to specific social activities. If we say, for example, 'Jones owns a car', then in the event of Smith, another car-owner, driving his vehicle so that it collides with Jones' car, the fact that Jones' interest in her car is one of 'ownership' will give rise to all kinds of possible relationships between Jones and Smith, turning on the questions as to what *rights* Jones may have in law against Smith, and what *duties* Smith may have infringed in respect of Jones and her damaged car. In this chapter, these basic legal concepts and the various attempts made by legal writers to analyse and classify them will be examined critically; in the second part of the chapter, the idea of 'legal personality', or what constitutes a 'person' in the eyes of the law, will be considered with various examples.

Rights and duties: problems of analysing legal concepts

> ... the law consists of certain types of rules regulating human conduct and ... the administration of justice is concerned with enforcing the rights and duties created by such rules. The concept of a right is accordingly one of fundamental significance in legal theory ...[1]

What do lawyers mean when they speak of 'legal rights'? There are a number of contexts in which the notion of 'rights' may arise.

1 J. Salmond, *Jurisprudence* (12th edn., ed. P. J. Fitzgerald, 1966, Sweet and Maxwell), p 215.

Human rights and the Human Rights Act 1998

We noted the difficulties of analysing the idea of 'rights' in the general context of 'human' or 'civil' rights in chapter 2, and we may stress once again here that the fact that a social group might recognise something as a 'moral right' does not necessarily imply that it is a *legally protected right*. Furthermore, when speaking of such 'human rights', we are making statements about a social group's adherence or non-adherence to a particular moral and political code which contains such principles. Such a code may or may not be applied, nor even recognised, in any given social group or society.[2] History reveals a number of examples of commitments to codes of rights – on the eve of the French Revolution in 1789, for example, those wishing to bring about radical change agreed upon the 'Declaration of Human Rights', which set out basic civil liberties for all French people. The first ten amendments to the American Constitution, ratified in 1791, comprise the 'Bill of Rights' which defines and protects specified civil liberties for all American citizens. More recently, Canada established its Charter of Freedoms in 1982; and in Europe, the European Convention on Human Rights, established in 1950, set out fundamental rights and freedoms which were in principle guaranteed by all those European states which ratified the Convention. Most of the European Convention has now been incorporated into English law by means of the Human Rights Act 1998. Schedule 1 to the Act sets out those Articles of the European Convention which are included, and this important development in English law requires further discussion.

Article 2 of the Convention deals with the right to life. All human life is to be protected by law, and no one may be deprived of their life except by means of capital punishment as may be provided by law.[3] It is, however, provided that no breach of this provision occurs if a person dies as a result of the use of necessary force used for the defence of any person from unlawful violence, for carrying out a lawful arrest, for preventing a lawfully arrested person from escaping, or for quelling a riot or insurrection. Article 3 provides for the prohibition of torture and inhuman or degrading treatment or punishment. 'Slavery and forced labour' are prohibited by Article 4, though it is provided that this term does not include work carried out by those held in lawful detention, such as work done in prison, work done as part of military activity, work carried out under emergency conditions or 'any work or service which forms part of normal civic obligations'.

Article 5 is a complex provision, dealing with the right to liberty and security. It states, in essence, that people have the right to liberty and personal security, and there shall be no deprivation of liberty unless by due process of law (which includes lawful arrest as well as detention on conviction, and also includes detention for the purpose of preventing the spread of infectious diseases, the detention of 'persons

2 On this see, for example, Lloyd's *Introduction to Jurisprudence* (7th edn. by M. D. A. Freeman, 2001, Sweet and Maxwell); J. Waldron (ed.) *Theories of Rights* (1984, Oxford University Press).
3 There is no such provision in Britain. Capital punishment was suspended in 1965 and this suspension was extended indefinitely in 1969.

of unsound mind, alcoholics or drug addicts, or vagrants' and the detention of those seeking to enter or leave a country illegally). This Article also provides for the rights of arrested persons to know the reasons for the arrest, and to be brought before relevant authorities (such as a court of law) within a reasonable time.

Article 6 provides for the right to a fair trial, and this will include an entitlement to a hearing by an 'independent and impartial tribunal established by law', and the right to be informed clearly of the nature of the accusation, to have adequate time to prepare a defence, to defend oneself in person or by means of legal assistance, to examine witnesses and to have the assistance of an interpreter, if necessary. The presumption of innocence – 'everyone charged with a criminal offence shall be presumed innocent until proved guilty according to law' – is specifically incorporated. Article 7 provides that no conviction or punishment be imposed unless as provided by law.

Article 8 provides for basic rights to respect for private and family life without any interference by any public authority 'except such as is in accordance with the law and is necessary in a democratic society in the interests of national security, public safety or the economic well-being of the country, for the prevention of disorder or crime, for the protection of health or morals, or for the protection of the rights and freedoms of others'. Freedom of thought, conscience and religion are dealt with by Article 9 – once again, these freedoms are to be limited only as prescribed by law – and freedom of expression is protected by means Article 10. Here, too, however, it is provided that this freedom is not unlimited: free expression may be affected by legal proscriptions 'in the interests of national security, territorial integrity or public safety, for the prevention of disorder or crime, for the protection of health or morals, for the protection of the reputation or rights of others, for preventing the disclosure of information received in confidence, or for maintaining the authority and impartiality of the judiciary'.

Similar limitations are imposed by Article 11, dealing with freedom of assembly and association; although Article 12, dealing with the right of all persons of marriageable age to marry, is much more straightforward. Article 13 prohibits any discrimination 'on any ground'[4] which would prevent the enjoyment of any of these rights and freedoms.

The Human Rights Act 1998 contains two further important elements. First, it is provided in s 3 that all legislation passed by the United Kingdom Parliament must be interpreted in such a way as is compatible with the above Articles of the Convention. If this is not possible, then the Act states that any higher court (that is, the House of Lords, the Privy Council, the Court of Appeal and the High Court) can declare that legislative provision to be incompatible, in which case it is up to

4 Article 14 expressly mentions discrimination on the ground of sex, race, colour, language, religion, political or other opinion, national or social origin, association with a national minority, property, birth or other status. It is likely that this Article would also cover discrimination on the ground of marital status or sexual orientation, though see the discussion on legal personality, below.

Parliament (which will usually mean a government minister) to take action to amend the law in order to achieve compatibility, and a special 'fast-track' procedure is provided for this purpose by s 10 of the Act. It should be noted that the Act empowers, but does not require, such remedial action to be taken, which means that, in practice, any such action (or inaction) will be the result of a political, rather than a legal decision.

Second, the Act provides (s 6) that it is unlawful for any 'public authority' to act in a way which is incompatible with the Convention, and it is clear that the term 'public authority' will include central and local government, health authorities, the police, the courts, education authorities and anyone acting on behalf of any of these organisations. Importantly, it is clear that any action by an organisation whose functions may be a mixture of public and private will be covered with respect to the 'public' functions which it discharges (though not to the 'private' ones). A university, for example, will normally receive public funding for the teaching of most of its undergraduate students, but will also typically engage in private contracts. It will therefore be treated as a 'public authority' with respect to the former function, but not to the latter.

Any public authority which acts in a way which is incompatible with the Convention may find itself being challenged before the English courts[5] by any person, group or organisation who is affected, directly or indirectly, by that breach of the Convention. If the public authority is found by a court to have acted in the manner which the claimant alleges, the claimant may receive any remedy which the court has power to award, and which the court considers 'just and appropriate'. Remedies may therefore include compensation and injunctions, which are orders of the court having the effect of restraining defendants from carrying out any further breach of the Convention.

It will be clear that the wording of the Articles of the Convention, together with the provisions as to compatibility, mean that the courts have a major task with regard to the detailed interpretation of this important statute. The Act has already triggered a considerable amount of case law and, although we cannot embark on any detailed analysis of this complex statute, reference is made in this book to those areas where the Act is likely to have a major impact.

Legal rights, legal duties and legal remedies

Let us now turn to the issue of the acknowledgement and protection of specific legal rights: what does it mean when we speak of X as 'having a right to be paid a debt owed by Y', or of A as 'having a right to compensation in respect of injuries caused by B'?

Legal writers have at various times offered different analyses of the concepts 'rights' and 'duties'.[6] Few of these analyses have met with unqualified acceptance by

---

5 And not, as was previously the case, before the European Court of Human Rights at Strasbourg.
6 For a detailed commentary and discussion on the various approaches to the analysis of rights and duties, see Lloyd, op. cit.

critics, but they have provided us with useful insights into the analytical problems involved. Let us look briefly at some of the many approaches to the problem in order to appreciate both the insights and the difficulties.

Salmond, whose *Jurisprudence* was first published in 1902,[7] regarded legal rights as being essentially connected with the idea of 'interests', which he defined as 'things which are to a man's advantage'. He pointed out that rights and interests are separate but connected: a right protects the interests 'which accordingly form the subject matter of [a man's] rights but are different from them'.[8] Certainly, it is easy to think of legal rules which appear to embody rights protecting interests – the right to defend oneself and one's property from attack and intrusion (the right to self-defence) may be seen as protecting one's interests in life and property, for instance. But Salmond himself admitted that not all interests are protected by legal rights (it may be in my interest to accumulate wealth by appropriating yours, but the law of theft prohibits my doing so). Moreover, the *trust* is an illustration of a case where a person may be able to exercise legal rights (as where trustees administer and manage property entrusted to their care) despite the fact that the person has no *personal* interests protected by those rights: where there is a trust, the interest in the property remains at all times in the beneficiary, on whose behalf the property is managed. The only way in which we can ascertain whether a particular interest is protected by a legal right, then, is to determine whether a legal rule affecting that interest exists at all, and then to discover the way in which that legal rule, if it exists, actually operates in relation to the particular interest in question.

Sometimes it has been argued that legal rights exist only where the holder of the right can enforce it by bringing an action in law. This proposition is based on the idea that whenever a person's legal right is infringed, a legal remedy will be available for that person in respect of that infringement. Against this, Hart[9] has argued that although a person may be physically incapable of preventing the unauthorised taking of his property, we do not conclude that he therefore has no legal right to the property as against the thief. This example may, however, be somewhat misleading. Although the disabled victim may be *presently* incapable of asserting his right to the property as against the thief, there is no doubt that he can subsequently take legal action for the recovery of that property. And we must take care to distinguish between legal rights and *moral* rights: even where a legal right may not exist (or may be extinguished), a moral right may well continue. For example, the possibility for an aggrieved party to bring certain legal actions only remains open for a limited period, after which time that party cannot sue the other person. Some debts are subject to this rule, and the effect is that after the given time-period has expired, the action in law is said to be 'statute-barred'. If Jones owes Smith money, and Smith is unable to bring a legal action against Jones to enforce his legal right to be repaid because the time-period has elapsed, then we may say that Smith's 'remedial right'[10]

---

7 Op. cit. See also R. Dworkin, *Taking Rights Seriously* (1977, Duckworth).   8 Ibid., p 217.

9 H. L. A. Hart, 'Definition and Theory in Jurisprudence' (1954) 70 LQR 37.

10 D. Lloyd, *The Idea of Law* (1991, Penguin), pp 312–314.

(the procedural right afforded in law for the provision of a legal remedy) is no longer available. This limitation does not, however, affect Smith's 'primary right' to be paid by Jones. This right will continue to exist despite the absence of a legal power by Smith to *enforce* that primary right. It would seem, then, that the connection between having a legal right and the power (physical or legal) to enforce it does not provide us with a key to understanding and analysing the concept of legal rights.[11]

A number of writers have linked the idea of 'rights' with that of 'duties'. To return to our example of the debt owed by Jones to Smith: if Jones owes Smith £100, then we say that Smith has a legal *right* to be paid £100 by Jones, and that Jones is under a corresponding legal *duty* to repay the money. The 'right' and the 'duty' in this case are, so to speak, opposite sides of the same coin. But does this necessarily mean that *all* legal rights imply corresponding legal duties, and vice versa? Certainly this was the view taken by Salmond: as the editor of the last edition of Salmond's *Jurisprudence* explained the position, 'on this view, every duty must be a duty *towards* some person or persons, in whom, therefore, a corresponding right is vested. And conversely every right must be a right *against* some person or persons, upon whom, therefore, a correlative duty is imposed'.[12]

The contrary view, that duties do *not* necessarily imply corresponding rights, was taken by Austin, among others, writing in the nineteenth century. He distinguished between *relative* duties which, as in our example of the debt, involve corresponding rights, and *absolute* duties, which are imposed by law without any corresponding rights being implied or involved. Examples of absolute legal duties may be found within the area of criminal law. We are all under legal duties not to commit crimes, but it is not easy to identify the subject of corresponding 'rights'. To the argument, 'it is the community, through the agencies of prosecution, which holds and exercises the right to deal with the offender', it may be replied that the prosecution of an offender may well be regarded as a *duty* rather than a right; and a criminal prosecution does not of itself present the victim of the crime, still less the community in general, with any form of *remedy* in recognition of any infringed right. Moreover, assuming that the criminal offender is caught, prosecuted and convicted, many would assert that the sentencing judge is under a legal duty to pass an appropriate sentence. Surely this cannot force us to the conclusion that the offender has a corresponding legal *right* to be fined or imprisoned?

Even if we accept the distinction between relative and absolute duties, we are left with the difficulty of ascertaining whether legal rights imply corresponding duties. It is here that the term 'rights' is perhaps at its most inadequate: one term cannot possibly accommodate the complex and varied situations within the law where a particular relationship between persons needs to be analysed. The problems of

---

11 This discussion may, however, help us appreciate the implications of current debates about 'animal rights'. The fact that animals are clearly incapable of exercising legal rights should lead us to question whether it makes sense to speak of such 'rights', and to recognise that a better approach might be to discuss the *obligations* (either legal or moral) upon *people* not to mistreat animals, or, for that matter, any other aspect of the environment.   12 Op. cit., p 220.

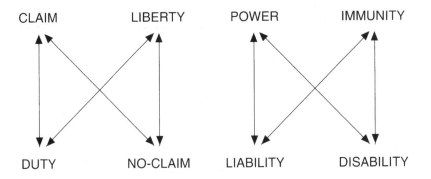

CLAIM   LIBERTY   POWER   IMMUNITY

DUTY   NO-CLAIM   LIABILITY   DISABILITY

analysing such cases, and specifying appropriate terms to describe such relationships, were confronted, in particular, by Hohfeld, an American legal writer whose
Fundamental Legal Conceptions appeared in 1913.[13] After pointing out the analytical dangers of using phrases such as 'rights' and 'duties' indiscriminately, and of
attempting to reduce all legal relationships to these unit-terms, Hohfeld proceeded
to elucidate his own classification of 'jural opposites and correlatives'. He substituted for the general terms 'rights' and 'duties' a set of alternative terms referring to
legally specific relationships. These jural correlatives and opposites have been presented diagrammatically[14] above.

The *vertical* arrows link jural correlatives. This idea may be stated thus: 'the
holding by X of a *claim* to be repaid money which s/he has lent to Y implies the presence of a *duty* in Y to repay the money to X'. The second pairing may be illustrated
by the statement 'the holding by X of a *liberty* to enter and remain on his own land
implies a *no-claim* in Y, who has no such liberty to enter and remain on X's land'. The
correlatives 'power' and 'liability' are shown in the example of a power held by a local
authority to purchase property compulsorily (provided by various legal enactments).
The authority may be said to hold a *power*, whilst the landowner whose property is
being purchased (whether he or she likes it or not) is said to be under a legal *liability* to have the land so purchased. The fourth pair of correlatives may be seen in the
example of the defence of 'privilege' in that part of the law of tort relating to defamation (libel and slander). It has been the case since the Bill of Rights 1688 that if a
Member of Parliament makes a defamatory statement in the course of Parliamentary
debate, the person defamed may not bring an action for defamation against the MP
who may, in Hohfeld's terminology, be said to enjoy an *immunity* from that legal
action, whilst the aggrieved person is under a legal *disability* in respect of that action.

The *diagonal* arrows connect jural opposites: this idea is somewhat simpler. If X
has a *claim* in relation to a person in respect of some matter, then X cannot at the

13 'Fundamental Legal Conceptions' (1913); see Lloyd's *Introduction to Jurisprudence*, op.cit.,
pp 355–8; R. Stone, *Textbook on Civil Liberties and Human Rights* (4th edn., 2002, Oxford
University Press), ch.1 for a discussion of the work of Hohfeld in the context of human rights.
14 G. Williams, 'The Concept of Legal Liberty' in R. Summers (ed.), *Essays in Legal Philosophy* (1968,
Blackwell).

same time have a *no-claim* in respect of that person or subject-matter; if Y is *liable* in respect of a given legal rule, then Y cannot at the same time be *immune* from falling under that legal rule, and so on.

Not even this complex classification, under which many legal relationships may be successfully pigeon-holed, has been immune from criticism. The terms used in the schema are in some cases (such as the idea of 'no-claim', or 'no-right') not legally recognised or used; and it may be argued that the seemingly simple notion of the 'legal power' may in fact denote quite different ideas. The 'legal power', or capacity, of the ordinary individual to marry, make a will or make contracts, none of which require any special status, may be contrasted with the 'legal powers' of specific officials or institutions, such as government ministers or local authorities, which may be better thought of in terms of 'authority'. The same kind of objection may be made concerning the single category 'duty': civil law duties differ in various ways from those of criminal law, for example, and arguably require a much more detailed analysis than Hohfeld provides.[15]

Despite these and other analytical problems, many of which might be remedied by elaboration of the original schema, Hohfeld's work throws valuable light on the problems of trying to elucidate 'legal rights' and 'legal duties'. So great have these problems proved, in fact, that the modern tendency is to reject the quest for an all-embracing catalogue or definition of the terms, and to turn instead to the exploration of the proposition that the meanings of these general terms will differ according to the contexts in which they are used.

This, broadly, is the argument put by Hart.[16] He tries to show how words such as 'rights' and 'duties' are simply not amenable to definition through mere synonym, but must be examined in the specific legal contexts in which they are commonly used, in order for their meanings in those contexts to be understood.[17] Hart has not been alone in pointing to the dangers of ambiguities of terminology. Glanville Williams showed[18] many years ago how words in common legal use, such as 'possession' and 'ownership' (both having provided headaches for would-be definers), are often used in different ways in different contexts. Lloyd, in the original Preface to his *Introduction to Jurisprudence*,[19] explains his own attraction to approaches which are sensitive to the importance of linguistic accuracy.

Taking Hart's approach as an example: he attempts to introduce a mode of elucidation of legal concepts by specifying particular contexts and conditions in which words such as 'right' and 'duty' are characteristically used. Thus, rather than

15 See Lloyd's *Introduction to Jurisprudence* op. cit.
16 H. L. A. Hart, 'Definition and Theory in Jurisprudence', op. cit.
17 See also H. L. A. Hart, *The Concept of Law* (1961, Oxford University Press) and 'Positivism and the Separation of Law and Morals' (1958) 71 *Harvard Law Review* (also in R. M. Dworkin, *The Philosophy of Law* (1977, Oxford University Press), pp 17–37. For a thorough critical discussion of Hart's work, see N. MacCormick, *H. L. A. Hart* (1981, Edward Arnold).
18 G. Williams, 'Language and the Law' (1945) 61 *LQR* at 71, 179, 293, 384.
19 Lloyd's *Introduction to Jurisprudence*, op. cit., esp. pp ix–x.

seeking a simple synonym for the word 'right', Hart instead presents the following as an elucidation of the expression 'a legal right':

(1) A statement of the form 'X has a right' is true if the following conditions are satisfied:
    (a) there is in existence a legal system;
    (b) under a rule or rules of the system some other person Y is, in the events which have happened, obliged to do or abstain from some action;
    (c) this obligation is made by law dependent on the choice either of X or some other person authorised to act on his behalf so that either Y is bound to do or abstain from some action only if X (or some authorised person) so chooses or alternatively only until X (or such person) chooses otherwise.
(2) A statement of the form 'X has a right' is used to draw a conclusion of law in a particular case which falls under such rules.[20]

This formula helps us fill in something of the formal legal contextual background to the statement 'X has a right', although it does presuppose the existence of a clear legal rule under which the rights and obligations can be seen to apply. Unfortunately, as Hart himself emphasised in another article,[21] there are many legal rules which are not, at any given moment, clear-cut as regards their application. Such a rule, to adopt Hart's own example, may forbid you to take a vehicle into a public park: 'Plainly this forbids an automobile, but what about bicycles, roller skates, toy automobiles? What about aeroplanes? Are these . . . to be called "vehicles" for the purposes of the rule or not?'[22] There is, within any given rule, a 'core' of plain and settled meaning; in such a case, Hart's formulation of the idea of 'a legal right' will be fitting. But what of the doubtful cases – those cases which, as Hart puts it, fall into the area of the 'penumbra' around the 'core' of meaning? There are many such 'grey areas' involved in legal rules where we cannot, with any certainty, make sense of the case by using Hart's elucidation, and where the scope of a rule is unclear then the scope of relations falling under that rule is also unclear.

When a new legal rule is created, for instance (either by Parliament or through judicial law-making in deciding cases), it is not immediately clear what the limits of the applicability of the rule are. Take the well-known case of *Donoghue v Stevenson*[23] in 1932, for example.

In this case, the plaintiff, Mrs Donoghue, had been bought a bottle of ginger-beer by a friend in a cafe. The ginger-beer, unknown to anyone, allegedly contained a decomposing snail which could not be detected by visual examination because the bottle was made of dark glass. The plaintiff had drunk some of the liquid, and then poured out the remainder, on doing which she saw the snail's remains, which floated out of the bottle. As a result of seeing this, coupled with the fact that she had already consumed part of the contents, she suffered shock and gastro-enteritis. She sued the manufacturer of the ginger-beer, Stevenson, on the ground that he owed

20 'Definition and Theory in Jurisprudence', op. cit., p 49.
21 'Positivism and the Separation of Law and Morals', op. cit.
22 Ibid. in Dworkin, op. cit., p 22.   23 [1932] AC 562.

consumers in her position a duty to ensure that such contamination did not occur, and that she therefore had a right to compensation in respect of her illness. Outside the law of contract (and there was no contract entered into by the plaintiff in this case) there was no clear ground on which such a legal action, in the tort of negligence, could be brought. The court decided that, on these facts, there was a good cause of action which might be brought against the manufacturer; but prior to that decision, if we asked, 'Has the plaintiff a right to compensation?' then, if we applied Hart's formula, the answer would have to be, in such an unclear area of law, 'Perhaps; perhaps not. It is not possible to give a firm answer.' Even after the decision in *Donoghue v Stevenson*, which decided that a manufacturer owes a duty to the ultimate consumer to take reasonable care over the preparation of the goods which he produces, it was not always possible to give a clear, unequivocal answer to a case where a consumer was asserting a claim of right against a manufacturer; for the law does not stand still, and legal rules are changed, extended, limited or modified in the course of future disputes which are decided by the courts.

Hart's analytical device, then, only takes us so far in understanding the nature of 'rights' in law. It does not explain the dynamic quality of legal rules (and hence of legal rights created through those rules). It does not explain the conditions under which new or modified rules may emerge.[24] Hart's contribution in his elucidation of the phrase 'a legal right' lies in the emphasis that words and phrases referring to legal concepts must be examined in their particular contexts and usages. These contexts, however, are constituted not only by the *formal* conditions of legal rules and the framework of legal institutions, but also *their* contexts in turn: the structure of legal, social, economic and political events, circumstances and developments. Here, we must ask a rather different kind of question from the ones to which Hart's formulation is addressed.

To understand what is meant by such terms as 'rights' and 'duties' in law, it is suggested that an approach is needed which takes into account certain fundamental requirements or conditions. In addition to considering the part played by *interests*, and by the possession or otherwise of physical or legal *power* to enforce rights, it is surely also important to clarify the relationship between the *legal* structure of rules, rights, duties and other legal phenomena, and the *social and political* settings from which these legal phenomena emerge. The approach taken here attempts to take account of these relationships, and of the dynamic aspect of laws, rights and rules. Rather than viewing rights, duties and rules, then, as static, presupposed phenomena, the changing nature of law and society is considered, and rights and duties are seen as part of a *continuing process* of legal regulation, during which those rights and duties will emerge, undergo modifications or extensions, or may, in time, be extinguished altogether. The 'legal right' is, after all, merely a symbolic term, referring to a continuing process of legal regulation of a given social activity, and it is

24 For cases of similar novel import, see for example *Rylands v Fletcher* (1868) LR 3 HL 330; *Home Office v Dorset Yacht Co Ltd* [1970] AC 1004 and *Hedley Byrne & Co Ltd v Heller & Partners Ltd* [1964] AC 465, both of which are discussed below; and perhaps *White v Jones* [1995] 1 All ER 691.

this legal regulation, together with the legal relationships which arise from that regulation – relationships which we speak of as involving 'rights' and 'duties' – which is the focus of our enquiry.

The adoption of this processual approach opens up three distinct stages in that process. First, there is the claim of right: when Mrs Donoghue, in the case discussed above, brought her legal action against the defendant Stevenson, she was in effect arguing that 'she ought to be accorded a right' in respect of her injuries. Note the two aspects to this claim: the plaintiff was claiming a right to a legal remedy (a 'remedial right') which, she argued, rested upon a basic right not to be injured through manufacturers' negligence (a 'primary right'). Such a primary right was previously unknown in law.[25] This plaintiff was therefore inviting the court to recognise her claim, and the House of Lords, by a majority of three judges to two, duly did so. Why did the court accept that Mrs Donoghue's claim was legitimate? In the absence of any general laws protecting the consumer in such situations as this, the court felt, as can be discerned from various passages in the leading judgment of Lord Atkin in the case, that the law *ought* to provide a remedy for such loss or injury:

> It is said that the law . . . is that the poisoned consumer has no remedy against the negligent manufacturer. If this were the result of the authorities I should consider the result a grave defect in the law . . . I do not think so ill of our jurisprudence as to suppose that its principles are so remote from the ordinary needs of civilised society and the ordinary claims it makes upon its members as to deny a legal remedy where there is so obviously a social wrong.[26]

The court was, as can be seen, recognising the general social need for some form of remedy for aggrieved consumers who suffer loss through negligence by manufacturers, and thus recognising Mrs Donoghue's claim of right as worthy of protection in law. This first stage, the *claim of right*, is invariably the start of the process whereby rights become embodied in legal rules. Such a claim may be brought before a court, as in this case, through litigation; or it may be presented before Parliament,[27] the objective being to secure new legislation which will recognise and protect the interests concerned through the provision of new rights and duties. Even when a legal rule already exists, a plaintiff who brings an action based upon that rule will also be exerting a claim of right, for, as we shall see in chapter 7 when we consider the operation in law of the doctrine of precedent and the problems of statutory interpretation, the courts are continually being invited by plaintiffs and by prosecutors to bring a novel situation within the ambit of an existing legal rule. Indeed, this is one way in which the law changes and is brought into line, where the judges think it appropriate, with changing social conditions.

---

25 Except for the established cause of action where a plaintiff was a party to a contract (in which case the action was in contract, not in tort), and cases in tort which involved articles which were either inherently dangerous (such as guns or poisons) or had a defect which was known to the manufacturer. See the dissenting judgment of Lord Buckmaster in *Donoghue v Stevenson* [1932] AC 562.
26 *Donoghue v Stevenson* [1932] AC 562 at 582.   27 See chapter 7.

The case of *Home Office v Dorset Yacht Co Ltd*[28] in 1970 serves to illustrate the point. Although many cases decided since *Donoghue v Stevenson* had widened the basic principle contained in that case so as to encompass situations involving relationships between persons other than just manufacturers and consumers,[29] this case raised an entirely novel proposition. A group of borstal trainees had been taken on a training exercise to an island in Poole harbour. They were supervised by three borstal officers who, in breach of their instructions, went to bed one night and left the trainees unsupervised. Seven of the boys escaped and went on board a yacht, which collided with the plaintiffs' yacht. The trainees then boarded the plaintiffs' yacht and caused considerable damage. The plaintiffs sued the Home Office, the supervisors' employer, claiming compensation for the supervisors' alleged negligence which, they argued, was the cause, in law, of the damage.

Among the various questions for the House of Lords was whether there was any duty owed by the defendants towards the plaintiffs, and, as Lord Diplock put it, 'this is the first time that this specific question has been posed at a higher judicial level than that of a county court'.[30] Although clearly far removed from the *Donoghue* situation, the House of Lords held, by a majority, that the Home Office was under a duty of care towards the plaintiffs. In the words of Lord Reid,

> where negligence is involved the tendency has been to apply principles analogous to those stated by Lord Atkin . . . (and) . . . I can see nothing to prevent our approaching the present case with Lord Atkin's principles in mind.[31]

Now, in terms of the first stage of the 'rights process', the plaintiffs were presenting a claim of right in a context in which the court, if it recognised and accepted that claim, had to apply the law of negligence[32] to a situation in which it had not been applied before. The fact that the court in this case was prepared to accept the validity of the plaintiffs' claim, and decide that on the alleged facts of the case there *could* be a duty owed by the defendants to the plaintiffs, brings us to consider the second stage in the process: that of legal *recognition* of the claimed rights. As implied above, such recognition will usually take the form of either a successful outcome for the plaintiff in a case brought before a court, or a new Act of Parliament which embodies the claimed rights in new legal rules. It must be said, however, that in the former case a court might recognise a claim of right without necessarily proceeding to the next stage in the process – that of *protection* of the primary right by the provision of a legal remedy in the case before the court.

A classic example of this was the case of *Hedley Byrne & Co Ltd v Heller & Partners*[33] in 1964. This was a decision of the House of Lords, and was the culmination of a long and complicated series of cases in the law of tort which concerned the question as to whether, and in what circumstances, a plaintiff might recover

---

28 [1970] AC 1004.
29 The duty of care has been held to apply to repairers, to car dealers, to surgeons and many others.
     See chapter 9.   30 [1970] 2 All ER 294 at 323.   31 Ibid., pp 297–298.
32 See chapter 9.   33 [1964] AC 465.

compensation in respect of financial loss suffered as a result of relying on a negligently made statement by the defendant. In the case itself, the plaintiffs were advertising agents who wished to ascertain the credit-worthiness of a potential client. They enquired about this matter to the client's bankers (the defendants) who replied that the client company was financially sound. Relying on these references, the plaintiff spent a considerable amount of money on behalf of the client, and when the latter went into liquidation they suffered a substantial loss. The statements made by the defendants had been untrue, and had been made negligently, although the defendants had made it clear that they accepted no responsibility for the statements they had made. The House of Lords acknowledged that in such (limited) circumstances, where there is a 'special relationship' between plaintiff and defendant (such as that between banker and legitimate enquirer), there *may* be liability for negligent misstatement: that is, the plaintiffs' *claim of right* was *recognised* by the court as capable of protection. On the specific facts of the case, however, the plaintiffs obtained no legal remedy (that is, no legal *protection*) because the defendants had explicitly denied any responsibility for the statements they had made.

It is necessary to bear in mind the possibility of a plaintiff's failing to obtain the protection, through a remedy, of a recognised right through legal technicalities or by reason of some other material factor in the case. In general, however, when we analyse a case in which a plaintiff is successful and obtains a legal remedy (be it compensation, an injunction restraining the defendant from pursuing particular activities, or some other form of redress) we shall see these stages in the 'rights' process: the initial claim of right, the recognition that the claimed right is capable and worthy of legal protection, and the provision of that protection through a remedy. Of course, in many cases a plaintiff will fail to convince the court that the claim involved is one which should result in legal rights and remedies. And it is also true that many interest-groups fail to secure the legislative enactments which they desire. Such failures indicate that, for some legal or political reason, the judges or legislators do not accept the claims of right, and do not therefore recognise or protect those claims through legal rules.

We may see something of this process in more detail when we turn to consider the important question of *who* may claim, possess and enjoy legal rights. It is by no means the case that the law, through its various regulatory and facilitative channels and mechanisms, treats everyone in exactly the same way. It may be that no distinction is made between one human being and another for the purposes of, say, the protections afforded through the criminal law; but in other respects, the law proceeds frequently upon the basis that people in society are treated according to the particular category in which, for many legal purposes, they fall.

Legal personality

The 'human being' is, of course, the most obvious entity to which legal rights and duties may be ascribed. The law, as we shall see presently, does treat other, non-human, entities as 'legal persons', but to begin with it is important to realise that even the 'basic unit' of the human being is a matter not wholly free from legal problems. The fundamental factors pertaining to human existence are, of course, life and death. It is crucial for the law to contain within it some form of test whereby the living existence of a human being may be definitively ascertained, for the most basic rights we enjoy may be affected. In the past, for example, the 'moment of death' has been, in law as elsewhere, accepted as the moment when the heart ceases to beat. But the development of advanced techniques in medical science have brought delicate problems: today, most of the body's functions, including the heartbeat, can be sustained by means of mechanical and electronic life-support systems. There have been cases in this country and elsewhere which have centred on the victims of tragic accidents which have resulted in comatose patients being, literally, kept alive by means of life-support systems. If such a patient can, in the opinion of medical experts, never be expected to regain consciousness, and life-functions could not continue independently of the support system, can that patient be said to be 'alive'? If the life-support system is switched off by doctors, even with the consent of the patient's relatives, are those doctors guilty of murder? Such ethical and legal problems may, in fact, have been resolved in most such cases by the recognition of the medical conception of 'brain-stem death': it is generally accepted that, though bodily functions may be maintained by life-support systems, the best test of whether life is present in the patient, independently of the support system, is the presence or absence of electrical activity in the brain. If there is none, then the patient is in effect already dead, for no life-supporting functions can operate independently of the support apparatus.

Apart from such practical considerations, there are clearly significant moral aspects to such cases – for example, is it always in the best interests of the patient to be kept alive, given the technical and human resources which are required to maintain that life? This question was among the many legal, moral and ethical problems discussed by the House of Lords in *Airedale National Health Service Trust v Bland*[34] where the court concluded, taking all the various arguments into account, that it was lawful for doctors to remove the life support treatment of one of the victims of the Hillsborough football stadium disaster, Anthony Bland, who had been in a persistent vegetative state for over three years with no possible hope of recovery. And in 2002, the High Court was directly approached by a patient (who came to be known as 'Miss B') who was being kept alive by means of a ventilator, asking for the legal recognition of her right to ask that her doctors switch off the ventilator equipment, which would of course end her life at her own request. In this case, which attracted substantial media interest, the judge approached the situation from the point of view of mental competence: if the applicant were mentally competent to take decisions concerning her medical treatment, then she would, in law, have the right to decline further medical treatment. Such a finding was in no way

34 [1993] AC 789, HL.

inconsistent with existing legal principle that a patient having the mental capacity to take such a decision has every right to refuse treatment of whatever kind, irrespective of the advice of doctors.

This case must be distinguished from the decision in the case of Diane Pretty, a sufferer from motor neurone disease, who unsuccessfully argued in 2001 that, as the disease left her incapable of ending her own life, she had the right to end her life by means of her husband's assisting her to die.[35] The law's response was that should this occur, there was no reason in principle why her husband should not be convicted of the offence of assisting suicide under the Suicide Act 1961, s2(1) of which clearly provides that 'a person who aids, abets, counsels or procures the suicide of another . . . shall be liable on conviction . . . to imprisonment for a term not exceeding fourteen years'. No guarantee could be given, said the court, that her husband might not be prosecuted under this Act were he to assist Diane Pretty to end her life. It is not particularly easy to reconcile these cases: it might be thought that a member of a medical team taking the necessary action to switch off a ventilator at the patient's request is acting in a way which is practically and ethically identical to a husband taking the necessary action to end his wife's life at her request.

As we saw in chapter 2 when discussing the similar dilemmas which had to be confronted by the courts in 2000, in deciding the legality of an operation to separate conjoined twins as a result of which, although one twin would be saved, it was inevitable that the other, weaker, twin would die,[36] it is by no means always possible to reach a conclusion which is legally, morally, and ethically immune from criticism.

If the ethical problems of life-support systems are difficult enough, then those surrounding the moment at which the embryonic human being becomes defined as having a sufficiently independent and formed existence to be treated as a person, with all the rights which a person enjoys, are even more complicated.

One example where this issue arose was the Thalidomide tragedy. The drug Thalidomide had been introduced as a 'safe' sedative, and had been prescribed for many pregnant women to help deal with tension which often accompanies pregnancy. Between 1959 and 1962, however, and (as it was later established) as a result of their mothers taking the drug, many children were born with severe deformities. The ensuing years saw a protracted out-of-court battle between Distillers Ltd, who had manufactured Thalidomide in this country, and the parents of the children who had suffered the handicaps. The liability of Distillers (which was, in the event, never tested before a court of law) depended upon the applicability or otherwise of the tort of negligence, which in turn raised many difficult questions. Among these questions was the extent to which, if at all, the manufacturers owed a duty of care to the unborn children – a difficult issue, given that many of the affected children were not even conceived at the time of the alleged negligence: how can a duty of care be owed to someone who does not yet exist?[37]

---

35 [2002] 1 AC 800.   36 *Re A (children) (conjoined twins: surgical separation)* [2001] Fam 147.
37 See, for more detail on the Thalidomide case, *The Sunday Times, The Thalidomide Children and the Law* (1973, Deutsch).

As a matter of policy, of course, there is no reason why such liability might not be imposed in such situations, but the attempt to solve such questions by the application of existing legal concepts of personality would raise problems which are virtually insoluble. This particular situation has been clarified somewhat by the Congenital Disabilities (Civil Liability) Act 1976, which provides that if the parent of a child is affected by an occurrence which results in the child being born disabled, then the perpetrator of that occurrence will be liable to the child if he would be liable in tort to the parent concerned.

Another problem which is centrally related to the issue of the unborn child is that of the acceptability or otherwise of abortion (see chapter 2). The law permits abortion in special, and limited, circumstances: on one side of the law there stands the lobby which argues for the extension of the right to an abortion, and on the other side is the lobby holding the firm belief that all abortion, at whatever stage of development of the foetus, is morally wrong. It is not easy to see how this particular problem will, if ever, be resolved.

In recent years the law has had to confront another difficult area: the question of sex. The possibilities exist for sex-change operations, due to advances in medical science and a growing awareness, at least in some quarters, of the fact that a person who, for instance, is biologically male may nevertheless regard him/herself subjectively (that is, in terms of emotions, and cultural and sexual predilections) as female. Here the law, as represented at least by the opinion of the court in the case of *Corbett v Corbett*[38] in 1971, appears to take a strictly limited and narrow view. The case involved the validity of a marriage ceremony between a man and a person who had been born a biological male, but who had undergone a sex-change operation in order to become female.[39] The court considered various aspects to the problem, and decided the issue on narrow biological grounds, holding that the person in question, despite the operation, was, and at all times since birth had been, male. Since neither English law nor the Church recognised the possibility of homosexual marriage, the result was that the marriage ceremony in question had not resulted in a valid marriage tie.

The same conclusion as that reached in *Corbett* was reached by the court in the criminal case of *R v Tan* in 1983,[40] and in 2002, the European Court of Human Rights considered the position of the United Kingdom on this issue in *Goodwin v United Kingdom*.[41] In that case, the court found that the UK was, in maintaining its legal position on the question of transsexuals, in breach of Articles 8 and 12 of the European Convention.

In *Bellinger v Bellinger* in 2003,[42] the petitioner had been born male, but had undergone gender reassignment surgery and treatment to become female. In 1982

---

38 [1971] P 110. See the Report of the Interdepartmental Working Group on Transsexual People (Home Office, 2000).

39 The issue of transsexual relationships must not be confused with the recent changes in the law making it possible to enter into a legally-recognised same-sex civil partnership, discussed above in chapter 2.   40 [1983] QB 1053.   41 (2002) 35 EHRR 18.

42 [2003] 2 AC 467; [2003] 2 All ER 593.

she had gone through a ceremony of marriage with a man, and she sought a declaration from the court that the marriage was valid. The issue turned on the meaning of the words 'male' and 'female' in s 11(c) of the Matrimonial Causes Act 1973 which provides that a marriage shall be void if 'the parties are not respectively male and female'. The House of Lords, through a series of not unsympathetic judgments, refused to grant the declaration, since the words in the 1973 statute were to be given their 'ordinary' meaning, and referred to a person's gender at birth. In the words of Lord Nicholls of Birkenhead, to decide in favour of the petitioner

> would represent a major change in the law, having far reaching ramifications. It raises issues whose solution calls for extensive enquiry and the widest public consultation and discussion. Questions of social policy and administrative feasibility arise at several points, and their interaction has to be evaluated and balanced. The issues are altogether ill-suited for determination by courts and court procedures. They are pre-eminently a matter for Parliament, . . .[43]

However, the House of Lords asserted that, given this interpretation of s 11(c) of the 1973 Act, that provision was a 'continuing obstacle' to the possibility of such relationships being recognised by English law as valid marriages, and was therefore incompatible with the right to respect for private and family life and the right to marry, as provided in Articles 8 and 12 of the European Convention on Human Rights.

The government had, at the time of this decision, signalled its intention to introduce legislation on the subject, and the Gender Recognition Act 2004 now provides that transsexual people can obtain legal recognition in their acquired gender by applying for, and being granted, a 'gender recognition certificate'.

Legally, it would seem that the matter is now resolved as regards the issue of legal personality, although some critics have argued that the problem encountered by transsexuals is not, in fact, physical or biological but is, rather, psychological, and that the Act fails to recognise this. Against this, it can be argued that a person's gender is as much a matter of personal identity and subjective feelings of alignment to a particular sex-role (irrespective of biological 'signposts') as it is a matter of biology. Certainly, many other countries have long provided full legal recognition of transsexuals' new identity,[44] and the recent changes to English law may be thought long overdue.[45]

The above examples show that, as far as legal definitions of situations are concerned, not even the most basic propositions about human beings can be taken for granted: questions as to what constitutes a human being may present difficult questions for the law to resolve. In the vast majority of cases, of course, there are no such problems for courts or legislators to resolve. More often, the issue concerns the

---

43 [2003] 2 AC 467 at p 478.   44 See report cited at footnote 38, above.
45 For further discussion see T. Walton, 'Transsexuals: the goals in sight' (1995) *NLJ*, 8 December; S. Whittle, 'An Association for as Noble a Purpose as Any' (1996) *NLJ*, 15 March; the *Guardian*, 6 February 1996.

status of a particular person, and the extent to which rights and duties attach to that person as a consequence of belonging to a particular class, group or category which is legally significant.

A person may, for the purposes of the law, perform a whole variety of social roles, any of which may or may not be legally significant. A person may be an employer or employee; a householder, a voter and a trade unionist; a husband, a father, a pensioner or a consumer; he or she may be anti-vivisectionist or gambler, disabled or blind, drug-addict or alcoholic. Each of these categories may or may not have legal rules associated with it, and the rules pertaining to a person's status as a member of one of these groups may be, and frequently are, legally unrelated to other aspects of that person's life. The role of 'father', for example, involves various rights and duties which are wholly unconnected with the same person's activities as a local councillor or a member of a political party. On the other hand, one aspect may affect others. For example, a parent's claim to state benefits and allowances may well depend upon that person's status as 'employee'. The point to be stressed is that, for legal purposes, the law *classifies* people: the response by the law to claims of right may depend upon race, occupation, sex, income, nationality, age *or any other individual or group characteristic perceived by law-makers as relevant*. The identification of individual or group characteristics in law will normally be followed by the provision of rules stating the conditions under which these categories of people will or will not be protected or made liable through the operation of those rules and the legal rights and duties embodied in them.

The fluctuations and complexities of the legal definitions and treatment of people falling into various categories will often be quite striking. The law has, for example, for many years recognised the categories 'landlord' and 'tenant' and, as we shall see in chapter 5, various statutes have provided explicitly for the legal regulation of the landlord-tenant relationship. During the nineteenth century, there was little or no legal control over the rights of landlords to lay down the terms on which they let their premises to tenants: they could charge whatever rent they liked, could evict tenants if they so desired, and could impose all manner of other, frequently oppressive, contractual terms upon their tenants. Over the years, however, the pendulum of legal protection has swung (albeit gradually and with some fluctuations) in the direction of providing legal protections for tenants through the passage of housing and rent legislation which provided for 'fair rents' and also gave protection against eviction, except in specific and well-defined situations. Any attempt by the landlord, moreover, to secure eviction through any form of harassment is a criminal offence. More recently, the pendulum has swung back in favour of the interests of landlords, largely through government policy which has been to attempt to leave the regulation of housing to market forces. We can see from this example how the interests of one category of person ('landlords') may at one time be recognised and protected through law by certain legal rights (or, more accurately in this case, by the absence of any regulatory or controlling legislation) and may at another time lose their dominance to the interests of another category ('tenants') who come to enjoy legal protection through various legal rules embodying new legal rights.

The way in which the law is used to embody rules involving rights and duties in such cases as this is, of course, a matter of policy as decided by Parliament, ministers, judges or subordinate law-makers. In the first case, it usually happens that important legislative enactments reflect government policies; political considerations can and do influence the content of the law. This becomes clear when we consider the ways in which the law has been used, at various times, to regulate group activity. Groups of people may be formed as a deliberate act by those people; or they may comprise diverse persons linked only by the ascription to them of certain rights or obligations. Some groups, like cricket clubs or rock bands, attract little or no legislative attention. Other groups and their activities, however, have often attracted the attention of governments, which have responded to the group and its activities in various ways. Obviously, whether or not there will be a response, and, if so, what form that response will take, are not legal but political questions whose answers will depend on the way in which particular governments perceive and define the group in question. There have been instances in history when the official response to a group and its activities, for instance, has been to declare that group an unlawful organisation. Such was the fate of the early organised groups of workers, the forerunners of our own trade unions, which, as we saw in chapter 1, were unlawful for many years, as were any forms of collective action by workers such as strikes or other pressures placed upon employers.

In 1854, for example, more than 3,000 workers were imprisoned for 'leaving or neglecting their work'[46] and although collective action was made lawful during the nineteenth century, many judges' attitudes remained hostile to unions and their activities well into the twentieth century.

Finally, another important way in which the law can be used to regulate group activity is for the group to seek and receive some form of special legal recognition. The best example of this is the legal device of *incorporation*, whereby a group is treated, in law, *as if it were a person*. Such treatment will often serve as a mechanism which facilitates certain activities by the group, as well as a form of regulation and control of those activities. We noted in chapter 3 the best-known example of the corporate body: the limited company – but there are many other examples of corporate bodies in existence. The British Broadcasting Corporation and local government bodies are but two other instances. Yet another special case involving 'artificial' legal personality is the trade union, which has a kind of 'hybrid' legal status. A union possesses certain benefits and liabilities which accrue to corporate bodies, but it is not treated in law as a fully corporate entity.

The Trade Union and Labour Relations (Consolidation) Act 1992 provides, in s10, that a trade union cannot become a corporate body, but that a trade union none the less has the power to enter into contracts, to sue and to be sued, in its own

---

46　See chapter 1.

name. Before 1982, the trade union enjoyed a certain degree of immunity from lia-bility in tort in respect of acts done in contemplation or furtherance of a trade dispute, but the Employment Act 1982[47] provided that this immunity is largely removed, and the trade union now stands in the same position with regard to tort liability as an ordinary individual, with the exception that there are limits imposed on the amount of compensation which may be payable by a union in any tort action.[48] Employers' associations have a similar legal status, except that such an association may choose for itself whether to remain an unincorporated association or to become a corporate body by registration as a company.

Summary

In this chapter it has been argued that legal concepts (especially those of 'rights', 'duties' and 'personality') which are frequently used in everyday legal practice are rarely simple to elucidate. In offering criticisms and limitations of some of the many contributions to the analysis of these concepts, we have suggested that these terms are best understood not by seeking alternative words or phrases to express different legal meanings, but rather by close examination of the social, economic and political contexts in which are created the legal rules which express certain rela-tionships in terms of these concepts. 'Rights', 'duties' and so on, it is suggested, are shorthand symbolic expressions of legal relationships which are subject to change and modification. In the next chapter we will see how one such concept has grad-ually been accorded a place of primacy in English law, and in the legal regulation of certain social and economic relationships. This is the concept of 'property' and the accompanying structure of legal rules which create 'property rights'.

47 Now Trade Union and Labour Relations (Consolidation) Act 1992, s 20.
48 Trade Union and Labour Relations (Consolidation) Act 1992, s 22.

5

Law and property

Legal rules are invariably related to social and economic conditions prevailing at a given period, and so we find that the legal normative expressions of the relationship between the holder of property rights and the objects of those rights have their basis in social and economic practice. We saw in chapter 3 the extent to which the law relating to business concerns itself predominantly with business property, and the regulation and transfer of that property, in accordance with the economic structure within which business operates, and we noted in chapter 2 the relationship between the law of theft and the demands of propertied classes for adequate legal protection of their property. Similarly, property concepts such as ownership and possession, leases and mortgages, contracts and trusts, are legal normative reflections of the economic activities and demands of individuals and classes at different periods.

In considering law and property, we must also bear in mind two further points. First, in our economic system, property rights are related to wealth, and when we speak of wealth and property we are usually implicitly acknowledging the unequal distribution of private property and property rights among social classes. Second, property is not treated in law as a homogeneous category. Because property objects have taken different forms and have represented differing degrees of value at different times, the law has developed a fairly specific classification of property, each type of which has particular legal rules attached to it. The most obvious form of property is land: it is the oldest and most permanent form of wealth and, as we shall see, the various rights which may exist with regard to land and its use may be traced back to feudal times. The emergence of legal rules pertaining to material, moveable objects (such as furniture, books or manufactured goods) may be seen as the reflection of developing capitalism, when such goods became increasingly important in an economic system which was coming to depend more and more upon manufacture and commerce: it is in the light of these economic developments, for example, that we may understand the development of the law of theft as we know it today. And a third legal category of property objects, called 'choses in action', refers to a type of property which is intangible, and which only exists in some symbolic form, such as bank accounts, copyright and negotiable instruments, which will be considered presently.

The legal system of a capitalist society will inevitably exhibit a comprehensive set of rules and rights concerning private property, because private property is of basic importance to such a society. The economic system depends upon the acquisition of private personal wealth, and so we may expect the legal system to be concerned to a large extent with the protection of that wealth, and with the framework within which such wealth can be invested, transferred and consolidated. The law purports, of course, to afford equality of treatment to everyone in society, regardless of social class, wealth or poverty; but it must be borne in mind that in a society where 'the percentage of wealth held by the richest one per cent increased from 18 per cent to 22 per cent between 1992 and 2000',[1] the law is used for the protection and transfer of property by only a very small proportion of the population. Similarly, with regard to transactions involving land: the law concerning land may be thought of as affecting a large number of transactions over a considerable quantity of houses, building land, industrial land and so on, but it is worth remembering that the total proportion of *urban* land in Britain is estimated at just over 10% of the whole,[2] the remainder comprising agricultural land and a much smaller proportion of forest and woodland. About half the agricultural land is owned by private individuals and concerns, the remaining half being owned by central and local government, the Church, the monarchy, and so on; such land will relatively rarely change hands. Of the 10% of urban land, a considerable proportion is taken up by uses other than housing (such as manufacturing, transport and amenities),[3] so, although land law is of great significance in the management of, and transactions relating to, landed property, such transactions affect only a small proportion of the total acreage of Britain.

The function of private property in capitalist society

It is illuminating at this point to consider something of the wider aspects of property and property rights in a capitalist society such as Britain, and to examine some of the views advanced by theorists in explaining the relationships between the economic system, property and law. Marx sought to show how civil law has developed side by side with the development of commerce and industrialisation,[4] and how various nations faced with new problems associated with these developments often adopted the civil law of ancient Rome as the basis for their own legal systems. Roman law was appropriate, argued Marx, because its legal system reflected its complex and rigid hierarchical 'class' system which centred on the distinction between the property-owners and the property-less.

Durkheim, too, was critical of private property in 'advanced' societies. Unlike Marx, he did not regard property as intrinsically productive of conflict and

1 D. Maxwell, *Fair Dues* (2004, Institute for Public Policy Research), p 12.
2 Source: Department for the Environmental, Food and Rural Affairs (2004) at www.defra.gov.uk/environment/statistics/land/lduse.htm.
3 See the Table in D. Massey and A. Catalano, *Capital and Land* (1978, Edward Arnold), p 59.
4 See K. Marx and F. Engels, *The German Ideology* in K. Marx and F. Engels, *Collected Works*, vol. 5 (1976, Lawrence and Wishart), esp. pp 89–92.

exploitative forces, but viewed certain forms of private property as tending to obstruct the realisation of a truly integrated society (that is, one having 'organic' solidarity). In particular, he was concerned to show how the continued presence of hereditary transmission of private property served to impede genuine equality of opportunity which would otherwise allow people to occupy positions in society commensurate with their abilities:

> If one class of society is obliged, in order to live, to take any price for its services, while another can abstain from such action thanks to resources at its disposal which, however, are not necessarily due to any social superiority, the second has an unjust advantage over the first at law. In other words, there cannot be rich and poor at birth without there being unjust contracts. This was still more the case when social status itself was hereditary and law sanctioned all sorts of inequalities.[5]

In Durkheim's general theory – especially on the impact of the division of labour, with the accompanying growth of civil law having the aim of restitution (compensation) – property occupies a central place.[6] Restitutive legal norms rest, by definition, upon the assumption that compensation awarded through law puts the aggrieved person, as far as practicable, in the position he or she would have been in if the transaction complained of (for example, a contract which the other party has breached) had not taken place. Compensation is peculiarly apt in cases of *material* losses – property damage, unlawful possession of another's goods, or failure to deliver goods specified by a contractual agreement – though the device is also used, albeit somewhat clumsily, for injuries of a *personal*, or bodily, nature.

The precise function of private property in Western society was the concern of the Austrian legal theorist Karl Renner, writing in the early years of the twentieth century. He sought to show how the social institution of 'private property' can undergo striking transformations in its features and functions, without any radical change in the original *form* of the legal norms concerning property-ownership. Writing from a Marxist perspective, Renner argued that in a capitalist system 'property, from a mere title to dispose of material objects, becomes a title to power, and as it exercises power in the private interest, it becomes a title to domination'.[7] How does this occur? Building on Marx's theoretical foundations, Renner explained that the original social function of private property in a pre-industrial society was merely to allow the owner to live, by using, exchanging or disposing of his own property – uses of property which were supported by legal norms. But, argued Renner, when private property developed into *capital*, which was used to set up enterprises in which the property-owner became the employer of workers, this original control of property became control over *people*: the owner/employer

5 E. Durkheim, *The Division of Labour in Society* (1964, Free Press, New York), p 384.
6 See the extract by E. Durkheim in V. Aubert (ed.), *Sociology of Law* (1972, Penguin).
7 K. Renner, *Institutions of Private Law and their Social Functions* (1949, reprinted 1976, Routledge and Kegan Paul), p 117; and see extract in Aubert, op. cit., p 39.

controlled the activities and tasks of his wage-labourers and supervised the execution of his commands as to the work to be undertaken.

The transformation of the function of property occurred, however, with no changes in the legal norms pertaining to property and ownership. In fact, said Renner, these developments, which led to domination over workers, took place regardless of legal rules and assumptions about 'freedom of contract' and 'contracts of employment' (see chapter 1). The reality is that the worker has choice only over *which* master is to dominate him; he cannot escape having to work for *someone.*

So, for Renner, legal norms continue basically unchanged, whilst the real nature and function of property become transformed. The law, Renner suggested, is in reality as irrelevant as the lawyers' assumptions about freedom of contract and of employment are illusory.

> The right of ownership . . . assumes a new social function. Without any change in the [legal] norm . . . a *de facto* right is added to the personal absolute-domination over a corporeal thing. This right is not based upon a special legal provision. It is the power of control, the power to issue commands and to enforce them.
>
> . . . This power of control is a social reality, but at the same time it is profitable to the owners – it establishes a rule not for the purposes of protection but for the purposes of exploitation, of profit.[8]

With the advantage of the ability to analyse social and economic developments in the period after Marx's work was done, Renner went on to argue that there has been, since the early stages of capitalism, a gradual but increasing transformation of private property into 'public utility', in the form of privately offered services, transport facilities, shops and so on: 'Private property has now become accessible to everyone, it is put at everybody's disposal . . . The sovereign power of private property has suddenly . . . been converted into a subject who has public duties . . .'[9] although these changes have been accompanied by legal changes as well. Still the basic legal assumptions about ownership and contract linger on, argued Renner, with law-makers and judges affording as much, and the same, protection through law to property interests as they ever did.

Renner's analysis has been criticised on several grounds. It has been suggested that he neglected the fact that in modern capitalism, 'in the overwhelmingly important field of corporate enterprise, the nominal owner, that is the shareholder, is becoming more and more powerless. He turns into a mere recipient of dividends'[10] while effective power is possessed by persons other than the legal owner.[11] This point refers to the developments in modern capitalism whereby there is, it is

---

8 Renner, op. cit., p 107; Aubert, op. cit., p 35.   9 Renner, op. cit., p 120; Aubert, op. cit., p 43.
10 W. Friedmann, *Law in a Changing Society* (1972, Penguin), p 101.
11 Ibid. And see R. Dahrendorf, *Class and Class Conflict in Industrial Society* (1959, Routledge and Kegan Paul), chapter 2. See also A. Sampson, *The Changing Anatomy of Britain* (1982, Hodder and Stoughton), chapters 21 and 22.

114 An Introduction to Law

argued, an effective separation between *ownership* of property and *control* of that property. This argument has been outlined thus:

> Growth in scale has necessarily entailed the rise and predominance of joint stock enterprise. Large business is typically owned, not by single individuals, families or partners who themselves run the enterprise, but by a multitude of shareholders. The shareholders are far too many and too scattered to exercise control . . . So, in the place once occupied by owner-entrepreneurs, there is now a power vacuum. Or there would be, were it not filled by those who are in position to exercise control: the 'managers'. Constitutionally only salaried officials – agents responsible through the board to the legal owners – in fact they acquire real power.[12]

This argument is frequently used to support the contention that in such a context of changes within capitalist structure, the older, Marxist argument that 'property equals power' falls down. The details of this particular debate are well outside the scope of this book, although we should note Westergaard and Resler's point that these changes are more apparent than real. In particular, they argue that 'middle management' may indeed have effective 'operational' control of the enterprise, in that this group takes day-to-day decisions in the running of the business (especially the larger corporate business structures), but when it is a matter of 'strategic' policy-making concerning questions of profitability and growth, investment, mergers, labour relations and relations with government, we find that these decisions are invariably taken at the top levels of the organisation – by the members of the boards of directors, who are themselves large *owners* of share capital in business organisations. The apparent division, then, between ownership and control is seen to be only partial, effective power still being concentrated in the hands of the few who usually own large slices of the organisation.[13]

As we saw in chapter 2, the centrality of the institution of property in our economic and political structure constitutes not only the criterion for possession of effective power, but also a criterion for the *legitimisation* of that power. Property has long been clothed with moral value: the ruling class in pre-industrial society ruled by virtue of its land-ownership, and this class widened out after the industrial revolution to include manufacturing and commercial classes whose claims to a legitimate role in government rested on their property-owning status. Essentially, the developing propertied middle classes claimed the right to a say in political affairs; it was upon them and their economic role that Western societies were becoming increasingly dependent with industrialisation, and so, as Gouldner explains, 'the new middle class held in highest esteem those talents, skills and energies of individuals that contributed to their own individual accomplishments and achievements. The middle-class standard of utility implied that rewards should be proportioned to men's personal work and contribution.'[14] The middle-class men

12 J. Westergaard and H. Resler, *Class in a Capitalist Society* (1976, Pelican) p 154.
13 Ibid., pp 150–171.
14 A. Gouldner, *The Coming Crisis of Western Sociology* (1971, Heinemann), p 63.

of property, then, equated their accumulation of wealth from rents and profits with social and economic 'usefulness', a stance from which their claims to political status and participation were made and fought for: 'The middle class insisted that property and men of property were useful to society and deserving of honour and other rewards because of this . . .'[15]

The law of property

Because the legal right is separate from the thing which is the object of that right, it is possible for all kinds of legal relationship between the property right and the property-object to exist. The most basic of all the various property rights is *ownership*, described by Lloyd as 'not a single category of legal "right" but . . . a complex bundle of rights'.[16] The concept of ownership has proved difficult to elucidate. Clearly, the owner of goods or land has a greater degree of legal right to deal with those goods or land than someone who is not the owner, but there are many common situations where the owner may not, in fact, be in a position to enjoy the property-object in question because the right to possession of that object has been voluntarily given up. A car-hire company, for example, enters into agreements with its customers to hire out cars to them. Here, the customer is lawfully in possession of the car for the period of the hire, and the car-hire company may not, for that period, take back possession of the car without the consent of the customer, or unless the customer has broken the terms of the hire agreement. In the absence of either of these factors, the company itself will be in breach of the hire contract (see chapter 11) if it retakes possession during the period of the hire. Despite this voluntary waiving of ordinary owner's rights to possession, however, the company remains at all times the legal *owner* of the car.

There is, then, a distinction in law between ownership and possession of property-objects. Although 'ownership' usually implies exclusive right to use and control the property-object, there are cases where 'possession' entitles the possessor of the property-object to exclude the legal owner, albeit for a limited period. A tenant of a flat, for instance, is usually entitled to exclusive possession of the flat for the period of the lease, during which time the tenant is legally entitled to exclude everyone, including the owner of the flat, from taking possession, subject to the terms of the lease.

Despite the importance of the idea of possession in law, however, the many and varied contexts in which the term is used make it impossible to define in a precise manner. Like the concepts of 'rights' and 'duties' discussed in chapter 4, we must examine what is meant by this term 'possession' by taking into account the specific situations in which the word is used. In the case which is regarded as the basis for our modern law of theft, the *Carrier's Case* in 1473, a carrier of goods was held by

15 Ibid., p 71.
16 D. Lloyd, *The Idea of Law* (1991 reprint, Penguin), p 323. See also S. Coval et al., 'The Foundations of Property and Property Law' (1986) 45 *CLJ* 457.

the court to have come into possession of those goods only when he broke open the bales which he was carrying on behalf of the owner, and appropriated the contents for his own unlawful purposes, although as a matter of common sense we would consider the carrier to have been in possession of both bales and contents from the moment of the giving over of them to him by the owner for the lawful purposes of carriage.

Again, in *Warner v Metropolitan Police Comr*[17] in 1969, a more recent case involving the offence of possession of prohibited drugs, the problem of possession was the central issue. Warner's defence was that, although he had known that two boxes in his possession contained something, he did not know that those contents were prohibited drugs; and that he had believed them to contain scent. Now, although the offence of unlawful possession of a prohibited drug has long been held by the courts to be one of *strict liability*, involving no requirement that the prosecution establish intention or even knowledge on the part of an accused (a policy issue, justified by the courts by reason of the perceived seriousness of the 'drug problem' – see chapter 10), the House of Lords in *Warner* nevertheless thought that the notion of 'possession' in this context *itself* required an element of knowledge on the part of the accused: he must at least know that he possesses *something*. You are not 'in possession' of a cigarette containing cannabis if someone slips it, unnoticed by you and without your knowledge, into your pocket. But could Warner be said to have been 'in possession' of the drug, if he thought that the contents of the boxes were scent? The House of Lords, in a somewhat confusing series of judgments, affirmed Warner's conviction on the grounds that, in the words of Lord Pearce, 'the term "possession" is satisfied by a knowledge only of the existence of the thing itself and not its qualities, and . . . ignorance or mistake as to its qualities is not an excuse'.[18] Warner, on this reasoning, was in possession of the contents of the boxes, *whatever those contents might turn out to be*. The decision, which does not now reflect the law,[19] is none the less useful in illustrating the problems posed in law by the notion of 'possession'. It may be that in Warner's case itself, the court was making a policy decision regarding the presence or absence, in law, of the defendant's 'possession' of the contents of the boxes; it is easy to appreciate that, had the decision been otherwise, the way would have been open in later cases for defences – perhaps spurious ones – to have been raised along the lines of asserting ignorance of the contents of containers,[20] leading, some might think, to the increased difficulty of controlling the use of prohibited drugs. Be that as it may, the case shows that the concept of 'possession' must be examined in specific legal contexts where it is used, and cannot be regarded as susceptible to an overall general definition.

17 [1969] 2 AC 256.   18 [1969] 2 AC 256, per Lord Pearce at 305.
19 Section 28 of the Misuse of Drugs Act 1971 has provided a defence to a charge of unlawful possession of prohibited drugs, provided that the accused can establish that he or she did not know or suspect, nor had any reason to suspect, that he or she was in possession of a controlled drug.
20 See also *R v Searle and Randolph* [1972] *Crim LR* 779; *R v McNamara* (1988) 87 Cr App Rep 246, CA; *R v Waller* [1991] *Crim LR* 381.

In most everyday situations where the concepts of ownership and possession are significant, however, these technical problems rarely arise. There are some very common transactions which involve this distinction – the case of the car-hire was mentioned above, and other examples are hire-purchase contracts (where the trader remains the legal owner until all instalments are paid, even though the customer enjoys possession of the goods – see chapter 11), and agreements between landlords and tenants for the lease of property, which we will consider later.

As noted above, the law classifies various forms of property-objects, and specific legal rules may or may not attach to these objects according to their classification. Tangible objects, such as the things we own and usually possess as part of our everyday life (furniture, books, food, cars and clothing, for instance) are termed, in law, 'personal property'.[21] Such property is not generally subject to special bodies of legal rules. We buy and sell articles and goods through the ordinary law of contract, and these objects (or rather, our rights in them) are given legal protection through the various criminal-law rules (forbidding theft, criminal damage and so on) and rules in the law of tort (providing civil remedies in the event of trespass to our goods, or of someone unlawfully keeping or selling our goods).[22]

The category 'personal property', however, includes not only these tangible property-objects, called *choses in possession*, but also property-objects which cannot be seen or carried away: these objects of personal property, called *choses in action*, include such things as company shares, copyright, patents, debts and negotiable instruments (cheques, bills of exchange and promissory notes). In a material sense, these property-objects exist only as pieces of paper; but they represent assets which are clearly of value to the owner. There are other important differences between choses in possession and choses in action, however. We may understand readily everyone's need for items which are basic to our very existence: we all need food, clothes, and the means whereby we may cultivate our food, make our clothes and so on. Choses in action, however, can be seen to originate not from such basic needs, but rather from pressures and problems within specific economic systems. Of course, many tangible objects cannot be said to be necessary to our existence – cars, furniture and television sets are examples of such objects – but choses in action are particular *forms* of property-object, created as responses to perceived problems of property and property-transfer at specific periods.

In particular, negotiable instruments (one of the most important kinds of choses in action) may be traced back to the appearance of banks during the sixteenth and seventeenth centuries, and the growing importance of money (rather than land) in a developing commercial economy. A negotiable instrument *represents* money or

---

21 See M. Bridge, *Personal Property Law* (3rd edn., 2002, Oxford University Press).
22 There are other, infrequently invoked, legal rules pertaining to these issues. One is the law relating to gifts: the donor of an alleged gift cannot change his or her mind and take it back from the recipient, as long as there was initially a clear intention on the donor's part to make the gift, and as long as there was *delivery* of the gift to the recipient by the donor (or an agent acting on the donor's behalf), or through some symbolic means, such as handing over a key to a safe containing the substance of the gift.

money's worth, but has none of the drawbacks which can attach to the use of money in business transactions; money is bulky, it is highly attractive to thieves and it has an anonymous quality – one banknote is similar to another banknote, and it may be difficult to establish that the possessor is truly entitled to it. Negotiable instruments, on the other hand, are convenient to despatch and handle, and they contain specific details as to the identity of the intended recipient. The definition of negotiable instruments may, then, be stated as 'written promises to pay money (or money's worth) to the holder, which can be freely transferred between individuals'. If A owes B money, and pays him by means of a cheque ('a bill of exchange drawn on a banker payable on demand'),[23] then B may transfer that amount to C by *endorsing* the cheque, that is, by writing on the back of the cheque 'please pay to C', signing his own name and delivering the cheque to C. C may use the same cheque to pay a debt to D, by means of a new endorsement, and so on.

Because of the somewhat complicated nature of negotiable instruments, and also because of the possibilities for fraud, the law was used to provide the framework within which these devices could be used to greatest advantage and with adequate security. Most of the relevant law is still contained in the Bills of Exchange Act 1882, but more recently the Cheques Act 1992 places restrictions on the transferability of cheques produced by banks, with the effect that crossed cheques bearing the phrase 'account payee' cannot be transferred simply by endorsement. They can only be paid into the account of the payee – the person originally named on the front of the cheque.[24] This measure was enacted as part of the effort to prevent fraud. The continuing development of the law relating to these property-objects and property rights reflect the significance of choses in action in commercial transactions, and the way in which the law is adapted to try to resolve novel problems.

Intellectual property and data protection

In recent years, developments in advanced electronics and information technology have brought new problems concerning *intellectual property* which the law has been called upon to help resolve. One of the most important issues in this area is the protection of the legal interest called *copyright*. Copyright refers to the legally-protected property-right in the original work which a person creates, and by virtue of the current statute governing this area, the Copyright, Designs and Patents Act 1988, copyright may subsist in literary, dramatic, musical or artistic work, and in sound recordings, films, broadcasts and publications. The creator of the work – the copyright owner – is legally and exclusively entitled by virtue of this right to control and exploit the use of his or her work. Why has information technology brought problems for this area?

---

23. Bills of Exchange Act 1882, s 73.
24 See, for coverage of these topics, R. Goode, *Commercial Law* (3rd edn., 2004, Penguin); L.S. Sealy and R.J. Hooley, *Commercial Law: Text, Cases and Materials* (3rd edn., 2003, Oxford University Press); or any other up-to-date standard text in this area.

To begin with, the huge increase in popularity of home computers, and the accompanying development and sales to consumers of commercial computer programs (notably, of course, computer games), has resulted in illegitimate 'pirate' copies of copyrighted programs being made. Similarly, the illicit 'pirating' and resale of films, the unauthorised recording of live concerts from which copies are made and sold ('bootlegging') and the far more commonplace home recording of television broadcasts and records by private individuals has given rise to widespread concern among the owners of copyright in these materials.

The development and increasing use of digital technology DVD ('digital video disc' or 'digital versatile disc'), which can contain high-quality video, audio and computer data, has virtually replaced the videotape cassette. Home entertainment DVD playback machines which can also record clearly bring further possibilities for unauthorised home recording of music and video material. When tape-to-tape machines became available during the 1980s, enabling the fast-dubbing of the content of one music cassette onto a blank cassette, the attempt was made – in *CBS Songs Ltd v Amstrad Consumer Electronics plc*[25] – to prevent their sale on the basis that they facilitated copyright infringement by home users. It was held by the House of Lords that there had been no copyright infringement, nor any other civil wrong, by the machine's manufacturers. The machines were capable of being used for lawful as well as for unlawful purposes, and the manufacturer had no control over the use to which a purchaser put the recording machine. Moreover, the company's advertising of the machines made it clear that the company had no authority to authorise any copyrighted recording, and so could not be said to have incited the infringement of any copyright.

The majority of problems in recent years, which the law has been used to try to address, have arisen from the rapid growth and availability of digital technology in relation to the use of home computers and the internet. The cassette-based 'tape-to-tape' recording facility has largely been replaced by the widespread home recording of pre-recorded CDs by means of computers onto blank disks ('burning') which has proved difficult to detect or prevent by the copyright owners (recording companies, music publishers, and artists).[26] Some organisations within, in particular, the music industry have attempted to incorporate copyright protection software (such as 'content scrambling systems') into their CDs, which in theory prevents their content being copied. These systems have proved difficult to operate in practice, however: in the case of Sony – one of the biggest record and music publishing organisations – the software made the user's computer vulnerable to attack by 'hacking' (illicitly gaining access to another's computer) – and in any case, virtually any such system is vulnerable to 'reverse engineering' whereby it can be analysed and programs can be designed which will counter and neutralise the protection software.

25 [1988] AC 1013.
26 In May 2006 the National Consumer Council reported the results of a survey which suggested that over half the survey respondents admitted copying CDs onto computers and MP3 players; and 59% of respondents thought it was legal to do so.

The other major concern of copyright-owners is the extent to which copyright material – in particular, music and films – can be downloaded by means of the internet. There has been a huge increase worldwide in the number of computer-users having access to the Internet (currently estimated at over 50% of households in the UK), and so the opportunities for downloading copyrighted material (either cheaply or for nothing), and possibly distributing it to friends and other users, have clearly become extensive. MP3 players, onto which large quantities of downloaded recorded music can be copied from a computer, have become hugely popular con-sumer products, dominated by the Apple iPod range, behind which is Apple's own online music store, iTunes. Such arrangements, like those of similar companies, are of course wholly legitimate, since they are created to comply with legal require-ments regarding copyright. In fact, so significant has this method of legally acquir-ing music become that a number of successful popular recordings have been made available *only* as internet downloads.

The difficulty is that, apart from legal music downloads, there are a number of internet websites which provide illegitimate music downloads (either commer-cially or through 'file-sharing'), and this is the problem against which the music industry seeks to protect itself and its artists. In a number of litigated cases in the USA, Australia, Britain and elsewhere, attempts have been made by large music cor-porations to combat file-sharing In the US case of *MGM v Grokster* in 2005,[27] a number of claimant companies, led by MGM, sued two internet file-sharing com-panies. The US Supreme Court held in the claimants' favour, deciding that file-sharing activity could indeed induce copyright infringement. Two months later, the Australian Federal Court came to a similar conclusion in a case brought against the file-sharing internet company Kazaa by a number of major recording companies.[28] Their argument was that Kazaa in effect encouraged massive copyright infringe-ment through users illegally downloading recorded music through its website. These cases may be contrasted with the *Amstrad* decision in that the courts did not accept the defence that the technology *might* be used for lawful, as well as unlawful purposes, and that the defendants could not control the use to which the technol-ogy was put by individual end-users.

In Britain, the British Phonographic Institute has taken legal action against dozens of individual file-sharers for breach of copyright, and although many were settled out of court, any cases which come before a court will result in such defen-dants being liable to pay considerable sums in compensation and in legal costs. The International Federation of the Phonographic Industry reports numerous actions taken against individuals and organisations involved in various aspects of music 'piracy' worldwide,[29] including legal action against almost 2,000 individuals in nine European countries for illegal file-sharing.

---

27 545 U.S., 125 S. Ct. 2764 (2005).
28 *Universal Music Australia Pty Ltd & Others v Sharman License Holdings Ltd & Others* (2005).
29 See www.ifpi.org for further information.

Clearly, the impact of internet downloading without copyright owners' permission cannot be ignored; though the type of interventions mentioned above clearly run counter to the original 'philosophical' view of the internet as an unrestricted 'cyber highway' which was unrestricted, free and open to all. What is clearly happening is that whilst the entertainment industry is engaged in policing the violations made feasible by digital internet technology, it is at the same time embracing that technology and using its potential for profitable commercial activity which can only continue to benefit the industry and the creative artists whose work is increasingly being sold on-line rather than through High Street record-shops.

The law concerning copyright, trade marks and patents – all choses in action – is clearly designed to protect the rights and interests of the *creators* of these materials – authors, computer-program writers, composers, artists, inventors and designers[30] – and the current law is contained principally in the Copyright, Designs and Patents Act 1988,[31] the Trade Marks Act 1994 and the Patents Act 1977.[32] The law on this subject is extremely complex, and what follows is a necessarily abridged and simplified account of the main provisions of the 1988 Act concerning copyright, in order to indicate the ways in which the law defines and regulates this type of property right.

Based on a government White Paper published in 1986,[33] and part of a complex web of international agreements and conventions, the Act of 1988 may be seen as a good illustration of what intellectual property law may cover. The Act deals with the rights of both the creators of original works and of those who produce, broadcast, publish or record them. These rights may be protected by means of copyright or design rights, depending on the nature of the work or object in question. The basic difficulty is that the proposition that the creator of original works should be entitled, whether through copyright, patent law or design rights, to legal protection through the exclusive right to exploit that work commercially is essentially anti-competitive. The logical result of unrestricted or unqualified protection, provided first to the creator and after that to the creator's estate, or to an assignee, would be the legal creation and maintenance of a monopoly in that work or design. As we saw in chapter 3, our economic system and indeed those of other European countries is based on the idea that monopolies are damaging to national economies because they restrict competition.

---

30 Or their employers. Under s 11 of the Copyright, Designs and Patents Act 1988, the 'first owner' of any copyright in a literary, dramatic, musical or artistic work produced by someone 'in the course of his employment', is his employer, subject to any agreement to the contrary in their employment contract.

31 As amended by Regulations and by the Copyright, etc., and Trade Marks (Offences and Enforcement) Act 2002.

32 Wrongful use of computers may involve criminal liability. Apart from the possibility of offences under the Theft Act 1968, the Computer Misuse Act 1990 creates three new offences: unauthorised access to computer material, unauthorised access with intent to commit or facilitate commission of a further offence and unauthorised modification of computer material. On this see M. Wasik, 'The Computer Misuse Act 1990' (1990) *Crim LR* 767.

33 *Intellectual Property and Innovation* (1986, Cmnd 9712, HMSO).

The law's response to this paradox is to grant the right of exclusivity to the creator of a legally protectable work, but only for a fixed time-period, and subject to some qualifications. At the end of the time-period the work is vested in the public domain, so anyone may then exploit the work for commercial purposes. Copyright cannot exist until the work has taken on some tangible form – there can be no copyright in mere ideas. But once the created work is recorded in some tangible form, copyright in that work automatically exists, so long as the work is original: there is no requirement that the author takes some further action to register the claim.[34]

The 1988 Act identifies three categories of materials which are protected by copyright – the property right which exists in relation to works created by authors. As indicated above, these categories are first, original *literary, dramatic, musical or artistic works*, second, *sound recordings, films, broadcasts or cable programmes*, and third, *typographical arrangements of published works*. Copyright in the first category lasts for 70 years[35] after the year of the author's death; in the second, copyright in photographs and films lasts for 70 years; and in the third category, where the copyright is owned by the publisher of the work, the period is 25 years from the year of first publication. During these periods, the protected copyright interest is such that no one except the copyright owner may copy,[36] publish, perform, show, broadcast or adapt the work without the owner's express permission. That permission may be given by means of a licence; or by means of assigning the entire right – like any property-right, copyright may be disposed of to another person by means of, for example, a contractual agreement. There are many examples in everyday life of situations in which copyright permission is routinely obtained for what would otherwise be cases of infringement – where a scene in a television play or film requires a hit record to be heard;[37] wherever background music is played in a public place such as a hotel or airport; whenever a local video shop hires out a videotaped movie; when a rock band plays in public its own version of another band's hit song; when a song is played down a telephone line whilst the caller is being queued for a connection; and so on. Note that the user of copyrighted material does not have to *intend* to breach the copyright: it is sufficient that the use is made of the protected material without the permission of the copyright owner. Infringement of copyright is a civil wrong, although the 1988 Act also provides criminal penalties where the copyright is infringed for commercial purposes and the infringers know, or have reason to believe, that they are infringing copyright.[38] Civil remedies for infringement include compensation[39] and injunctions to restrain further infringement.

---

34 It is however advisable for the author to indicate that copyright is held in the work (for example, through the use of the symbol ©. The presence of such an indication also makes a plea of innocence by an infringer difficult to sustain).

35 Council Directive 93/98/EC *Harmonising of Copyright Duration*.

36 Subject to the exceptions noted below.

37 Though the deliberate use of such material must be distinguished from the 'incidental inclusion' of copyrighted material which is *unintentionally* included in, for example, a documentary, televised sporting event or news reporting. Such incidental inclusion is not an infringement of copyright: Copyright, Designs and Patents Act 1988, s31.   38 Section 107.

39 Based on the principles of the law of tort: see chapter 9.

The Act provides that home-taping of a broadcast programme 'solely for the purpose of enabling it to be viewed or listened to at a more convenient time' (the concept of 'time-shifting') does not constitute an infringement of copyright, though this still leaves unanswered the problem, taken very seriously, as we noted above, by record and film publishers, of illicit taping for other purposes than simply time-shifting. Burning a CD from a friend's original purchased copy, copying a hired DVD film, or downloading copyrighted files from the Internet, will constitute copyright infringements, since these situations do not fall into the categories of either 'broadcasts' or 'time-shift purposes'. Various ways of protecting the economic interests of music and film publishers have been considered, ranging from the proposed imposition of a levy on blank audio and video tapes to the installation of anti-copying technology within hi-fi and video hardware. We noted earlier that the latter solution has so far proved impracticable because of the availability of methods of counteracting the protective technology, although the 1988 Act provides that anyone who makes counteracting devices available may be proceeded against as a copyright infringer.

The copying of material for educational or research use is dealt with by the 1988 Act through a number of mechanisms. Section 36 provides that, in the absence of any licensing agreement, multiple copies of up to 1% of any literary, dramatic or musical work may be made in any three-month period by an educational institution for educational purposes. In practice, it is likely that licensing agreements will regulate such copying, rather than the statutory provision; disputes concerning such licensing agreements and schemes are heard and resolved by the Copyright Tribunal, a body created by the Act which is given the task of determining proceedings involving licenses, royalty payments, and various other aspects of copyright. Section 29 provides that a literary, dramatic, musical or artistic work may be copied for the purposes of research or private study, though multiple copies may not be made; and s 30 deals with 'fair dealing' with a work for the purposes of criticism or review, or the reporting of current events: if accompanied by a 'sufficient acknowledgement', these uses are not treated as infringements.

If the rapid development of technology has created problems for the copyright owner, then the same may be said of the ordinary citizen whose personal details may, through computer data files, be easily communicated to others for all kinds of reasons and purposes. The interest at stake here is a person's interest in information about themselves and what may be done with it, and, we might say, an interest in personal privacy. The Data Protection Act 1998 represents an attempt to recognise and protect people's interests in *personal information* relating to them. There are many situations in which data concerning private individuals are filed on computers or stored in manual filing systems by both public and private organisations. This may be done for commercial purposes (as where a person's creditworthiness is assessed and filed by a bank or finance company) or administrative purposes (as where a government department or agency retains data relating to tax, motor vehicles or television licences). Problems which have arisen over such records include the difficulty for the citizen in gaining access to these records; the possibilities of erroneous or out-dated information being retained; and the general threat to individual privacy posed by the collection, processing and transferring of personal information. Once again, we are dealing here with a statute of considerable complexity, but the main legal provisions may be discussed briefly.

The Data Protection Act 1998 supersedes the earlier Act of 1984, and implements Council Directive 95/46/EC on the protection of individuals with regard to the processing of personal data and on the free movement of such data. Essentially, any person or organisation (the *data controller*) collecting and processing personal data (that is, data which relate to a living individual who can be identified from those data, and includes any expression of opinion about the individual) must register with the Information Commissioner,[40] and must specify various items of information about the data collected and the uses to which the data will be put.

The principles on which the Act is based are that (i) personal data should be processed[41] fairly and lawfully; (ii) personal data shall be obtained only for one or more specified and lawful purposes, and shall not be further processed in any manner incompatible with that purpose or those purposes; (iii) personal data shall be adequate, relevant and not excessive in relation to the purpose or purposes for which they are processed; (iv) personal data shall be accurate and, where necessary, kept up to date; (v) personal data processed for any purpose or purposes shall not be kept for longer than is necessary for that purpose or those purposes; (vi) personal data shall be processed in accordance with the rights of data subjects under this Act (vii) appropriate technical and organisational measures shall be taken against unauthorised or unlawful processing of personal data and against accidental loss or destruction of, or damage to, personal data; (viii) personal data shall not be transferred to a country or territory outside the European Economic Area, unless that country or territory ensures an adequate level of protection of the rights and freedoms of data subjects in relation to the processing of personal data.

Perhaps not surprisingly, although it applies to both private commercial enterprises and public bodies, including government departments, the Act contains certain exemptions. Principally, data pertaining to national security, the prevention or detection of crime, the apprehension or prosecution of offenders, or the assessment or collection of any tax or duty or of any imposition of a similar nature, among other matters, are exempt from some or all of the provisions of the Act. Although it may be thought sensible to exclude police information and some security information in the interests of national security or crime prevention and detection, the Secretary of State is given considerable further powers under the Act to grant various additional exemptions from the provisions of the Act.

40 The Data Protection Act 1998 referred to the 'Data Protection Commissioner' but the office was renamed 'Information Commissioner' by s 18 of the Freedom of Information Act 2000: see below.
41 The definition of 'processing' in the Act is wide, and includes 'obtaining' and 'disclosure' of the data.

Finally in this section, we should note the main provisions of another statute relating to information – the Freedom of Information Act 2000.[42] There had for many years been heavy criticism of the secrecy with which British government was carried out, and a mounting campaign to introduce freedom of access to official information along the lines adopted by many other countries.[43] In Labour's election manifesto in 1997, a bill on freedom of information was promised, and this was followed after the election by a White Paper, *Your Right to Know*.[44] In due course, a Freedom of Information Bill was published in 1999, after an extensive consultation process. That consultation process seems to have led the government to dilute its previously liberal proposals, no doubt after pressure from the anti-access lobbies within Whitehall: it has been remarked that the Bill 'heralded the end of a liberal approach to freedom of information and open government'.[45] The Freedom of Information Act 2000 appears to make so much information exempt from its access provisions that it may be thought to have made virtually no changes, for practical purposes, at all.

The Act provides for a general right of access to information held by public authorities, with provision as to time limits within which those authorities must comply with requests for information, and advice and assistance to be given to applicants. If access to information is refused, the authority denying the access has to state the basis for the refusal of the request. The Act is enforced overall by the Information Commissioner and the Information Tribunal, both of which also have enforcement functions under the Data Protection Act 1998. An applicant who is refused access to requested information may apply to the Commissioner, who must decide whether the authority in question has or has not acted in compliance with the Act. If the Commissioner decides that the authority has failed to comply, he or she may issue a decision notice or an enforcement notice. Authorities may appeal against the Commissioner's decision to the Information Tribunal, and from the tribunal, on a point of law only, to the High Court.

Perhaps the most significant and disappointing aspect of the Act is Part II, which provides that numerous categories of information are exempt from the Act's disclosure requirements. The main areas for exemption cover information which is accessible to applicants by other means; information intended for future publication (such as research findings which will be published anyway in due course); information supplied by, or relating to, bodies dealing with security matters, information relating to national security, defence, international relations, or relations between

---

42 For discussions see N. Johnson, 'The Freedom of Information Act 2000' (2001) *NLJ*, 13 July; M. Supperstone and T. Pitt-Payne, *The Freedom of Information Act 2000* (2001, Butterworths); P. Birkinshaw, *Freedom of Information: The Law, the Practice and the Ideal* (3rd edn., 2001, Butterworths); P. Birkinshaw, 'Freedom of Information in the UK and Europe: Further Progress?' *Government and Information Quarterly* (2002) vol., 19.

43 See, for example, the critical accounts in D. Wilson (ed.) *The Secrets File: The Case for Freedom of Information in Britain Today* (1984, Heinemann); and N. S. Marsh (ed.) *Public Access to Government-Held Information* (1987, Stevens).

44 (1997) Cm 3818.   45 Johnson, op. cit.

public administrations in the United Kingdom; information which might prejudice the economic interests of the United Kingdom; information relating to criminal proceedings, the prevention or detection of crime, the apprehension or prosecution of offenders, the administration of justice, or court records; information held by a government department relating to the formulation or development of government policy, ministerial communications, the provision of advice by any of the Law Officers or any request for the provision of such advice, or the operation of any ministerial private office; information relating to communications with Her Majesty, with other members of the Royal Family or with the Royal Household; information which would, or would be likely to endanger the physical or mental health of any individual, or endanger the safety of any individual; information subject to legal professional privilege; and information comprising a trade secret.

Given this array of categories of exempt information, it is hard to imagine that any public body wishing to prevent access to information would have any problem in justifying its refusal of access by insisting that one or other of these exemptions applied. Although the Act will not be fully implemented until 2005, the signs are that the Freedom of Information Act 2000 will not go far to create a long-overdue openness in government.

Land and the law

So far we have discussed the two legal categories of *personal* property, choses in possession and choses in action. In both cases, the law has been used, wherever it was thought appropriate, to regulate and protect the interests of property-holders by means of legally enforceable rights, and by means of a protective code of legal rules contained in the general criminal and civil law. In general, it is true to say that, apart from intervening in the ways just described, the state has never found it necessary to interfere in a *restrictive* manner in the field of personal property; rather, it has left individuals and business organisations relatively free to enjoy and dispose of their personal property in whichever ways they wish, and this is, of course, quite consistent with the demands of a free market economy and the competitive *laisser-faire* philosophies which underpin our economic structure.

When we turn our attention to the law relating to land, or *real property*, however, we see that it is quite a different matter. We have seen at various points the clear historical relationship between land-ownership and the possession of effective economic and political power; the traditional ruling class in England has long been the land-owning class. The extremely complicated structure of land law cannot be understood without an appreciation of both the peculiar nature of land itself and the connections and tensions between land-ownership and use, and economic interests and inequalities.

Land, unlike goods, is immovable, permanent and – apart from the effect of natural forces such as coastal erosion – indestructible. It cannot be taken away by thieves and it cannot be protected by locking it away in a bank vault. Moreover, it may be said to be the sole and original form of wealth, not least because it is a fixed and *limited* commodity. The control of land brings with it considerable social and economic power, for its very scarcity, coupled with the fact that everyone must, in order to live, have access to some land, however small, means that the landholder has the power to gain substantial economic benefit from that land by, for example, granting others certain rights over it in exchange for rents.

These characteristics of land have given rise to specific forms of social and political relations and institutions over different periods in history, although English land law still bears traces of the extremely complex social relations of feudal England. Under feudalism in the Middle Ages, land was ultimately owned by the sovereign (technically this is still the case, though of no practical significance today), and portions of land were given into the possession of those who served the sovereign, typically by rendering military services, in return for those services. At the time of the Norman Conquest, these rewards to knights and followers meant that a new political order was imposed on the pre-existing structure whereby peasants lived on the land and worked the soil for the benefit of Saxon lords. As Simpson points out, however:

> In general the effect of the Norman Conquest was only to substitute a new, alien lord for his Saxon predecessor. What a tenant in chief acquired by the King's grant was not the enjoyment of land so much as the enjoyment of rights over land and services due from peasants who cultivated that land; to the peasant it may not have seemed that anything very momentous had occurred.[46]

The structure of rights and titles whereby land was held by various individuals was very complex, involving many different forms of *tenure* based on the particular form of service rendered to the sovereign. 'Tenure signifies the relation between lord and tenant, and what it implies is that the person whom we should naturally call the owner does not own the land, but merely holds it as tenant of the Crown or some other feudal superior. But if he is not owner of the land, what is the nature of the interest that he holds?'[47] The answer to this is found in the doctrine of *estates*. An estate is the specific type of interest which the landholder has, and which the law recognises and protects. The feudal system of land law recognised a bewildering and complex array of different types of estates, onto which the jurisdiction of the Court of Chancery, administering rules of equity (see chapter 7), grafted a number of separate *equitable* interests. At common law, there were two types of landholding: the *term of years* (the original version of the modern *lease*) – whereby land was granted to someone for a specific period, which was not really regarded as a form of estate at all – and the *freehold*. Freehold estates were of three types: the *fee simple estate*, which approximated to ownership, subject to the limitations of the

---

46 A. W. B. Simpson, *An Introduction to the History of the Land Law* (2nd edn., 1986, reprinted 1996, Oxford University Press), pp 4–5.
47 G. C. Cheshire and E. H. Burn, *Modern Law of Real Property* (16th edn. by E. H. Burn, 2000, Oxford University Press), p 25.

principle of tenure; the *estate in fee tail,* whereby land could be passed on to the male heirs of the landholder; and the *life estate,* whereby land was held by a person for life, or during the life of another. Equity recognised a number of interests in land which the common law did not, most of which were connected with the *trust,* whereby land was held by one person (the *trustee*) on behalf of and for the benefit of another (the *beneficiary*). Land-holding was thus structured upon a complicated system of legal rules and concepts under feudalism, and although important developments took place over the years, the basic scheme endured until the important land legislation of 1925.

Three conclusions follow from this structure of land-holding under feudalism. First, there was nothing equivalent to our system whereby land and houses might be bought and sold. Land-holding rights sprang from tenure, and the multiplicity of services (both already rendered and continuing as conditions of tenure)[48] were usually of a *personal* nature not easily transferred from one person to another. Second, the social relations of the feudal structure were static: peasants were tied to the land held by their lord, and in exchange for services and produce from the land were allowed by that lord to eke out their own living. Social status was not a matter of personal industry, talent and competitiveness, as much as a question of accident of birth. The feudal system is, then, the basis of the landed aristocracy in England as we understand the term in more modern times.

Third, the morass of technicality which comprised feudal land law plagued English law for the next eight or nine hundred years, a long period which saw the decline of feudalism and the rise of commerce and industry culminating in the period we know as the industrial revolution. It was not until the landmark Law of Property Act 1925 that the old system of tenure was removed from the rules and principles of English land law. As Cheshire says,

> The real property law as it existed in 1922 might justly be described as an archaic feudalistic system which, though originally evolved to satisfy the needs of a society based and centred on land, had by considerable ingenuity been twisted and distorted into a shape more or less suitable to a commercial society based on money.[49]

The legislation of 1925 did much to simplify and bring up to date the law relating to real property. Much still depends upon the distinction between legal and equitable interests and remedies, however, and the legislation is still far from straightforward. The essential point of the reforms of 1925, however, apart from simplification, was to render the *transfer* of land easier by reducing the number of separate interests which might exist in a given piece of land. The old doctrine of tenure had long since fallen from use, thanks to earlier statutory reforms, but the classification of estates was still extremely complicated. In an economy which by the twentieth century had come to rest predominantly upon industry and commerce, with the attendant fluctuations in national and personal fortunes, it was

48 See Simpson, op. cit., chapter 1.   49 Cheshire and Burn, op. cit., p 6.

clearly of the utmost importance to seek as high a degree of flexibility as possible in matters concerning land and its transfer.

The remaining equitable remedies are mainly to do with the hereditary transmission of property, through devices such as the trust, the strict settlement and other interests recognised in equity. Space does not permit a detailed examination of these equitable interests, and the reader is referred to materials providing full coverage of these matters.[50] What is more important for our purposes is the discussion of the legal estates in land – the fee simple, the holder of which is for all practical purposes the owner of the land; and the lease, whereby a landlord lets the land to a tenant in exchange for rent. Something must be said about these forms of legal estate, and the developments which have taken place around them.

Land and its use: private or public control?

One of the recurring themes of legal development during the twentieth century is that of increasing state intervention, through legal machinery, in areas of social and economic life which in previous times were the sole preserve of the private individual. Under the all-embracing banner of the 'welfare state', we have witnessed in this country, especially since the Second World War, a flood of legislative provisions concerning all aspects of our lives, frequently providing the citizen with new rights, such as social security and unemployment benefits, but equally often imposing new responsibilities and legal duties. This interventionist current is particularly clear in the law relating to land-use.

Planning

The adage 'an Englishman's home is his castle' may once have had real, and for some Englishmen literal, meaning. There was a time, up to the introduction of the first planning controls, when owners of land could do much as they pleased with it. They could build upon it, demolish existing structures, or let it out by means of the lease to tenants and receive income in the form of any rent they cared to charge. Today, the holder of land will find that before any substantial alteration can be made to the land or to the buildings on it, planning permission may be required from the local authority; and if the land or buildings are let out to tenants, then, subject to certain exceptions contained in the current rent legislation, the landholder will encounter controls in the matters of the amount of rent that may be charged, and the possibility of evicting those tenants should he or she so desire.

---

50 For example, Cheshire and Burn, op. cit.; D. Hayton, *The Law of Trusts* (4th edn., 2003, Sweet and Maxwell); Sir R. Megarry, *Manual of the Law of Real Property* (8th edn. by A. Oakley, 2002, Sweet and Maxwell); E. H. Burn, Maudsley and Burn's *Land Law: Cases and Materials* (8th edn., 2004, Oxford University Press); M. Thompson, *Modern Land Law* (2nd edn., 2003, Oxford University Press); K. Gray and S. Gray, *Elements of Land Law* (4th edn., 2004, Oxford University Press); J-A. McKenzie and M. Phillips, *Textbook on Land Law* (10th edn., 2004, Oxford University Press); A. Stroud, *Making Sense of Land Law* (2005, Oxford University Press); or any of the other standard texts in this area.

The public control of land-use through town and country planning legislation is a creature of welfare state philosophy. The first major planning legislation was the Town and Country Planning Act 1947, directed towards the need to rebuild city centres shattered by wartime bombing, and to restrict the unregulated growth of suburban development by effectively taking away from individuals the right which they had previously enjoyed to develop land, and vesting this in the state. Thus the concept of planning permission for development was born. These regulative developments gave local authorities a vital role from the very beginning, and later legislation, notably the Town and Country Planning Acts of 1968 and 1971, as amended in 1972, required local authorities to prepare and submit to the ministry for approval 'structure plans' and 'local plans' – forming a positive aspect to planning policy in contrast to the more negative regulatory requirements for the acquisition of planning permission for changes in land-use or building structures.

The current law is contained principally in the Town and Country Planning Act 1990 (as amended by the Planning and Compensation Act 1991) and the Planning and Compulsory Purchase Act 2004.[51] In essence, within the parameters of general regional and local plans, drawn up by Regional Planning Bodies and local government planning authorities, respectively, individual developers, whether they own the land or not, must apply for planning permission for any new development, including changes in use of land, and permission will be granted (often with conditions attached) or refused, depending on how the proposed development fits in with, or affects, the development plans. Breaches of any of the conditions, or more generally breaches of the law concerning what is done on the land by the developer or occupier, are regulated by means of the local authority's serving of an enforcement notice, and it is a criminal offence not to comply with such a notice. If an application for planning permission is refused, there is a right of appeal to the Secretary of State, who makes the final decision.

Many critics have pointed to problems associated with planning legislation. First, as with nearly all interventionist legislation, the point of greatest tension is the point at which individual wishes encounter official policies. In planning, as elsewhere, mechanisms have always been provided within the legislative and administrative structure for both public consultation and individual dispute-solving. The Act of 1990 provides, for example, for drafts of local plans to be publicised and for objections to be formally made by members of the public; in the event of such objections being made, the local authority must hold a public inquiry, at which objectors have the right to appear. Similar inquiries may be held to deal with objections to specific proposals for development.

If a citizen wishes to complain about alleged *maladministration* by a local planning department within a local authority, it is possible to approach the 'local Ombudsman', or Commissioner for Local Administration (see chapter 6) though

51 See major texts on planning law, such as A. Telling and R. Duxbury, *Planning Law and Procedure* (13th edn., by R. Duxbury, 2005, Oxford University Press); V. Moore, *A Practical Approach to Planning Law* (9th edn., 2005, Oxford University Press).

the ombudsman does not act as a court of appeal and has no power to assess a planning decision on its merits or demerits. In the event of maladministration by a planning authority at *central* government level, the Parliamentary Commissioner for Administration (the Parliamentary 'Ombudsman') (see chapter 6) has power to investigate complaints alleging such grievances, although this power is circumscribed by the procedures for instigating such an enquiry (they may only be approached through an MP), and by limitations upon the action he or she may take (they cannot alter decisions, but may only submit a report on the problem to Parliament if he or she finds that an injustice has been caused by maladministration).

Another means of resolving individual disputes is the provision, in many areas of planning, for appeal to a higher authority (we have already noted the example of an appeal to the minister against a planning decision by a local authority planning department): in some cases, there may also be grounds for bringing an action in court if the problem falls within the supervisory jurisdiction of the courts, as, for example, in the case of an alleged breach of natural justice or where the complainant alleges that the planning authority has exceeded its statutory powers (acting *ultra vires*).[52] The difficulties with this course of action are considerable, however, not least because of the delay and expense of litigation, but also because of the cumbersome and out-dated procedural and remedial aspects of this particular procedure.

Pollution control

Closely linked to the issue of planning, and possibly one of the most significant developments over the past 20 years, the growing concern over pollution and its effects on the environment is causing governments all over the world to rethink their policies on pollution control. Depletion of the ozone layer, poisonous waste, global warming, the effects of acid rain, threats to the rain forests and to the survival of many species of animal, bird, marine and plant life, and many other harmful consequences of both industrial and domestic pollution have been at the forefront of such developments as the emergence of the Green Party in the United Kingdom and elsewhere in Europe, the activities of organisations such as Friends of the Earth and Greenpeace in various parts of the world, the formulation of policy statements at national and international conventions, and the various stated commitments of governments worldwide to tackle the problems of pollution.

In this country as elsewhere, there have been a number of attempts to control pollution and its effects, and these are largely, but not exclusively, incorporated in legal provisions. It should not be assumed, however, that concerns about pollution, and attempts at its control, are wholly new: as far back as the nineteenth century, statutes such as the Public Health Act 1848 were designed to confront and control the environmentally (and personally) damaging effects of industrialisation. It is

---

52 See chapter 12.

true to say, however, that statutory controls over more aspects of environmentally damaging industrial and domestic practices have accelerated in recent years, as more and more evidence has emerged of the potentially devastating effects of uncontrolled pollution, and as technology has produced increasing amounts of toxic and radioactive substances and applications.

The law on environmental control is vast and complex, and its development has been piecemeal and uncoordinated, though it is becoming less piecemeal with the introduction of major legislation such as the Environmental Protection Act 1990, and with the development of integrated systems such as Integrated Pollution Control and Integrated Pollution Prevention Control, all of which are discussed below. It would be impossible here to detail the many legal provisions in this area, as many attempts have been made over the years to combat specific problems through the use of law (see, for example, the Sea Birds Preservation Acts 1869–80, the Protection of Birds Act 1954, the Conservation of Seals Act 1970 and the Badgers Act 1973) and once again the reader is referred to specialist texts in the area.[53] Our purpose here is to explore briefly some of the problems and evaluate the ways in which those problems have been dealt with, frequently though law.

Many questions arise when any individual pollutant, or polluting activity, is under discussion. What evidence is there that the activity in question *does* lead to the environmental damage which is alleged? How serious is that damage and its consequences, assuming that the causal link is established? What should be the balance between the conflicting public interests in, on the one hand, controlling or preventing the polluting activity, and on the other, the economic advantages of allowing that activity to continue? What *level* of pollution is deemed unacceptable? Who decides? Should the law be used, or could the industry in question effectively police itself? Who should enforce pollution control legislation, and by what mechanisms? Who should pay for the effects of pollution? And ought Britain to control a particular polluting activity if other countries do not?

Clearly, many of these are political and economic, not legal, questions, and require consideration of complex technical scientific data. Although space does not allow consideration of all the various forms of pollution, and the ways in which controls have been attempted, it is possible, by focusing on one aspect of the problem – atmospheric pollution – to gain some understanding of the difficulties in this field. A number of general propositions are explored below with particular reference to air pollution, though the point must be stressed that these propositions are equally applicable to water, land, and other types of pollution.

Pollution can take many forms and result from many types of activity

The law was first used to combat air pollution as early as 1273, when a law was passed to control the emission of smoke in London, though it was not until the

---

53 Leading texts on environmental law include S. Bell and D. McGillivray, *Environmental Law* (6th edn., 2006, Oxford University Press); S. Wolf and N. Stanley, *Environmental Law* (4th edn., 2003, Cavendish); D. Hughes, N. Papworth et al., *Environmental Law* (4th edn., 2002, Butterworths).

development of the various processes used in the manufacturing industries, and the widespread use of coal-burning fires and furnaces in the eighteenth and nineteenth centuries, that attempts to control smoke pollution became more widely used. Apart from smoke pollution, the common use in industry of a process which produced soda, but which caused the emission into the atmosphere of hydrogen chloride gas, became a serious problem: the gas, when combined with rain, formed hydrochloric acid – acid rain. The Alkali Acts of 1863 and 1874 were passed to try to combat this problem by requiring that factories prevented any hydrogen chloride emissions in excess of 0.2 grains per cubic foot, which remains the present legal limit. The consolidating Alkali, etc Works Regulation Act 1906 required the 'best practicable means' to be taken to prevent the escape of these gases. Smog is yet another form of seriously damaging air pollution: one of the worst incidents occurred in London in December 1952, when a heavy fog was affected by smoke, soot, carbon dust and gaseous waste.

> Nothing unusual was noticed until prize cattle at the Smithfield Show started to suffer from respiratory problems. The smog got everywhere, even inside the Sadler's Wells Theatre, which resulted in the stoppage of a performance because of the difficulty of seeing the stage. When the smog had lifted it was estimated that at least 4,000 people had lost their lives as a consequence of the smoke and other emissions.[54]

The enquiry which followed led eventually to the passage of the Clean Air Act 1956, which was followed in subsequent years by further legislation regulating smoke and other emissions from the country's factory and domestic chimneys. The height of factory chimneys, in particular, is seen as critical: the theory is that the higher the chimney, the more widely the gases are to be dispersed, and the more diluted the pollutant when it finally falls – in whichever form – to earth. A side-effect of this policy, however, is that gases produced from factory chimneys in England can be carried long distances, causing pollution problems elsewhere. Scandinavian countries in particular have suffered from deposits of sulphur dioxide and acid rain originating in Britain, and this has been the subject of a continuing dispute, which efforts were made through negotiations in the 1980s to resolve.

Despite the controls mentioned so far, and the more recent Clean Air Act 1993, the continuing use in industry of processes which lead to the emission of carbon dioxide (from fossil fuel burning), and other 'greenhouse gases', coupled with the contribution to the levels of these gases through car exhausts, has led to international concern about the 'greenhouse effect' leading to higher temperatures – global warming. This, it is thought, could spell worldwide disaster in many forms: melting ice-caps, rising sea-levels, unpredictable weather patterns, and the loss of homes, jobs and food-production capacity. Linked to this problem – and also caused by the emission of gases (in this instance, chlorofluorocarbons, or CFCs) – is the depletion of the ozone layer of the earth's atmosphere. This layer absorbs ultra violet

54 S Bell and D McGillivray, op. cit. p 632.

(UV) radiation from the sun's rays, and massive holes in the ozone layer have the result that more UV radiation reaches the earth, possibly leading to, among other problems, an increase in the number of cases of skin cancer.

We can add other atmospheric pollutants to this depressing list: airborne lead particles from vehicle exhausts, for example, leading to lead poisoning, which has led to the widespread use of vehicle engines designed to use unleaded fuel; concerns with particulate emissions from diesel-engines; and smoke produced by means other than factory and domestic chimneys, such as stubble-burning by farmers, which is now controlled by the Environmental Protection Act 1990.[55] There are new problems relating to air quality, involving, for example, volatile organic compounds, which are gases emitted from various activities including vehicle exhaust systems, paint and glue, and other compounds.

Attempts to control pollution have been piecemeal and complex, and a number of different agencies have been charged with enforcing control measures

Generally speaking, the pattern has been for new measures to be introduced as and when new pollution-related problems have arisen, or more accurately, have been perceived by government as sufficiently serious to warrant some form of control. Since the Alkali Act 1863, no fewer than nine separate Acts have been passed, along with innumerable regulations which provide detailed guidance, for instance, about permitted levels of pollution, and which often specify the various activities which are wholly or partially exempted from controls. To take just one or two examples: the Clean Air Acts empowered the Secretary of State to make regulations concerning the emission of smoke and other substances from chimneys. Among the regulations made were the Dark Smoke (Permitted Periods) Regulations 1958, which provide for specific periods of time during which dark smoke may be emitted from factory chimneys; and the Clean Air (Emission of Grit and Dust from Furnaces) Regulations 1971 incorporates the definition of 'grit', which is in turn distinct from 'dust'. The problems caused by emissions from vehicle exhausts were tackled in the Road Traffic Act 1988, together with amendments to the Construction and Use Regulations to take in European Community initiatives.

Not only are the legislative provisions, and regulations made thereunder, extremely detailed, technical and complex: a number of separate agencies have, over the years, been charged with the enforcement of these controls. The Alkali Acts created the Alkali Inspectorate to enforce the law relating to chemical emissions from factory chimneys. But smoke controls, provided in public health legislation from 1875 onwards and the Clean Air Acts of the 1950s, were placed in the hands of local authorities, which may be involved in their role in planning and development control, and/or their role in environmental protection. From the point of

---

55 See S. Payne, 'No Smoke Without Precautions' (1991) *NLJ* 16 August.

view of someone wishing to complain about a problem involving air pollution, it may not have been clear as to which was the appropriate body to approach.

In 1995, the important Environment Act was passed, which, among other things, created the new Environment Agency,[56] which carries out the various functions previously performed by Her Majesty's Inspectorate of Pollution, the National Rivers Authority and waste disposal authorities. In essence, the new Agency deals with water pollution and land drainage, waste disposal, the control of radioactive waste and also Integrated Pollution Control and Integrated Pollution Prevention Control. The 1995 Act introduced provisions for dealing with contaminated land, after substantial consultation,[57] by means of amendments to the Environmental Protection Act 1990. Contaminated land is defined in the 1995 Act as land which may lead to 'significant harm' or the 'significant possibility' of such harm to human health or property, other living organisms, or controlled waters. Responsibility for identifying such land and ensuring that it is cleaned up is placed upon local authorities, though if the harm is likely to be serious, the land is designated as a 'special site' and is dealt with directly by the Environment Agency.

Controls have, to date, met with differing degrees of success in tackling pollution

There are many reasons why attempts through law to combat pollution may not be successful. First, the law may not be regarded as an appropriate method of control, though other methods may not be particularly effective. There has been no attempt, for example, at legal control regarding the ozone layer problem. Instead, there has been some progress by means of international agreements, and by the rapid phasing-out by some manufacturers of the use of CFCs – most notably perhaps the reduction in the amount of domestic aerosol products using CFC gases. Second, a particular legal provision may turn out to be inadequate because it is found not to cover a particular activity. For instance:

> Attempts were made to control the emission of smoke through such Acts as the Public Health Act 1875, the Public Health (Smoke Abatement) Act 1926 and the Public Health Act 1936 but these generally dealt with smoke nuisances. These powers could not rid industrial cities of the problems of smoke pollution. The physical evidence of this pollution could be seen on blackened buildings, and by the frequency of smog . . .[58]

Third, as we saw in the case of acid rain, solving a problem in one locality could really mean only shifting it to somewhere else. Fourth, there may be resistance to proposals for change, particularly from manufacturers who deny that their activity causes pollution, and from politicians who may place pollution and the need to control it fairly low on their list of priorities: legislation may in such cases be slow to appear, and in the event may prove inadequate. Fifth, the technical nature of the

56 For Scotland, the Act creates the Scottish Environmental Protection Agency.
57 See Department of the Environment, *Paying for our Past* (1994) and *Framework for Contaminated Land* (1994).   58 Bell and McGillivray, *Environmental Law*, op. cit., p 632.

problem, and of the industrial processes concerned, means that industry itself will be involved in the negotiations concerning controls: solutions which identify an 'acceptable' level of pollution and prohibit any excess over that level may fail to be effective if the 'acceptable' level does not prevent further pollution. Finally, there are inherent difficulties in imposing criminal liability on companies for pollution offences. Where liability for a criminal offence depends on proof that the polluter intentionally, or at least knowingly, carried out the polluting activity, it may be extremely difficult, if not impossible, to prove that the persons who control the company – nowadays regarded as the human embodiment of the corporate 'will' – possessed the relevant degree of knowledge or intent. Most offences involving 'causing' are now however offences of strict liability (see chapter 10) although even though this may mean that there may be fewer problems in securing convictions, the only available criminal sanction for corporate bodies is the fine, and this may not be sufficient to deter companies from further offences.

Pollution control measures have been modified in a number of recent statutes, designed to achieve a more integrated system of control

The recent changes have been heavily influenced by public concern, media attention to environmental issues, the international community and, most especially, European Community initiatives (see chapter 8). Among recent legislation are the Town and Country Planning Act 1990, the Wildlife and Countryside Act 1981, the Environmental Protection Act 1990, and a number of statutes concerning water in 1991. Noise pollution is dealt with under the provisions of the Noise and Statutory Nuisance Act 1993.

Atmospheric pollution, along with that of water and land, is dealt with by the Environmental Protection Act 1990, although the control of smoke continues to be provided for by other legislation specifically dealing with clean air. Part One of the 1990 Act deals with what are termed 'Integrated Pollution Control (IPC) and Air Pollution Control by Local Authorities (APCLA)' and these constitute two separate systems of control, which must be seen alongside more recent developments extending the principles of IPC – notably the Pollution Prevention and Control Act 1999.

The current legislation provides very considerable powers of enforcement regarding air pollution control. Conditions may be attached to authorisations, and the enforcement agency may vary or revoke authorisations, or issue enforcement or prohibition notices. They have powers of entry, search and seizure, and may take legal proceedings to secure compliance with notices. The Secretary of State also has wide powers under the Acts, ranging from the power to prescribe the processes and substances to be controlled, to establishing standards, and directing the enforcement agencies as to the exercise of their powers. All authorisations will be subject to a general provision that 'best available techniques not entailing excessive cost' (a phrase now in common use, and usually abbreviated to BATNEEC) should be used, although the phrase is abbreviated, under the integrated Pollution Prevention Act 1999, to 'best available techniques' (BAT).

Aspects of the current legislation are derived from European Community initiatives: the BATNEEC formula, for example, comes from a number of European Community Directives, and the Act itself – especially Part I – constitutes the writing into English law of the Directives, including the specification of emission limits. The same is true of the Integrated Pollution Prevention Act 1999. Other influences on the Act include various internationally agreed Conventions and Protocols on such aspects of atmospheric pollution as sulphur dioxide emissions and ozone layer depletion.

The modern tendency is for controls to be less *reactive* and more *positive* – for example, to lay down standards to be adhered to in the future, rather than waiting until a problem reaches crisis proportions before tackling it. It remains to be seen how effective all these measures and new initiatives will prove in the long run. Whilst the European Community is dedicated to increasing pollution controls, some see the progress made by the international community on issues such as toxic waste and the ozone layer problem as worryingly slow. Whether the environment is to be better protected through law or through international agreement, it remains the case that environmental protection is essentially a political matter: no doubt governments will need to be continuously pressed into further action, continuously reminded of the threat to the world we live in, and continuously urged to rethink political priorities so that better and more effective environmental protection remains high on their political agendas.

Housing

The fact that private property developers have chosen to deal in terms of commercial developments rather than house-building is reflected in the diminished rate of house-building over the years. The number of public and private housing units completed in Britain in 1965 was 382,000;[59] in the financial year 2004–05 the number of completions was 206,000.[60] The greatest proportion of these – 89% – were private enterprise developments. Of the remainder, the vast majority – about 22,000 – were built by housing associations, and only a very small number built by public sector bodies[61] – local authorities, new towns, government departments and other providers. The term 'social housing' is used to refer to housing provision which is at least partly funded by public funds; such housing is typically provided by housing associations, local authorities, housing trusts or development corporations.

The legal device whereby many people occupy houses, office blocks and other buildings is, of course, the *lease*. The lease, it will be recalled, creates a tenancy which is the only legal estate in land apart from the fee simple. The use of the lease enables the property-owner to render the land profitable in terms of revenue

---

59 Housing and Construction Statistics.
60 The total number has been rising, with some fluctuations, since the end of the 1980s. The figure for 2000–2001 was 167,500, and for 2002–3 184,000.   61 www.statistics.gov.uk .

income by contracting with the tenant so that the latter enjoys possession of the land in exchange for the payment of rent to the land-owner.

In the housing context, tenants occupy rented property which is owned by private individuals or companies, or public bodies. The precise rights and obligations of the landlord and the tenant will depend upon the terms of individual leases, subject to the conditions which have been imposed by statute (such as those provisions in the Rent Acts and Housing Acts which provided tenants with rent control and security of tenure, making it difficult for the landlord to evict them). Here again, state intervention in the hitherto private area of rented housing has made a considerable difference over the years not only to living conditions (through slum clearance, building regulations which improve health and safety, and planning programmes) but also to housing and property-owning patterns in Britain.

In the nineteenth century and before, the vast majority of houses were privately owned by landlords and rented out, or were tied to jobs. During the twentieth century, there was an enormous decrease in the proportion of privately rented accommodation. Why did this decrease come about?

In the first place, there was of course a huge increase in the number of people in a position to buy their own home. Owner-occupiers account for about 70% of the total number of householders today, and this increase has been due to a number of factors, including the growth and accessibility of banks and building societies; easier access to borrowing; the housing policies of government administrations which have aimed to return housing provision to the open and deregulated competitive market; and the coming of the 'affluent society', in which increased income and improved standards of living have enabled more people to buy into the culture of our society which prizes home-owning so highly. Banks and building societies are politically and economically very powerful: locally, they may be unwilling to advance loans for property in certain deteriorating parts of a town or city, or areas which are predominantly commercial in nature, and may on the other hand be keen to invest in other, more 'up market' areas. In this way, building societies, which it should be remembered are private- not public-sector organisations, may dramatically influence local development patterns.

Although there has been a massive increase in home-ownership through mortgage loans with banks and building societies, it should not be forgotten that homes can be repossessed by the lenders in the event of failure to maintain mortgage payments. In the long period of recession at the end of the 1980s and the early 1990s, with its usual accompaniments of high rates of redundancy and unemployment, repossessions of houses reached record levels – in 1992, there were 68,500 repossessions, and 58,500 in 1993,[62] causing untold misery for many families facing, in many cases, the prospect of having no roof over their heads. The number of repossessions has remained fairly steady throughout the 1990s, but fell during the 2000s: in 2004

---

62 *Key Data 1995–96* (1995, HMSO), p 77.

the figure stood at 6,230. Apart from repossessions, about 1.5 million home-owners found, during the recession, that their houses were worth less than they had paid for them ('negative equity'), clearly causing financial insecurity.

Apart from the growth in owner-occupation, two other critical developments – public sector housing provision and the legal protection of tenants in the private rented sector – have changed the pattern of residential accommodation over the last 80 or 90 years, and both these developments are part of the movement towards increased state intervention in the realm of property and property-rights.

In 1914, local authority rented housing accounted for only 1% of residential accommodation, whereas in 1974 the figure was 33%. This figure has been falling quite dramatically: between 1981 and 2004 the number of rented local authority homes fell by over 50%.[63] The social class background of most council house tenants is working class – the very social class for whom *privately* rented accommodation was usual in the nineteenth century. This factor clearly accounts to some extent for the decline of the private landlord, though other factors should be mentioned such as slum clearance programmes, rent control and increased protection for tenants against eviction, discussed further below. Council housing may be seen as one very important aspect of welfare state philosophy whereby housing was recognised during most of the twentieth century as a basic necessity and taken on in the policies of successive governments as part of welfare state provision.

The current law[64] is contained in the Housing Act 1985, as amended, in particular, by the Housing Act 1996. Council house tenants enjoy in essence, the same protections against eviction as those enjoyed by private tenants by virtue of the Rent Acts, and additional rights such as the right to carry out minor repairs and improvements and the right to take in lodgers. The tenant has *security of tenure*, and the Housing Act 1980 further provided for the 'right to buy', which has recently been amended by the Housing Act 2004. Now, all secure tenants who have been public sector tenants for five years or more have the right (subject to some exceptional circumstances as provided in the 2004 Act) to purchase their house (or in the case of council flats, the long leasehold) from the council. Substantial discounts are available under the 'right to buy' system.

The Housing Act 1985 also provided the statutory right to a mortgage (s 132), provided by the council if necessary, but this right was abolished by the Leasehold Reform, Housing and Urban Development Act 1993, which, among other things, substituted the notion of 'rent into mortgage', whereby a tenant may continue to make rental payments, but have those payments treated, in effect, as buying a

---

63 *Social Trends No 36* (2006, The Stationery Office). The decline in this part of the housing sector has however been accompanied by an increase in the number of homes rented from registered social landlords (mainly housing corporations).

64 On which see, for example, A. Arden and C. Hunter, *Manual of Housing Law* (7th edn., 2002, Sweet and Maxwell); J. Morris, *Principles of Landlord and Tenant Law* (2nd edn., 1999, Cavendish); S. Garner and A. Frith, *A Practical Approach to Landlord and Tenant* (4th edn., 2004, Oxford University Press).

'share' of the property, with the right to pay the balance at some point in the future by means of an ordinary mortgage. This scheme has not been widely taken up.

The right-to-buy provisions were based upon the government's assumption that owner-occupation is a status to which everyone aspired, and that the public housing sector was over-subsidised by central government. It was strongly argued by supporters of the legislation that selling council houses would reduce public expenditure by increasing revenue to local councils through mortgage repayments and through councils being relieved of the costs of maintenance. It was urged, on the other hand, by opponents that public money would not, in fact, be saved in this way, because whereas rents can be increased to take account of inflation, the real value of mortgage repayments actually falls over a period of time.[65] As far as the individual purchaser is concerned, it may well be that mortgage repayments will exceed the amount otherwise payable as rent, and in many cases this will have been a disincentive for tenants to buy their homes, especially if there are uncertainties about possible redundancy and the prospect of unemployment which faced, and still faces, many potential buyers.

In connection with the latter point, it was argued that only better-off council tenants, in the more desirable houses on popular estates, would find the purchase of their house an attractive proposition, leaving a considerable amount of council housing stock on poorer estates and unpopular sites such as high-rise flats, containing tenants too poor to purchase, and consisting of property which tenants would not find particularly desirable anyway.[66] With drastic reductions in council house building programmes as a result of new legal frameworks and restrictions, together with public expenditure cuts, this has arguably exacerbated existing housing problems, such as quality and availability of housing stock, long waiting lists and homelessness.

By the end of March 1982, more than 400,000 right-to-buy claims from about 9% of council tenants had been received. However, there was considerable regional variation in this overall figure: the more urbanised the area, and the greater the proportion of high-rise flats, the lower the proportion of tenants who claimed the right to purchase their houses. Since that initial surge in council house sales, there have been peaks and troughs, though after falling steadily since about 1989, sales rose during the latter half of the 1990s. A considerable amount of local authority housing stocks were, since the late 1980s, sold off to housing associations by virtue of provisions in the Housing Act 1985. In 2004, there were about 75,000 sales. The letting of houses by housing associations and other 'social landlords' reflects the continuing need for substantial rented housing in the 'social housing' sector.[67]

---

65 R. Forrest and A. Murie, *Selling the Welfare State: The Privatisation of Public Housing* (1988, Routledge and Kegan Paul).

66 For discussions see D. White, 'The Council House Buyers', (1982) *New Society*, 19 November ; articles in *Critical Social Policy* (1981), vol. 1, no. 2 and (1982), vol. 1, no. 3; Forrest and Murie, op. cit.

67 On social housing see, in particular, D Hughes and S Lowe, *Public Sector Housing Law* (3rd edn., 2000, Butterworths).

The legislation affecting tenants in the *private* housing sector is extremely complex, with various types of tenancies held through private leases to which somewhat different sets of rules apply. The differential positions of landlord and tenant in terms of their respective bargaining power, together with the various manifestations of that differential power, such as high rents, have been recognised by legislators for many years, and some form of rent control has been in force, through a long series of statutes, since 1915. The area has long been fertile ground for party political battles, with Conservative governments tending to attempt to restore protection and freedom to private landlords which Labour governments have tried to place under legal controls and restrictions. The most far-reaching in this series of enactments, the Rent Acts of 1968 and 1974, provided considerable protection for the private tenant through a system of rent regulation ('fair rents' being fixed, on application by landlord or tenant, by rent officers, their decisions being subject to appeal to rent assessment committees) and a system of security of tenure, whereby the tenant enjoyed, by virtue of the protection provided by the Acts, possession of the property without danger of eviction save in a number of specified circumstances. Recent changes in the legislation have had a significant impact on the rent-control and security of tenure issues.

The detailed analysis of the statutory provisions in this area is outside the scope of this book, and readers seeking detailed information on this complex area of law must refer to more specialised texts.[68] To gain a general understanding of the ways in which the law is used to regulate private rented housing, however, we may however briefly outline the law as follows. Leases may be of two kinds, fixed-term and periodic. Fixed-term leases are for specified periods of time (long leases are for 21 years or more, and are frequently for much longer periods), whereas with periodic leases (the most common arrangements between landlords and tenants) rent is payable on a periodic basis, usually each week or each month.

Leases created prior to January 1989 are still governed by the Rent Act 1977. Under this statutory regime, for periodic leases, if a landlord wishes to evict a tenant, a written *notice to quit* must be issued by the landlord to the tenant. It must give at least four weeks' notice, and must inform tenants of their rights under the Rent Acts. Before any tenant can be required to leave the property, however, a county court possession order must be obtained by the landlord. With some exceptions such as cases where the rent includes payment for board or attendances; or those where the landlord is resident in the same building, or has let the property for holiday purposes, or is a public body such as a local authority or housing association, all tenancies are *protected* by virtue of the Rent Act 1977, Part I, as amended by the Housing Act 1980.

These statutory protections provide the private tenant with *security of tenure*. This means that, although the contractual agreement between landlord and tenant

---

68 For more detailed coverage of the law relating to the private rented sector, G. Randall, *Housing Rights Guide* (updated annually, Shelter) is strongly recommended. See also D. Cowan (ed.), *The Housing Act 1996: A Practical Guide* (1996, Jordans); and references at n 64, above.

may be terminated by means of a notice to quit, the statutory protections take over, transforming the original contractual tenancy into a *statutory tenancy* with the same rent and conditions. A landlord may gain possession in such cases only by obtaining a court order (Rent Act 1977, s 98); such an order will be awarded either where the court is satisfied that there is suitable alternative accommodation available, or where the landlord has established that the tenancy falls into one or more categories provided in Sch 15 to the Rent Act 1977. By virtue of this Schedule, a court may order possession if the tenant is in arrears with rent or has broken an obligation of the tenancy, or is causing a nuisance, or has, by waste or neglect, accelerated the deterioration of the premises, or furniture therein, or has assigned or sub-let the whole of the premises without the landlord's permission, or is sub-letting at a rent in excess of that fixed by a Rent Officer or Rent Tribunal. Additionally, an order may be granted if the landlord, having previously occupied the premises, reasonably requires them again for him or herself or a member of their close family, providing that such possession will not throw the tenant into even greater hardship.

The Schedule also provides conditions which, if met, mean that the court *must* order possession. These conditions are, principally, that the landlord who previously occupied the premises now requires them again for him or herself or a close family member, or wishes to sell the property if the house is no longer suitable for their needs, provided that notice of such an intention was given to the tenant before the tenancy was created; that the landlord bought the premises to retire into and now wishes to move in or sell, provided, again, that appropriate notice was given; that the lease was for 8 months or less of premises used for holidays during the holiday seasons and notice was given to the tenant before the tenancy was created; that the lease was for 12 months or less of premises used for student accommodation, and notice was given to the tenant; that the tenancy was used for a minister of religion, an agricultural worker or a member of the armed forces, who was given notice before the tenancy was created.

The policy behind the Housing Act 1988, as amended by the Housing Act 1996, was to facilitate increased returns on investment in the private rented sector. This Act created 'assured tenancies' (which might be *fixed-term*, involving a tenancy created for a fixed period; *periodic*, involving regular payment of rent over an indefinite period; and *assured statutory periodic*, which occurs when a fixed-term tenancy comes to an end); and 'assured shorthold tenancies'. Rent increases desired by the landlord may be referred by the tenant to rent assessment committees, who will determine the appropriate market rent. The 'market rent' may differ from a 'fair rent' in that when assessing the former, not only factors such as the size and condition of the premises, but also local availability of accommodation may be taken into account: this may well have the effect that the 'market' rent is higher than what might previously have been fixed as 'fair', and in many cases is certainly higher than that which would be charged for similar accommodation in council housing by local authorities.

A landlord may only terminate a periodic or assured statutory periodic tenancy by means of a court order, though an assured fixed-term tenancy may be terminated by the landlord's exercising their power contained in the agreement, in which case the tenancy automatically becomes a 'periodic' tenancy, after which the landlord may only gain possession, after giving proper notice, by means of a court order, after proving one of the following grounds for eviction: where the building society, bank or other mortgagee requires possession of the property for sale if the mortgage was granted before the start of the tenancy; where the landlord intends to demolish, rebuild, or carry out substantial work on the property; where the landlord requires possession from a succeeding tenant (though this does not include that tenant's spouse) within a year of the death of the assured periodic tenant; and where the tenant is in at least eight weeks' rent arrears at the time of both the giving of the notice to quit and the actual court hearing. Additional situations in which the court has a *discretion* as to ordering repossession include: where there has been persistent delay in payment of rent; where the tenant has suitable alternative accommodation; where the tenant or someone else living in the property has damaged furniture provided by the landlord or has caused a nuisance or annoyance to neighbours or has been convicted of using the property for illegal or immoral purposes; or where the tenant induced the landlord to grant the tenancy by means of a false statement made knowingly or recklessly.

The shorthold tenancy was a major change first brought about by the Housing Act 1980. This, too, was an attempt to stimulate what was then the dwindling private rented sector: the effect of the statutory provisions is to allow landlords to let property to tenants for a fixed term. This form of renting did not at first prove particularly popular among landlords, even though, from their point of view, it avoided the situation in which an undesirable tenant who could not be brought within Sch 15 to the Rent Act 1977 remained in possession of the premises against the wishes of a landlord who could not remove that tenant. The 'assured shorthold tenancy' was created by the Housing Act 1988, and the indications are that these have become more widely used because there is no security of tenure at all beyond the fixed period of the agreement. The introduction of this type of tenancy seems to have succeeded in stimulating the private rented sector (for the first time in many years) by deregulating the landlord-tenant relationship, though this is not without cost in terms of a higher degree of insecurity for tenants, and of payments by the state in housing benefit.

Assured shorthold tenancies were introduced from January 1989, and most tenancies created since that date have been assured shortholds. In essence, this type of tenancy is identical to an 'assured tenancy' in all respects except that the tenant may be evicted once the period of the tenancy has expired, as long as this is at least six months after the commencement of the tenancy. By virtue of the Housing Act 1996, however, the tenancy will *automatically* be an assured shorthold tenancy unless the situation falls within one of a number of specified categories, the most important of which is that the landlord states explicitly that the tenancy is *not* to be an assured shorthold tenancy. This will effectively reduce tenants' security of tenure. The tenancy is subject to the mandatory and discretionary grounds for eviction for assured tenancies outlined above, and s 21 of the 1988 Act provides that once the fixed term has expired, a court *must* normally order repossession, as long as the landlord has given the tenant at least two months' notice.

We noted above the tendency in recent years towards a fall in the amount of house-building, and a decline in the private rented sector. By the early 2000s, however, the house-building industry had begun to revive. A government-sponsored review of housing was completed in 2004,[69] recommending, among other things, an increase in the amount of house-building in order to meet demand and to help stabilise the spiralling cost of homes which made it increasingly difficult for aspiring home-owners to obtain affordable homes of their own. The government response to the review was a commitment to encouraging house-building and making housing more affordable, so that new buyers could more easily become property-owners, to improving the quality and choice of homes for those in the rented-home sector, promoting 'mixed, sustainable communities' (defined as places where people want to live and work, offering a high quality of life and remaining sensitive to the environment) and supporting programmes of urban and 'neighbourhood' renewal. 2004 also saw the passage of the important Housing Act.

The Housing Act 2004 affects both the private and social rented housing sectors in various ways. Once again, specialised texts should be consulted for full details of the Act, but some of the main features may be noted here. First of all, it provides greater powers to local authorities' housing departments to deal with poor housing conditions, which includes cases where there are health and safety hazards in the home. There is a new Housing Health and Safety Rating System, and the Act lists almost 30 hazards, ranging from excess cold to electrical dangers and risks of structural collapse.

Second, the Act introduces mandatory licensing of houses 'in multiple occupation', which is generally defined as a property occupied by more than one household and more than two people. This will include houses split into bedsits and shared houses (occupied, for example, by groups of students). Initially, the Act was to apply to multiple occupation properties comprising three or more floors, and occupied by five or more people. Before a license can be granted, the property-owner must satisfy the local housing authority that there are adequate facilities, that the property owner is a 'fit and proper' person, that the property is not overcrowded and that the property is safe in a number of key respects (that is, with regard to means of escape, fire, gas and electrical safety, and other factors). Local housing authorities also have powers under the Act to extend licensing requirements to other types of property.

The Act also introduced 'Home Information Packs'. For many years, the purchase of a house by intending owner-occupiers has been a complex, expensive and

---

69 Kate Barker, *Review of Housing Supply: Delivering Stability – Securing our Future Housing Needs* ((2004) HMSO).

lengthy process, involving a number of separate checks on such factors as the title to the property, whether the property is, or will be, affected by developments such as new road schemes and of course the physical condition of the property. There are many situations in which the lengthy business of negotiating the details of the sale of a house has foundered at some point over the appearance of some adverse information about a property, by which time a considerable amount of time and expenditure may have been incurred.

The Home Information Pack scheme is intended to make the process of providing information more straightforward by making it mandatory (from early 2007) for the seller of a house to prepare a Home Information Pack comprising a set of documents available to potential buyers covering all this, and more, information about the property. The pack will include details of the survey of the property, and the new 'Home Condition Report' (at a cost of around £350) will be prepared by qualified Home Inspectors: this report can then be used by buyers, sellers, and of course those advancing money through loans and mortgages for the purchase of the property.

The Housing Act 2004 also makes changes to the right-to-buy scheme (noted above) and contains provision to ensure better treatment of and protection for mobile home owners *vis-à-vis* site owners, and for travelling people, against, in particular harassment and eviction.

Finally in this section, we need to consider another legal basis for the occupation of property – the *licence*.

In law, a licence is simply permission given by one person to another, which allows that other to enter upon land. The licence may be 'bare', as where a householder allows the next-door neighbour to make use of a back yard; or 'contractual', as where one pays to enter a cinema or theatre in order to watch the performance. The differences between the lease and the licence may be stated quite simply: a lease involves exclusive possession of the premises by the tenant, but a licence does not; a lease is a property interest which can bind subsequent owners of the premises (a landlord may sell the premises to another, but the 'sitting tenants' will retain their rights irrespective of that transaction, subject to the provisions discussed above), but a licence is usually held to be a purely *personal* right, held by the licensee and enforceable only against the individual landlord who granted the licence; and perhaps most important of all, a licence does not attract Rent Act protection for the licensee, and so anyone living in accommodation under a licence is not protected by those statutory provisions.

The contractual licence became popular with many landlords as a means of hiring out accommodation which avoided the protections given to tenants by the Rent Acts, especially after the decision in the case of *Somma v Hazlehurst* in 1978,[70] where an unmarried couple each signed a separate (though identical) agreement with the owner of the premises. Each agreement stated that it was a licence, and

70 [1978] 2 All ER 1011.

included a term to the effect that the owner himself had the right to share the premises and to introduce one other licensee to share the use of the premises. It was held that neither of the couple had exclusive possession, nor did they share exclusive possession (because of the owner's stated right to share); the agreement was therefore held not to be a tenancy, and was outside Rent Act protection.

This use of licences was, however, fundamentally affected by the House of Lords' decision in *Street v Mountford* in 1985.[71] This case concerned an agreement, entitled a 'licence agreement', granting occupancy of two rooms subject to termination by 14 days' notice, and to certain conditions in the agreement. The occupant had signed a declaration to the effect that she understood that the agreement did not give her a tenancy protected by the Rent Acts. The occupant and her husband had exclusive possession, and this was conceded by the landlord. The question for the court was whether this agreement was indeed a licence, or whether the arrangement constituted, in law, a tenancy agreement. The court held that it was a tenancy, and stated that where residential accommodation had been granted for a term at a rent with exclusive possession, the grantor providing neither attendance nor services, the legal consequence was the creation of a tenancy, notwithstanding the statements in the agreement. On the question of *Somma*, Lord Templeman stated that in that case the agreement signed by the couple constituted the grant to them 'jointly of exclusive possession at a rent for a term . . . and the agreement therefore created a tenancy'[72] and went on to say:

> Although the Rent Acts must not be allowed to alter or influence the construction of an agreement, the court should, in my opinion, be astute to detect and frustrate sham devices and artificial transactions whose only object is to disguise the grant of a tenancy and to evade the Rent Acts. I would disapprove of the decision [in *Somma v Hazlehurst*].[73]

Henceforth, said the court, the only question in such cases would be whether the occupier was a lodger or a tenant. The case would seem therefore to have put paid to the use of the contractual licence for residential accommodation, at least where the agreement specifically made it clear that the occupier was to enjoy exclusive possession. But what about the situation where the landlord inserted into the agreement a clause to the effect that the occupation was non-exclusive?

In *Antoniades v Villiers* and *AG Securities v Vaughan* in 1988[74] the House of Lords had to deal with this issue. In the first case, the two occupiers had moved into a small flat comprising one bedroom, a bed-sitting room, a kitchen and a bathroom. They had signed separate agreements, each containing non-exclusive possession clauses, though it was understood that they would be living together as husband and wife. The agreements purported to be licences, and the occupiers licensees; and there was an explicit statement to the effect that the intention of the parties was to create a licence which would not fall under Rent Act protection.

71 [1985] AC 809.   72 Ibid., at 890.   73 Ibid.   74 [1990] 1 AC 417.

In the second case, four occupiers moved at different times into a four-bedroom flat with a sitting-room, bathroom and WC. They signed separate agreements with the owners, each for a six-month period, stating that there was no right to exclusive possession, and that the occupiers were licensees.

The House of Lords, in deciding what the true legal position in these cases was, stated that the basic question as to whether the agreement was a lease or a licence depends on the matter of exclusive possession, to be decided by reference to the intention of the parties to the agreement. In *Antoniades*, the court held that the nature of the accommodation was such that neither party could realistically have contemplated that the owner would use or share part of the flat, or put anyone else in to share. It follows that in this case the true intention was the creation of a tenancy. But in *AG Securities*, the occupants entered into different agreements at different times and for different rents. Each agreement could be terminated without reference to those of the other three. Here, in the court's view, there was a common intention that the occupiers *should* be licensees, and certainly not joint tenants.

In *Bruton v London and Quadrant Housing Trust* in 1999,[75] B became the occupier of a flat in a block owned by a local authority. The authority, intending ultimately to demolish the building, allowed a charitable trust, by means of a licence agreement, to use it to provide short-term accommodation for homeless people. B's agreement was stated to be a short-term licence agreement which made it clear that, among other things, B was to vacate the property on being given reasonable notice, and B agreed to allow the trust's staff and certain other people to enter the flat for purposes connected with the trust's work, and to ensure that the flat was being kept clean and in good repair. This agreement was held to be a tenancy – the key factor once again was the exclusivity of possession, and this was so even though the trust itself only held the property on licence from the local council. If these decisions have finally resolved the vexed issue of the attempted use of licences by landlords to avoid Rent Act protection, then what might at first seem like a legal victory for tenants has to be seen against the 'assured shorthold' provisions of the Housing Act 1988, discussed above, which may well serve landlords' interests even better than this short-lived use of the licence.[76]

What emerges is that, as governments try to stimulate the market for provision of private rented accommodation, adjustments have been made, over the years, to the difficult balance between the rights of tenants (security of tenure, fair rents) and those of landlords (control over their property, returns on investment). The resulting law is, as can be appreciated even from the very general discussion above,

---

75 [2000] 1 AC 406.
76 It remains the case that many people still live in certain types of accommodation as licensees. Examples established by case law are: those living in old people's homes; those living as lodgers in premises where the licensor has total access to and use of the premises for the provision of attendance and services; those living in hostels without separate accommodation within that hostel; and those who enter premises initially as squatters who are temporarily allowed to remain there on the clear understanding that no intention to create a tenancy exists.

extraordinarily complicated. The legal complexities were addressed by the Law Commission in 2002 in a consultation paper produced with a view to creating 'a framework that is simpler and more flexible than current arrangements'.[77] The Law Commission project was:

> the result of a number of pressures. In his review of the Civil Justice System, Lord Woolf complained that the very complexity of housing law constituted a considerable barrier to access to justice. Housing associations have been calling for a single form of social tenure. Landlord interest groups have been developing ideas for new approaches to the regulation of the private rented sector.[78]

The stated objective, then, was to simplify the law, whilst making it more flexible, by reducing the number of types of occupation and the differences between them. The Consultation Paper identified four basic principles – security of tenure in appropriate circumstances; repossession of property only after due process of law; a more 'consumer' orientation to housing law, based on written and fair contractual arrangements; and recognition of the impact of the European Convention of Human Rights. The Law Commission was in no doubt that these matters could not be left to the free-market contractual arrangements between landlords and occupiers – 'the past 150 years demonstrate that there are potential imbalances in the relationship between landlords and occupiers which cannot be corrected solely by the operation of market forces. There remains an important role for Government in the regulation of that relationship'[79] – and was hopeful that the proposed new, simplified arrangements would not only govern future renting arrangements but might be mapped onto existing tenancy relationships.

At present, with the accent firmly on the policy of pursuing deregulation in this, as in other, sectors of the economy, the legal provisions give reduced protection for the tenant in the interests of boosting the private-rented housing sector. The various ways in which property can now be let may well have rendered the financial prospects of letting property more attractive, though the high cost of the upkeep of the property (usually the contractual responsibility of the landlord and subject, in the case of tenancy agreements, to statutory provision, for example in the Housing Acts 1985 and 1996), and the impact of tax on rents received, may still mean that many landlords feel they no longer have the control over their own property which they, as owners, feel they should have. Although the right to get rid of tenants whom landlords feel to be unsuitable is provided by statute (especially the Housing Act 1988, as amended by the Housing Act 1996), the amount of rent they charge may well be challenged by application to rent officers or tribunals. At the same time, however, there remains a significant section of the population – migrant workers, students, the poor, minority ethnic groups – for whom home ownership or council housing is unavailable or inappropriate, and it is this – very vulnerable – section which depends most upon the private housing sector.

77 Law Commission, *Renting Homes – 1: Status and Security: A Summary* (2002, Law Commission Consultation Paper No 162), para 5.   78 Ibid., para 1.   79 Ibid., para 12.

The housing issue – in both private and public sectors – has long been a political football, being made the subject of the political ideologies of successive governments since the First World War when the council housing system became well-established. In the 1990s, the public housing sector continued to be squeezed through cuts in public spending, and the private sector remains on the ever-swinging pendulum which at times has swung in favour of landlords, at times in favour of tenants', protection. We saw the attempt to revitalise private sector housing, through, for example, the introduction of the shorthold lease in 1980. And in the meantime, the problem of homelessness in modern Britain grows more and more acute. The numbers of homeless individuals and families has been rising for many years, despite the passage of the Housing (Homeless Persons) Act 1977, as amended by later legislation, which placed responsibility for finding accommodation for the homeless upon local authorities. Unfortunately, there is little – if any – reason to believe that government will resolve the problem, for whatever the causes of homelessness – and they are many and varied – it seems that only the provision of some form of *affordable* housing will help, and this implies a government commitment to such provision through public spending.

Conclusion

Our brief discussion shows that the type and degree of regulation will depend very much upon the dominant political and ideological complexion of any given period. We have explored the relationships between law, property and economic and political power, and noted the main legal forms of property rights, and the various types and uses of property-objects. The basic contention after our brief survey must be that property-ownership continues to be regarded as a fundamental value in our society, and that the law continues to be called upon to protect the interests of those who own and control that property. In some respects, such protection is unobjectionable, but in other respects, such as planning, property development and housing, the unfettered freedom of private property-owners to use their property as they wish has raised serious social problems which the state, through planning, pollution controls and housing legislation, has intervened to try to resolve. In the end, however, it is true to say that the marriage of welfare state legislation with the older body of property law represented in the Law of Property Act 1925 has reflected the social and political chasm between those who own and control property and those who do not; between the private landlord and the tenant; between the property-owner and the homeless; between the polluter and the victims. In a society where there is still such a great gulf between rich and poor, it becomes all the more important to ensure that measures enacted by the state through law should serve the interests of the latter, and not subjugate them to the power of the former.

6

Law and the settlement of disputes

Every social group contains within it the elements and conditions in which disputes will arise. Even the smallest social group will experience disputes between its members, and, as we would expect, the larger and more complex a social group becomes, the more varied and, perhaps, frequent will be the disputes which crop up within it. Hardly a day goes by in people's everyday lives without some problem occurring, some argument arising or some resentment or frustration being felt by one person or group over the activities of another. Family rows, arguments with friends, confrontations at work and so on are familiar to most people, as are the various solutions which we use to deal with those disputes.

The simplest disputes are dealt with by various informal, often quite good-natured, means. Within family units, there may be an invocation of an established family custom or rule, or the calling-in of a third party to mediate in the dispute. Rarely would family squabbles result in the initiation of any kind of formal proceedings to settle the matter. Similarly, the social and economic world outside such small units as friends or family rests upon various types of relationships between, for example, business enterprises, employers and employees, traders and consumers, and citizens and government agencies. When considering the frequency with which something goes wrong with the smooth running of these relationships, and a dispute arises, it is important to appreciate that the informal resolution of the problem, through concession or compromise, is by far the most usual way of settling the matter.

This mode of settling disputes through concession or compromise is especially important where the parties to the dispute are in some long-standing or permanent relationship with each other. In domestic situations, feuding neighbours will rarely resort to litigation to solve their disputes, partly because theirs is a continuing relationship, as is the relationship between employer and employee, or landlord and tenant. In the sphere of commercial agreements and business contracts, research by Macaulay, among others,[1] has suggested that people in business rarely invoke the law as a means of resolving business disputes over their contractual agreements, mainly because this is seen as having the effect of perpetuating the conflict and

---

1 S. Macaulay, 'Non-Contractual Relations in Business' (1962) *Amer Soc Rev*. See chapter 11.

polarising the disputants, instead of resolving the particular problem without damaging the continuing business relationships of the parties.

Often, a dispute will be settled by invoking some kind of rule.[2] The rule in question may be peculiar to a particular family;[3] or it may be established by people entering into a specific relationship, so that anticipated difficulties may be resolved without too much friction (as when those entering into business contracts insert into those contracts clauses which specify that, should a certain event occur, then by agreement certain results will follow – see below and chapter 11); or the rule may be a rule of *law*, which provides some form of solution to the particular type of dispute which has arisen. What is certain is that, just as the complexities and fluctuations of smooth-running social and economic relationships must inevitably raise problems which we call disputes, so the social structural arrangements within a social group will invariably contain *dispute-settling*, as well as *dispute-prevention*, mechanisms.

Although the vast majority of disputes are settled by informal means, there will, at least in more complex and technologically developed societies, be various official, formal institutions and agencies whose purpose is the resolution of disputes. The clearest examples in our own society of such agencies are, of course, the courts of law and tribunals, one of whose most important functions is the authoritative settlement of disputes through the application of legal rules. These agencies will be considered later in this chapter.

The prevention and settlement of disputes in modern society

The last century has seen a considerable growth in the potential for disputes between individuals, groups and state agencies. To begin with, the expansion of agencies created for the implementation of state interventionist policies in, for example, the field of welfare provision, has created in turn the potential for disputes between individuals and social security officials, and between property-owners and planning authorities. Frequently, as we shall see, the legislation which has established the machinery for implementing such policies has also set up the institutional framework within which disputes in particular fields are to be resolved; and it is significant that in many such cases, the dispute-solving mechanisms adopted have not been ordinary courts of law, but rather specialised *tribunals*, which we will discuss in more detail later. In other areas, disputes which were once a purely private matter between the individuals concerned have been subject to regulation through new legal procedures and legal rules. Let us look briefly, by way of an example, at the area of industrial relations.

Until the turn of the last century, disputes at work were usually settled on an individual basis between employer and employee, and rarely to the latter's advantage.

2 On rules in general see chapter 1.
3 See W. Twining and D. Miers, *How to Do Things with Rules* (4th edn., 1999, Butterworths), chapter 1.

With the growth of trade unionism and the consequent increase in unions' bar-gaining-power, especially during the course of the twentieth century, many individual problems over pay, conditions of work and so on were resolved by means of *collective bargaining* between management and trade unions.[4] This is not to say, of course, that all trade unions had equal bargaining-power, nor that employees in all industries were able to turn to their unions to negotiate on their collective (or individual) behalf.[5] Some unions were larger and more powerful than others, whilst in some industries, especially those in which the labour force was predominantly casual or part-time, there was often little union presence. In addition, employers might have been in some cases unwilling to encourage, or even to recognise, trade unions in their particular business enterprise. Despite these factors, for many industries in the years following the Second World War, industrial relations in this country were characterised by an emphasis on voluntary collective bargaining between unions and management, and *relatively* little involvement by the state through regulatory legislation.[6]

In this environment, disputes in the workplace, which inevitably occurred from time to time, tended to be resolved not on the basis of seeking redress for workers on an *individual* basis, but rather by means of negotiating and renegotiating *collective* agreements with management, the terms of which would be incorporated into individual workers' employment contracts. The sanctions which trade unions could – and did – impose on reluctant or unco-operative management included, of course, calling the labour force out on strike, but,

> from the government's point of view, a highly prized feature of the . . . system of collective bargaining was its institutionalisation of the inevitable conflicts of interests created by the labour market and the subordinate position of the employee in the employment relationship. The disruption caused by strikes, lock-outs, and other forms of industrial action was a price to be paid for a system which resolved the majority of conflicts without resort to either overt industrial action or state intervention.[7]

The importance of *individual* employment contracts gradually grew in the 1960s and 1970s, through a series of statutes which placed emphasis on employment protection for workers *individually* by requiring that certain contractual terms (for example, regarding minimum periods of notice, compensation in the event of redundancy and the right not to be unfairly dismissed) be specifically written into contracts of employment. In the 1970s, too, measures were introduced in the

---

4 See S. Deakin and G. S. Morris, *Labour Law* (4th edn., 2005, Hart Publishing); M. Curthoys, *Governments, Labour and the Law in Mid-Victorian Britain* (2004, Clarendon Press); P. Davies and M. Freedland, *Labour Legislation and Public Policy* (1993, Oxford University Press).
5 See Deakin and Morris, op. cit.; G. Pitt, *Employment Law* (5th edn., 2003, Sweet and Maxwell); C. Barrow, *Industrial Relations Law Textbook* (2nd edn., 2002, Cavendish); R. Upex, R. Benny and S. Hardy, *Labour Law* (2004, Oxford University Press).
6 Working conditions, especially in factories, had been regulated since the nineteenth century by a series of Factory Acts; and legislation provided for minimum wages for certain industries, and health and safety in the workplace.   7 Davies and Freedland, op. cit., p 645.

attempt to ensure equal pay between men and women engaged in 'like work', and to prohibit discrimination in the workplace on the grounds of sex or racial or ethnic origin.[8]

During the same period, in which there was considerable industrial unrest, with disputes often becoming bitter and involving substantial periods of time lost to strikes, politicians began to recognise the limitations of leaving industrial relations problems to the mechanism of collective bargaining. Attempts were made to curb the power of trade unions during the 1970s: union activity, especially the use of strikes as a means of settling collective industrial conflicts, was directly confronted by formal legal controls in the Conservative government's Industrial Relations Act 1971, the failure of which was followed in turn by the attempt in 1974 by the incoming Labour government to set up a less rigid procedure for settling disputes at work between unions and management, as part of an overall strategy for industrial harmony.[9] One aspect of this strategy was the introduction, in the Employment Protection Act 1975,[10] of the Advisory, Conciliation and Arbitration Service (ACAS), an administrative agency funded by, but operating independently of, government. We will say more about the work of ACAS presently. The Conservative government which took office in 1979 regarded union activity as being crucially responsible for the economic problems facing the country at that time: as the government saw it,

> If productivity was low or efficiency poor, the problem could not lie with the free enter-
> prise basis of British capitalism; rather it must lie with externally imposed constraints
> on its operation. And in 1979 those constraints seemed self-evident. They were trade
> unions and their malevolent influence on wages and productivity levels . . . trade
> unions caused inflation by pressing for unjustified wage rises; trade unions obstructed
> management from introducing new technology and raising productivity; they caused
> high taxation by insisting on unreasonable wages in the public sector; they locked
> Britain into the cycle of inflation, lost competitiveness, poor productivity, devaluation,
> low growth and yet more inflation.[11]

During the 1980s a number of measures were introduced which significantly curtailed trade union activities with regard to, among other things, picketing, secondary industrial action and 'closed shop' disputes (see chapter 3). Today, the trade union movement has been dramatically weakened as a result of the statutory measures, and collective bargaining as a means of resolving industrial disputes has given way to a legal framework centred on workers' *individual* employment contracts.

With regard to *collective* disputes at work, ACAS has an important role. One of the statutory functions of the service is to try, where possible, to effect a solution to the dispute by means of discussion and negotiation followed by an agreed settlement

---

8 Equal Pay Act 1970; Sex Discrimination Act 1975; Race Relations Act 1976.
9 See Davies and Freedland, op. cit.   10 Now the Employment Rights Act 1996.
11 W. Hutton, *The State We're In* (1996, Vintage), p 82.

between the parties. In this way, the hope is that direct industrial action such as strikes may in many cases be avoided. The service has an important similar function, however, with regard to *individual* grievances and disputes between employer and employee. In the sphere of individual employment law, many such disputes may be brought before an employment tribunal for formal settlement. The number of applications received by employment tribunals[12] rose steadily and dramatically in the 1990s, reaching a total of around 120,000 in 2001–2. Since then, the total number of applications has fallen somewhat – in 2004–5, just over 86,000 claims were received. Of these applications, however, only about one-third actually culminated in a tribunal hearing.[13] The jurisdiction of these tribunals includes claims for unfair dismissal[14] (accounting for about half the number of applications), claims arising from redundancy payments, claims for unpaid wages, allegations of discrimination at work on the grounds of sex, race, or disability, and disputes arising from matters involving health and safety at work. The Employment Relations Act 1999 added to this list the right not to be victimised on the grounds of pregnancy, child birth or maternity.

Before a claim is heard by an employment tribunal, however, it is statutorily provided that the dispute must be referred to ACAS, once again in the hope of settling the matter through conciliation or mediation[15] without recourse to the tribunal. Available figures suggest that, at least with regard to unfair dismissal cases (by far the largest single category of such disputes), the vast majority of claims are settled by means of intervention by an ACAS officer.

From this brief discussion, we can see that state intervention through legal rules and frameworks may enter the arena of dispute-prevention and settlement in a number of ways. First, under a regime of collective bargaining, in many cases of potential dispute the parties effectively *prevent* disputes from disrupting their relationship by specifying, within collective bargaining agreements, agreed procedures and solutions should certain problems arise. Second, the law may provide basic criteria (such as definitions of 'trade dispute' or 'unfair dismissal') whereby a dispute is recognised as having particular features, or as setting in motion particular procedures for settlement. Third, the law may dictate the means whereby a dispute may be settled. This may take a *negative* form, as where governments may, through legal measures, attempt to curb certain industrial action such as strikes; or it may take a *positive* form, as where special agencies, such as ACAS or employment tribunals, are created in order to resolve the dispute through discussion and conciliation and, if these fail, official resolution and the award of a remedy where appropriate.

12 Previously known as Industrial Tribunals: the title of these tribunals was changed by the Employment Rights (Dispute Resolution) Act 1998.
13 Source: *Employment Tribunals Service Annual Report, 2004–5.*
14 On this see, for example, S. Anderman, *The Law of Unfair Dismissal* (3rd edn., 2001, Butterworths).
15 The difference between the two is that conciliation involves bringing the disputing parties together and helping them settle the dispute themselves; through mediation, a third party makes specific recommendations to the parties in the attempt to resolve the dispute, though it is up to the parties themselves to accept any solution which will settle the matter.

If we look at the machinery of dispute-prevention and settlement in modern society more generally, we can see that there are many other areas in which one or more of these legal responses have been introduced. Sometimes, changes in the nature and structure of society and in dominant social attitudes have brought certain areas of dispute out into the open rather more clearly than previously, and new dispute-settlement agencies have been established to deal with these disputes and grievances. Several such agencies are worthy of particular note, in so far as they substantially supplement (and to a certain extent may supplant) traditional legal solutions and the provision of remedies through litigation. First, the Sex Discrimination Acts of 1975 and 1986 prohibit discrimination on the ground of sex in the fields of employment, housing, education and the provision of goods and services. This legislation enacted the European Union Directive on equality of treatment in the workplace and the right not to be discriminated against on the ground of sex. The body responsible for administering the provisions of this Act is the Equal Opportunities Commission – one example of what have come to be known as 'quasi-autonomous non-governmental organisations' ('quangos') set up to deal with specific areas.[16] This commission has the power to investigate alleged discrimination, and can take steps to order such discrimination to cease. The Act provides that court proceedings can ensue, but by and large the commission has powers to secure remedies for victims of sex discrimination without recourse to courts by issuing 'non-discrimination notices' to the respondent, requiring the cessation of the discriminatory practice. In addition, individuals complaining of discrimination can take complaints to the county court (or to the employment tribunal, if the complaint concerns discrimination in employment).

Second, the Race Relations Act 1976 makes similar provision in the area of race discrimination. The Commission for Racial Equality can enquire into alleged racial discrimination in various fields, and here, too, individuals may take cases alleging discrimination to the county courts or, where appropriate, to an employment tribunal.

Third, the Disability Discrimination Act 1995 provides that it is unlawful to discriminate on the grounds of disability[17] in the field of employment or in the provision to the public of goods, facilities or services (including education). The 1995 Act was followed by the Disability Rights Commission Act 1999, which created the Disability Rights Commission.[18] This body is charged with working towards the elimination of discrimination against disabled persons in the fields of employment, the provision of goods and services, and the management and disposal of premises. The Commission must promote equal opportunities for the disabled, and encourage good practice in their treatment. In furtherance of these aims, the DRC may

---

16 Other examples are the Civil Aviation Authority, the Council on Tribunals, and the Food Standards Agency.

17 Defined in s 1 as 'a physical or mental impairment which has a substantial and long-term adverse effect on (the) ability to carry out normal day-to-day activities'.

18 This body supersedes the previous National Disability Council.

initiate investigations into discriminatory practice which infringes the 1995 Act, and may issue 'non-discrimination' notices which require the offending person or body to stop its discriminatory practice. In the event of non-compliance with such an order, a court order may be sought by the DRC which compels compliance.

Often, disputes and claims which *could* be the subject of court hearings are dealt with by some other, non-litigious, agency or procedure. One major device for dealing with disputes, and claims arising from disputes, is insurance, discussed more fully in chapter 9. It is theoretically possible to insure against any eventuality, but for most people, insurance usually covers such contingencies as burglary, property damage, injury at work and road accidents.

Another example is the Criminal Injuries Compensation Authority (CICA). The functions of this body were originally carried out by the Criminal Injuries Compensation Board (CICB), set up in 1964 to award payments out of public funds to those injured as a result of crime. The CICA replaced the CICB in 1996, and the Authority is charged with the implementation of the version of the scheme introduced in 2001.[19] Although the victim of a crime would have a good claim in civil law against the offender, such actions have always been rare, and the majority of victims wishing to claim compensation have done so by applying for Criminal Injuries Compensation. In 1999–2000, the CICA received over 78,000 applications. Many applications are rejected each year, as explained below, but in 2002–3, just over 42,000 applicants received payments totalling about £132 million. Appeals against decisions of the CICA may be made to the Criminal Injuries Compensation Appeals Panel, which dealt with about 2000 cases in 2002–3.[20]

What kind of crimes may attract awards from the CICA? The wording of the original scheme used the phrase 'crimes of violence', though the interpretation of this phrase by the board caused many problems. The current scheme simply refers (in para 6) to applicants who have 'sustained a criminal injury', and this term is defined in para 8 as personal injury attributable to crimes of violence, to the offence of trespass on a railway, or to the apprehension (or attempted apprehension) of an offender or suspected offender, the prevention (or attempted prevention) of an offence, or to the giving to help to a constable who is engaged in any such activity.

Certain types of injuries are expressly excluded from the scheme. Allowable claims in respect of 'mental injury' or 'mental illness', attributable to a crime of violence but occurring without any physical injury, are very narrowly defined; and all traffic offences causing injury are excluded from the scheme, except where the vehicle is driven deliberately at the victim – perhaps in a situation we now refer to as 'road rage' – and is therefore being used as a weapon.

---

19 For a full discussion of the present scheme, see D. Miers, *State Compensation for Criminal Injuries* (1997, Oxford University Press) and 'Criminal Injuries Compensation: The New Regime' (2001) 4 *Journal of Personal Injury Litigation* at 371. More details about the scheme and the Authority can be obtained at www.cica.gov.uk.
20 Source: Criminal Injuries Compensation Authority Annual Report, 200–3.

A claim must normally be brought before the Authority within two years of the incident itself, although the Authority has power to waive that time-limit if 'by reason of the particular circumstances of the case, it is reasonable and in the interests of justice to do so' (para 18). Under the old scheme, the CICB was reluctant to exercise its power to waive the time-limits, and one consequence of this, for which the Board was strongly criticised, was that child victims of sexual abuse which may have taken place over a long period of time, and in respect of which the perpetrators may have been convicted only after the victims have reached adulthood, were denied compensation on the ground that their claims are out of time. There was a substantial increase during the 1990s of claims from applicants alleging physical or sexual abuse taking place when they were children, and there is, under the present scheme, no reason in principle why such claims should not be successful, although it must be remembered that the essence of a number of sexual offences is the absence of consent by the victim. It follows that problems may arise in cases where the victim may be said to have consented – for in such cases no crime will have been committed – although in this area the law insists that consent must be genuine, and not the result of deception or improper pressure by the assailant.

Another difficulty with such cases is the problem of establishing, to the satisfaction of the CICA, the allegations of criminal injury. After a long period of time it may not be possible to corroborate the allegation with any hard evidence – the alleged abuser or abusers may have disappeared or died, making it virtually impossible for any investigation to take place to verify the claim. And this particular issue is linked to a general provision in the scheme: the CICA is empowered to refuse or reduce an award if, after taking account of the claimant's own behaviour, it is considered that an award – or a full award – would be inappropriate. Thus, para 13 empowers a CICA claims officer to withhold or reduce an award if the applicant did not take all reasonable steps to inform the police (or other appropriate body) of the offence, failed to co-operate with the police or other authority or failed to give all reasonable assistance to the CICA; or if the applicant's conduct 'before, during or after the incident giving rise to the application' or their character 'as shown by his criminal convictions . . . or by evidence available to the claims officer' make it 'inappropriate that a full award or any award at all be made'.

In considering 'conduct', the claims officer may consider whether 'excessive consumption of alcohol or use of illicit drugs by the applicant contributed to the circumstances which gave rise to the injury' make it inappropriate for an award, or a full award, to be given. It is clear that under the scheme, 'undeserving applicants'[21] may well find their claims rejected. But it is also possible that abuse-victims who have failed, possibly through fear of retaliation by the perpetrator, to co-operate fully with the police, may find their claims reduced or even rejected.

The other major change introduced after the 1995 Act was the introduction of a 'tariff' of payments for specified types of injury. Injuries are allocated to a specific

---

21 Some of whom are discussed by Miers, op. cit.

point on the tariff, attracting a fixed compensation sum. The scheme introduced in 2001 incorporates a classification of some 400 physical injuries, each of which is allocated a sum of money. For example, burns affecting over 25% of skin area, with significant scarring, would attract compensation of £33,000, whereas burns to the face causing 'minor disfigurement' would attract £2,000; a fractured hand resulting in 'substantial recovery' would attract compensation of £2,000, whereas the loss of, or 'equivalent loss of function' of one hand would attract £44,000. The tariff includes mental as well as physical injury, and incorporates a detailed classification of physical and sexual abuse of both adults and children. The maximum amount payable under the tariff is £250,000, this sum being tied to paralysis of all four limbs, or 'extremely serious' brain damage (that is, no effective control of functions).[22] Three applicants received the maximum sum in 2002–3.

The establishment of a detailed tariff of injuries and amounts of compensation means, of course, that the overall cost of the system is subject to greater control by government than a system in which the compensating body has complete discretion as to amounts payable. It is interesting to note that over half of the successful claimants in 2002–3 only received between £1,000 and £2,000, and some 85% of successful claims received £5,000 or less.

Apart from 'criminal injuries', the victim of *any* crime may recover compensation, not from public funds, but through a court order made against the convicted wrongdoer. This avenue for obtaining compensation is provided by the Powers of Criminal Courts (Sentencing) Act 2000, and is much wider than the jurisdiction of the CICA: the victim has, in principle, more chance of recovering *some* compensation because the Act covers all crimes ranging from those causing personal injury or damage to property, to financial losses sustained as a result of false trade descriptions (see chapter 11). The court is required by the Act to take into account the means of the convicted person when considering an order, though interestingly it is provided in s 130(3) that if a court does *not* make a compensation order in any case where it has the power to do so, it must give reasons for not doing so. A compensation order is quite separate from any criminal sanction, such as a fine or imprisonment, which the court may also impose upon the convicted offender. One important effect of these provisions is that for many victims of crime, a compensation order imposed upon the convicted offender may well be a satisfactory alternative to taking a separate civil action against the perpetrator in order to obtain compensation – and it is expressly provided in s 134 of the Act that in any subsequent civil proceedings whereby the victim claims compensation against the perpetrator, the claimant's compensation will be calculated to take into account the sum awarded in the earlier compensation order – it is not possible to be compensated twice!

The compensation order made by a criminal court may be seen as a way of reducing the number of civil claims for compensation made before the civil courts.

---

22 In addition, to this, a maximum of £250,000 is payable in respect of lost earnings and/or special expenses. This overall maximum of £500,000 was paid in four cases in 2002–3.

The general tendency over the last 20 years or so has been to create or encourage methods of resolving disputes of various kinds without having recourse to expensive and time-consuming litigation. One of the reasons for the encouragement of these 'Alternative Dispute Resolution' (ADR) schemes is to reduce the huge cost of the legal system, which we explore later. For the moment, we need to acknowledge some of the other major forms of ADR currently in operation.

To turn briefly to a dispute-resolution system of quite a different kind: we noted in chapter 5 the Parliamentary Commissioner for Administration (PCA) and the Commissioners for Local Administration: the 'Ombudsmen'.

The word 'ombudsman' is Swedish in origin, and the first such official was established by the Swedish government in 1809, as a means of monitoring and checking government activity. The idea of having an independent person with the authority to receive and investigate complaints against 'officialdom' was first introduced into the United Kingdom in 1967, when legislation created the Parliamentary Commissioner for Administration. Though there is no statutory definition of 'maladministration', a common working definition is 'poor administration or the wrong application of rules'. There is now a substantial network of ombudsman-type officers covering many areas, and it is important to be aware of the more important ones.

Complaints relating to central government

Complaints alleging maladministration at central government level in England may be referred, through an MP, to the Parliamentary Commissioners for Administration. The number of complaints received in 2004–5 by the PCA for England was 2,214 – an increase compared to previous years.[23] Of these, the highest proportion of complaints related, as they have tended to do in previous years, to the Department of Work and Pensions (most of which related to the Child Support Agency), the Home Office and the Inland Revenue. The Commissioner's Report for 2004–5 also highlights the incidence of problems and disputes connected with the Legal Services Commission and the tax credits scheme.

In Scotland, there has been since 2002 a single Public Services Ombudsman, covering the Scottish Executive, the health service in Scotland, social housing (see chapter 5) and local government. In 2004–5, the Ombudsman received a total of 2,377 complaints, 61% of which related to local government-related issues. A further 14% related to the health service in Scotland.[24] For Wales, the Welsh Administration Ombudsman, created in 1999, received 63 new cases in the year 2003–4.[25]

The Ombudsman for Northern Ireland was established in 1969, though the current powers and duties of the Northern Ireland Ombudsman were defined

23 *Parliamentary and Health Service Ombudsman Annual Report, 2004–5*. In 2000–1, the Parliamentary Commissioner received 1721 complaints.
24 Source: *Scottish Public Services Ombudsman, Annual Report 2004–5*.
25 Source: *Welsh Administration Ombudsman, Annual Report 2003–4*.

in 1996.[26] Technically, the Northern Ireland Ombudsman operates as two distinct officers – the Assembly Ombudsman for Northern Ireland and the Northern Ireland Commissioners for Complaints. Essentially, however, the role is to receive complaints from those claiming to have suffered injustice through maladministration by government departments and certain other public bodies in Northern Ireland. In 2004–5, this Ombudsman received a total of 541 complaints.[27]

Complaints relating to local government

The Commissioners for Local Administration ('local government Ombudsmen') were created in 1974. At present there are three local commissioners for England (each responsible for one of the three areas into which England is divided for this purpose). The situation in Scotland, where the ombudsman system was reformed in 2002, has been discussed above. In Wales, a similar unification of the various public services ombudsmen will be put into place during 2006.[28]

For England, the Commissioners received a total of 18,698 complaints about local government in the year 2004–5[29] – more or less the same number as the previous year. The Commissioners identified planning, social services and highways as being particular 'growth' areas for complaints. Figures for Scotland for 2004–5 are given above; and in the same year 492 complaints relating to local government in Wales were received.

Health Service Commissioners

In 1973, Health Service Commissioners for England and Wales were created (the Scottish equivalent having been established in 1972) to investigate failures to provide services leading to injustice. Although a separate jurisdiction, this function is in fact carried out by the Parliamentary Commissioners (or equivalents) for England, Scotland, Wales and Northern Ireland. In July 2004, the Healthcare Commission undertook the role of dealing with NHS complaints prior to their being passed on to the Ombudsman, though for England, during 2004–5, 1,937 complaints against NHS bodies and practitioners were nonetheless received by the Ombudsman, compared with 2,595 in 2000–1. For Scotland in the same year, 321 complaints were received (compared with 224 in 2000–1) and for Wales, 209 complaints were received in 2003–4 compared with 162 in 1999–2000. The Northern Ireland Ombudsman received 74 complaints in 2004–5 relating to the health service in that province.

It is clear from the annual reports published by these various Commissioners that although complaints brought to the attention of the various ombudsmen often highlight areas of specific difficulty or inefficiency in some aspect of central or local

---

26 In the Ombudsman (Northern Ireland) Order 1996 and the Commissioner for Complaints (Northern Ireland) Order 1996.
27 Source: *Northern Ireland Ombudsman Annual Report, 2004–5.*
28 Public Services Ombudsman (Wales) Act 2005.
29 *Annual Report of Commission for Local Administration in England, 2004–5.*

administration, or in some area of health service provision, most complaints are resolved to the satisfaction of the complainants. It must be remembered that the general jurisdiction of the various ombudsmen discussed so far involves complaints of 'maladministration', which refers to the *manner* in which a decision is taken, and may include bias, incompetence, arbitrariness, failure to consider relevant facts, unfair discrimination or unjustifiable delay in reaching a decision. The ombudsmen have no power to enquire into the *substance or merits* of a decision. There is, moreover, no power to investigate matters in respect of which the complainant has a right to take his or her case before a tribunal, before a court of law, or before a minister by way of appeal against the decision, unless the Commissioner is satisfied that in the particular circumstances of the case, it would be unreasonable to expect the complainant to pursue any of these avenues for resolution of the dispute. This proviso applies to both the Parliamentary and the local commissioners.

One controversial feature of the British ombudsmen system (unlike other countries operating similar systems) is the requirement that complaints to the Parliamentary Commissioner for Administration must be filtered through MPs: there is no direct right of access. In practice, however, the parliamentary commissioners receive many complaints sent directly to them by aggrieved citizens. Since 1978 such direct communications have been sent to the complainant's MP requesting consent to investigation (which is usually given). During the 2004–5 Parliamentary session, the Parliamentary Commissioner (Amendment) Bill was introduced into the House of Lords which, if passed, would have removed the necessity for the 'MP filter' and have allowed direct access by the complainant to the Commissioner. This bill failed, however, to reach the statute-book on that occasion.

Complaints may be sent directly to local commissioners by virtue of the Local Government Act 1988, s 29: this was a significant and welcome change to the previous procedure whereby complaints had to be referred through local councillors. Previously, complaints sent directly to the local commissioner instead of going through the 'filter' of local councillors were simply returned to the aggrieved person, pointing out the correct procedure – a practice which inevitably resulted in many potentially sound complaints subsequently being dropped.

In August 2005, the Government issued a consultation paper entitled 'Reform of Public Sector Ombudsmen Services in England' which invited consultation on a series of proposed reforms to the English Ombudsman system. The paper explains that

> Under existing legislation, the Ombudsmen are restricted in their ability to work together, thereby preventing them, in cases which cross more than one Ombudsman jurisdiction, from providing a fully joined-up and coherent service for the citizen. Therefore the Government, which has worked closely with the public sector Ombudsmen on this, wishes to remove some of the existing legislative constraints . . .

The stated intention is to provide more of a 'one-stop shop' for the complainant, and is in line, certainly, with the 2002 reforms already implemented in Scotland.

The Government's consideration of the responses to the consultation exercise will take place during 2006.

Other Ombudsman schemes

In 1990, the Legal Services Ombudsman was established to deal with complaints against solicitors and barristers. In 2000, a number of complaint-handling schemes within the financial services industry were combined to form a single Financial Ombudsman Service, dealing with complaints from consumers relating to mortgages, banks, insurance and investment firms. There are ombudsman schemes covering estate agents, funeral services, pensions, and the prison and probation services. There is an ombudsman for the European Parliament whose function is to investigate complaints of maladministration on the part of any institution of the European Community. And apart from systems bearing the (formal or informal) label of 'ombudsman', there are, of course, many other systems whose function is to deal with and investigate complaints – for example, the Broadcasting Standards Commission and the Police Complaints Authority.

In all the cases discussed above, dispute-settlement through courts of law may be regarded, for a number of reasons, as inappropriate, and although in many (though not all) cases, courts constitute 'last resort' forums of dispute-settlement, court hearings comprise only a tiny proportion of resolutions of disputes. In addition to the examples already mentioned, two other major alternative methods of avoiding and resolving disputes must be noted: arbitration and dispute-avoidance in business or commercial contracts, and the use of tribunals.

Business disputes: avoidance and arbitration

We stated earlier that there is within the business and commercial world a general reluctance to call on lawyers and the courts for the solution of contractual disputes. Tillotson has noted that 'in the mid-nineteenth century contract litigation occupied a significant amount of the time of the civil courts. . . . A century later, a survey of reported cases for 1957–66 revealed only 56 cases which were determined on the basis of points of contract-law.'[30] There are various reasons for this decline in the use of the courts as a means of dealing with business disputes. As we have noted, the stable continuation of business relationships between companies may be impaired by recourse to courts; additionally, litigation is extremely expensive, especially if the dispute involves complex contractual documents, a large number of witnesses or substantial amounts of time in the courtroom dealing with technical aspects of a business contract. Third, the basic common-law rules of contract (discussed in chapter 11) have been largely and increasingly superseded by specialised and technical statutory provisions requiring corresponding specialism in dispute-prevention and settlement devices and techniques.

---

30 J. P. Tillotson, *Contract Law in Perspective* (3rd edn., 1995, Cavendish), p 235.

Finally, business contracts almost always contain within them the agreed means of solving certain specified problems, should they arise. Suppose, for example, that X Ltd, a manufacturer of fitted kitchen furniture, agrees to supply Z Ltd, a discount furniture retail store, with a large quantity of kitchen units at an agreed price, the goods to be delivered by an agreed date. If X's workforce then takes industrial action, with consequent delays in production, or if X's source of raw materials is affected by, say, the sinking of a ship which is carrying a shipment of supplies for X, with the result in either case that X Ltd is unable to meet the contractually agreed delivery date, then how is this problem to be resolved? If Y Ltd sues X Ltd for breach of contract, difficult questions may arise as to whether the doctrine of frustration may apply (see chapter 11). An expensive and possibly protracted court action will be avoided, however, if the parties have inserted into their original contract a clause which states what shall happen if, for some specified reason, one of the parties is unable to fulfil the contract through no fault of their own. Such a clause is called a *force-majeure* clause, and the kinds of incidents which may be foreseen in such clauses might include strikes, the outbreak of war, fire, flood or any other occurrence which is outside the control of the parties and which may affect the performance of the contract. Should one of these incidents prevent or delay performance, then the agreed clause will specify what the consequences will be: the clause may provide that one or other party may terminate the contract (with agreed provisions as to which party shall bear any financial losses), or that the delivery date shall be extended for the duration of the adverse circumstances. This kind of clause is a very important means of dispute-prevention in business, for it provides the means of avoiding expensive, time-consuming and possibly detrimental litigation.

What happens, however, if the parties cannot agree on the applicability of a *force-majeure*, or some other, clause within the contract – for example, because of difficulties over the interpretation of the clause? Here again, recourse to the courts is unlikely. It is far more probable that the contract will contain provisions to the effect that in such an event the dispute is to be referred to *arbitration*. Arbitration is essentially intended to be an informal, private and speedy alternative to court hearings, and has the additional advantage of flexibility: the parties are free to stipulate the identity and, if appropriate, the qualifications and experience of the arbitrator; they can decide how many arbitrators – one, two or perhaps three – will be called upon to deal with the dispute (though in some instances, known as institutional arbitration, the proceedings are governed by rules and practices of a trade association to which the contracting parties may belong). The arbitrator is under a duty to act impartially and to observe any relevant rules of procedure (such as the obligation to ensure that each party is given the opportunity to put their side of the case). In general, an arbitration hearing is a private, less formal version of a court action, following much the same line of procedure.

Arbitration can be invoked in a number of situations involving business contractual disputes – where there is a dispute of fact (such as whether, in our hypothetical example above, the industrial action by the workforce actually accounted for the failure to meet the contractual delivery date), where there is a dispute of law (such as whether the relevant contractual clause, properly interpreted, actually covers the eventuality of the sinking of the ship carrying raw materials), or, more frequently, where a dispute involves both fact and law (requiring both the finding of facts and the application to them of the relevant law). Whichever kind of arbitration is required, and whoever acts in the capacity of arbitrator, however, the conduct and outcome of the arbitration proceedings are subject to the overriding control of the law.

It may at first seem odd that a dispute-settlement mechanism which is primarily regarded as informal, private and structured largely according to the contracting parties' own desires, is none the less subject to an overriding legal control. There are, however, a number of reasons for the fact that, as one judge explained,

> it is the policy of the law in this country that, in the conduct of arbitrations, arbitrators must in general apply a fixed and recognisable system of law, which primarily and normally would be the law of England, and that they cannot be allowed to apply some different criterion such as the view of the individual arbitrator or umpire[31] on abstract justice or equitable principles.[32]

First of all, no matter how detailed contractual specifications may be, there may well be gaps in the contractual provision which neither party anticipated, but which may prove significant. In such an event the general law of arbitration will fill such gaps. Second, there is a general principle within the law of contract that it is against public policy for any contractual term to oust or exclude the jurisdiction of the ordinary courts,[33] this being a well-established limitation on the otherwise much-vaunted and traditional judicial notion of 'freedom of contract'.[34]

Third, the legislation relating to arbitration in Britain contains specific provision concerning the courts' involvement in arbitration matters. The Arbitration Act 1950 provided that, in order to ensure that an arbitration award was not based upon an error of law, either party to the arbitration could request that difficult points of law could be taken before the High Court by means of the 'case stated' procedure. The same Act provided that the court had the power to set aside an arbitration award if there was any error of fact, law or procedure revealed on the face of the award – although the court could not 'look behind' the award itself. Both of these provisions caused problems, however. There was a tendency for the 'case stated' procedure to be abused, with the sole intention by one party of delaying payment of sums awarded against them by the arbitration award. The appeal procedure caused additional delays and expense; and judicial review was made difficult by reason of many arbitrators' omitting their reasons from the awards, so that

---

31 An umpire may be brought in to adjudicate if, where there is an arbitration panel of two, there is disagreement between the arbitrators.

32 *Orion Compania Espanola de Seguros v Belford Maatschappij voor Algemene Verzekgringeen* [1962] 2 Lloyd's Rep 257 at 264, per Megaw J.

33 See, for example, *Baker v Jones* [1954] 2 All ER 553; and for a case on this point involving an arbitration agreement, see *Scott v Avery* (1856) 5 HL Cas 811.   34 See chapter 11.

awards were made less likely to be set aside. Both the 'case stated' and the appeal procedures had the effect of transforming the arbitration procedure into a fully fledged court action, with the accompanying problems of delay and expense, and it was clearly the case that much financially lucrative arbitration work (including arbitrations on foreign disputes which is arguably a 'valuable invisible export')[35] was being lost.

To solve these and certain other problems, the Arbitration Act 1979 changed the law relating to judicial review. The 'case stated' procedure was abolished by this Act, which also limited the right to appeal from an arbitration decision to a court of law. The right of appeal was further limited by the Arbitration Act 1996, which now contains the relevant law in this area. Unless the parties otherwise agree, there may be an appeal, subject to certain conditions, on a question of law; and by s 68(1) of this Act, a party may challenge an arbitration award in a court of law on the ground of 'serious irregularity', which includes (s 68(2)) the arbitrators' failing to abide by their general duty to act fairly and impartially and to give each party a reasonable opportunity to state their case; exceeding their powers; failing to run the proceedings in the way the parties have agreed; or failing to deal with the relevant issues put to them. If either of the parties have, however, continued with the proceedings without objecting to such irregularity, then the right to appeal will be lost. Arbitration proceedings will always be open to challenge on the basis of judicial review (see chapter 12).

Apart from arbitration over disputes arising from contracts between businesses, there is often provision for aggrieved *consumers* to have their complaints against manufacturers or retailers dealt with by arbitration. Many businesses, through their trade associations, have introduced codes of practice approved by the Office of Fair Trading (OFT), which, among other things, often include conciliation and arbitration schemes for consumer complaints. Clearly, such schemes do not, and indeed cannot, exclude the right of a consumer to take legal action against a retailer or manufacturer, but in many cases the consumer may well find that such schemes provide satisfactory solutions to the problem without the need to incur expense and suffer the delays of court actions. Thus, for example, among the many codes of practice currently in operation with OFT approval is the ABTA Code of Practice, drawn up by the Association of British Travel Agents. This deals, among other things, with the requirement under the code for brochures and booking forms to contain clear and comprehensive information, for arrangements for refunds on cancellation of bookings and for a conciliation and arbitration scheme to deal with consumer complaints. Similar schemes are found in the Code of Practice for the Motor Industry and the code operated by the Radio, Electrical and Television Retailers' Association. The attempts at conciliation are not intended to operate by means of strict adherence to what the parties' rights would be in law, but to reach a satisfactory settlement (which may often be a compromise solution) without invoking strict legal rights. If

---

35 Tillotson, op. cit., p 240.

conciliation fails, then the dispute can be referred to arbitration, which is carried out under the provisions of the Arbitration Acts. For many consumers, these schemes are a useful method of resolving problems and, of course, from the traders' point of view they help maintain good relations with consumers.

These conciliation and arbitration schemes are quite separate from the 'small claims' procedure in the county court, introduced in 1973 as a means of dealing with consumers' claims against traders over transactions involving relatively small amounts of money. In such cases, a court action will usually be wholly inappropriate as a means of settling the dispute, and the 'small claims' procedure was designed as an appropriate alternative.

The operation of the scheme is now part of the new civil procedure system, introduced in 1998. Under the Civil Procedure Rules 1998, claims involving amounts below £5,000 are normally allocated to the 'small claims track' and the dispute is dealt with by means of a 'small claims hearing'. There were 55,836 small claims hearing in the year 2000, though this had fallen to 46,100 for the year 2004.[36] The initiative for bringing the claim lies with the aggrieved party, and it remains the case that many ordinary people may be put off by the prospect of arguing their own case through the small claims procedure. Legal aid is not available for such claims, although an adviser with some expertise, such as a member of a Citizens' Advice Bureau, is allowed to help present the case.

The growth of tribunals

Apart from the example of employment tribunals mentioned earlier, there exists a vast and complicated undergrowth of various other tribunals, all of them created by means of legislation designed to implement state policies and schemes during the twentieth century. It is with regard to the kind of work handled by these agencies that the increased potential for disputes in the public sector – between groups, and between individuals, groups and state institutions – can best be appreciated.

The state in Britain has provided various benefits for, as well as controls upon, the life of the ordinary citizen. Social security benefits, unemployment benefit ('job seekers' allowance'), industrial injury compensation, unfair dismissal provisions, compulsory purchase, the resolution of problems between landlord and tenant – these areas, and many more, have either come into existence through welfare state philosophies and policies (such as state benefits for unemployment) or, as a result of those philosophies and policies, been taken out of the hands of private individuals and regulated by means of state interventionist policies. All these areas are breeding-grounds for disputes and conflicts between the parties and agencies concerned. A worker may wish to challenge the grounds of a dismissal as being unfair; an employee injured at work may wish to claim compensation from the employer; a citizen claiming supplementary benefit may want to challenge the

36 *Judicial Statistics, 2001* and *2004.*

refusal of officials to allow the claim. If such disputes were taken before courts of law for resolution, there is no doubt that the court system would collapse under the weight of work; and in any case, the courts are, for many of these cases, inappropriate organs to deal with the dispute.

It would, for example, be somewhat out of place for a county court to have to hear a claim by a social security claimant where the claim may only amount to a few pounds per week, and where the usual delays affecting court cases would operate very harshly on the claimant, who might need a much more immediate decision.

To provide a means whereby such disputes may be dealt with without the trappings of the court of law, various governments have, through legislation, introduced a network of administrative tribunals designed to provide 'instant' justice cheaply, efficiently and with minimum delay and formality. These tribunals comprise not highly paid judges, but panels, with a chairperson who is (usually) legally qualified[37] and two other, non-legally qualified, people who have expertise in the particular field over which the tribunal has jurisdiction. Thus, social security appeal tribunals decide appeals at the instance of an aggrieved claimant; valuation tribunals deal with disputes between property-owners and local councils concerning valuation of property for council tax; and employment tribunals deal with claims from ex-employees that their dismissal was unfair, that their redundancy amounted to unfair dismissal, or that they were discriminated against on the grounds of race or sex. Apart from these examples, there are many specialised tribunals dealing with problems of compulsory detention of mentally ill people in hospital (Mental Health Review Tribunals), appeals against decisions by the Home Secretary on matters concerning immigration (Immigration Appeal Tribunals) and appeals concerning pensions (Pensions Appeal Tribunals). Special tribunals also deal with complaints about services provided by various occupations and professions, such as the Solicitors' Disciplinary Tribunal and the Disciplinary Committee of the General Medical Council. In all, there are about 70 different types of tribunal, hearing about a million cases per year – many more than the number of disputes heard by courts of law.

Tribunals are invariably creations of Acts of Parliament. Unfortunately, however, the pattern of their development has been piecemeal. A statute creating, for example, the social security system will also create the tribunals pertaining to social security appeals; and Mental Health Review Tribunals are the creation of the Mental Health Act 1959.[38] The resulting diversity between tribunals was one of the problems discussed in the *Report of the Committee on Administrative Tribunals* (the

---

37 The Franks Committee, reporting in 1957, (see below) thought that chairpersons of appeal tribunals should be legally qualified, and chairpersons of other kinds of tribunals preferably so qualified. Although these recommendations were not incorporated into the Tribunals and Inquiries Act 1992, it is generally the case that statutes creating tribunals require the chairperson of an appeal tribunal to be a lawyer.
38 These tribunals are now governed by the consolidating provisions of the Mental Health Act 1983.

Franks Committee) in 1957,[39] which was followed in 1958 by the Tribunals and Inquiries Act. The provisions of this and later enactments are now consolidated in the 1992 Act of the same name. Whilst this diversity has led to a confusing network of tribunals dealing with different areas and incorporating different procedures, it must be remembered that tribunals are *specialised* bodies, each dealing with a limited area. This specialisation may be contrasted with courts of law, many of which, such as the county courts, must be 'jacks of all trades', having jurisdiction to hear many kinds of dispute involving various different fields of law. This specialisation has inevitably meant the tailoring of particular tribunal procedures to the contingencies arising in the specific area of the tribunal's jurisdiction.

The Franks Committee said that tribunals should be characterised always by openness, fairness and impartiality, and made various recommendations towards this aim, most of which were implemented by the 1958 Act. The Council on Tribunals, for example, which was recommended by the Franks Committee, has the task of keeping under review the constitution and working of tribunals; a second recommendation was that those who chair tribunals should be legally qualified, and this is normally required by Acts which create tribunals. Further recommendations which were implemented were that representation should be possible before all tribunals, if necessary by a qualified lawyer; and that tribunals must give reasons for their decisions.

In 2001, the report was published of a major review by Sir Andrew Leggatt of the working of tribunals. The report begins by stating that:

> Together [tribunals] constitute a substantial part of the system of justice in England and Wales. But too often their methods are old-fashioned and they are daunting to users. Their training and IT [information technology] are under-resourced. Because they are many and disparate, there is a considerable waste of resources in managing them, and they achieve no economies of scale. Most importantly, they are not independent of the departments that sponsor them.[40]

On the issue of the independence of tribunals, Leggatt pointed out that:

> there . . . is an uneasy relationship between most tribunals and the departments on whose decisions they are adjudicating. In those tribunals which are paid for by the sponsoring departments, the chairmen and members feel that they cannot be seen as independent, however impartial they are, and however scrupulous departments are. Indeed, plainly they are not independent. Even in tribunals which are no longer paid for by 'their' departments, there can be an unhealthy closeness. For example, the General Commissioners of Income Tax, although now sponsored by the Lord Chancellor's Department, are still wholly dependent on the Inland Revenue for case listing and for the flow of information to enable them to take their decisions.[41]

39 Cmnd 218 (1957, HMSO).
40 Sir A. Leggatt, *Tribunals for Users: One System, One Service* (2001), 'Overview', para 1.
41 Ibid., chapter 1, para 1.19.

The question of independence is particularly important, not only because of intrinsic value as a principle underpinning any system which is supposed to secure justice, but also because of the importance placed by the review upon 'user-friendliness' and the stress throughout upon the proposition that citizens should be in a position to obtain all necessary advice to enable them to present their own cases before tribunals. The review team were in no doubt as to their view of the main purposes of tribunals:

> There should be one guiding principle. In origin, many tribunal functions started within the administrative process. Tribunals were established because it was clear that the citizen needed an independent means of challenging possible mistakes and illegalities which was faster, simpler and cheaper than recourse to the courts. Tribunals are an alternative to court, not administrative, processes. They will keep the confidence of users only in so far as they are seen to demonstrate similar qualities of independence and impartiality to the courts.[42]

To enhance the independence of tribunals and to create a single organisational structure for all tribunals, the review proposed the establishment of a Tribunals System, which would unify all tribunals, with one or two exceptions,[43] into a single co-ordinated structure. This structure would operate by means of grouping tribunals into 'divisions', and by reforming appeal channels into a 'rational and clearly defined' route. The system would be administered by a single Tribunals Service, which would be the responsibility of the Lord Chancellor and based within the Lord Chancellor's Department. The Council on Tribunals would continue to have an important role in overseeing tribunals and their work, and should also, according to the review's proposals, take on new roles of monitoring the development of the new Tribunals System, and check that the practices and procedures of government departments are compatible with the requirements of the Human Rights Act 1998. The operation of a unified service would make it possible, among other things, to ensure appropriate training for those responsible for staffing tribunals; to improve the information technology systems through which the work of tribunals must, like any other modern organisation, operate; and to encourage 'a new culture, starting with improved recognition of just how daunting the tribunal experience is for first-time users, as most are'.[44]

The review presented detailed sets of proposals as to how the Tribunal System might be made more 'user-friendly'[45] and more efficient through the use of IT and through efficient case-management, and – inevitably – examined the related question as to whether citizens using tribunals should be able to obtain any state-subsidised assistance with, in particular, the cost of legal advice and possibly legal representation.

---

42 Ibid., chapter 2, para 2.18.
43 For example, Patent Office tribunals on the basis of their specialised and technical nature and the Investigatory Powers Tribunal, which deals with matters of security.
44 Sir A. Leggatt, op. cit., Overview, para 31.   45 See, in particular, chapter 4.

aid or other state subsidisation of the cost to the citizen of
…iscussed presently, but in the context of the tribunal system,
…ople wishing to take cases before tribunals need, at the very
…ance, and possibly representation if they are unable to
…here is evidence to suggest that representation at tribunals
…erable difference to the outcome of the case.[46] The Leggatt review
…unals noted that the Community Legal Service and the Legal Services
Commission[47] can provide advice and assistance short of actual representation
(called 'legal help'), though there is financial means-testing.

It is with regard to legal representation that the review of tribunals was perhaps
at its most cautious. Although the review acknowledged the evidence that citizens
appearing before tribunals benefit significantly from representation, the reviewers
stated their conviction that:

> Representation not only often adds unnecessarily to cost, formality and delay, but it
> also works against the objective of making tribunals directly and easily accessible to the
> full range of potential users. We accept that that objective is challenging and will not
> always be achievable. But measures in this report are designed to achieve it for most
> people in most cases and, therefore, should radically reduce the need for representa-
> tion whilst meeting human rights requirements. A combination of good quality infor-
> mation and advice, effective procedures and well conducted hearings, and competent
> and well-trained tribunal members should go a long way to helping the vast majority
> of appellants to understand and put their cases properly themselves.[48]

The difficulty, of course, lies in attempting to define the characteristics of those citizens who *cannot* put their cases properly themselves, and in putting into place
effective provision which will ensure that such citizens are not disadvantaged or in
some way denied the opportunity for a hearing at which they can put their side of
the case. The review team acknowledged that there may be a need for representation in particular cases, and recommend the development of 'specific criteria' (para
4.23) through which such cases may be identified. Thus,

> no public funding should be considered unless a case has a reasonable prospect of
> success . . . Given that prospect of reasonableness, help with representation should be
> provided where it is required because applicants' personal circumstances (such as inad-
> equate knowledge of English, or mental or physical disability) or the complexity
> of the case in fact or law, make it unreasonable to expect them to present the case
> themselves.[49]

The government, receiving the Leggatt Report in March 2001, stated its belief that
tribunals already fully meet the standards of independence and impartiality

---

46 H. Genn and Y. Genn, *The Effectiveness of Representation at* Tribunals (1989, Lord Chancellor's
    Department) ; J. Baldwin, 'The Adjudication of Claims' (1992) *NLJ*, 5 and 12 June.

47 See below.

48 Ibid., chapter 4, para 4.21. See also H. Genn, 'Tribunals and Informal Justice' (1993) 56 *MLR* 393.

49 Ibid., chapter 4, para 4.23.

required by the Human Rights Act 1998, but undertook a consultation exercise on the report's recommendations. In the White Paper of 2004 in which the Government announced its plans for reform, it was recognised that the existing arrangements were

> highly fragmented, with each department, agency or tribunal responsible for trying to make improvements within its own sphere of operation. We believe that we need an approach and institutions which span the whole of government, joining up best practice and driving improvement forward.[50]

As a major first step towards developing a new, more integrated system, a new Tribunals Services was launched in April 2006. Based within the Department for Constitutional Affairs, this unified Service will, by 2008, administer a large number of tribunals (including Employment Tribunals, the Asylum and Immigration Tribunal, and the Criminal Injuries Compensation Appeals Panel). It is intended that the new system will address the issue of perceived lack of independence of tribunals, discussed by Leggatt, as well as forming a major plank in the government's stated objective, in the 2004 White Paper, of creating a 'joined-up' system of dispute-resolution. The need for proper training of tribunal panel members was recognised, and the White Paper speaks of

> a strong emphasis placed on training in judgecraft skills for all judges and members, based around the skills, knowledge and attributes identified for the judicial role. This role in itself is likely to evolve as new forms of dispute resolution grow up. Members may need to learn mediation skills and how best to use staff to help resolve disputes without the need for formal hearings.[51]

Although in the case of a number of tribunals (though not all of them) it is possible to appeal against the tribunal's decision to an appeal tribunal, it must be remembered that the courts, too, may have a role to play. Although the courts do not operate as additional courts of appeal, re-hearing the substantive arguments involved in the dispute, the High Court has long exercised, by means of the *judicial review* procedure, a supervisory jurisdiction over the activities of tribunals. This may be invoked if a problem involving a point of law or a breach of procedural rules is alleged by an aggrieved claimant to have occurred at a tribunal hearing. This jurisdiction is discussed more fully in chapter 12, but its main features are that first, if the claimant alleges that the tribunal in question exceeded its statutory authority and acted beyond its powers (*ultra vires*), or second, if it is alleged that a breach of the rules of natural justice occurred – that is to say that the complaining party was given no opportunity to present his or her side of the case, or that the presiding chairperson was in some way biased or partial, or that there was a possibility of such bias, as regards the case and its outcome, then the court may set aside that decision through the granting of a *quashing order*, or grant some other appropriate remedy.

---

50 *Transforming Public Services: Complaints, Redress and Tribunals* (Dept for Constitutional Affairs, 2004) para. 6.1.   51 Ibid., para. 6.74.

Although the government's White Paper of 2004 explicitly acknowledges that to remove this 'historic supervisory role' altogether would be a 'highly contentious constitutional proposition',[52] it was proposed therein to create – in addition to any existing appeal mechanisms – a new 'layer' of appeal, in the form of the 'administrative appeal tribunal'. This new mechanism would, it was argued, serve to keep tribunal-related matters within the tribunal system rather than bringing them before courts of law, though, if necessary, a final 'statutory review' by a judge of the Court of Appeal might be available.

On the vexed question of the provision of providing state-subsidised financial assistance (legal aid) for those wishing to bring cases before tribunals, and more particularly wishing to make use of legal representation at those hearings, the White Paper, not surprisingly, reiterates the long-standing government view that 'full-scale legal representation at the taxpayer's expense in every administrative dispute or tribunal case would be disproportionate and unreasonable'.[53] Pointing out that already, substantial amounts of public money are used to fund representation at certain tribunal hearings (notably the Mental Health Review Tribunal and the Immigration Appeal Tribunal), as well as funding for local advice agencies and law centres, the White Paper stressed that the paramount need is for better-quality decision-making by administrative agencies, which would go a long way towards preventing the disputes which eventually require resolution before tribunals. Similar benefits would result from improved and clearer information, provided by decision-makers to those affected by those decisions. Many disputes, furthermore, might be appropriately dealt with through mechanisms such as complaints procedures, or possibly approaches to a relevant Ombudsman, rather than by means of tribunal hearings. Only in those cases where a person 'cannot represent his or her own case and the tribunal is resolving a matter of great importance to the individual' will there be, in the government's view, a need for representation, and funding for representation in such 'exceptional cases' representation is already available under the Access to Justice Act 1999. A Courts and Tribunals Bill was introduced in the 2004–5 parliamentary session in order to implement those White Paper proposals requiring legislation, but the Bill failed to be passed in that session.

Some recent developments

In relation to the civil justice system in England, radical changes have taken place in recent years, which we will discuss presently. For the moment, bearing in mind the contemporary emphasis on 'alternative dispute resolution' – that is, ways of resolving disputes without recourse to courts of law – let us focus on some aspects of civil procedure in order to appreciate the pressures and some of the ways in which the system has, to date, responded to those pressures.

52 Ibid., para 7.28.   53 Ibid., para 10.3.

In an article published in 1993, Lord Hoffmann reviewed the numerous changes which had affected both the character and the practical operation of the civil justice system in England over the previous 20 years.[54] He noted that, first, there had been a huge increase in the number of cases where there was no substantive legal dispute between the parties, but rather where the plaintiff 'only wants access to the coercive power of the state in order to enforce his undoubted legal rights' because the defendant (typically a company) is 'delaying payment to improve his cash flow or because he is unable to pay his debts but wants to stave off liquidation or bankruptcy'.[55] The problem was that the appropriate procedure, as provided under the existing Rules of the Supreme Court, was far too slow, possibly taking months. There was a quicker method whereby plaintiffs could act, and that was to initiate proceedings to wind up the company, thus inflicting 'irremediable commercial damage' on the defendant. In the face of the increased number of such petitions, the Companies Court[56] 'has tried to protect itself . . . by making the winding up route a high risk strategy. It is in any event more expensive than (the other, more appropriate, procedure) and if it fails the Companies judge will dismiss the petition and order the creditor to pay the company's costs . . .'[57] The point stressed by Lord Hoffmann with this example is that:

> it shows how the system comes under pressure from market forces. If the standard procedure is not providing an adequate remedy, the ingenuity or desperation of the parties will divert the force of the current into some other procedure which may not be wholly appropriate . . . the situation which I have described demonstrates that something is wrong and clearly what is wrong is that the (relevant RSC procedure) is not functioning as efficiently as it should.[58]

Lord Hoffmann gave other examples of the ways in which existing rules have been adapted to deal with new situations coming before the courts. In actions in the early 1970s, seeking the removal of squatters from private property, the existing procedure was beset by the problems of delay and the difficulty of serving writs on identifiable defendants; so a new rule was created which provided a remedy for property-owners quickly and against unnamed defendants. In the 1980s, similar adaptability was shown in order to deal with the unidentifiable sellers of counterfeit tee-shirts and other souvenirs at pop concerts. In 1975, a new court order – the *Mareva* injunction[59] – was created to prevent defendants from avoiding payment to plaintiffs by simply moving their assets out of the country; this was first applied only to foreign defendants but was rapidly developed through decisions in the Commercial Court[60] to United Kingdom defendants who were thereby prevented

---

54 Sir Leonard Hoffmann, 'Changing Perspectives on Civil Litigation' (1993) 56 *MLR* 3.
55 Ibid., p 297.
56 Part of the Chancery Division of the High Court: see below.   57 Ibid., p 298.
58 Ibid., p 299.
59 See *Mareva Compania Naivera SA v International Bulk Carriers SA* (1975) 2 Lloyd's Rep 509.
60 Part of the Queen's Bench Division of the High Court: see below.

from making their assets unavailable within the United Kingdom.[61] In 1976, the *Anton Piller* order[62] was created to enable plaintiffs to enter and search the premises of defendants in possession of – in particular – unauthorised copies of copyrighted works (such as 'pirate' videotapes), thereby obtaining necessary evidence against such defendants; these orders may be applied for without the need for the defendants to be party to the proceedings, making them an extremely effective means of obtaining evidence before the defendants can remove the goods elsewhere.[63] And the problem of obtaining evidence necessary before a trial can be commenced was confronted in 1974 in the *Norwich Pharmacal* case[64] in which the House of Lords decided that a third party, who had been involved in a wrongdoer's activity but who was not a party to the litigation, could be required to provide information in advance of the trial which would identify the actual wrongdoers thus, literally, making a trial possible.[65] Thus, says Lord Hoffmann,

> We have therefore a range of weapons which have been developed over the last twenty years to assist plaintiffs to establish their rights in cases of commercial fraud . . . They are executive remedies of the kind one would expect the police to have, for tracking down and retrieving the proceeds of fraud. The plaintiff will in the first instance make his application *ex parte*; the first the defendant will hear of the matter is when his premises are raided under the *Anton Piller*, his bank accounts are frozen by the *Mareva* and his companies in receivership.[66]

Lord Hoffmann acknowledges that there are questions of fairness and effectiveness involved in this 'forensic *blitzkrieg*', and indeed that the new procedures 'often fit very uneasily' with existing civil procedure. The very useful analysis of the origin and use of the new mechanisms enables us to appreciate the ways in which the legal system can respond to pressures emanating from socio-economic change and technological advances, but such piecemeal changes have now been incorporated into a much more fundamental reform and modernisation of the civil justice system itself.

In 1994, Lord Woolf was appointed by the Lord Chancellor to examine the civil justice system with a view to improving access to justice and reducing the cost of litigation, reducing the complexity of the procedural rules. His final report, published in July 1996,[67] contained many radical and far-reaching proposals, and a new system of civil procedure, implementing the Woolf proposals, was introduced through the Civil Procedure Act 1997 and the new Civil Procedure Rules 1998, which came into effect in 1999.

Lord Woolf listed eight principles which the civil justice system should meet in order to ensure access to justice. In his view, the system should 'be *just* in the results

---

61 Under the Civil Procedure Rules 1998, the *Mareva* injunction has become an 'order to freeze a company's assets'.   62 See *Anton Piller AG v Manufacturing Processes Ltd* [1976] Ch 55.

63 Under the Civil Procedure Rules 1998, the *Anton Piller* order has become an 'order to search premises'.   64 *Norwich Pharmacal v Comrs of Customs and Excise* [1974] AC 133.

65 See also *British Steel Corpn v Granada Television Ltd* [1981] 1 All ER 417.   66 Op. cit., p 302.

67 The Right Honourable the Lord Woolf, Master of the Rolls, *Access to Justice: Final Report* (1996, HMSO).

it delivers; be *fair* in the way it treats litigants; offer appropriate procedures at reasonable *cost*; deal with cases with reasonable *speed*; be *understandable* to those who use it; be *responsive* to the needs of those who use it; provide as much *certainty* as the nature of particular cases allows; and be *effective*: adequately resourced and organised'.[68]

The three major strands of the new system are first, the 'track' system to which cases are allocated depending on their claim-value; second, the introduction of a case-management system which places responsibility for overseeing the progress of cases in the hands of the judges, with the whole system in charge of a senior judge designated Head of Civil Justice; and third, the radical reform and simplification of the Rules of Court.

The track system

Under the new system there are three tracks. Cases involving a claim-value of £5,000 or less are allocated to the small claims track; straightforward cases involving between £5,000 and £15,000 are allocated to a 'fast track' procedure with strictly limited procedures, fixed timetables of about 30 weeks up to the start of the trial, a maximum of one day for the trial, and fixed costs; and a 'multi-track' procedure for cases involving more than £15,000, in which directions and case-management are matched to the needs of the individual case.

The multi-track procedure deals with more complex cases and/or those with the highest claim-values, though even on the multi-track, Lord Woolf envisaged that the more straightforward cases might be dealt with by means of a streamlined procedure involving, among other things, limited expert evidence, a short timetable, limited trial time and a system of controlled costs. The type of cases which might go through such a procedure would include small medical negligence claims and intellectual property cases involving parties of unequal financial means. Every aspect of a case on the multi-track would be taken into account in the course of case-management, including the extent to which the parties had explored, or might still explore, alternative means of resolving the dispute.

Case management

The notion of placing the management of cases in the hands of judges, as opposed to the traditional system whereby the case was handled by the parties' legal advisers, was one of the most radical proposals in the Woolf Report, although the Report noted that case management had already been adopted in some courts in England and Scotland, and that similar developments had occurred in the United States, Canada, Australia and New Zealand.[69]

What does case management involve, and are the judges adequately equipped to undertake it? According to Lord Woolf,

68 Ibid., p 2.   69 Ibid., p 14.

I do not see the active management of litigation as being outside a judge's function. It is an essential means of furthering what must be the objective of any procedural system, which is to deal with cases justly. Case management includes identifying the issues in the case; summarily disposing of some issues and deciding in which order other issues are to be resolved; fixing timetables for the parties to take particular steps in the case; and limiting disclosure and expert evidence. These are all judicial functions. They are extensions backwards in time of the role of the trial judge . . . I envisage that the function of procedural judges will usually be taken by Masters and district judges, although in more complex cases Circuit judges and High Court judges will perform the task.[70]

The Civil Procedure Rules (CPR) provide details of 'the court's duty to manage cases' and states, in CPR, r 1.4(2), that 'active case management' includes:

(a) encouraging the parties to co-operate with each other in the conduct of the proceedings;
(b) identifying the issues at an early stage;
(c) deciding promptly which issues need full investigation and trial and accordingly disposing summarily of the others;
(d) deciding the order in which issues are to be resolved;
(e) encouraging the parties to use an alternative dispute resolution procedure if the court considers that appropriate and facilitating the use of such procedure;
(f) helping the parties to settle the whole or part of the case;
(g) fixing timetables or otherwise controlling the progress of the case;
(h) considering whether the likely benefits of taking a particular step justify the cost of taking it;
(i) dealing with as many aspects of the case as it can on the same occasion;
(j) dealing with the case without the parties needing to attend at court;
(k) making use of technology; and
(l) giving directions to ensure that the trial of a case proceeds quickly and efficiently.

The court's case-management powers are spelled out in Part 3 of the CPR. Rule 3.1 specifies a wide range of powers for active case management – the court may, for example, adjust the time for parties' compliance with any rule, practice direction or court order; adjourn or bring forward a hearing; require a party or a party's legal representative to attend the court; hold a hearing and receive evidence by telephone or by using any other method of direct oral communication. Apart from these and other specified powers, CPR, r 3.1 also provides a general power that the court may 'take any other step or make any other order for the purpose of managing the case and furthering the overriding objective'.

The reform of the Rules of Court

Lord Woolf's Final Report was accompanied by a draft set of new rules to replace the existing Rules of the Supreme Court and County Court Rules. In his report, Lord Woolf identified a number of problems with the existing rules, among them unexplained specialist terms, over-elaborate language and piecemeal amendment

---

70 Ibid., pp 14–15.

and development. Rather than having multiple sets of rules, each specifically designed to deal with particular cases involving particular actions in particular courts, Lord Woolf's stated aim was to create more general rules of broader application, which are less complex and thus more accessible to users of the legal system.

The new Civil Procedure Rules, following Woolf's recommendations, were implemented in April 1999, though there have been many updates and amendments since that date. The emphasis on encouraging parties to resolve their dispute without recourse to the formality and expense of a court of law is built into the new rules – it is specifically mentioned in CPR, r 1.4(2) above, for example.

Lord Woolf's proposals attracted criticisms: some were sceptical, in particular, as to the Report's anticipation of the extent to which the cost of civil justice might be reduced. Apart from the cost factor, some questioned whether the new system would be sufficient to dissuade lawyers, in particular, from introducing complexities into cases which make them longer to resolve and which contribute substantially to their cost:

Although it is still too early to judge the overall success or otherwise of the reformed civil justice system, the Lord Chancellor's Department issued an evaluation of the civil justice reforms in March 2001. Among the key findings were that there had been a fall in the number of claims issued with respect to county courts and Queen's Bench Court, in the types of claim where the new Civil Procedure Rules have been introduced; that there had been an increase in the number of cases in which alternative dispute resolution was used, which suggests that parties are more likely to try alternative means of settling claims rather than going to court; and that it was too early to state whether there had been any significant cost savings in the system. In 2002, a research report published by the Law Society and the Civil Justice Council reported that on the basis of interviews with lawyers, insurers and claims managers working in the areas of personal injury, clinical negligence and housing disrepair, 'most practitioners regarded the Woolf reforms as a success. The reforms were liked for providing a clearer structure, greater openness and making settlements easier to achieve.'[71]

The English courts: the constitutional position

At the beginning of this chapter we noted that the vast majority of disputes which occur in modern society will be resolved satisfactorily without recourse to any formal dispute-settlement agency; we then considered the establishment of specialised agencies to deal with various types of disputes, either through advice and attempts at conciliation, or through other 'alternative dispute resolution' methods such as tribunal hearings which are designed to provide solutions to certain disputes without the encumbrances and expense of courts of law.

71 T. Goriely, R. Moorhead and P. Abrams, *More Civil Justice: The Impact of the Woolf Reforms on pre-action Behaviour* (2002, Law Society/ Civil Justice Council), p 7.

It is not surprising to find, then, that although the court may be regarded as the clearest instance of official means of dispute-settlement in modern society, in fact only a tiny proportion of disputes are ever aired before the courts. In fact, the total number of cases coming before courts of law is extremely small when compared with the frequency with which disputes – many of which may involve legal aspects – occur and are settled without recourse to legal proceedings.

The court is, nevertheless, perhaps the central institution within the English legal system; the pronouncements of the higher courts, in particular, have great significance for, among other things, the substance of the law itself; dominant social and political attitudes and values are communicated through judicial utterances in the courts; and the courts of law are the ultimate arenas where disputes which cannot be settled in any other way may be taken. The courts are also a feature of the state, connected with, but in certain important ways independent of, other agencies of state and government. For these reasons, it is important to consider in more detail the present position of the courts of law within the legal system and within the social structure.

Constitutional lawyers used to regard as fundamental the doctrine of the 'separation of powers', whereby the courts, the legislature (Parliament) and the executive (government) are constitutionally separate, thus serving democratic ideals by ensuring that no one of these 'arms of the state' becomes all-powerful, through complex 'checks and balances' of each arm by the other two. Thus, in theory, the judges operate independently of party politics, and in a manner untainted by political bias. The doctrine may be challenged, however, on both constitutional and other grounds; the degree to which the judges may be seen as politically neutral will be discussed in chapter 14, but in the present context consideration of the flaws in the doctrine of the separation of powers will serve to illustrate various features of the English courts.

The doctrine involves three propositions, each of which, it is argued, is open to question. First, the doctrine requires that the same persons should not occupy positions in more than one of the three arms of the state – judiciary, legislature and executive. In practice, however, as is well known, members of the Cabinet (executive) are invariably members of one or other House of Parliament (legislature). Cabinet government as we know it in the United Kingdom could not possibly work without this convention, and this is one example of departure from the strict doctrine; as is the case of the Lord Chancellor, who until recently was not only a Cabinet minister, but also a judge, president of the House of Lords in both its legislative and judicial capacities, and involved in the appointment of other judges. The mixture, in one appointment, of judicial, legislative and executive functions was striking,[72] and did not go uncriticised. In 1998, a number of MPs called for the creation of a new office of Minister of Justice to replace the Lord Chancellor, and

---

72 See J. A. G. Griffith's analysis of the judiciary in *The Politics of the Judiciary* (5th edn., 1997, Fontana), chapter 9; and see S. Lee's assessment of Lord Hailsham in *Judging Judges* (1988, Faber and Faber), chapter 19.

further criticism of the mixture of the Lord Chancellor's powers came from the Council of Europe in 2003. Accordingly, under the Constitutional Reform Act 2005, the office of Lord Chancellor remains, but will no longer carry out any judicial functions. Instead, the Lord Chief Justice will be responsible for the judiciary as a whole, and the functions of the Lord Chancellor will be, in essence, political rather than judicial. The Act explicitly places a duty on all government ministers, including the Lord Chancellor, to uphold and maintain the independence of the judiciary, and provides for the continuing maintenance of the constitutional principle of the rule of law. The Lord Chancellor himself has the ministerial role of Secretary of State for Constitutional Affairs.[73]

Second, the doctrine of the separation of powers requires that each arm of the state exercises its functions independently of any control or interference from the others. Again, this requirement is not fulfilled. The House of Commons (part of the legislature) in theory controls the executive, but with a majority government the House can be effectively controlled, in fact, by the executive.[74] Either way, the requirement is breached, though there appears to be little or no attempt to influence the judicial function, at least regarding court hearings, today. It seems that this was not always so. Paterson's research[75] clearly suggests that as late as the nineteenth century, judicial appointments were intimately linked with candidates' party political allegiances.

Formally, it is firmly established constitutionally that Parliament is the supreme law-making body in this country, so that the judges' task when confronted in court by a statutory rule is theoretically limited to the interpretation and application of that rule; they have no power to change it or declare it invalid (see chapter 7). However, it should be noted that by virtue of s 4 of the Human Rights Act 1998, the High Court, Court of Appeal or the House of Lords[76] may declare that a statute, or some provision within a statute, is incompatible with the provisions of that Act. Such a declaration of incompatibility does not render the enactment invalid, or indeed have any *legal* effect, but rather creates a *political* challenge: the minister responsible for the incompatible rule may (though is not required to) amend the offending provision so as to remove the incompatibility with the Human Rights Act 1998. Should the decision be made to amend the enactment, the Human Rights Act 1998 provides for a 'fast-track' procedure involving an order laid before and approved by both Houses of Parliament.

Third, the doctrine requires that one organ of the state should not exercise the functions of either of the others. In practice, the distinction between functions may be seriously blurred. To take the outstanding illustration, an Act of Parliament may empower a minister of the government to make rules having legal effect; this is

---

73 For further and more detailed discussion, see chapter 14.
74 In practice, a minority government may be overturned by the House of Commons. An example of this occurred in 1979 with the successful vote of 'no confidence' brought against the Labour government, resulting in a general election.
75 A. Paterson, 'Judges: A Political Elite?' (1974) 1 *British Journal of Law and Society* 2.
76 These are the higher courts in the court hierarchy, discussed below.

known as *delegated legislation*, and it is arguable that in some cases this device amounts to a minister's having law-making power (as opposed to mere power to make regulations *in furtherance of* parliamentary enactments). Important examples of delegated legislative powers are the powers given to ministers under the European Communities Act 1972 to make regulations implementing European Community policies which do not have automatic direct effect (see chapter 8); the wide powers given to the Lord Chancellor to amend or repeal rules relating to the provision of legal services under the Courts and Legal Services Act 1990; and the rule-making powers delegated to the Secretary of State for Education and Employment under the Education Reform Act 1988. As we have seen, it is one of the functions of the courts to ensure, through their supervisory jurisdiction, that powers entrusted to ministers, tribunals or other executive or administrative agencies are not abused or exceeded.

Apart from the case of delegated legislative powers, which may be seen as a legislative function being exercised by a member of the executive, there is virtually no situation in which one arm of the state exercises the powers of either of the others, though we must note that the House of Lords has both a legislative and a judicial capacity:[77] in practice, the judicial members of the House are judges, not politicians, whose role is to sit when the House operates in its judicial capacity. They rarely sit in legislative debates, and by the same token, the political members of the Lords do not participate in judicial hearings. There is, then, a separation of judicial and legislative functions in this particular institution.

Commenting on the separation of powers, Drewry neatly summarises the position:

> The point is that there are some aspects of 'separation of powers' which are eminently sensible. For example, it is probably a good idea to have a judiciary which is somewhat aloof from the rough and tumble of party politics. And words like 'legislative', 'executive' and 'judicial' are a useful shorthand way of describing a lot of things that go on in government, provided we remember that the boundaries between them are indistinct and that they are all functionally inter-related.[78]

The English court structure

English courts are arranged in a structure according to three sets of criteria. First, does the court deal with *civil* or *criminal* matters? This division is central to English law, though it is not easy to explain with any precision. Criminal law rules cover offences such as murder, theft and assaults, offences against the consumer (food and drugs offences, false trade descriptions – see chapter 11), offences involving firearms and other weapons, crimes against public order and state security and, of

---

77 The House of Lords is, constitutionally, one of the two Houses of Parliament: legislatively, the law-creating body is 'The Queen in Parliament' – that is, the sovereign, the House of Lords and the House of Commons.   78 G. Drewry, *Law, Justice and Politics* (2nd edn., 1981, Longman), p 4.

course, the many road traffic offences. These cases may be seen as disputes between the alleged offender and the state, representing the community at large.

Civil law comprises all legal rules which are not part of the criminal legal code, but the dividing line is difficult to draw. It is sometimes said that whilst criminal proceedings are brought by the state, civil proceedings are brought by private individuals[79] against other individuals. Thus, a *claimant* sues a *defendant*. Criminal proceedings are often said to be public, and civil proceedings private, but this 'public-private' distinction is by no means watertight. Certainly, we speak of 'private law' remedies being available in civil actions for, say, breach of contract, and of criminal proceedings being brought on behalf of the public; but there are many occasions when *public* bodies may be party to civil actions, and *private* individuals may initiate criminal prosecutions. An example of the former would be an action between a local authority and a private company over a contract for the supply of goods; an example of the latter would be a prosecution of a shoplifter by the store concerned. Until 1985, in England and Wales the prosecution of criminal offences was carried out by the police: the Prosecution of Offences Act 1985, however, created the Crown Prosecution Service, an agency independent of the police operating under the Director of Public Prosecutions (DPP), who has the function of designating regional areas, each with its own Chief Crown Prosecutor. The possibility of a privately initiated prosecution was, however, specifically retained in the 1985 Act. In some cases the Attorney-General (a government official) alone has the authority to prosecute, and for certain other offences prosecution must be authorised by the DPP, who also has the power to take over the prosecution of serious offences.

A second distinguishing feature is often said to lie in the different aims of the two branches of the law. The traditional aims of the criminal law are the apprehension and disposition of wrongdoers, whilst the aims of civil law are usually stated to be those of restitution, or compensation.[80] The problems with this distinction appear when we consider that there are some cases in which civil awards may be intended by the court to be punitive. Such cases are rare, but may arise, for example, when a defendant may make a profit from wrongful conduct, over and above the amount of compensation which he or she must pay to the claimant. The publishers of a defamatory book, for example, may enjoy more profits than might otherwise accrue, simply because publicity surrounding the case might induce more people to buy the offending book. And there are instances in criminal law where compensation may be payable by a convicted person to the victim: we noted above that the Powers of Criminal Courts (Sentencing) Act 2000 provides that compensation orders may be made by criminal courts against any person convicted of damaging other people's property or causing some other type of loss.

79 Including public bodies, such as local authorities, and other incorporated bodies, such as companies.   80 See chapter 1.

Despite these difficulties, there remains, for practical purposes, a broad distinction between civil and criminal law along the lines of their respective aims and remedies, and this distinction is firmly embedded in the court structure.[81] The civil courts, with one or two exceptions, deal exclusively with civil matters; the most important exception is probably the Queen's Bench Division of the High Court, which has some criminal jurisdiction by way of appeals from magistrates' courts and Crown Courts through the 'case stated' procedure. Here, the appeal is made by either defendant or prosecution (the only instance where the latter can appeal from an acquittal) over a point of law raised by, say, the interpretation of a statute, where a decision of a higher court is required to clarify the matter. On the criminal side, magistrates' courts have some civil jurisdiction, mainly involving liquor, gaming and betting licences, and actions for certain debts, as well as some family law matters, notably separation orders upon marriage breakdown and questions of custody and adoption of children.

The second criterion affecting the position of a given court in the overall structure is that concerning the *extent* of the court's jurisdiction. The county court, for instance, at the lowest rung of the civil court ladder, deals with actions in contract and tort, proceedings involving mortgages, estates of deceased persons and other equity matters. Although there is now no financial restriction on the jurisdiction of the county court (that is to say, cases involving any amount of claim-value may be heard there), the Civil Procedure Rules 1998 provide that, with one or two exceptions, civil claims involving no more than £5,000 will be dealt with by means of the 'small claims track', as opposed to the 'fast track' or 'multi-track' which are intended for cases involving higher claim-values and/or greater complexity. On the criminal side, the magistrates' court, dealing in the main with minor criminal offences, has a limited jurisdiction regarding the imposition of sanctions for cases heard in that court. The consolidating Powers of the Criminal Courts (Sentencing) Act 2000 contains provision for sentences for various crimes which may attract imprisonment or fines. Such provisions, it must be stressed, relate to the court's *summary* jurisdiction, and the vast majority of criminal cases, being of a relatively minor or trivial nature, are dealt with by these courts. For offences of a more serious nature, and in those cases where the accused elects to be tried *on indictment* (that is, with a jury), the case must go before the higher Crown Court.[82] We may note here that magistrates' courts also hold *preliminary examinations* in *all* criminal cases. This is a procedure to ascertain whether, on the face of the evidence, there is a case against the accused. If so, then the case will be dealt

---

81 See R. Ward and A. Wragg, *Walker and Walker's English Legal System,* (9th edn., 2005, Oxford University Press); S. H. Bailey, M. Gunn, and D. Ormerod, *The Modern English Legal System* (4th edn., 2002, Sweet and Maxwell); G. Slapper and D. Kelly, *The English Legal System* (7th edn., 2004, Cavendish).

82 The Report in 2001 by Sir Robin Auld on the *Review of the Criminal Courts* proposed, among other things, that a new criminal court structure should be introduced, and that the decision as to which court was to deal with a case would no longer be taken by the accused, but by a magistrates' court, which would take into account the seriousness of the offence.

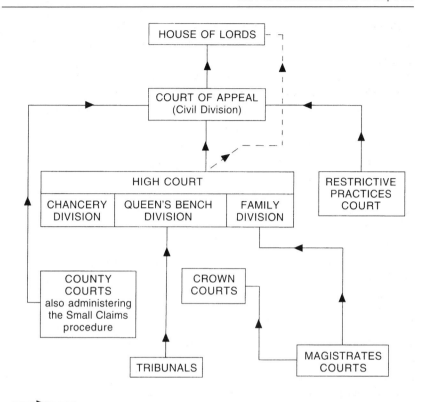

Channels of appeal from lower to higher courts. Appeals from tribunals are available only in rare cases, although the supervisory jurisdiction of the Queen's Bench Division may be invoked if a breach of natural justice, or an *ultra vires* decision, is alleged.

This is the 'leap-frogging' procedure introduced by the Administration of Justice Act 1969, whereby appeals may be made directly from High Court to House of Lords: (a) where both parties agree, and (b) where the trial judge grants leave, which he may do only if a point of law of public importance is involved concerning either the interpretation of a statute or a previous decision by which he considers himself bound. Final leave to appeal must also be granted by the House of Lords itself.

Figure 1 The Civil Courts

with either summarily or on indictment, depending on the offence and upon the circumstances.[83]

The third criterion affecting the position of a court in the hierarchy is the question whether the court is one of *first instance* (where the original trial takes place) or whether it is a court of *appeal*. Magistrates' courts and county courts are both courts of first instance; and the Court of Appeal and the House of Lords are both

83 Again, the Auld proposals would abolish the concept of 'committal' in favour of a system whereby cases would be handled in their entirety by one court only.

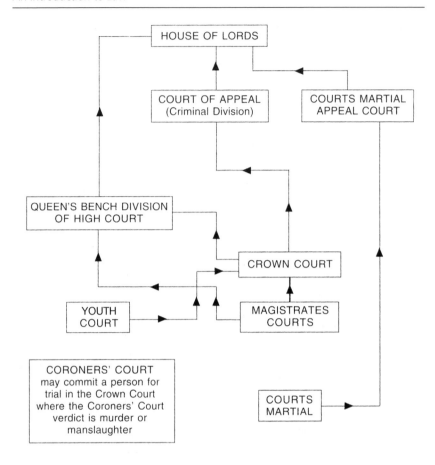

Channels of appeal from lower to higher courts.

Figure 2 The Criminal Courts

appellate courts only. The courts which lie in between these levels of the structure may, depending on the case before them, be either of first instance or appellate jurisdiction. The three Divisions of the High Court – Chancery, Queen's Bench, and Family – are civil courts (excepting the criminal jurisdiction of the Queen's Bench as noted above) which deal, in the main, with first instance trials. In the Chancery Court, disputes over property, trusts, wills, revenue, bankruptcy and company matters are heard, and this court includes the Company Court and Patents Court. In the Queen's Bench are heard contract and tort cases which cannot be dealt with in the county courts below, and this division includes the Admiralty Court and the Commercial Court; and the Family Division hears divorce cases and other matrimonial matters. But the Family Division may also hear appeals from magistrates' courts acting in their civil capacity over matrimonial and other family affairs; and the Queen's Bench may hear appeals by way of case stated and also, in the limited circumstances where they are permitted by statute, appeals from tribunal decisions.

The diagrams on pages 183 and 184 indicate the relative positions of, and channels of appeal between, the main courts of law in this country.[84]

The courts and society

The court structure is designed, through its appeal channels, to ensure that justice is done in all cases, although the suggestion has been made, perhaps not too seriously, that this appeal system could be somewhat modified:

> The institution of one Court of Appeal may be considered a reasonable precaution; but two suggest panic. To take a fair parallel . . . our surprise would be great if, after the removal of our appendix by a distinguished surgeon, we were taken before three other distinguished surgeons, who order our appendix to be replaced: and our surprise would give place to stupefaction if we were then referred to a tribunal of seven distinguished surgeons, who directed that our appendix should be extracted again. Yet such operations . . . are an everyday experience in the practice of the law.[85]

Be this as it may, the system whereby the Court of Appeal and the House of Lords may hear appeals from lower courts tends to maintain, first, the idea that justice is being done, and second, the keeping of the judicial finger on the pulse of social and moral currents within society. The common law, which is law made by the judges through decided cases (discussed fully in chapter 7), has developed through the doctrine of *precedent*. This doctrine requires that, in theory, decisions of the higher courts are *binding* on all courts below them in the hierarchy. In practice, the strictness of the formal doctrine is diluted by the judges' use of a large number of interpretative techniques whereby the following of previous decisions (precedents) may be avoided.[86] To take a well-known example, in 1932 the House of Lords, in the case of *Donoghue v Stevenson*,[87] decided that a manufacturer of goods owes a legal duty of care towards the ultimate consumer of those goods, assuming that there has been no reasonable opportunity for them to have been interfered with in the transition from factory to consumer.

The impact of this decision, thanks to the doctrine of binding precedent, has been that in cases since then a consumer who is injured or harmed in similar circumstances is able to recover compensation from the manufacturer, irrespective of the place in the court hierarchy where the case is heard, because that House of Lords decision in 1932 *bound* all lower courts to follow it. The case was examined by the courts over the ensuing years in later cases in such a way as to bring not only

---

84 The reader is referred for more detailed descriptions to works on English Legal System – see n 81, above.   85 A. P. Herbert, *Wigs at Work* (1966, Penguin), pp 92–93.

86 See Twining and Miers, op. cit., esp. chapter 8.   87 [1932] AC 562. See chapter 9.

manufacturers but also repairers[88] and car-dealers,[89] not only bottles of ginger-beer but also various other articles, within its ambit.[90]

The doctrine of binding precedent is said to have the outstanding advantage of ensuring that the law is kept up to date, through authoritative pronouncements from the top of the judicial tree through the system of appeals, whilst at the same time maintaining stability within the law by requiring all other courts to follow higher courts' decisions. The extent to which these aims are achieved, and the extent to which the formal doctrine of precedent hides what may be, in fact, a considerable degree of judicial creativity in handling precedents, will be discussed in later chapters (in particular, chapters 7 and 14).

The dispensing of justice in dispute-solving, the maintenance of stability in the law through precedent, the keeping of the law at least minimally in touch with the needs of a changing society – these are the main and ostensible functions of the courts, as usually expounded by jurists and legal commentators. We might add another, less obvious, social function, however: that of *social control*. It is through the decisions of the higher appellate courts in particular that dominant ideological currents on morality, law and order, and other contemporary problem areas are propagated.[91] The received pronouncements constitute a kind of patchwork quilt of judicial decisions, each of which contains within its reasoning and premises some aspect of the judicial assumptions about social consensus and the importance of upholding such 'consensual values' in the dispensation of justice. We see these processes most clearly in the case of criminal law, where one fundamental function of the courts is the trial and disposition of those whom the law labels 'criminally deviant'.

According to some writers, the criminal justice system represents not simply the trial and disposition of the offender; it represents the systematic destruction of the accused's social identity. Garfinkel[92] wrote in 1956 of the court as a 'degradation ceremony', whereby 'the public identity of an actor is transformed into something looked on as lower in the local scheme of social types . . .'.[93] In other words, the court process involves mechanisms and procedures which have the effect of revealing a convicted person as having all the *negative* characteristics of a 'criminal', a 'deviant', an 'outsider' – characteristics which the accused is 'seen' to have had all along. The accused stands revealed 'as he or she really is', and is invested with the stigma of criminality, which in turn brings all sorts of social consequences: 'We exercise varieties of discrimination, through which we effectively, if often

---

88 For example, *Haseldine v Daw* [1941] 2 KB 343.
89 *Andrews v Hopkinson* [1957] 1 QB 229.
90 Cases have involved such items as hair dye, tombstones and underwear: see chapter 9.
91 See, for example, the discussions of the judges in *Roberts v Hopwood* [1925] AC 578; *Bromley London Borough Council v Greater London Council* [1983] 1 AC 768; *Ward v Bradford Corp* (1971) 70 LGR 27 (see chapter 14); and other cases referred to in chapters 2 and 14.
92 H. Garfinkel, 'Conditions of Successful Degradation Ceremonies' (1956) *American Journal of Sociology*, p 420. Abridged version in C. Campbell and P. Wiles (eds), *Law and Society* (1979, Martin Robertson), p 189.   93 Garfinkel, op. cit., p 420; Campbell and Wiles, op. cit., p 189.

unthinkingly, reduce his life chances. We construct a stigma theory, an ideology to explain his inferiority and account for the danger he represents, sometimes ratio-nalising an animosity on other differences, such as those of social class.'[94] For we, the observers, remain 'normal', and within the boundaries of assumed consensual social standards of behaviour and values, whilst the convicted person is shown to be 'different', and apart from the rest of us.

A good example of these processes is the number of difficulties encountered by ex-prisoners, on release, in finding social acceptance, accommodation and, most importantly, employment. Studies have shown[95] that not only ex-prisoners, but in fact *anyone* who has come into contact with the criminal justice system through investigation and arrest, even though *no* subsequent charge or conviction ensues, has extreme difficulty in being accepted for employment if the applicant's history is known to the potential employer. The Rehabilitation of Offenders Act 1974 which provides that when a person's conviction has been 'spent', that person should suffer no discrimination in applying for or securing employment and does not have to admit to a conviction before a prospective employer, may make some difference to the problems of ex-offenders in obtaining jobs, although this Act does not apply to certain occupations and clearly does not guarantee non-discrimination in cases where the conviction is known by a prospective employer.

The criminal justice system, then, as epitomised in courtroom procedure, is geared not simply to establishing a deviant trait, weakness or aberration in the person appearing before it; rather, the discovery of the criminally deviant act for which the accused is before the court is presented as indicative of a *total* deviant identity. As Garfinkel points out,[96] this process must, to be effective, be presented as carried out in the name of communally held social values against which the accused has offended; the judge must be seen to represent the community in upholding those values which are embodied in the law, and various writers have expanded on the ways in which this essentially *symbolic* representation is carried out.

Carlen, for example, has discussed the effect of the highly theatrical atmosphere of the magistrates' court.[97] The accused is physically removed from the rest of the proceedings and is therefore dislocated from the 'normal' people in the courtroom, with the exception of the magistrates whose physical position fulfils quite a different symbolic function: 'the magistrate sits raised up from the rest of the court. The defendant is also raised up to public view but the dock is set lower than the magisterial seat, whilst the rails surrounding it are symbolic of the defendant's captive state.'[98]

The trial proceeds by way of formalities, set procedures, and ritualism, the whole ceremony being 'maintained partly to facilitate physical control of defendants and

94 E. Goffman, *Stigma* (1968, Pelican), p 15.
95 See, for example, R. Schwartz and J. Skolnick, 'Two Studies of Legal Stigma' (1962) 10 *Social Problems* at 133; R. Boshier and D. Johnson, 'Does Conviction Affect Employment Opportunities?' (1974) 14 *Br J Crim.*   96 Op. cit.
97 P. Carlen, *Magistrates' Justice* (1976, Martin Robertson).   98 Ibid., p 21.

any others who may step out of place and partly to refurbish the historically sacred meanings attached to law'.[99]

Furthermore, the accused person is immediately stripped of all the characteristics of an autonomous, participating individual:

> He is of interest only as a 'case'. The 'case', in turn, becomes the object of negotiation among the leading players in the courtroom. The defendant, although formally the focus of the bargaining is, in practice, excluded from participating. He is 'represented' and must wait patiently for the outcome of the deliberations of others. He is a man taken out of his world and transposed to the world of others.[100]

The position is significantly worse if the defendant is *not* represented by a lawyer, for in all probability the defendant will have little or no legal knowledge, and will frequently be unable to appreciate fully what is expected when he or she is asked to speak (see chapter 13).

It is significant that Garfinkel, in specifying the 'conditions of successful degradation ceremonies', is careful to note that the 'rules of the game' must be accepted by all the participants; the procedure and ceremony of the courtroom must be taken as 'given' by lawyers, judge, witnesses and defendant, and it is interesting that there have been occasions where failure by the defendants to accept the legitimacy of these 'ground rules' has resulted in what may be seen as unsuccessful degradation ceremonies. In 1969, for example, seven young political radicals were tried in Chicago for 'conspiracy to cross state lines with the intention of organising, promoting or encouraging a riot'. They had, in fact, planned in 1968 to arrange a protest demonstration at the Democratic Convention in Chicago, and it is important to remember that this was a period of political criticism and unrest among students, radicals and many others in Europe and in the United States.

The trial which followed is interesting not so much for the substantive offences charged, but rather for the way in which the defendants consistently and systematically refused to accept the very basis on which the trial was being conducted: there were frequent interruptions of counsel and judge by the defendants, usually to the effect that the latter were the victims not of a legal battle, but of political repression:[101]

> the judge expressed a positive conception of his role as upholder of the orderly legal process, one who was attempting to be an impartial arbiter despite attacks by the defendants and the media . . . [the defendants] viewed the court in illegitimate terms, seeing it as the expression of a corrupt legal, political and social order which they desired to alter radically.[102]

---

99 Ibid., p 25. See also D. Hay, 'Property, Authority and the Criminal Law' in D. Hay et al., *Albion's Fatal Tree* (1977, Peregrine); E. P. Thompson, *Whigs and Hunters* (1977, Peregrine); Z. Bankowski and G. Mungham, *Images of Law* (1976, Routledge and Kegan Paul), chapter 4.

100 Bankowski and Mungham, op. cit., p 88.

101 See *Contempt* (1970, Swallow Press, Chicago); T. Hayden, *Trial* (1970, Jonathan Cape).

102 R. J. Antonio, 'The Processual Dimension of Degradation Ceremonies: The Chicago Conspiracy Trial: Success or Failure?' (1972) *British Journal of Sociology*.

The result was that the trial: '*failed* as a degradation ceremony. If there was any appreciable change in status, it was the court which was degraded rather than the defendants. Because of the mass violation of ceremonial rules the court was unable to act in the tradition of efficiency and fairness which gives it definition.'[103] It is, moreover, interesting that this trial attracted considerable publicity, by no means all of which was uncritical of the ways in which the judge conducted the proceedings.

Although, as noted above, it is important that the *symbolic* meanings of law and courtroom procedure are maintained, there is also a public expectation that courts provide *practical justice.* In recent years we have seen a number of cases in which the objective of securing justice appears, at least to many observers, to have failed, and the status of the court – and indeed the legal system itself – has been undermined. The wrongful convictions of the four defendants in the Carl Bridgewater murder case, and those of the Guildford Four and the Birmingham Six (in which the defendants were wrongly convicted of offences connected with terrorist bombings) highlighted weaknesses in the criminal justice system in this country,[104] and, in particular, raised issues concerning methods of police investigation and the courts' ability to test the reliability of prosecution evidence. In the attempt to identify and rectify miscarriages of justice, and under the provisions of the Criminal Appeal Act 1995, the Criminal Cases Review Commission was set up in 1997.

The Commission's main responsibilities are to review suspected miscarriages of justice, and to refer convictions, verdicts or sentences to the appropriate Court of Appeal when the Commission considers that there is a real possibility that it would not be upheld; to investigate and report to the Court of Appeal on any matter referred by that Court to the Commission; and to consider and report to the Home Secretary on any matter referred to the Commission arising from consideration of whether or not to recommend exercise of the Queen's prerogative of mercy in relation to a conviction. To be eligible for consideration by the Commission, a case must have exhausted the possibilities of appeal within the normal court system. By 2006, the Commission had received over 8,000 applications, of which there were 955 in 2004–5. Many of these applications are excluded on the basis of showing no new evidence or argument, and in 2004–5, 45 cases were referred to appeal courts.[105]

103 Ibid., pp 295–296.
104 For a discussion of these and other cases, see S. Greer, 'Miscarriages of Criminal Justice Reconsidered' (1994) 57 *MLR* 1.
105 *Criminal Cases Review Commission Annual Report, 2004–5.* And see R. Nobles and D. Schiff, *The Criminal Cases Review Commission: Reporting Success?* (2001) 64 *MLR* 2.

7

The making of legal rules

One of the most important functions of any legal system is the authoritative statement of the normative legal code – the legal rules – by which the society in question is to operate. As we have seen, legal rules are not necessarily the only normative
codes which prescribe social behaviour (morals and etiquette are others), but legal
rules are distinct in that they constitute the *official* code which has the backing of
state powers of enforcement and sanctions. In this chapter we examine the principal sources in modern society whereby legal rules are created.

Parliamentary legislation: politics, pressures and public policy

According to the constitution, Parliament or, more correctly, the 'Queen in
Parliament', is the sovereign law-maker in Britain. This means that although the
judges have a role in the law-making process, they must bow to the superior powers
of the legislature who may override judge-made 'common law' rules by Acts of
Parliament. Britain's membership of the European Community has brought dramatic consequences for this constitutional doctrine, as we will see in chapter 8. In
this chapter, however, we will concentrate on the domestic law-making processes
of the UK, and in this first section we consider the procedural aspects of legislation
and discuss the background to and impact of legislative enactments.

Acts of Parliament proceed through the various stages of enactment as 'bills', of
which there are several kinds. A public bill, dealing with matters affecting the public
generally, may be introduced either by a minister – in which case it is termed a government bill – or by a private member of Parliament, when it is called a Private
Member's bill. This should not be confused with a private bill, dealing with limited
or sectional interests such as matters affecting a single local authority, which is promoted by the body concerned by *petition* to Parliament. Our main interest is with
public bills and the procedural stages through which they must pass.

Government bills may originate in various ways. To begin with, the proposed
legislation may derive from the party manifesto on which the party in power based
its general election campaign (such as the enactment in 2000 of the Freedom of
Information Act which implemented the Labour party's 1997 manifesto commitment); or it may be introduced as a means of implementing government policy

once elected to power (such as the Scotland Act 1998, which made provision for the elected Scottish Parliament, or the Sexual Offences (Amendment) Act 2000 which, after some years of controversy, lowered the age of consent for homosexual sexual activity to 16). Legislation may be passed because of some national emergency or crisis which has occurred during the government's period in office. The Anti-Terrorism, Crime and Security Act 2001, passed by Parliament after the terrorist attacks on New York and Washington on 11 September of that year, was such a measure.

On occasion, issues arise over which there may be public disquiet, or about which the government may feel the need for special investigation and, possibly, recommendations for new legislation. Such issues might be investigated in several ways: a Parliamentary Select Committee, or a departmental (or inter-departmental) committee, may be established to look into the matter; or the government may set up a Royal Commission, whose terms of reference will specify the area and extent of its investigative brief.

Royal Commissions report to Parliament, usually with recommendations for legislation which may or may not be taken up as part of the government's legislative programme. The findings of several Royal Commissions, some of which led to no legislative changes at all, are noted in this book, among them the Royal Commission on Civil Liability for Personal Injuries and Death (see chapter 9), established in 1973 to enquire into existing provision for compensation in the areas of industrial injuries, motor accident injuries, injuries arising from defective products and congenitally handicapped children; the Royal Commission on Legal Services (see chapter 13), established in 1976 as a result of considerable public criticism of lawyers, their work and their remuneration. In recent years Royal Commissions have been used very infrequently, the most recent examples being the Royal Commission on Criminal Procedure (the Phillips Commission), which reported in 1981, the Royal Commission on Criminal Justice (the Runciman Commission), which reported in 1993, and the Royal Commission on Reform of the House of Lords (the Wakeham Commission) which reported in 2000, and on whose recommendations on changes to the House of Lords the government broadly accepted, though politically, the task of implementing those changes proved extremely difficult.[1]

Another source of legislation is the recommendations of the Law Commission, created in 1965 in order to review and make recommendations about any areas of the law which the commission felt to be in need of reform. This is not the only body charged with proposing changes to the law – there is also the Law Reform Committee and the Criminal Law Revision Committee – but the work of the Law Commission is probably the most wide-ranging. Such reform might be achieved by means of repealing obsolete statutes, the codification of the law in specific areas,

---

1 See Lord Windlesham, 'The Constitutional Reform Act 2005: Ministers, Judges amd Constitutional Changes' [2005] *Public Law* 806; and Lord Windlesham, 'The Constitutional Reform Act 2005: The Politics of Constitutional Reform' [2006] *Public Law* 35.

the reduction of the number of separate statutes in a given area, or the removal of anomalies within the law. Law Commission proposals, which are presented to Parliament, often have draft bills appended, although these are by no means always implemented.[2]

It is from such sources as this that legislative measures are passed which do not necessarily create new law, but which are designed to amend or consolidate existing legal provision. The Trade Union and Labour Relations (Consolidation) Act 1992, the Employment Rights Act 1996 and the Powers of the Criminal Courts (Sentencing) Act 2000 are examples of such Acts. Finally, every government will introduce bills dealing with finance, such as the annual Finance Act which gives effect to the Budget proposals, and other bills which concern taxes and public expenditure.

Private Members' bills may be the result of an MP being approached for support for a proposal put forward by particular interest-groups operating outside Parliament (see chapter 2), but a substantial number originate from the government, which may suggest to an MP that he or she propose a particular measure. The amount of Parliamentary time allocated to Private Members' bills, however, is strictly limited. It has been noted that the amount of time permitted by successive governments in recent years for debate on Private Members' bills has been diminishing.[3] It has been suggested that 'private members' bills which are opposed do not pass unless they are given government time. This is because . . . time is restricted and any concerted opposition can talk a bill out.'[4] Another difficulty is that Private Members' bills do not, in general, enjoy the same facilities for discussion with civil service departments, drafting by the parliamentary draftsmen or strong governmental support, as government bills, although a government may on occasion provide help and support for a Private Member's bill of which it approves. A government which does not wish to see such a bill enacted will use its powers to prevent the passage of the proposed legislation. In these circumstances it is not surprising that the majority of Private Members' bills fail: in the session 2004–5, out of a total of 54 Private Members' bills introduced, none were passed, compared with 34 government bills which were introduced in the same session, of which 20 were passed.[5]

As far as government bills are concerned, these will have 'usually been firmly shaped in a process of departmental and inter-departmental or Cabinet discussion and consultation with outside interests. Accommodations will have been reached

2 In its Annual Report for 2004–5, the Law Commission stated that at the end of March 2005, four new Law Commission reports had been accepted by the government and introduced in Parliament; 16 reports had been accepted by the government with legislation yet to be introduced; and 13 reports were awaiting decisions by the government. At that point there were 29 reports (some of which had been published some years previously) which awaited implementation.

3 D. Marsh, P. Gowin and M. Read, 'Private Members Bills and Moral Panic: The Case of the Video Recordings Bill 1984' (1986) 39 *Parliamentary Affairs* at 179.

4 D. Marsh, M. Read and B. Myers, 'Don't Panic: The Obscene Publications (Protection of Children, etc.) Amendment Bill 1985' (1987) 40 *Parliamentary Affairs* at 73. See also A. Mitchell MP, 'A Home Buyer's Bill: How not to pass a Private Member's Bill' (1986) 39 *Parliamentary Affairs* at 1.

5 *House of Commons Sessional Information Digest* (2004–5).

and bargains struck.'[6] Such compromises are a remarkable (though not unique) feature of our legislative system, and it is important to note that many of these discussions and consultations take place *before* the bill is introduced into Parliament: although we usually speak of Parliament as the law-making assembly, in practice, most bills already have their initial shape and content clearly set out before their appearance in Parliament. Some critics question whether Parliament is not effectively by-passed in the modern law-making process.

If we consider briefly the various parliamentary stages of legislation, we see that the opportunities for change and amendment to proposed measures may be considerable. After a formal 'first reading' of a bill in the House where the proposal originates (this may be either the Commons or the Lords), there is a 'second reading', which is a full statement of the objectives of the bill. This is followed by a debate in which MPs, particularly, of course, opposition MPs, may table amendments to the bill. Frequently, the second reading stage is the point at which public attention becomes drawn to the proposal, through press coverage and, on occasion, vociferous campaigns for and against the measure by pressure-groups affected by the proposal. The bill then passes to the 'committee stage', where proposed amendments are discussed in detail: some will be incorporated, others will be rejected. For bills originating in the House of Commons, the committee which carries out these discussions – usually one of a number of Standing Committees – comprises MPs representing the different political parties roughly in proportion to the overall composition of the House. There will therefore be a government majority on the committee, though the attempt is made to ensure representation by minority parties. On rare occasions, such as when a bill proposes fundamental constitutional change, the committee comprises the full House. Another variation, if discussions on the proposed bill require detailed analysis, possibly with witnesses being called, is for the bill to go before a Select Committee. If the bill originates in the House of Lords, there is a less strict procedure, and the Lords have no Standing Committees.

When the committee reports back to the House, further amendments may be tabled. After this stage (and after any further proposed amendments have been dealt with) the bill is given its 'third reading'. The next step is for the bill to go through similar procedures in the other House, after which it is returned, with any proposals for amendments which may have been made in that other House, to the originating House. Finally, when this lengthy process is over, the bill receives the Royal Assent and becomes an Act of Parliament.

Of course, some amendments may be made for purely practical reasons, such as the need to simplify an otherwise over-complicated clause. But as often as not, amendments derive from our system of government which comprises not just one governing political grouping, having the power to realise whichever policies it pleases, but rather a number of political parties, whose presence in Parliament

---

6 C. Turpin, *British Government and the Constitution: Text, Cases and Materials* (5th edn. 2002, Butterworths, p 397).

ensures, in theory and usually in practice, that no political party coming to power after an election may gain absolute control over the affairs of the nation. The basic task of the opposition, after all, is to *oppose* the policies of the government. This system is supposed to ensure the free discussion by all sides of all matters concerning government, including legislative proposals; it also results in the fact that much legislation is to some extent a political *compromise*: very few Acts emerge without some amendments being made on their way through the parliamentary process, though at the same time it must be acknowledged that very few government bills are actually defeated:

> The procedure for the enactment of a public bill is not without its hazards for the government. Even if it has a sufficient majority to overwhelm opposition parties, they may by exploiting the procedures of Parliament cause trouble for the government in its efforts to get a bill enacted, intact and on time. The government's own back-benchers cannot always be coerced by the Whips,[7] and in recent years numbers of them have shown a robust willingness to vote in the Opposition Lobby. Minority governments are especially vulnerable . . .
>
> But in ordinary circumstances the obstacles of the parliamentary process can be overcome. Governments have usually enjoyed the support of mainly loyal majorities in the House of Commons; opposition parties are usually open to bargaining, and if persistently obstructive can be curbed by use of the guillotine . . . or of the closure . . .[8] In a full session the government can generally achieve the passage of between 40 and 60 bills, substantially or entirely in the form in which they are wanted.[9]

Once a measure has gained the Royal Assent (these days, merely a formality) and has become an Act, there may then be a considerable time before the Act is actually *implemented*, that is, brought into force. There may be inadequate resources available to fulfil the Act's provisions immediately; bodies affected by the Act may require time to adjust their procedures and practices so as to enable them to meet the Act's requirements; special machinery may have to be set up before the Act can be properly enforced. For such reasons as these, the implementation of statutes may be delayed, or the provisions of statutes implemented gradually, on a piecemeal basis. Such piecemeal or delayed implementation causes confusion to lawyers and lay people alike. To take just one example: the Consumer Credit Act 1974 was an extremely complex and wide-ranging statute, regulating all aspects of consumer

---

7 'The role of the whips is of crucial importance in conveying the views of the rank and file to the leadership and vice versa; in keeping members informed . . . of forthcoming parliamentary business; in giving the expected times of divisions in order to secure a high attendance – by underlining the matter once, twice or thrice; failure to comply with a three-line whip without a very good excuse is often to be construed as an act of rebellion against the leadership. . . and in helping to impose party discipline by suasion, admonition and, if necessary, threats that the party whip may be withdrawn . . .': S. A. de Smith and R. Brazier, *Constitutional and Administrative Law* (8th edn. by R. Brazier, 1998, Penguin), p 266.

8 'Closure' is a parliamentary procedural device for bringing debate to an end, involving a member of the government moving that 'the question be now put'. The 'guillotine' also has the effect of limiting the time spent on debate, by means of a resolution allocating a specific number of days for debate on each stage of a bill.   9 C. Turpin, op. cit. pp 399–400.

credit from hire-purchase to bank overdrafts. It contains nearly 200 separate sections, uses new terms which require definition and familiarity among lawyers, brings together legal regulation of various transactions previously contained in a number of separate statutes – and took over ten years from its passage through Parliament to being fully implemented!

Some measures towards improving this state of affairs were announced in 1982, when the government stated that where an Act contains neither a date of commencement (the preferred alternative) nor provision for a commencement order, then the Act should itself provide that it should come into force not less than two months after the Royal Assent.

As we noted in the last chapter, another important form of law is *delegated* (or *subordinate*) legislation. An Act of Parliament may authorise a specific body to enact rules having the force of law, in accordance with the power vested in that body by the parent statute. For example, local authorities may make by-laws 'for the good rule and government of the whole or part of the district or borough . . . and for the prevention and suppression of nuisances therein' by virtue of s 235 of the Local Government Act 1972. Another common example of delegated legislation is that of powers conferred on government departments to make regulations affecting a given issue: in chapter 6 we noted, as examples, the powers conferred on relevant ministers by the European Communities Act 1972 and the Courts and Legal Services Act 1990. Social security and housing legislation similarly contains provision empowering the relevant Secretary of State to make orders and regulations; and the important regulations affecting the construction and use of motor vehicles are made under the authority of s 41 of the Road Traffic Act 1988, a measure consolidating earlier provisions which conferred similar powers on the Secretary of State responsible.

It must not be thought, however, that parent statutes give a blank cheque to subordinate legislators. There are various controls which, in theory at least, may be exerted over delegated legislation. The first is that Parliament itself must approve the initial parent statute which confers law-making powers on a particular body; the relevant sections in the parent Act may also provide that any delegated legislation made by virtue of that Act must be affirmatively resolved by Parliament. More usually, however, there is no requirement that the regulation (usually a Statutory Instrument) must be affirmatively resolved, but simply must be 'laid before Parliament' for a certain period (usually 40 days) during which MPs may raise questions on the measure, and possibly press for a resolution to annul it, but in practice such a response is infrequent: a government would rarely grant parliamentary time for such a debate. It might be thought that parliamentary scrutiny of delegated legislation is not as rigorous as it might be, given that authority to create such legislation derives from Parliament itself.

The courts have the power to review delegated legislation in the event of its validity being challenged, and to declare it invalid if it is found to have been made *ultra vires* ('beyond the powers of') the authority being challenged. Delegated legislation may be *ultra vires* either because the authority has, literally, gone beyond the powers conferred on it by the parent Act, or because that authority has acted in a manner not in accordance with *procedures* laid down in the parent Act.

To say that no single political party can control the affairs of the nation, however, is not the same as saying that no single political or economic group, however loosely constituted, may gain such control in legislative or policy terms. We will see in chapter 14 how notions such as 'public policy' and the 'national interest' can obscure the social, political and economic divisions and interests in society. The same problem is inherent in the idea that legislation 'reflects public opinion', for public opinion is almost impossible to define or measure. The constitutional lawyer Dicey, writing at the turn of the century, stated that 'there exists at any given time a body of beliefs, convictions, sentiments, accepted principles, of firmly-rooted prejudices, which, taken together, make up the public opinion of a particular era . . . [which] has, in England, if we look at the matter broadly, determined, directly or indirectly, the course of legislation'.[10] He seems to have had some doubts, however, about the strength of his proposition, as is seen by his use of the qualifying phrases 'broadly' and 'directly or indirectly'. Dicey recognised the connections between legislation and powerful classes and interest-groups quite clearly, and must not be taken to have posited the existence of a blanket consensual 'public opinion' of the kind frequently referred to by judges and politicians. Dicey's answer to the problems raised by these facts is interesting:

> Individuals . . . and still more frequently classes, do constantly support laws or institutions that they deem beneficial to themselves, but that certainly are in fact injurious to the rest of the world. But the explanation of this conduct will be found, in nine cases out of ten, to be that men come easily to believe that arrangements agreeable to themselves are beneficial to others. A man's interest gives a bias to his judgment far oftener than it corrupts his heart.[11]

There is, in other words, a tendency to presume that what is good for one group is good for all groups, and this is certainly the thrust of the ideological currents which dominate modern legislative and political activities and permeate all other groups in society through channels such as the media, political speeches and, of course, judicial pronouncements.

It must be acknowledged that despite attempts by politicians and judges to justify policies on the grounds of 'public opinion', this notion is analytically elusive and, on any given issue, impossible to assess. For Parliament is much more than merely a debating-chamber for the discussion and implementation of policies supported by popular opinion. Often the parliamentary process itself represents only the most superficial element in the law-making process. Given the predominance of government bills, much legislative preparation, consultation and discussion occurs *outside* Parliament, within government departments, among members of

10 A. V. Dicey, *Law and Public Opinion in England* (1905, Macmillan); extract in V. Aubert (ed.), *Sociology of Law* (1969, Penguin), p 74.   11 Ibid.

the civil service, and between MPs, civil servants and interested outside groups. Some such groups – 'interest-groups' – exist for the purpose of permanently representing particular interests in all manner of ways, including making their views known on legislative proposals. Thus, there may be consultation with groups such as the Confederation of British Industry, the Trades Union Congress, the Law Society, the police and the British Medical Association, if the interests of the members of such groups stand to be affected by the proposals in question. Other groups – 'cause groups' or 'pressure-groups' – exist simply to campaign for a particular cause or issue, such as prison reform, divorce law reform or civil liberties. Whether, and at what stage, such groups will be consulted by government departments for their views on a particular matter is a complex question.

To begin with, we must take into account the dimension of *political power* in the consultative process. Some groups enjoy more power than others; if a proposal concerned the provision of social housing owned and managed by local authorities, it is probable that local authorities' views would be sought, but far less likely that local tenants' federations would be consulted. If the proposal concerned changes in the prison system, it is unthinkable that the Prison Officers' Association would not be listened to, but most improbable that the views of a prisoners' rights organisation would be heard. And even if interest groups manage to present their arguments, it does not necessarily follow that their views will actually be taken into consideration: much will depend upon the political power and prestige, the general 'credibility', the level of organisation and the degree of political skill possessed by particular groups.

Of course, as most commentators and researchers acknowledge, legislation is sometimes enacted which seems to be *dis*advantageous to powerful interest-groups and social classes. Examples are the measures designed to control and combat industrial pollution by the use of criminal sanctions, and the statutes which date back, in various forms, to the last century which impose stringent controls and requirements on those concerned in the management of factories to maintain standards of safety. How are such statutes to be explained?

Various answers may be given. First, if we consider the extent to which most such laws are actually *enforced* with any rigour, we often see that they are rather weak weapons against the proscribed activity. Various studies have suggested that prosecution of offenders is a rarity, the use of warnings often being a preferred solution.[12] Second, there may be a reluctance to launch a criminal prosecution unless there is a good chance of conviction, and in many of these areas, the chances of conviction are assessed as low, sometimes because of the complexity of the case, sometimes because of lack of hard evidence, or even victims: for example, in cases of

---

12 W. G. Carson, 'Some Sociological Aspects of Strict Liability and the Enforcement of Factory Legislation' (1970) 33 *MLR* 396; R. Cranston, *Regulating Business: Law and Consumer Agencies* (1979, Macmillan); N. Gunningham, *Pollution, Social Interest and the Law* (1974, Martin Robertson). See also W. Chambliss and R. Seidman, *Law, Order and Power* (2nd edn., 1982, Addison Wesley).

corporate fraud, where the victims will usually be shareholders, their losses may not be immediately felt.

Moreover, it is not always the case that such legislation adversely affects powerful interests, despite appearances to the contrary. Carson's research into the origins of the factory legislation which was introduced during the nineteenth century reveals, in his view, how the powerful factory-owners who were close to the legislative process realised that legal controls might operate to their advantage by forcing competitors out of business.[13] It is possible to perceive the same kind of attitude today on the part of manufacturers and advertisers towards legislative controls which we call 'consumer protection'. Here, the ostensible objective of, say, legal controls on advertising (designed to secure minimum standards of truthfulness and decency) is to protect the consumer from irresponsible and misleading claims; but one latent function may very well be the maintenance of an acceptable and respectable public image of an industry which is shown publicly to be operating in the interests of truth, honesty and the consumer interest. The actual extent of stringent control may be questioned, especially in the light of the fact that the standards of advertising, and the enquiries into complaints about advertisements, are dealt with by the Advertising Standards Authority, which is itself composed of members of the advertising industry.

The legislative process, then, is far from being one in which interests common to everyone are protected and promoted. We have repeatedly seen how values and interests differ immensely among various groups and classes in society, and that it is consequently impossible to identify any single 'public interest'. Rather:

> The output of the legislature means rags or riches, servility or power, weakness or strength, to every interest group in the country. The institution which produces such extraordinary benefits or detriments cannot in its very nature be a merely impartial framework for struggle. Like every bureaucratic organization, it responds to the pressure of the powerful and the privileged.[14]

Of course, a significant proportion of the legislative output is, to a great extent, uncontentious in party political terms, and much welfare state legislation, providing benefits and pensions, local authority services and other similar provisions, *does* operate to the benefit of the less powerful groups in society. None the less there are periods when such provision falls victim to the influential voices of the economically powerful groups and individuals wishing to see, for instance, cuts in public expenditure and the relocation of national resources towards private industry and enterprise. Overall, it is hard to avoid the conclusion, when considering the legislature, that the democratic ideal, in terms of government and law-making, is far from being a political and social reality.

---

13 W. G. Carson, 'Symbolic and Instrumental Dimensions of Early Factory Legislation' in R. Hood (ed.), *Crime, Criminology and Public Policy* (1974, Heinemann); see also extract in C. Campbell and P. Wiles (eds), *Law and Society* (1979, Martin Robertson).

14 W. Chambliss and R. Seidman, *Law, Order and Power* (1st edn., 1971, Addison Wesley), p 73.

Precedent and policy I: the common law

Judge-made law, as developed through the doctrine of binding precedent, or *stare decisis*, is one of the oldest and most fundamental features of the English legal system. The doctrine of precedent states that a decision made by a court in one case is *binding* on other courts in later cases involving similar facts. In this way, uniformity within the law is, in theory, to a large extent maintained, and one of the most basic demands of our conception of justice is met by the treating of like cases in like manner.

Allen,[15] in his review of the history of the doctrine, presents evidence that English judges were making use of previously decided cases as guides as early as the thirteenth century. But it was not until the sixteenth century that the availability of reports of decided cases – and some of the earlier series of law reports were grossly unreliable and inadequate[16] – brought any certainty or consistency into the operation of what gradually became the doctrine of binding precedent.

Precedent is the basis of the common law: that body of law emerging from cases as they are decided by the judges. We have seen several examples of cases[17] containing points of sufficient legal importance to constitute precedents, notably *Donoghue v Stevenson* in 1932,[18] containing Lord Atkin's statement of the 'neighbour principle' which was to become the foundation stone of the later cases involving negligence, and so on. What we are concerned with here is precedent in theory and in practice: how the *practical* operation of precedent compares with the *formal rules* of the doctrine.

To understand the doctrine of precedent we must recall the hierarchical structure of the English courts, and the appeal system.[19] At the lowest levels are the courts of first instance, then further up are the Divisional Courts, followed by the Court of Appeal; at the top of the structure is the ultimate court of appeal, the House of Lords. Cases reach the higher, appellate courts by reason of their being taken there on appeal by the party to the dispute who loses in the court below. The most authoritative decisions, then, are those of the higher courts – the Court of Appeal and the House of Lords – and it is these decisions which tend to constitute precedents, although it must be noted that High Court decisions can sometimes be regarded as authoritative.

Given this structure, the basic rules of the doctrine of precedent are fairly easily stated. First, all courts are bound to follow the previous decisions of courts which are *higher in the hierarchy* in cases which are similar to those previously decided cases. Thus, a decision of the Court of Appeal is binding on all courts below it, but

15 C. K. Allen, *Law in the Making* (7th edn., 1964, Oxford University Press), chapter 3. Also R. Cross and J. Harris, *Precedent in English Law* (4th edn., 1991, Oxford University Press); but for a more up-to-date discussion see M. Zander, *The Law-Making Process* (6th edn., 2004, Cambridge University Press).   16 See examples given in Allen, op. cit.

17 See especially chapters 2–4 above.   18 [1932] AC 562. See chapters 4 and 10.

19 See chapter 6.

is not binding on the House of Lords; a decision of the House of Lords is binding on all other courts; and, at the bottom of the structure, a decision of the county court is binding on no other court. Second, the binding nature of a precedent applies to all future cases which have like facts, and as we shall see presently, this feature of the doctrine may give rise to difficult problems of interpretation for the courts.

To what extent is one court's decision binding on itself? Beginning with the High Court: this court is technically not bound by its own decisions though, in practice, High Court judges will usually follow previous High Court decisions unless there are good reasons not to do so. The Court of Appeal is, generally speaking, and subject to certain exceptions, bound by its own decisions. In *Young v Bristol Aeroplane Co Ltd* in 1944,[20] the Court of Appeal explained the situations in which it might depart from its own previous decisions, these being: first, where the court is faced with two conflicting decisions of its own, it may choose which one to follow; second, the court is not bound to follow one of its own previous decisions which is inconsistent with a later House of Lords' decision; and third, the court is not bound to follow a decision of its own which was given *per incuriam*, that is to say, a case which was decided without taking into account some statutory provision or precedent which would have affected the decision.[21]

Despite the attempts of Lord Denning, whilst Master of the Rolls, to free the Court of Appeal from the constraints of the doctrine of precedent[22] the House of Lords made it clear in no uncertain terms that, subject to the exceptional circumstances as stated in *Young*, the Court of Appeal remained bound by its previous decisions.[23]

With regard to the House of Lords: until 1966 this court considered itself bound by its own decisions (see chapter 14). This could mean that unless Parliament stepped in and changed the effect of a House of Lords' decision by statute, such a decision, at least in theory, could never be modified, limited, extended or overruled, because there is no higher court to which such a decision might be taken on appeal. The essence of the doctrine of precedent is, again in theory, both certainty and flexibility: the possibility should always exist for judicial pronouncements to be modified or even removed, if the decision proves unjust, inadequate or outdated. Although there are contained within the doctrine of precedent mechanisms whereby earlier decisions *may* not be followed (see below), there could none the less be 'blockages', where a House of Lords' decision

20 [1944] 2 All ER 293.
21 In *R (on the application of Kadhim) v Brent LBC Housing Benefit Review Board* [2001] 2 WLR 1674, the Court of Appeal declined to follow its earlier decision in *Thamesdown BC v Goonery* (Unreported, February 13, 1995) on the basis that the court in the earlier decision had erroneously assumed that a proposition of law, which had not been the subject of argument before that court, had been correct. This may now constitute a further basis on which the Court of Appeal may depart from its own previous decisions.
22 See *Gallie v Lee* [1969] 2 Ch 17; *Barrington v Lee* [1972] 1 QB 326.
23 See in particular *Davis v Johnson* [1979] AC 264.

bound all courts, including itself, thus preventing or at least seriously impeding the possibilities for change.

In 1966, the Lord Chancellor announced that henceforth the House of Lords would consider itself empowered to depart from its own previous decisions. The Practice Direction explaining this change[24] states that:

> Their Lordships . . . recognise that too rigid adherence to precedent may lead to injustice in a particular case and also unduly restrict the proper development of the law. They propose therefore to modify their present practice and, while treating former decisions of this House as normally binding, to depart from a previous decision when it appears right to do so.
>
> In this connection they will bear in mind the danger of disturbing retrospectively the basis on which contracts, settlements of property and fiscal arrangements have been entered into and also the especial need for certainty as to the criminal law.

This was undoubtedly a sensible, if overdue, development, although it should be added that such departures are fairly infrequent.[25] It is arguable that the stability and continuity of the law would suffer if such departures 'appeared right' too often (see chapter 14). This limited slackening of the grip of the doctrine of precedent nevertheless, it is to be hoped, increases the court's ability to ensure that the principles enshrined in previous cases are not permitted to dictate injustice, and that legal principles and rules are kept in line with the demands of changing social and economic conditions.

But surely, it may be objected, no two cases are ever exactly alike? How 'alike' does a later case have to be before a court must follow a given precedent? The *practical* answer to these questions will be discussed in due course; but the *theory* of precedent rests upon the proposition that the similarity between any two cases derives not just from their specific facts, but rather from their respective 'law-and-fact' content. In law, every case has two aspects. First, there is the particular dispute itself – a fact-situation which the court must resolve with reference to relevant legal rules. For example, a consumer alleges injury suffered because of a faulty product; a motorist is prosecuted for driving whilst drunk; a husband brings an action against his wife for divorce. The second aspect is the precise legal issue which these facts raise: the circumstances provided in law whereby the consumer obtains a remedy, the legally prescribed conditions of liability under which the motorist may be convicted, or the legal grounds which must be shown before a divorce can be granted. It is to these issues that legal argument and the citation of precedents are directed. If the consumer's injury is caused by a defective bottle of shampoo, for instance, we do not have to search the Law Reports for previous cases in which a

---

24 [1966] 1 WLR 1234. See A. Paterson, *The Law Lords* (1982, Macmillan/SSRC); Zander, *The Law-Making Process*, op. cit., pp 196–203.

25 Two significant departures from previous decisions discussed in this book are *Murphy v Brentwood District Council* [1990] 2 All ER 908 (see chapter 9) and *R v G and another* [2003] 4 All ER 765 (see chapter 10).

bottle of shampoo caused injury. It is enough that we discover a legal authority, through precedents, for the general legal proposition that a consumer may in appropriate circumstances recover compensation for injury caused by a defective product. The actual item which features in previous cases might be a car,[26] underwear,[27] or a bottle of ginger-beer;[28] what really matters is the legal principle involved, and not the specific facts of the previous case. This legal principle – the *ratio decidendi* – is the part of the decision which constitutes the binding precedent.

This seems a simple enough proposition, and it *would* be, if it were possible to state firmly and clearly what the *ratio* of a given case is. The fact is that different judges may interpret the judgments given in previous cases quite differently, and conclude that in their opinion the 'correct' reading of a case provides a *ratio* which may be wider or more restrictive (or compatible or incompatible with the case in hand) than the interpretation of their colleagues on the bench. There are some cases in which it is extremely difficult, if not impossible, to ascertain precisely the *ratio* of the case,[29] and to distinguish the *ratio* from the *obiter dicta* (the judges' statements which are not part of the points of legal principle and therefore not binding). As Twining and Miers point out, 'talk of *finding* the *ratio decidendi* of a case obscures the fact that the process of interpreting cases is not like a hunt for buried treasure, but typically involves an element of choice from a range of possibilities'.[30]

There is a strong connection between the facts of a case and the legal rules or principles which judges derive from those facts; and differences of fact between otherwise similar cases may have important consequences for the final decision in a new case. The doctrine of precedent allows for such situations by mechanisms whereby a judge may depart from a particular line of precedent, for the doctrine does not require that judges are mere slaves to the past. Indeed, one of the advantages claimed for the doctrine is that the judges have the freedom, or at least the discretion, to treat precedents with some flexibility.

The first such mechanism is inherent in the court structure itself: a court is free to *overrule* a decision of a court lower than itself, if it is of the opinion that the previous case was wrongly decided or has become out of date. Hence the Court of Appeal may overrule a decision of the High Court, and the House of Lords may overrule a decision of the Court of Appeal – and sometimes a previous decision of its own. Another device whereby precedents may be avoided (open to all courts irrespective of their place in the hierarchy) is known as *distinguishing on the facts*. This means that if a judge thinks that a precedent which otherwise covers the case

---

26 *Andrews v Hopkinson* [1957] 1 QB 229.   27 *Grant v Australian Knitting Mills* [1936] AC 85.
28 *Donoghue v Stevenson* [1932] AC 562.
29 Some examples of difficult cases are *Suisse Atlantique Société d'Armement SA v NV Rotterdamsche Kolen Centrale* [1966] 2 All ER 61, a case in the law of contract; and *Bromley London Borough Council v Greater London Council* [1982] 2 WLR 62, which concerned the legality of the General London Council's levying a supplementary rate on the London boroughs in order to subsidise its policy of reducing London Transport fares, discussed below in chapter 12.
30 Twining and Miers, op. cit., p 335.

in hand is nevertheless different in some *material* particular, then that precedent may be distinguished and not followed. Take, for example, the treatment of *Donoghue v Stevenson*[31] in the later *Evans v Triplex Safety Glass Ltd.*[32] In the latter case, a car windscreen had shattered, due to some unexplained cause, and had injured the occupants of the car. The court refused to follow *Donoghue v Stevenson* and hold the manufacturers of the windscreen liable in negligence because, unlike the faulty product in that previous case, the windscreen might have been interfered with, and the defect introduced, by any of a whole range of possible agencies other than the original manufacturer. This possibility of alternative cause was held to be a sufficiently material difference for the court to distinguish *Donoghue* (which nevertheless, of course, remained perfectly good law) and to conclude that the case before the court should be decided in favour of the respondent manufacturer.

Having explained the formal mechanisms of precedent, we must now consider how precedent works *in practice.*[33] Precedents constitute the common law; they contain the legal rules which the judges interpret as emerging from decided cases. Until a few years ago, many judges denied that they properly had any creative role at all, and even in recent times some judges have insisted on keeping judicial creativity within strict limits.[34] There were times in the past when the common law was explained by the judges as something which they merely 'declared'; the rules and principles themselves were held out to be always existing, albeit in unstated form, awaiting 'revelation' through the judges by means of some mystical process of reasoning. Law creation was thought to be exclusively the job of Parliament, not the judiciary. Thus Lord Esher could state in 1892: 'There is . . . no such thing as judge-made law, for the judges do not make the law, though they frequently have to apply existing law to circumstances as to which it has not previously been authoritatively laid down that such law is applicable.'[35]

Nowadays, the debate between adherents of this declaratory theory and those arguing, or accepting, that judges *do* make law is somewhat arid and fruitless, despite the arguments presented by Dworkin to the effect that judges always decide within existing limits of rule and principle and that there is always a 'right answer' if only it can be discerned.[36] Such views run against the tide of modern opinion, and indeed of judicial acknowledgments of their law-making activity. Most judges and commentators accept that judges create new law, and concentrate on the far more important issues regarding the *manner* and *extent to which* judges create legal rules, and the limitations which may operate on this creative judicial function.[37] We will explore these questions further in chapter 14, but at this stage several important aspects of judicial law-making must be noted. To begin with, modern judges have to acknowledge explicitly the role played by their conceptions of public policy in influencing their decision-making. Lord Denning in particular repeatedly

31 Op. cit.   32 [1936] 1 All ER 283.   33 See Twining and Miers, op. cit., chapter 9.
34 See, for example, Lord Devlin, *The Judge* (1979, Oxford University Press), chapter 1.
35 Cited in Allen, op. cit., p 308.   36 See R. Dworkin, *Taking Rights Seriously* (1978, Duckworths).
37 Devlin, op. cit.. And see chapter 14.

pointed out[38] that the older, fictional ideas among judges and lawyers about the 'mere application of rules to facts' should give way to the immediate necessity of shaping the law to fit the needs of modern society. As Friedmann, in a thorough comparative review of the relationship between judge and doctrine in modern society, put it some years ago: 'What would be fatal and illusory, would be any attempt to return to the nineteenth-century myth of a judiciary that simply interprets statutes or precedents, in accordance with legal logic, but need not concern itself with the deeper struggles and agonies of society.'[39] At the same time there may be good reasons, and indeed substantial social and political pressures, in response to which a particular judge fights shy of making policy decisions too explicit, or another judge insists on upholding some or other aspect of the fictions within the 'declaratory' theory of precedent. As the American writer Jerome Frank said,:

> The reason for the judges' reluctance to admit their creativeness is not far to seek. The theory of our democratic government is that. . .the legislature expresses the popular will, legislation is the voice of the people. . .the courts would seem to be acting beyond their powers were they frankly to legislate. Fear of popular denunciation of illegal usurpation of power accordingly has led judges to obscure by words what they actually did, what they could not help doing.[40]

Sometimes, when faced with a case of novel implications which are not covered by precedents, judges justify and legitimise their decisions by an appeal to the 'public interest', discussed above and in chapter 14; but in cases of lesser import, we may find that the 'application' of precedents to cases is by no means as straightforward as might be thought. There are many reasons why a judge may find himself in the position of what Twining and Miers have called 'the puzzled interpreter', a number of which are discussed by those authors,[41] but one important reason may be the presence of conflicting precedents. One of the peculiarities of the common law is that, in general, for every precedent cited by counsel in support of a client's case, the opposing side will have discovered, among the many thousands of reported cases, precedents of similar weight which will support the *other* party's case. It is often such clashes of precedent, giving rise to at least *arguable* propositions of law by counsel on both sides, which bring cases before the appeal courts in the first place, for if a case is directly and uncontentiously covered by a previous decision, there is little point in appealing. The issue then becomes – and it must be stressed that we are here discussing, in the main, the activities of the higher courts – *how* the presiding judges handle these arguments and the previous cases on which they are based.

Many judges would assert that the manner in which they select the relevant precedent is based upon logic: the idea that the law contains within it the solution to

---

38 See esp. *Spartan Steel and Alloys Ltd v Martin and Co (Contractors) Ltd* [1973] 1 QB 27.
39 W. Friedmann, *Law in a Changing Society* (1972, Penguin), p 74.
40 J. Frank, 'Words and Music: Some Remarks on Statutory Interpretation' (1947) 47 *CLR* at 1267.
41 Twining and Miers, op. cit., esp. chapter 4.

almost any fact situation which may arise, which the judges must decide in line with what the law prescribes. There is some debate as to what is meant by the term 'legal logic'. One meaning is simply that the judges must decide 'rationally': this may just refer to the need to decide in a non-arbitrary manner, or it may refer to the use of certain principles of reasoning, such as that the judge *deduces* the solution to a case by applying a legal rule to the facts before him, or that he uses *inductive* reasoning (finding the facts in a case, then seeking out the relevant legal rule and 'fitting' it to that case).[42] Another meaning of 'legal logic' may take the law to be a 'closed system', whereby the 'correct' answer to any question may be derived from the legal rules (see chapter 1). These views miss one essential point. In referring to concepts like 'logic' the impression may often be given that the mode of reasoning used by judges is somehow scientific and demonstrable: that a conclusion follows 'logically' (that is, *inevitably*) from a given premise: given X, then Y logically must follow.

In law, however, this is not the case. The judge must make a *selective* decision as to which of two (or more) conflicting lines of precedent should apply to a case. Some years ago, Campbell argued that 'legal logic' is not the logic of scientific demonstration, but 'it is the logic of rhetoric. In the court situation the lawyer, by use of the logic of argumentation, seeks to persuade his audience, the judge'.[43] Twining and Miers, after considering the various techniques with which lawyers and judges handle precedents, acknowledge that judges use a wide variety of reasons for their preference for one line of argument/precedent as against another, such as that a given rule is firmly established, or serves a useful function, and so on. They maintain that these stated reasons for choosing one solution as against any other constitute a set of constraints operating to control the exercise of discretion in deciding cases.[44]

The picture, then, unfolds: the judge, required by convention and a conception of justice to make decisions in line with previous cases which justify his conclusions objectively, must nevertheless make creative selections from the mass of precedents which may be cited. It is this essentially creative activity which is obscured by the 'declaratory theory', and by the use of the formal device of 'distinguishing on the facts', for, as we shall see in our illustrations shortly, the interpretation of facts by counsel and judges is as much a matter of contention as is the interpretation of the precedents themselves.

The different styles of individual judges may be attributable, then, to the extent to which their essentially creative role in handling precedents is acknowledged, and one useful analytical model whereby we may appreciate different modes of judicial behaviour is the distinction presented by an American writer, Karl Llewellyn. He suggested[45] that, over substantial periods of time, it is possible to discern patterns

42 Allen, op. cit., pp 161–163.
43 C. Campbell, 'Legal Thought and Juristic Values' (1974) 1 *British Journal of Law and Society* at 18; see also J. Shklar, *Legalism* (1964, Harvard University Press), chapter 1; Twining and Miers, op. cit., chapter 10; and see Zander, op. cit,. ch.5.   44 Twining and Miers, op. cit., chapter 9.
45 K. Llewellyn, *The Common Law Tradition: Deciding Appeals* (1960, Little, Brown).

or styles of the judicial use of precedent. He distinguished between what he called the 'Grand' style of judging, where the judge bases his decision upon grounds of public policy, or with a view to the consequences of his decision, and takes a view of precedent which allows for creativity and flexibility; and the 'Formal' style of judging – the 'orthodox ideology'[46] – where 'the rules of law are to decide the cases; policy is for the legislature, not for the courts, and so is change even in pure common law'.[47]

Whilst these 'styles of judging' will not be found in any pure or absolute form at any period, and should not be taken as literal and accurate descriptions of judicial practice in a given era,[48] this distinction does help us understand something of the differences in decision-making between different judges, and some of the problems which can crop up and recur within the body of case law. We have seen something of the work of judges whom we might term 'Grand style': judges such as Lord Atkin and Lord Denning, who have been responsible for some of the landmark cases in English law, such as *Donoghue v Stevenson* and many others. Even cases which have been heavily criticised, such as *Shaw v DPP*, must be acknowledged as constituting firm statements by judges of new, or at least up-dated, common-law principles and rules. The impact of such cases need not be repeated here. But what examples may be given of 'Formal style' judging, that is, where the mode of judicial reasoning comprises adherence to the 'orthodox ideology' of precedent, an insistence on a strict application of legal and doctrinal rules, and a reluctance to admit the creative interpretative function of the judges?

A first illustration is the dissenting judgment of Lord Buckmaster in *Donoghue v Stevenson* itself.[49] His Lordship began by stating that:

> the common law must be sought in law books by writers of authority and in judgments of the judges entrusted with its administration. The law books give no assistance, because the work of living authors however deservedly eminent, cannot be used as authority, though the opinions they express may demand attention; and the ancient books do not assist. I turn, therefore to the decided cases to see if they can be construed so as to support the appellant's case.[50]

Having explained the doctrinal position, his Lordship then went on to examine a number of previous cases, and concluded that, on his reading of the precedents, none supported Mrs Donoghue's case, except for *George v Skivington*[51] which, Lord Buckmaster clearly suggested, ought not to be followed in the present case. Because he was, therefore, unable to tease out of the precedents any principle or rule which would tend towards making the ginger-beer manufacturer liable in negligence, his Lordship's conclusion was that the claim should fail.

46 Ibid., p 38.
47 Ibid. See also A. Paterson, *The Law Lords* (1982, Macmillan/SSRC), chapter 6, esp. p 130.
48 Paterson, op. cit. See also Lloyd's *Introduction to Jurisprudence* (7th edn. by M. D. A. Freeman, 2001, Sweet and Maxwell); W. Twining, *Karl Llewellyn and the Realist Movement* (1973, Weidenfeld and Nicolson); R. Stevens, *Law and Politics* (1979, Weidenfeld and Nicolson), p 78.
49 [1932] AC 562 at 566–578.   50 Ibid., at 567.   51 (1869) LR 5 Exch 1.

In complete contrast, Lord Atkin's leading judgment in *Donoghue*, to which we have already referred,[52] contains passages which indicate that his Lordship was fully aware of the fact that he was advocating a dramatic extension to the common law:

> It is said that the Law of England and Scotland is that the poisoned consumer has no remedy against the negligent manufacturer. *If this were the result of the authorities,*[53] I should consider the result a grave defect in the law . . .[54]
>
> I do not think so ill of our jurisprudence as to suppose that its principles are so remote from the ordinary needs of civilized society and the ordinary claims it makes upon its members as to deny a legal remedy where there is so obviously a social wrong.[55]

A second example of contrasting judicial styles concerns a series of cases in the law of contract, all of which revolve around a similar basic fact situation: A has something to sell, and is approached by B, who is a con-man; B tells A that B is someone else, and A parts with the goods to B in exchange for B's worthless cheque. B then re-sells the goods to C, who buys innocently and with no knowledge of B's fraud. B makes off with C's money, and A brings an action against C for the recovery of the goods.

The problem for the court is which of two innocent victims, A or C, should win, and keep the goods. The legal issue revolves around the nature of the original deal between A and B. This transaction cannot be a perfectly lawful contract, for it is tainted with B's fraud. Is that transaction, then, *void*, so that it has no legal validity whatsoever and the property in the goods cannot pass to B? Or is it *voidable*, that is, valid unless and until it is terminated (or 'avoided') by the injured party A, in which case, assuming that A does *not* terminate, the property in the goods passes from A to B, and B can then give a good title to those goods to C? If the first solution is taken, then A recovers the goods; if the second is adopted, then C retains the goods. This problem has resulted in some interesting manipulation of precedents.

In *Phillips v Brookes*, in 1919,[56] a con-man walked into the plaintiff's jewellery shop and took away a valuable ring, leaving a cheque bearing the name 'Sir George Bullough'. The plaintiff had heard of Bullough, and accepted the cheque. The con-man then pledged the ring as security for £350 from the defendant, and made off with the money. In this case, the court adopted the second solution outlined above, on the basis that a shopkeeper is happy to sell goods to anyone entering the shop, whatever the identity of that person may be. The contract between the plaintiff and the rogue was held to be voidable, and as the former had not terminated the transaction before the rogue had made the deal with the defendant, good legal title to the goods had passed to the defendant, who won the case.

On the basis of this case, one would have predicted that the court would make a similar decision in *Ingram v Little* in 1961.[57] Here, the con-man called himself 'P G M Hutchinson', a businessman, during negotiations with the plaintiffs, who were elderly ladies, over the sale of their car to him in exchange for a cheque. Eventually

---

52 See chapter 4.   53 Italics added.   54 *Donoghue v Stevenson*, op. cit., at 582.
55 Ibid., at 583.   56 [1919] 2 KB 243.   57 [1961] 1 QB 31.

the cheque was accepted and the con-man took the car, which he then sold to the defendant, who bought innocently and in good faith. But the Court of Appeal sought to distinguish *Phillips v Brookes* on the basis that, since the ladies had taken the (rather inadequate) step of looking up 'P G M Hutchinson' in the telephone directory and checking that such a person did reside at the address which the rogue had given them, this showed that they had intended to sell the car to Hutchinson, and only Hutchinson. Since the con-man was not Hutchinson, there could be no contract at all: the title to the car did not pass to the rogue or to the defendant, and so the plaintiffs here recovered their property.

These conflicting cases had to be dealt with in 1972 in the case of *Lewis v Averay*[58] in the Court of Appeal. Again, the fact-situation is virtually identical. Here, the con-man claimed to be Richard Greene, the film-star of the 1950s TV series *The Adventures of Robin Hood*, and produced a studio pass as evidence of this. Both the pass and the cheque which he presented in exchange for the plaintiff's car had been stolen, and the car was later traced to the defendant. Lord Denning, in the Court of Appeal (which, it will be recalled, is normally bound by its own decisions), noted that the two precedents were quite irreconcilable, and referred critically to the 'distinctions without a difference' created by the courts in the previous cases; in Lord Denning's view, such distinctions 'do no good to the law'. *Ingram v Little* was said to be a case with which the court would not agree, and *Phillips v Brookes* was followed. As Lord Denning said, it was regrettable that one of two innocent people had to suffer the loss, but the seller of the car must be taken to have contracted with the person before him, and it was up to him to assure himself of the creditworthiness of that person. If he failed to do so adequately, then he must take the consequences. The 1972 decision, then, broke with the fine distinctions and formalism of the previous cases on the point, the court preferring to face the problem squarely and refusing to perpetuate a complicated debate based on precedents containing propositions of dubious helpfulness.[59]

There are, of course, many hundreds of examples which could be cited to show how different judges have approached the problems raised by precedents. The issues, however, are clear: ought judges to hold themselves rigidly bound by previous cases, whatever the outcome? If they wish to reach a conclusion other than that apparently dictated by strict interpretation of the precedents, how are they to justify that conclusion? The 'Formal style' answer rests upon the tendency to tease out differences in the facts of cases, and make distinctions within the parameters of a legal principle, which may in the end only complicate and confuse the law. The 'Grand style' answer is based on the capacity to recognise the policy issues facing the courts in the disputes before them, and to reach decisions through a sound appreciation of the place within the common law of common sense, justice and a responsible creative role.

58 [1972] 1 QB 198.
59 But see now *Shogun Finance Ltd v Hudson* [2002] 2 WLR 867, another 'rogue buyer' case which makes it clear that this part of the law is still unsettled.

Equity and the common law

So far in this chapter, we have considered two sources of English law – parliamentary legislation and the common law. The latter is so called because of the gradual change, during the Middle Ages, from separate systems of local customary law in various regions to a uniform legal code *common* to the entire country. As we have seen, common law is case law; that is to say, it is the body of legal rules and principles contained in the decisions of the judges (particularly those at the higher levels of the court hierarchy) in cases coming before them.

Under the old common law of five centuries ago, however, there were various problems for the litigant. A plaintiff had to ensure that the case was presented by means of the correct *writ* (the plaintiff's statement of claim) and that all particulars entered on the writ were correct, otherwise the case might be lost because of procedural defects. Apart from this, however, there could be other, more substantial, problems. For instance, the common-law courts only provided the remedy of *damages*, which in some cases was an inappropriate remedy – a plaintiff might wish to have the defendant prevented from continuing some activity, or to force him or her to carry out an obligation, for example, but such remedies were not available as a general rule in the common-law courts. Neither did the common law recognise simple breaches of contract as actionable. Breaches of contractual agreement could result in a remedy for the aggrieved plaintiff only if the action could be framed as a writ for debt or detinue (an action brought against someone wrongfully detaining the goods of another); the common-law courts had no conception of actions for breach of contractual promise *per se*. Furthermore, the common law did not deal adequately with the problems which stimulated the development of the *trust*. A trust is one means whereby property can be held by one person on behalf of another. A father, for example, who wishes to leave his property upon his death to his infant child may provide that the property shall be left in the hands of *trustees* who hold and administer that property for the benefit of the child, who will come into possession of the property on reaching the appropriate age. At common law, if such an arrangement occurred, then the property was deemed to be a gift to the trustees, and no beneficial rights of the child could be enforced in law.

Gradually, it became the practice for litigants who could not obtain satisfaction at common law to petition the Lord Chancellor, an official close to the sovereign and originally an ecclesiastic, for a remedy which could not be obtained in the common-law courts; as James puts it, 'The Chancellor could remedy these defects; he was one of the chief royal officials, and being closely associated with the king, he was bound by neither the rules nor the procedure of the common-law courts; nor was he likely to be over-awed by any man.'[60] By the sixteenth century, the practice whereby the Lord Chancellor came to administer 'real' justice where the common

---

60 *James' Introduction to English Law* (13th edn. by P. Shears and G. Stephenson, 1996, Butterworths), p 27.

law failed, had become established. The Court of Chancery, where these petitions were heard, gradually formulated a set of rules and principles known as 'equity', which supplemented the common law and proceeded side by side with it. Equitable relief includes the remedies of *rectification*, whereby a written contractual agreement which, due to a mistake, does not reflect the intentions of the contracting parties, may be amended; *rescission*, which allows a person to terminate a contract which she was misled into making; *specific performance*, which has the effect of compelling defendants to carry out or perform specified activities; and the *injunction*, whose effect is to prevent defendants from carrying out specified activities. The device of the trust came to be enforced in equity, not simply because of common-law defects, but because the Court of Chancery was concerned with providing justice according to the merits of a given case: for this reason, equitable remedies were, and still remain, discretionary remedies in the hands of the courts. Today, as a result of the Judicature Acts 1873–75, the rules and maxims of equity are administered and applied in the same courts as the common law, although the distinctions between these bodies of law are still very much alive. In particular, the discretionary nature of equitable remedies continues to place the judges in positions where their subjective views as to the substantial justice of a particular claim will make a considerable difference to the outcome, although the building-up of case law and the operation of the doctrine of precedent has resulted in a situation where today the jurisdiction of equity (originally an inherently flexible tool for providing remedies where the common law gave none) has become stultified by procedural complexity and technicalities. Although it may be argued that the concern of equity to provide *substantial* justice has, over the years, given way to a preoccupation with the dictates of *formal* justice, it is possible to discern equitable influences on developments in modern law: the *Mareva* injunction and the *Anton Piller* order, discussed in chapter 6, are but two recent examples of such developments.

Precedent and policy II: statutory interpretation

A large proportion of the work of the judiciary in deciding cases consists of making decisions as to the interpretation of statutory law – does a particular statute cover the case before the court? – and here again, questions of precedent and policy arise. The doctrine of precedent also applies to statutory interpretation. For example, once the words 'mechanically propelled vehicle' in the Vehicles (Excise) Act 1949 have been interpreted to include 'cars', then that interpretation stands for future cases where the status of a car is in issue for the purposes of that Act.

The operation of the system of statutory interpretation is to a great extent fashioned by factors similar to those influencing the common law, discussed above, although the materials from which the judges must make their interpretative decision may be such that the range of possible interpretations is more limited. There may be dozens of precedents having a bearing on a case at common law, but perhaps only one or two conflicting statutory provisions to be considered by the court in a given case. The courts define their role in interpreting statutory provisions as (i) applying the statute to the facts before them, and (ii) giving effect to the intentions of Parliament, as expressed in that statute. There are then two basic issues: what were the intentions of Parliament in passing a particular statute? And do the facts in the present case before the court fall within the ambit of the provisions of the statute in question?

For many years the courts consistently refused to enter the world of parliamentary politics when dealing with the first question. They denied themselves access to the one document which might throw considerable light on the intentions of Parliament – the reports of debates in *Hansard*[61] – in order, among other reasons, to avoid political 'contamination'; and worked instead on the assumption that those intentions were expressly stated in the statute before them. Unfortunately, as anyone who has studied almost any modern statute will know, such an assumption is far from justified. Statutes are extraordinarily complicated documents, often because of poor draftsmanship, and their construction and terminology may raise all kinds of problems. In *Pepper v Hart* in 1993[62] the House of Lords broke with the conventional view on using *Hansard*, and held that in some – probably highly exceptional – cases this would be permitted as a source of assistance in the process of statutory interpretation if the legislation in question contained ambiguous wording. Lord Browne-Wilkinson, giving the leading judgment in the case, explained that even in such circumstances, *Hansard* should only be used if it was clearly helpful in 'disclosing the mischief aimed at or the legislative intention lying behind the ambiguous or obscure words'. His conclusion, therefore, was that the rule excluding consideration of *Hansard*:

> should be relaxed so as to permit reference to parliamentary materials where: (a) legislation is ambiguous or obscure, or leads to an absurdity; (b) the material relied on consists of one or more statements by a minister or other promoter of the Bill together if necessary with such other parliamentary material as is necessary to understand such statements and their effect; (c) the statements relied on are clear. Further than this, I would not at present go.[63]

In cases heard since *Pepper v Hart*, some judges have gone further than this restrictive framework, having referred to *Hansard* on occasions where there is no particular ambiguity in the statutory language and where the reference to *Hansard* merely confirmed the interpretation which the court had adopted in any case.[64]

Of course, as is well known, the courts have evolved for themselves various techniques of interpretation, apart from the limited assistance provided by the Interpretation Act 1978, and these common-law techniques may be simply stated.[65]

---

61 See D. Pannick, 'The Law Lords and the Needs of Contemporary Society' (1982) 53 *Political Quarterly* 3; Twining and Miers, op. cit.; Zander, op. cit.   62 [1993] 1 All ER 42.   63 Ibid.
64 See Zander, op. cit., pp 170–179; Twining and Miers, op. cit., pp 287–296; *Three Rivers District Council v Bank of England (No 2)* [1996] 2 All ER 363, esp. the comments by Clarke J at 366–368; *Wilson v First Country Trust* [2003] 4 All ER 97.
65 See R. Cross, *Statutory Interpretation* (3rd edn. by J. Bell and G. Pringle, 1995, Butterworths).

First, the 'Literal Rule' requires that words in statutes should be given their ordinary literal meaning; second, the 'Golden Rule' is designed to ensure that, in interpreting words literally, no absurdity or inconsistency results; and third, the 'Mischief Rule' is the principle whereby the courts may ask themselves what the 'mischief' was that the statute seeks to remedy. There is more form than substance to these 'rules', however, 'partly due to vagueness, but also because in many cases where one principle appears to support one interpretation, there is another principle, often of equal status, which can be invoked in favour of an interpretation which would lead to a different result'.[66]

In the vast majority of cases reaching the courts, there will be no ambiguity over the applicability or otherwise of a statutory provision to the case in hand. Such situations fall into the category of what Hart has termed 'core' meanings and applications. It is the minority of cases, reaching appeal courts, where a statute is vague or open to alternative interpretations, which cause problems for the courts. In such cases, using Hart's phrase, the statute and the fact-situation will be in that grey, blurred, 'penumbral' area where clear meanings do not exist. For, as Hart says,

> fact situations do not await us neatly labelled, creased, and folded, nor is their legal classification written on them to be simply read off by the judge. Instead, in applying legal rules, someone must take the responsibility of deciding that words do or do not cover the case in hand with all the practical problems involved in this decision.[67]

It is at this point that the question as to the intention of Parliament may well merge with the question of the applicability of rules to facts, and with that of judicial attitudes to public policy. To begin with, the meanings and applications of a statute may well differ according to the objectives behind that statute. To take a hypothetical example: consider the meaning and scope of the word 'dwelling'. Clearly, this would include houses and flats; but would it include caravans or tents? If the statute in question used the term in connection with, say, assessment of a property for the purposes of local authority rates, then arguably, a tent, being movable and temporary accommodation, would fall outside the scope of the term. But if the statute prohibited the erection of a 'dwelling' at the side of a road, then it could be held that the putting up of a tent and staying in it might well contravene the statute.

It is clear, then, that there is a complex relationship between the meanings given to words, and the purposes of a given statute under consideration by a court. Statutory interpretation must be recognised as involving just as much a creative function, in many instances, as does the interpretation of previous cases – and, as hinted above, judicial attitudes to public policy may enter into the deliberations of the court.[68]

---

66 Twining and Miers, op. cit., p 278.
67 H. L. A. Hart, 'Positivism and the Separation of Law and Morals' (1958) 71 *Harvard Law Review* 593 at 607.
68 See for example *R v Greater London Council, ex p Bromley London Borough Council* [1983] 1 AC 768, and see the discussion of the interpretation by the court in this case of the relevant statute – the Transport (London) Act 1969 – by J. A. G. Griffith in *The Politics of the Judiciary* (5th edn., 1997, Fontana). pp 126–33.

In the interpretation of statutes, as in the development of the common law, much depends upon the outlook, vision and ideologies of those entrusted with the development and administration of the law. And clashes may occur between the judges themselves as to the 'correct' way to deal with lacunae or areas of ambiguity within statutory provisions. Some judges, notably Lord Denning, have argued for a *creative* role for judges, taking on for themselves the task of ascertaining the purpose of an Act and, to paraphrase Lord Denning, 'ironing out the creases' which may appear.[69] Others, including Viscount Simonds, who explicitly condemned Lord Denning's approach in a case in 1952, argue against such a creative role, preferring to leave all aspects of the legislative function to Parliament: 'if a gap is disclosed, the remedy lies in an amending Act'.[70]

The modern tendency is, as we have seen in the context of *Pepper v Hart*, to adopt an approach to statutory interpretation which emphasises the importance of the *context* of the statute – and particularly its *purpose* – as opposed to the narrow concentration on the literal meanings of words. In *Pepper v Hart* itself, Lord Griffith stated that 'the courts now adopt a purposive approach which seeks to give effect to the true purpose of legislation'.[71] That said, however, it may well be that a purposive approach to statutory interpretation is as problematic as any other:

> One should not be misled into thinking that to adopt a purposive approach necessarily means that there is a single purpose to be found, or that different judges will agree on what the purpose(s) of a disputed provision might be, or how formulated; or, indeed, that judges are agreed on what the adoption of a purposive approach might entail. In short, one should not think that the adoption of a purposive approach will resolve all problems of interpretation.[72]

The impact of the law of the European Union and the European Court on English judges and their practices is bringing more changes in the judicial attitude to such matters as precedent and statutory interpretation. For one of the characteristics of Community law is the use of *general* statements of principle, rather than precise and detailed language. As Lord Denning pointed out some years ago in *H P Bulmer Ltd v J Bollinger SA*[73] in 1974, the English courts, when faced with the task of interpreting European legislation, 'must follow the European pattern', and 'divine the spirit of the Treaty and gain inspiration from it. If they find a gap, they must fill it as best they can. They must do what the framers of the instrument would have done if they had thought about it.'[74]

Whether the United Kingdom Parliament could consider it wise to follow the European practice of phrasing legislation in wide and general terms, leaving the

---

69 See the judgment of Lord Denning in *Seaford Court Estates Ltd v Asher* [1949] 2 KB 481.
70 In *Magor and St Mellons Rural District Council v Newport Corpn* [1952] AC 189.
71 [1993] 1 All ER 42 at p 50.
72 Twining and Miers, op. cit., p 284. And see the discussion in T. Ingman, *The English Legal Process* (9th edn., 2002, Oxford University Press) pp 368–383.   73 [1974] Ch 401.
74 Ibid., at 425. See also V. Sacks and C. Harlow, 'Interpretation European Style' (1977) 40 *MLR* 578; and see in particular the discussion in Zander, op. cit., ch.3.

judges to fill in any gaps and to develop the detailed application of such legislation, is an interesting question. Ought judges to be given such a clear legislative function? Would this not run counter to the constitutional idea of parliamentary sovereignty? To what extent might judges interpret such provisions restrictively and thus frustrate the intentions of Parliament? And through what controls – legal or political – might such judicial activity be monitored or checked? Moreover, the present methods of interpretation and development of the law by the judges – both in the common law and through the interpretation of statutes – have not always led to consistent or clear statements of law, as we shall see when we examine specific areas of law. Before moving on to examine the important areas of tort, criminal law, contract and administrative law, however, it is now necessary to build on our coverage of English legal institutions and law-making processes by considering the impact of the European Community on English law.

8

The European dimension of English law

On 1 January 2002, 12 member states of the European Union – Germany, France, Spain, Ireland, Italy, Luxembourg, Belgium, the Netherlands, Austria, Portugal, Finland and Greece – adopted the euro as their official currency. This event was significant in a number of important respects, the main ones being first, that it marked an important stage in the move towards European economic and monetary union; second, that some member states of the European Union – Britain, Denmark and Sweden – chose *not* to join the common currency at that time (and this remains the case). Third, the fact that Europe is split on the euro issue is an indicator of the extent to which the European Union has embraced what has been termed a 'twin-track' situation in which some member states, through powers to opt out of European Union initiatives, choose to move towards European objectives at a different speed than others. This issue has become more acutely marked since the accession to the European Union of ten new member states in 2005 – Cyprus, the Czech Republic, Estonia, Hungary, Latvia, Lithuania, Malta, Poland, Slovakia, and Slovenia.

The history of the European Union has been one of gradual expansion of both its membership and its agenda. In terms of its member states, the original European Economic Community, created through the Treaty of Rome in 1957, consisted of six members – Germany, France, Italy, Belgium, the Netherlands and Luxembourg – who came together with the purpose of creating closer economic relationships. In 2006, the European Union comprises 25 member states, including Britain, with applications currently under consideration from other European countries including Bulgaria, Romania, Croatia and Turkey. Arrangements were put into place in the Treaty of Nice (2000) to accommodate this enlarged membership, which involves European states of a much more disparate nature, in terms of size, population, relative economic development and wealth, than was previously the case. Several new members (and applications under consideration), for example, are from what used to be known as 'eastern bloc' countries during the long period in the twentieth century of Russian domination of eastern Europe: countries such as Hungary, Romania, Poland and the Czech Republic.

As regards the objectives and aspirations of the European Union, the Treaty of Rome, together with the Single European Act 1986, provided for, among other things, the harmonisation of the legal codes of member states to the extent required for the proper functioning of the common market. What was originally an *economic* community, however, has increasingly moved towards both monetary and political union: the Treaty on European Union (the Maastricht Treaty) of 1992 established the European Union, and contains provision for closer ties on matters including foreign policy, national security and defence. As we have seen, monetary union has been achieved for most member states, although the issue remains highly controversial for those member states – including Britain – who are currently outside the 'euro zone'. There is little doubt that Britain's membership of the still-developing European Union will generate domestic political upheavals for some time to come, especially given the controversies which surround the question of Britain's adoption of the euro (which will involve not only the satisfaction of the government's economic tests, but also a referendum which will sound out the views of the electorate) and the question of the ratification of the European Constitution which, if adopted, would provide the new constitutional framework for the EU, reflecting the increased membership and replacing many of the treaties which, over the years, have affected the structure and the policies of the Union.

The European Constitution was formulated in 2004, but before it can come into force, it must be ratified by all member states. In 2005, in referenda in both France and the Netherlands, voters rejected the Constitution, and many believed that this effectively killed off (or at any rate, postponed indefinitely) any real chance that the Constitution would be ratified by EU members. In the UK, the prime minister has indicated that there would be a referendum on this matter, though as at mid-2006, there are no signs that this is imminent.

The Maastricht Treaty of 1992 was important for creating the current structure of the European Union, which is said to comprise the three 'pillars' of the Economic Community, the common Foreign and Security Policy, and co-operation in justice and home affairs. The latter 'pillar' was re-designated 'police and judicial co-operation in criminal matters' by the Treaty of Amsterdam in 1997. The first 'pillar' actually refers to three European 'communities' – the European Community (originally the economic community), the European Coal and Steel Community and the European Atomic Energy Community. Given the three 'pillars', the general aim of the European Union, as originally set out in the Treaty of Rome and amended by Article 2 of the Maastricht Treaty[1] is as follows:

> . . . by establishing a common market and an economic and monetary union . . . to promote throughout the Community a harmonious and balanced development of economic activities, sustainable and non-inflationary growth respecting the environment, a high degree of convergence of economic performance, a high level of employment and of social protection, the raising of the standard of living and quality of life, and economic and social cohesion and solidarity among the Member States.

---

1 Originally Article B. This was amended by the Treaty of Amsterdam: see below.

The Maastricht Treaty signified the broadening-out of the European Union agenda to include, in particular, social policy as well as economic. The Treaty originally included the 'social chapter' which covered, among other things, extended legal protection of workers' rights. The government of the United Kingdom was opposed to these provisions, and refused to endorse them, with the result that they were removed from the Treaty and contained within a Protocol to the Treaty, signed by all the other member states. It was not until the New Labour government came to power in 1997 that the United Kingdom signed up to the social chapter, which became fully part of the EC Treaty in 1999 by means of the Treaty of Amsterdam.

This 'opting out' by Britain is another example of the way in which the European Union allows the 'twin tracking' referred to above. Another more recent illustration of this is in relation to the Treaty of Amsterdam in 1997. This Treaty incorporated what are known as the Schengen Agreement arrangements whereby member states of the European Union agreed on the removal of border controls in order to implement fully the policy of free movement of individuals within the European Community. The United Kingdom and the Republic of Ireland both opted out of these arrangements, insisting on the importance of retaining border controls and passport checks.

> In most continental Member States immigration controls have, for a great many years, been of a post-entry type, involving registration and identity cards, because borders with other Member States were largely unpoliced, except at road crossing points. The effect of the United Kingdom's island geography, however, has been that the emphasis has been very much on the entry process and the granting or refusing of leave at the point of entry.[2]

Clearly, closely connected with the United Kingdom's position here is the concern about illegal immigration to the United Kingdom and the perceived need for continued vigilance at all points of entry, especially – given the problems of smuggled illegal entrants by means of road transport vehicles – at seaports and at the Channel Tunnel terminal.

In the Treaty of Nice 2000, provision is made for the expansion of the membership of the European Union, by means of changes to the arrangements regarding individual member states' voting power, and this will increase the voting strength of the larger states. This Treaty also made provision, in the context of the second pillar of foreign and security policy, for the European 'rapid reaction force', a military unit comprising 60,000 personnel to be deployed mainly for peace-keeping missions. This is another example of the extent to which the policies of the European Union have moved well beyond the strictly 'economic'.

Britain's membership of the European Union means that the legal provisions contained in the Treaties are part of the law of the United Kingdom, and there is also provision for the output of the European legislative bodies, discussed below,

---

2 C. Vincenzi and J. Fairhurst, *Law of the European Community* (3rd edn. 2002, Longman), p 321.

to be incorporated into English law. There are various kinds of European Community legislation in addition to the Treaties, the most important of which are the Regulation and the Directive.

Principal institutions of the European Community

Before we discuss in more detail the forms which European Community law-making may take, and the implications for domestic law in Britain, it is important to appreciate the principal institutions of the European Community. It is by means of these institutions that the political representatives of member states are able to register the positions taken and views adopted by the governments of the Community countries.

The Council of the European Union, created by Article 204 of the EEC Treaty,[3] comprises one representative of the government of each member state. The Council, which prior to the Maastricht Treaty was known as the Council of Ministers, is essentially a co-ordinating body with regard to general European Community economic policies. It should not be thought that Britain's representative on the Council is always the same person: exactly which government minister represents Britain's interests will depend on the issue under discussion – if it is transport policy, for example, then it will be the British Minister for Transport who represents the country. The Council is presided over by the representatives of member states, each holding office for six months, and rotating in a strict cycle.

The Council is distinguishable from the *European Council*, which refers to the meetings of the heads of government of all the member states – in fact, what we would normally understand by the term 'summit meetings'. These essentially political and rather more high-powered meetings date back only as far as 1974, when the heads of government first agreed to meet regularly three times a year. The Maastricht Treaty now provides, rather more formally, that the European Council 'shall bring together the Heads of State . . . of the Member States and the President of the Commission . . . assisted by the Minister of Foreign Affairs of the Member States and by a Member of the Commission' (Article 4). The council is to meet at least twice a year. The European Council

> Is, essentially, a political forum in which the heads of government, meeting at least twice a year, accompanied by their foreign ministers, thrash out the political agenda for the Community in the ensuing months and years. These meetings are often referred to as European Summits.[4]

Although the Council can initiate European Community legislation, it is common for such initiatives to originate with the *Commission*. This body originally comprised 20 Commissioners who, though citizens of member states, were chosen for their

---

3 The Treaty provisions were re-numbered by the Treaty of Amsterdam. Throughout this chapter, the new numbers are given.

4 J. Fairhurst, *Law of the European Union* (5th edn., 2006, Pearson), p 81.

known competence and independence. It is not the function of Commissioners simply to represent the interests of their own country but to act independently; and member states must respect their independence and not try to influence them. A member state must have one Commissioner, but may not have more than two, and the larger states – France, the United Kingdom, Germany, Spain and Italy – have had two Commissioners (in practice, one from the party in government and one from the opposition parties) while the remaining states have had one. With the enlargement of the European Union in 2004, the number of Commissioners was increased to 30, with one new Commissioner for each of the new member states. After 2005 the Commission includes one person from each member state, which effectively reduces the membership of each of the five largest states to one.

The Commissioners' period of office is five years, though this period is renewable. Although individual Commissioners may well undertake special responsibilities within the Commission (rather like ministers of the government), responsibility for the acts of the Commission is collective, not individual. The Commission is divided into 36 sections known as *Directorates General,* each one headed by a Director General who is responsible to the relevant Commissioner for the work of that section. The Commission has considerable administrative support: it is backed up by some 20,000 staff, including a large body of interpreters and, in addition, each Commissioner has a private staff.

The functions of the Commission, in essence, are to initiate and co-ordinate European Community policy and to act as the executive body of the Community. In the process of initiating and formulating policies, the Commission engages in consultation with interested parties from across the whole Community, including industry, trade unions and the civil service equivalents of each member state: it is clear that such consultation should ensure that the positions taken on any given matter by member states' governments are brought to the Commission's attention. The Commission's role includes the specification of detailed practical aspects of policy, and the final policy statements of the Commission go to the Council for deliberation.

The executive powers of the Commission include both the making and the enforcement of rules of European Community law, these powers deriving either from the general terms of the Treaty, or in some instances through specific delegation by the Council to the Commission of law-making powers with regard to specific areas, such as the common agricultural policy. The Single European Act 1986 has strengthened this law-making role as delegate of the Council. As to general law-making powers, Article 249 of the EC Treaty provides that:

> In order to carry out their task . . . the European Parliament acting jointly with the Council, the Council and the Commission shall make regulations and issue directives, take decisions, make recommendations or deliver opinions.

We will examine this provision in more detail below. With regard to the enforcement of European Community rules, the Commission has a major role in investigating alleged breaches of European Community law, and notifying the defaulting member state of the breach. In practice, it is usually the case that the member state concerned takes steps to remedy the problem well before the completion of an investigation. The Commission's enforcement powers extend to individuals (such as companies) who are in breach of, for example, community competition law, and it has powers to bring legal action against such individuals which may result, in the case of breaches of competition law, in substantial fines.

In addition to these important functions, the Commission also prepares the preliminary draft budget, which then goes to the Council and duly becomes the draft budget, which in turn is placed before the European Parliament. The latter, as we will see, has considerable powers to require amendments or modifications to the draft budget, and ultimately has the power to reject it: the draft budget was in fact rejected by the European Parliament in 1979 and 1984. Finally, the Commission is also the body which acts as negotiator in the process of making treaties.

At this point it will be clear that a considerable amount of output from the Commission must be referred for further deliberation and/or action to the Council. Given the fluctuating composition of the latter body, and its relatively infrequent meetings, there was established a body sitting, so to speak, between the Council and the Commission: this is a Committee of Permanent Representatives of the member states, normally known as COREPER (an acronym derived from the French term for this committee). COREPER is a permanent, full-time committee whose function is to sift and filter proposals coming from the Commission to the Council. Through this filtering process, only issues involving major problems or controversies actually come before the Council: the unproblematic and uncontentious proposals are effectively dealt with by COREPER, though the Council always has the final say.

Originally known as the European Assembly, an unelected body with few powers and certainly never meant to be a law-making body, the *European Parliament* (so called since the Single European Act 1986) has undergone significant change and since 1979 has comprised members democratically elected by the electorate of each member state.

Over the years, the role and powers of the European Parliament have been considerably extended, and those powers have been extended further by the provisions of the Maastricht Treaty which came into force in 1993. There are now 732 Members of the European Parliament (MEPs) elected from the member states and each serving for five years. Germany elects 99; the United Kingdom, France and Italy each elect 78; Spain 54; the Netherlands 27; Belgium, Portugal and Greece 24; Sweden 19; Austria 18; Denmark, Finland and Slovakia 14; Ireland and Lithuania 13; Latvia 9; Estonia and Slovenia 7; Cyprus and Luxembourg 6; and Malta 5. The Treaty of Nice, which made provision for changes in the numbers of MEPs to allow for representation by new member states, reduced the numbers allocated to all of the pre-2004 member states except for Germany, which, because of the size of its population, retains its 99 members. MEPs are not mandated by their home governments but, rather, operate on a personally independent basis. Not surprisingly for a political body, however, MEPs make political alliances, though these are political groupings which reflect European, as opposed to domestic, political stances. The essential and original function of the European Parliament is to act as a consultative body; however, since the introduction of elections for MEPs in 1979, the Parliament has sought and won wider powers with regard to the legislative functions of the European Community. On some issues, the European Parliament must be consulted as part of the Community's specific procedural requirements, and it has been known for legal rules made by the Council to be annulled on the grounds that the latter failed to consult the European Parliament on the matter.[5]

If the European Parliament, having duly considered and discussed a proposal, rejects it, or wishes to propose amendments, then the Council will normally reconsider its proposal in light of the reasons for the rejection or proposed amendments. Clearly, the Council may accept and implement the amendments, but should it not wish to do so, or if it considers that the proposal should take effect despite rejection by the European Parliament, then it may pass its original proposal, provided that it does so unanimously and (in the case of a rejection) within three months (Single European Act 1986). There are other procedures whereby the European Parliament participates in the legislative function, the most recent of which is the 'co-decision' procedure. This was created by the Treaty of European Union and is a mechanism whereby, with regard to certain specified European Community matters, the Parliament may veto Council proposals – this is the first time such a power has been vested in the European Parliament, and arguably increases the degree of democratic representation within Community institutions, which according to some critics had hitherto been overly dominated by the Council of Ministers. However, on the other side of this 'democratic deficit' argument, it might be said that democratic control of the Community, and in particular of the members of the Council, ultimately lies with the electorate of each member state through the national election procedures of each member state.

One of the most important powers of the European Parliament is that of political control over the Commission. It discusses the reports of the Commission; it may question individual Commissioners, who must answer either orally or by a written response; and it has power, ultimately, to dismiss the entire Commission by a vote of censure. This power, though threatened on occasion, has never been used. The European Parliament has no direct powers of control over the Council, although it has been held by the European Court that the European Parliament may bring an action against either the Council or the Commission if either of these bodies fails to act in circumstances where it should have done so.[6] In 1999, following criticism by the European Parliament, the Community's Court of Auditors reported that the

5 See Case 138/79 *Roquette Frères SA v EC Council* [1980] ECR 3333 and Case 139/79 *Maizena GmbH v EC Council* [1980] ECR 3393.
6 See the *Roquette Frères* case above; and Case 13/83 *European Parliament v EC Council* [1986] 1 CMLR 138; Case C-70/88 *European Parliament v EC Council (Chernobyl)* [1990] ECR I-2041.

Commission had been responsible for fraud and mismanagement. The entire Commission resigned – indeed, if it had not done so, the Parliament would have exercised its powers to remove Commission members. Following the re-establishment of the Commission by mid-1999, the new Vice-President, Neil Kinnock, took on the responsibility for reforming the Commission, and the proposals put forward to achieve this were adopted by the Commission in 2000.

The *European Court of Justice*,[7] comprising 25 judges (one from each member state) and the President, has as its main task the responsibility of 'ensuring that in the interpretation and application of this Treaty the law is observed' (Article 220). The role and functions of the court have been concisely summarised thus:

> It is the supreme authority on all matters of Community law, and in this capacity may be required to decide matters of constitutional law, administrative law, social law and economic law in matters brought directly before it or on application from national courts. Its jurisdiction is principally over the acts of the institutions and Member States within the Communities' sphere of activity . . . In its practices and procedures the ECJ draws on Continental models; in developing the substantive law it draws on principles and traditions from all the Member States.[8]

The judges are assisted by eight Advocates-General, chosen for their personal and guaranteed independence, whose primary function is to prepare analyses of cases coming before the court and make recommendations to the court on matters arising from those cases. The court differs from English courts of law in a number of respects, not least being the fact that the European Court is not bound by a doctrine of precedent (see chapter 7), and that the general outlook taken by the court is far more creative and proactive in its interpretations of the general provisions of the Treaties than that of its English counterparts.

The Single European Act 1986 created a new court – the Court of First Instance – which is intended to relieve the European Court of some of its very heavy workload, and which presently deals with a limited number of disputes, including those arising between the European Community and its staff. There is provision for appeal from the Court of First Instance to the European Court, and, because there are very many such appeals, the creation of the Court of First Instance has had little effect on the case load of the European Court.

Article 234 provides that:

The Court of Justice shall have jurisdiction to give preliminary rulings concerning:

(a) the interpretation of this Treaty;
(b) the validity and interpretation of acts of the institutions of the Community;
(c) the interpretation of the statutes of bodies established by an act of the council, where those statutes so provide.

---

7 The European Court of Justice must not be confused with the separate European Court of Human Rights, created under the European Convention on Human Rights. This court, located in Strasbourg, deals with alleged violations of the convention by European states against individuals.
8 J. Steiner and L. Woods, *Textbook on EEC Law* (8th edn., 2003, Oxford University Press), p 35.

Article 234 also provides that, where such a question arises in any case before a court or tribunal[9] within any member state, that court or tribunal may refer the question to the European Court for a ruling. This jurisdiction is essentially one of preliminary rulings on matters of interpretation of European law (not the domestic law of member states). The European Court hears and decides disputes concerning matters of Community law arising from Article 234 references from domestic courts, and so has an important function regarding matters of interpretation of the Articles of the Treaty.

Now, given that European law takes precedence over the domestic law of the member states, it can happen that a legal rule of the European Community is in direct conflict with a rule of domestic law. What is the consequence of this for English law, and the constitutional doctrine of the supremacy of Parliament? Can we still, in Britain, speak of the constitutional 'sovereignty' of our own Parliament, given the relationships between our own law and legislation and that of the European Community?

It will be recalled that, according to the constitution, the Westminster Parliament is the 'supreme law-making body' of the United Kingdom. All this has meant, historically, is that the courts had no power to override, or declare invalid, a properly enacted statute or its contents. The implication of European Community membership is that, to a large extent, the Westminster Parliament may no longer be said to be the supreme law-making body in the United Kingdom (at least in so far as its legislative provision on matters affecting Community issues is concerned), for the Community legislature has superiority.

The point is well illustrated by considering the *Factortame* case in 1989–90.[10] The European Court had in 1964 stated, in the context of a case originating in Italy,[11] that:

> The transfer by the States from their domestic legal system to the Community legal system of the rights and obligations arising under the Treaty carries with it a permanent limitation of their sovereign rights . . .

The facts of *Factortame* were that, in 1988, the Westminster Parliament had passed a statute – the Merchant Shipping Act 1988 – which provided for the registration of British fishing vessels whose catches of fish would, after registration, count as part of the British fish quotas allowed by the European Community. The Act laid down that only British-owned ships managed and controlled from the United Kingdom could be registered as British fishing vessels; 95 fishing ships, previously registered as British under a previous statute, but managed and controlled from Spain, were held to be excluded from registration.

---

9 Defined as any body exercising a judicial function: that is to say, having a jurisdiction concerning the rights and duties of individuals.

10 *Factortame Ltd v Secretary of State for Transport* [1989] 2 All ER 692; refd sub nom *R v Secretary of State for Transport, ex p Factortame Ltd (No 2)*: C-213/89 [1991] 1 AC 603. Case 246/89R *EC Commission v United Kingdom* [1989] ECR 3125.

11 Case 6/64 *Costa v ENEL* [1964] CMLR 425.

The owners of the ships challenged the validity of the 1988 Act, arguing that it was contrary to Community law, which, of course, applied in the United Kingdom. The English Divisional Court, hearing the claim, sought a preliminary ruling under Article 177 (now Article 234) from the European Court on the point of Community law involved in the case. Because it was expected that the European Court would take about two years to give a ruling on the point, and the owner of the boats concerned would clearly suffer hardship if they could not fish during that time, the Divisional Court in the meantime granted the owners an interim remedy, ordering that the relevant provisions of the Merchant Shipping Act 1988, and regulations made under it, should be 'disapplied' and that the responsible minister should not enforce the provision of this Act pending the ruling from the European Court.

On appeal, both the Court of Appeal and the House of Lords held that the Divisional Court had no power under English law to make such an interim order: constitutionally, the courts have no power to override the provisions of a duly enacted statute – but the House of Lords was unsure as to whether any principle of European law gave English courts such a power.

In a separate action, the European Commission had brought proceedings in the European Court against the United Kingdom over the Merchant Shipping Act 1988, alleging that the United Kingdom had failed to observe its EC Treaty obligations by imposing the nationality requirement for registration. The European Court responded to this allegation by ruling that the United Kingdom must suspend the nationality requirements contained in the 1988 Act; the government of the United Kingdom duly complied with this decision.

The pincers finally closed on the United Kingdom government in the eventual ruling by the European Court in 1990,[12] in which the court briefly stated that:

> Community law must be interpreted as meaning that a national court which, in a case before it concerning Community law, considers that the sole obstacle which precludes it from granting interim relief is a rule of national law must set aside that rule.

The House of Lords, on receipt of this ruling, went on to confirm the grant of interim relief to Factortame. In *Kirklees Borough Council v Wickes Building Supplies* in 1991,[13] in which Kirklees Council sought to prevent Wickes from continuing to open its stores for normal trading on Sundays, alleging that this was contrary to British Sunday trading law, the Court of Appeal acknowledged the implications of the *Factortame* decision, and required the plaintiff council to enter into an undertaking for the payment of compensation to the defendant company in the event of the British Sunday trading laws being found to be in contravention of European Community law. And in *R v Secretary of State for Employment, ex p Equal Opportunities Commission*[14] the House of Lords stated that some provisions of the Employment Protection (Consolidation) Act 1978 were incompatible with Community law, and issued a declaration to that effect.

---

12 *R v Secretary of State for Transport, ex p Factortame Ltd (No 3)*: C-221/89, above.
13 [1991] 4 All ER 240.   14 [1995] 1 AC 1.

Despite the implications of these decisions for the sovereignty of the Westminster Parliament, and indeed the English courts, it must always be remembered that the decision to join the European Community was a political one. This means that, strictly speaking, if political or economic policy so required, the United Kingdom could leave the Community, which would have the effect of restoring full legislative supremacy to the Westminster Parliament. It may be true that the constitutional law-making supremacy of our own Parliament has been eroded, but there is no international agreement or provision which could affect Britain's right to decide to end its membership, and then to proceed with political and economic policies in complete legal independence of the European Community. Having said this, it is the case that Britain is now so firmly enmeshed in the policies and laws of the Community that pulling out is not a realistic possibility: although to be sure, much political debate centres on the extent to which Britain should accept or adopt Community policies (for example, on the single European currency) *above and beyond* the original economic objectives of the Community, few serious politicians suggested outright withdrawal – and anyway, as we have seen, the acceptance of 'twin tracking' within the European Union enables member states, if they so wish, to proceed towards European Union objectives more cautiously or at a slower pace than others.

European Community law and the principle of direct effect

As we have said, the EC Treaties themselves are part of English law, and as Lord Denning stated in *H P Bulmer Ltd v J Bollinger SA* (1974)[15] 'any rights or obligations created by the Treaty are to be given legal effect in England without more ado'. Any rights or obligations *enjoyed by or imposed on any individual by the Treaties, therefore, are actionable in the English courts,* and this is essentially the meaning of the terms 'direct effect' and 'direct applicability', as interpreted by the European Court. It is not always clear, however, exactly which provisions in the Treaties are in fact capable of being of direct effect:

> Some provisions are regarded as binding on, and enforceable by, States alone; others are too vague to form the basis of rights or obligations for individuals; others are too incomplete and require further measures of implementation before they can be fully effective in law. Whether a particular provision is directly effective is a matter of construction, depending on its language and purpose as well as the terms on which the Treaty has been incorporated into domestic law.[16]

Apart from the substantive content of the Treaties, however, Article 249 of the EEC Treaty provides, as noted above, that the Council and the Commission may make rules and recommendations, and deliver opinions. Article 249 further provides that:

> A regulation shall have general application. It shall be binding in its entirety and directly applicable in all member States.

---

15 *Bulmer v Bollinger SA* [1974] Ch 401.   16 Steiner and Woods, op. cit., p 89.

> A directive shall be binding, as to the result to be achieved, upon each member State to which it is addressed, but shall leave to the national authorities the choice of form and methods.
>
> A decision shall be binding in its entirety upon those to whom it is addressed.
>
> Recommendations and opinions shall have no binding force.

Regulations, like the Treaties, are of direct effect and are directly applicable. Upon enactment, they immediately and automatically become binding law in all member states. Directives, which may or may not be of direct effect (see below), must usually be specifically implemented by the governments of member states. For example, the Directive concerning liability for defective products was enacted into English law by means of the Consumer Protection Act 1987, discussed in chapter 9.

Regulations and Directives are the most important of these various measures, since, as can be seen, these may well affect the domestic law of each member state either by – in the case of a Regulation – raising actual or potential conflict between the European Community rule and a pre-existing domestic law or by – in the case of Directives – requiring the member state to enact the contents of the European rule in new domestic legislation or by some other method which will have the effect of rendering the Directive part of domestic law.

In the process of deciding the many cases brought before it, the European Court has filled in some of the detail – left open by the general terms of the Treaty – as to the implications of the terms 'direct effect' and 'direct applicability' regarding the provisions of the Treaty and European Community regulations. It has been held that where a provision is of direct effect, then individual citizens of member states may initiate legal action against the government of that state. This is known as 'vertical' direct effect: the Treaty obligation is imposed on the member state, and affects the relations between the state and its citizens. Thus in the important *Van Gend en Loos* case in 1962,[17] the court was asked, by means of an Article 234 (previously Article 177) reference, about the enforceability by individuals of a Treaty provision which prohibited member states from 'introducing between themselves any new customs duties on imports or exports'. The European Court ruled that, since the Treaty conferred rights and duties on individuals, in the sense that its provisions might well affect the relations between individuals and their national governments, then those rights and duties were enforceable at the suit of the individuals affected as long as certain conditions were satisfied. These conditions were stated in *Van Gend en Loos* to be first, that the provision in question must be clear and unconditional, and second, that the implementation of the provision is not dependent upon any subsequent action having to be taken by the member state.

'Horizontal' direct effect is the term used to refer to situations where European Community law affects *interpersonal* relations, and where one individual may initiate an action under Community law against another *individual.* Thus in *Defrenne*

---

17 Case 26/62 *Van Gend en Loos v Nederlandse Administratie der Belastingen* [1963] CMLR 105.

v Sabena,[18] Ms Defrenne sought compensation from Sabena Airlines, her employer, in relation to the unequal pay which she had received compared with the company's male workers. This, she argued, infringed the obligations on the employer contained in Article 141 (previously Article 119) of the Treaty, which provides that member states must ensure and maintain 'the application of the principle that men and women should receive equal pay for equal work'.

The question for the European Court was whether this provision of the Treaty was enforceable as between individuals. In its ruling, the court stated that 'the fact that certain provisions of the Treaty are formally addressed to the Member States does not prevent rights from being conferred at the same time on any individual who has an interest in the performance of the duties laid down' and that therefore Ms Defrenne had the capacity in law to enforce those rights as against the defendant, since the defendant company had obligations towards her in respect of sex equality law enacted by the Belgian government in compliance with Article 141.

As stated above, European Community Regulations are always of both horizontal and vertical direct effect (Article 249). What about the status of Community Directives?

Article 249 provides that Directives are binding as to their aims and objectives, but leaves it open to member states as to exactly *how* the content of a Directive is to be incorporated into domestic law. At first sight, therefore, it would seem that Directives cannot by their nature be of direct effect: the European Court has held, however, that it is possible for a Directive to have direct effect.

The question arose in *Van Duyn v Home Office* in 1974.[19] Article 39 (previously Article 48) of the Treaty is concerned to guarantee the right of free movement of workers between member states, subject to limitations on the grounds of public policy, public security or public health. A Council Directive of 1964 provided that member states only had a limited power to invoke the 'public policy' proviso to prevent workers from another member state from entering the country, and this Directive stated that such decisions must be based 'exclusively on the personal conduct of the individual concerned'.

Miss Van Duyn, a Dutch national, wished to come to the United Kingdom in order to work for the Church of Scientology. In previous instances the British government had decided that Scientology was not to be particularly encouraged, with the result that known members of the Church of Scientology were normally refused admission into the country.[20] Miss Van Duyn was duly refused entry, the government seeking to justify the exclusion on the grounds of the public policy proviso. She then brought proceedings against the British government, in the English courts, and the question arose as to whether Article 39 and the Directive in question had direct effect. Miss Van Duyn argued that Article 39 had direct effect; that she was therefore entitled to rely on its provisions before the English courts; and

18 Case 43/75 [1976] 2 CMLR 98.   19 Case 41/74 [1975] 1 CMLR 1.
20 See *Schmidt v Secretary of State for Home Affairs* [1969] 2 Ch 149.

that the British government was not justified in refusing her entry, because since the public policy proviso (as defined in the Directive) was confined to matters of 'personal conduct', the simple fact of membership of the Church of Scientology had nothing to do with 'personal conduct'.

Ruling on the direct applicability of these provisions, the European Court held first, that Article 39 was of direct effect; and second, that the Directive in question was also directly effective. The court stated that:

> If . . . regulations are directly applicable and, consequently, may by their very nature have direct effects, it does not follow from this that other categories of acts mentioned in [Article 249] can never have similar effects . . . In particular, where the Community authorities have, by directive, imposed on member States the obligation to pursue a particular course of conduct, the useful effect of such an act would be weakened if individuals were prevented from relying on it before their national courts and if the latter were prevented from taking it into consideration as an element of Community law . . .

On the particular facts of the present case, the European Court acknowledged that what counted as being justifiable 'grounds of public policy' would vary between member states, but made it clear that the conduct of the individual concerned need not actually be illegal within a given country in order to fall foul of the public policy proviso: it is enough if the conduct in question is generally regarded by the member state as socially harmful. Since *Van Duyn*, however, it has been held that the principle of *commonality between member states* of grounds of public policy should be developed.[21]

It is clear, then, that a Directive can have direct effect once the time-limit for implementation of that Directive by a member state has expired (but not before),[22] though some member states' courts have refused to accept this binding effect[23] on the ground that in Article 249 only Regulations, and not Directives, are explicitly stated to have direct effect. Against this, it is argued that, since there is no doubt that Directives impose obligations on member states to ensure that the objectives of Directives are achieved, the mandatory nature of Directives would be

21 Later cases – in particular Case 30/77 *R v Bouchereau* in 1977 and Cases 115 and 116/81 *Aduoi and Cornuaille v Belgian State* in 1982 have adopted a rather more restrictive approach to this issue. In the former case, involving the proposed deportation by the British government of a French national who had been convicted of unlawful possession of drugs, the courts stated that the use of the public policy proviso 'presupposes . . . the existence, in addition to the perturbation of the social order which any infringement of the law involves, of a genuine and sufficiently serious threat to the requirements of public policy affecting one of the fundamental interests of society' and in the latter case, concerning the refusal of the Belgian government to admit two French women on the grounds that they were allegedly prostitutes, the court said that 'a Member State may not (by means of the public policy proviso) expel a national of another Member State from its territory or refuse access to its territory by reason of conduct which, when attributable to the former State's own nationals, does not give rise to repressive measures or other genuine and effective measures intended to combat such conduct'.
22 Case 148/78 *Pubblico Ministero v Ratti* [1980] 1 CMLR 96.
23 *Minister of the Interior v Cohn-Bendit* [1980] 1 CMLR 543 (France); *O'Brien v Sim-Chem Ltd* [1980] ICR 429 (Britain); *Re VAT Directives* [1982] 1 CMLR 527 (Germany).

undermined if there were no means of enforceability in the event of non-implementation. Certainly, action might be taken against defaulting states by the Commission, but the argument adopted by the European Court in cases such as *Van Duyn* is that there is no reason why action cannot be taken in such circumstances by affected individuals.

What of instances where Community obligations fell not on public bodies such as government departments, but upon private employers, such as obligations concerning equal pay? Can a Directive have direct effect on private organisations (that is, horizontal direct effect) as well as on governments?

Through a number of cases before the European Court during the 1980s –*Becker*,[24] *Marshall*,[25] *Van Colson*[26] and others – these issues were debated and various alternatives discussed. In *Marshall v Southampton and South West Hampshire Area Health Authority* in 1986, the applicant had been dismissed by her employer, the Area Health Authority, when she was 62 years old. She argued that, since the retiring age for men was 65, this was sex discrimination contrary to Council Directive 76/207/EEC, which required equality of treatment between the sexes, but which had not been implemented in Britain even though the deadline for implementation had been passed. The question was whether Mrs Marshall could bring proceedings before an English court, based on the relevant Directive.

The European Court held that the different retirement age was indeed in breach of the Directive, but that because Article 249 specified that Directives were addressed to member states and not to individual employers, it followed that individuals could not base proceedings against the employer on the Directive in question.

The result, prior to 1990, was that where a Directive was held to have direct effect, an affected individual might bring proceedings against a member state (that is, there might be vertical direct effect) but not against another private individual or organisation (that is, no horizontal direct effect). The decision in *Marshall* and similar cases, however, left some questions unresolved. The idea of bringing an action against a 'state' does not in itself provide a clear and definitive dividing-line between a 'state' and a 'private' individual, body or agency. In *Foster v British Gas plc* in 1990[27] for example, which once again concerned differentials in retirement ages between male and female employees, the question arose whether British Gas plc, operating as a privatised industry created by statute and carrying out statutory duties, was a public or a private concern. The court ruled that Directives may have vertical direct effect in the case of agencies which were 'subject to the authority or control of the State or had special powers beyond those which result from the normal relations between individuals'.[28] The court held that a Directive could give rise to a claim by individuals against a 'body, whatever its legal form, which has been made responsible, pursuant to a measure adopted by the State, for providing

24 Case 8/81 *Becker v Finanzarnt Münster-Innenstadt* [1982] 1 CMLR 499.
25 Case 152/84 *Marshall v Southampton Area Heath Authority* [1986] 1 CMLR 688.
26 Case 14/83 *Van Colson and Kamann v Land Nordrhein-Westfalen* [1986] 2 CMLR 430.
27 [1990] 2 CMLR 833.   28 Paragraph 18.

a public service under the control of the State . . .' British Gas plc was held to be such a body.[29] This remains an area of uncertainty: in a case in 1993, the court reiterated the *Marshall* position with regard to vertical direct effect, though pointed out that in insisting that Directives could not have horizontal direct effect, the Court was not thereby denying remedies to individuals affected by private organisations: alternative avenues for redress in many cases might be available either through the principle of *indirect effects,* or by virtue of the decision in 1990 in the case of *Francovitch v Italian Republic.*[30]

The principle of indirect effect was developed by the European court in the cases of *Von Colson v Land Nordrhein-Westfalen*[31] and *Harz v Deutsche Tradex GmbH*[32] whereby the court invoked Article 10 (previously Article 5) of the EC Treaty which provides that member states must take 'all appropriate measures' to fulfil their Community obligations. The court in these cases emphasised that such measures included member states placing obligations on their own courts to ensure, where appropriate, that the objectives of Community Directives are achieved. This means, in effect, that national courts must interpret domestic statutes which are passed in implementation of Directives, and since 1990 even those which are not,[33] in such a way as to ensure compliance with European Community law.

The *Francovitch* case provides another method whereby individuals may obtain redress in connected with Directives. Here, a number of employees of two Italian private companies brought proceedings against the Italian government. Some were owed wages by their employers when the company was declared insolvent, and Mr Francovitch was owed part of his salary by his employer. All the applicants had failed to obtain what was due to them, and they brought these proceedings against the government on the basis that the Italian government had failed to implement Council Directive 80/987/EEC, which stated that member states were required to take the necessary measures to ensure that workers received pay arrears if their employers became insolvent.

The European Court had already ruled that Italy was in breach of its Treaty obligations for having failed to implement this Directive, and now the group of workers sued the Italian government for *compensation.* The European Court held that member states were indeed liable to compensate individuals who suffered damage as a result of a failure to implement a Directive where three conditions were met. First, the Directive in question must confer rights on individuals; second, the content of those rights must be determinable by reference to the provisions of the Directive; and third, the damage suffered by the individuals concerned must be *caused* by the state's failure to implement a Directive, or even, it has been suggested, by an incorrect or inadequate implementation.

---

29 But see *Doughty v Rolls-Royce plc* [1992] IRLR 126, in which Rolls-Royce (at the time 'under the control of' the state) was held not to fall into this category of organisations because it did not provide services to the public or operate by means of special statutory powers.
30 [1992] IRLR 84.   31 [1986] 2 CMLR 430.   32 [1986] 2 CMLR 430.
33 *Marleasing SA v La Comercial Internacional de Alimentación SA* [1992] 1 CMLR 305.

The effect of the *Francovitch* decision was to reduce somewhat the significance of the debate as to the direct effectiveness of Directives. The ruling places the responsibility for damage suffered on the state, and not on the private-sector employer. The type of issue which lay at the heart of cases such as *Marshall*, above, it would seem, is no longer of great relevance: as has been suggested with reference to the facts of *Marshall*,

> *Francovitch* . . . cuts right through the continuing debate on this issue by having the effect that private sector employees who were subjected to discriminatory retirement age between August 1978 (when the UK Government was required to correctly implement Equal Treatment Directive 76/207) and 7 February 1987 (when the prohibition on discriminatory retirement ages in the Sex Discrimination Act 1986 came into force) can sue the UK Government for compensation for the loss they suffered (by losing their jobs) as a result of the UK's failure to implement the Directive correctly.[34] This ability to sue the member state for compensation if the conditions laid down in *Francovitch* are satisfied raised a further series of questions, however. Many of the issues raised by the ruling were discussed by the court in 1993 in the cases of *Brasserie du Pêcheur SA v Germany* and *Factortame v United Kingdom*.[35] The outcome of the court's deliberations in these cases is that the principle laid down in *Francovitch* is applicable to *any* breach by a member state of Community law – not just failure properly to implement Directives. Further, the conditions laid down in *Francovitch* were recast, with a new condition that the breach of the legal rule must be 'sufficiently serious', the test for which was stated as whether the agency concerned has 'manifestly and gravely exceeded the limits of its discretion'. The court explained that, in considering this question, a number of factors would be taken into account, including:
>
> > the clarity and precision of the rule breached, the measure of discretion left by that rule to the national or Community authorities, whether the infringement and the damage caused was intentional or voluntary, whether any error of law was excusable or inexcusable, the fact that the position taken by a Community institution may have contributed towards the omission, and the adoption or retention of national measures or practices contrary to Community law.[36]

The approach so far taken by the court in applying this test may be considered in *R v HM Treasury, ex p British Telecommunications plc*[37] in which British Telecom argued that a particular Directive had been wrongly implemented in regulations produced by the United Kingdom government. In assessing whether the breach was 'sufficiently serious', the European Court stated that the wording of the Directive itself was unclear, and that this made the UK's action excusable. In contrast, in *R v Minister of Agriculture, Fisheries and Food, ex p Hedley Lomas (Ireland) Ltd* [38] the claimants alleged that they had suffered losses as a consequence of a ban imposed by the United Kingdom on the export of sheep to Spain. The ban had been imposed because of allegations that Spanish slaughterhouses were run in a manner which was inconsistent

---

34 [1992] IRLR at 53.   35 [1996] All ER (EC) 301.   36 Paragraph 56.
37 [1996] All ER (EC) 411.   38 [1996] All ER (EC) 493.

with the relevant European Directive. The court found that the United Kingdom ban was in breach of the EC Treaty, and was not justified under Article 36 of the EC Treaty (which allows for measures such as export bans to be implemented if certain conditions are met, such as public morality, public security, the protection of health and life of humans, animals or plants) because the United Kingdom did not produce evidence of a breach of Community law by Spain which would threaten animal health. The United Kingdom's breach was held to satisfy the 'sufficiently serious' condition, and liability under the *Francovitch* principle was made out. The reasoning – and conclusions – of the court in this case appear to be somewhat stricter than in the *British Telecommunications* case, and would seem to have significant implications for the potential liability of member states under the *Francovitch* principle.

Finally in this section, the two other types of act – Decisions and Recommendations – may briefly be explained. Decisions, which may be addressed to member states or to individuals, are generally not directly applicable, although the European Court has held that, if the conditions for direct effect are satisfied, then a particular decision may be of direct effect. As Steiner and Woods point out, however, this matter 'does not pose the same theoretical problems as Directives, since [Decisions] will only be invoked against the addressee of the Decision. If the obligation has been addressed to him and is "binding in its entirety", there seems no reason why it should not be invoked against him.'[39]

Recommendations are not binding and cannot be relied upon as the basis of proceedings before any courts.

European Community law: an overview

It is not possible in one chapter to examine in any detail the considerable body of substantive law of the European Community, contained in the various Treaties, Regulations and Directives, and all the domestic legislation through which Directives are implemented: for this, the reader should consult the specialist texts.[40] Some idea of the nature and scope of European Community policy can be gained by a brief overview of the main areas, but before presenting that overview, it is useful to consider briefly the *general principles* whereby Community law is interpreted.

These principles include the principle of *certainty* (the proposition that community law must be clear and unambiguous, and should not operate retrospectively), and the principle of *equality*, which both requires that citizens should be treated in the same way unless there is justification for different treatment, and also recognises prohibition of discrimination on the grounds of nationality, sex, religion, disability, age or sexual orientation. A third principle is that of '*legitimate expectation*', which

39 Steiner and Woods, op. cit., p 103.
40 See, in particular, Steiner and Woods, op. cit.; Fairhurst, op. cit.; Vincenzi and Fairhurst, op. cit.; M. Horspool, *European Union Law* (3rd edn., 2003, Oxford University Press); J. Tillotson and A. Cygan, *Text, Cases and Materials on European Union Law:* (5th edn., 2007, Routledge Cavendish); J Hanlon, *European Community Law* (3rd edn., 2003, Sweet and Maxwell).

means that community law must not infringe the legitimate expectations of people affected by that law, unless there is justification deriving from overriding public interest. Furthermore, the principles of *natural justice*, deriving from English administrative law and discussed further in chapter 12, are applicable if procedural rights are not otherwise provided for in European Community legislation. Natural justice in this context has been held to mean that a person has a right to a hearing which is free from bias, and that a court or tribunal must give reasons for its decision.

The principles of *proportionality* and *subsidiarity* also require brief explanation. 'Proportionality' involves the idea that public bodies must not impose obligations or sanctions which are beyond those necessary and appropriate to achieve a particular purpose.[41] This principle is well illustrated in the case of *R v Intervention Board, ex p Man (Sugar) Ltd* in 1985.[42] The Board was the agency responsible for the regulation of the sugar market, as provided by Community legislation. M, a sugar dealer, submitted to the Board tenders for the export of sugar to states outside the European Community. Under the relevant legislation, M had lodged securities amounting to over £1.5 million with a bank. M should have applied for export licences by noon on 2 August 1983, but was almost four hours late in doing so because of staffing problems within M's organisation. The Board, acting under applicable Community regulations, declared that M forfeited the money lodged as securities. M claimed that this penalty was too severe – that it was a disproportionate response to a trivial error. The European Court ruled that the forfeiture of the entire sum was indeed a disproportionate act following a trivial breach of the deadline.

Subsidiarity in the context of European law derives from the Maastricht Treaty. It has been explained as follows:

> Put simply [it] means that decisions should be made at the lowest level where possible. If an adequate solution can be obtained by a Member State there is no reason why that decision should be taken by a Community institution. It is about the allocation of responsibility between different levels of administration in the Community.[43]

The extent to which the principle of subsidiarity may form the basis of claims before the European Court has yet to be decided by that court, though it has been suggested that, at the very least, the principle is admissible as an aid to interpretation of European Community legislation, especially in the light of the Protocol to the Treaty of Amsterdam, whereby in deciding whether action is best taken by individual states, or by Community institutions, the guidelines should be (a) whether the issues in question have transnational aspects which cannot be adequately decided by member states; and/or (b) whether actions by member states would conflict with Treaty requirements; and/or (c) whether the Council is satisfied that action at Community level would result in clear benefits compared with action at the level of member states.

41 Case 181/84. See chapter 12 for discussion of the extent to which the concept of proportionality is having an increasing impact on English administrative law.   42 [1985] ECR 2889.
43 J. Hanlon, *European Community Law*, op. cit., p 10.

The final principle to be considered is that of *fundamental rights*. This may be thought to be particularly important, given the enactment into English law of the European Convention on Human Rights by means of the Human Rights Act 1998.[44] In fact, the histories of the European Convention (and the European Court of Human Rights), and the European Community, are quite distinct. The European Convention on Human Rights (1953) is an international treaty having as its objective the protection of human rights. Not all European countries fully committed themselves to that Convention – the United Kingdom is a good example, in that although it was a signatory to the Convention, it did not incorporate the Convention into English law until 1998.

As we saw earlier, the origin of the European Community was the coming together of a number of European countries to pursue an integrated *economic* policy. Although the European Court of Justice has, in a number of decisions, made reference to the European Convention, it was the relatively recent Treaty of Maastricht in 1992 which incorporated the statement that 'the Union is founded on the principles of liberty, democracy, respect for human rights and fundamental freedoms, and the rule of law, principles which are common to the Member States'; and the Council of the European Union is empowered to suspend the voting rights of member states found to be in serious breach of this provision.

At the European Council meeting in Nice in 2000, the Charter of Fundamental Rights was signed by 15 member states – and it must be recognised that in some respects this Charter overlaps with the European Convention:

> The Charter combines in a single text the civil, political, economic, social and societal rights which have previously been laid down in a variety of international, European and national sources. It includes rights of dignity (e.g. the right to life); freedoms (e.g., respect for private and family life; freedom of assembly and of association); equality (e.g, respect for cultural, religious and linguistic diversity); solidarity (e.g. right of collective bargaining and action); citizens' rights (e.g. freedom of movement and residence); and justice (e.g. presumption of innocence and right of defence).[45]

The essential point concerning 'fundamental rights' is to recognise that the European Court of Justice has acknowledged that there are a number of sources of 'fundamental' or 'human' rights which may have significance in the application of European Community law. In *J Nold v Commission*[46] the court stated that it was 'bound to draw inspiration from constitutional traditions common to the member states, and it cannot therefore uphold measures which are incompatible with fundamental rights recognised and protected by . . . those states. Similarly, international treaties for the protection of human rights on which the member states have collaborated or of which they are signatories, can supply guidelines which should be followed.'

Given these principles, we need to outline the nature and scope of European Community policy. Originally, the European Economic Community was solely

44 See chapter 4.   45 Vincenzi and Fairhurst, op. cit., p 119.
46 Case 4/73 [1974] 2 CMLR 338.

concerned with economic, commercial and business matters, creating legislation designed to unify, and remove barriers between, the economic practices of the various member states, and business organisations operating within them. Article 18 of the EEC Treaty, as amended by the Single European Act 1986, defined the internal European market as 'an area without internal frontiers in which the free movement of goods, persons, services and capital is ensured'. The principal means of achieving this aim is by the adoption of common systems of, for example, customs tariffs across all member states, and of prohibitory legal rules designed to prevent inequality and discrimination. The *free movement of goods* is sought by means of removing barriers in the form of individual national customs duties on goods exported and imported, and no member state may discriminate against the goods or products of any other member state by means of the imposition of taxes on those goods in excess of any taxation imposed on any similar domestic version of the product.

As we saw above, however, it is provided in Article 30, that these provisions referred to above shall not preclude

> prohibitions or restrictions on imports, exports or goods in transit justified on grounds of public morality, public policy or public security; the protection of health and life of humans, animals or plants; the protection of national treasures possessing artistic, historic or archaeological value; or the protection of industrial and commercial property. Such prohibitions or restrictions shall not, however, constitute a means of arbitrary discrimination or a disguised restriction on trade between member States.

Taking just one of these grounds as an example: in the case of *Conegate Ltd v Customs and Excise Commissioners* in 1985[47] the ground of 'public morality' was considered. The facts were that the British customs seized a number of inflatable rubber dolls, described as 'love dolls', as well as other articles imported from Germany of the type which are sold in Britain in sex-shops. HM Customs was of the view that these articles were indecent and obscene, and that their importation was therefore illegal. The importers challenged this seizure, arguing that it was in breach of Article 28 (previously Article 30), which deals with measures which totally or partially restrain imports, exports or goods in transit. Additionally, the importers argued that such goods are not banned in the United Kingdom, and that therefore the seizure was discriminatory.

The public morality ground was, of course, considered in the arguments before the European Court. It had already been decided in a case in 1979[48] that the public morality ground in Article 30 could justify a ban on importing pornography: such a ban was not disguised protectionism for the United Kingdom's own market, since there was no lawful market in pornography in the United Kingdom. Could the same be said of the goods in the *Conegate* case?

The European Court held that there was nothing unlawful in the United Kingdom about making and marketing goods such as those seized, and the British

47 Case 121/85 [1987] QB 254, [1986] 2 All ER 688.
48 Case 34/79 *R v Henn and Darby* [1980] 1 CMLR 246; [1981] AC 850.

government had done little to prevent such goods being sold. That being so, the applicants' argument succeeded, and the court held that the seizure of the goods was not justified under Article 30. The various grounds stated in Article 30 have been held to justify, among other things, the import and export of gold collectors' coins (public policy), the imposition of restrictive requirements on importers of petroleum oils (public security), and the inspection on health grounds of imported apples as part of pest control procedures (health and life of humans).

The *free movement of persons* is the subject of Articles 39–41 (previously Articles 48–50), providing for individual workers' right to enter, reside and work in any member state, subject to restrictions imposed by those states on the grounds of public policy, public security or public health (see the *Van Duyn* case, discussed above). 'Worker' is not defined in the European provisions, but the term certainly excludes self-employed and professional persons, for whom provision is made through the provisions in Articles 43–48 (previously Articles 52–58) *on freedom of establishment*; in order that professionally qualified people (such as lawyers and accountants) should be able to enjoy the same freedom as any other workers, it is necessary that the professional qualifications recognised in each member state carry equal validity and recognition in other states. Litigation before the European Court has included an Article 234 reference from Belgium on the matter of the transfer fee system operating within member states whereby footballers are, in effect, bought and sold by football clubs.[49] The court's ruling was that Article 39 prohibits all discrimination against workers, and this includes the transfer fee system because it impeded the free movement of professional footballers from one member state to another.

Articles 49–55 are concerned *with freedom to provide services*, and here again, the realisation of a Community-wide freedom depends on the harmonisation of national domestic laws in various respects. In Britain, statutes dealing with company law and financial services have been implemented partly to bring Britain's legal regulatory framework in these areas into line with those elsewhere in the Community.

In line with the free movement of people, Article 42 seeks to ensure that the social security systems of member states are co-ordinated in order to provide protection for workers from other member states.

As will quickly be appreciated, the establishment of a common market required that Community-wide competition policy be put into place (see chapter 3). Article 3 of the Treaty states that there must be 'the institution of a system ensuring that competition in the common market is not distorted', and the main general provisions setting out European Community competition law are Articles 81 and 82. Article 81 provides that:

> All agreements between undertakings, decisions by associations of undertakings and concerted practices which may affect trade between member States and which have as

---

49 See P. E. Morris, S. Morrow and P. M. Spink, 'EC Law and Professional Football: *Bosman* and its Implications' (1996) 59 *MLR*.

their object or effect the prevention, restriction or distortion of competition within the common market

are prohibited. Any such agreement is 'automatically void', although there is provision for certain agreements to be exempt. These are, in general terms, agreements which contribute to improving the production or distribution of goods or promoting technical or economic progress, while allowing consumers a fair share of the resulting benefit (Article 81(3)). 'Undertakings' include any persons or organisations, whether operating as sole traders, corporations (including local authorities) or partnerships (see chapter 3). There need be no formal agreement: the European Court held in a case in 1970 that a 'gentleman's agreement' can be 'sufficient'. 'Concerted practices' means some co-ordinated co-operation between undertakings, the co-ordination being achieved through direct or indirect contact. Note that an agreement between two linked organisations, such as a parent company and its subsidiary, will not fall foul of Article 81. It must be shown that the action taken noticeably restricts competition within the Community: Article 81 does not prevent *all* agreements between businesses, but only those which affect competition to some significant degree (the *de minimis* principle).

Agreements which are caught by Article 81 would include agreements to fix prices or orchestrate price increases (for example, *Re Aniline Dyes Cartel* [50] and the consequent *ICI Ltd v Commission* [51]), or to divide up the market artificially between organisations party to the agreement.

Article 82 concerns abuse of a dominant position, and deals with monopoly and near-monopoly trading. Specifically, it states that:

> any abuse by one or more undertakings of a dominant position within the common market or in a substantial part of it shall be prohibited as incompatible with the common market in so far as it may affect trade between member States.

It will be noted that this Article does not prohibit monopolies in themselves, but rather aims at 'dominant' undertakings involved in anti-competitive conduct. The rule will apply to more than one undertaking in the same market group which, when combined, create a dominant position (the 'enterprise entity' principle). The operation and effect of Article 82 can best be appreciated by means of a case example. [52]

It is an important part of the Commission's function to investigate suspected breaches of community law, and to bring proceedings against suspected violators. United Brands Co, a worldwide concern trading in the cultivation, distribution and sale of bananas, had been found by the Commission to have abused its dominant position in the banana market within Europe. In *United Brands Co v EC Commission* in 1976, [53] a case which contains some important points of principle, the company sought to have that decision annulled.

---

50 [1969] CMLR D23.   51 [1972] CMLR 557.
52 For more recent cases see *Tetra Pak International SA v Commission* [1996] ECR 1- 5951.
53 Case 27/76 [1978] 1 CMLR 429.

238 An Introduction to Law

The first task for the court was to establish what the relevant market was. The approach to this is by means of the concept of 'product substitution', which refers to the extent to which consumers can buy, and producers supply, products similar to, or acceptable as substitutes for the product in question (in this case, bananas). Having established this, the second question was whether United Brands Co dominated the relevant market; the third, if so, whether the company had abused that dominant position in breach of Article 82. In confronting these questions, the Court had to investigate various aspects of the banana market within the European Community. As to the definition of the relevant market, could there be said to be a 'banana market' (as the Commission contended), or was the relevant market in fact better defined as a 'fresh fruit' market (as the company argued) in which bananas were sold alongside other fruit such as apples, oranges, peaches, strawberries and so on? If the court adopted the latter solution, then clearly the company's position in such a wider market would be substantially diminished. In the event, the court decided in favour of the Commission's position: that there was indeed an identifiable 'banana market' quite distinct from the more general 'fresh fruit market'. The following extracts from the court's decision indicate the reasoning which led to this conclusion:

> The applicant submits . . . that bananas compete with other fresh fruit in the same shops, on the same shelves, at prices which can be compared, satisfying the same needs: consumption as a dessert or between meals . . .
>
> The Commission maintains that there is a demand for bananas which is distinct from the demand for other fresh fruit especially as the banana is a very important part of the diet of certain sections of the community.
>
> The specific qualities of the banana influence customer preference and induce him not to readily accept other fruits as a substitute. For the banana to be regarded as forming a market which is sufficiently differentiated from other fruit markets it must be possible for it to be singled out by such special features distinguishing it from other fruits that it is only to a limited extent interchangeable with them and is only exposed to their competition in a way that is hardly perceptible. The ripening of bananas takes place the whole year round . . .
>
> Throughout the year production exceeds demand and can satisfy it at any time.
>
> Owing to this particular feature the banana is a privileged fruit and its production and marketing can be adapted to the seasoning fluctuations of other fresh fruit which are known and can be computed.
>
> There is no unavoidable seasonal substitution since the consumer can obtain this fruit all the year round.

The court considered further economic aspects of the production of and trade in bananas and concluded:

> The banana has certain characteristics, appearance, taste, softness, seedlessness, easy handling, a constant level of production which enable it to satisfy the constant needs of an important section of the population consisting of the very young, the old and the sick . . .

It follows from all these considerations that a very large number of consumers having a constant need for bananas are not noticeably or even appreciably enticed away from the consumption of this product by the arrival of other fresh fruit on the market . . .

Consequently the banana market is a market which is sufficiently distinct from the other fresh fruit markets.

The next question for the court was whether United Brands Co had a dominant position in the banana market. Noting that there was considerable variation between member states as to import, distribution and sales arrangements, the court none the less held that six member states which the Commission had defined as the relevant market[54] 'form an area which is sufficiently homogeneous to be considered in its entirety'. The term 'dominant position' was defined by the court as:

a position of economic strength enjoyed by an undertaking which enables it to prevent effective competition being maintained on the relevant market by giving it the power to behave to an appreciable extent independently of its competitors, customers and ultimately of its consumers.

The court considered the various features of the company's structure and systems of production, quality control (the company had perfected new banana-ripening methods in which it instructed the distributors/ripeners of the particular type of banana involved), transportation (the company was the only company of its kind capable of carrying two-thirds of its exports by means of its own fleet of ships), advertising, and so on; after taking into account the company's competitors and noting that 'an undertaking does not have to have eliminated all opportunity, for competition in order to be in a dominant position', the court observed that the company's market share was between 40 and 45% (several times greater than its nearest rival) and concluded that, taking all these factors and more into account: 'The cumulative effect of all the advantages enjoyed by UBC thus ensures that it has a dominant position on the relevant market.'

Finally, the court then had to consider the question as to whether United Brands Co had abused its position. The Commission had found that the company had forbidden its distributors from reselling bananas while still green: this the Commission found to be an abuse, because it effectively stopped inter-state trade in green bananas. Further, the company routinely supplied fewer bananas than the market demanded, preventing distributors from penetrating new markets: this amounted to controlling the structure of the market. The company had also stopped supplying a Danish distributor, after finding that the distributor had promoted a rival brand of banana. And finally, the Commission had argued that the company's selling prices, which differed according to the customer's member state and which were imposed at the port of entry, were unacceptable. Because these prices were fixed at the point of entry, the discrepancies could not be due to transportation costs.

---

54 Because of special factors concerning the market for bananas in these countries, Britain, France and Italy were excluded from the Commission's view of the relevant geographical market.

The court had little difficulty in holding that the company's prohibition on the resale of green bananas was an infringement of Article 82, as was the refusal to supply the Danish distributor. Of the latter, the court had this to say:

> Although it is true, as the applicant points out, that the fact that an undertaking is in a dominant position cannot disentitle it from protecting its own commercial interests if they are attacked, and that such an undertaking must be conceded the right to take such reasonable steps as it deems appropriate to protect its said interests, such behaviour cannot be countenanced if its actual purpose is to strengthen this dominant position and abuse it.
>
> Even if the possibility of a counter-attack is acceptable that attack must still be proportionate to the threat taking into account the economic strength of the undertakings confronting each other . . .
>
> Such a course of conduct amounts therefore to a serious interference with the independence of small and medium-sized firms in their commercial relations with the undertaking in a dominant position . . .

As to the fixing of differential prices at ports of entry, the court held that this practice enabled the company 'to apply dissimilar conditions to equivalent transactions with other trading parties, thereby placing them at a competitive disadvantage', and that this was, once again, an abuse of its dominant position.[55]

The *United Brands* case illustrates, among other things, the complexity of most cases brought before the European Court: it is not surprising that such cases take a considerable time to reach their conclusion.

In this chapter we have been able only to touch on the main provisions of European Community law, but it can be readily appreciated from our brief examination how far these various provisions affect the domestic legal system of the United Kingdom. In many respects, the original *economic* objectives of the European Union have for some time been spreading further into the realms of *other political* and *social* contexts. In Britain, the political debates continue about the possibility of a federal Europe, which may or may not entail a single government, economic policy and currency. Although it seems unlikely that the progress made so far towards European integration can be reversed, and it appears that the future of the European Community will involve the continued pursuit of commonality of goals – economic, social and political – between member states, the political divisions between and within member states and their governments make the extent and speed of these developments extremely difficult to predict.

---

55 Now see also *Microsoft Corporation v Commissioners* (Case T-201/04, Court of First Instance in which the Court held that Microsoft, having a dominant position in certain aspects of computer operating systems, had abused that position by, among other things, insisting that its 'Windows Media Player' software be incorporated into every sale of 'Windows' software. Microsoft was fined nearly 500m euros, though the eventual outcome of the case depends upon the result of a long-drawn-out appeal process. And early in 2006, it was announced that a number of European airlines, including British Airways, were under investigation for anti-competitive behaviour.

9

Liability in English law: the law of tort

One of the most basic functions of law in any society is to specify the situations in which a person may be legally liable, that is, answerable to the law, for his or her acts or omissions. In English law, the major areas containing the fundamental principles of liability are crime, tort and contract, all of which, together with the important area of *public-law* regulation, have been briefly introduced in earlier chapters. In this chapter and the three following, the question to be discussed may be stated as follows: in what circumstances will the infringement of a legal obligation involve the imposition of legal liability, and hence some form of legal sanction, upon the violator?

The law of tort, or *civil wrongs*, incorporates as a basic general condition of liability the proposition that a defendant is only liable if that person is in some way 'at fault'. As we saw in chapter 2, the proposition 'no liability without fault' is a general characteristic of English law: how, then, is this idea built into the law of tort?

Tort and capitalism

The high-water mark of the principle of 'no liability without fault' in English law was undoubtedly the nineteenth century. We have repeatedly noted how, in the twentieth century, the state intervened to regulate more and more areas of social and economic life, but the nineteenth century – the period of economic individualism and *laisser-faire* – saw minimal state interference with the business and commercial life of the community. The best example of *laisser-faire* as reflected in the law is probably the law of contract, discussed fully in chapter 11. Contract law, as developed by the judges during the period, rested on the assumption that private individuals were best left to regulate and look after their own affairs and interests, the law only intervening where there had been some breach of legal obligation by a person who had voluntarily undertaken that obligation through a freely negotiated contract.[1]

With regard to the development of conditions of liability in tort, Fleming has pointed out that the nineteenth century saw an increase not only in traffic

---

1 See P. S. Atiyah, *The Rise and Fall of Freedom of Contract* (1979, Oxford); and see chapter 11.

accidents, but also, and at the time perhaps more importantly, in accidents at work.

> Both posed serious problems for the law of torts whose main preoccupation had hitherto been occasional assaults, defamation, boundary disputes, noxious neighbours, trespassing cattle and the like. Because Parliament was otherwise preoccupied, it fell to the courts to deal with the challenges of the new industrial society. By and large, their response was to try and contain the flood by raising the barriers to recovery.[2]

As far as industrial accidents were concerned, the area of tort which was usually invoked in the attempt to gain compensation was *negligence*, and in dealing with such claims, the courts worked on the same assumptions that underpinned the development of the law of contract: individuals entered into employment contracts voluntarily and freely, and therefore must be taken, in some cases, to have voluntarily taken on the risk of injury. Having done so, they were to be debarred from complaining about it later by the courts' application of the maxim *volenti non fit injuria*.[3] In other cases, the victims' own carelessness (or *contributory* negligence), which frequently contributed to their accidents, was held to prevent their recovering compensation;[4] whilst the development of the doctrine of *common employment*, whereby an employer could not be held liable to an employee for the wrongful acts of a fellow employee, effectively prevented many victims of industrial accidents from gaining compensation.[5] These responses, which rendered the law of tort rather less effective than it might have been in the provision of compensation for personal injury, were not merely the outcome of legalistic assumptions about the contract of employment; an equally important reason for these judicial responses was grounded in economic considerations. If these actions for compensation were to be allowed to succeed, who was to bear the cost, and on what principles?

> It was felt to be in the better interest of an advancing economy to subordinate the security of individuals, who happened to become casualties of the new machine age, rather than fetter enterprise by loading it with cost of 'inevitable' accidents. Liability for faultless causation was feared to impede progress because it gave the individual no opportunity for avoiding liability by being careful and this confronted him with the

---

2 J. G. Fleming, 'The Pearson Report: Its "Strategy"' (1979) *MLR* at 250.
3 See, for example, *Thomas v Quartermaine* (1887) 18 QBD 685; and *Membery v Great Western Rly Co* (1889) 14 App Cas 179.
4 Under the old law, the loss lay where it fell: the establishment of the plaintiff's contributory negligence was a bar to recovering any compensation. Today, the position is as provided by the Law Reform (Contributory Negligence) Act 1945, whereby a negligent plaintiff is not precluded from recovery, although damages will be reduced in proportion to the extent to which the plaintiff is held to be to blame for the accident. For examples, see *Froom v Butcher* [1976] QB 286 (passenger's failure to wear car seat-belt held to be contributory negligence); *Sayers v Harlow UDC* [1958] 1 WLR 623 (plaintiff, trapped in a public lavatory by a faulty door lock, attempted to climb out; held contributorily negligent not for attempting to escape, but for the manner in which she attempted it).
5 See *Priestley v Fowler* (1837) 3 M & W 1; also *Hutchinson v York, Newcastle and Berwick Rly Co* (1850) 5 Exch 343.

unpalatable choice of either giving up his projected activity or shouldering the cost of any resulting injury.[6]

The law of tort as a means of allocating responsibility for harmful activity has attracted much attention from economists, who have produced analyses of tort law seeking to assess the efficiency of the law from the point of view of economic theory.[7] The 'economic approach to law' proceeds from the basic economic theory of supply and demand: in a perfect competitive market within a capitalist system, if demand for a particular commodity exceeds supply, then the price of that commodity will rise, and if supply exceeds demand, the price will fall, until the point is reached where supply and demand are in equilibrium and customers obtain the goods they want at a price they are prepared to pay. Naturally, this model assumes that the price of the commodity reflects the cost of producing that commodity, and takes into account the cost of raw materials, resources used in production and so on. If the price does not reflect such factors then the price will be too low, and this means that there has been an inefficient use of resources.

Suppose, however, that X, the manufacturer of a particular commodity, produces a certain amount of pollution in the process of manufacture, and this pollution has a harmful effect on Y, who occupies land adjoining X's factory. In the absence of any legal rules regarding liability for the pollution, how would X and Y deal with the situation? According to Coase,[8] in a perfectly competitive market situation, the harm caused to Y would lead Y to negotiate with X for a reduction in the level of pollution. From X's point of view, the installation of equipment to prevent pollution would incur a cost, which in turn would have to be incorporated into the price of the product, which might lead to a fall in sales, and hence to a decrease in profit. Similarly, if X were to offer to compensate Y for the harm, then that compensation, too, would have to be taken into account in the price of the product, with identical results. But suppose Y were to pay X in exchange for a reduction in pollution by X? Here, if Y's payment exceeded the cost to X of reducing the level of pollution, then X would accept that payment and reduce the pollution, because X's profits would not be affected. X and Y would bargain along these lines until an agreement was reached whereby Y's payment to X corresponded with the cost to X of reducing – the point of equilibrium, and the point at which X would be said to be operating with the 'socially efficient' level of pollution (that is, an allocation of resources which is efficient from the point of view of all concerned).

Continuing Coase's analysis: suppose now that the law becomes involved, and requires X to compensate Y for the harm caused by the pollution. X must now consider the cost of compensating Y, as compared with the profit made by means of the pollution-causing production process. Coase argued that when *all* the profit had to

6 J. G. Fleming, *The Law of Torts* (9th edn., 1998, Sweet and Maxwell), p 7.
7 See P. Burrows and C. G. Veljanovski (eds), *The Economic Approach to Law* (1981, Butterworths), esp the introductory essay by the authors; Atiyah's *Accidents, Compensation and the Law* (6th edn. by P. Cane, 1999, Butterworths), chapter 18.
8 R. Coase, 'The Problem of Social Cost' (1960) 3 *Journal of Law and Economics.*

be paid to Y as compensation, X would cease to increase the level of pollution, and once again, the 'socially-efficient' level of harm would be produced. It should be noted that 'socially efficient' does *not* imply the complete cessation of pollution: that would be inefficient from X's point of view. From the 'Coase theorem', a number of conclusions follow. First, the analysis suggests that the intervention of law and the allocation of legal duties and rights to compensation would not affect the final outcome, because the parties would continue to bargain around the legal provisions until the 'social efficiency' level was reached. Second, the theorem assumes that the parties negotiate within a perfectly competitive market situation. This assumes in turn that there are no costs to the parties incurred within the process of negotiation itself ('transaction costs'). In practice there will be a number of costs attaching to the transaction, such as the cost of obtaining information, and perhaps the retention of lawyers to conduct the negotiations and so on. It is true to say that this analysis draws particular attention to the factor of transaction costs and acknowledges that the law may have a role to perform in regulating the allocation of such costs, but it is not clear which criteria might be used in the process of allocation.

Third, the analysis fails to take into account any values other than economic ones. For example, it might be the case that as a matter of general social policy it is preferable for the law to strive to eradicate all industrial pollution in the interests of the environment, rather than to permit a level of pollution which is decided by means of an economic efficiency criterion. Fourth, it often happens that those at risk from harm caused by others are in no position to bargain, either because they lack sufficient bargaining-power or because (as in the case of most road accidents) their relationship is not a permanent one, but is casual, fortuitous and fleeting. The 'Coase theorem' may be thought to underplay the role of the law in favour of 'market regulation' mechanisms, but surely the law in this area has a part to play in the allocation of liability; that is, in the allocation of resources to be used to compensate for or prevent harmful activities? Many would argue, for instance, that the law of tort fulfils, to some extent at any rate, a *deterrent* function: by imposing liability on those who might cause harm, such persons are encouraged to take steps to prevent that harm and so avoid liability.

Calabresi[9] pursued this approach in the field of law relating to accidents, arguing that the 'principal function of accident law is to reduce the sum of the cost of accidents and the cost of avoiding accidents'.[10] The law of negligence, he argues, does this by imposing liability on the 'cheapest cost avoider'.[11] This view amounts to the proposition that the law here constitutes a deterrent to potential accident-causers by imposing liability on those who are in the best position to avoid the accidents. Thus,

9 G. Calabresi, *The Costs of Accidents: A Legal and Economic Analysis* (1970, Yale University Press).
10 Ibid., p 24.
11 Defined by Calabresi as the party who is in the best position to make the cost-benefit analysis between accident and accident avoidance, and to act on that decision once it is made.

If we can determine the costs of accidents and allocate them to the activities which cause them, the prices of activities will reflect their accident costs, and people in deciding whether or not to engage in particular activities will be influenced by the accident costs each activity involves. They will be influenced without having to think about it, for the accident costs will simply be a part of the price which will affect whether they buy one product or engage in one activity rather than another . . . if manufacturers of cars without seat belts were charged the accident costs which resulted from the absence of belts, no federal law would be needed requiring seat belts. A beltless car would save the cost of the belt, but bear the accident costs which resulted; a car with a belt would save on accident costs but bear the cost of putting in a belt. The decision as to whether belts were worth it would be made by buyers in the light of the price of each kind of car. The question whether safety sells would be given a market answer rather than the purely conjectural one to which we have become accustomed.[12]

For such a theory to work, we must be able to identify the activities which cause the accidents, and the extent of these activities must be responsive to the price mechanisms.[13] Atiyah argued that there are many forms of harm (such as diseases) which cannot be traced to particular activities; and some forms of harm which, though attributable to particular activities, are not reducible by means of general deterrence because the activity in question is not susceptible to the price mechanisms. To use his example: smoking is known to be a cause of lung cancer, but continuous price increases on cigarettes through taxes have not appeared to affect sales very much.

Furthermore, it may be very difficult, at the outset, to place costs on particular activities or the harm they create: in many cases, placing a price upon an activity or a harmful effect is highly artificial. And again, exactly who is to bear these costs? Taking the example of road accidents, from the fourth edition of Atiyah's *Accidents, Compensation and the Law*:

> . . . why should we treat motoring as an activity, rather than break it down into various sub-categories, such as driving for pleasure, driving to the pub, driving to work . . . and so forth. Secondly, many road accidents involve non-motorists, such as pedestrians, or cyclists. What, if anything, enables us to say that these accidents should be treated as part of the activity of motoring rather than walking or cycling? . . . In terms of 'cause' . . . vehicle manufacturers and designers and road makers are just as responsible as motorists for most road accidents. There is a good deal of evidence to suggest that the number and costs of road accidents could be reduced more effectively by concentrating on road improvements and on vehicle design, than by worrying about the motorist. How then can general deterrence work, unless we have some idea how to allocate the cost of road accidents between these various activities and causes?[14]

So far, theories such as those of Calabresi have received much critical appraisal, though little, at least in the United Kingdom, in the way of practical application. It

---

12 G. Calabresi in R. Keeton, J. O'Connell and J. McCord (eds), *Crisis in Car Insurance* (1968, University of Illinois Press), pp 243–244.
13 Atiyah, 6th edn. by P. Cane, op. cit., chapter 18.   14 Atiyah, 4th edn., op. cit., p 512.

may well be that the tort system does, in fact, incorporate within its framework and functions the objectives of general deterrence, at least in so far as is compatible with the principles of fault liability; but the law has not yet gone so far as to impose any generalised duties or liabilities upon enterprises which can often be shown, at least in part, to have contributed to accident causation. Some of the reasons for this, perhaps, can be found in the analysis of the relationship between tort law and capitalism presented by Abel.

Abel has argued that there is a particular relationship between tort law and capitalism.[15] Though basing his discussion on American tort law, he suggests that his critique is equally applicable to other capitalist societies. His thesis is that, 'because capitalists have to maximise profit in a competitive market, they must sacrifice the health and safety of others – workers, consumers, those affected by environmental danger'.[16] Thus capitalism encourages injury, and tort law reflects this in various ways.

One effect of capitalism, argues Abel, is to reduce interpersonal relationships to those based on capitalist economics (the employment contract, whereby workers sell their labour for wages; the lawyer-client relationship, whereby the lawyer's services are bought and sold; and private health care systems – the norm in the United States, and increasingly encouraged in Britain despite the well-established National Health Service – whereby medical services, too, are subject to market forces operating on a privatised system). In addition, mass production and consumer consumption of goods thus produced creates an environment in which money and property are seen as the commodities having the highest value: 'hence money damages come to be seen as adequate compensation'.[17] Finally, says Abel, the logic of the use of money damages for injury is extended to compensation for pain, suffering, emotional distress, wrongful death and loss of consortium. Thus 'tort law under capitalism equates money with labour, possessions, care, emotional and physical integrity, and ultimately love'.[18]

Abel's argument, deriving from Marxism, is summarised thus:

> The lawyer . . . combines his expertise with the victim's injury (as the capitalist combines his capital with the worker's labour) to create a tort (a commodity) that has exchange value both in the state-created market (the court) and in the dependent markets it spawns (negotiated settlement). The lawyer (like the capitalist) exercises total control over this process; the victim (like the worker) has virtually no say over which torts are produced or how they are produced. When the transaction is complete, the victim receives the bare minimum necessary for survival (or less) and the lawyer takes the rest as a fee (the capitalist expropriation of surplus value) . . .[19]

It may be that Abel overstates his case here. To begin with, the English experience does not seem to bear out the idea of victims accepting only 'the bare minimum'. Cane has noted that 'awards in cases of serious and long-term injuries causing

15 R. L. Abel, 'Torts' in D. Kairys (ed.), *The Politics of Law: A Progressive Critique* (1982, Pantheon Books).   16 Ibid., p 188.   17 Ibid., p 187.   18 Ibid.   19 Ibid., p 188.

severe disablement are very great indeed. The largest lump sum awarded in a personal injuries action to date is in the region of £9 million'[20] and although he acknowledges that such increases are no more than might be expected if awards are to stay in line with the cost of living, it remains true that those receiving compensation through the tort system gain much more than those receiving compensation or benefit through any other system. Second, is it accurate to speak of the lawyer having 'total' control over the tort process? There is a great deal of control, but the victim/client initiates the proceedings, and is the one who decides, albeit on the lawyer's advice, whether to accept or refuse any out-of-court settlement which the defendant may offer. Third, we might question the extent to which the tort system and the legal procedures involved therein are unique to capitalism. Arguably the relationship between lawyers and clients which, as we will argue later (see chapter 13), is one based largely on power, is likely to be found in any society having a developed legal system relying on the provision of expert advice and representation, whatever its economic system.

Abel goes on to identify and discuss three general features of tort law under capitalism. First, there is the question of discrimination on the grounds of class, race and gender. Those less well off may for various reasons be less inclined to consult lawyers in the event of an actionable injury than the well-to-do (see chapter 13); different social classes and sections within them differentially face the risk of injury in the workplace and the home, and in terms of the risks inherent in goods and services which may be of poor quality but are all that can be afforded. Industrial injuries are more likely to be channelled into industrial injury compensation schemes than the tort system, the benefits being rather less than might be the case after a successful tort action,[21] and those injured at home are unlikely to have any redress from the tort system unless the injury fell within a known head of liability, such as injury caused by defective goods. There is inequality, too, between road-users of different social classes:

> Imagine a car crash between A, who is unemployed and drives a worthless jalopy, and B, who owns a Rolls-Royce and earns a high income. If A is negligent and B non-negligent, A will have to pay for the damage to the Rolls and to B's earning capacity. But if B is negligent and A non-negligent, B will have to pay virtually nothing . . . If we make the hypothetical more realistic by giving both parties liability insurance the inequality remains: A's insurance premium will have to reflect the possibility of injury to B, and be higher than would be necessary to protect A and others like him, whereas B's premium will reflect the possibility of an injury to A, and be lower than would be necessary to protect a world of Bs. A thus pays part of the cost of protecting the privileges of B.[22]

---

20 Atiyah, 6th edn., by P. Cane, op. cit., p 143.   21 Abel, op. cit., pp 284–290.
22 Abel, op. cit., p 190. Also noteworthy is the fact that legal aid is not available for actions brought for defamation: it might be said that only those who can afford legal services have the privilege of protecting their reputation through the law.

On examination, these assertions cannot stand without some qualification. The first part of the argument may be true; but if we consider the second proposition concerning insurance premiums payable by A and B, the reality is that there are far more As than Bs, and so the insurance premiums payable by both parties will reflect the statistical likelihood of damage to Rolls-Royce cars as compared with cars of far less value, thus tending to *depress*, not inflate, A's premium. And let us not forget that B's insurance premium too must reflect the possibility of damage by B to *another* Rolls-Royce, as well as 'worthless jalopies'! We all know that, in fact, A will pay far less in insurance premium than will B: the reality of the situation is thus far less unequal than may first appear, although it must be conceded that the relative wealth of A and B will be such as to reduce the impact of the cost to B as compared to A.

Turning to a second concern – that of the production by capitalism of illness and injury – Abel considers that the pursuit of profit, and the accompanying drive to minimise expenditure in ways which will *not* return profit, mean that 'the capitalist . . . *must* be as unsafe as he can get away with being'.[23] To the extent that business entrepreneurs may be held liable for injury which is caused by their negligence, the financial compensation payable to the victim will in most cases be no deterrent against further negligence by the entrepreneur, because the amount paid out is recoverable in most cases by passing on the liability costs to the consumer in the form of higher prices for the goods or services which that entrepreneur provides. And businesses will tend to weigh the cost of safety against the cost of legal liability. It may be cheaper to pay out compensation in the event of injury caused by a faulty product than to incur expenditure in withdrawing or modifying that product and making it safe. Thus – using Abel's illustrations – the Ford Motor Corporation in the United States manufactured a car with a petrol tank it knew to be unsafe, and American Airlines flew a DC-10 plane which later crashed, despite their knowledge of a faulty component. As Abel argues:

> The capitalist response to the threat of tort liability is to strive to externalise accident costs by concealing information . . ., threatening retaliation against those who seek compensation, and using the enormous resources of the enterprise . . . to coerce victims into accepting inadequate settlements, to overwhelm them in litigation, and to pass legislation that immunises the enterprise from liability costs . . .[24]

The latter device is not far removed, of course, from the common-law responses to industrial injury claims in nineteenth-century England: to prevent their success by means of the doctrine of common employment, and the principles of contributory negligence and voluntary assumption of risk.

The third aspect of tort law and capitalism which Abel discusses is that of the reproduction of bourgeois ideology. Centrally, the insistence within tort law upon

---

23 Abel, ibid., p 190.
24 Ibid., p 192. The Ford Pinto case is reported as *Grimshaw v Ford Motor Co* (1981) 174 Cal Rep 348. For a discussion of other multiple disasters where negligence on the part of corporations has been alleged, see C. Pugh and M. Day, 'Toxic Torts' (1991) *New Law Journal*, 15 and 22 November.

proof of a defendant's fault reinforces the element within bourgeois ideology of *individualism*. In fact, says Abel, tort law sustains individualism at the expense of social and economic reality: the fact that wrongs are caused 'by the confluence of multiple, ongoing, collective entities'.[25] Furthermore, tort law, by compensating property-owners for property damage, upholds the capitalist conception of private property and its place as a central social value: 'tort law proclaims the class structure of a capitalist society: you are what you own, what you earn, and what you do'.[26] And tort law, by providing money damages for non-pecuniary losses (such as pain and suffering), also translates human experiences into commodities having a cash value.

A recurring theme throughout Abel's critique is the way in which tort law functions on the premise that money compensation is appropriate for the victims of tortious acts or omissions. The main remedies available in tort will be discussed presently, along with some proposals for reform, but it is appropriate at this point to say more about the more important heads of tortious liability.

Liability in tort

Tort – the law of civil wrongs – encompasses a wide range of different heads of liability, each with its own conditions of liability. It includes liability for trespass (the intentional[27] invasion of personal or property-rights); for statements which damage someone's reputation (libel and slander); for damage caused by animals or by fire; for loss resulting from false statements (deceit, negligent misstatements[28]); and for loss or damage caused by dangerous premises. The tort of private nuisance is concerned with the *unreasonable interference* by one person with another's enjoyment of his or her land, and frequently involves not an intentional and intrinsically unlawful act of a defendant as much as the unreasonable encroachment by the defendant upon a plaintiff's enjoyment of property caused by the former's *lawful* activity.[29] For example, in *Sturges v Bridgman* in 1879[30] the defendant operated a confectioner's business and the plaintiff alleged that the noise from the defendant's machinery interfered with his practice as a physician. The court held that such interference was indeed unreasonable and amounted to nuisance. It is true, however, that a defendant may commit this tort by means of

25 Ibid., p 194.   26 Ibid., p 195.
27 In *Fowler v Lanning* [1959] 1 QB 426 it was suggested that trespass to the person may be committed negligently. On the basis of dicta in the later cases of *Letang v Cooper* [1965] 1 QB 232, per Lord Denning and *Wilson v Pringle* [1987] QB 237, however, the better view seems to be that unintentional (ie negligently inflicted) injury would attract liability in negligence, leaving trespass exclusively concerned with intentional harm. See the recent case of *Blake v Galloway* [2004] EWCA Civ 814.
28 *Hedley Byrne & Co Ltd v Heller & Partners Ltd* [1964] AC 465; negligent misstatement is discussed more fully below.
29 See C. Gearty, 'The place of private nuisance in a modern law of torts' (1989) *CLJ* 214.
30 (1879) 11 Ch D 852. And see, for example, *Halsey v Esso Petroleum Co* [1961] 1 WLR 683; *Bridlington Relay Ltd v Yorkshire Electricity Board* [1965] Ch 436; *Cambridge Water Co Ltd v Eastern Counties Leather plc* [1994] 1 All ER 53.

an element of deliberate maliciousness, as where the neighbour of a music teacher, resenting the noise made in the course of music lessons, retaliated by making various cacophonous noises during the lessons simply to annoy the teacher (*Christie v Davey*, 1893).[31]

Space does not permit a detailed discussion of all the heads of tortious liability, and the reader is referred to the various texts in this area.[32] Probably the single most important area of tort liability today, however, is that of *negligence*, concerned with liability for personal injury caused not intentionally, but through the defendant's negligent acts or omissions. The numerical predominance of claims arising from personal injury over those involving other, older areas of tortious liability was established in the nineteenth century, and this pattern remains today; the great majority of tort claims concern either accidents at work or injuries sustained in road accidents.[33] We shall see later that tort is one of a number of systems for providing compensation for injury. However, before considering the place of the tort system in the context of these other systems, it is important to appreciate the specific conditions of liability in negligence, as developed, in the main, by the courts, in order to understand the importance of this area of law in modern society.

The classic formulation of the law of negligence is that of Alderson B in *Blyth v Birmingham Waterworks Co* in 1856: 'Negligence is the omission to do something which a reasonable man, guided upon those considerations which ordinarily regulate the conduct of human affairs, would do, or doing something which a prudent and reasonable man would not do.'[34] The negligent person, then, not only could but *should* have adopted an alternative course of action or inaction from the one which was followed. The fact that a person followed a wrongful or 'unreasonable' course of conduct is, then, evidence of *fault* – of 'negligence'.

The requirement that fault should constitute the basic condition of liability in negligence, although well established many years previously, received its most lucid and well-known formulation in 1932 in the case of *Donoghue v Stevenson* (see chapter 4). The case concerned the liability of a manufacturer to a consumer injured as a result of a defective product, and the relationship between the plaintiff and the defendant was explained by Lord Atkin in the House of Lords:

> The rule that you are to love your neighbour becomes in law, you must not injure your neighbour; and the lawyer's question, who is my neighbour? receives a restricted reply. You must take reasonable care to avoid acts or omissions which you can reasonably foresee would be likely to injure your neighbour. Who, then, in law is my neighbour?

31 [1893] 1 Ch 316. See also *Hollywood Silver Fox Farm v Emmett* [1936] 2 KB 468.
32 See, for example, *Winfield and Jolowicz on Tort* (17th edn. by W. V. H. Rogers, 2006, Sweet and Maxwell); J. Murphy, *Street on Torts* (11th edn. 2003, Oxford University Press); V. Harpwood, *Modern Tort Law* (6th edn. 2005, Cavendish); M. Jones, *Textbook on Torts* (8th edn. 2002, Oxford University Press); B. Markesinis and S. Deakin, *Tort Law* (5th edn. 2003, Oxford University Press); M. Lunney and K. Oliphant, *Tort Law: Text and Materials* (2nd edn. 2003, Oxford University Press).
33 See the *Report* of the Royal Commission on Civil Liability and Compensation for Personal Injury (the Pearson Report) (Cmnd 7054, 1978, HMSO); and Atiyah, op. cit.
34 (1856) 11 Exch 781 at 784.

The answer seems to be – persons who are so closely and directly affected by my act that I ought reasonably to have them in contemplation as being so affected when I am directing my mind to the acts or omissions which are called in question.[35]

His Lordship went on to formulate the general legal principles of liability for negligently manufactured products:

a manufacturer of products, which he sells in such a form as to show that they left him with no reasonable possibility of intermediate examination, and with the knowledge that the absence of reasonable care in the preparation or putting up of the products will result in an injury to the consumer's life or property, owes a duty to the consumer to take reasonable care.[36]

Now, we noted previously that this principle has been modified through later cases, and that liability has been extended to cover various articles and to persons other than just manufacturers. Although, as we shall see later, manufacturers' liability for injuries caused by defective products is now regulated by statute, the general principle enunciated in *Donoghue v Stevenson* has for many years governed claims for compensation for injuries suffered by consumers as a result of defectively made, serviced or repaired products, and has also formed the basis of the modern law of negligence generally.

The key words in the above quotations from Lord Atkin's judgment are 'duty', 'reasonable care' and 'reasonably foreseeable'; and these are the concepts which the judges have used to decide liability in later cases. For example, a negligent motor-cyclist who had caused a serious road accident was held to owe no duty to a plaintiff who suffered injuries as a result of seeing the aftermath of the accident because no risk of direct physical harm to her was 'reasonably foreseeable' (*Bourhill v Young*, 1943).[37] In another case, injuries were suffered by a blind person who fell into a hole in the street, dug by the defendants' workmen, around which there were, it was held, inadequate precautions for the protection of blind people. The defendants were held liable to the victim because a sufficient number of blind people walk on the streets to make it 'reasonably foreseeable' that such an injury would ensue if adequate precautions were not taken (*Haley v London Electricity Board*, 1965).[38] In a third case, damage caused to the plaintiff's yacht by a number of borstal trainees who escaped from supervision owing to the alleged negligence of the borstal officers was held to be actionable because a duty of care was owed by the officers to the plaintiffs (*Home Office v Dorset Yacht Co*, 1970).[39] In the recent case of *Vowles v Evans*[40] in 2002 it was held that the referee of a rugby game owed a duty of care to the players to take steps to enforce the rules of the game: it was held to be fair, just and reasonable (see below) that players should rely on the referee to ensure that the rules of such a potentially dangerous game are enforced. And as a final example: it has been held in a number of cases that if someone by their negligence creates a dangerous situation which

35 [1932] AC 562 at 580.   36 Ibid., at 599.   37 [1943] AC 92.   38 [1965] AC 778.
39 [1970] AC 1004. See chapter 4.   40 [2002] EWHC 2612 (QB).

harms, or threatens to harm, someone, then not only is a duty owed to that 'primary' victim, but also to someone who comes along to try to rescue that victim, as long as such an act by the rescuer is reasonably foreseeable.[41] The duty to the rescuer is quite independent of the duty owed to the primary victim.[42]

In recent cases the courts have pointed out that the way in which the duty principle has been extended to new situations has generally been by examining the new case in the light of previous decisions – developing the law case-by-case and by analogy with the precedents. Given a particular set of facts and the established case law, the courts would ask whether the defendant, given the foresight of a 'reasonable man', ought to have appreciated that by failing to take 'reasonable care', he or she might 'reasonably foreseeably' have caused injury to the plaintiff.

Signs of a more generalised approach first appeared in 1970, in the *Dorset Yacht* case, noted above, in which Lord Reid, discussing Lord Atkin's formulation of the duty principle, expressed the view that 'the time has come when we can and should say that [the Atkin test] should apply unless there is some justification or valid explanation for its exclusion'.[43] This view was taken further in the judgment of Lord Wilberforce in *Anns v Merton London Borough Council* (1978)[44] as follows:

> First one has to ask whether, as between the alleged wrongdoer and the person who has suffered damage, there is a sufficient relationship of proximity or neighbourhood such that, in the reasonable contemplation of the former, carelessness on his part may be likely to cause damage to the latter – in which case a prima facie duty of care arises. Secondly, if the first question is answered affirmatively, it is necessary to consider whether there are any considerations which ought to negative, or to reduce or limit the scope of the duty or the class of person to whom it is owed, or the damages to which a breach of it may give rise.[45]

This formulation, it will be noticed, treated as synonymous the concepts of 'proximity' and 'neighbourhood', both rooted in Lord Atkin's concept of 'reasonable foreseeability'. In essence, this general test would place a duty of care on all defendants where it was reasonably foreseeable that their carelessness might cause damage to the plaintiff, *unless* considerations such as those of public policy persuaded the court otherwise.

In a series of negligence cases during the 1980s, the *Anns* formulation came under increasing attack. In *Governors of the Peabody Donation Fund v Sir Lindsay Parkinson and Co Ltd* in 1984,[46] Lord Keith stated that the test as to whether a duty existed in any given case was dependent upon an analysis of the *specific* facts of the case, and that a material consideration would be whether it was 'just and reasonable'[47] to impose such a duty. This narrowing-down of the *Anns* test was reiterated by the House of Lords in 1987 in *Curran v Northern Ireland Co-Ownership Housing*

---

41 See *Haynes v Harwood* [1935] 1 KB 146; *Baker v T. E. Hopkins & Son Ltd* [1959] 3 All ER 225.
42 *Videan v British Transport Commission* [1963] 2 QB 650.   43 [1970] AC 1004 at p 1027.
44 [1978] AC 728.   45 [1978] AC 728 at pp 751–752.   46 [1984] 3 WLR 953.
47 [1984] 3 WLR at p 960.

Association Ltd,[48] and in *Yuen Kun-yeu v A-G of Hong Kong,*[49] where Lord Keith suggested that:

> the two-stage test formulated by Lord Wilberforce for determining the existence of a duty of care in negligence has been elevated to a degree of importance greater than it merits, and greater perhaps than its author intended . . . Foreseeability of harm is a necessary ingredient of . . . a relationship [which may give rise to a duty of care] but it is not the only one. Otherwise there would be liability in negligence on the part of one who sees another about to walk over a cliff with his head in the air, and forbears to shout a warning.[50]

His Lordship stressed that everything depended upon all the circumstances of any particular case, and that in addition there may well be public policy considerations which may negative a duty of care: given a particular set of facts, *ought* the law to impose a duty upon the defendant?

We have already seen examples of the operation of public policy considerations. Lord Keith's hypothetical situation of the careless cliff-walker above can be accommodated by the principle of policy that in negligence there is in general (and subject to some exceptions) no duty to act positively for the benefit of others, no matter what the morality of the situation may require. This point was reiterated in *Stovin v Wise (Norfolk County Council, third party)*[51] in 1996, though there are recent cases which suggest that, at least in certain circumstances, a duty to act positively may arise,[52] and it may be that the matter will need reconsideration in the light of the Human Rights Act 1998, at least in respect of public bodies. We will discuss further the impact of the Human Rights Act presently.

Other examples of cases clearly involving public policy would include *Donoghue v Stevenson* itself; and in the *Dorset Yacht* case (considered above, chapter 4), the court had to consider the defendants' argument that the imposition of a duty of care upon borstal supervisors might impede the proper functioning of the borstal system (supervisors would be reluctant to take trainees out of the institutions as part of their training for fear of legal repercussions should any damage be done) and that this would, clearly, militate against the public interest in the efficient operation of the borstal system. The position of the police and the emergency services has been considered in a number of recent cases in which public policy has played a prominent part, and these decisions are reviewed separately, below.

Clearly, it is well-established that public policy considerations may be taken into account by the courts in deciding whether a duty of care exists, and that such considerations may, indeed, negative, reduce or limit the scope of the duty of care in particular circumstances. The *Anns* formulation of the test for the duty received a further major blow by the House of Lords in *Caparo Industries plc v Dickman*

48 [1987] 2 All ER 13.   49 [1987] 2 All ER 705.   50 [1987] 2 All ER 705 at p 710.
51 [1996] 3 All ER 801. And see J. Conaghan and W. Mansell, *The Wrongs of Tort* (1993, Pluto Press), esp. chapter 2.
52 See, for example, *Kent v Griffiths and others* [2001] QB 36; and see discussion below on the liability of emergency services.

in 1990,[53] where Lord Bridge, discussing the major decisions where the test for the duty of care was considered, concluded that:

> Since *Anns*'s case a series of decisions of the Privy Council and of your Lordships House, notably in judgments and speeches delivered by Lord Keith, have emphasised the inability of any single general principle to provide a practical test which can be applied to every situation to determine whether a duty of care is owed and, if so, what is its scope . . . What emerges is that, in addition to the foreseeability of damage, necessary ingredients in any situation giving rise to a duty of care are that there should exist between the party owing the duty and the party to whom it is owed a relationship characterised by the law as one of 'proximity' or 'neighbourhood' and that the situation should be one in which the court considers it fair, just and reasonable that the law should impose a duty . . .[54]

It is most important, when considering this passage, to bear in mind that Lord Bridge was not here discussing the special problems of negligent misstatement causing financial loss (the issue with which the facts of *Caparo* were concerned) but rather the *general* test for the duty of care in negligence.

Anns was finally killed off in the summer of 1990 by the House of Lords in *Murphy v Brentwood District Council*[55] in which *Anns* was 'departed from', and the earlier decision in 1972 of the Court of Appeal in *Dutton v Bognor Regis UDC*[56] was held to have been wrongly decided. Lord Wilberforce's test for the duty of care has not survived. The present test for the existence of a duty of care is that of Lord Bridge in *Caparo*, and so it is necessary to consider that formulation in a little more detail. According to Lord Bridge three components must be present before a duty of care will be owed. These are:

(i)   the foreseeability of damage;

(ii)   the relationship of 'proximity' between defendant and plaintiff; and

(iii)   the proposition that it is fair, just and reasonable to impose a duty upon the defendant as regards the plaintiff in the circumstances of the case.

The first and third elements of this formulation give rise to no particular conceptual difficulty. Foreseeability of damage has, ever since *Donoghue v Stevenson*, been accepted as an essential ingredient, and the 'fair, just and reasonable' element is another way of stating the established proposition that public policy plays an important part in the deliberations of the courts in deciding whether a duty should or should not be owed. In fact, the first and third elements of Lord Bridge's formulation are very similar indeed to Lord Wilberforce's formulation in *Anns*.

It is the second element – the 'proximity' relationship – which poses problems for a number of reasons. First of all, many cases involving physical harm[57] from *Donoghue* onwards have proceeded on the basis that 'proximity' is synonymous with 'reasonable foreseeability'. It is clear, however, that Lord Bridge regards the

---

53 [1990] 1 All ER 568.   54 [1990] 1 All ER 568 at 573–574.   55 [1991] 1 AC 398.
56 [1972] 1 QB 373.   57 As opposed to economic loss or psychological harm: see below.

two concepts as having distinct meanings. This is consistent with the determined separating-out of the two concepts by the judges in England and elsewhere[58] throughout the 1980s. But it begs the question as to how, precisely, 'proximity' is defined.

The judgments in *Caparo* offer little by way of help on this point. Lord Bridge himself acknowledges that 'the concepts of proximity and fairness embodied in these additional ingredients are not susceptible of any such precise definition as would be necessary to give them utility as practical tests'.[59] There is no doubt that the use by Lord Bridge of the term 'proximity' in his formulation of the requirements for a duty in negligence has muddied these conceptual waters considerably. It is true enough that a number of passages appear in judgments in various recent cases which stress that the notions of 'foreseeability', 'proximity' and 'fair, just and reasonable' are merely pragmatic conceptual tools which are not susceptible of precise definition and which simply highlight the essentially flexible nature of the legal notion of 'duty' in tort generally. The following example is typical:

> Indeed, it is difficult to resist a conclusion that what have been treated as three separate requirements are, at least in most cases, in fact merely facets of the same thing, for in some cases the degree of foreseeability is such that it is from that alone that the requisite proximity can be deduced, whilst in others the absence of that essential relationship can most rationally be attributed simply to the court's view that it would not be fair and reasonable to hold the defendant responsible.[60]

Indeed, it is strongly arguable that in negligence cases involving physical harm where, *despite foreseeability*, no duty was held to exist, the reasons for this conclusion have almost invariably been 'public policy' considerations.[61] Certainly, some judges seemed, immediately after *Caparo*, to be of the opinion that the three-pronged test in that case was inapplicable to cases involving physical harm. Thus in *B v Islington Health Authority* in 1991,[62] a case involving physical harm, Potts J in the High Court alluded to the *Caparo* speeches by Lord Bridge and Lord Oliver, pointed out that that case (not the speeches!) was concerned with economic loss, and continued:

> Thus I proceed on the basis that the nature of the duty of care in cases involving physical injury and consequential loss remains as it was before the decisions of the House

---

58 Two Australian cases are worthy of mention here. In *Jaensch v Coffey* (1984) 54 ALR 417, a case concerning liability for psychiatric harm, there is in the judgment of Deane J an interesting but tortuous argument in support of the alleged distinction between foreseeability and proximity in Lord Atkin's speech in *Donoghue*; and in the course of his judgment in *Sutherland Shire Council v Heyman* (1985) 60 ALR 1, Brennan J said that 'it is preferable, in my view, that the law should develop novel categories of negligence incrementally and by analogy with established categories, rather than by a massive extension of a prima facie duty of care restrained only by indefinable "considerations which ought to negative, or to reduce or limit the scope of the duty or the class of person to whom it is owed"' – a statement which clearly calls for a return to the case-by-case approach, and which it seems to have become *de rigeur* for the English judiciary to cite with approval.   59 [1990] 1 All ER 568 at 574.
60 *Caparo v Dickman*, op. cit., per Lord Oliver at p 585.
61 See, for example, *Osman v Ferguson* [1993] 4 All ER 344, discussed further below.
62 [1991] 2 WLR 501.

of Lords in *Caparo Industries plc* and *Murphy v Brentwood District Council* . . . In *Donoghue v Stevenson* . . . the foresight of a reasonable man was accepted as a general test as to whether a duty of care existed. In *Bourhill v Young*[63] . . . Lord Macmillan said, at p 104: 'The duty to take care is the duty to avoid doing or omitting to do anything the doing or omitting to do which may have as its reasonable and probable consequence injury to others, and the duty is owed to those to whom injury may reasonably and probably be anticipated if the duty is not observed.' This formulation of the duty is appropriate in the present case and I respectfully adopt it.[64]

But in *Marc Rich & Co AG v Bishop Rock Marine Co Ltd and others* in 1995,[65] the House of Lords made it clear that the *Caparo* formulation applied to *all* cases in which the court was called upon to decide the duty question, including those involving physical harm. The *Caparo* test has thus brought the element of proximity firmly into the equation as an apparently separate concept, though not without considerable criticism. It has been suggested that an element of circular reasoning has thus crept into the law – 'there is a duty of care where there is proximity, and proximity means that the facts give rise to a duty of care'[66] – and the present law has also been criticised on the grounds, *inter alia*, that:

> 'proximity' is an excellent example of a normative concept masquerading as a factual one and causing nothing but confusion as a result . . . The point is not that questions about the normative relevance of 'proximity' could not sometimes, or even always, be satisfactorily answered in some way. The point is that, in practice, answers are never given, with the result that judgments based on 'proximity' seem at best off the point and at worst arbitrary.[67]

It seems, moreover, as we will see later, that the term 'proximity' may mean different things, depending on the particular context: the use of the term in cases involving psychological harm (the 'nervous shock' cases) seems to be quite different from its use in cases involving financial loss caused by negligent misrepresentation. It remains to be seen whether the judges will, in later cases, present a more precise indication of the meaning of 'proximity' in these various contexts, or whether the term will turn out to be redundant, as adding little or nothing to the more familiar and well-established notions of 'reasonable foreseeability' and 'public policy', which would signify, of course, a return to the Lord Wilberforce approach in *Anns*. Why were the courts during the 1980s and 1990s so determined to replace this with a more cautious incremental approach?

An answer may be found if we look behind the doctrinal confusion. The willingness to expand the categories of negligence liability which characterised many of the judicial statements in cases during the 1970s[68] gave way during the 1980s and

---

63 [1943] AC 92.   64 [1991] 2 WLR 501 at p 507.   65 [1996] AC 211.
66 R. Martin, 'Professional Negligence and Morgan Crucible' (1991) 7 *Professional Negligence* 37, p 38.
67 D. Howarth, 'Negligence after Murphy: Time to Re-Think' (1991) 50 *CLJ* 58, p 71.
68 See, for example, *Home Office v Dorset Yacht Co.* op. cit.; *Dutton v Bognor Regis Urban District Council*, op. cit.; *Anns v Merton London Borough Council*, op. cit.

early 1990s to a clear judicial desire to keep negligence liability within narrower limits. Howarth has suggested that:

> The English law of negligence appears . . . to be confused and aimless for three main reasons. First, the judges seem to have no clear idea of what the law of negligence is for; secondly, they harbour vague fears about Americanisation; and thirdly, their conceptualisation of the law rests on an idea that, if not inherently flawed, at least invites confusion and misuse, namely the duty of care.[69]

There has, without doubt, been a resurgence of the fear of the opening of 'floodgates': it has frequently been argued by some judges that once one particular step is taken towards widening the availability of remedies in negligence, then the 'floodgates of litigation' will open. Such an argument was used, for example, in 1932 by Lord Buckmaster in his dissenting judgment in *Donoghue v Stevenson*, and it is well for the development of the law of negligence that it found little support in the majority opinion in that case. The floodgates did not, of course, open after 1932. They rarely do.

Even if we acknowledge, however, that the general test as stated by Lord Wilberforce in *Anns* was too wide, and that it is sensible for the courts to impose limits on the applicability of the law of negligence to new situations, then we might none the less argue that the courts ought to create those boundaries in a straightforward, clear and logical manner, rather than by concealing their strategies of containment in a fog of highly complex conceptualisation which serves only to confuse the law in this area.

• Once it is established that a duty exists, a plaintiff must then prove that the defendant has been in breach of that duty – or to put it another way, has acted in a manner in which a reasonable person, in the circumstances, would not act. Whether there has been a breach of duty is established by means of the so-called 'objective test' of the 'reasonable man': in essence, did the defendant's behaviour measure up to that of the hypothetical 'reasonable man'? If so, then the defendant was not negligent. If not, then, on the face of it, the defendant acted negligently. Obviously, everything depends upon the circumstances of the case: the act or omission of the defendant must be judged in the light of available knowledge at the time (*Roe v Minister of Health*, 1954[70]); the status of the defendant must be taken into account – if the defendant is a skilled person such as a surgeon, then 'the test is the standard of the ordinary skilled man exercising and professing to have that special skill'[71]; the reasonableness of the defendant's behaviour in the light of risk of injury

---

69 Op. cit., p 91.

70 [1954] 2 QB 66. The court held that there was no liability for the failure by an anaesthetist to see a hair-line crack in a glass container during an operation carried out in 1947: the medical profession had not been made aware of the risk of such invisible cracks until it was brought to their attention in 1951.

71 *Bolam v Friern Hospital Management Committee* [1957] 2 All ER 118 at 121, per McNair J. See M. Khan and M. Robson, 'What is a Responsible Group of Medical Opinion?' (1995) 11 *Professional Negligence* 4.

will be taken into account – not only in terms of the *likelihood* of the injury occurring (for example, *Bolton v Stone*, 1951[72]) but also of the *seriousness of the injury*, should it materialise (for example, *Paris v Stepney Borough Council*, 1951[73]). Whether it would have been practicable for the defendant to have taken further precautions against the injury might be a consideration (for example, *Latimer v AEC*, 1953[74]), and in some cases the courts have weighed the risk to the plaintiff against the social or public importance of the defendant's activity – was the latter sufficiently important to justify taking the risk of harm to the plaintiff, as in *Watt v Hertfordshire County Council* in 1954?[75]

Ultimately, the court must decide whether the injury to the plaintiff was 'reasonably foreseeable', and whether or not the defendant acted with 'reasonable care'. These terms have frequently created problems for the courts in deciding issues of liability in negligence. The law, it has been said, requires that we 'guard against reasonable probabilities, not fantastic possibilities'[76] and there are many examples in the case law of judges' attempts to maintain the dividing-line between possibility and reasonable probability.[77] This dividing-line is essential if fault is retained as a criterion for liability, for it is only the person who acts unreasonably who is held by the law to be culpably negligent.

The difficulties are well illustrated in the case of *Whitehouse v Jordan* in 1981.[78] Here, a senior hospital registrar had been in charge of the delivery of a baby (the plaintiff) after a high-risk pregnancy. An attempt had been made by the registrar to carry out a forceps delivery; he had pulled the baby with the forceps several times and then, conscious of the risk to the mother's safety, proceeded to carry out a Caesarean section, which was done successfully. The plaintiff was born with severe brain damage resulting, it was alleged, from the negligent pulling of the head with the forceps. This action was brought against the registrar, claiming compensation in respect of the damage which was caused, it was claimed, by the registrar's pulling too hard and too long with the forceps. There was considerable expert medical

---

72 [1951] AC 850. The court had to consider the likelihood of cricket-balls being hit out of the defendants' ground and hitting people in the road outside; this was considered too remote to require the defendants to have taken additional precautions, for example, by building a higher perimeter fence around the ground. Compare *Miller v Jackson* [1977] QB 966.

73 [1951] AC 367. The court considered here the seriousness of eye injury to a one-eyed plaintiff as compared with a normal-sighted person; the seriousness of such an injury was held to be such as to have required the defendants to have provided goggles.

74 [1953] AC 643. The defendant factory owners were held to have acted reasonably in cleaning up after a flood; despite the clean-up, the plaintiff fell on the slippery floor and was injured. The defendants need not, as the plaintiff claimed, have closed down the factory: the risk of injury did not require so great a precaution.

75 [1954] 1 WLR 835. Here, a heavy jack was being carried on a vehicle to free a trapped woman; the jack fell onto and injured the plaintiff fireman. The court held that the attempt by the fire service to save life was of sufficient importance as to justify the taking of the risk of injury to the plaintiff. See also *Daborn v Bath Tramways Motor Co Ltd* [1946] 2 All ER 333; *Griffin v Mersey Regional Ambulance* [1998] PIQR P34.

76 *Fardon v Harcourt-Rivington* (1932) 146 LT 391 at 392.

77 See, for example, *Bolton v Stone*, above.

78 [1981] 1 All ER 267. And see *Shakoor v Situ* [2000] 4 All ER 181.

opinion to the effect that it was a matter of clinical judgment as to how to use forceps in such cases, and also evidence from one of the defendant's colleagues who had been present at the delivery that the defendant had not used the forceps violently or wrongly.

The plaintiff succeeded at first instance; on appeal by the defendant the Court of Appeal held that the registrar's conduct was an 'error of judgment' and not negligence. Indeed, in the opinion of Lord Russell in the House of Lords (on appeal by the plaintiff), the Court of Appeal seemed to consider that an error of judgment could never amount to negligence. In the event, the House of Lords found for the defendant, but made it plain that in the view of that court, an error of judgment could amount to actionable negligence if it constituted a lapse from the standard of skill and competence required in the making of clinical judgments. In other words, a doctor who, by the proper use of his or her professional skill and judgment simply makes a mistake will not for that reason alone be guilty of negligence; a doctor whose mistake results from a failure to use proper skill and judgment, however, may well be held to have been negligent, because that would amount to a departure from the standards of the 'reasonable' doctor.

The test as stated by McNair J in the important case of *Bolam v Friern Hospital Management Committee*[79] in 1957 is 'the standard of the ordinary skilled man exercising and professing to have [the] special skill. A man need not possess the highest expert skill . . . it is sufficient if he exercises the ordinary skill of an ordinary competent man exercising that particular art.'[80] In *Bolitho v City and Hackney Health Authority* in 1997[81] a two-year-old boy in hospital suffered brain damage after cardiac arrest caused by the obstruction of his bronchial passages. Although a doctor had been called to attend, she failed to do so. The failure to attend amounted to negligence, which the defendants admitted, and it was also admitted that, if the doctor had attended and had intubated (that is, inserted a tube into the boy's larynx to provide a clear airway) the respiratory failure and subsequent brain damage would have been avoided. The defendants contended, however, that if the doctor had attended, she *would not have carried out the intubation procedure*, and adduced evidence from an expert witness that such a procedure would have been inappropriate in this case. The plaintiff's expert witnesses, however, disagreed, and testified to the effect that intubation would have been reasonably required in these circumstances.

There was a clear conflict of expert testimony, and the trial judge, applying the *Bolam* test, accepted the defendant's expert witness's testimony as constituting a body of responsible medical opinion, with which the doctor's behaviour was consistent – the failure to intubate in this case was not out of line with a body of medical opinion, even though there was another body of medical opinion holding the contrary view. In the House of Lords, however, the *Bolam* decision was considered, and the court took the view that in some cases, even if there was an acknowledged body

79 [1957] 2 All ER 118.   80 Ibid., p 121.   81 [1997] 4 All ER 771.

of medical opinion supporting a particular course of action, a defendant might still be held to have been negligent. In the words of Lord Browne-Wilkinson,

> in cases of diagnosis and treatment there are cases where, despite a body of professional opinion sanctioning the defendant's conduct, the defendant can properly be held liable for negligence . . . In my judgment that is because, in some cases, it cannot be demonstrated to the judge's satisfaction that the body of opinion relied upon is reasonable or responsible. In the vast majority of cases the fact that distinguished experts in the field are of a particular opinion will demonstrate the reasonableness of that opinion. In particular, where there are questions of assessment of the relative risks and benefits of adopting a particular medical practice, a reasonable view necessarily presupposes that the relative risks and benefits have been weighed by the experts in forming their opinion. But if, in a rare case, it can be demonstrated that the professional opinion is not capable of withstanding logical analysis, the judge is entitled to hold that the body of opinion is not reasonable or responsible.[82]

Bolitho thus makes it clear that a court is not bound to exonerate a defendant simply because a body of medical opinion would support his action. The final decision as to the appropriateness or otherwise of the defendant's conduct, in other words, is unambiguously stated to be that of the court; the court's role is not mere acceptance of that conduct just because it happens to be supported by a body of professional opinion.

The *Bolam/Bolitho* test is generally applicable to anyone professing to use special knowledge or skill. It will be appreciated that, in many cases, the kind of distinctions described above will be very difficult to draw, and it can be seen that one major hurdle for a plaintiff is to convince the court that the situation in which the injury occurred was one in which the defendant ought to have foreseen the likelihood of injury.

There has, moreover, long been controversy over the *extent* of the damage for which the negligent defendant is to compensate. In *Re Polemis* in 1921,[83] stevedores negligently dropped a plank into the hold of a ship. Unfortunately, the dropping of the plank somehow caused a spark which ignited inflammable benzine vapour which had leaked from tins in the hold. Fire resulted, and the ship was destroyed. The dropping of the plank was found to have been negligent; but there was a finding of fact that the *fire* was not a reasonably foreseeable consequence of that negligent act. In the event, the defendants (the employers of the stevedores) were held liable for *all* the damage, including the damage by fire. The case may be taken to have decided that once there was a negligent act having some *foreseeable* consequences (such as, in this case, physical damage caused by the falling plank), then the defendants are liable for *all* the damage which actually ensues, both foreseeable and *un*foreseeable.

In 1961, the Privy Council decided the case of the *Wagon Mound (No 1)*,[84] another case concerning a ship. Here, the defendants had negligently allowed fuel

---

82 Ibid., p 779.   83 [1921] 3 KB 560.   84 [1961] AC 388.

oil to leak from their ship onto the waters of a harbour. The oil caught fire, in an unforeseeable manner, and the plaintiffs' wharf was extensively damaged by the fire. In this case the court held that the defendants were liable *only for the foreseeable damage*, and not for the (unforeseeable) fire damage. This case has been accepted as representing the law on this point, although later cases have complicated the issue somewhat by the introduction of distinctions between *kinds* of damage. The implications of such distinctions have been stated as follows:

> It is not necessary that the precise concatenation of circumstances should be envisaged. If the consequence was one which was within the general range which any reasonable person might foresee (and was not of an entirely different kind which no one would anticipate) then it is within the rule that a person who has been guilty of negligence is liable for the consequences.[85]

In *Bradford v Robinson Rentals Ltd* in 1967,[86] for example, the plaintiff, who was employed by the defendants, was driving an unheated van in the course of his job; the weather was extremely cold, and the plaintiff suffered severe frostbite as a result. The court held that he was entitled to recover compensation, despite the fact that frostbite was thought to be unlikely and hence unforeseeable; the defendants were held liable because frostbite was part of the general *kind of harm* which might be expected to result from exposure to extreme cold.[87]

The decision as to whether or not damage is within a 'general range' of foreseeable consequences in any given case may, however, give rise to difficulty. Consider the case of *Tremain v Pike* in 1969[88] – a case which both illustrates the difficulties in this specific area and also highlights some aspects of the doctrine of binding precedent (see chapter 7). The plaintiff worked on the defendants' farm, where the rat population had been allowed to become too large. The plaintiff had come into contact with rats and had contracted a rare[89] disease called leptospirosis, caused by contact with rats' urine. Because of this, the plaintiff sued the defendant, alleging that he had been negligent in failing to keep the number of rats on the farm under proper control, and that as a result the plaintiff had suffered injury.

The problem was whether or not the disease fell into a category of injuries which a reasonable person could foresee might result from a failure to control the number of rats on a farm. This is an issue which is clearly not susceptible of any precise delineation, but in the opinion of the judge, Payne J, the various precedents were

85 *Stewart v West African Terminals Ltd* [1964] 2 Lloyd's Rep 371 at p 375.
86 [1967] 1 WLR 337.
87 See also *Hughes v Lord Advocate* [1963] AC 837; *Muirhead v Industrial Tank Specialities Ltd* [1986] QB 507 at pp 531–533.   88 [1969] 1 WLR 1556.
89 In 1990, in reply to a parliamentary question, the Secretary of State for Employment reported that in the period 1985–89 there were 299 cases of leptospirosis in England and Wales, of which 180 were known to have been occupationally related; 139 of these were connected with agricultural and abattoir workers. In the same period there were 15 reported deaths from the disease. Currently there are about 50 cases per year in the UK. Apart from the 'at risk' occupations, it is now usual for enthusiasts of some water-sports, notably canoeing, to be issued with leaflets explaining and warning about the disease.

distinguishable from the present case. He referred to *Bradford v Robinson Rentals Ltd* in his judgment, quoting Rees J in that case as referring to 'cold injuries'[90] and noting that Rees J had, in the earlier case, resolved in the plaintiff's favour the question of whether frostbite was 'the type and kind of injury which was reasonably foreseeable'.[91] Payne J, however, went on to dismiss *Bradford*'s applicability to the case as being concerned only with *degrees* of harm caused by cold.[92] The judge then held that leptospirosis was not simply a matter of *degree* of harm caused by rats, but was injury of a completely different *kind* from that which might have been foreseen – notably rat bites and poisoning resulting from contamination of food by rats. The plaintiff therefore failed in his claim.

Various questions might be raised about the learned judge's mode of reasoning in this case, and his use of the precedent of *Bradford v Robinson Rentals Ltd*. First of all, Rees J, in *Bradford*'s case, very clearly and explicitly referred to frostbite in terms of its 'type and kind' and *not* simply in terms of *degrees* of cold injury, as Payne J seems to infer. Second, in an area where the precision sought by Payne J is so elusive, would it not have been better to acknowledge a generalised category of harm called 'rat injuries', just as Rees J had referred in *Bradford* to 'cold injuries'? The decision did not go to appeal, and we are left with a rather odd conclusion. If the case is to be taken as authority, farm-workers should note that the success of any claim they might make for injuries caused by rats might well depend upon which end of the rat they make contact with! Had the case gone to the Court of Appeal, the result might well have been different, for as Winfield suggests, 'the case may be out of line with the general trend of the decisions on personal injury since *The Wagon Mound*'.[93] Clearly, everything depends upon the degree of generality with which a court approaches the question of 'types of harm'. In *Jolley v Sutton London Borough Council*[94] in 2000, the plaintiff, then a schoolboy aged 14, and his friend had been attempting to repair an old and abandoned boat which had been lying on ground belonging to the defendant council for over two years. Using a car-jack borrowed from the plaintiff's father (though without his knowledge or consent) the boys had raised the front of the boat in order to try to repair holes in the bottom. The boat collapsed and fell onto the plaintiff as he was working underneath it, causing him serious back injury which resulted in his being confined to a wheelchair. The case raised a number of legal issues, one of them being whether the injury was of a type or kind which was outside the realm of foreseeability by the defendants. The trial judge held that the type of accident and injury was reasonably foreseeable and, taking the other issues into account, found for the plaintiff. The

90 Ibid., p 1562.   91 Ibid.   92 Ibid., p 1563.
93 *Winfield and Jolowicz on Tort* (16th edn. by W V H Rogers, 2002, Sweet and Maxwell), p 229. As an interesting postscript to the discussion of this case: in 1988, a building worker who contracted leptospirosis during the construction of a canal bridge through contact with rats' urine sued his employer for damages, claiming that the defendant should have taken steps to kill the rats which were known to be present on the site, and should have warned the workers to take precautions. The plaintiff was successful in his claim and was awarded £125,000 compensation. See the *Guardian*, 2 November 1988.   94 [2000] 2 Lloyd's Rep 65.

Court of Appeal, however, took a narrower view, and held that although it would have been reasonably foreseeable for the boys to have sustained injury by, for example, falling through the boat's rotten planking, the falling of the boat after being jacked up, and the consequent injury to the plaintiff, was an accident of a different type or kind from that which the defendants could reasonably have foreseen. The defendants' appeal was allowed.

In the House of Lords, it was observed that 'in this corner of the law the results of decided cases are inevitably very fact-sensitive'.[95] The substantive judgments of both Lord Steyn and Lord Hoffmann are to the effect that the original conclusion of the trial judge, taking a more generalised view of the 'type or kind' of accident involved, was the correct one – Lord Hoffmann in particular said that the judge's 'broad description of the risk as being that children would "meddle with the boat at the risk of some physical injury" was the correct one to adopt on the facts of this case. The actual injury fell within that description and I would therefore allow the appeal.'[96]

Though the principle of 'reasonable foreseeability' may be seen to be linked to the idea of 'fault liability' and thus firmly embedded in the law of negligence, it is clear that no hard and fast test exists whereby a court can simply conclude that there was or was not a duty of care, that there was or was not negligence, or that the damage was or was not foreseeable. The necessary flexibility of approach can be appreciated from the cases discussed above, as can the important role played of judicial conceptions of public policy. Some recent decisions, however, make it necessary for us now to consider what might be termed 'sub-sets' of the tort of negligence, each with problems and principles additional to the basic requirements of 'duty', 'breach' and 'damage'. These sub-sets are (i) liability involving the police and emergency services; (ii) liability for acts or omissions causing purely economic loss; (iii) liability for statements causing economic loss; and (iv) liability for psychological, or psychiatric, harm.

Liability in negligence in cases involving the police and emergency services

It is useful to treat this area as involving some special considerations for a number of reasons. First of all, as the courts have emphasised, there may be important issues of public policy involved. Second, as has recently been made clear by the European Court of Human Rights, questions of liability in this area may well involve important questions concerning the applicability of the Human Rights Act 1998. And third, there are important implications of recent case law with regard to the law relating to rescuers.

The position of the police in this context is particularly noteworthy. The Court of Appeal in *Hill v Chief Constable of West Yorkshire*[97] in 1987 denied the

95 Lord Steyn, ibid., p 70.   96 Ibid., p 73.   97 [1988] QB 60.

possibility of a claim for compensation against the police by the mother of the last victim of the perpetrator of a series of murders. The court stated that the police owed no special duty of care to the victim to apprehend the offender, over and above their general public duty to enforce the law and suppress crime, and it is clear from the judgments in the case that this decision was largely the result of considerations of public policy. *Hill* was clearly accepted by the courts as giving the police virtual immunity[98] from negligence liability in such cases. In *Ancell v McDermott*[99] for example it was held, on grounds of public policy, that the police had no duty towards road users to protect them from, or warn them against, hazards on the road which had been created by others. The 'immunity from suit' approach was most dramatically seen in 1993 in *Osman v Ferguson*[100] where the facts were that a school-teacher had developed an obsession with a pupil, then aged 15, and had even changed his name to that of the boy. The teacher, who had been dismissed from his job, was interviewed by the police about vandalism at the Osman home. He had warned the police that he was in danger of doing 'something criminally insane'. Two days later, the police went to arrest him for criminal damage but he was not there. The teacher then obtained a stolen shotgun, shot and killed the boy's father, injured the boy, and killed the head teacher of the school where he had worked, also injuring the head teacher's son.

In this action, the plaintiffs alleged negligence by the police in failing to arrest the teacher before the tragic shootings could occur. The Court of Appeal, despite stating that there was an arguable case for a very close degree of proximity between the police, the Osman family and the teacher, concluded that the situation was governed by *Hill*, which, said the court, gave the police immunity from negligence actions in the matter of the investigation of crime; and the claim was struck out as disclosing no cause of action. We might pause to comment that whilst the identity of neither victim nor perpetrator were known to the police at the relevant time in *Hill* (and that fact alone might justify the refusal to impose a duty of care), the acknowledged degree of proximity/foreseeability in *Osman* could have led the court to distinguish *Hill* and find for the plaintiffs. It is hard to see how such a decision would have had a particularly wide-ranging effect on the police, given the particular circumstances of the case, and even harder to see how any flood-gates argument might be sustained. The decision is explicable only on the grounds of public policy considerations.[101]

The House of Lords having refused leave to appeal, Mrs Osman and her son took their case to the European Court of Human Rights, alleging a number of violations

---

98 Though not total immunity: see *Swinney v Chief Constable of Northumbria Police* [1997] QB 464, where the court explained that there could be public policy considerations which counterbalance the need for police immunity from negligence actions.

99 [1993] 4 All ER 355. See also *Alexandrou v Oxford* [1993] 4 All ER 328; *Clough v Bussan* [1990] 1 All ER 431. But see the reasoning which led to a duty being imposed upon the police in the Scottish case of *Gibson v Orr* 1999 SC 420.   100 Op. cit.

101 See M. Tregilgas-Davey, '*Osman v Metropolitan Police Commissioner*: The Cost of Police Protectionism' (1993) 56 *MLR* 732.

of their rights under the European Convention of Human Rights – now incorporated into English law by means of the Human Rights Act 1998. The European Commission, and subsequently the European Court, found that there had indeed been a breach of Article 6 of the Convention, involving the right to a fair trial. The striking-out of the claim at an early stage in the proceedings on the basis of assuming a 'blanket immunity' from actions in negligence on the part of the police constituted the breach of the right to a fair trial: the European Court of Human Rights stated that the striking-out of the claim had deprived the applicants of the opportunity for an 'adjudication on the admissibility and merits of an arguable claim that they were in a relationship of proximity to the police, that the harm caused was foreseeable, and that in the circumstances it was fair just and reasonable not to apply the exclusionary rule outlined in the *Hill* case'.[102] The court took the view that the circumstances of the case were such that the merits of the plaintiffs' claim needed to be examined and explicitly weighed against the competing public policy arguments in favour of immunity from suit. In other words, the principle of proportionality had relevance here – the denial of any right conferred by the European Convention must be proportionate to the plaintiffs' injuries or loss. It might be that, after due consideration both of the plaintiffs' claim and of the arguments for police immunity, the court decided in favour of the latter: the point however was that the applicants in this case had been denied the opportunity for such judicial consideration to take place, and this was a breach of Article 6.[103]

The liability of the police in negligence, then, would seem now to depend upon the specific facts of any particular claim, and the consideration by the court of those facts together with any public policy considerations which might have a bearing on the case. The notion of a simple blanket immunity in negligence would seem, according to *Osman*, to fall foul of the European Convention, and therefore of the Human Rights Act 1998.

Similar policy considerations have been influential, too, in the courts' treatment of claims involving other emergency services. In 1997, three appeals involving the fire service were heard together by the Court of Appeal.[104] In *John Munroe (Acrylics) Ltd v London Fire and Civil Defence Authority*, fire-fighters had responded to an emergency call, and had arrived at the scene of a fire. Mistakenly believing that they had extinguished the fire, the fire-fighters left the scene. Unfortunately the fire re-ignited, causing further damage. In *Church of Jesus Christ of Latter Day Saints (Great Britain) v Yorkshire Fire and Civil Defence Authority*, the plaintiffs' chapel was

---

102 *Osman v United Kingdom* [1999] 1 FLR 193, para 139. And see now *Brooks v Commissioner of Police for the Metropolis* [2005] UKHL 24, which in essence reiterates the basic position in *Hill*.

103 It is noteworthy that in *Barrett v London Borough of Enfield* [2001] 2 AC 550, where the claimant brought an action against the local authority alleging that it had been negligent in making fostering arrangements when he was a child in the care of the authority, the House of Lords, though critical of the European Court of Human Rights' decision in *Osman*, none the less felt that it would not be prudent to accede to the defendant authority's application to have the claim struck out as disclosing no arguable cause of action, and that the striking-out procedure ought not be to used where the case was not clear-cut.

104 All three cases are reported at [1997] 2 All ER 865.

destroyed by fire which fire-fighters had failed to extinguish owing to a lack of a proper supply of water. The plaintiffs claimed damages against the defendant fire authority for negligence and for breach of statutory duty under the Fire Services Act 1947, which requires fire authorities to ensure an adequate supply of water for fire-fighting purposes. In these two cases, the Court of Appeal held that the defendant authorities owed no duty of care. Despite foreseeability of harm, there was an insufficient degree of proximity between claimants and defendants – the mere fact that an emergency call had been made to the fire service did not establish such proximity[105] – and the statutory context in which the fire service operated did not give rise to a common-law duty of care in negligence. There was no guarantee that attendance at a fire would always successfully extinguish the fire or prevent harm or damage, and it was thought inappropriate to expose the fire services to actions from distressed or disappointed fire victims. Moreover, the imposition of a common-law duty might lead to 'defensive' fire-fighting, that is, only taking that action which would keep the fire-fighters 'legally safe' from any possible litigation. It was also argued that there was a danger that the 'floodgates' of litigation would open. It was said, therefore, that: 'the fire brigade are not under a common law duty to answer the call for help, and are not under a duty to take care to do so. If, therefore, they fail to turn up, or fail to turn up in time, because they have carelessly misunderstood the message, got lost on the way or run into a tree, they are not liable.'[106]

But in the third case – *Capital and Counties plc v Hampshire County Council* – it was held that on the facts of the case the fire brigade *did* owe a duty to the claimant. Here, the fire-fighting crew having arrived at the scene of a fire at the claimants' premises, one of the fire officers gave orders that the water sprinkler system in the building be turned off. The result was that the fire spread and caused further damage. In this case, although – as is invariably the case – the initial outbreak of fire was not caused by the fire brigade, they had, by their positive act in turning off the sprinklers, made the situation worse and caused more extensive damage than would otherwise have occurred. In such a situation, it was well-established that a duty existed, breach of which could result in liability.[107] This decision was not based on any special factors peculiar to the fire service, but was rather the result of the application of general principles.

What about other emergency services? In *Kent v Griffiths, Roberts and London Ambulance Service*[108] after an emergency telephone call, an ambulance took over half an hour to reach a patient, when the journey should have taken them about nine minutes. By the time the ambulance arrived and collected the patient, the medical emergency had worsened, and the patient developed respiratory arrest which led to brain damage. This would have been avoided had the ambulance arrived sooner. No explanation was ever given for the delay, though there was evidence that the ambulance crew had attempted to cover up the matter by falsifying

---

105 Following *Alexandrou v Oxford*, above.   106 [1997] 2 All ER 865 at 1030.
107 See *Sheppard v Glossop Corpn.* [1921] 3 KB 132; *East Suffolk Rivers Catchment Board v Kent* [1941] AC 74.   108 [2001] QB 36.

the log. The Court of Appeal held that a duty of care is owed by an ambulance service, once the service has accepted the call for assistance. The court preferred to adopt the analogy of the clear duty owed to patients turning up at a hospital accident and emergency department, rather than making comparisons with the fire and other emergency services.

In *OLL Ltd v Secretary of State for Transport*[109] in 1997, the liability in negligence of the coastguard service was at issue. The facts were that a group of children were in a small boat and adrift at sea. Rescuers in a lifeboat and in a helicopter were attempting to locate them, and it was alleged that the coastguard had negligently provided them with misleading information as to the likely whereabouts of the missing boat. It was held that there was no duty owed by the coastguard: their action had not exacerbated the situation – the misdirection had not, unlike the switching off of the sprinkler system in *Capital and Counties plc*, caused additional injury.

In so far as these cases imply any generalised notion of immunity from negligence actions for these emergency services, the impact of the *Osman* decision in the European Court of Human Rights will no doubt be highly relevant, and it remains to be seen how this decision, and also now the Human Rights Act 1998, will affect the courts' approach to dealing with allegations of negligence against these services and, indeed, other public bodies such as local authorities where policy considerations have weighed heavily with the courts in litigation in recent years.[110] It is also important to remind ourselves of the duty imposed by the Human Rights Act 1998 on all public bodies not to act 'in a way which is incompatible with a Convention right':[111] it will be interesting to see how this provision will be interpreted by the courts in relation to the work of organisations such as the police and local authorities.

Negligent acts or omissions causing economic loss

The common-law development of the tort of negligence has proceeded on the basis that, if a plaintiff is to succeed and recover compensation from a defendant, not only must proof of fault be established but also physical injury or material loss to the plaintiff's person or property. Once this injury or loss is shown, then it is well established that the plaintiff can recover damages in respect of any financial losses which are consequent on that physical or material loss. In actions for personal injury, then, there may be awards of compensation in respect of pain and suffering and loss of amenity, as well as an amount for the injury itself. These will be discussed in more detail presently. But apart from these physical losses, the plaintiff may recover medical expenses and any other financial loss which is

---

109 [1997] 3 All ER 897.
110 See in particular *X and others (Minors) v Bedfordshire County Council* [1995] 2 AC 633; *Barrett v London Borough of Enfield* [2001] 2 AC 550; *JD v East Berkshire Health NHS Trust; MAK v Dewsbury Healthcare NHS Trust; RK v Oldham NHS Trust* [2005] UKHL 23. And see P. de Prez, 'Proportionality, symmetry and competing public policy arguments: the police force and civil immunity' (1999) 15 *PN* 217.   111 Section 6(1). See chapter 4.

attributable to that injury, such as loss of earnings or earning capacity suffered as a result of the injury.

But it has long been held by the courts that financial losses suffered through someone's negligence are not recoverable if there has been no physical damage or injury. This was settled in 1875 in *Cattle v Stockton Waterworks Co*,[112] and has been reaffirmed on many occasions since then. In *Spartan Steel and Alloys Ltd v Martin & Co (Contractors) Ltd* in 1973,[113] the defendants negligently damaged an electricity cable, cutting off power to the plaintiffs' factory. At the time, there was work in progress in the plaintiffs' furnace, and the material then in the furnace depreciated in value. Apart from claiming in respect of this damage, the plaintiffs claimed for further losses of profit on materials which they were unable to produce because of the power cut. They recovered compensation in respect of the material which was actually in the furnace, but were unable to recover in respect of the further losses of profit. The court gave various reasons for this decision, Lawton LJ relying on the authority of *Cattle*'s case, and Lord Denning providing various policy reasons for holding that purely economic loss was not recoverable. He felt that one important consideration was the possibility that if this claim were allowed, many others would follow: 'Some might be genuine, but many might be inflated, or even false. A machine might not have been in use anyway, but it would be easy to put it down to the cut in supply. It would be well-nigh impossible to check the claims.'[114]

In *Junior Books Ltd v Veitchi Co Ltd*[115] in 1982 the position was reconsidered by the House of Lords. The defendant flooring specialists had been specifically nominated by the plaintiffs' architects as sub-contractors to lay the floor in the plaintiffs' new factory, which was being built by the main building contractors. There was no contract between the plaintiff and the defendants, but the plaintiffs alleged that they had placed reliance on the defendants, as specialists, to ensure that the floor was properly laid. About two years after the floor had been laid, cracks began to appear in it, and had continued to appear in it ever since. The plaintiffs alleged that the defendants had been negligent in laying the floor and claimed £206,000 as being the cost of replacing it, together with a number of costs incidental to the replacement work. These included the cost of storage of books and removal of machinery during the work, loss of profits due to disturbance of business, wages of employees and overheads.

---

112 (1875) LR 10 QB 453.   113 [1973] QB 27. See also *Londonwaste Ltd v Amec Civil Engineering Ltd* (1997) 53 Con LR 66.

114 Ibid., at p 38. This is, of course, the 'flood-gates' argument once again. The fallaciousness of the argument in the present context, it might be thought, lies not so much in the fact that more cases might be brought before the court – for any new development in the law must bring new claims – as in the fact that such claims are somehow thought difficult, or 'impossible to check'. Why should scrutiny of claims brought in respect of economic loss be any more difficult than claims brought in respect of personal injury? One view might be that, as such loss is far more amenable to evaluation than is, say, the worth of a broken leg or the loss of an eye, the task of the court would in some ways be easier; problems of evidence and proof of facts would surely be no more difficult, and claims no more dishonest or frivolous, than is already the case with personal injury, or for that matter any other, litigation. See the dissenting judgment of Lord Justice Edmund Davies in *Spartan Steel*.   115 [1982] 3 All ER 201.

Although there was, in this case, no danger of physical damage either to persons or to property, the House of Lords unanimously agreed that there could be liability for these losses, on the basis that the relationship between plaintiff and defendant was sufficiently close (in terms of the reliance by the plaintiffs on the defendants as flooring specialists) to justify the imposition of a duty of care upon the defendants towards the plaintiffs.

Orthodoxy was, however, reaffirmed by the Court of Appeal in *Muirhead v Industrial Tank Specialities Ltd*[116] in 1985. Here, the plaintiff, a wholesale fish merchant, contracted with Industrial Trade Specialities Ltd to install a tank in which to store live lobsters. To keep the lobsters alive, sea-water had to be pumped continuously through the tank to oxygenate the water. The pumps for this operation were supplied by ITT, the second defendants, and powered by electric motors made by a French company and supplied through their English subsidiary, Leroy Somer Electrical Motors Ltd, the third defendants.

The electric motors continually cut out, and the plaintiff frequently had to call out electrical engineers to re-start them, incurring costs in so doing; if the motors failed during the night, this would not be discovered for some time, and this was particularly problematic since if the re-circulation and oxygenation stopped, the lobsters would die within 90 minutes. On one occasion, indeed, the whole stock of lobsters died, and the plaintiff incurred more costs in salvaging and refrigerating the dead lobsters.

Eventually, it was established that the cause of the problem was the inability of the motors to handle the full voltage range of the United Kingdom supply. The plaintiff claimed compensation in respect of various losses incurred, these being the cost of the pumps; the costs incurred as a result of electrical engineers having to attend to the defective equipment; loss of interest on capital; loss of the lobsters; and loss of profits on intended sales of lobsters, the latter sum being estimated at £127,375. One of the main problems was whether, and to what extent, the manufacturers of the motors were liable in negligence to the plaintiff.

The Court of Appeal considered that *Junior Books* was distinguishable from the present case. The 'very close relationship'[117] which existed between the parties in *Junior Books* – said by Lord Roskill in that case to be 'as close as it could be short of actual privity of contract'[118] – did not exist between the parties in the present case. The plaintiff could, then, recover compensation for his material losses, but not for the loss of profits ultimately arising from the faulty motors.

It is clear from *Muirhead* and subsequent cases[119] that there is still in general no liability in negligence for acts or omissions causing purely economic loss. This will apparently be so even though there may be close relationships – along *Junior Books* lines – between plaintiff and defendant. In *Greater Nottingham*

---

116 [1986] QB 507.   117 Ibid., p 528.   118 [1982] 3 All ER 201 at 214.
119 For example, *Simaan General Contracting Co. v Pilkington Glass Ltd. (No 2)* [1988] 1 All ER 791.

Co-Operative Society v Cementation Piling and Foundations Ltd[120] the owner of a building sued the defendant sub-contractor over delay in completing work on the building. There was here an actual contract between the parties which had required the defendants to take reasonable care. This relationship, though closer even than that in *Junior Books*, was held by the Court of Appeal not to give rise to a duty of care in tort regarding the financial losses of the plaintiffs: the parties ought to have sorted their respective obligations and liabilities out by means of their contract, and in the absence of such contractual stipulations, it was not open to the plaintiff to allege liability in tort. Such attempts to use tort actions to disturb or subvert contractual obligations have been condemned in a number of cases.[121]

The picture has been considerably complicated through a series of cases involving defective buildings.[122] The basic scenario of most of these cases is as follows. A builder constructs a building in such a way that it is defective. During the building operation, however, the local authority becomes involved through one of its employees, such as a building inspector or surveyor, carrying out an inspection of the architects' plans and/or the actual site in pursuance of its statutory powers to do so. The operation is passed by the inspector as being sound. Some years later, when the fundamental defects in the building – which may be foundations dug insufficiently deep,[123] an inappropriate drainage system[124] or some other deep-seated defect in the structure – have caused visible problems, such as cracking walls and floors, the owner and/or occupier of the building sues the local authority (the builder being typically no longer available to sue[125]) in respect of the allegedly negligent inspection which ought to have revealed the original defect in the construction process.

The first problem is the nature of damage suffered in these cases. The courts have insisted – in most of[126] the cases referred to in the paragraph above – that the plaintiffs' losses were economic, and not physical. Why? The answer may be found by comparing the typical facts of these 'defective building' cases with those of *Donoghue v Stevenson*. In the latter case, the defendant negligently created a dangerously defective product which subsequently caused physical harm to the plaintiff. In the 'buildings' cases, even if the defendants did cause a dangerously

---

120 [1989] QB 71.
121 See *Simaan General Contracting Co. v Pilkington Glass Ltd.*, above; *Pacific Associates Inc. v Baxter* [1990] 1 QB 993; *Marc Rich & Co. v Bishop Rock Marine*, op. cit.
122 The principal decisions are *Dutton v Bognor Regis UDC* [1972] 1 QB 373; *Anns v Merton London Borough Council* [1978] AC 728; *Peabody Donation Fund v Sir Lindsay Parkinson & Co Ltd* [1985] AC 210; *Investors in Industry Commercial Properties Ltd v South Bedfordshire District Council* [1986] 1 All ER 787; *D & F Estates Ltd v Church Comrs for England* [1989] AC 177; *Murphy v Brentwood District Council* [1991] 1 AC 398.
123 As in *Anns v Merton London Borough Council* [1978] AC 728 and *Investors in Industry Commercial Properties Ltd v South Bedfordshire District Council* [1986] 1 All ER 787.
124 As in *Peabody Donation Fund v Sir Lindsay Parkinson & Co Ltd* [1985] AC 210.
125 Though in *D & F Estates* the builder was sued.
126 Except for *Anns*, where the loss was held – wrongly, according to *Murphy* – to be physical.

defective building to be constructed, that building had not, at the time of the action, gone on to cause physical harm to anyone:

> If a dangerous defect in a chattel is discovered before it causes any personal injury or damage to property, because the danger is now known . . . the defect becomes merely a defect in quality. The chattel is either capable of repair at economic cost or it is worthless and must be scrapped. In either case the loss sustained by the owner . . . is purely economic.
>
> I believe that these principles are equally applicable to buildings. If a builder erects a structure containing a latent defect which renders it dangerous to persons or property, he will be liable in tort for injury to persons or damage to property resulting from that dangerous defect. But if the defect becomes apparent before any injury or damage has been caused, the loss sustained by the building owner is purely economic. If the defect can be repaired at economic cost, that is the measure of the loss. If the building cannot be repaired, it may have to be abandoned as unfit for occupation and therefore valueless. These economic losses are recoverable if they flow from breach of a relevant contractual duty, but, . . . in the absence of a special relationship of proximity they are not recoverable in tort.[127]

On this point, then, the 'defective buildings' cases can be brought into line with the orthodox position on economic loss.[128]

A broader issue is the degree of legal protection now afforded to home-owners who are the victims of the original builders' negligence. *Dutton v Bognor Regis*[129] and *Anns v Merton London Borough Council*[130] provided the occupier with a potential remedy against the local authority whose employee had been negligent. *Murphy* denies them such a remedy:

> It must, of course, be kept in mind that the decision (in *Anns*) has stood for some 13 years. On the other hand, it is not a decision of the type that is to a significant extent taken into account by citizens or indeed local authorities in ordering their affairs. No doubt its existence results in local authorities having to pay increased insurance premiums, but to be relieved of that necessity would be to their advantage . . . To overrule it is unlikely to result in significantly increased insurance premiums for householders . . . The decision is capable of being regarded as affording a measure of justice, but as against that the impossibility of finding any coherent and logically based doctrine

127 *Murphy v Brentwood District Council* [1990] 3 WLR 414 at 435–436, per Lord Bridge.

128 The reasoning begs questions, however. If, whilst digging in my garden, I negligently throw a spadeful of rocks over my garden wall, and these damage my neighbour's car parked in his driveway, what is the loss suffered by my neighbour? Surely, the answer must be the cost of repairing the car. I cannot deny that I have caused physical damage, or that I would be liable to recompense my neighbour were he to sue me in negligence. But that is not the point. It remains true that his actual loss is purely economic!

129 [1972] 1 QB 373. In *Dutton*, Lord Denning said (at 397–398): 'It was (the council inspector's) job to examine the foundations to see if they would take the load of the house. He failed to do it properly . . . The council should answer for his failure. They were entrusted by Parliament with the task of seeing that houses were properly built. They received public funds for the purpose. Their very object was to protect purchasers and occupiers of houses. Yet they failed to protect them. Their shoulders are broad enough to bear the loss.'   130 [1978] AC 728.

behind it is calculated to put the law of negligence into a state of confusion defying rational analysis . . .

. . . I would hold that *Anns* was wrongly decided as regards the scope of any private law duty of care resting upon local authorities in relation to their function of taking steps to secure compliance with building byelaws or regulations and should be departed from . . .[131]

Murphy has been criticised for, inter alia, this aspect of the decision, and indeed has not been followed in other common-law jurisdictions.[132] It has been argued that local authorities ought to shoulder this type of liability precisely because they are in the best position to check that the foundations, drains, and so on, are sufficient or adequate before those features of the building are covered over and lie hidden, slowly wrecking the building above, for 10 or 15 years. Liability might be an additional spur to ensure that inspections are properly carried out, especially, it has been suggested, if the construction industry is prone to save money by cutting corners on non-obvious aspects of the building work. There are, in other words, important policy aspects of the *Dutton/Anns/Murphy* scenario which the court in *Murphy* did not, it might be thought, adequately address.

Negligent statements causing economic loss

The principle that purely economic loss is irrecoverable in negligence was modified significantly in 1964 in the important case of *Hedley Byrne & Co Ltd v Heller & Partners Ltd*[133] which we noted in chapter 4. In that case Lord Devlin drew attention to the artificiality of the distinction between physical and economic, as opposed to purely economic, loss. The effect of *Hedley Byrne* was to make possible the recovery of compensation for financial loss sustained through reliance by the plaintiff upon statements made negligently by the defendant, but only where there exists a 'special relationship' between the parties. *Hedley Byrne*-type liability is, it must be stressed, confined to liability for negligently made statements, and is best regarded as an exception to the general 'economic loss' rule. The phrase 'special relationship' has in recent cases in this area been recast in terms of a 'relationship of proximity': it must be carefully noted that, although 'proximity' has been discussed already in a more general context, the term is used in this section with reference only to the law relating to negligent misstatement.

The term 'special relationship' which must exist between plaintiff and defendant before there can be liability was not defined with any degree of precision in *Hedley Byrne* itself. In this context, it is certain that reasonable foreseeability alone will not suffice to found a duty of care; Lord Reid spoke of:

---

131 [1990] 3 WLR 414 at 432–433, per Lord Keith.
132 See *Invercargill City Council v Hamlin* [1996] 1 All ER 756 (New Zealand); *Winnipeg Condominium Corpn No 36 v Bird Construction Co Ltd* (1995) 121 DLR (4th) 193 (Canada); *Bryan v Maloney* (1995) 128 ALR 163 (Australia).   133 [1964] AC 465.

those relationships where it is plain that the party seeking information or advice was trusting the other to exercise such a degree of care as the circumstances required, where it was reasonable for him to do that, and where the other gave the information or advice when he knew or ought to have known that the inquirer was relying on him.[134]

Lord Morris of Borth-y-Gest said that:

if, in a sphere in which a person is so placed that others could reasonably rely on his judgment or skill or on his ability to make careful inquiry, a person takes it on himself to give information or advice to, or allows his information or advice to be passed on to, another person who, as he knows or should know, will place reliance on it, then a duty of care will arise.[135]

Lord Devlin pointed out that, had there been payment to the bank in exchange for the information, then the solution in law would have been clear: there would have been liability for breach of contract if the information provided was wrong. Payment would also constitute 'very good evidence that (the advice) is being relied on and that the informer or adviser knows that it is'.[136] But in the absence of payment:

it will be necessary to exercise greater care in distinguishing between social and professional relationships and between those which are of a contractual character and those which are not . . . I do not think it possible to formulate with exactitude all the conditions under which the law will in a specific case imply a voluntary undertaking, any more than it is possible to formulate those in which the law will imply a contract. But in so far as your lordships describe the circumstances in which an implication will ordinarily be drawn, I am prepared to adopt any one of your lordships' statements as showing the general rule . . .[137]

It was asserted by Lord Oliver in the later case of *Caparo Industries plc v Dickman*[138] that it can be concluded from the judgments in *Hedley Byrne* that:

the necessary relationship between the maker of a statement or giver of advice ('the adviser') and the recipient who acts in reliance upon it ('the advisee') may typically be held to exist where (1) the advice is required for a purpose, whether particularly specific or generally described, which is made known, either actually or inferentially, to the adviser at the time when the advice is given; (2) the adviser knows, either actually or inferentially, that his advice will be communicated to the advisee, either specifically or as a member of an ascertainable class, in order that it should be used by the advisee for that purpose; (3) it is known either actually or inferentially, that the advice so communicated is likely to be acted upon by the advisee for that purpose without independent inquiry; and (4) it is so acted upon by the advisee to his detriment. That is not, of course, to suggest that these conditions are either conclusive or exclusive, but merely that the actual decision in the case does not warrant any broader propositions.[139]

---

134 [1964] AC 465 at p 486.   135 [1964] AC 465 at p 503.   136 Ibid., at p 529.
137 Ibid., at pp 529–530.   138 [1990] 1 All ER 568.   139 Ibid., at p 589.

It will quickly be appreciated, however, that an immense – perhaps infinite – number of communications between people may satisfy these conditions. Because of this, and the courts' abiding concern to avoid a situation where there may be liability 'in an indeterminate amount for an indefinite time and to an indeterminate class',[140] judges in later cases have been at pains to keep the generality of the basic *Hedley Byrne* proposition within limits.

In *Mutual Life and Citizens' Assurance Co Ltd v Evatt*, a Privy Council decision in 1971,[141] the plaintiff, a policy holder in the defendant company, asked for advice from the defendants about the financial soundness of another company with which the defendants were closely associated. Relying on the information provided, the plaintiff invested money in the other company. Because the information was incorrect, the plaintiff lost his money. The court held by a majority that the plaintiff had failed to establish that a duty of care existed on the facts, because he had neither alleged that the defendants were in the business of supplying such information or advice, nor that they claimed any special qualification, skill or competence to do so. If such a requirement were necessary, this would have the effect of limiting the duty of care to professional advisers such as accountants. The minority opinion in the case – which has been preferred in later cases to that of the majority – was however of the view that:

> when an enquirer consults a businessman in the course of his business and makes it plain to him that he is seeking considered advice and intends to act upon it in a particular way, any reasonable businessman would realise that, if he chooses to give advice without any warning or qualification, he is putting himself under a moral obligation to take care . . . (it is) within the principles established by the *Hedley Byrne* case to regard his action in giving such advice as creating a special relationship between him and the enquirer and to translate his moral obligation into a legal obligation to take such care as is reasonable in the whole circumstances.[142]

It is plain that the duty will not arise where the information is given in a purely social or informal context, such as off-the-cuff statements at a party. But the real difficulty lies in establishing exactly what requirements must be satisfied, on any given set of facts, in order for the court to deduce that the maker of the statement owed a duty of care to the recipient. The cases decided in recent years do not, unfortunately, generate a coherent body of legal principle.

Throughout the judgments in recent cases, we can discern the influence of public policy considerations, and in particular a determination to keep within limits the types of situation which might give rise to liability. Consider the important decision of the House of Lords in *Caparo Industries plc v Dickman*[143] in 1990. The defendants were auditors who had audited the accounts of a company in which the plaintiff company owned shares. The plaintiffs made a successful take-over bid

---

140 Cardozo CJ in the American case *Ultramares Corpn v Touche* 255 NY Rep 170 (1931).
141 [1971] 1 All ER 150.   142 [1971] 1 All ER 150 at 163, per Lords Reid and Morris.
143 Op. cit.

for the company, only to find that the target company's assets were substantially less than the accounts had indicated. They brought this action against the auditors, alleging negligent misstatement causing financial loss to the plaintiffs. The central question of law raised by the case was whether auditors owed a duty, in the preparation of the audited accounts, to shareholders who might rely on those accounts for the purpose of buying shares in the company. In the House of Lords, it was held that no such duty was owed by auditors to either actual or potential shareholders. The statutory purpose of the auditor's task was to protect existing shareholders as a body, and to facilitate their effective and informed control of the company; it was not to provide information which might enable individual shareholders to purchase more shares and make a profit. Clearly, the refusal to open up liability to 'an indeterminate class' can be seen at work here.

Judgments in *Caparo* refer to the requirements not only that the statement must be relied on, and of course that the recipient of the statement must suffer financial loss as a result, but also that defendants must have knowledge that their statement would both be communicated to, and be relied on by, the plaintiffs. It is not clear whether this must be actual knowledge[144] or whether knowledge may be inferred from the circumstances.[145] The former requirement would be highly restrictive, and there are certainly cases which would support the latter proposition.[146] The trouble is that even after *Caparo*, the requirements for liability for negligent misstatement could not be isolated with anything approaching precision. In *James McNaughton Paper Group Ltd v Hicks Anderson & Co*[147] in 1991, Neill LJ in the Court of Appeal referred to a number of factors which might be relevant in establishing whether a duty of care existed. Accepting Lord Oliver's statement of conclusions from *Hedley Byrne*, cited above, his lordship went on to note as relevant:

> (1) the purpose for which the statement is made . . . (2) the purpose for which the statement was communicated . . . (3) the relationship between the adviser, the advisee and any relevant third party . . . (4) the size of any class to which the advisee belongs . . . (5) the state of knowledge of the adviser . . . (6) reliance by the advisee . . .[148]

Several more considerations might be linked to this list of factors. For example, how far might it be said that the relationship between adviser and advisee is 'akin to contract'?[149] Did the advisee's reliance on the statement actually cause the loss?[150] What about if the person asking for advice is himself an expert in the matter?[151]

---

144 See the judgment of Lord Bridge: [1990] 1 All ER 568 at p 576; and see *JEB Fasteners Ltd v Marks Bloom & Co* [1981] 3 All ER 289.   145 See the judgment of Lord Oliver, quoted above.
146 See, for example, *Smith v Eric S Bush* and *Harris v Wyre Forest District Council* [1990] 1 AC 831.
147 [1991] 2 WLR 641.
148 [1991] 2 WLR 641 at 651–652. This list was described as 'helpful' in *Morgan Crucible Co plc v Hill Samuel Bank Ltd* [1991] 1 All ER 148.
149 See the *Bush* and *Harris* cases, above, n 146. But see *Commissioner of Police for the Metropolis v Lennon* [2004] EWCA Civ 130.
150 *White v Taylor* [2004] EWCA Civ 1151; and see the *JEB Fasteners* case, above.
151 *Valse Holdings Ltd v Merill Lynch* [2004] EWHC 2471.

Central though many of these questions have been held to be, few of them were specifically addressed in either *Spring v Guardian Assurance plc*[152] or *Henderson v Merrett Syndicates Ltd.*[153] In both these cases, detailed discussions of the basic issue were put by Lord Goff, and his approach in both cases was to attempt to discern the basic principles arising from *Hedley Byrne*. In *Spring*, the plaintiff, having been dismissed by the second defendant, C Ltd (who had been taken over by the first defendant), had attempted to set up his own business selling the life assurance policies of another company. That other company – the Scottish Amicable Life Assurance Society plc – was bound by the rules of LAUTRO, the self-regulatory body for the financial services industry, to obtain a reference on the plaintiff from his previous employer. On the basis of that reference, Scottish Amicable refused to deal with him. The reference stated that the plaintiff kept the best business for himself, that he was a man of little or no integrity and could not be regarded as honest, and that he had handled the sale of a policy in such a way as to make a very substantial commission for himself at the client's expense. The plaintiff had similar experiences at the hands of two other life assurance companies which he approached.

He brought this action against his former employers alleging (i) breach of an implied contractual term that the defendants would prepare any references with reasonable care and would provide a full, frank and truthful reference, and (ii) negligence in providing an unsatisfactory reference. The trial judge held that there was no contract with Guardian Assurance plc, and no such implied term in the contract with C Ltd; but held that the defendants owed a duty of care, and that they had been negligent. The defendants appealed, and the plaintiff cross-appealed on the contract issue. The Court of Appeal allowed the appeal, holding that no duty of care existed towards the plaintiff; that his only remedy lay in defamation; and that there was no implied term in the contract with C Ltd. The plaintiff now appealed to the House of Lords.

The appeal was allowed. Lord Goff stated the issue as involving two questions: first, was there a prima facie duty ('in contract or in tort') owed to the plaintiff, and second, if so, whether such a duty would none the less be negatived because it would undermine the policy underlying the defence of qualified privilege in the law of defamation. On the first question, Lord Goff felt there *was* a duty of care owed to the plaintiff. On principles derived from *Hedley Byrne*, there was 'an assumption of responsibility by those companies to the plaintiff in respect of the reference, and reliance by the plaintiff upon the exercise by them of due care and skill in respect of its preparation'[154] and Lord Goff went on to say that:

> All the members of the [House of Lords in *Hedley Byrne*] spoke in terms of the principle resting upon an assumption or undertaking of responsibility by the defendant towards the plaintiff, coupled with reliance by the plaintiff on the exercise by the defendant of due care and skill. Lord Devlin . . . said that 'the essence of the matter in the present case and in others of the same type is the acceptance of responsibility'.

152 [1995] 2 AC 296.   153 [1995] 2 AC 145.   154 [1994] 3 All ER 129 at 143.

> Where the plaintiff entrusts the defendant with the conduct of his affairs, in general or in particular, the defendant may be held to have assumed responsibility to the plaintiff, and the plaintiff to have relied on the defendant to exercise due skill and care, in respect of such conduct.[155]

The special skill here embraces 'special knowledge': 'the employer is possessed of special knowledge, derived from his experience of the employee's character, skill and diligence'.[156] And the reference is also for the benefit of the employee, not just the enquirer:

> The provision of such references is a service regularly provided by employers to their employees; indeed, references are part of the currency of the modern employment market . . . It is plain that the employee relies on [the employer] to exercise due skill and care in the preparation of the reference before making it available to the third party . . . All the elements requisite for the application of the *Hedley Byrne* principle are present.[157]

And Lord Goff expressly denied that this decision would in any way affect the general practices of giving references: 'the vast majority of employers will continue, as before, to provide careful references. But those who, as in the present case, fail to achieve that standard, will have to compensate their employees who suffer damage in consequence. Justice, in my opinion, requires that this should be done, and I . . . cannot see any reason in policy why that justice should be denied.'[158]

It is noteworthy that Lord Keith in a dissenting judgment based his concerns on issues of public policy, feeling that employers would, as a result of this decision, be apprehensive of negligence actions and may not provide the full and frank references which business requires. Lord Keith also noted that in this case there was *no* reliance by the plaintiff on any statement – an issue to which we will return presently.

The facts of *Henderson v Merrett Syndicates Ltd* concerned the claim by a number of Lloyd's 'names' who were members of syndicates managed by the defendant underwriting agents, and who had suffered considerable financial losses following a series of substantial claims against Lloyd's. The relationships between the plaintiffs and the defendants were contractual ones, and it was accepted that it was an implied term in the various contractual agreements that the agents would exercise due care and skill in the exercise of their function as agents. The plaintiffs wished to establish, however, because of limitation implications, whether there was also a duty of care in negligence owed to them by the agents, or by sub-agents. It was decided, in the trial of the substantive claims by the names, that the plaintiffs should succeed. Clearly, the losses involved were purely economic. The defendants argued, *inter alia*, that the existence of a tortious duty was inconsistent with the contractual relationship between the parties – a point which, as we have already seen, has been regarded by the courts as significant in a number of recent cases.

---

155 Ibid., at p 145.   156 Ibid., at p 146.   157 Ibid., at p 147.   158 Ibid., at p 151.

In the leading judgment, Lord Goff once again went straight to *Hedley Byrne*, and indeed discussed very few other cases in any detail. He placed much emphasis again on the passages in that case concerning *reliance* on a person's special skill, and the *voluntary undertaking* by the provider of information or advice to give information or advice to persons when he knows, or should know, that those persons will rely on it. Those circumstances, it was said in *Hedley Byrne*, will give rise to a duty. Lord Goff referred to Lord Devlin's statement in *Hedley Byrne* to the effect that there are relationships which, but for the absence of consideration, are 'equivalent to contract', and went on to say that:

> we can derive some understanding of the breadth of the principle underlying the case. We can see that it rests upon a relationship between the parties, which may be general or specific to the particular transaction, and which may or may not be contractual in nature. All of their Lordships spoke in terms of one party having assumed or undertaken a responsibility towards the other . . . Although *Hedley Byrne* was concerned with the provision of information and advice, the example given by Lord Devlin of the relationship between solicitor and client . . . show(s) that the principle extends beyond the provision of information and advice to include the performance of other services.[159]

His Lordship stressed the need for the element of reliance, which may include cases 'where the plaintiff entrusts the defendant with the conduct of his affairs . . . [and where] . . . he may be held to have relied on the defendant to exercise due skill and care in such conduct',[160] giving, as an example of this, the relationship between a solicitor and a client.

Lord Goff recognised that the courts in some recent cases, in trying to impose reasonable boundaries around the scope of the tort, have tended to criticise the notion of 'assumption of responsibility' as being 'unlikely to be a helpful or realistic test' (*Smith v Eric S Bush*). But here, he felt, there was no reason not to use the concept, 'which appears after all to have been adopted, in one form or another, by all of their Lordships in *Hedley Byrne*'; he continued:

> If a person assumes responsibility to another in respect of certain services, there is no reason why he should not be liable in damages for that other in respect of economic loss which flows from the negligent performance of those services. It follows that, once the case is identified as falling within the *Hedley Byrne* principle, there should be no need to embark upon any further inquiry whether it is 'fair, just and reasonable' to impose liability for economic loss – a point which is, I consider, of some importance in the present case.[161]

Did the *Hedley Byrne* principle apply to the present case? Lord Goff clearly felt that it did. Noting that the group of persons to whom the case has been applied has widened,[162] Lord Goff could see no reason why a duty should not be imposed on

---

159 [1994] 3 All ER 506, p 520.   160 Ibid.   161 Ibid., p 521.

162 See the cases cited above. For a recent, and unsuccessful, attempt to widen the applicable categories still further, see *Goodwill v British Pregnancy Advisory Service* [1996] 2 All ER 161.

the defendants here. Indeed, 'the relationship between name and managing agent appears to provide a classic example of the type of relationship to which the principle in *Hedley Byrne* applies'.[163] There is an *assumption of responsibility* and there is *reliance*:

> The managing agents hold themselves out as *possessing a special expertise* to advise the names on the suitability of risks to be underwritten; the names, as the managing agents well knew, placed implicit *reliance* on that expertise, in that they gave authority to the managing agents to bind them to contracts of insurance and reinsurance and to the settlement of claims. I can see no escape from the conclusion that, in these circumstances, *prima facie* a duty of care is owed in tort by the managing agents to such names.[164]

Although the 'voluntary assumption of responsibility/reliance' equation may have cut through much of the doctrinal confusion arising from some of the earlier cases, it leaves several questions unanswered. For example, although it clearly covers the basic situation where A makes a statement to B and B relies on it to his detriment, does it cover the case where there may be lots of Bs (and, in particular, where those Bs are *not* related by contract to A) – the situation, for example, in *Caparo*? Does Lord Goff's rehabilitation of 'voluntary assumption of responsibility' cover this situation? Presumably an auditor or accountant does not voluntarily undertake responsibility as regards indeterminate large numbers of Bs. What about the case where A makes a statement to B, which is relied upon by C to C's detriment? Could 'voluntary assumption' also cover this? To answer this question, we would have to return to the statements in *Caparo* and other cases in which the courts have addressed the question as to the degree of knowledge which A must possess regarding C.[165]

The issue of 'reliance' is equally problematic. The meaning of 'reliance' in both *Spring* and *Merrett* is much wider than that in *Hedley Byrne*, or for that matter in *Caparo* and other recent cases, where the 'reliance' relates to a specific *statement* made by the defendant.[166] In *Spring* and *Merrett*, it must be acknowledged that the meaning of the term is much more generalised. And in *White v Jones* in 1995,[167] another case in which Lord Goff invoked the *Hedley Byrne* principle, there cannot be said to have been any 'reliance' by the plaintiff at all.

In *White v Jones*, the facts were that a testator had, after a family quarrel, made a will which excluded his daughters from any bequest upon his death. A few months later there had been a reconciliation, and the testator had instructed the defendant solicitors to draw up an amended will in order to leave gifts of £9,000 each to his daughters. The solicitors had negligently failed to amend the will, and the testator died without the earlier will being amended. As a result, the two daughters – the plaintiffs in this action – failed to receive the intended gifts, and brought this action alleging

---

163 Ibid., p 522.   164 Ibid.
165 See, for example, *Harris v Wyre Forest District Council* [1988] 1 All ER 691.
166 See, for example, *Lambert v West Devon Borough Council* (1997) 96 LRG 45.
167 [1995] 1 All ER 691.

negligence by the solicitors. The trial judge held that there was no duty; the Court of Appeal allowed the appeal; there had been a breach of the solicitor's professional duty and there had to be a remedy in such cases because in the event of negligence by a solicitor, the testator, once deceased, could not seek any remedy. It was just and reasonable, then, in the court's view, that the intended beneficiary should be able to sue.

On appeal by the defendants to the House of Lords, it was held by a majority (Lord Keith and Lord Mustill dissenting) that a duty of care *was* owed by a solicitor to a testator in these circumstances, though this conclusion was reached only by explicitly making an extension to the existing law. Lord Keith recognised that there was a contractual duty between the testator and the defendants, but stressed that no contract existed between the plaintiffs and the defendants. To allow the plaintiffs to succeed would therefore have infringed the privity of contract principle (see chapter 11). As far as allowing the claim based in negligence was concerned, his lordship stated that he 'found the conceptual difficulties involved in the plaintiffs' claim. . . . to be too formidable to be resolved by any process of reasoning compatible with existing principles of law'.[168]

In his judgment, Lord Goff discussed the situation in other countries, noting that such claims as the present one were allowable in some, though not in other, jurisdictions. There were a number of conceptual difficulties involved in the claim: first, a solicitor arguably owes a duty of care only to the client, on the basis that that relationship is almost always a contractual one. Second, it is arguable that no tortious duty can be owed to the beneficiary because the latter's loss is purely financial: apart from cases falling within *Hedley Byrne*, no such liability is generally recognised in tort.

Third, if liability *were* to be recognised in cases such as this, 'it would be impossible to place any sensible bounds to cases in which such recovery was allowed'.[169] This is, of course, the floodgates argument. And, furthermore, there was no act by the solicitor which could be characterised as negligent: the solicitor simply did nothing for a period of time. As we have seen, the general rule, subject to some exceptions, is that there is no liability in negligence in respect of the defendant's omission.

Lord Goff, having recognised these problems, went on to discuss what he termed 'the impulse to do practical justice'[170] and he summarised his views on this point thus:

(i)   In the forefront stands the extraordinary fact that, if such a duty is not recognised, the only persons who might have a valid claim (i.e. the testator and his estate) have suffered no loss, and the only person who had suffered a loss (i.e. the disappointed beneficiary) has no claim . . . This I regard as being of cardinal importance in the present case.

(ii)   The injustice of denying such a remedy is reinforced if one considers . . . the right of citizens to leave their assets to whom they please . . .

(iii)   . . . the solicitors' profession cannot complain if such a liability may be imposed upon their members. If one of them has been negligent in such a way as to defeat his client's

168 Ibid., p 695.   169 Ibid., p 700.   170 Ibid., p 702.

testamentary intentions, he must regard himself as very lucky indeed if the effect of the law is that he is not liable to pay damages in the ordinary way.

(iv) That such a conclusion is required as a matter of justice is reinforced by consideration of the role played by solicitors in modern society.[171]

His Lordship, after discussing a number of possible approaches to the problem, each of which he found problematic for one or more reasons, turned to tort for a solution, and held that:

> your Lordships' House should in cases such as these extend to the intended beneficiary a remedy under the *Hedley Byrne* principle by holding that the assumption of responsibility by the solicitor towards his client should be held in law to extend to the intended beneficiary who (as the solicitor can reasonably foresee) may, as a result of the solicitor's negligence, be deprived of his intended legacy in circumstances in which neither the testator nor his estate will have a remedy against the solicitor.[172]

This solution, he argued, does not contravene any contractual principles; nor does any problem arise by reason of it being economic loss. Lord Goff was not impressed by the floodgate arguments, stating that, though there must of course be limits to liability, it was up to the courts in future cases to delimit the boundaries on a case-by-case basis, rather than to deny practical justice in any particular instance.

Lord Browne-Wilkinson agreed with Lord Goff, stressing the importance of the notions of 'assumption of responsibility' and 'reliance' in *Hedley Byrne* itself. Although, as he acknowledged, the intended beneficiary could not be said to have relied upon the solicitor, 'the solicitor who accepts instructions to draw a will knows that the future economic welfare of the intended beneficiary is dependent upon his careful execution of the task'.[173] And the solicitor, by accepting the client's instructions, has 'assumed responsibility for the task of procuring the execution of a skilfully drawn will knowing that the beneficiary is wholly dependent upon his carefully carrying out his function'.[174] This reasoning is interesting, since it subtly shifts the emphasis away from 'reliance' (which is, so to speak, something which the *plaintiff* does) to 'knowledge of the beneficiary's dependence', which is, or ought reasonably to be, something in the mind of the *defendant*.[175]

This case clearly represents, as the majority in the House of Lords acknowledged, an extension of the law, and this in more ways than one. To begin with, despite basing this extension on the foundation-stone of *Hedley Byrne*, it is clear that the situation is some way removed from the original notion of a negligent *statement* which is relied on by the plaintiff: here, the defendants made no statement, but rather did nothing at all. It must therefore also be viewed as an extension of the law relating to liability for omissions, the path having been paved for this extension by *Henderson* and also to an extent (though it did not figure in this case) by *Spring*: see in particular the judgments of Lord Goff in both cases on the issues of *assumption of responsibility* and *reliance*.

171 Ibid., pp 702–703.   172 Ibid., p 710.   173 Ibid., p 717.   174 Ibid., p 718.
175 See *Gorham v British Telecommunications plc* [2000] 1 WLR 2129.

As the law now stands, it is not possible to provide a definitive statement as to when a duty might arise in this area of law. As we have seen, the judges have by no means been unanimous in regarding the 'voluntary assumption of responsibility' factor as particularly significant, and the notion of 'reliance' has proved problematic in some cases. It is difficult not to have sympathy with the courts' desire to keep this developing area within bounds, but at the same time it is very difficult to discern much consistency in the recent case law.

Negligent acts or omissions causing psychiatric illness

Subject to what has been said regarding the current judicial thinking on the duty of care, the basic principles governing liability for physical damage or loss resulting from someone's negligence are fairly well-established. There is, similarly, little difficulty where a plaintiff suffers psychiatric illness consequent upon physical harm. But what of the case where someone suffers no physical harm at all, but claims that as a result of a defendant's negligent act or omission, he or she has suffered some form of psychiatric illness: what the courts for many years referred to as 'nervous shock'?

To begin with, it has long been the case that 'nervous shock' must be distinguished from 'ordinary' distress or grief. The latter is not recoverable in negligence:

> The driver of a car . . . even though careless is entitled to assume that the ordinary frequenter of the streets has sufficient fortitude to endure such incidents as may from time to time be expected to occur in them . . . and is not to be considered negligent towards one who does not possess the customary phlegm.[176]

although exactly what the difference comprises has never been clear. Apart from this, the history of liability for 'nervous shock' is characterised by two features. First, we must recognise that until relatively recently the nature and causes of psychiatric harm were little enough understood by the medical profession, let alone the judiciary; and second, it is true to say that judicial reluctance to open the doors to recovery for such harm was, and remains, due to a degree of suspiciousness on the part of the judges as to the authenticity of such claims. How could it be established, for example, that a plaintiff was suffering from a clinically diagnosable psychiatric condition, as opposed to 'normal' distress or grief? How might fraudulent claims be avoided? Even if such a condition were to be established, how could it be shown to have been *caused* by a defendant's negligence?

Thus in 1888, in *Victoria Railway Comrs v Coultas*[177] a level-crossing attendant negligently allowed a pregnant woman to cross the railway line in her carriage in front of an oncoming train. She suffered nervous shock and a miscarriage. The Privy Council refused her claim on the basis that such damage was simply too

---

176 *Bourhill v Young* [1943] AC 92 at 117, per Lord Porter.   177 (1888) 13 App Cas 222.

remote a consequence. By 1901, however, in *Dulieu v White*,[178] a more positive approach began to develop, though still reflecting caution by the courts. Here, a pregnant barmaid suffered nervous shock when a negligently driven van crashed into the pub where she was working behind the bar. It was held that this harm was recoverable, as long as the shock was sustained by reason of the plaintiff's reasonable fear for her own personal safety.

In *Hambrook v Stokes Bros* in 1925,[179] a mother saw a lorry out of control, careering down a hill from around a bend round which her three children has just gone on their way to school. She suffered severe nervous shock through fear that her children had been injured. Once again, compensation was allowed, the Court of Appeal being of the view that the qualification in *Dulieu* was too narrow. This decision established first, that a plaintiff need no longer be in fear of physical injury to herself; second, that a claim might succeed where the harm was suffered after the disaster had occurred (as opposed to being about to occur); and third, that there was a qualification on the right to recovery, this being that the plaintiff's shock had to result from what she had seen with her own unaided senses, and not as a result of what someone else had told her.

The House of Lords in *Bourhill v Young* in 1943[180] denied liability to a woman who suffered both physical and psychiatric damage. She had been alighting from a stationary tram when, on the other side of the tram, a motor-cyclist negligently collided with a car. The plaintiff had heard the crash (in which the motor-cyclist was killed) and a little later on witnessed the scene and saw blood on the road. It was as a result of these experiences, she alleged, that she had suffered the damage complained of. The exact *ratio* of the case is not clear, though it was noted that the plaintiff did not witness the crash itself with her own eyes and ears, and was never in any physical danger herself from the crash (being protected, as it were, by the tram), and that therefore she was, as far as the motor-cyclist was concerned, an unforeseeable plaintiff.

Boardman v Sanderson,[181] decided in 1964, was more in line with *Hambrook*: the defendant had negligently reversed his car over the foot of the plaintiff's young son. The plaintiff was within earshot and heard the boy's screams, though did not actually witness the accident himself. Again, the plaintiff recovered compensation.[182]

In *Dulieu*, the plaintiff was put in fear of physical harm to herself; in the other cases discussed so far, the plaintiffs were 'secondary' victims, in the sense that they suffered harm as a result of apprehending harm to someone else – the 'primary' victim. This distinction was emphasised in *Page v Smith* in 1995[183] in which the driver of a car, which had been involved in a minor accident with a vehicle driven by the defendant, had suffered no physical injury but had suffered, as a result of the collision, a recurrence of his pre-existing myalgic encephalomyelitis (ME). It was

---

178 [1901] 2 KB 669.   179 [1925] 1 KB 141.   180 [1943] AC 92.
181 [1964] 1 WLR 1317.   182 See also *Hinz v Berry* [1970] 1 All ER 1074.
183 [1996] AC 155.

held that, as regards *primary* victims, there was no distinction in principle between physical and psychiatric harm; the issue was one of reasonable foreseeability, and, as has long been established in cases of physical injury, the defendant must take the plaintiff as he finds him.[184]

It will no doubt have been noticed that in most of these cases where recovery was allowed, there was a close family tie between plaintiff and the primary victims of the incidents in question. There are, however, cases in which plaintiffs have recovered despite the lack of close ties. In *Chadwick v British Railways Board* in 1967, for example,[185] the plaintiff became ill after helping in the rescue of passengers in a terrible railway accident. The court held that the circumstances of the injuries to the passengers and of the accident in general were such that it was reasonably foreseeable that those witnessing its results would suffer psychiatric harm. And in *Wigg v British Railways Board* in 1986,[186] it was held that it was reasonably foreseeable that a train driver who stopped the train and got down to help a passenger who had fallen in front of the train, owing to the negligence of the guard in giving the starting-signal, but who had in fact died, might suffer nervous shock. These cases are, however, explicable by virtue of the fact that in both cases the plaintiffs were classed as 'rescuers'. As pointed out above, defendants who, by their negligence, create a dangerous situation which threatens primary victims, may also owe a duty towards those who might reasonably foreseeably come along to try to rescue those victims, and who themselves succumb to the danger.[187] We will say more about the current position of rescuers presently.

In *McLoughlin v O'Brian* in 1983,[188] a mother received news, whilst at home, that her family had just been involved in a road accident in which their car had been in collision with a lorry. The crash had been caused by the defendant lorry-driver. Mrs McLoughlin was taken to the hospital, where she was informed that one of her children had been killed and that her husband and other children had been seriously injured. She saw the injured members of her family in the state in which they had been brought to hospital and before they had received any medical treatment: these circumstances were described by Lord Wilberforce as 'distressing in the extreme and . . . capable of producing an effect going well beyond that of grief and sorrow'.[189] The mother subsequently suffered severe shock, organic depression and a change of personality, in respect of which she brought this action against the lorry-driver.

In the House of Lords, two views emerged from the judgments. In the opinion of Lord Bridge, liability here should depend, quite simply, on the test of whether the injuries were reasonably foreseeable, although he added the qualification that the illness would have to amount to more than the degree of shock which a person

---

184 Though see the critique of this case by Lord Goff in the course of his judgment in *White v Chief Constable of South Yorkshire* [1999] 2 AC 455.   185 [1967] 2 All ER 945.
186 [1986] *NLJ Rep* 446n.   187 See the 'rescue' cases cited above, but see also the important qualifications to the law on rescue in *White v Chief Constable of South Yorkshire* [1999] 2 AC 455, discussed below.   188 [1983] 1 AC 410.   189 [1983] 1 AC 410 at 417.

of reasonable fortitude might suffer. He specifically rejected the 'floodgates' argument as being greatly exaggerated.

Lord Wilberforce, however, stated what has become known in these 'nervous shock' cases as the 'aftermath' principle. On his view, recovery was allowed, but only where the shock came through sight or hearing of the event or its 'immediate aftermath'; on the facts, arrival at the hospital some two hours after the crash was held to be within the 'immediate aftermath'. Furthermore, in his lordship's view, there must be a close relationship between the plaintiff and the primary victim (subject to the qualification regarding 'rescuers', noted above):

> As regards the class of persons (who may recover), the possible range is between the closest of family ties, of parent and child, or husband and wife, and the ordinary bystander. Existing law recognises the claims of the first; it denies that of the second, either on the basis that such persons must be assumed to be possessed of fortitude sufficient to enable them to endure the calamities of modern life or that defendants cannot be expected to compensate the world at large . . . The closer the tie (not merely in relationship, but in care) the greater the claim for compensation. The claim, in any case, has to be judged in the light of the other factors, such as proximity to the scene in time and place, and the nature of the accident.[190]

In the autumn of 1991 came the House of Lords decision in the litigation arising from the Hillsborough Football Stadium tragedy in Sheffield in April 1989, reported as *Alcock and others v Chief Constable of South Yorkshire Police*.[191] It is necessary to outline the facts in some detail.

On the day of a semi-final FA Cup football match between Liverpool and Nottingham Forest, to be played at Sheffield Wednesday's Hillsborough Stadium, the South Yorkshire police allowed a large crowd of intending spectators into the ground, and into an area reserved for Liverpool supporters which was already full. In the resulting crush, 95 people were killed and over 400 injured. The match was to have been televised live, and scenes of the disaster were broadcast during the course of the disaster. It was acknowledged that the television broadcasts were carried out in line with television broadcasting guidelines: none of the television pictures depicted the suffering or dying of any recognisable individuals. The defendant admitted liability in respect of those killed and injured in the disaster. The plaintiffs in this action all claimed compensation for the psychiatric illness they suffered as a result of either seeing the television broadcasts or actually being present in other parts of the stadium, and knowing that their relatives or friends might be killed or injured in the crush. The defendant denied liability to these plaintiffs on the ground that he owed them no duty of care.

In fact, of the original 16 plaintiffs in the litigation, only ten appealed to the House of Lords. Nine of these plaintiffs had lost relatives; the tenth had lost her fiancé. All but two of them had witnessed either television or radio broadcasts of

---

190 [1983] 1 AC 410, p 422.   191 [1992] 1 AC 310.

the tragedy; the others had been at the stadium, though not in the affected part of the ground – they had witnessed the tragedy at first hand. One of these two plaintiffs had learned of his two brothers' deaths by telephone the next morning; the other plaintiff, who lost his brother-in-law, identified the latter's body in the temporary mortuary at the football ground at around midnight the same night.

The plaintiffs were unsuccessful for a number of reasons. Lord Keith, considering the three elements said to be inherent in any claim of this kind – 'the class of persons whose claims should be recognised; the proximity of such persons to the accident; and the means by which the shock is caused'[192] – felt that with regard to the first factor, reasonable foreseeability should be the guide: he 'would not seek to limit the class by reference to particular relationships such as husband and wife or parent and child', because the key issue was 'close ties of love and affection' rather than specific relationships; even an unrelated bystander might not be excluded from the range of reasonably foreseeable victims of shock 'if the circumstances of a catastrophe occurring very close to him were particularly horrific'.[193] As to the element of 'proximity', he stressed the need for the plaintiff to be close to the accident 'in time and space', either through actual presence or through coming upon the 'immediate aftermath'. And Lord Keith reiterated the requirement that the means whereby the shock is caused should be by sight or hearing of the event or its immediate aftermath, and not by receiving the news through a third party.

On this basis, Lord Keith rejected the claims of the plaintiffs who were present at the stadium on the grounds that neither had shown evidence of particularly close ties of love or affection with the deceased. On the same basis he rejected the claims of those not at the stadium, with the exceptions of those who had lost a son and the woman who had lost her fiancé. However, these three plaintiffs had witnessed the event on television; in Lord Keith's opinion,

> the viewing of these scenes cannot be equiparated with the viewer being within 'sight or hearing of the event or its immediate aftermath' . . . nor can the senses reasonably be regarded as giving rise to shock, in the sense of a sudden assault on the nervous system. They were capable of giving rise to anxiety for the safety of relatives known or believed to be present in the area . . . and undoubtedly did so, but that is very different from seeing the fate of the relative or his condition shortly after the event. The viewing of the television scenes did not create the necessary degree of proximity.[194]

Lord Ackner pointed out that the plaintiffs in this case were effectively seeking to extend the principles governing liability for shock beyond previous case law and stressed that in this area of law there was a real need for some limitation upon the extent of admissible claims. He too would not confine the class of potential plaintiffs to those within specific named relationships, but stressed the essential requirement for 'close ties of love and affection'. As to 'proximity to the accident', his lordship felt that in the case of the plaintiff who had identified his brother-in-law at the makeshift

192 Ibid., p 912.   193 Ibid., at p 914.   194 Ibid., p 915.

mortuary at the stadium the same night, the fact that some eight hours had elapsed since the event which had caused the death meant that this could not possibly be described as part of the 'immediate aftermath'.

The other plaintiff who had been at the football ground, and who had lost two brothers, was dealt with fairly briefly, and his claim dismissed, on the apparent ground that his claim had not been presented 'upon the basis that there was such a close and intimate relationship between them as gave rise to that very special bond of affection which would make his shock-induced psychiatric illness reasonably foreseeable by the chief constable' and that, as there was therefore 'no evidence to establish the necessary proximity which would make his claim reasonably foreseeable'[195] his claim was not valid.

As regards the plaintiffs who had witnessed the event on television, Lord Ackner agreed that this could not be equated with 'sight or hearing of the event of its immediate aftermath'.

In the course of his judgment, Lord Oliver, too, stressed the need to establish the requisite degree of 'proximity' between plaintiff, primary victim and the accident itself. Largely echoing the speeches of Lords Keith and Ackner, his lordship spoke of the need to establish that there was, as between primary victim and plaintiff, an 'affectionate relationship'.[196] Once again, receipt of the information by means of television was dismissed as not providing the necessary 'degree of immediacy',[197] and Lord Oliver pointed out that all of the plaintiffs except for the two who were present at the stadium received news of the deaths 'second hand and many hours later'.[198] In the case of the two plaintiffs who were at the ground:

> their perception of the actual consequences of the disaster to those to whom they were related was again gradual. In my judgment, the necessary proximity was lacking in their cases too . . . but . . . there is also lacking the necessary element of reasonable foreseeability.[199]

Interestingly, Lord Oliver referred at several points to the lack of logic – in his view inevitable – in this area of law, and concluded that the policy considerations inherent in the 'nervous shock' decisions could be better stated by means of legislative enactment.

The other two judgments, by Lord Jauncey and Lord Lowry, add little to the reasons already outlined for rejecting the plaintiffs' appeals.

The current state of the law has been criticised as profoundly unsatisfactory. In terms of the issues which future plaintiffs must address, and on which they must satisfy a court, the following are among the problems which the case raises.

First, for exactly how long, in terms of hours, does an 'immediate aftermath' last? Two hours in *McLoughlin* was held to be admissible; eight hours in *Alcock* was held to be too long. Where is the cut-off point? In *Galli-Atkinson v Seghal*[200] the plaintiff

---

195 Ibid., p 921.   196 Ibid., p 930.   197 Ibid., p 931.   198 Ibid.
199 Ibid., pp 931–932.   200 [2003] EWCA Civ 697.

had arrived at the scene of a road accident about one hour after the accident had occurred. She was told by a police officer that her 16-year-old daughter, who had been involved in the accident, was dead. Later at the mortuary, some two hours after the accident, the plaintiff saw her daughter's body. The plaintiff claimed damages in respect of a psychiatric condition which ensured. In this case the Court of Appeal held that the immediate aftermath extended from the moment of the accident until the moment when the plaintiff saw and held her daughter's body in the mortuary. The Court took the view that the 'aftermath' of such an incident could comprise a number of components, provided that overall there was sufficient 'proximity' to the original accident. Second, if the relationship between the plaintiff and the primary victim is not to be specified, but must none the less be one involving 'close ties of love and affection', what exactly must a plaintiff establish? We may assume that such ties will easily be demonstrated in the case of spouses or as between parents and children; but how may the evidentiary burden be discharged in cases involving less obviously close relationships?[201]

Third, although perception of the event by means of television was rejected as insufficiently proximate by all the judges in *Alcock*, Lord Ackner somewhat confusingly suggested that there might well be cases where such perception would be 'the equivalent of the actual sight or hearing of the event or its immediate aftermath'. He cited the example of Nolan LJ in the Court of Appeal as:

> an example of a situation where it was reasonable to anticipate that the television cameras, whilst filming and transmitting pictures of a special event of children travelling in a balloon, in which there was media interest, particularly amongst the parents, showed the balloon suddenly bursting into flames . . . Many other such situations could be imagined where the impact of the simultaneous television pictures would be as great, if not greater, than the actual sight of the accident.[202]

Why, logically, should there be any distinction between such a hypothetical case and that which actually occurred? And might it not be argued that the perception of a live television broadcast could in fact be a greater stimulus to shock than physical presence at the event? The awareness of not being present, and the inability to do anything to help or save the victims, might well be more of a trigger inducing psychiatric illness.

In *McFarlane v EE Caledonia Ltd*[203] in 1994, the plaintiff had been a worker on the *Piper Alpha* oil-rig which was destroyed by fire in 1988, resulting in the death of 164 men. The plaintiff had at the time been off-duty, and was on a ship some 100 metres from the rig. He had watched the destruction of the oil-rig and believed that he himself was in physical danger (though the court held that he had never been in any physical danger himself).[204] He argued that he should recover

---

201 In two cases decided since *Alcock*, relatives of Hillsborough victims were held to have satisfied the criterion of 'close ties of love and affection' and were successful in their claim for damages.

202 [1991] 4 All ER 907, p 921.   203 [1994] 2 All ER 1.

204 See also *Hegarty v EE Caledonia Ltd* [1997] 2 Lloyd's Rep 259, where the facts were virtually identical to those in *McFarlane*. In *Hegarty* Brooke LJ remarked that: 'The law does not . . .

for the psychiatric harm which he suffered as a result of witnessing this horrific event on the ground, *inter alia*,[205] that it had been recognised in *Alcock* that even a bystander might recover in such circumstances. The plaintiff's argument failed: the court held that individuals' reactions to disastrous events were wholly subjective and hence, from a defendant's point of view, unforeseeable. Indeed, it was pointed out that many bystanders gather at accident scenes simply to witness those events. In order to succeed, the plaintiff would have had to establish the criteria laid down in *Alcock*, which, in this case, he had failed to do. A similar conclusion was reached in *Robertson v Forth Road Bridge Joint Board (No 2)*[206] in 1994. It is doubtful whether the comments in *Alcock* regarding bystanders can now be regarded as creating any exception to the specific requirements defined in that case.[207]

It is clear that the courts are determined to confine the boundaries of liability in this area of law by means of the 'aftermath' doctrine: several of the judgments in *Alcock* made it clear that liability does not simply depend on foreseeability. The area is replete with difficulties of 'drawing the line' which can only perpetuate uncertainty in the law; and it has been suggested that recent cases do little to indicate judicial awareness of modern psychiatric knowledge of shock, or post-traumatic stress disorder.[208]

In *White v Chief Constable of South Yorkshire Police*[209] in 1999, a number of police officers who had suffered psychiatric disorders after assisting at the Hillsborough football stadium disaster sued the Chief Constable on the basis that the relationship between themselves and the defendant was equivalent to that of employment. Three of the officers had been on duty at the time, and had been involved in dealing with the victims; two other officers had arrived at the scene somewhat later, but also witnessed horrific scenes. A sixth officer had not been present at the football stadium, but had dealt with hospital staff and relatives. In the Court of Appeal, it was held that although no duty was owed to the last-mentioned officer, who had not been close to the immediate scene of the disaster, the first five officers could recover, either on the basis that they had witnessed exceptionally horrific scenes in the course of their employment, or that they were rescuers – and it made no difference that they might be described as 'professional rescuers' – and were therefore owed the same duty of care as the 'primary' victims, that is, the football supporters at the stadium.

accommodate people who are not directly threatened but who genuinely and irrationally believe they are, because their dilemma is not reasonably foreseeable. This is one of the control mechanisms the law has created . . .'
205 The plaintiff also argued that he was in the position of a rescuer. The court rejected this argument, since he had played no part in any attempt at rescue.   206 [1994] SLT 568.
207 See also *Hunter v British Coal Corporation* (1998) 42 BMLR 1.
208 For further reading see A. Ritchie, 'Damages for Psychiatric Injuries' (1994) *NLJ*, 9 December; D. W. Robertson, 'Liability in Negligence for Nervous Shock' [1994] 57 *MLR*; M. Napier and K. Wheat, *Recovering Damages for Psychiatric Injury* (1995, Blackstone); H. Teff, 'Liability for Negligently Inflicted Psychiatric Harm: Justifications and Boundaries' (1998) 57 *CLJ* 91.
209 [1999] 2 AC 455.

The House of Lords, however, disagreed. As quasi-employees, the officers were subject to the normal rules of negligence, and would have had to satisfy the control devices in *Alcock* – close ties of love and affection, proximity in time and space, and direct perception of the accident or its immediate aftermath. Clearly, the police officers did not satisfy all these tests. And with respect to their claim as rescuers, the court made it plain that rescuers were in no special position: in Lord Hoffmann's view,

> References in the authorities to rescuers sometimes give the impression that they are a category of persons who would not qualify for compensation under the strict rules of the law of negligence but receive special treatment on grounds of humanity and as a reward for altruism . . . In fact, . . . the cases on rescuers are . . . quite simply illustrations of the application of general principles of foreseeability and causation to particular facts. There is no authority which decides that a rescuer is in any special position in relation to liability for psychiatric injury.[210]

This is, in effect, stating that the law of rescue requires that the rescuer should *himself* have been in danger of foreseeable physical injury when effecting or attempting the rescue – a proposition with which not all members of the House of Lords agreed,[211] but which seems now to constitute the law on this point. Lord Hoffmann acknowledged that there could be an extension to the law so that rescuers in the position of the police officers did not need to establish that they were in physical danger, but in his Lordship's view there was at least one further important consideration, which several members of the House of Lords explicitly discussed. This was the danger of a public perception of unfairness if the police officers' cases succeeded when those of the relatives of the Hillsborough victims had failed. Lord Hoffmann felt that the 'ordinary person':

> would think it unfair between one class of claimants and another, at best not treating like cases alike and, at worst, favouring the less deserving against the more deserving. He would think it wrong that policemen, even as part of a general class of persons who rendered assistance, should have the right to compensation for psychiatric injury out of public funds while the bereaved relatives are sent away with nothing.[212]

Furthermore, added Lord Hoffmann:

> It seems to me that in this area of the law, the search for principle was called off in *Alcock v Chief Constable of South Yorkshire Police*.[213] No one can pretend that the existing law, which your Lordships have to accept, is founded upon principle . . . Consequently your Lordships are now engaged, not in the bold development of principle, but in a practical attempt, under adverse conditions, to preserve the general perception of the law as a system of rules which is fair between one citizen and another.[214]

---

210 Ibid., at pp 508–509.
211 Lord Goff and Lord Griffith dissented on the point about rescuers. See L. Lomax and .S Treece, 'Liability to the professional rescuer: who pays?' (1999) 15 *Professional Negligence* 139.
212 Op. cit. at p 510.   213 Op. cit.   214 Op. cit., p 511.

Clearly, as Lord Hoffmann's comment about the 'search for principle' reveals, the law in this area is in serious need of reform. The Law Commission, in its report on *Liability for Psychiatric Illness*[215] in 1998, made a number of recommendations for changes to the law, the main ones being the creation of a new statutory duty of care (alongside existing common-law duties) whereby a person suffering reasonably foreseeable psychiatric illness as a result of the 'death, injury or imperilment' of a person with whom the person had a 'close tie of love and affection' would be entitled to recover compensation. There would be no need to establish either 'proximity in time and space' or that the person had directly perceived the accident or its aftermath with their own unaided senses. The Law Commission proposals include a detailed specification of the relationships which would be automatically presumed to involve 'close ties of love and affection' although relationships outside this list could be established by means of appropriate evidence as entailing such a 'close tie'. The Law Commission did not exclude the possibility of liability where the defendant is also the initial victim, although in *Greatorex v Greatorex*,[216] where a fireman, in the course of his employment, had attended a road accident caused by his son's careless driving, and in which the son himself had been injured, it was held that, on public policy grounds, there could be no duty owed by the son to the father in respect of psychiatric harm suffered by the latter after attending to the accident. To hold otherwise might open up the possibility of actions in negligence arising from domestic accidents; and furthermore 'a duty to take care of oneself so as not to shock others would impinge upon the defendant's right of self-determination'.[217]

Summary

Although the law relating to liability for negligence causing physical harm may remain relatively straightforward, this certainly cannot be said of recent decisions relating to economic loss (whether caused by acts, omissions or statements) or psychiatric illness. These decisions have as a common theme the judicial desire to keep within limits the number and types of situations in which negligence liability may arise, and this is clearly sensible, as long as the law remains clear as to where those limits lie. The trouble is that the resulting case law is, as we have seen, difficult, highly technical and on occasions inconsistent. Fine distinctions abound, and it is hard to resist the conclusion that in the recent use of the term 'proximity' the courts have fashioned for themselves a formidable weapon whose very vagueness and imprecision provide them with a means of reaching conclusions in new cases which owe more to judicial determination to pursue the policy of keeping negligence liability within limits, than to the case-by-case 'reasoning by analogy' approach which the higher courts claim to have resurrected.

215 Law Com No 249 (1998).   216 [2000] 4 All ER 769.
217 *Winfield and Jolowicz on Tort*, op. cit., p 185.

It is clear that our phrase 'conditions of liability' must be explained not simply in terms of the application of clear rules of law, to be applied to cases as they occur. Rather, it must be explained in terms of broad principles resting upon the foundation of fault liability; and subject to the interpretation and creativity of the judges, and the part played by judicial conceptions of what is 'reasonable and just', 'the best policy' or 'the just solution'. Hopefully, cases decided in the near future will, however, reduce some of the complexities discussed in this section to something approaching a clearer set of legal principles.

Liability for defective products[218]

Although the modern law of negligence may be said to have grown from the celebrated dicta of Lord Atkin in *Donoghue v Stevenson* in 1932, the law of negligence as it relates to a manufacturer's liability has been criticised on a number of grounds. The Thalidomide tragedy, for example (see chapter 4), was a situation where, had the issue been fully argued before the courts, it is by no means clear that the makers of the drug would have been held liable under the common law of negligence. Did the manufacturers owe a duty of care to the unborn children? And even if they did, had they been in breach of that duty? If it were established that they had researched and tested the drug according to the then accepted standards for testing within the pharmaceutical industry, then presumably they might be said to have acted 'reasonably', and had not been negligent.

Again, the somewhat arbitrary distinction between the legal rights of a buyer of defective goods and those of the consumer who was not the buyer seemed to many to be of dubious justification in the modern world. A buyer of defective goods – whether suffering injury or not from those goods – has a remedy against the seller for breach of contract (see chapter 11). For such a breach, the seller is strictly liable: the buyer has a remedy against the seller without having to prove negligence. If the consumer is not the buyer, however, then the doctrine of privity of contract prevents that person from suing for breach of contract, because only parties to a contract can bring an action arising from that contract. Could the non-purchaser sue the manufacturer in tort? The answer must be, only if that person could establish, first, that he or she had suffered injury or loss as a result of the defective goods and, second, that the manufacturer had been guilty of a breach of the duty to take reasonable care, that is to say, had been negligent.

Establishing negligent manufacture is often difficult enough, but the problem is compounded by the fact that many defective goods causing injury are not manufactured in this country, but are made overseas and imported for sale. Given the clear problem posed by attempting to sue a manufacturer in, say, Hong Kong, the

---

218 See J. Stapleton, *Product Liability* (1994, Butterworths); D. Fairgrieve (ed.), *Product Liability in Comparative Perspective* (2005, Cambridge University Press); C. Hodges, *European Regulation of Consumer Product Safety* (2005, Oxford University Press); C. Miller and R. Goldberg, *Product Liability* (2nd edn., 2004, Oxford University Press).

only alternative then would be to attempt to fix liability upon a British defendant – the importer, distributor or seller – and, once again, this could only be done (in the absence of a contract) by establishing that such a person or organisation owed a duty of care and had been negligent.

For some years, therefore, there was mounting pressure by consumer organisations and others for reform of the law which would provide a remedy for consumers injured by defective goods (whether or not they had bought the goods) which would not depend upon proof of negligence, or fault. The Law Commission proposed in 1977[219] that producers' liability in tort for injury or death caused by defective products should be strict, and these proposals were echoed, in general, by the Royal Commission on Civil Liability and Compensation for Personal Injury (the Pearson Commission), which reported in 1978.[220] More important was the European Directive on product liability,[221] adopted by the Council of the European Communities in 1985, whose provisions were enacted into English law in Part I of the Consumer Protection Act 1987.

The Act imposes strict liability for personal injury or property damage upon the 'producer' of 'defective goods' (the latter specifically including electricity, gas and water). The producer may be the manufacturer or the importer of the goods, or anyone who puts their name or mark on the goods: this means that a supermarket chain which packages and sells goods carrying its own label, even though not the manufacturer of those goods, will be strictly liable should those goods prove defective and cause injury or damage. In certain circumstances the ordinary retailer of the goods may count as 'producer' for the purposes of this Act: if the injured person requests from the seller the name of the producer, and this information is not given within a reasonable time, then the seller becomes liable as 'producer'. The injured consumer need not be the purchaser of the goods: the person who receives the defective product as a gift is protected in exactly the same way as the consumer who buys the product.

It is still necessary to establish that the damage or injury was caused by the defective article, and that the article was indeed defective. A product is defective, as provided by s3 of the Act, when its safety is not such as persons generally are entitled to expect. 'Safety' includes safety in the context of risk of damage to property as well as risk of death or personal injury. Factors which can be taken into account when determining this are the manner in which, and the purposes for which, the product has been marketed, its presentation, the use of any mark in relation to the product and any instructions or warnings included with the product; what might reasonably be expected to be done with or in relation to the product (ie the use to which it might be put); and the time when the product was supplied by its producer – though the existence of a defect may not be inferred simply because the product has since been superseded by a better product, for example, a 'Mark II' model. It

219 Law Com No 82, *Liability for Defective Products*, 1977.   220 Op. cit.
221 Council Directive 85/374/EEC.

seems clear from the wording of this part of the Act that the common-law concept of 'reasonableness' is likely still to have relevance in establishing whether an article was indeed defective. There would be few problems in establishing the defectiveness of, say, an electrical appliance which was faulty and which electrocuted the user when switched on; but suppose that a person obtains an electric hot-air paint-stripper and uses it to dry their hair, suffering burns as a result. If the manufacturer did not include in the packaging a warning against such a use, would that make the article 'defective'? Or would such a warning be thought unnecessary because 'persons generally' (the reasonable person?) would appreciate that such a use would be highly dangerous? Such questions await decision by the courts.[222]

One of the more controversial aspects of the Act is the inclusion, among other defences,[223] of the 'state of the art', or 'development risk' defence. This defence, which the European Directive made optional for member states to enact, provides, as enacted by the United Kingdom, that the producer shall not be liable if 'the state of scientific and technical knowledge at the relevant time[224] was not such that a producer of products of the same description as the products in question might be expected to have discovered the defect if it had existed in his products while they were under his control' (s 4(1)(e)). It is thought that this will enable many manufacturers to escape liability. Consider once again the Thalidomide case. As suggested above, it may well be that the manufacturers could have escaped liability in negligence by establishing that all reasonable care was taken in testing and manufacturing the drug, in accordance with the then established knowledge and practices of the pharmaceutical industry. Would not the manufacturers similarly escape liability under the Consumer Protection Act 1987 by invoking this defence?[225]

There is an absolute ban on actions brought under Part I of the Act after ten years of the supply of the product; and actions must be brought not later than three years after the date of the existence of the cause of the action, or of the consumer's knowledge of the damage, whichever is the later: this latter time-period, as mentioned above, applies by virtue of the Limitation Act 1980 to actions for personal injury in any case. This Act applies the limitation period to actions for property damage brought under the 1987 Act.

In appropriate cases, plaintiffs injured by defective products will almost certainly be more ready to bring legal actions than were plaintiffs when the area of manufacturers' liability was exclusively within the domain of the tort system. At the

---

222 See *Richardson v LRC Products* [2000] Lloyd's Rep Med 280; *A v National Blood Authority* [2001] 3 All ER 289.

223 Other defences are (i) that the defect did not exist at the time of supply (the 'relevant time'); (ii) that in the case of a defective component contained in a product, the defect was solely attributable to the design of the other product of which it formed part; (iii) that the defect is solely attributable to compliance with a legal obligation; (iv) that the defendant neither supplied the goods in the course of a business nor produced them for profit; or (v) that the producer did not supply the goods to anyone.

224 The 'relevant time' is the time when the product was put into circulation.

225 Interestingly, the German version of the Act specifically provides that pharmaceutical manufacturers may not avail themselves of the 'development risk' defence.

same time, the greater likelihood that a strict liability regime will result in more decisions against manufacturers may well urge potential defendants to settle disputes out of court – not least through insuring against such losses – and this might be one reason why litigation in this area has yet to reach the higher courts in the United Kingdom. Some of the other reasons why potential plaintiffs might view an action based in negligence with some trepidation are implicit in the above discussion; we may add, however, that from the point of view of a prospective plaintiff considering bringing an action in tort, there may well be a considerable degree of unpredictability as to the outcome of a dispute involving personal injury, or financial or property damage. We must remember at all times that the tort system requires that negligence is established before liability ensues. Given what may be substantial uncertainty about this, many injured plaintiffs may well look elsewhere for compensation. The major alternative sources of financial benefit which have developed alongside the tort system are insurance and the social security system. The first of these has had particular importance in the law of tort because of the development of the doctrine of vicarious liability.

Vicarious liability and the role of insurance

In *Bayley v Manchester, Sheffield and Lincolnshire Rly Co*[226] the wrongdoer was a railway porter, employed by the defendant company, and the plaintiff was a passenger intending to travel on a train bound for Macclesfield, his destination. The porter, however, mistakenly believing that the train was going elsewhere, seized the plaintiff and pulled him off the train, causing him injury. The plaintiff could, of course, have brought an action directly against the over-zealous porter, but instead sued the railway company for the wrongful act of their employee in the course of his job, and the company was held liable for that wrongful act.

The doctrine which allowed the plaintiff to do this is that of vicarious liability, which is of great importance in modern tort law. It is the principle, applicable only in certain circumstances, of holding one person liable for the wrongs of another. In the above example, the railway company (a legal 'person') was held liable for the tortious act of their employee, the porter. From the employer's point of view, of course, this might seem to be an imposition of strict liability in the sense that the employer himself was not at fault. But the doctrine rests on the notion that liability is transferred from the actual wrongdoer – in the above case, the porter – to the employer of that wrongdoer. Indeed, for the doctrine of vicarious liability to apply, the plaintiff must prove – in addition to establishing the specific conditions of liability attaching to the tort which the wrongdoer has allegedly committed – that the wrongdoer was *employed* by the defendant,[227] and that the injury occurred in the course of the wrongdoer's employment.

226 (1873) LR 8 CP 148.
227 The doctrine only applies if the wrongdoer and defendant are in a relationship of employment: it does not apply if the wrongdoer is an independent contractor. On this distinction, see chapter 1.

On the face of it, this may seem rather odd. Surely, it might be argued, this runs against the fundamental idea of 'no liability without fault' which is supposedly the very basis of tortious liability? Might it not be seen as unjust to hold a person liable in this way?

To answer these questions: 'justice' is a particularly difficult and elusive concept, and its meaning and scope are wholly dependent upon definitions and contexts. Vicarious liability only seems 'unjust' as long as we continue to base our general conditions of tortious liability on fault. Once it is appreciated that the idea of vicarious liability is founded upon notions quite distinct from that of fault, it is possible to explain and justify the doctrine in various ways. Atiyah has analysed a number of justifications for the doctrine, and, finding most of them wanting, concludes that 'the most rational justification that can be offered for vicarious liability today'[228] is that of loss distribution, an idea closely connected with that of insurance.

In the great majority of cases an employer who has to pay damages for the torts of his servants does not in fact have to meet these liabilities out of his own pocket. The cost of the liabilities is distributed over a large section of the community, and spread over some period of time. This occurs partly because of the practice of insurance, and partly because most employers are anyhow not individuals but corporations. Where the employer insures against his legal liabilities he will charge the cost of insurance to the goods or services which he produces. In general, this cost will be passed on by the employer in the form of higher prices to the consumer.[229]

It has been suggested that the traditional confinement of the doctrine of vicarious liability to those cases where the defendant was the employer of the wrongdoer is in need of modification, if the principle of loss distribution is not to be undermined. McKendrick has pointed out[230] that there has been a large increase in the number of self-employed workers in Britain in recent years, rising from about 1,950,000 in 1979 to around 3,345,000 in 1990. This increase is explicable in large part by:

> the desire of employers to evade the scope of employment protection legislation and by the tax advantages offered to self-employed workers. Many of these self-employed workers are in no better position than employees to pay compensation to an injured party and they are unlikely to be carrying appropriate insurance cover.[231]

In addition, there is a large number of part-time, temporary and casual workers who are not regarded in law as being employed under a contract of employment.[232] McKendrick has argued that, even though not technically in an employment contract in the eyes of the law, the employer is still, in these cases, usually in the best position to bear the burden of compensation, through insurance and the ability to pass on the costs through the pricing of his products. The law therefore ought to

---

228 P. S. Atiyah, *Vicarious Liability in the Law of Torts* (1967, Butterworths), p 13.
229 Ibid., pp 22–23.
230 E. McKendrick, 'Vicarious Liability and Independent Contractors – A Re-examination' (1990) 53 *MLR* 770. See also the discussion in Winfield and Jolowicz, op. cit.   231 Ibid., p 771.
232 See, for example, *O'Kelly v Trusthouse Forte plc* [1983] ICR 728.

recognise this, and extend the conditions under which vicarious liability will apply to these situations which fall short of comprising strict employer/employee relationships as conventionally understood.

The role of insurance must not be underestimated. As we saw in chapter 6, very few disputes having a legal element actually come before courts of law, and most claims for compensation for personal injury (if they are not dealt with through the separate system of social security benefit, the industrial injuries compensation scheme or some other alternative system) are handled by means of insurance. Even if a case comes before a court, the bodies which stand to win or lose are actually the insurance companies, for both motorists and employers are required by law[233] to insure against the risk of legal liability for accidents caused through negligence.

It must be understood that frequently the insured person is insured against legal liability, and so if the defendant is not liable according to the conditions contained in the law, the insurance company will not have to compensate the injured person. An insurance policy is

> an agreement whereby, in return for a premium, the insurer agrees to indemnify the insured against a loss – in this case, certain types of legal liability . . . It is the insured who pays the cost of the insurance because it is the insured who gets the benefit of it; . . . From the insured's point of view, then, liability insurance is a protective device. From the plaintiff's point of view, it is a vital means of ensuring that persons injured by another's tort obtain compensation' and in the context of personal injuries, this is how liability insurance is now viewed. Indeed, insurance against liability to third parties in respect of personal injury is now compulsory under the Road Traffic Act and under the Employers' Liability(Compulsory Insurance) Act; and this is not for the protection of drivers and employers but for the protection of injured road users and employees.[234]

The statutory obligation upon drivers and employers to insure underlines the fact that loss distribution is a principle of social policy. Compensation through insurance payments is made to the aggrieved person, not by one individual but, ultimately and in small doses, by a sizeable section of the community. Such a philosophy is far removed from the *laisser-faire* individualism which underpinned the establishment of individual fault as a primary condition of liability in tort a century ago, and which is now increasingly giving way to other, competing notions regarding compensation for injury. The main point of focus has become the injured person, rather than the blameworthy defendant. The development of insurance which has taken place, so to speak, alongside but outside the scope of the law of tort, is one important factor leading many critics of the tort system to cast doubt on the adequacy of that system as a means of providing compensation in modern society. In recent years, the connection, explained above, between insurance and tortious liability has given rise to new and potentially serious problems, especially in the United States. There, the

233 The current statutes are the Road Traffic Act 1988, s143(1), as amended, and the Employers' Liability (Compulsory Insurance) Act 1969.   234 P. Cane, op. cit., p 191.

298 An Introduction to Law

introduction of strict liability imposed on manufacturers for defective products has encouraged litigation which, coupled with the massive awards of compensation by American courts, has created a crisis within the insurance industry, and among the corporate and individual clients of that industry. Since liability insurance is intended to reflect the risk of liability, many corporations (and, indeed, individuals such as, in particular, medical practitioners) have been faced with enormous increases in annual insurance premiums, reflecting the insurance companies' apprehension regarding legal liability and huge awards of damages. Similarly huge rises in medical practitioners' annual insurance premiums have taken place in England. In some cases, it is reported, the cost of insurance premiums has become so high as to force some commercial enterprises to close down, and to persuade individuals such as dentists and doctors to carry out only the most minimal and 'safe' treatments upon their patients, for fear of subsequent actions for negligence should something go wrong. It remains to be seen how this crisis will be resolved.

Apart from the development of insurance, welfare state legislation has, over the years, provided a fairly comprehensive scheme for the provision of benefits for certain accidents and illnesses. This exists completely separately from the tort system. First, legislation has provided that an employee who is injured at work in circumstances 'arising out of and in the course of his employment' may claim compensation from the Department for Work and Pensions. There is no need for the claimant to establish any negligence: the simple fact of injury at work is sufficient for entitlement to benefit. This state-run 'no-fault' scheme runs side-by-side with the tort system, so that an injured employee may have a claim against the employer in negligence or some other claim in tort, as well as a claim for benefit under the state scheme. Second, the social security system, created and modified by means of a long series of statutes, provides various benefits and allowances for non-industrial sickness and disability. There is a major difference between pursuing claims from the Department and taking legal action through the tort system, however, apart from the distinction concerning fault: the state payments are considerably less than the lump-sum compensation payment which a successful claim in tort may bring, though the certainty of a successful claim from the Department for Work and Pensions is far greater than the risky business of establishing a claim in negligence in a court of law.

In recent years, criticism has mounted of the tort system as a primary means of providing compensation for the victims of injury. Compelling arguments for reform have been presented, pointing out that the tort system is cumbersome, expensive and slow, and full of technicalities and pitfalls which have the result that many injured people are unable to obtain compensation for their injuries.[235] The Thalidomide tragedy in the 1970s was largely responsible for triggering a major review of the English systems for compensation for personal injuries by means of

---

235 See, for example, T. G. Ison, *The Forensic Lottery* (1967, Staples Press); P. S. Atiyah, *Accidents, Compensation and the Law* (6th edn., by P. Cane, 1999, Cambridge University Press).

a Royal Commission set up in 1973 under the chairmanship of Lord Pearson. The Commission reported in 1978,[236] and its report covered three major areas, in addition to the recommendations on strict product liability discussed above. These areas were compensation for industrial injuries, for motor accident injuries and for handicapped children. Regarding injuries at work, the Commission felt that the existing system of state-controlled benefit paid through the social security system was basically sound, and recommended no major changes in that system. It recommended, however, modifications to the system of compensating severely handicapped children, proposing that a special benefit should be payable to parents and guardians of such children, as an addition to the child benefit provisions already in force, and payable through the (then) Department of Health and Social Security; and the introduction of a new state-run, no-fault system of compensating the victims of road accidents. These recommendations, however, met with a lukewarm reception[237] and were not implemented.

To a certain extent, the introduction of strict liability for injuries caused by defective products by means of the Consumer Protection Act 1987, discussed above, may go some way towards improving the situation, but many problems remain. A survey carried out in the mid-1970s by the Oxford Centre for Socio-Legal Studies[238] revealed that only about 12% of accident victims receive compensation through the tort system. Most victims in the sample never even considered claiming compensation, and of those who did, many did not pursue claims because of ignorance about the law and the legal profession, problems raised by the need to produce evidence of fault, delays in the legal process and the substantial costs involved in litigation. In 1988, the Report of the Review Body on Civil Justice[239] found that High Court cases could often take up to five or six years from the original incident to the courtroom conclusion, and county court cases, involving disputed sums of less than £3,000, could take three years or more; and in a successful High Court action, the legal costs could swallow up half or even more of the damages awarded. In the county court, it was found that legal costs could even exceed the sums awarded as damages.

Of course, on an analysis such as that of Abel, discussed above, nothing short of radical socio-economic change in society would adequately meet many of the shortfalls of the processes both of accident causation and of injury compensation. Many have, none the less, been concerned to propose reforms of the English tort

---

236 *Report of the Royal Commission on Civil Liability and Compensation for Personal Injury* (the Pearson Report) (1978, Cmnd 7054, HMSO); see also the *Civil Justice Review* (1988, Cm 395, HMSO).

237 See J. F. Fleming, 'The Pearson Report: Its "Strategy"' (1979) *MLR* at 250; N. S. Marsh, 'The Pearson Report on Civil Liability for Death and Personal Injury' (1979) *LQR* at 513; D. K. Allen et al, *Accident Compensation after Pearson* (1979, Sweet and Maxwell).

238 D. Harris et al., *Compensation and Support for Illness and Injury* (Clarendon Press, 1984). And see Atiyah, op. cit., chapter 1.

239 Cm 394 (1988, HMSO). See chapter 6 for a discussion of recent changes in civil litigation procedure which are designed to address problems such as these.

system, and have looked approvingly at systems for personal injury compensation elsewhere. In particular, the system which has been introduced in New Zealand has attracted considerable attention. In 1967, proposals were put forward in that country by a Royal Commission on Compensation for Personal Injury (the Woodhouse Commission),[240] and these proposals were implemented in 1974. The effect of the New Zealand system is that liability in tort for personal injuries has been abolished, and in its place there is a comprehensive system whereby all persons injured in accidents at work, on the road or as a result of criminal attack, or who suffer occupational diseases, receive compensation from the state, as of right and without having to prove fault. The state funds are provided by means of employers' contributions, contributions from self-employed people, levies payable in respect of motor vehicles and general taxation. Although the New Zealand scheme has its limitations, many critics of the English system have urged that some such state-administered, no-fault, comprehensive system for compensation be introduced in this country to replace the existing 'plethora of systems' whereby claims for accident compensation may be made.

It is clear that there has been at least a partial shift in attitudes to personal injuries caused by accidents.[241] The focus, once upon the necessity of proving fault on the part of the defendant, has shifted to the injured victim and the social desirability of providing compensation for that injury, whether it arises from an accident at work, on the road or through some tragic misfortune such as the side-effects of drugs. Over the last few years, however, there has been some criticism of the operation of the tort system, linking it to the rise of a 'compensation culture' in the UK.[242] This phrase is normally used to mean either an increased tendency to engage in litigation seeking compensation, and/or an associated 'risk aversion' on the part of those who might potentially face such actions. In *Better Routes to Redress,* published in 2004, the Better Regulation Task Force[243] (an independent body whose function is to advise government) argued that it was not so much the existence of a 'compensation culture', as much as a *belief* or *perception* that such a culture existed, and that

> It is this perception that causes the real problem: the fear of litigation impacts on behaviour and imposes burdens on organisations trying to handle claims. The judicial process is very good at sorting the wheat from the chaff, but all claims must still be assessed in the early stages. Redress for a genuine claimant is hampered by the spurious claims arising from the perception of a compensation culture. The compensation culture is a myth; but the cost of this belief is very real.
>
> It has got to be right that people who have suffered an injustice through someone else's negligence should be able to claim redress. What is not right is that some people should be led to believe that they can absolve themselves from any personal responsi-

---

240 *Report of the Royal Commission of Inquiry into Compensation for Personal Injury in New Zealand* (1969, NZ Government Printer).
241 See, for example, the judgment of Lawton LJ in *Whitehouse v Jordan,* op. cit.
242 See esp. K. Williams, 'State of Fear: Britain's "compensation culture" reviewed' (2005) *Legal Studies* 499.   243 Now called the Better Regulation Commission.

bility for their actions and then expect someone else to pick up the pieces when something goes wrong, regardless of whose fault it was.[244]

Thus, there have been media stories about the reluctance of schools to arrange trips and outdoor activities for pupils, and local authorities closing public spaces for fear of litigation in cases of accident. In fact, as suggested by the Report, the available evidence seems to suggest that there has been no increase in the number of personal injury claims, though there is concern on the part of government and other organisations (such as the Bar Council) about 'claims farmers' – claims management companies who are perceived as exploiting the victims of accidents by encouraging them to sue (on a 'no win, no fee' basis), even though the majority of such claims have little chance of success.

In 2005, the Compensation Bill was introduced into the House of Lords. This proposal became the Compensation Act 2006, and set out to address the 'compensation culture' issues. It contains, first, a provision that a court may consider, when deciding a negligence claim, whether a judgment that additional steps should have been taken by the defendant might have the effect of preventing a 'desirable activity' from taking place, or might discourage people from organising such 'desirable activity'. This proposal caused considerable controversy, partly on the grounds that it might lead to an upsurge in litigation to test out the meaning and scope of 'desirable activity', and partly because, some argued, the courts already took such factors into account in appropriate cases.

As an illustration of the latter point: in *Tomlinson v Congleton Borough Council and Another* in 2004,[245] a young man had been seriously injured after diving into a lake, managed by the defendant council, which formed part of a popular local beauty-spot. Although various recreational activities took place on and around the lake, swimming was not allowed, and there were notices to that effect. In practice, many people disregarded the warning notices. The claimant sought in this action to establish the liability of the council for failing to take further action to prevent people from entering the water to swim. The claim was rejected in the House of Lords, principally on the basis that the claimant had chosen to undertake the risks involved. Lord Hobhouse stated quite firmly that

> it is not, and should never be, the policy of the law to require the protection of the foolhardy or reckless few to deprive, or interfere with, the enjoyment by the remainder of society of the liberties and amenities to which they are rightly entitled. Does the law require that all trees be cut down because some youths may climb them and fall? Does the law require the coastline and other beauty spots to be lined with warning notices? Does the law require that attractive waterside picnic spots be destroyed because of a few foolhardy individuals who choose to ignore warning notices and indulge in activities dangerous only to themselves? The answer to all these questions is, of course, no. But this is the road down which your Lordships, like other courts before, have been invited to travel . . . In truth, the arguments for the claimant have involved an attack

244 *Better Routes to Redress* [2004], p 3   245 [2004] 1 AC 46.

upon the liberties of the citizen which should not be countenanced. They attack the liberty of the individual to engage in dangerous, but otherwise harmless, pastimes at his own risk and the liberty of citizens as a whole fully to enjoy the variety and quality of the landscape of this country. The pursuit of an unrestrained culture of blame and compensation has many evil consequences and one is certainly the interference with the liberty of the citizen.[246]

The other major issue covered by the Compensation Act is the subjection of claims management firms to a regime of regulation. A new Regulator will authorise and regulate the conduct of such firms, with criminal penalties in cases where such firms operate outside the regulatory scheme. The insurance industry by and large welcomed the Act, though with the qualification that the introduction of this measure should be followed by a more radical reform of the UK's compensation system.

Remedies in the law of tort

Although the tendency, over the centuries, has been the absorption of older self-help remedies into the law, there are situations today in which the law itself provides self-help remedies without the aggrieved person having to sue. Although the old forms of retaliation and satisfaction for wrongs, such as feuds and duelling, have long been outlawed in the interests of preserving public order, there are still cases where 'such force as is reasonable in the circumstances' may be used by any person in the course of preventing a crime. This provision, now contained in s 3 of the Criminal Law Act 1967, replaces the old common-law rules about self-defence. There is no doubt, however, that the law places limits on the amount of force which may legitimately be used in self-defence; it may not be out of proportion to the force used or threatened by the attacker. Again, in the law of tort, a trespasser on someone's land who refuses to leave on request may be ejected, using only reasonably necessary force; and the law of private nuisance provides that a sufferer from a nuisance may take steps to abate that nuisance. The best-known instance of this is perhaps the right of an occupier of land to cut off branches of a neighbour's trees which overhang that land (although the cut foliage belongs to the neighbour). As Winfield has said, however, 'self-help is apt to be a perilous remedy, for the person exercising it is probably the worst judge of exactly how much he is entitled to do without exceeding his rights'.[247]

Today, it is far more likely in cases of private nuisance (see above) that the aggrieved person will make an initial complaint to the local authority, for various statutes have provided that where waste disposal, atmospheric pollution, noise or unhealthy premises amount to a nuisance, the local authority will have either a power or a duty to take steps to regulate the activity in question or require that it ceases altogether. Where a local authority has no such power to intervene, or is

---

246 Ibid., pp 96–7.   247 Op. cit., p 794.

unwilling to do so, the plaintiff must ask a court to grant an injunction. Originally available only in equity, the injunction is now (like all equitable remedies) available in all courts, and its effect is that the defendant is ordered by the court to cease the activity complained of. Although perhaps most often thought of as a remedy for private nuisance, the injunction is available for all torts except false imprisonment and negligence, and is given at the court's discretion. Though clearly useful and appropriate in many cases in tort, it is none the less true that the most frequently sought remedy in tort is not the injunction, but the award of damages.

Damages – financial compensation for loss suffered – is, historically, the only remedy which the old common law offered, and so the development of the rules governing awards of damages is to a great extent the result of judicial deliberation in cases coming before them.[248] In many cases, an award of damages, if adequately assessed, may be a wholly appropriate remedy, particularly where the loss sustained is of a material nature. In the law of contract, damages for loss through a breach of contract will usually be relatively easy to assess, especially if the parties have inserted into their contract a 'liquidated damages' clause, which is an agreed estimate of the financial liability of each party in the event of a breach. In tort, however, the damages claimed by a plaintiff are 'unliquidated damages', or sums of money awarded at the court's discretion which are not predetermined.

To award financial compensation in cases of personal injury, however, is quite a different matter. It is highly artificial in the sense that money cannot actually compensate for the loss of a leg, an eye or a life. To be fair, the judges have long recognised this problem;[249] none the less, they have the task of estimating a fair and just figure to compensate, as far as money can compensate, for a plaintiff's injuries. There is the distinction between 'general' and 'special' damages alleged by the plaintiff; the former being non-quantifiable damage such as the injury itself, the latter being quantifiable damage such as loss of earnings, which must be specified by the plaintiff in the statement of claim. There are various heads of damage, moreover, within each category. Non-pecuniary damage, in cases of personal injury, will include, where relevant, separate sums of money in respect of pain and suffering,[250] loss of amenity (awarded where a plaintiff, because of the injury, is no longer able to enjoy particular activities), and of course the injury itself.[251] Pecuniary loss, apart

248 Some statutory provision has affected the common law in this area, notably the Fatal Accidents Act 1976 (consolidating previous enactments) which provides that in the event of the death of a person by reason of another's tort, the deceased's dependants may bring an action against the wrongdoer if the deceased would have had a right of action had he or she lived; and the Administration of Justice Act 1982, considered below. See Winfield, op. cit., chapter 22.
249 See the cases cited in Winfield and Jolowicz, op. cit., pp 762–788.
250 No damages are recoverable under this head if the plaintiff is unable to experience pain or suffering (for example, because of unconsciousness).
251 On these matters, see P. Barrie, *Personal Injury Law: Liability, Compensation, Procedure,* (2nd edn., 2005, Oxford University Press); Judicial Studies Board, *Guidelines for the Assessment of General Damages in Personal Injury Cases* (7th edn., 2004, Oxford University Press); J. Munkman, *Damages for Personal Injury and Death* (11th edn. by G. Exall, 2004, Lexis Nexis Butterworths). Up-to-date information as to current amounts awarded for various injuries may be found from time to time in the *New Law Journal* and in *Current Law.*

from loss of earnings, includes medical expenses (both past and future) and other incidental financial losses.

Some types of damages are intended not to compensate, but to meet other objectives. Damages may be nominal, in cases where no specific harm or injury is alleged apart from the bare breach of the plaintiff's legal right. Nominal damages must be distinguished from contemptuous damages, awarded where the court, though deciding in favour of the plaintiff, has formed so low an opinion of the plaintiff's case that, traditionally, the award comprises the smallest coin of the realm – and the plaintiff may well not be awarded costs. (This means that the plaintiff's legal costs are met by the plaintiff, and not the defendant.[252]) Exemplary and aggravated damages occur when an award is increased by reason of the defendant's malicious or otherwise reprehensible motives or conduct.[253] These distinctions and categories do not greatly affect the substantive legal rules and principles within the law of tort, but they do affect procedure and formality, and may well have consequences for the kind and amount of damages a plaintiff will eventually claim, as can be seen from the cases referred to above.

Such considerations may well make it difficult for legal advisers to predict the outcome of a case with any accuracy, and such uncertainties are enhanced by the problems attendant on the artificiality of putting a monetary figure upon physical injuries. In practice, the judges work to a fairly uniform scale of awards for particular injuries, but in some respects the predictability factor is not easily calculable. This may be important, for an injured plaintiff may well have to decide whether to take the claim before the court – where there may potentially be a very high award of damages – or before, say, an industrial injuries tribunal, where the success of the claim may be more certain, but the amount of compensation less than might be the case in a court hearing. Or the plaintiff may have to weigh up the advantages of accepting an out-of-court offer of a settlement from the defendant or the defendant's insurers, against the possibilities of obtaining more money, if the claim is successful, in a court action.

Some heads of damages are notoriously less certain then others. Prior to 1982, the award of damages for 'loss of expectation of life' involved an extremely speculative judgment by the courts as to the amount which was appropriate for this loss. Section 1 of the Administration of Justice Act 1982, however, abolished the head of loss of expectation of life, thus removing at least one of the uncertainties in the law. The same Act also went some way towards dealing with another difficulty in this area. Before the 1982 Act, the rule was that damages were awarded as a lump sum, given once and for all to the injured plaintiff. This meant that the plaintiff's medical advisers had to make a very careful assessment of the chances of any worsening of the plaintiff's condition in years to come, for should an injury prove, in the course of time, to be more serious or more complicated than was originally thought, there

---

252 See *Dering v Uris* [1964] 2 QB 669; *Pamplin v Express Newspapers Ltd (No 2)* [1988] 1 All ER 282.
253 See *Rookes v Barnard* [1964] AC 1129; *Cassell & Co Ltd v Broome* [1972] AC 1027; *A B v South West Water* [1993] 1 All ER 609.

was no possibility of bringing a further action for more money. The Administration of Justice Act 1982 confronted this problem by providing, in s 6, that where the condition of a plaintiff may seriously deteriorate, or where the plaintiff may as a result of the tortious act or omission develop a serious disease in the future, rules may be made so that the court may assess damages provisionally, on the assumption that such deterioration or disease will not occur. Further damages may then be awarded at some future date if the deterioration or disease in fact occurs.

In all the circumstances, it is not surprising that the common-law rules governing the award of damages have been criticised. Possible reforms might include the removal of compensation for personal injury from the arena of tort law altogether, and the substitution of a state-run system of insurance to replace the existing role of tort. Of course, such reforms cannot solve the problems identified by Abel, for whom the only solution to the inequalities of the tort system within a capitalist economy which cultivates accidents and injuries is a socialist alternative, which ensures 'that those at risk regain control over the threat of injury and illness'[254] and that the risk of injury is spread more equally. But as Abel acknowledges, such a transformation cannot be made without changing not only the law but society itself. The difficulties of such a project are, perhaps fortunately, well outside the scope of the present discussion, but it remains true that the tort system and its capacity (and willingness) to provide compensation is just as much a reflection of social and economic developments as is any other institution or procedure of law.

254 Abel, op. cit., p 208.

10

Liability in English law: crime and the criminal justice system

We have seen, at various points in this book, the ways in which certain activities and values come to be incorporated into law; such incorporation may be positive, as where the law is used to protect specific interests and values, or negative, as where the law, especially the criminal law, is used to proscribe certain activities because they offend certain dominant values (such as the sanctity of private property or the values attaching to particular moral beliefs), or because they are seen as an affront to the very foundations of social existence (such activities would include murder, rape and other violent behaviour). Definitions of 'deviant behaviour', then, are not something 'pre-social', that is, eternal, permanent and deriving from periods prior to social life as we know it; rather, they are dependent upon particular social structural arrangements at given periods of history. Whatever the origins of particular legal rules proscribing 'unacceptable' behaviour may be, those legal rules do have certain things in common, one of the most important of which is that they invariably provide for some form of legal sanction to be visited upon the offender upon conviction by a court.

A second feature is that, through the operation of ideological currents as reflected in the mass media, judicial pronouncements and political policies (as enunciated in and implemented by legislation), the criminal offender who has infringed or flaunted dominant moral and ideological norms (we are not here speaking of the speeding motorist or car-parking offender) comes to be seen publicly as a marginal individual, acting in a way which is antagonistic or threatening to the lives, property or values of everyone else. We will discuss this in more detail later, but the corollary of this phenomenon is that the role of the legal personnel who administer the criminal justice system (police, magistrates, judges, prison and probation officers, and so on) is seen to be the apprehension, conviction, condemnation and disposal of these deviants on behalf of the rest of the social group – the 'public'.

This presentation of the criminal deviant as marginal, anti-social and reprehensible is achieved partly by the ritualism, ceremony and awe-inspiring atmosphere and procedures of the courtroom, and partly by the condemnatory attitudes which have traditionally been a hallmark of the judges presiding in criminal courts: 'I think it highly desirable that criminals should be hated, that the punishments inflicted upon them should be so contrived as to give expression to that hatred, and to justify it so far as the provision of means of expressing and gratifying a healthy and natural sentiment can justify and encourage it.'[1] Those words were written in 1883, but we find similar expressions in more recent statements by certain members of the judiciary: 'It is a mistake to consider the objects of punishment as being deterrent or reformative or preventive and nothing else . . . The ultimate justification of any punishment is not that it is a deterrent, but that it is the emphatic denunciation by the community of a crime.'[2]

Well away from the sphere of judicial utterances, we find that within certain schools of thought in social science, similar kinds of notion, stripped of the emotive impact of judicial pronouncements, have been presented. One of the best-known expositions of the relationship between criminal law and popular morality is that of Durkheim, who argued, first, that 'The totality of beliefs and sentiment common to average citizens of the same society forms a determinate system which has its own life: one may call it the collective or common conscience',[3] and second, that 'an act is criminal when it offends strong and defined states of the collective conscience'.[4]

In previous chapters, we have criticised strongly the idea that social values can be characterised in our own society as consensual, but certain facts nevertheless stand out. First, such a view is firmly held within the legal system itself, especially by the judges;[5] second, it is undeniable that our everyday ideological and common-sense attitudes and experiences tell us that most of us do adhere to a certain core of ideas about such activities as violent behaviour and theft, no matter how subtly these ideas may have been inculcated through our learning processes and through the various other institutions, such as the media, which are concerned with the presentation of dominant ideological currents. Third, there is within social science a line of thought and reasoning among some writers (notably Talcott Parsons[6]) which posits ideas about crime and the criminal legal code resting upon these notions of consensus. Some of the consequences and doubts about such assumptions, especially when held by those involved in the administration of the criminal justice system, are discussed later in this chapter, but to begin with it is necessary to examine some of the fundamental principles and conditions of liability in criminal law.

Liability in criminal law

The element of fault, which we have already discussed in the context of tort law, has similar prominence in criminal law as regards the general conditions of liability, except in specific circumstances. Consideration of the distinction between criminal law and tort may reveal why fault continues to be defined by legislators and judges as of fundamental importance to the criminal justice system.

1 J. Stephen, *A History of the Criminal Law of England* (1883).
2 Lord Denning, in *Report of the Royal Commission on Capital Punishment* (1953, Cmnd 8932, HMSO), p 18.
3 E. Durkheim, *The Division of Labour in Society* (1964, Free Press, New York; Macmillan, London), p 79.   4 Ibid., p 80.   5 See chapter 14.
6 See, for example, T. Parsons, *The Social System* (1951, Routledge and Kegan Paul).

Tort claims, and other civil proceedings, are instituted by individuals or bodies in order to obtain compensation from, or some other private remedy against, other individuals or bodies. Criminal proceedings are generally (though not invariably: see chapter 6) brought under public authority – nominally the Crown – against the wrongdoer. The legal sanctions differ too: the objectives of the criminal justice system[7] may be punishment, deterrence, rehabilitation, or a mixture of all three, and these are sought to be achieved in a significant number of cases by deprivation of liberty, through confinement in prison or some other institution such as the detention centre. Criminal sanctions, therefore, are generally to be regarded as more severe than civil sanctions, in that they adversely affect a person's liberty, reputation and opportunities, for example, in relation to employment and other activities (see chapter 6). Because of this – and because, indeed, one aim of the system may be seen as the deliberate stigmatisation of the offender as reprehensible – lawyers have in general steadfastly maintained the principle that only the blameworthy or morally guilty person should be subjected to those sanctions.

The general conditions of liability in criminal law reflect this principle by requiring that the prosecution in a criminal trial establish, beyond reasonable doubt,[8] not only that the accused brought about the prohibited situation, but also that this was done in a manner which shows the accused's guilt or blameworthiness. These two aspects of liability are present, as we shall see, in most, though not all, criminal offences as defined in the law. They may be seen as distinct elements, both of which must be established before a criminal conviction can follow. The all-important expression is the Latin maxim *actus non facit reum nisi mens sit rea*, roughly translated as 'the act is not blameworthy unless the mind is guilty'. To recap: the distinction is made in criminal law between the criminal act[9] and the element of guilty mind in the commission of a crime, and in general both must be present for there to be criminal liability.

The first element, known as the *actus reus*, refers to the observable 'doing' or 'bringing about' of the prohibited consequence. In murder, for example, it is the bringing about of someone's death; in theft, the appropriation of someone's

---

7 On which see, for example, A. Ashworth, 'Sentencing' in M. Maguire, R. Morgan and R. Reiner (eds), *The Oxford Handbook on Criminology* (3rd edn., 2002, Oxford University Press); D. Thomas, 'The Sentencing Process' in M. McConville and G. Wilson, *The Handbook of the Criminal Justice Process* (2002, Oxford University Press); A. Ashworth, *Sentencing and Criminal Justice* (3rd edn., 2000, Butterworths).

8 This is the standard of proof which must be attained by the prosecution in a criminal case. The term has been defined and explained by judges to juries in various ways, some of which have met with disapproval from the appellate courts. In 1952 the Court of Criminal Appeal thought that juries should be told that to convict, they should be 'satisfied so that they can feel sure' of the guilt of the accused. Today, the term is usually explained to juries in terms of 'being sure' of guilt. The standard of proof is rather less in civil cases: plaintiffs must establish their case 'on a balance of probabilities', so that it is more likely than not that the plaintiff's version is the true one. See C. Tapper, *Cross and Tapper on Evidence* (10th edn., 2004, Oxford University Press); A. Keane, *The Modern Law of Evidence* (6th edn., 2005, Oxford University Press); I. Dennis, *Law of Evidence* (3rd edn., 2006, Sweet and Maxwell).

9 The term *actus reus* may also include omissions to act, and states of affairs. See below.

property; in criminal damage, the destruction or damaging of someone's property; and so on. If, then, X is charged with criminal damage after having thrown a stone through P's window, or with the theft of P's car, it must be established by the prosecution that these acts – the *actus reus* in each case – were in fact done by the accused. The commission of these acts must be shown to have been voluntary and for this reason, someone committing a prohibited act whilst in a state of unconsciousness, such as a trance, or a lapse of consciousness brought about by a physical illness,[10] will normally be excused because the act is not the outcome of the accused's rational will. Such a person is said to be in a state of 'non-insane automatism', or 'acting like a robot'.

For example, in *R v Bailey* in 1983,[11] the accused was a diabetic and received insulin treatment. After his girl-friend had left him and begun an association with another man, the accused went to see the man. During that meeting, the accused said he felt unwell, and drank some sugar and water, but ate nothing. A few minutes later, he struck the other man on the head with an iron bar, causing severe injuries. Charged with the offence of causing grievous bodily harm contrary to s 18 of the Offences Against the Person Act 1861, the accused in his defence claimed that he had acted in a state of automatism, caused by hypoglycaemia following his failure to take food after drinking the sugar and water. Following his conviction at the Crown Court, the accused appealed, and the Court of Appeal held that, in these circumstances, the defence of automatism could be appropriately pleaded. It is important to stress that the defence of automatism is concerned with those cases where the accused can be said to have acted involuntarily: in *Broome v Perkins* in 1987,[12] the defendant drove his car several miles, in a hypoglycaemic state, and was convicted of the offence of driving without due care and attention – though he may not have been aware of what he was doing, his condition was not, in the view of the court, one of automatism because he clearly had some command of the controls of the car.[13]

The defence of automatism must be distinguished from the general defence of insanity, discussed presently. Moreover, the state of automatism may be induced by causes other than medical ones: a car-driver may be attacked by a swarm of bees, or struck by a stone from the road, and in such cases, it has been suggested,[14] the driver cannot sensibly be said to be acting voluntarily.

It must not be thought that the *actus reus* is invariably a positive act. Everything depends upon the definition of the offence. It may be constituted by an omission such as a failure to take out insurance on a car contrary to the road traffic legislation. Less obviously, in *Airedale National Health Service Trust v Bland*[15] in 1993, the House of Lords had to decide on the lawfulness of doctors' withdrawal of the feeding-tube from an unconscious patient. The patient – a victim of the

---

10 *R v Charlson* [1955] 1 All ER 859.   11 [1983] 2 All ER 503.   12 (1987) 85 Cr App Rep 321.
13 See also *A-G's Reference (No 2 of 1992)* [1994] QB 91, where, on similar facts, the court stated that there must be a *complete* lack of voluntary control.
14 *Hill v Baxter* [1958] 1 QB 277 at 286, per Pearson J.   15 [1993] 1 All ER 821.

Hillsborough football stadium disaster[16] – was in a persistent vegetative state, with no prospect of improvement or recovery. The withdrawal of the feeding-tube would result in death. The court stated that the fundamental issue was whether keeping the patient alive artificially was in the patient's best interests, and that to prolong the patient's life when there was no prospect of any improvement was not in those interests. Withdrawal of the feeding-tube, in the court's view, would constitute an omission to feed, rather than a positive act, and it was held that in these circumstances the doctors would not be acting unlawfully in withdrawing the treatment. It was stressed, however, that euthanasia by means of a positive act would be unlawful. Clearly, in this case the distinction between a positive act and an omission to act was a subtle one. In *R v Stone and Dobinson*[17] it was held that a couple were liable for the death of the sister of one of them, who lived with them and who had become infirm and unable to care for herself. Her death was due to neglect by the couple, and the Court of Appeal held that as the couple had undertaken the duty of looking after her, the neglect of that duty which led to her death could constitute the offence of manslaughter.

For some offences, the *actus reus* may comprise a state of affairs such as being in possession of prohibited ('controlled') drugs.[18] And in some cases, the definition of an offence, and its interpretation, may lead to peculiar results. In the odd case of *Winzar v Chief Constable of Kent*[19] the accused was convicted of the offence of being found drunk in the highway. He had been on the premises of a hospital, and, having been discovered to be drunk, had been told to leave. The police were called, and they removed him into their police car parked on the highway outside the hospital. It was this act by the police which constituted the commission of the offence by the accused, who had carried out no voluntary act whatsoever!

The second vital element in the vast majority of criminal offences refers to the mental state of the accused at the time of the offence, and this is known as *mens rea*. This is sometimes called the 'guilty mind', 'evil intent', 'guilty knowledge' or just the 'mental element'. The latter is, arguably, preferable, as it is perfectly possible for an accused to satisfy this condition of liability without having acted in an 'evil' way. A person might act out of pity, sympathy or compassion, but still be guilty of an offence: the motive of the accused is, in general, irrelevant to the question of liability. Someone administering a lethal overdose of drugs to a dying relative in severe pain, in order to save that person from further suffering, is committing murder; some may think the motive laudable, but in law there has been an intentional taking of another's life. Motive is, however, certainly admissible, and indeed often cogent, evidence at the trial as tending to show guilt.

The test of *mens rea* has traditionally been thought of as subjective: the rules of criminal liability involve an enquiry into the state of mind of the accused. This subjective test may be contrasted with the objective test applied in the law of negli-

---

16 See chapter 9.   17 [1977] 2 All ER 341.   18 Misuse of Drugs Act 1971, s 5.
19 (1983) *Times*, 28 March. See also *R v Larsonneur* (1933) 24 Cr App Rep 74.

gence, discussed in chapter 9, which asks the question, did the defendant's conduct measure up to that of a hypothetical 'reasonable' person? Though previous authority suggested otherwise,[20] the Criminal Justice Act 1967 provides, in s 8, that a court or jury:

(a) shall not be bound . . . to infer that (an accused) intended or foresaw a result of his actions by reason only if its being a natural and probable consequence of those actions; but

(b) shall decide whether he did intend or foresee that result by reference to all the evidence drawing such inferences from the evidence as appear proper in the circumstances.

It is important to appreciate that, again in contrast to civil cases which are almost always tried by a single judge, criminal cases are tried either by magistrates, who are not trained lawyers, or, in serious cases in the Crown Court, by a judge with a jury. The presiding judge must explain to the jury the relevant law in the case, and because of the difficulties which this task can involve, quite a few criminal convictions are appealed on the basis of alleged misdirections by judges to juries.

Liability depends upon the *actus reus* and the *mens rea*: how may the latter be defined? The 'state of mind' to which the term *mens rea* refers will differ from offence to offence. Generally speaking, the clearest state of mind is an *intention* by the accused to bring about the prohibited consequence (*actus reus*), though sometimes the definition of the offence makes it clear that only a *specific intention* to bring about the *actus reus* will suffice; for many offences, the requirement as to *mens rea* will be satisfied by showing that the person brought about the *actus reus* either *intentionally* or *recklessly*. The latter term may for the moment be defined as 'the taking of an unjustified risk', though this statement, as we will see presently, needs further elaboration.

At common law, a person who brought about prohibited consequences through their negligence – which is clearly a somewhat less blameworthy mental state than intention or recklessness – was not normally held to have satisfied the requirement for *mens rea*, but today we must qualify this by reason of the fact that a number of statutory offences may be committed through negligence (notably careless and dangerous driving) and there is, within the law of homicide, the special case of the offence of manslaughter through *gross* negligence.[21] Finally, we might note that harm might be caused by someone through blameless inadvertence. Criminal liability will not normally attach to someone in such circumstances, although as we shall see presently, it is possible for a person to be criminally liable even though their state of mind is wholly blameless, if the offence concerned is one which does not require proof of *mens rea* at all – an offence of strict liability.

A few words must be said at this stage about the meaning and scope of the terms introduced above, along with several other expressions, such as 'wilfully' and 'maliciously', in the statutory definition of various offences.

20 *DPP v Smith* [1961] AC 290.   21 See *R v Adomako* [1995] 1 AC 171.

'Intention'

Although this is a common and everyday word, its meaning in the context of criminal liability has given rise to difficult problems. Perhaps the clearest and most basic
example of intention is where the accused commits the offence with the specific
purpose of doing so. For example, D loads a gun and fires it directly at P, with the
specific purpose of killing P. Here, the accused's intention is obvious, and the test
of *mens rea* will clearly be satisfied. But suppose that D places a bomb on an aircraft, timed to explode when the plane is in mid-air, with the purpose of claiming
insurance money in respect of the destroyed cargo: it is virtually inevitable that the
explosion will kill the crew, but can D be said to have intended their deaths? D's
purpose is not to kill, but to profit financially. We would none the less be surprised
if D were to escape liability on this basis, but can D's action here be termed 'intentional'? Most of us would agree that in this example the virtual certainty of death
would lead us to assert that D must have 'intended' this result, and would be guilty
of murder,[22] which is said to be a crime of 'specific intent', that is to say, the *mens
rea* of murder requires an intention to kill or cause grievous (that is, serious) bodily
harm – recklessness will not suffice.

Consider next the facts of *Hyam v DPP*.[23] Here, the accused set fire to a house
with the purpose of frightening a woman into leaving the area. The woman's children were killed in the fire. Did the accused intend the deaths of the children? The
trial judge directed the jury that if they were satisfied that 'when the accused set fire
to the house she knew that it was highly probable that this would cause death or
serious bodily harm then the prosecution will have established the necessary
intent'. This direction would imply that knowledge that a consequence was highly
probable amounts, in law, to an intention to bring it about. On appeal, the House
of Lords considered carefully the direction to the jury. The House affirmed the conviction, but offered somewhat differing views as to the meaning of 'intention' relating to the law of murder.

The difficulty is whether foresight of probable consequences can amount to
intention. And, to compound the issue, if it is accepted that such can be the case,
then how probable must those consequences be? Would a 51% chance be sufficient
probability? Or only probability amounting to 'virtual certainty'? The use by judges
of phrases such as 'highly probable' and 'highly likely' do nothing to clarify the
issue. The House of Lords in *Hyam* appeared to accept that foresight of 'highly
probable' consequences could amount to intention in the crime of murder, but the
position was certainly not clear.

The opportunity to clarify the matter arose in *R v Moloney* in 1985.[24] The
accused was charged with murder, having fired a shotgun at close range at his stepfather after a drunken and heated discussion about their skill with guns. The
defence was that there had been no intent to injure or kill, and that the accused had

22 So thought Lord Hailsham in *Hyam v DPP* [1975] AC 55.
23 [1975] AC 55, [1974] 2 All ER 41.   24 [1985] AC 905.

not realised that the gun was pointing at his stepfather. In the leading judgment in the House of Lords, Lord Bridge acknowledged that the law on this point was confusing, and pointed out that the crime of murder is one of 'specific intent', that is to say, a crime which requires proof of intent, either direct or 'oblique' (as in blowing up the aircraft). Offences of 'specific intent' stand in contrast to those of 'basic intent', where either intention or recklessness will suffice.

Lord Bridge pointed out that, in general, judges should, when directing juries as to the law concerning crimes of specific intent, avoid 'any elaboration or paraphrase of what is meant by intent, and leave it to the jury's good sense to decide whether the accused acted with the necessary intent',[25] explaining that it would only be in rare cases that additional direction was needed which referred to foresight of consequences. He went on to lay down 'guidelines'[26] on this point for courts' future reference. In essence, these guidelines emphasise that the significance of the accused's foresight of consequences is a matter of evidence on the basis of which a jury draws its inference, and Lord Bridge continued:

> In the rare cases in which it is necessary to direct a jury by reference to foresight of consequences, I do not believe it is necessary for the judge to do more than invite the jury to consider two questions. First, was death or really serious injury in a murder case (or whatever relevant consequences must be proved to have been intended in any other case) a natural consequence of the defendant's voluntary act? Secondly, did the defendant foresee that consequence as being a natural consequence of his act? The jury should then be told that if they answer yes to both questions it is a proper inference for them to draw that he intended that consequence.[27]

The matter was further considered by the House of Lords in 1986 in *R v Hancock and Shankland*.[28] The facts of the case, which arose during the miners' strike of 1984, were that the defendants, who were two striking miners, had pushed two blocks of concrete off a bridge spanning a motorway. On the motorway below, a taxi was carrying another miner to work. In front of, and behind, the taxi were police vehicles forming a convoy. One of the concrete blocks hit the taxi, and the driver was killed. The defendants claimed that they had no intention of killing or injuring anyone, since they thought that the blocks would fall onto the middle motorway lane, and that the taxi was being driven in the nearside lane. The trial judge directed the jury in terms of the guidelines in *Moloney*, and the accused were convicted. On appeal, the Court of Appeal stated that the term 'natural consequence' in Lord Bridge's guidelines in *Moloney* was potentially misleading, in that the term should have been elaborated by the trial judge to indicate that it meant 'highly likely' (an elaboration which was indeed given in *Moloney* by Lord Bridge, but in another passage in his judgment) and not just 'something which followed in an unbroken causal chain from the initial event, whether it was highly likely or not'.[29] The Court of Appeal allowed the appeal.

25 Ibid., at 926.   26 Ibid.   27 Ibid., at 929.   28 [1986] AC 455.
29 Ibid., at 460.

In the House of Lords, Lord Scarman, in his leading judgment, had sympathy with this view. His Lordship, who stated that cases in which additional explanation as to foresight of consequences were unlikely to be so rare as was suggested by the House in *Moloney*, reiterated the view expressed in that case that the 'foresight of consequences' factor is 'no more than evidence of the existence of intent',[30] and stressed that the probability of a consequence of an act is an important matter for the jury to consider. Although Lord Scarman recognised that Lord Bridge had emphasised the importance of probability, but admitted that reference to this element was missing in the paragraph containing the 'guidelines'; he went on to explain his own doubts about the value of elaborate guidelines, given that 'juries are not chosen for their understanding of a logical and phased process leading by question and answer to a conclusion but are expected to exercise practical common sense'.[31] Certainly, when foresight of consequences is an important part of prosecution evidence, juries should be told of the importance of the probability factor: in view of the absence of such an explanation in the trial judge's direction in the present case, the Crown's appeal should be dismissed.

In *R v Nedrick* in 1986[32] the suggestions as to directions to juries on this difficult point given by the Lord Chief Justice in the Court of Appeal might be thought to be rather clearer than the cases discussed above. In that case (which involved facts very similar to those in *Hyam*), Lord Lane CJ stated that, in the rare cases where the probability factor is in issue,

> When determining whether the defendant had the necessary intent, it may . . . be helpful for a jury to ask themselves two questions. (1) How probable was the consequence which resulted from the defendant's voluntary act? (2) Did he foresee that consequence?
>
> If he did not appreciate that death or serious harm was likely to result from his act, he cannot have intended to bring it about. If he did, but thought that the risk . . . was only slight, then it may be easy for the jury to conclude that he did not intend to bring about that result. On the other hand, if the jury are satisfied that at the material time the defendant recognised that death or serious harm would be virtually certain (barring some unforeseen intervention) to result from his voluntary act, then that is a fact from which they may find it easy to infer that he intended to kill or do serious bodily harm, even though he may not have had any desire to achieve that result.[33]

And in a passage which was later to be regarded by the House of Lords[34] as a model direction, it was said that:

> Where the charge is murder . . . the jury should be directed that they are not entitled to infer the necessary intention unless they feel sure that death or serious bodily harm was a virtual certainty (barring some unforeseen intervention) as a result of the

---

30 Ibid., at 471.   31 Ibid., at 473.   32 [1986] 3 All ER 1.

33 Ibid., at 3–4. And see *R v Walker and Hayles* (1989) 90 Cr App Rep 226, where the court stated its preference for the phrase 'virtual certainty' in directions to juries.

34 In *Woollin* [1998] 4 All ER 103.

defendant's actions and that the defendant appreciated that such was the case . . . The decision is one for the jury to be reached on a consideration of all the evidence.[35]

In *Woollin*[36] the facts were that the accused had lost control when his baby son choked on his food. He threw the child several feet across a room, causing injuries from which he died. The accused was charged with murder. He denied that he had either intended to kill, or thought that he would kill the baby. The prosecution contended that he must have realised that his action was virtually certain to cause the baby grievous bodily harm. In his direction to the jury, the trial judge explained that the accused would have the necessary intent to cause grievous bodily harm if they were satisfied that he must have realised that there was a 'substantial risk' that he would cause such harm. The accused was convicted, and appealed unsuccessfully to the Court of Appeal. In the House of Lords, the conviction for manslaughter was substituted for one of murder. That court held that the use by the trial judge of the phrase 'substantial risk' was wrong, and that the direction to the jury should have been in accordance with that in *Nedrick*. The only refinement which the House of Lords made to that 'model' direction (through the judgments of Lord Steyn and Lord Hope) was that it would be clearer to use the term 'to find', rather than 'to infer', in the passage from *Nedrick* cited above.[37]

The complexities of the debate on 'intention' and 'foresight of consequences' also have implications for the law relating to the definition of 'recklessness', as will be seen presently; for the moment, however, it should be noted that the modern approach to *mens rea* incorporates within the concept of 'intention' the terms 'maliciously', 'knowingly' and 'wilfully'. The word 'maliciously' has repeatedly been held simply to import a requirement for *mens rea* in the sense of 'basic intent', that is, intention or recklessness. In some statutory definitions, the term 'knowingly' appears; the word has been variously interpreted, but would seem to require that *mens rea* as to the elements of the *actus reus* of the particular crime must be proved. The word 'wilfully' is capable of two interpretations. Some cases have interpreted it simply as reiterating the need to prove the voluntariness of the accused's conduct, whilst others have read the term as importing a requirement of full *mens rea*. Recent decisions seem to support the first interpretation of the term.

'Recklessness'

It will be recalled that for crimes of basic intent, the requirement of *mens rea* will be satisfied on proof that the accused acted intentionally or recklessly. Like 'intention', however, the term 'recklessness' has been subjected to judicial deliberation in

---

35 *Nedrick*, op. cit., at 4.   36 Op. cit. And see *R v Matthews and Alleyne* [2003] 2 Cr App Rep 30.
37 For critical discussions of this difficult area of law, see esp. Card, Cross and Jones, *Criminal Law* (16th edn. by R. Card, 2004, LexisNexis/Butterworths), pp 92–101; M. Jefferson, *Criminal Law* (7th edn., 2006, Pearson), pp 95–104; *Smith and Hogan's Criminal Law* (11th edn., by D. Ormerod, 2005, Oxford University Press) pp 93–102; M. Allen, *Textbook on Criminal Law* (8th edn., 2003, Oxford University Press), pp 54–66.

recent years, with less than satisfactory results. Prior to 1981, it was settled law that a person was reckless if he or she foresaw that harm might be done as a consequence of an act, but none the less went on to take that risk. The leading case, decided in 1957, was that of *R v Cunningham*.[38] The facts were that the accused, in order to steal the contents of a gas meter in an unoccupied house, tore the meter from the wall, leaving gas leaking from the pipe. The gas seeped into the house next door, and was inhaled by a person living there. The accused was charged with, and convicted of, maliciously administering a noxious thing so as to endanger life, contrary to s23 of the Offences Against the Person Act 1861. On appeal, the Court of Criminal Appeal held that the trial judge had misdirected the jury by telling them that 'malicious' simply meant 'wicked'. In the opinion of the court, 'malicious' in a statutory definition of a crime imported a requirement either for specific intention (discussed above), or wilful taking of a known risk – recklessness – that the harmful consequence might ensue. In other words, *Cunningham* decided, or at least was taken to have decided, that 'recklessness' for the purposes of *mens rea* in criminal law necessitated a knowledge by the accused of the risk that was being taken, and that the risk was unjustifiable.

In 1981, however, the House of Lords decided the case of *Metropolitan Police Commissioner v Caldwell*.[39] Here, the accused, who bore a grudge against the proprietor of a hotel, decided whilst drunk to get his own back. He broke into the hotel, and started a fire inside. The fire was quickly put out. The accused was charged with arson under the provisions of the Criminal Damage Act 1971. Section 1(1) of that Act provides that 'a person who without lawful excuse destroys or damages any property belonging to another intending to destroy or damage any such property or being reckless as to whether any such property would be destroyed or damaged shall be guilty of an offence'. Lord Diplock, in the House of Lords, discussed the meaning of recklessness within this subsection, and stated that:

> a person charged . . . under s.1(1) of the 1971 Act is 'reckless as to whether any property would be destroyed or damaged' if (1) he does an act which in fact creates an obvious risk that property will be destroyed or damaged and (2) when he does the act he either *has not given any thought to the possibility of there being any such risk* or has recognised that there was some risk involved and has none the less gone on to do it.[40]

This passage, to which italics have been added, was clearly a departure from the older 'subjective' test of recklessness as enunciated in *Cunningham*. Under the test in *Caldwell*, the accused need not be shown to have known of the unjustifiable risk being taken, and the *Caldwell* criteria were thus considerably wider in scope, though it has been emphasised that the risk must be an unjustifiable one.[41]

The *Caldwell* test of recklessness raised serious questions about the relationship between recklessness and negligence. The law usually drew the line of criminal

---

38 [1957] 2 QB 396, [1957] 2 All ER 412.
39 [1982] AC 341, sub nom *R v Caldwell* [1981] 1 All ER 961.   40 [1981] 1 All ER 961 at 967.
41 See *R v Reid* [1992] 3 All ER 673.

liability between recklessness and negligence (the reckless person being liable, the negligent person not being liable). An inadvertent risk-taker, however negligent the inadvertence might be, was not liable under the *Cunningham* test; but the *Caldwell* test would clearly appear to imply the criminal liability of one who was unaware of the (obvious) risk, but ought to have known about it – that is, a person who was negligent. The *Caldwell* decision was much criticised over the following 20 years or so, not least because it undermined the traditional subjective enquiry into the accused's state of mind, and replaced this in certain instances with an objective test as to the blameworthiness of the accused. To make matters worse, *Caldwell* did not overrule *Cunningham*, and so two quite different tests of recklessness sat side-by-side within the criminal law, with a considerable degree of uncertainty as to which test applied to which criminal offence.

After some years of criticism of *Caldwell*, the Law Commission proposed in 1989, in its draft Criminal Code for England and Wales,[42] that recklessness be redefined statutorily in terms of the pre-*Caldwell* formulation. The unsatisfactory state of the law on this point was resolved, however, not by statutory definition, but as a result of the decision in *R v G and Another* in 2003.[43] In this case, the defendants were two boys aged 11 and 12. They had gone into the back yard of a shop and set fire to some newspapers which they found there. They threw the burning paper under a large plastic rubbish bin. They left the yard without putting out the fire. The rubbish bin set on fire, and the fire spread, eventually to the shop, which also caught fire, causing about £1 million worth of damage. The boys were charged with arson contrary to s.1 of the Criminal Damage Act 1971.

They argued that they had expected the newspapers to burn up, but that the fire would then go out on the concrete surface of the yard. It was accepted that they had not appreciated that there was any risk at all of the fire spreading in the way that it did. At their trial, the boys were convicted, the court applying *Caldwell*. The Court of Appeal turned down their appeal, bound, as it was, by the *Caldwell* decision.

The House of Lords considered once again the implications of its own decision in *Caldwell*, which had decided in cases like this that a defendant would be held to have been reckless, and hence liable, if he had either known about a risk and gone on to take that risk, or if he had created a risk which would have been obvious to an ordinary reasonable person, even though he himself had not given any thought to there being such a risk. This was the *objective* test of recklessness. The House of Lords felt that *Caldwell*, which had caused much controversy and criticism, must be overruled. Lord Bingham in his leading judgment gave a number of reasons for this. He pointed out that a genuine failure to appreciate that a risk exists is not something so blameworthy that it should carry the risk of imprisonment; that the court should not be oblivious to the fact that *Caldwell* had attracted so much criticism from academic lawyers and from legal practitioners, including judges; and

42 Law Commission, *A Criminal Code for England and Wales* (1989, Law Com No 177).
43 [2003] 4 All ER 765; [2003] 3 WLR 1060.

that the interpretation of the word 'recklessly' by the court in *Caldwell* was in fact a *mis*interpretation of the term as used in the Criminal Damage Act 1971.

Lord Bingham stated the correct principle to be as stated and recommended by the Law Commission in 1989:

> A person acts recklessly within the meaning of section 1 of the Criminal Damage Act 1971 with respect to –
> (i)   a circumstance when he is aware of a risk that it exists or will exist;
> (ii) a result when he is aware of a risk that it will occur;
> and it is, in the circumstances known to him, unreasonable to take the risk.

As a result, the law on recklessness has been returned to the *Cunningham* position, with the clear requirement that to be held to have been reckless for the purposes of criminal liability, the accused must be shown to have *known about* the risk involved: the subjective test has been reinstated.

Strict liability

We have seen from the preceding discussion how important individual words and phrases within statutory definitions may be. The crucial importance of ascertaining the meaning and scope of such words becomes clearer still when we consider the impact of strict liability offences, which require discussion in a little detail.

So far in this chapter, the criminal offences discussed have been offences which require proof of both *actus reus* and *mens rea*. They reveal the importance which lawyers have always attached both to the voluntariness of the action and to the mental state of the accused at the time of an alleged offence. There are, however, many offences,[44] usually (though not invariably) created by statute, which do not require proof of the mental element. Such offences are called 'strict liability' offences, and an accused charged with such an offence is liable to conviction on proof of *actus reus* alone.

We are faced here with the problem of reconciling the deeply embedded principle of 'no liability without fault' with a body of legal rules which appear to render liable a person who may not have been 'at fault', in that there may be a conviction for a strict liability offence despite the absence of intention or recklessness on the part of the accused. As with the development of the doctrine of vicarious liability in tort, this apparent paradox in the law is explicable only by examining the changing content and functions of criminal law in modern society. Traditional views as to the function of the criminal law, as expressed, in particular, by the judges, have tended to focus upon the social necessity of protecting the public from such harmful acts as violence and unauthorised interference with, or appropriation of, private property. More generally, the criminal law is seen as protecting the community at large from acts which are held to be injurious, for example, to state

---

44 Currently thought to be about half of the total number of criminal offences: see Jefferson, op. cit., ch.4; Card, op. cit., ch. 5.

security. These views have, in general, rested upon ideas connecting 'crime' and 'wickedness'. Lord Denning, for example, suggested many years ago that for centuries, 'in order that an act should be punishable it must be morally blameworthy. It must be a sin.'[45] And Hart has suggested that a crime is 'conduct which, if duly shown to have taken place, will incur a formal and solemn pronouncement of the moral condemnation of the community'.[46] The doctrine of *mens rea* is, of course, the test whereby we establish the extent to which an accused has, in fact, acted in a way which is morally blameworthy.

Strict liability offences are those which do not require proof of *mens rea*. How do these offences come to be defined in this way? Given that the majority of these offences are created by statute, the first part of the answer is that, quite simply, in creating such offences, Parliament has omitted from the statutory provisions any words such as 'knowingly' or 'intentionally', or phrases such as 'with the intention of . . .', any of which would normally indicate that *mens rea* is required. This, however, is only part of the answer. Statutory provisions fall to be interpreted by the courts, and, faced with such statutory provisions, the courts have in some instances been prepared to 'read in' a *presumption* of *mens rea*, as if Parliament had actually intended this. In other situations, however, the courts have been prepared to interpret the statute as imposing strict liability.

By way of case-examples: in the old case of *Sherras v De Rutzen* in 1895, the landlord of a public house had been charged with 'supplying liquor to a constable on duty', an offence contrary to s 16(2) of the Licensing Act 1872. The words of the relevant section did not specifically require the prosecution to show that the defendant had acted 'knowingly', but the court took the view that, as there was no clear way in which the landlord could have established whether the constable was on- or off-duty, it was not possible for pub landlords in this position to avoid criminal liability if faced with this situation: the effect of this was to *imply* the requirement for proof of knowledge into s 16(2) of the Act.

Sherras is often contrasted with another case involving a conviction under the same statute – *Cundy v Le Cocq* in 1884. [47] Here, a pub landlord was accused and convicted of the offence of selling intoxicating liquor to a drunken person (an offence whose wording contained no '*mens rea*' words), and his conviction was upheld despite his argument that he did not know, and had no reason to believe, that the customer was drunk. In the court's view, given the wording of the statute, it was enough that he had sold alcohol to a drunken person – his state of knowledge or belief were not relevant.

It is not easy to reconcile these two decisions,[48] and it is not easy to explain why the courts have been prepared to infer a requirement for knowledge in some cases

---

45 Lord Denning, *The Changing Law* (1953, Stevens), p 112.
46 H. L. A. Hart, 'The Aims of the Criminal Law' (1958) 23 *Law and Contemporary Problems* at 405.
47 (1884) 13 QBD 207.
48 See also the contrasting cases of *R v Prince* (1875) LR 2 CCR 154 and *R v Hibbert* (1869) LR 1 CCR 184.

but not in others. Judges have on occasion alluded to a 'presumption' that *mens rea* is not to be taken as excluded in the absence of very clear statutory wording. In *Sweet v Parsley* in 1970,[49] the accused was the tenant of a cottage which she sub-let to a number of other people. She did not live there herself – she lived in a flat some miles away – but when it was discovered that her sub-tenants had been smoking cannabis in the cottage, she was charged with the offence of 'being concerned in the management of premises which were used for the purpose' of taking drugs, contrary to s5(b) of the Dangerous Drugs Act 1965. She had no knowledge of the drug-use, and exercised no control over the sub-tenants. On conviction, she appealed eventually to the House of Lords, where Lord Reid regarded the conviction as an 'obviously unjust result'.[50] Her appeal was allowed, the court being of the view that despite the silence of the statute as to a requirement for knowledge on the part of the accused, proof of such knowledge was necessary for a conviction under this section. Lord Reid said that

> there has for centuries been a presumption that Parliament did not intend to make criminals of persons who were in no way blameworthy in what they did. That means that, whenever a section is silent as to *mens rea*, there is a presumption that, in order to give effect to the will of Parliament, we must read in words appropriate to require *mens rea*.[51]

And in the same case, Lord Diplock stated that the implication of *mens rea*

> stems from the principle that it is contrary to a rational and civilised criminal code . . . to penalise one who has performed his duty as a citizen to ascertain what acts are prohibited by law . . . and has taken all proper care to inform himself of any facts which would make his conduct unlawful[52]

When considering whether an offence should be interpreted as importing strict liability, it is clear that the judges take into consideration not simply the literal wording of a statutory provision, but also the surrounding context. In *B v DPP*, in 2000,[53] Lord Nicholls stated that relevant factors included 'the language used, the nature of the offence, the mischief sought to be prevented and any other circumstances that might assist in determining what intention was properly to be attributed to Parliament'.[54]

The courts' views as to the desirability or necessity of interpreting statutory provisions as requiring strict liability have fluctuated over the years but in recent cases, the judges have shown a discernible reluctance to infer strict liability in the absence of clear wording, at least in this area of the law concerned with sexual offences.[55]

---

49 [1970] AC 132   50 Ibid., at p 148.   51 Ibid.   52 Ibid., at p 162.
53 [2000] 2 AC 428 (HL).   54 Ibid., at p 464.
55 *B. v. DPP*, above; and see *K(Age of Consent: Reasonable Belief)* [2002] 1 AC 462 (HL); *R v Kumar* [2005] 1 WLR 1352. Note, however, the effect of the Sexual Offences Act 2003 on these decisions: there is now clearly strict liability as to the age of those involved in this type of sex offence. But among many examples of cases in which judges have been prepared to impose strict liability are *St Margaret's Trust Ltd* [1958] 2 All ER 289. *Maidstone Borough Council v Mortimer* [1980] 3 All ER 502; *R v Greener* (1996) 160 JP 265; and *Harrow London Borough Council v Shah* [1999] 2 Cr App Rep 457 (CD).

But why should Parliament, in its enacted legislation, remain silent as to *mens rea* for some offences, but not for others? There has never been any failure, for example, to include *mens rea* words in statutes concerning homicide or theft. Part of the answer lies in the argument that many strict liability offences fall into the category of what have been called *regulatory* offences. In some areas of social and economic activity, the criminal law, it is argued, is not used to deliver criminal sanctions for 'moral wrongdoing', but is used as an instrument of social policy to encourage the maintainance of high standards of, for example, safety in factories and on the roads,[56] purity and hygiene in the preparation of foodstuffs and other edible goods,[57] and honesty and fair dealing in matters such as the provision of professional services and commercial transactions with the consuming public.[58] Almost invariably, offences connected with these activities are ones of strict liability. It is more important that such offences should be strictly punished than that conviction should be contingent upon proof of moral 'guilt'.

The point is that these offences may be said to comprise a special category within criminal law. They are not so much concerned (as is the conventional criminal offence) with punishing an offender for blameworthy conduct, as with the establishment of standards which must be continuously observed.

The difficulty is that the dividing line between 'traditional' crimes and strict liability or 'regulatory' crimes is not easy to draw, as is shown in some of the cases cited above involving certain sex offences, which have little to do with public welfare or the maintenance of safety or hygiene standards. Judges may also be influenced by their view of the seriousness of the offence in question, and the amount of social danger associated with that offence. This has meant, for example, that legislation concerning prohibited drugs has been interpreted by the judges as involving offences of strict liability,[59] as once was the offence of bigamy,[60] neither of which would seem to constitute 'public welfare' offences.

In *Gammon (Hong Kong) Ltd v A-G of Hong Kong* in 1985,[61] Lord Scarman stated that:

(1) there is a presumption of law that *mens rea* is required before a person can be held guilty of a criminal offence; (2) the presumption is particularly strong where the offence is 'truly criminal' in character; (3) the presumption applies to statutory offences, and can be displaced only if this is clearly or by necessary implication the effect of the statute; (4) the only situation in which the presumption can be displaced is where the statute is concerned with an issue of social concern; public safety is such an issue; (5) even where a statute is concerned with such an issue, the presumption of *mens rea* stands unless it can also be shown that the creation of strict liability will be

---

56 See Health and Safety at Work etc Act 1974.   57 See Food Safety Act 1990.
58 See Trade Descriptions Act 1968.
59 *Yeandel v Fisher* [1966] 1 QB 440; *Warner v Metropolitan Police Comr* [1969] 2 AC 256, though *Sweet v Parsley* is an exception to this approach.
60 *R v Wheat and Stocks* [1921] 2 KB 119, a case based on a particular interpretation of *R v Tolson* (1889) 23 QBD 168. *R v Gould* [1968] 1 All ER 849 has made it clear that the offence is not one of strict liability.   61 [1984] 2 All ER 503.

effective to promote the objects of the statute by encouraging greater vigilance to prevent the commission of the prohibited act.[62]

As a matter of a balance of social values, it may be thought acceptable that certain 'public welfare' offences are interpreted as implying strict liability; especially when, as frequently happens, the accused is not an ordinary individual but a company or corporation for whom the sanction will – on the rare occasions on which they are prosecuted – almost invariably be a fine (as in the case of breaches of factory legislation or pollution control legislation).[63] Many consider it far less acceptable for the criminal law to embark upon a course of development whereby in other circumstances an individual is rendered criminally liable, and possibly subject to sanctions of extreme gravity,[64] without the necessity of establishing some form of *mens rea*. At present, criminal liability continues, for the most part, to insist upon *mens rea* as a condition of liability, subject to the exceptions noted, and though (as we shall see later in a somewhat different context) some have argued for the complete abolition of the *mens rea* requirement, it is pertinent to ask whether departures from the conventional general conditions of liability for any criminal offence should be left to the fluctuating tides of judicial interpretative thought.

Defences

It follows from the foregoing discussion that if the defence can show that the accused in a criminal trial did not commit the *actus reus* then there must be an acquittal; the same is true – leaving aside strict liability offences – if the accused did not have the requisite *mens rea*, because 'the act is not blameworthy unless the mind is guilty'. For example, the harm or damage may have been caused purely accidentally, with no intention or recklessness on the part of the accused; or the accused may have been labouring under a mistake as to the facts alleged. A man charged with theft, for instance, who took another's property in the genuine, though mistaken, belief that it was his own, will not be guilty of a criminal offence. The mistake as to fact must be such as to render innocent the accused's actions had the facts been as he believed them to be: a man charged with unlawful possession of heroin (a controlled drug) cannot argue his innocence on the basis that he was under the mistaken impression that the substance in his possession was cocaine, for cocaine is also a controlled drug! A mistake as to law is no defence. Everyone is presumed to know the law (as long as this has been published so that it can be known), and ignorance of the law is no defence. If this were otherwise, it is argued, everyone charged with criminal offences could escape liability by pleading ignorance of the law.

---

62 [1984] 2 All ER 503 at 508.   63 See chapter 7.

64 Offences under controlled drugs legislation carry possible sentences of imprisonment, as do various road traffic offences, such as causing death by dangerous driving, held in *R v Ball and Loughlin* (1966) 50 Cr App Rep 266 to be an offence of strict liability.

In some special circumstances, it may be established that the accused was incapable of forming criminal intent sufficient, in law, for a conviction. There is a presumption, for example, that children below the age of criminal responsibility are incapable, because of immaturity, of distinguishing between right and wrong, and are therefore not capable of forming *mens rea*. The age of criminal responsibility has been changed over the years, the trend being to raise the age; at present, the age of responsibility is ten. Prior to 1998, children between ten and 14 could be found guilty of an offence only if sufficient evidence was forthcoming that the child did, in fact, appreciate that what they had done was seriously wrong. As Card explains it, this rule:

> gave rise to the odd result that children from 'good' homes were more likely to be found guilty than children from 'bad' homes, since children from 'good' homes are more likely to have known the serious wrongfulness of their conduct than children from 'bad' homes, although the latter may be more in need of the corrective treatment which can follow a finding of guilt.[65]

The presumption that a child aged between ten and 14 could not form the requisite *mens rea* unless rebutting evidence was produced by the prosecution, was judicially criticised,[66] and was abolished in 1998.[67] None the less, it has been argued that despite the 1998 Act, if it can be proved that a child did not appreciate the serious wrongfulness of his action, there would still be a defence.[68] The issue awaits judicial clarification.

Normally a person has no defence if the offence is committed whilst he or she is drunk or under the influence of drugs: an exception to this may be a case where the offence charged requires proof of specific intent (see above) and the intoxication prevented the accused from forming the necessary intent. For crimes of basic intent, the House of Lords in *DPP v Majewski*[69] held that the voluntary consumption of alcohol did not prevent the accused from acting voluntarily, and so having the necessary basic *mens rea*. There are, once again, clear policy reasons for limiting the extent to which intoxication may constitute a defence in criminal law.

More difficult are those cases where the accused pleads lack of responsibility for actions by reason of some mental illness or disability. In law, 'insanity' constitutes a defence to any charge, and the rules as to insanity in law remain as laid down by the judges in *M'Naghten's Case* in 1843.[70] Under these rules, every person is presumed sane unless the contrary is proved, and it is a defence to show that, at the time of the commission of the offence charged, the accused had 'such a defect of reason resulting from a disease of the mind as not to know the nature and quality of his action; or if he did know it, that he did not know he was doing wrong'.

---

65 Card, op. cit., p 717.
66 *C v DPP* [1995] 2 All ER 43, in which the House of Lords was highly critical of this principle, and
    recommended a change in the law.   67 Crime and Disorder Act 1998, s 34.
68 N. Walker, 'The End of an Old Song' (1999) 149 *NLJ* 64.
69 [1976] 2 All ER 142, [1976] 2 WLR 623.   70 (1843) 10 Cl & Fin 200.

Modern psychiatric diagnosis has long overtaken this antiquated approach to mental illness, and the formula has caused problems for judges and expert psychiatric witnesses alike. The basic difficulty is what constitutes a 'disease of the mind'. This is not a phrase used by psychiatrists, and there are conflicting judicial decisions about the conditions which may or may not fall into the category. Does a physical illness having repercussions on the brain, and hence upon consciousness, constitute a disease of the mind?[71] Does minor mental illness, such as depression, constitute a disease of the mind within the *M'Naghten* test? In *R v Clarke* in 1972[72] the answer was that such a depressive state which involved fits of absent-mindedness and confusion was not a disease of the mind. In *R v Sullivan* in 1984[73] the accused had attacked someone whilst suffering from an epileptic seizure during which he had temporarily lost consciousness. The House of Lords held that this fell within the *M'Naghten* Rules as being a 'disease of the mind', in that there was impairment, however temporary, of the accused's faculties of reason, memory and understanding. Lord Diplock, however, expressed his reluctance at using the term 'insanity' to describe such a physical and mental state as that of the accused, suggesting that it lay within the powers of Parliament to change the terminology involved in such cases.

Many have criticised the present law on this matter: fundamentally, judges are not well qualified to analyse issues involving mental illness, and indeed psychiatry itself has been criticised for its inability to provide precise definitions of mental illnesses. Nevertheless, the judges have insisted upon retaining the out-dated *M'Naghten* test for the purposes of liability in criminal law, although legislation in recent years has gone some way towards alleviating the problems by providing measures specifically designed for the treatment, if necessary in secure conditions, of offenders found to be suffering from mentally abnormal conditions such as psychopathy and psychosis. In particular, the Criminal Procedure (Insanity and Unfitness to Plead) Act 1991 amended the earlier Criminal Procedure (Insanity) Act 1964 to the effect that if an accused is found not guilty by reason of insanity the court must either make an order admitting the accused to a hospital, or make a guardianship order, a supervision and treatment order, or an absolute discharge. If the charge was one of murder, however, the court *must* make a hospital admission order. In such a case, the hospital authorities make the decision, in due course, about the accused's release, unless the court makes a restriction order (which may specify a minimum period for detention, or an indefinite period) in which case the decision as to release lies with the Home Secretary. In cases of murder, an indefinite restriction order must be made.

With regard to this defence, it must also be borne in mind that until the suspension of the death penalty in England in 1965, a successful defence of insanity

---

71 See *Bratty v Attorney-General for Northern Ireland* [1963] AC 386; *R v Charlson* [1955]; *R v Sullivan* [1984] AC 156; *R v Kemp* [1957] 1 QB 399.
72 [1972] 1 All ER 219. See also *R v Quick* [1973] 3 All ER 347; *R v Burgess* [1991] 2 All ER 769.
73 [1984] AC 156.

might be the only means of avoiding execution for murder: since the abolition of capital punishment, murder has carried a mandatory sentence of life imprisonment, which may, if necessary, be served in an institution for the criminally mentally ill. Perhaps because of this, since 1965, there has been a fall in the numbers pleading insanity in cases of murder. It has been pointed out that 'there were two successful pleas in 1974, three in 1978, three in 1981, none in 1988, one in 1990, two in 1991, three in 1992 and 11 in 1996'.[74]

Additionally, the Homicide Act 1957 provides a *partial* defence linked, like insanity, to abnormality of mind, though this defence is available only for charges of murder. This is the defence of 'diminished responsibility' which, although not a complete defence, has the effect of *reducing* the charge of murder to the lesser charge of manslaughter.[75] To establish the defence of diminished responsibility, the defence must prove that, at the time of the offence, the accused was 'suffering from such abnormality of mind (whether arising from a condition of arrested or retarded development of mind, or any inherent causes, or induced by disease or injury) as substantially impaired his mental responsibility'.[76] The practical effect of a successful plea of diminished responsibility[77] is to avoid the mandatory sentence of life imprisonment attracted by a conviction for murder, and to allow the sentencing judge to pass a sentence appropriate to the circumstances and gravity of the offence (see below).

Finally in this section, it is necessary to refer briefly to the question as to whether criminal law recognises as defences necessity and duress. Duress may be defined as a situation in which the accused is forced by another – perhaps at gunpoint or because of threats to his life – to commit an offence. Necessity covers the situation where someone is not under threat from another person, but where failure to commit the offence would result in some disastrous consequence for the perpetrator. Although some have suggested that there is little difference between a threat posed by a person and one posed by a circumstance the law none the less has always made such a distinction. Necessity has never been recognised as a general defence,[78] although duress has been accepted as available as a defence to any criminal charge with the exception, until 1987, of that of murder as a principal – that is, as the actual killer. If it is accepted as a general proposition that the distinction between duress and necessity is 'a distinction without a difference, since . . . duress is only that species of the genus of necessity which is caused by wrongful threats',[79] then the law

---

74 Jefferson, op. cit., p 326.
75 For detailed discussions on the difficult area of manslaughter, see the main texts on criminal law: for example Smith and Hogan, op. cit.; Jefferson, op.cit.; and Card, Cross and Jones, op. cit.
76 Homicide Act 1957, s 2.
77 A similar result will follow if in a murder case the accused successfully pleads that the killing took place in circumstances in which he was provoked to 'lose his self-control' (Homicide Act 1957, s 3). The provocation must, however, be sufficient to make a 'reasonable man' do as the accused did. For discussion see texts on criminal law, above.
78 See the well-known case of *R v Dudley and Stevens* (1884) 14 QBD 273. For a superb discussion of this case and its background, see A. Simpson, *Cannibalism and the Common Law* (1984, Penguin).   79 *R v Howe*, op. cit., at 429.

is clearly illogical. As to the availability of the defence of duress in murder cases, it was long held that this defence was not available to the actual perpetrator. The House of Lords held in 1975 in *DPP for Northern Ireland v Lynch*,[80] that the defence of duress was available where the charge was murder as a *secondary party*: in that case, the accused was threatened with being shot if he refused to drive another offender to a place where the latter intended to kill a police officer. The House of Lords in 1987, however, in *R v Howe*[81] decided that *Lynch* was wrongly decided, and should be overruled.[82] In the leading judgment of Lord Hailsham, there are passages which make it clear that the decision is at least partly the result of considerations not of precedent but of public policy,[83] and the effect of this decision is to deny the defence to duress on any charge of murder, whether as a principal or as a secondary party, or attempted murder.[84]

Of course, the courts recognise that different degrees of culpability (even in homicide) may exist, and that trial courts may take lesser degrees of culpability into account when deciding the appropriate sentence to impose on the convicted offender. It is to a consideration of the post-conviction process – sentencing – that we now turn.

The criminal justice system

The judges' main concern in sentencing convicted offenders is (and always has been) stated to be 'the protection of the public' and the reflection in their sentencing policies of what they take to be the social condemnation of offence and offender concerned. The element of strong moral condemnation must not be underemphasised, for as we have seen, it occupies a central place in legal ideology: the very basis of criminal liability involves the requirement that in the majority of criminal offences there must be proof of the 'guilty mind', or *mens rea*, before conviction can ensue. This is the means whereby the moral responsibility of the offender and the voluntariness of his or her acts are written into the conditions of liability within the criminal law, and the requirement of moral blame is deeply rooted in our ideas about what constitutes a criminal offender. This is one of the main reasons why, as we have seen, there has at times been reluctance on the part of judges and other lawyers to admit principles of liability based on 'strict liability' or 'liability without fault'.

Given this background, the main general objectives of sentencing in our legal system have usually been presented as falling into three categories: retribution, deterrence and rehabilitation.[85]

---

80 [1975] AC 653.   81 [1987] AC 417.
82 As to the House of Lords' ability to reverse its own previous decisions, see chapter 7.
83 See, for example, Lord Hailsham's judgment at 433–435.
84 *R v Gotts* [1992] 1 All ER 832, HL. For further discussion see major texts, and also A. Reed, 'The Need for a New Anglo-American Approach to Duress' [1996] *Jo of Criminal Law* 209.
85 Though these are commonly discussed as the 'aims of sentencing', it is possible to identify other possible aims, notably 'reparation', or making good the loss suffered by the victim, or 'incapacitation', which aims simply to make the offender incapable of re-offending. Lord Bingham suggests

Retribution is straightforward punishment inflicted on the offender in response to the offence. It is sometimes called the principle of 'just deserts'; it is the type of legal sanction which Durkheim called 'repressive' (see chapter 1) and is perhaps the oldest type of sanction, having its Old Testament justification in the phrase 'an eye for an eye'. Examples of retributive sentences might include the Great Train Robbery case in 1965[86] which attracted sentences of 30 years for the participants; and the judicial comments in the 'Angry Brigade' trial and the IRA bomb trials in the 1970s reveal that retributive principles were at least partly at work in the assessment of the sentences in these cases.[87] Retributive principles underlie the main statute which currently governs sentencing practice, the Powers of Criminal Courts (Sentencing) Act 2000.[88]

Until recently it was generally accepted that the principal sentencing policy of the courts tended to be not retribution, but deterrence. Deterrence is a double-edged principle. It should, of course, deter offenders themselves from committing further crimes, but also, and very importantly, it has been seen by the judges as serving to inhibit the rest of the community from indulging in criminal behaviour. The message is, simply, 'if you do this, this is what you can expect'. The deterrent principle has for some years been widely used, though whether or not the policy works in these ways is somewhat debatable. There has been much research on this matter, which, according to Walker and Padfield, enables us to say only that:

> Naive claims that deterrent policies are highly effective – or totally ineffective – have been replaced by the less exciting realisation that *some* people can be deterred in *some* situations from *some* types of conduct by *some* degree of likelihood that they will be penalised in *some* ways; but we do not yet know enough to enable us to be very specific about the people, the situations, the conduct, or the likelihood or nature of the penalties.[89]

To begin with, in order to be effective, a deterrent sentence must be publicised among the community, and although most crimes, serious and petty, are covered in national and local media, how many of us have any idea of the sentence we might expect if we were caught, for example, shoplifting or stealing from cars? Probably

---

that 'the maintenance of public confidence' might be added to this list (T. Bingham, *The Business of Judging* (2000, Oxford University Press), p 302). For full and very detailed discussion on these, and indeed all aspects of sentencing and penal policy, see A. Ashworth, *Sentencing and Criminal Justice* (4th edn., 2006, Cambridge University Press); N. Padfield, *Text and Materials on the Criminal Justice Process* (3rd edn., 2003, Oxford University Press); S. Easton and C. Piper, *Sentencing and Punishment: The Quest for Justice* (2005, Oxford University Press).

86 *R v Wilson and others* [1965] 1 QB 402.

87 Other examples might include the trial of the Kray twins, that of Sutcliffe (the 'Yorkshire Ripper'), the exemplary sentences given out to young people convicted of 'mugging' offences in the early 1970s (on which see S. Hall, C. Critcher et al., *Policing the Crisis* (1978, Macmillan)) and perhaps the sentence in 2002 of 60 days' imprisonment (reduced on appeal to 28 days) imposed on a mother for failing to prevent her daughters' truancy – the first time such a sentence had been imposed, and occurring at a time when the government was expressing concern over the alleged connection between truancy and youth crime.

88 As amended by the Criminal Justice Act 2003.

89 N. Walker and N. Padfield, *Sentencing: Theory, Law and Practice* (2nd edn., 1996, Butterworths) p 101.

very few people have any accurate knowledge of the kinds of sentences such activities might attract, and it is only the sensational and unusual cases which attract much publicity. Research carried out in the aftermath of the exemplary 20-year sentence handed down to a young Birmingham man for a mugging offence in 1973 showed that, despite extensive publicity given by the media to this case, the frequency of 'mugging' offences did not appear to diminish.[90]

Apart from this, doubts have been raised about the efficacy of deterrence in sentencing policies upon potential offenders within the community at large. To take the most prominent example, that of capital punishment for murder: this is believed by many to be the 'ultimate deterrent', but available evidence does not support the proposition that the death penalty is any more effective a deterrent than long periods of imprisonment; and, proportionately, there is no evidence that the suspension of the death penalty in 1965 has resulted in an appreciable increase in the murder rate in Britain, as many at the time of suspension feared it would. And the 1990 Conservative government White Paper *Crime, Justice and Protecting the Public* thought that it was 'unrealistic to construct sentencing arrangements on the assumption that most offenders will . . . base their conduct on rational calculation. Often they do not.'[91]

The third principle which may underlie criminal sanctions is that of rehabilitation. Now, whilst the principles underlying the aims of retribution and deterrence are to some extent compatible, in that in both cases the gravity of the sentence imposed is related to the seriousness of the offence committed, the aim of rehabilitation involves considerations which are quite different, and must be regarded as an objective quite distinct from the first two. Essentially, the rehabilitative sentence is tied not to the offence and its gravity, but to the offender and his or her 'needs': the sentencing judge must make a choice in any given case as to whether to pass a sentence linked to the offence (retributive or deterrent) or an individualised rehabilitative sentence, designed to reform or 'treat' the offender for an identified 'problem'.

Which of these principles is most prominent today? Whilst the attitude of the judges has tended to remain generally retributivist,[92] in the current edition of *Smith and Hogan's Criminal Law* the point is made, with regard to legislation in this area, that

> Parliament has regarded various of these theories as being more influential at one time or another, and its failure to adopt a single principled approach to sentencing for any sustained period has become a matter of concern in recent years. The shift in attitude is illustrated by comparison of the sentencing provisions of the Criminal Justice Act 1991 with those of the Criminal Justice Act 2003. In the 1991 Act the overriding principle was that criminals should 'get their just deserts'. . .. . .Under the 2003 Act, deterrence has assumed a more significant role.[93]

90 See M. Cavadino and J. Dignan, *The Penal System: An Introduction* (3rd edn., 2005, Sage), p 35.
91 Cm 965, para 2.8.   92 *Smith and Hogan's Criminal Law*, op. cit., p 4.   93 Ibid., p 5

There has also been in recent years a noticeable move towards what has been called 'restorative justice', some examples of which we will examine presently; this approach has been explained as one which:

> seeks to engage offenders in a variety of processes that require them to reflect on the harm they have caused to others and encourages them to try to make amends for what they have done. Some of these processes involve some form of dialogue between victims and offenders . . . Others involve . . . techniques that do not necessarily involve the participation of a victim. One feature that both sets of processes have in common is that they rely on the use of *internal sanctions* which operate on the basis of an offender's conscience rather than the application of external sanctions of the kind that characterise most conventional forms of punishment.[94]

In any particular period, the principles underpinning the operation of the criminal justice system – and certainly of those aspects which are concerned with sentencing policy – can be identified partly with the enduring concerns of the judiciary, noted above, but more substantially with the stance taken by the government of that period and enshrined in legislation. The importance of the 'politics of law and order', and the links between politicians' assumptions and beliefs about crime and sentencing and their parties' ideological positions has often been noted; and certain historical trends since the 1960s have been identified, some having argued that the Conservative Party has traditionally been the 'party of law and order', whilst the Labour Party has traditionally been portrayed by its parliamentary opponents as being 'soft on crime'.[95] It has recently been observed, however, that the main political parties in England – in the context of rising crime rates – have converged in recent years in emphasising the importance of tackling problems of crime, law and order in modern Britain.[96]

The Conservative government's 1990 White Paper, *Crime, Justice and Protecting the Public* led to the Criminal Justice Act 1991[97] which was underpinned by the clear policy of attempting to keep offenders out of prison,[98] unless a custodial sentence was warranted by the seriousness of the offence; and the promotion of non-custodial sentences, and in particular community orders – probation, community service,[99] attendance centre, supervision and curfew orders,[100] together with

---

94 M. Cavadino and J. Dignan, op.cit., p 167.
95 See, for example, D. Downes and R. Morgan, 'Dumping the "Hostages to Fortune"? The Politics of Law and Order in Post-War Britain' in Maguire, Morgan and Reiner, op. cit.; and see I. Taylor, *Law and Order: Arguments for Socialism* (1981, Macmillan).
96 See in particular Downes and Morgan, ibid.
97 As amended by the Criminal Justice Act 1993 and the consolidating Powers of Criminal Courts (Sentencing) Act 2000 – see below.
98 Though this policy was clearly at odds with government pronouncements over the ensuing five years to the effect that imprisonment was effective in combating crime and would be used more.
99 Introduced by the Powers of Criminal Courts Act 1973, as amended by s 68 of the Criminal Justice Act 1982, this is an order which may be made in respect of a person aged 16 or over, convicted of an offence which might be punishable with imprisonment. The community service order requires the person to perform unpaid work 'for the community' for a specified number of hours.
100 As amended by the Anti-Social Behaviour Act 2003, s 88.

combination orders, combining probation with a requirement to carry out a specified number of hours of unpaid work. Over the five years following the Act,
however, the government made substantial changes to the 1991 framework, with
the result that by 1996 there seemed little coherence in the over-arching policy of
the criminal justice system. Certainly, the notion of attempting to keep offenders
out of prison had been abandoned in favour of the proposition that, in the words
of the then Home Secretary Michael Howard in 1993, 'prison works'. Indeed, following the 1996 White Paper *Protecting the Public*, the Crime (Sentences) Act 1997
envisaged substantially greater use of imprisonment by providing, among other
things, for mandatory life imprisonment for a second 'serious offence',[101] seven
years' imprisonment for a third offence involving Class A drugs, and three years' for
a third offence of burglary. These ideas were, of course, variations of the 'three
strikes and you're out' philosophy developed in the United States; the Labour Party
had supported these proposals during the passage of the bill in 1997, and indeed
implemented them on taking office in 1997.

The judiciary, however, were less supportive, regarding these provisions as
undermining their discretion in sentencing. The Court of Appeal effectively neu-
tralised the mandatory life imprisonment provision in 2000, in a case in which the
court adopted a liberal interpretation of the statutory provision that the mandatory
life sentence need not be imposed in 'exceptional circumstances'; and 'the "three
strike" sentences have proved equally unpopular with sentencers, who in these cases
already had the benefit of a wider "get-out clause" in the original legislation, being
empowered to pass a lighter sentence if the one prescribed is "unjust" '.[102]

Under the New Labour administration which came to power in 1997, little was
done to affect the rising prison population, which rose from just over 55,000 in
1996 to 65,000 in 2000, and to over 70,000 by March 2002. In spring 2006, the figure
stood at 77,000. Despite this, the New Labour government set about the radical
overhaul of the criminal justice system, and initially, particular attention was paid
to 'youth crime'. The 1997 White Paper *No More Excuses – A New Approach to
Tackling Youth Crime in England and Wales* described the measures proposed,
which were subsequently embodied in the Crime and Disorder Act 1998.[103] The
Home Secretary made the government's intentions clear:

> For too long we have assumed that young offenders will grow out of their offending if
> left to themselves. The research evidence shows that does not happen . . . an excuse
> culture has developed within the youth justice system. It excuses itself for its inefficiency,
> and too often excuses the young offenders before it, implying that they cannot help their
> behaviour because of their social circumstances. Rarely are they confronted with their

---

101 Defined in s2(5) as attempt, conspiracy or incitement to commit murder, soliciting murder,
manslaughter, wounding or causing grievous bodily harm with intent, rape or attempted rape,
sexual intercourse with a girl under 13, robbery involving a real or imitation firearm, and other
offences involving firearms.
102 M. Cavadino and J. Dignan, *The Penal System* (3rd edn., 2002, Sage), p 106.
103 See N. Padfield, *A Guide to the Crime and Disorder Act 1998* (1998, Butterworths).

behaviour and helped to take more personal responsibility for their actions . . . This White Paper . . . sets out a new approach to tackling youth crime.[104]

It is important to consider briefly some of the main provisions of the Crime and Disorder Act 1998, since by doing so we can gain some appreciation of government thinking in this difficult area. The 'health warning' must be given, however, that the law, policy and practice of sentencing is extremely complex, and this brief discussion cannot provide a comprehensive account.[105]

It is also important to appreciate that the specific 'youth crime' problems addressed by the 1998 Act must be seen in the context of the government's wider political agenda which involved, among other things, tackling the problems of social exclusion, introducing measures to support families, allocating substantial resources to improve education, introducing programmes to tackle drug use and attempting to provide new opportunities for training and employment. New Labour's approach, in other words, was to ensure that 'joined-up thinking' linked the problem of youth crime to the related issues of the problematic life-experiences of a substantial number of young people in order to confront not just crime, but also the perceived 'causes of crime'. Such an approach requires a role not only for the police and the courts, but also parents, local education authorities, social services and other organisations, and we can perceive the necessary multi-agency approach in various aspects of the Crime and Disorder Act 1998.[106]

The Act itself provided for a number of measures intended to prevent criminal activity. The *anti-social behaviour order (ASBO)*, for example, is an order made by a magistrates' court, on application by a local authority, with regard to any person aged ten or above who has acted in an anti-social manner, that is, 'in a manner that caused or was likely to cause harassment, alarm or distress to one or more persons not of the same household as himself',[107] where the order is necessary to prevent further similar behaviour. Such an order, which specifies the conduct in which the offender is prohibited from engaging, lasts for at least two years, and any breach of the order may be followed by a fine or imprisonment imposed by the magistrates' court. In the period up to March 2006, a total of 7,356 ASBOs had been made, of which 3,135 were made in respect of people aged between 10 and 17. The substantial use of the ASBO has, however, been criticised on a number of grounds. To begin with, it has been argued that there are many examples of cases in which the behaviour complained of, though undoubtedly eccentric, and in some cases disturbing, has not in itself been criminal, and there have been cases in which it is at least arguable that the issue of an ASBO was a singularly inappropriate method of handling the situation:

> Magistrates in Bath served an Asbo on a 23-year old woman who repeatedly tried to kill herself. She has been rescued from the River Avon three times, found 'hanging by

---

104 *No More Excuses* (1997, Cm 3809).
105 Readers wishing to explore the detail of this fast-developing area should consult specialised and up-to-date texts.
106 This Act must be read in the light of the Powers of Criminal Courts (Sentencing) Act 2000.
107 Section 1(1)(a).

her fingertips' from a railway bridge and has been loitering at the top of multistorey car parks. The magistrates considered it an appropriate response to issue an Asbo banning the suicidal woman from going near railway lines, rivers, or bridges.[108]

Second, ASBOs are issued by magistrates' courts on application by local authorities: they are essentially *civil* orders, but non-compliance by the person subject to the order can result in *criminal* penalties, including, potentially, imprisonment. Ought such sanctions to be imposed without an appropriate criminal trial? The Howard League for Penal Reform has argued that, at least with regard to the use of ASBOs for children,

> current legislation has the effect of widening the net of the criminal justice system, by criminalizing naughty children and their parents, the mentally ill and those in social housing. Anti-social behaviour legislation relies on a low burden of proof. It does not rely on an objective test of behaviour but on the reaction to that behaviour by others. Yet anti-social behaviour legislation uses the criminal justice system if the original order is breached. There is a blurring of the boundaries between civil and criminal law which [has] serious implications for due process and the rights of the child.[109]

In line with the government's belief that parents must take responsibility for the provision of proper care and control of their children, the Crime and Disorder Act introduced the *parenting order*, whereby the parents of any offending child or young person may be required to comply with any requirements specified in the order (such as making sure that their child attends school every day) and also to attend counselling or guidance sessions for up to three months. Again, criminal sanctions in the form of a fine may be applied in the event of non-compliance with such an order.

On application by a local authority, a magistrates' court may make a *child safety order* in respect of any child under ten – the age of criminal responsibility. Such an order may be made where the child has committed any act which, in the case of a person aged ten or over, would have constituted a criminal offence; or where the order is necessary to prevent the commission of such an act; or where the child has already contravened a curfew notice (see below); or where the child has behaved in a manner that caused or was likely to cause harassment, alarm or distress to anyone not of the same household as him- or herself. The effect of a child safety order is that the child is placed, for a period not exceeding three months (or in exceptional cases, 12 months), under the supervision of a social worker or a member of a youth offending team (see below).

The 1998 Act made provision for local *child curfew schemes*,[110] to be made by local authorities (after consultation with local police and other appropriate bodies,

---

108 The *Guardian*, 7 June 2005. This article cites several other cases in which the issue of an ASBO has been criticised. And see S. Macdonald, 'A Suicidal Woman, Roaming Pigs and a Noisy Trampolinist: Refining the ASBO's Definition of Anti-Social Behaviour' (2006) *MLR* 143.
109 Press Release, 5 April 2005.
110 General powers to impose curfews on convicted offenders (part of a range of community orders) were introduced in the Powers of Criminal Courts (Sentencing) Act 2000.

and with the approval of the Home Secretary) whereby children under ten may be prohibited from being in a specified public place between 9 pm and 6 am unless they are with a parent or other responsible adult. Any child found to be in contravention of such a curfew order may be taken home by a police officer.[111]

The 1998 Act places additional specific responsibilities upon local authorities and others: every local authority and chief officer of police is required to draw up and implement, every three years, a 'strategy for the reduction of crime and disorder in the area'[112] and in doing so must act in co-operation with police and probation authorities, and with any other person or organisation which the Home Secretary may specify. In formulating the strategy, the local authority must produce and publish an analysis of crime and disorder in their area, and must obtain the views of the local community (possibly by holding public meetings). The strategy must include a statement of objectives and performance targets for measuring the attainment of those objectives.

The 1998 Act set out to reform substantially the youth justice system, in line with the White Paper commitment to deal with what had hitherto been 'a lack of consistent direction' and 'confusion about the purpose' of that system. After making it clear that 'it shall be the principal aim of the youth justice system to prevent offending by children and young persons' (s 37), the Act requires local authorities, working with chief police officers and probation and health authorities, to ensure that all youth justice services are available in their area, and to set up, for their area, 'youth offending teams'. These teams must include at least one probation officer, social worker and police officer, and must also include representation from the local health authority and local education authority. Once again, the multi-agency approach favoured by the government is clear. The youth offending team is responsible for the co-ordination of the provision of youth justice services in the area, and for carrying out such functions as are assigned to them in the annual 'youth justice plan' which must be drawn up by each local authority, and which must set out the details of the provision and funding of youth justice services in the area. The local authority's youth justice plan must be submitted to a new body established by the Act (s 41) – the Youth Justice Board – a non-departmental body reporting to the Home Secretary, comprising people appointed by the Home Secretary on the basis of their 'extensive recent experience of the youth justice system'. The Board's functions are, principally, to monitor the operation of the system, and to advise the Home Secretary as to the operation of the system and any further steps that might be taken to prevent offending by children and young persons.

But attempts at prevention will not always be successful, and provision is made in the Act for new measures for dealing with young offenders. There are new procedures for reprimanding or warning young 'first-time' offenders, replacing the

---

111 If the officer has reasonable cause to believe that the child would be likely to suffer significant harm by being taken home, it is the duty of the local authority to investigate the circumstances and take appropriate action to safeguard the child's welfare: Children Act 1989, s 47, as amended by the Crime and Disorder Act 1998.   112 Section 6 (1).

previous system of 'police cautions'. As the White Paper explained the new procedure:

- a first offence might be met by a police reprimand, provided it was not serious. Any
  further offence would have to result in a Final Warning or criminal charges: in no circumstances should a young offender receive two reprimands;
- if a first offence results in a Final Warning, any further offence would automatically lead
  to criminal charges, except where at least two years have passed since the Final Warning
  and the subsequent offence is minor; and
- for any offence the police would have the option of pressing charges.[113]

Following a warning, the young person is referred to a youth offending team, who
must assess the offender and, unless they consider it inappropriate to do so, arrange
for a rehabilitation programme for that person.

The *reparation order* was a new non-custodial measure introduced by the Act
which is available to the youth court, whereby the convicted offender may be
ordered to make reparation either to the victim of the offence, or to the community at large. The intention was that for offenders aged between ten and 17, reparation orders would 'substantially displace' the conditional discharge[114] for 'less
serious offences'. The government's thinking behind this order was that:

> by allowing the offender to undertake some form of practical reparation activity which
> will benefit the victim (if the victim so wishes it), it is hoped that the victim will gain
> a greater insight into the reasons for the offence, and will therefore be able more easily
> to come to terms with the offence, and put it behind them. Reparation to the victim
> will also help the offender to realise the distress and inconvenience that his or her
> actions have caused, accept responsibility for those actions, and have the opportunity
> to make some amends either directly to the victim, or to the community as a whole . . .
> Reparation . . . is intended to challenge the young offender's behaviour and attitudes.
> It should not be a mechanistic process based upon an 'eye for an eye' approach . . .[115]

The other new non-custodial measure introduced in the 1998 Act was the *action
plan order*. This is a community sentence for offenders aged between ten and 17,
convicted of relatively serious offences, whereby the offender must undertake to
comply with a structured series of requirements regarding his or her actions and
whereabouts for a three-month period. During that time the offender is under the
supervision of a probation officer, social worker or member of a youth offending
team, and the conditions attached to the order may require the offender to participate in specified activities (such as anger management classes or drug or alcohol

---

113 Op. cit., para 5.13.
114 Generally, an 'absolute discharge' means that the offender goes free, a technical conviction
     having been recorded; a 'conditional discharge' is also a discharge from court, but conditions are
     attached, the most common one being that the offender must not commit any further offence
     for a specified period or else he or she will be liable to be dealt with in a sentence reflecting the
     new offence and also the one for which the conditional discharge was given.
115 *Crime and Disorder Act Guidance Document: Reparation Order* (2000, Home Office), paras
     2.3–2.4.

misuse programmes), to report to specified people at certain times and places, to attend an attendance centre for a specified number of hours, to stay away from specified places (such as car parks or amusement arcades), to comply with any specified educational arrangements (such as a requirement to attend school), to make reparation (see above) or to attend any hearing to review progress and make any adjustments to the plan.

The major change introduced by the 1998 Act with regard to custodial measures for young offenders was the creation of the *detention and training order*. This is intended to be a 'constructive and flexible custodial sentence providing a clear focus on preventing offending'.[116] Intended for offenders aged between ten and 17,[117] this order may only be imposed if the offence is so serious that only a custodial sentence is justified. The idea is that the court imposes a detention and training order for a period ranging from four to 24 months, and the first half of that period is served in a secure institution. When the first half is over, the offender is released, and spends the remaining half of the detention and training order period under supervision by a probation officer, a social worker or a member of a youth offending team.

Further provision for young offenders was made in the Youth Justice and Criminal Evidence Act 1999, which according to the Home Office 'Introduction' to the Act, continued to build into the youth justice system the key principles of restorative justice:

- making restoration to the victim;
- achieving reintegration into the law-abiding community;
- the offender taking responsibility for the consequences of their behaviour.[118]

The Act created a new sentence for young first-time offenders of referral to a *youth offender panel*.[119] Unless the youth court considers that an absolute discharge or a custodial sentence is called for, the offender is referred to the youth offender panel, comprising people from the local community with an interest or expertise in dealing with young people, and including a representative from the local Youth Offending Team. The panel works with the young offender, and will:

> agree a contract with the offender and their family aimed at tackling the young person's offending behaviour and its causes. The contract will set out clear requirements that they will have to fulfil. These might include an apology and some form of reparation to their victim, carrying out community work, taking part in family counselling or drug rehabilitation. In fulfilling the contract the young person will have to face both what they have done and its consequences. If they fail to agree or breach the terms of a contract the young person will be returned to the court for sentencing for the original offence.[120]

116 *No More Excuses*, op. cit., para 6.11.
117 Though offenders aged between 12 and 14 must be 'persistent offenders'; and a detention and training order may only be imposed on a person under 12 if the court considers that only a custodial sentence would be adequate to protect the public from further offending by that person.
118 Home Office 'Introduction to the Act', at www.homeoffice.gov.uk/yjceact/yopanel1.htm .
119 The scheme is further and substantially elaborated in the Powers of Criminal Courts (Sentencing) Act 2000, Part III.   120 Ibid.

It has been suggested that, as far as youth justice is concerned, the present policy on youth justice, with its array of weaponry and procedures designed to deal with young offenders, 'continues . . . to contain an at times uneasy balance between welfare and punishment'.[121]

More generally, the programme of reform and modernisation of the criminal justice system continued in the Criminal Justice and Court Services Act 2000, which dramatically changed the framework of the probation service and created the Children and Family Court Advisory and Support Service. This Act also re-named certain orders in order to make them more easily understood, and extended the use of electronic monitoring ('tagging') of offenders subject to curfews. In addition, the Act increased the maximum penalties for offences relating to indecent photographs of children, extended powers for compulsory drug testing of offenders, further extended electronic tagging of offenders and tightened protections against sex offenders and violent offenders; and substantial provision was made in the Criminal Justice and Police Act 2001 for dealing with disorderly behaviour, drunkenness in public places or in licensed premises, drug trafficking offenders, and other related issues. The pre-existing framework of sentencing law and policy was consolidated and amended by the Powers of Criminal Courts (Sentencing) Act 2000.

And the government pursued its campaign against 'anti-social behaviour' with the Anti-Social Behaviour Act 2003, providing local authorities and the police with greater powers to deal with activities defined as 'anti-social'. This wide-ranging statute covers powers for dealing with premises used for drug-dealing; provides local authorities, housing action trusts and social landlords with new measures for dealing with anti-social behaviour in, or in the vicinity of, their housing stock; prohibits the carrying of real or imitation firearms and tightens the regulation of the possession of air weapons; and extends powers for dealing with excessive noise, 'raves'[122] and other 'public assemblies',[123] graffiti and fly-posting. The Act even makes provision for the making of complaints by householders about high hedges on someone else's land – a 'high hedge' being defined (s66) as a barrier to light or access created 'wholly or predominantly' by a 'line of two or more evergreen or semi-evergreen trees or shrubs' which rises to a height of more than two metres above the ground.

Yet more government legislative activity culminated in the Criminal Justice Act 2003, designed to reform the criminal justice system by streamlining it and making it more efficient. The White Paper which preceded the Act incorporated the

---

121 M. Davies, H. Croall and J. Tyrer, *Criminal Justice: An Introduction to the Criminal Justice System in England and Wales* (3rd edn., 2005, Pearson Education), p 223.

122 A 'rave' may now, by virtue of s58 of this Act, comprise gatherings of 20 or more people. Previously the minimum number present had to be 100 in order to comprise a rave' (Criminal Justice and Public Order Act 1994, s63).

123 The Act re-defines 'public assembly' which was, by virtue of the Public Order Act 1986, previously defined as a group of '20 or more persons'. The term now covers any 'group' of more than two people.

proposals from two reports published in 2001 – Sir Robin Auld's *Review of the Criminal Courts of England and Wales* and John Halliday's review of the sentencing framework of England and Wales, *Making Punishment Work* (2001).

The Criminal Justice Act 2003 is substantial, complex and wide-ranging, containing nearly 340 sections and 38 Schedules. The intention is to create a comprehensive, flexible and clear sentencing framework, and though many parts of the Act effectively re-enact earlier legislation (in particular, the Powers of Criminal Courts (Sentencing) Act 2000) there are a number of features which are new, one or two of which may usefully be noted here. To begin with, The Act creates a new Sentencing Guidelines Council, chaired by the Lord Chief Justice and comprising seven other judges and four non-judicial members (who must have experience in one or more of the areas of police work, criminal prosecution, criminal defence, or the welfare of victims of crime). The Council's brief is to produce sentencing guidelines for all criminal courts, which the courts must in turn take into consideration when determining appropriate sentences.

The Act contains detailed statements as to the aggravating factors which will tend to increase the severity of sentences, and in addition to the existing ones (such as previous convictions or where the aggravating factors are racial or religious) the Act adds additional aggravating factors which involve hostility on the part of the accused with regard to a victim's disability or sexual orientation.

If an offence is too serious to be dealt with by means of a fine, or a conditional or absolute discharge, the Act provides that a 'community sentence' may be made, though in the case of offenders under 18 this is called a 'youth community order'. The new 'community sentence' replaces the pre-existing variety of different community orders into one concept, and the requirements now available with a generic community sentence include compulsory (unpaid) work, participation in specified activities, programmes aimed at changing offending behaviour, prohibition from certain activities, the imposition of a curfew, prohibition on entering certain areas, residence requirements, mental health, drug, or alcohol treatment (with the consent of the offender), supervision, and, for offenders under 25, attendance at an attendance centre.

With regard to sentences of imprisonment, the Act made some changes to the existing framework of available sentences (including an increase in the maximum penalties for certain drugs offences, driving offences causing death, and some road traffic offences), and introduced several new forms of custodial sentence. Two of the most important changes are new provisions relating to prison sentences of less than 12 months, and the introduction of the 'indeterminate sentence of imprisonment for public protection'.

Prior to the Act, offenders serving a prison sentence of less than 12 months were released half way through their sentence, with no conditions attaching to the remaining time. Under the 2003 Act, a new sentence, often referred to as 'custody plus', replaces most prison sentences of under 12 months. 'Custody plus' comprises up to 3 months in prison, followed by at least six months' supervision in the community. The court will determine, at the point of sentencing, the lengths of each part, and may attach requirements, based upon those available under the generic community sentence, to the supervision period of the sentence. And at the other end of scale of seriousness, the indeterminate sentence of imprisonment for public protection may only be passed by a court if an offender is convicted of any of a large number of specified sexual or violent offences which carry a maximum sentence of ten years or more. To attract such an indeterminate sentence, the court must be of the opinion that the offender poses a significant risk of serious harm to the public.

Many of the provisions of the 2003 Act have been controversial, not the least of which is the reform of the 'double jeopardy' rule. Hitherto, it was not possible for a person who had been acquitted of a criminal offence to be re-tried for that same offence. Under the Act, there may now be a re-trial in cases of serious offences where compelling new evidence subsequently comes to light against the acquitted person. Such evidence may comprise DNA evidence, or the evidence of new witnesses not present at the original trial. In such cases, the procedure is for the case to be considered by the Court of Appeal, who, if it considers it appropriate, may quash the original acquittal and order a re-trial. The whole process must have the approval of the Director of Public Prosecutions, and it should be noted that the possibility of re-trial after acquittal is only available for certain specified serious offences carrying a maximum of life imprisonment[124] – murder, manslaughter, rape and certain other serious sexual offences, serious drugs offences, criminal damage endangering life, war crimes, and terrorism offences.

One of the more controversial aspects of much post-1997 criminal justice legislation is the extent to which the complex framework of criminal justice as it is applied to youth and adult offenders alike incorporates a number of aims. We noted earlier that the Criminal Justice Act 2003 tends to embrace the principle of deterrence, though in s 142 of that Act, the 'purposes of sentencing' are identified as including punishment, the reduction of crime, reform and rehabilitation, the protection of the public, and reparation. It has been questioned whether a sentencing judge can possibly take all these into account, especially as, as we have already pointed out, it is not easy to see how some of these aims can be mutually compatible. The mixture in measures such as 'custody plus' of retribution (the period of imprisonment) and rehabilitation (the period of supervision) reflects the multi-agency approach favoured by the present government, which may be thought to encroach on the 'traditional' role of the sentencing judge or magistrate – how far do the new provisions assist, and how far do they restrict, the conventional 'discretionary power' of the sentencing judge to decide on the appropriate sentence? Certainly, for many years it has been common practice for reports such as social enquiry reports and probation reports to be provided at the pre-sentence stage for the sentencing judge. The new provisions reflect, however, a commitment by government to the idea that multi-agency inputs are not simply aids to arriving at

---

124 As specified in Schedule 5 of the Act.

an appropriate sentence, but rather constitute essential 'joined-up thinking' as to the most appropriate disposal, especially with a view to crime prevention.

But for many – especially adult – offenders, sentencing judges still retain substantial discretion. The fundamental principle of proportion remains: the sentence must be proportionate to the gravity of the offence, and the Court of Appeal will reduce (and in some cases increase)[125] a sentence which it feels is out of proportion.

The statutory definitions of criminal offences provide some guidance for the court by stating a maximum amount of fine or length of imprisonment which a judge may give out for that offence.[126] Below this maximum, however, the judges have a considerable amount of discretion as to precisely where on the scale of gravity of sentencing measures the offender is placed. There are statutory guidelines and policy directives, and there are, in addition, restrictions in the form of statutory provisions. The Powers of Criminal Courts (Sentencing) Act 2000, for example, provides that no court may pass a sentence of imprisonment on a person under 21.

Within these constraints, the sentencing judge has a considerable amount of discretion. The maximum sentence will be reserved for the most serious manifestations of a particular offence; 'average' examples will attract somewhat lesser sentences; and cases thought to be less serious than the 'average' will attract lesser sentences.

In the case of an offence whose seriousness may range from the very trivial to the most grave, such as theft, the range of sentences at the disposal of the court may start from non-custodial measures (such as fines or conditional discharges) at the bottom of the scale, to substantial periods of imprisonment where large amounts of money are involved. It must be remembered, however, that much depends upon the precise offence with which the accused is charged by the police. Many statutes contain a whole series of substantive offences, each with its own stated maximum sentence, and detailing specific offences involving the presence or absence of aggravating factors. The Theft Act 1968, for instance, contains not only the 'master definition' of theft in s 1, but also provides for a number of offences, all related to theft in the sense that they involve the unlawful appropriation of others' property, but differing in the additional factors which they involve: 'robbery' (s 8) is, basically, theft plus the element of force or violence, whilst 'blackmail' (s 21) concerns unwarranted demands for money or property belonging to another 'with menaces'.

The precise position of the sentence upon the scale for a given offence will be the result of 'fine tuning' by the judge; this is to say that after having considered the seriousness of the offence, and after having decided on the appropriate type of sentence, the judge will consider factors presented in mitigation by the accused or his or her counsel, such as the accused's background, age, domestic or emotional circumstances. Reports concerning the offender, prepared by probation officers or social workers, together with any psychiatric or other medical evidence,

---

125 In some cases a case may be referred to the Court of Appeal by the Attorney-General if a sentence is regarded as too lenient. In such cases, the Court of Appeal may increase the sentence: Criminal Justice Act 1988, s 36.

126 Note that there is a mandatory sentence of life imprisonment on conviction for murder.

if appropriate, will be taken into account; and although there is no obligation on the judge to act upon any recommendations made by any of these experts, the judge will usually incorporate such reports into the final decision as to sentence.

Recent criminal justice legislation, whilst retaining principles of retributive sentencing linked to the offence, none the less reflects an acceptance that in many instances it is appropriate to work towards an offender's rehabilitation – an aim clearly consistent with the objective of crime prevention. We have noted examples of this above, in the context of youth justice. The essence of rehabilitation is that the offender is not subjected to straightforward punitive measures, but instead to measures intended to reform, treat or cure the 'criminal deviance'. We are not simply referring here to the mentally abnormal offender, diagnosed as suffering from some medically defined mental condition. The rehabilitation view, at its strongest, is that all offenders commit crime for some identifiable reason, or some cause. It is also important to realise that although some measures are specifically designed for an offender diagnosed as having some medically treatable problem, such as Hospital Orders under the Mental Health Act 1983, it is by no means unknown for a court to pass an indeterminate sentence of imprisonment (that is, a 'life' sentence) designed to allow for the offender's release at some future unspecified date. Release is dependent upon the 'improvement' of the offender's condition, where the offender is not found to fall within the ambit of the Mental Health Act 1983 and where the offence indicates none the less that the offender is dangerous to the public. Many have argued that the aim of rehabilitation should be adopted as a general objective on practical and humanitarian grounds, but there are considerable practical and theoretical problems with this policy.

The essence of rehabilitation is the assumption that the offender committed the criminal act as a result of some 'cause' which can in some way be countered or treated. If treatment is thus prescribed by the court, it follows that there must be something to treat: this may be diagnosed as a response to social or emotional pressures, or some psychological or psychiatric condition, or even some external causal factor such as the influence of environmental pressures upon the offender's behaviour.

The fundamental problems which such a view raises for the criminal law can be fairly simply stated. Criminal liability in our legal system depends upon the offender's guilt. Guilt, as we saw earlier, is measured in law by means of the doctrine of *mens rea* – did the accused intentionally or recklessly commit the prohibited act? This in turn raises the assumption that, had the offender chosen to do so, he or she could have avoided doing the prohibited act; it is the very fact that the accused chose to commit it that makes that person criminally liable. Criminal liability, then, rests upon the assumption that our behaviour is the outcome of our freedom of will: we act as we do because we choose to, not because of any compelling or determining factors which dictate our behaviour for us. This 'free will' model of human behaviour is the bedrock of our legal system, and especially the criminal justice system.

Now, if the commission of the offence is said to be the result of causal factors such as psychological or environmental pressures, then it cannot be said that the offender chose to do the prohibited act. We have no direct control over such pressures, and therefore such behaviour cannot be said to be the result of 'free will'. The rehabilitative ideal, then, is built upon a conception of human behaviour which we may call 'causal' or 'deterministic' as opposed to 'free will', and the contradiction between the legal model and the rehabilitative, deterministic model is clearly seen at the level of the trial. At the conviction stage, the proceedings rest upon the idea of voluntaristic free choice by the accused, but at the sentencing stage, after conviction, the assumption changes if a rehabilitative measure is being considered by the court. Instead of 'freedom of choice', the underlying assumption becomes one of determinism: the view that behaviour is not the outcome of free will and free choice, but is caused by factors over which the accused has little or no control. As various writers have pointed out,[127] the main thrust of the social sciences, including psychology and psychiatric theories about crime – which, as Cohen and Clarke stress,[128] have had most effect upon the criminal justice system – is deterministic:

> The greater the detail in which circumstances are investigated and the greater the weight that is consequently given to the offender's environment, perhaps going back over many years, the more does the offence appear to be the natural and 'inevitable' outcome of the chain of circumstances so uncovered, and hence the less the apparent responsibility of the offender.[129]

In the courtroom, deterministic influences may appear in the use of psychiatric, probation and social enquiry reports; and at higher, policy-making levels, deterministic influences may become reflected in policies and legislative provisions through the involvement of social scientists concerned with crime – especially criminologists with expertise in psychiatry – in institutions such as the Home Office.[130]

The reaction by many lawyers, steeped in the traditional ideas about criminal responsibility and liability, is often one of suspicion and disquiet at the influence in the criminal courtroom, and the penal system generally, of these 'non-lawyers'. Not only is there suspicion about the basis and accuracy of much criminological theory, so much of which has been criticised on empirical or theoretical grounds,[131] but

---

127 See, for example, P. Bean, *Rehabilitation and Deviance* (1976, Routledge and Kegan Paul); M. Clarke, 'The Impact of Social Science on Conceptions of Responsibility' (1975) 2 *British Journal of Law and Society* 1; S. Cohen, 'Criminology and the Sociology of Deviance in Britain' in P. Rock and M. McIntosh (eds), *Deviance and Social Control* (1974, Tavistock).   128 Op. cit.
129 Clarke, op. cit., p 32. See also N. Lacey, 'Legal Constructions of Crime', in M. Maguire, R. Morgan and R. Reiner, *The Oxford Handbook of Criminology*, 3rd edn, 2002, Oxford University Press).
130 See D. Garland, 'Of Crimes and Criminals: The Development of Criminology in Britain' in M. Maguire, R Morgan and R Reiner, op.cit.; A. E. Bottoms, 'Reflections on the Criminological Enterprise' (1987) 46 *CLJ* 240; R. Walters, *Deviant Knowledge: Criminology, Politics and Policy* (2003, Willan).
131 See the critical surveys of criminological research in, for example, I. Taylor, P. Walton and J. Young, *The New Criminology* (1973, Routledge and Kegan Paul); see also S. Cohen, *Visions of Social Control* (1985, Polity Press); D. Garland, *Punishment and Modern Society* (1990, Oxford University Press); S. Hester and P. Eglin, *A Sociology of Crime* (1992, Routledge); W. Morrison, *Theoretical Criminology: from modernity to post-modernism* (1995, Cavendish); M. Cavadino and J. Dignan, *The Penal System* (3rd edn., 2002, Sage).

also there is a worry among many lawyers, concerned with issues of justice and fairness, about the degree of discretion placed in the hands of psychiatrists, social workers and others involved in the rehabilitation processes.

The dichotomy between punishment and rehabilitation is, then, far wider and deeper than a concern with merely practical issues. Reflected within it are strong ideological currents and commitments by the experts on both sides of the debate, with paternalism, rehabilitation and discretion on the one side, and a concern for 'due process of law', justice and 'free will' on the other. Whilst the 'just deserts' and 'taking responsibility for one's actions' ideas may represent victory for the 'justice model', history suggests that the post-1997 legislation is unlikely to be the last word on sentencing policy and practice, and we can expect the debates to continue.

Perhaps the root problem is that we know very little indeed about criminal behaviour, and there are many divergent theories and assumptions about crime and the penal system. It is true that very few of the measures introduced by Parliament for dealing with criminal offenders seem to have any lasting effect on the propensities of many offenders. One of the great difficulties with research into crime is the multiplicity of factors which may or may not explain why person X never offends at all, person Y never offends again after receiving a small fine for shoplifting, and person Z appears before the courts time and time again, despite a series of ever-increasing periods in prison. Why do we know so little about criminal behaviour?

Criminology and the criminal justice system

In examining and assessing the study of criminal behaviour – criminology – it is hard to avoid the feeling that not only the answers, but also many of the questions produced by this area of study are extremely misleading. To understand the complexities in the area, it is essential to grasp the underlying assumptions and the ideological implications on which criminological study has often been based, and to understand the multidisciplinary nature of this area of study.[132] Psychiatrists, psychologists, sociologists, lawyers and even biologists have at one time or another presented theories purporting to 'explain' criminal behaviour, and usually the objective – apparent or latent – underlying much of this body of theory has been an overriding concern with the eradication of crime and how best to achieve it: what has been called the 'correctional' perspective.[133] In this respect, of course, the aim of criminology coincides with the stated aims of law-makers, law-enforcers and judges.

But in other respects, social science and law diverge. The determinist criminologist, searching for 'causes of crime', cannot accept what the law takes for granted: that an offender need not have acted in the unlawful way, that he or she could have chosen

132 For an excellent survey, see K. S. Williams, *Criminology* (5th edn., 2004, Oxford University Press).
133 D. Matza, *Becoming Deviant* (1969, Prentice-Hall).

to act otherwise. And if the determinist criminologist is correct, there is neither point nor justification in punishment, which becomes irrelevant. The only consideration is to change, through treatment and/or rehabilitation, those causal factors which 'propel' the offender towards criminal behaviour.

But what are these 'causal factors' which are supposed to precipitate delinquency? The fact is that despite the impressive quantity of research undertaken over the years, and the vast amounts of money and labour utilised to produce it, criminology has so far failed to identify any such 'causes' with any precision or consistency. Psychologists and psychiatrists have claimed to have found the 'causes' in mental illness, personality defects or inadequate socialisation;[134] biologists have claimed to have discovered that some crimes are triggered by genetic abnormality;[135] and sociologists have argued that the causes of crime are environmental (slum conditions, economic deprivation, peer-group influence and so on) rather than emanating from 'inside the offender's head'.[136] No convincing confirmation of any of these ideas, many of which (though not all) have been attempts to find 'the' cause of crime, has yet been established:

> The fallacy of regarding 'crime' as a homogeneous social phenomenon which could conceivably have a unified explanation should be as plain as the naivety of seeking a single explanation of 'disease' or 'poverty'. What is less obvious, but equally true, is that not even a fairly specific type of offence is in every case attributable to the same state of mind, let alone the same process of causation. Even indecent exposure, or sadistic killings, are committed in varied moods, with varied intentions, and as a result of different kinds of experience.[137]

Why is criminology in this state, and along what lines might we proceed if we are to come closer to understanding criminal behaviour? Interestingly, it was not conventional criminology which provided new perspectives about crime and criminal behaviour, but a body of theory and empirical data which arose from a reaction *against* the assumptions of determinist criminology: the sociology of deviance. Matza provides a useful analytical framework with which to appreciate the

---

134 H. J. Eysenck, *Crime and Personality* (1970, Paladin); C. R. Hollin, *Psychology and Crime* (1989, Routledge and Kegan Paul).

135 See the theories of C. Lombroso in *L'Uomo Delinquente* (5th edn., 1876, Bocca, Turin); S. Mednick, T. Moffitt and S. Stack, *The Causes of Crime: New Biological Approaches* (1987, Cambridge University Press); the debate as to genetic abnormalities regarding chromosomal structure is discussed by T. Sarbin and J. Miller, 'Demonism Revisited: The XYY Chromosomal Anomaly' (1970) *Issues in Criminology* at 195.

136 For examples see W. Bonger, *Criminality and Economic Conditions* (1969, Indiana Free Press); D. Matza, *Delinquency and Drift* (1964, Wiley); D. Sutherland and D. Cressey, *Principles of Criminology* (1966, Lippincott); A. Turk, *Criminality and the Legal Order* (1969, Rand McNally); S. Box, *Recession, Crime and Punishment* (1987, Macmillan); R. Davidson, *Crime and Environment* (1981, Croom Helm).

137 Walker and Padfield, op. cit., p 39. See also N. Walker 'Lost Causes in Criminology' in R. Hood (ed.), *Crime, Criminology and Public Policy* (1974, Heinemann); and see also the discussions in S. Hester and P. Eglin, *A Sociology of Crime* (1992, Routledge) and M. Maguire, R. Morgan and R Reiner, op.cit.

problems of study. He has argued that three specific charges may be laid against conventional criminology.[138]

First, says Matza, criminology has concentrated upon the offender rather than the nature of the criminal law which symbolises the division between offender and law-abiding citizen. Second, criminology has been based upon a quest for a 'scientific' basis, and for 'laws' about human behaviour; and, third, criminology has insisted upon stressing that the offender, having committed an offence, is somehow 'abnormal', or 'different' from the rest of the community.[139]

Writers associated with the sociology of deviance have argued that these assumptions, among others, are unfounded. Deterministic ideas about human behaviour have been challenged, as have the assumptions about 'scientific method' in the study of criminal behaviour. Human behaviour, argue critics, is not subject to scientific 'laws' in the same way as are, say, gravity or electricity. People *do* make choices, albeit within constraints imposed by social structural and other circumstances; and moreover, the apparent motivation for an action may not necessarily be the real motivation, for people act out of stubbornness, maliciousness and greed whilst explaining their deeds in terms of more acceptable motivations. Arguably there is a substantial degree of conscious planning of behaviour, and this element of consciousness or voluntarism must be taken into account when studying criminal deviance.

Another argument presented by some critics is that it is misleading to characterise certain types of behaviour, such as juvenile violence or vandalism as 'senseless' or 'irrational': although such acts may seem meaningless in terms of the values and experiences of the observer, they may well have meaning, sense and purpose to the perpetrator. Such behaviour may represent, for instance, a felt need to assert masculinity or prove toughness among a peer-group,[140] or it may be a manifestation of what have been called 'subterranean values',[141] which in fact reflect the social values of the dominant adult middle-class groups in society. Thus, within 'delinquent' attitudes may be seen a search for thrills and excitement, a disdain for work and a degree of aggressiveness which have their parallels in middle-class society, with its quest for adventure through leisure pursuits, its lack of attachment to hard work and fondness for the 'soft job', and the general social acceptance of, and even taste for, violence as seen in the apparently insatiable public appetite for aggression in films and television. On this analysis, the aggressive juvenile may appear somewhat less irrational and certainly less alien than the image presented by conventional analyses.

---

138 Matza (1964), op. cit. See the discussion of Matza's work in K.S. Williams, op. cit., pp 323–6.

139 On this, see the discussion of the work of Garfinkel, Carlen etc in chapter 6, above.

140 See W. Miller, 'Lower-Class Culture as a Generating Milieu of Gang Delinquency' (1958) *Journal of Social Issues*; J. B. Mays, *Crime and its Treatment* (2nd edn., 1975, Longman). More recent research in this area includes M. Farnworth, T. Thornbury, M. Krohn and A. Lizotte, 'Measurement in the Study of Class and Delinquency: Integrating Theory and Research' (1994) *Journal of Research in Crime and Delinquency*, vol. 31.

141 D. Matza and G. Sykes, 'Juvenile Delinquency and Subterranean Values' (1961) *Amer Socio Review* at 712.

Sociologists, then, have argued that the deviant person must be recognised not only as having control over his or her own behaviour, but also as having the capacity to invest that behaviour with social meaning, which may not always be apparent to researcher, judge or social worker.

To what extent is it misleading to regard convicted or apprehended offenders as 'different' from law-abiding people? It has been argued that the distinction between deviant and non-deviant may in many cases be due only to the fact that the person defined by a court as 'deviant' happens to have been caught. How many people regarded as 'normal' and 'law-abiding' have in fact committed offences at one time or another without being caught? The use of 'self-report' studies, in which subjects are asked, in confidence, to indicate whether they have acted unlawfully at any time has revealed that most, if not all, of us commit offences at some point in our lives.[142]

Moreover, some studies reveal similarities between behaviour defined as 'against the law' and behaviour which, though not illegal, often has the same type of consequences: 'It is not only labelled vandals who break other people's property, not only professional con-men who con others into believing or parting with something, not only blackmailers who exploit a position of strength . . . [We] need to be alerted to similarities between deviant and normal transactions.'[143] Illustrations might include the practices of debt-collection agencies which, literally, may frighten people into parting with money they may or may not owe;[144] misleading advertisements which persuade people to part with money on the strength of ambiguous and exaggerated claims for their products; and motorists who damage others' property through their inattention to the road. None of these is usually officially labelled 'criminal', but in all these cases the money is none the less lost, the property no less damaged. Even in cases of 'corporate crime' where the offending organisations might appear to have acted unlawfully, it has often been found by researchers that prosecutions are rare. Examples include the well-documented case of the family car manufactured and sold by Ford which, to the knowledge of the corporation, contained a dangerous design defect which resulted in many serious accidents (see chapter 9); and the suggestion by Carson that many of the fatal accidents on off-shore installations in the North Sea were due to lower safety standards.[145] As Box put it:

. . . deaths, injuries, and economic losses caused by corporate acts are not the antics of one or two evil, or mentally disturbed, or relatively deprived senior employees. Rather they represent the rational choices of high-ranking senior employees, acting in the

142 See, for example, J. F. Short and F. I. Nye, 'The Extent of Unrecorded Juvenile Delinquency' (1958) *Journal of Criminal Law, Criminology, and Police Science* at 256; More recent studies include S. Anderson et. al., *Cautionary Tales: Young People, Crime and Policing in Edinburgh* (1994, Avebury) and T. Budd et. al., *Offending in England and Wales: First Results from the 2003 Crime and Justice Survey* (2005, Home Office). For a discussion of such reports and their validity see S. Jones, *Criminology* (2001, Oxford University Press) pp 70–73.
143 S. Cohen, 'Introduction' in *Images of Deviance* (1971, Penguin), p 20.
144 See P. Rock, *Making People Pay* (1973, Routledge and Kegan Paul).
145 W. Carson, *The Other Price of British Oil* (1981, Martin Robertson).

corporation's interests, who intend directly to violate the criminal law or governmental regulations, or to be indifferent to the outcome of their action or inaction, even though it might result in human lives obliterated, bodies mangled, or life-savings lost.[146]

The sociology of deviance, which grew and flourished in the 1970s, had by the late 1980s and 1990s itself been subjected to substantial critical debate. Sumner has presented a number of critical arguments which lead to his conclusion that the 'sociology of deviance' cannot be accepted as providing coherent analyses of crime and deviance.[147] He puts forward a number of reasons for this, ranging from the internal contradictions and incoherence of many of the propositions deriving from this body of research and theory, to the fact that:

> Since 1975 there has been an inadvertent coalition between left and right within criminology to abandon aetiological analysis of spurious behavioural concepts – it has become more manageable or politically realistic to focus on crime prevention, police accountability and victims.[148]

Sumner acknowledges, however, that the sociology of deviance, despite its weaknesses, achieved positive results in terms of our thinking about crime and deviance, in that it 'took us away from the psychopathology of degeneracy, threw attention on to the agencies of social regulation, taught us that most social deviation is merely the clash of differences in complex societies and urged us to think twice before stigmatising people, especially when our own interests were involved'.[149]

Are there, then, any more useful and illuminating perspectives through which we can attempt to understand criminal activity? One of the more persuasive recent approaches in the UK is 'left realist' theory – 'left' because it situates crime within the context of capitalist class society, and 'realist' as distinct from the 'left idealism' of writers within the area of 'sociology of deviance' and many theorists writing from a Marxist perspective. In particular,

> Left Realists consider that Left Idealists, in their search for an ideal society, have failed to address the very real problem of crime being encountered on a daily basis, particularly by poor and disadvantaged people living in run-down inner-city areas. Left Realists have expressed a concern to 'take crime seriously'. It is clear that working-class people – especially women – are the main victims of working-class crime.[150]

As far as the causes of crime are concerned, this approach acknowledges that there is no single cause of crime, although a number of long-established theoretical approaches are recognised as having valuable insights. If any such approach is viewed by Left Realism as particularly important, it is the concept of 'relative deprivation': in its classic form, this term refers not to deprivation or poverty in an *absolute* sense, but to the proposition that

---

146 S. Box, *Power, Crime and Mystification* (1983, Tavistock), p 25.
147 C. Sumner, *The Sociology of Deviance: An Obituary* (1994, Open University Press).
148 Ibid., p 311.   149 Ibid., p 315.
150 S. Jones, *Criminology* (3rd edn., 2006, Oxford University Press), p 267.

Some individuals see their present position as comparing unfavourably with others; they desire more; they often feel they deserve more; but if there seems to be no legitimate chance of acquiring more, they may use illegitimate means. Thus if relative deprivation is present, feelings of envy and injustice will be present and might influence behaviour.[151]

Thus, *relative* deprivation may be experienced by some individuals or groups even in times of overall socio-economic affluence – even though, as many writers have acknowledged, the majority of poor people do not, in fact, indulge in criminal behaviour, and a fair number of those who are comfortably well-off are not averse to tax evasion, questionable business deals and other unlawful (though rarely prosecuted) activities.[152]

One of the leading advocates of the 'Left Realist' approach, Jock Young, presented some years ago a conceptualisation of crime which stresses the dynamics of both the event and the ways in which it is experienced and perceived:

> (there are) four definitional elements of crime: a victim, an offender, formal control, and informal control. Realism, then, points to a square of crime involving the interaction between police and other agencies of social control, the public, the offender, and the victim. Crime rates are generated not merely by the interplay of these four factors, but as *social relationships* between the various points on the square. It is the relationship between the police and the public which determines the efficacy of policing, the relationship between the victim and the offender which determines the impact of the crime, the relationship between the state and the offender which is a major factor in recidivism . . .[153]

What kind of actions does this approach advocate in order to combat crime and its effects? Given the recognition of the complexities involved, it is not surprising that on this approach, there must be a multi-dimensional strategy, involving the police, the involvement of the community, and recognition of the situation of the victim. Not only this, but also, according to Left Realist theorists,

> Society needs to provide the more deprived with jobs, housing, and such community facilities as hostels, youth-clubs, drop-in centres, clinics, nurseries, etc . . . [but] . . . changing deep-seated attitudes like relative deprivation takes time measured in decades rather than days. Even then it depends on the nature of the positive input and on the make-up of the area in age, sex, race and in long-term unemployed, structural unemployment, and youths who have never worked. Many factors will bear upon recovery, just as many have a bearing on criminality and the choice to offend.[154]

This serves to remind us that by considering the kinds of factors linked to causal theories of crime which concentrate on characteristics of the individual offender – and especially those analyses which tend to present the offender as some kind of 'victim'

151 K. S. Williams, *Textbook on Criminology*, op. cit., p 313. And see R. Hopkins Burke, *An Introduction to Criminological Theory* (2nd edn., 2005, Willan), ch.16.
152 See also J. Young, 'Crime and Social Exclusion', in M. Maguire, R. Morgan, and R. Reiner, op. cit.
153 J. Young, 'Left Realist Criminology: Radical in its Analysis, Realist in its Policy' in M. Maguire, P. Morgan, and R. Reiner, The Oxford Handbook of Criminology, (2nd edn., 1997, Oxford University Press), p 485.   154 K. S. Williams, op. cit., p 437.

of society – we may be blinded to the social reality of crime, and to its impact upon individuals and the community. The necessity for agencies such as Rape Crisis Centres and women's refuges, and studies of the victims of crime – including the British Crime Surveys which began in 1982, but which now take place annually,[155] and the Islington Crime Surveys in 1986 and 1990[156] – have reinforced the idea that 'correctional' approaches to crime and criminal offenders cannot simply be dismissed.[157] These and other studies have shown that many vulnerable sections of the community – women, ethnic minority groups, and the elderly – have a fear of crime which, although perhaps based on an exaggerated belief as to its true incidence, is based on a perfectly rational appreciation of their vulnerability and of the harsh reality of criminal behaviour and its consequences. The heightened awareness in recent years of sexual violence against women, and the physical and sexual abuse of children (not new phenomena, but ones which for many years were hidden from the public eye) has brought home to many professional and lay people the need to take the necessary steps to protect the victims of violence and abuse.

Almost all commentators and practitioners, then, accept the need to 'take crime seriously' and to incorporate the problem within the political agenda. It remains to be seen whether current government policies and reforms will be successful; but there can be no denying the social, economic and political importance of crime in modern society. Given the uncertainty as to how best to understand and confront the problem, it remains vital, as most commentators emphasise, to continue to stress and explore further the connections between crime and the structural conditions of society: what significance has social class, age, sex or ethnic background? How are these linked to police practices? What impact do high rates of unemployment – particularly among the young – have on criminal behaviour? To what extent are rape and other sexual offences linked to, for example, the availability of pornography, the persistent oppression of and violence towards women – in employment, in the media, as parents and so on? What of 'street crime'? And what about corporate crime and its consequences?

Understanding crime, and building a rational criminal justice system geared to respond to and deal with the problems generated by crime, depends now more than ever before upon the ability not only to appreciate the problem at the level of individual behaviour and of the experiences of crime by its victims, but also to attempt – as objectively as possible – to locate and analyse it within its social and economic contexts.

155 Further information and research findings from the latest surveys can be found on the Home Office website at http://www.homeoffice.gov.uk/rds/bcs1.html .
156 T. Jones, M. McLean and J. Young, *The Islington Crime Survey: Crime Victimisation and Policing in Inner City London* (1986, Gower); A. Crawford, T. Jones, T. Woodhouse and J. Young, *Second Islington Crime Survey* (1990, Middlesex Polytechnic). See also M. Maguire and J. Pointing (eds), *Victims of Crime: A New Deal* (1988, Open University).
157 Though theoretical approaches which are overly simplistic or whose research evidence may be unconvincing will continue to attract criticism: see the discussions of the (largely US-based) 'Right Realist' approach to analysing crime and criminality in K.S. Williams, op. cit., pp 421–7, S. Jones, op. cit., pp 262–6; R. Hopkins Burke, op. cit., ch.3.

11

The development and role of the contract

The contract is the legal cornerstone of all transactions in business and consumer life. It is the legal device which facilitates *exchange* of goods or services between individuals and groups (such as businesses) in our society, and may be defined as a legally binding agreement between two parties whereby each party undertakes specific obligations or enjoys specific rights, conferred by virtue of that agreement. The expression 'breach of contract' refers to the fact that the agreement is legally binding: if one party fails to honour his or her part of the bargain, then the other can sue, and obtain a remedy through the courts for that breach.

Of course, not every agreement is a legally binding contract. Purely social or domestic agreements, mere requests by one party for information, a series of negotiations between two parties and collective agreements between trade unions and employers have been held by the judges not to constitute contracts,[1] and the judges have also refused to regard lotteries or football pools transactions as legally enforceable contractual relationships.[2] Regarding social and domestic arrangements, the courts have asserted that the parties to the agreements did not intend to enter into a legal relationship, and this 'intention to create legal relations' is often said to be one of the legal conditions for the formation of a contract. However, as one leading textbook on the law of contract states, 'in commercial agreements it will be presumed that the parties intended to create legal relations and make a contract'.[3] Whether such a presumption is realistic under modern business conditions will be discussed presently, but for the moment it is important to deal with one or two common misconceptions about the legal notion of the contract.

First, it is often supposed that only a *written* agreement can constitute a contract in law. Nothing could be further from the truth. Every time we buy a newspaper,

---

1 See, for example, *Balfour v Balfour* [1919] 2 KB 571 (agreement between husband and wife); *Ford Motor Co Ltd v Amalgamated Union of Engineering and Foundry Workers* [1969] 2 All ER 481 (agreement between management and union). The latter case has statutory backing in the Trade Union and Labour Relations (Consolidation) Act 1992.
2 *Jones v Vernon's Pools Ltd* [1938] 2 All ER 626 (pools agreement held binding 'in honour only').
3 G. Cheshire, C. Fifoot and M. P. Furmston, *Law of Contract* (14th edn. by M. P. Furmston, Oxford University Press, 2001), p 126.

a postage stamp or a packet of washing powder, we make a legally binding contract, which has just as much legal significance as a complex written contract such as an agreement to buy a house or a car, or a hire-purchase transaction. Second, it is often believed that a contract is concluded whenever we enter a shop and ask for a specific item. 'The shopkeeper is offering to sell goods', runs the argument, 'and the customer walks in and accepts that offer'. Such an argument might be heard when an aggrieved customer has been told that the goods in a shop window, for example, are wrongly priced, and the customer cannot understand why he or she cannot insist on being sold the goods at that (wrongly) marked price.

The reason why no contract exists in this situation lies in the rules of contract themselves. The judges, who have been responsible for developing this part of the law, have distinguished between a genuine *offer* (an essential part of every contract) and an *invitation to treat.*

They have stated on a number of occasions that placing goods in a shop window,[4] or advertising goods in newspapers,[5] are *not* offers to sell, but are invitations from the trader to the customer to make the trader an offer to *buy* the goods. Thus, in the leading case of *Pharmaceutical Society of Great Britain v Boots Cash Chemists Ltd* in 1952,[6] the defendants operated a self-service store where, as is usual, customers collected from open shelves the goods they intended to purchase, and took them to the cash-desk. At the defendants' cash-desk was a registered pharmacist. The Pharmacy and Poisons Act 1933 made it unlawful to sell any specified poison unless 'the sale is effected under the supervision of a registered pharmacist'. The issue for the court was the point at which the 'sale' took place: if it took place when customers put articles from the self-service shelves into their baskets, then there was no supervision by a pharmacist, but if the sale took place at the cash-desk, then there was such supervision. The Court of Appeal decided that the sale took place at the cash-desk, and not before; the presence of the goods on open shelves was in the court's opinion only an invitation to treat, and the customer, by presenting the goods at the cash-desk, was making an offer to buy them.

What about purchases made through the Internet? Here, the customer typically browses through a catalogue on the trader's website, chooses goods, and orders and pays for them (by credit card) by means of an entirely online transaction. It is thought that, logically, a trader's website is the equivalent of goods in a shop window or mail-order catalogues. The website would thus be regarded in law as an invitation to treat, and browsers who wish to purchase online then make an 'electronic offer' to the trader to buy the goods specified – usually by specifying goods in the buyer's 'virtual shopping basket'. This offer then must, of course, be accepted by the trader, and this is normally done by means of some electronic confirmation

---

4 *Fisher v Bell* [1961] 1 QB 394 (placing a flick-knife in a shop-window did not constitute 'offering it for sale').
5 *Partridge v Crittenden* [1968] 2 All ER 421 (a private 'classified' advertisement in a magazine was not an 'offer to sell'). Note, however, the exceptions of 'unilateral' contracts: see in particular *Carlill v Carbolic Smoke Ball Co* [1892] 2 QB 484.   6 [1952] 2 All ER 456.

to the buyer, once credit-card details have been provided, that the transaction has been completed. Such an application of ordinary contract-law principles would seem sensible: it would mean, of course, that traders could refuse to sell in the event of goods being described at the wrong price – as happened with the Argos store in 1999 when television sets were mistakenly described on its website as costing £2.99 instead of £299.[7]

Because of the legal principle that the customer makes the offer to the trader, who is then free to accept or reject that offer, the trader can, perfectly legally at common law, refuse to serve any customer on any grounds. In the realm of consumer contracts, statutory intervention has introduced some restrictions on this right. An example of this is the Trade Descriptions Act 1968, which forbids false or misleading descriptions being attached to goods, for example, on price-tags or in advertisements. Generally, however, the right to refuse service remains.[8] Such a rule clearly operates for the trader's protection, and it has been suggested, by way of justification for the rule, that shopkeepers should be able to favour their regular customers, especially in times of shortages. Against this, however, it might be argued that the principle of 'first come, first served' would be fairer: if shopkeepers present themselves as being in the business of selling goods, they should be held bound to sell items they stock at the prices marked. Atiyah has pointed out[9] that the courts have never discussed questions such as this, though some possible justifications for the legal position can be identified: if goods in a shop window were to constitute, in law, an offer, then

> the shopkeeper would be obliged to sell to every person who accepted such an 'offer', even where supplies had run out. In the case of displays on shelves in a self-service shop . . . it is said that if the display were an offer, once an article was selected and placed in the receptacle, the customer would have no right to change his mind. Another reason is that if a display was an offer a shopkeeper might be forced to contract with his worst enemy . . .[10]

It has also been suggested that it would facilitate fraud by customers who could switch prices on goods and then claim that they had accepted the shopkeeper's 'offer' to sell the goods at those prices. This may be a real possibility, but what if an unscrupulous *shopkeeper* switches prices, or claims untruthfully that an article has been wrongly priced? The real answer, it seems, is that the common law has always been more ready to protect the interests of businesses than those of the ordinary

---

7 The Electronic Commerce (EC Directive) Regulations 2002 provide that certain aspects of internet trading are mandatory, such as clarity to the customer of the nature of the transaction, and of the steps to be taken to establish the contract, and the provision of receipts to purchasers. These regulations do not, however, replace the basic common-law rules of contract-formation.

8 This right is subject to certain statutory restrictions, notably the Race Relations Act 1976, the Sex Discrimination Act 1975 and the Disability Discrimination Act 1995, which provide, among other things, that customers may not be refused service on grounds of, respectively, race, sex, or disability.

9 P. S. Atiyah, *Introduction to the Law of Contract* (6th edn., 2006, Oxford University Press), chapter 3.

10 Anson's *Law of Contract* (28th edn. by J. Beatson, (2002) Oxford University Press), p 33.

consumer; as we shall see, it has taken a whole series of statutes to create a legal environment of adequate protection for the consumer. Such biases in the law can only be clearly understood by examining the relationship between the law of contract and the economic and political context in which the law was developed.

The contract is, in essence, an exchange of promises. Sometimes the agreement refers to a promise to be fulfilled by one party in the future (an *executory* contract), though more often in everyday contracts the exchange is instantaneous and the contract completed straightaway (as in the case of ordinary purchases in shops): these are called *executed* contracts. The willingness of judges to award remedies for a broken contractual promise dates back to the fifteenth and sixteenth centuries, when a legal action called *assumpsit* was developed to enable a plaintiff suffering loss or damage through the defendant's breach of promise to recover compensation. The writ of *assumpsit* is the basis for the modern law of contract, developed by the judges in the eighteenth and, more particularly, nineteenth centuries. It is only relatively recently that Parliament has intervened in the basic common-law area of contract.

Economically, the last century saw the rapid expansion of trade and industry, bringing increased numbers of commercial disputes, often involving novel complexities. The courts of law were frequently looked to for the solution of such commercial and business disputes. The rules of contract law were not confined to dispute-solving, however; to a large extent, clear rules about commercial agreements meant that people in business could *plan* their activity and enterprises by reference to consistent and certain rules of law. They could calculate and predict the best ways of dealing, of buying and selling, in the knowledge that the rules they adhered to were also binding on those with whom they had business relations. The law of contract, then, was developed in response to the changing needs of business, and this continues to be so in modern society.

So far we have been looking mostly at the development of contract law by way of common law. Generally, in no area of law, especially when developed by the judges, is there a very high degree of clarity or consistency, and the law of contract is no exception. Though some would argue that this allows flexibility, Parliament has stepped into the area of contract law, as it has in many other areas. An early example in the nineteenth century was the Sale of Goods Act 1893 (now re-enacted, with amendments, as the Sale of Goods Act 1979), which was introduced in response to problems arising in the common law of contract. The Sale of Goods Act 1893 was designed to codify existing common-law rules, though despite its origin as a codified body of law for the guidance and protection of those in business, it has frequently been used to provide remedies for the consumer, as we shall see later.

The law of contract, then, developed through the cases, was designed as a framework for the solution of disputes and the efficient planning and running of business enterprises. The classical model of the contract as developed by the judges enabled them to disentangle and make sense of agreements which might well have involved long negotiations, complex documentation and ambiguous statements of rights and obligations. The legal model of the contract is characterised by the notion of an agreement between two parties, whose constituent elements (which must always be present if the contract is to be legally recognised as such) are an *offer*, an *acceptance* of that offer, an *intention to create legal relations* (discussed above) and *consideration*.

The phenomena of offer and acceptance are readily understood if we are speaking of agreements, but as we have seen, offers must be distinguished from invitations to treat, and from stages in negotiations where an apparent offer might be interpreted by the court as mere request for information[11] or as merely one stage in a continuing series of negotiations. It is, for example, established[12] that in cases concerning the sale of land, where the typical transaction is complex and protracted, the courts will not readily hold that a firm offer exists unless there is very clear evidence to the contrary. Acceptance in the law of contract is best understood by examining, first, what constitutes acceptance of an offer and, second, what constitutes effective communication of that acceptance – for the acceptance of the offer must be communicated to the offeror.

Acceptance may be explicitly made by written or oral statements, and such acceptance usually poses no particular problem. However, acceptance of an offer may be inferred by a party's conduct. In the leading case on this point, *Brogden v Metropolitan Rly Co* in 1877,[13] Brogden had supplied the railway company with coal for some years without there being any formal agreement between them. They decided to put their business relationship on a formal basis, and the company sent a draft form of agreement to Brogden. He added the name of a person who was to act as arbitrator in the event of a dispute, signed the form and returned it marked 'approved'. Nothing more was done in the matter by either party, though both carried on their business with each other thereafter in accordance with the terms of the draft agreement. When a dispute arose between the parties, Brogden denied that any contract existed between them. The problem here was that raised by the general rule in contract which stipulates that an acceptance must exactly fit the offer. If the draft agreement sent to Brogden was an offer, then by adding in the name of the arbitrator Brogden had added a new term to that draft, and so by returning it was probably making a new offer to the company, which it was up to the latter to accept, reject or modify. As the company did nothing more about the matter, however, and certainly did not do anything which could be said to constitute explicit acceptance of Brogden's offer, was there at any time an acceptance? The House of Lords held that the acceptance of the offer was constituted by the subsequent conduct of the parties in carrying out their business arrangements in a manner which showed that they both approved the terms of the draft agreement, and that the contract came into existence either when the company ordered its first load of coal from Brogden on these terms, or when Brogden supplied it.

11 See, for example, *Harvey v Facey* [1893] AC 552.
12 *Harvey v Facey*, op. cit.; *Clifton v Palumbo* [1944] 2 All ER 497. But compare *Bigg v Boyd Gibbins Ltd* [1971] 2 All ER 183. And contrast *Gibson v Manchester City Council* [1979] 1 All ER 972 with *Storer v Manchester City Council* [1974] 3 All ER 824.   13 (1877) 2 App Cas 666.

The facts of *Brogden*'s case also illustrate another problem concerning offer and acceptance. As we have said, an acceptance, to be effective in law, must exactly fit the offer, rather like two pieces of a jigsaw puzzle which fit each other exactly. If an apparent acceptance did not thus fit the offer, then that apparent acceptance was regarded by the courts as a *counter-offer*, whose legal effect was to destroy the original offer. If we take the following statements:

1. 'I will sell you my car for £1,500.'
2. 'That's too much. Will you take £1,400?'
3. 'No.'
4. 'Very well, then, make it £1,500.'

and examine them, it looks at first sight as though there is, eventually, a contract. But in law, statement 1 is an offer, which is refused in statement 2. The second statement also contains an offer, however, and this is the *counter-offer* which destroys the original one. In statement 3, that counter-offer is rejected. What, then, is the status of statement 4? It *looks* like an acceptance of the offer in statement 1, but as that offer has been destroyed, it cannot constitute an acceptance of anything! Following the logic of the law of contract, the status of statement 4 is that of *yet another offer*, which may or may not be accepted by the seller of the car. There is no contract in existence in this example.[14]

Moving to the matter of communication of the acceptance: it would be illogical to hold people bound by transactions they know nothing about, and so, although an offer may be made to the whole world,[15] anyone accepting that offer must make that acceptance known to the offeror. It may be that the offeror specifies a particular way in which the acceptance is to be communicated, in which case the acceptor must respond in the manner specified. In many cases, acceptance of an offer will be immediate, by means of spoken words, but most business contracts are made by letter or other posted documents. If acceptance is made by sending a letter by post, the legal rule is that the acceptance is complete as soon as the letter is posted;[16] the same applies to telegrams, but not to telex communication, where the acceptance is complete only when actually received by the offeror.[17] *Mere* silence can never constitute acceptance,[18] though the everyday situation in which we pass a supermarket cashier, paying for our goods and carrying them away without a word being said, is a good example of the cashier's acceptance of our offer to buy the goods (remembering the rule about invitations to treat!) by conduct.

What happens if the offeror has a change of mind and wishes to withdraw the offer? The courts have developed, through the cases, a series of rules covering this situation. First, an offer may be stated to be open for a specified time: it may

---

14 *Hyde v Wrench* (1840) 3 Beav 334.   15 *Carlill v Carbolic Smoke Ball Co* [1892] 2 QB 484.
16 *Adams v Lindsell* (1818) 1 B & Ald 681.
17 *Entores Ltd v Miles Far East Corpn* [1955] 2 All ER 493.
18 *Felthouse v Bindley* (1862) 11 CBNS 869, though for recent suggestions as to situations in which silence might constitute acceptance see *Re Selectmove Ltd* [1995] 1 WLR 474.

stipulate, for example, that it is to be open for three days. After that time, if no acceptance is forthcoming, the offer will lapse. If there is no specific period stated, then the offer will normally remain open for a reasonable time. This is, of course, a sensible rule, for if it were otherwise, an offer could theoretically be open for years on end – long after the unwanted car, for instance, had rusted away.

Second, the offeror may wish to take positive steps to indicate the revocation of the offer, in which case the withdrawal of the offer must be communicated to the person to whom it has been made; the revocation must be carried out before the offer has been accepted. In *Byrne v Van Tienhoven* in 1880,[19] an interesting situation arose where the plaintiffs telegraphed their acceptance of the defendants' offer when they received it; unknown to the plaintiffs, however, the defendants had previously posted a letter withdrawing their offer. The court here held that there was a binding contract, because the defendants' withdrawal was not received until after the acceptance had been made – a stricter rule, it will be noted, than the 'postal rule' for acceptance.

The doctrine of *consideration* has long been shrouded in mystique by lawyers and judges, and generations of students have been perplexed by the tortuous language of definitions of the term, such as that in *Currie v Misa* in 1875.[20] In this case, 'consideration' was stated to be 'some right, interest, profit or benefit accruing to one party, or some forbearance, detriment, loss or responsibility given, suffered or undertaken by the other'. In essence, consideration encapsulates the idea of the contract as a two-way arrangement, each party giving and receiving something of value, whether of a monetary nature or not. It is this exchange of 'something of value' which constitutes consideration, and the term may thus be thought of as the price paid for goods or services received: such an approach is 'easier to understand, it corresponds more happily to the normal exchange of promises and it emphasises the commercial character of the English contract'.[21]

Usually, the consideration will comprise money or cheques given in exchange for valuable goods or services, but the courts will regard as good consideration anything which they perceive as having value to the parties. Thus, in *Chappell & Co Ltd v Nestlé Co Ltd* in 1960,[22] the defendant company offered records of a tune called 'Rockin' Shoes' for the sum of 1s 6d (7.5 pence) plus three wrappers from their chocolate bars. The main purpose of this 'special offer' was, of course, to advertise their chocolate, and the wrappers were discarded by the defendants on receipt. The plaintiffs owned the copyright in the tune, and were thus entitled to a royalty payment of 6.25% of the retail price of each record sold. The defendants in fact offered the plaintiffs 6.25% of the sum of 1s 6d, but this was refused, the plaintiffs arguing that the chocolate bar wrappers were also part of the price. The House of Lords accepted this argument, holding that the wrappers were indeed part of the consideration, irrespective of the fact that the defendants threw them away: 'a contracting party can stipulate for what

19 (1880) 5 CPD 344.   20 (1875) LR 10 Exch 153.
21 Cheshire, Fifoot and Furmston, op. cit., p 82.   22 [1960] AC 87.

consideration he chooses. A peppercorn does not cease to be good consideration if it is established that the promisee does not like pepper and will throw away the corn.'[23] The rule as usually stated is that 'consideration must be sufficient, but need not be adequate'. What this rather obscure term means is that as long as the courts recognise the consideration as having some value to the parties, they will not concern themselves as to whether that consideration in fact reflects the true economic worth of the subject-matter of the bargain. The judges have always insisted that their role is to uphold agreements made voluntarily, and not to enquire into the economic soundness or sense of those agreements. This is why, if A promises to sell B a brand new Rolls-Royce for the sum of £1, A will be legally bound by that promise, for money is always good consideration, irrespective of whether the amount actually represents the market value of the car.

Through the cases, the judges have evolved a series of rules concerning consideration and its sufficiency in law, and the main rules can now be briefly set out.

Past consideration is insufficient consideration

If my neighbour, whilst I am away on holiday, decides to do me a good turn by mowing my lawn, and upon my return I gratefully promise to pay her £5 for what she has done, then she cannot sue me for the money if I fail to pay. This is because, although she may have *hoped* for payment, she did the work without actually discussing payment with me; legally, consideration must be made with an existing bargain in mind. In this example, the 'consideration' is said to be *past*, and is insufficient in law.

Past consideration must, however, be contrasted with *executed* and *executory* consideration, both of which are perfectly valid in law. Executory consideration is given when the parties make an agreement, the completion of which is to be at some point in the future. For instance, X offers to sell his car to Y for £1,200, and Y accepts, promising to pay the money within a week. Here, there is an exchange of promises, both parties agreeing that the exchange will be made at some future point. The consideration here is the promise to pay – it is executory consideration, and is valid in law. The usual example of executed consideration is that of a reward offered for the return of a lost dog. If A offers £5 to anyone who will find and return her lost dog, and B returns the dog to her, B's act is both the acceptance of A's offer and also the required consideration, and so B can claim payment of the reward.[24]

Can performance of an existing duty be sufficient consideration?

Suppose that A's alleged consideration in respect of an agreement with B, is in fact something which A is already under an obligation to do. Is this valid consideration? In general, the consideration must contribute to the agreement in some way, and the cases dealing with this point can best be approached from this point of view. It is generally settled that a duty imposed by the general law cannot be good consideration,

---

23 Ibid., at 114, per Lord Somervell.   24 See also *Carlill v Carbolic Smoke Ball Co*, op. cit.

though if a party does *more than* that legal duty, then this may be valid consideration. In *Glasbrook Bros v Glamorgan County Council* in 1925,[25] a colliery company,
threatened by a strike which it was thought might involve violence, approached the
police for protection of the mine. The police took the view that a mobile body of
officers would be sufficient to protect the mine, but the colliery management wanted
a police guard stationed at the mine. The police authorities agreed to provide such a
guard for the sum of £2,200. The colliery company refused to pay this sum and, when
sued for it, argued that, as the police had done no more than they were legally obliged
to do, there was no consideration. The House of Lords held that, whilst the police
were certainly under a public duty to provide protection as far as was necessary, they
had in this case done more, by complying with the company's request, than they were
legally obliged to do, and had therefore given valid consideration.

The point was illustrated more recently in *Harris v Sheffield United Football Club
Ltd,*[26] where the dispute concerned a claim against the football club for payment for
the substantial police presence at football matches. The club argued that the police
were doing no more than their existing public duty in providing protection and
enforcing law and order at football grounds, and that the police were therefore not
entitled to payment for this. The court held that the provision of police at the football club during matches went beyond what the club was entitled to have provided
in pursuance of their public duties; that the police were under no public duty to
protect against the 'mere apprehension' of possible crime; and that therefore the
club were obliged to pay for this 'special provision'.

Similarly, in *Ward v Byham* in 1956,[27] an unmarried man and woman entered
into an agreement whereby the woman undertook to look after their child in
exchange for a payment of £1 a week from the man, on conditions stipulated by the
latter that the child would be 'well looked after and happy' and would be 'allowed
to decide for herself' whether or not she wished to live with the mother. When the
mother married another man, the weekly payments ceased, and she sued for breach
of contract. Although it was clear that by virtue of the National Assistance Act 1948
there was an existing legal duty on the mother of an illegitimate child to maintain
that child, the Court of Appeal held that the mother had undertaken to do more
than her legal duty by agreeing to 'look after the child well' and to allow the child
to decide with whom she wanted to live.

Apart from an existing legal duty, however, there are cases where an existing *contractual* duty has been alleged to be good consideration. It has until recently been
taken as settled law that if the plaintiff only does what is already required by an
existing contract with the defendant, this cannot suffice as consideration for a new
agreement. Thus in *Stilk v Myrick* in 1809,[28] the plaintiff was a seaman. In the course
of a voyage on which he had worked, two sailors had deserted the ship, and the
captain had promised the rest of the crew extra money if they would work the ship
short-handed. On failing to receive the extra wages, the plaintiff sued for them. The

25 [1925] AC 270.   26 [1988] QB 77.   27 [1956] 2 All ER 318.   28 (1809) 2 Camp 317.

court held that his claim failed, because he and the rest of the crew were already bound by their original contract to deal with normal emergencies of the voyage, and were doing no more than their existing contractual duty in working the ship back home. The court acknowledged, however, that if they had exceeded their duty, it would have been different.[29]

However, through its decision in *Williams v Roffey Bros and Nicholls (Contractors) Ltd* in 1990,[30] the Court of Appeal has – to say the least – modified this basic proposition. The defendants, who were building contractors, contracted to refurbish a block of 27 flats. They sub-contracted the carpentry work to the plaintiff, the agreed price being £20,000, and the plaintiff was to receive interim payments at reasonable intervals as the carpentry work progressed. After receiving a total of £16,200, the plaintiff ran into financial difficulties, partly because he had not properly supervised his workers, but partly because the carpentry work had been underpriced from the outset. The defendants, who would have been liable under a penalty clause in the main contract if the work was not finished on time, were aware of the plaintiff's circumstances, and they agreed to pay the plaintiff an extra £10,300 to ensure that the carpentry work continued and was duly completed on time. The plaintiff then carried on the work, and duly received one further payment of £1,500. The plaintiff then stopped work on the remaining flats and brought an action against the defendants claiming £10,847.

The case appeared to be – in the words of one of the judges in the Court of Appeal[31] – 'a classic *Stilk v Myrick* case', in that the new agreement was unsupported by fresh consideration: the plaintiff was to receive extra money for carrying out his existing contractual obligation, while the promisor (the defendant) received no new or additional benefit. Counsel for the defendants conceded that, in practical terms, the defendants obtained the benefits of (i) seeking to ensure that the plaintiff continued work, (ii) avoiding the penalty for delay, and (iii) avoiding the trouble and expense of engaging someone else to complete the carpentry work. However, it was argued for the defendants, these *practical* advantages did not amount to 'additional benefits' in law, since the plaintiff was only promising to do what he was already contracted to do.

However, both Glidewell LJ and Purchas LJ denied that the present situation was covered by *Stilk v Myrick*: both referred to the modern concept of economic duress, whereby one party obtains a benefit from the other by taking unfair advantage of the other's difficulties, and suggested that *Stilk* and similar cases might be explained better as examples of economic duress rather than cases turning on the issue of consideration. In the words of Purchas LJ, cases like *Stilk*:

> involved circumstances of a very special nature, namely the extraordinary conditions existing at the turn of the eighteenth century under which seamen had to serve their contracts of employment on the high seas. There were strong public policy grounds at

29 See *Hartley v Ponsonby* (1857) 7 E & B 872.   30 [1991] 1 QB 1.
31 [1990] 1 All ER 512 at 527, per Purchas LJ.

that time to protect the master and owners of a ship from being held to ransom by disaffected crews. Thus, the decision that the promise to pay extra wages . . . was not supported by consideration is readily understandable.[32]

Glidewell LJ, after discussing the modern notion of economic duress, summarised the law as follows:

> (i) if A has entered into a contract with B to do work for, or supply goods or services to, B in return for payment by B and (ii) at some stage before A has completed his obligations under the contract B has reason to doubt whether A will, or will be able to, complete his side of the bargain and (iii) B thereupon promises A an additional payment in return for A's promise to perform his contractual obligations on time and (iv) as a result of giving his promise B obtains in practice a benefit, or obviates a disbenefit, and (v) B's promise is not given as a result of economic duress or fraud on the part of A, then (vi) the benefit to B is capable of being consideration for B's promise, so that the promise will be legally binding.[33]

There was no suggestion that economic duress played any part in the facts of the present case, and, that being so, the court had no difficulty in holding that the second agreement was binding in law.

The case is open to comment on a number of grounds, not least that of the reasoning process of the court. It has been suggested that the court may have been 'guided less by technical questions of consideration than by questions of fairness, reasonableness and commercial utility'[34] and that this case, along with other recent cases in contract law, reflects a judicial change of approach which is moving away from analyses based on the technical rules of consideration, towards an approach which fully recognises, and acts on, the hard commercial reality which motivates parties such as those in *Williams v Roffey Bros*. It remains to be seen how far the courts will extend the reasoning behind the decision in *Williams*; does it matter whether the plaintiff or the defendant initiates the 're-negotiation'? Or whether the modification is positive (that is, promising more money for the same work) or negative (the same money for less work)? As always, we must await future decisions.

A related situation is that in which A pays, or promises to pay, part of a debt already owed by A to B, in return for which B promises to release A from the balance of the debt. The general rule is that B is not bound by that promise, and can sue A for the balance, because A has provided no fresh consideration for the new bargain. Although it has been suggested that this rule should, logically, be modified in the light of *Williams v Roffey*,[35] it has been well-established since *Pinnel's* case in 1602,[36] and is usually called 'the rule in *Pinnel's* case'. In order for A to be discharged from the remainder of the debt, it follows that A must provide consideration other than mere part-payment of the existing debt. There are a number of ways in which such

---

32 [1990] 1 All ER 512 at 526.   33 [1990] 1 All ER 512 at 521–522.
34 J. Adams and R. Brownsword, 'Contract, Consideration and the Critical Path', (1990) 53 *MLR* 536
    at 537.   35 See Adams and Brownsword, ibid., esp. pp 540–541.
36 (1602) 5 Co Rep 117a.

valid consideration may be provided. A may agree, for example, to pay the smaller sum, at B's request, before the date on which the debt is due, or at a different place; or the part-payment may be accompanied by some other item, given by way of an additional gift, again at B's request. Another situation where the rule in *Pinnel's* case will not apply is where the amount of the debt to B is in doubt, or is disputed – for here, there is the possibility that the part-payment offered by A is in fact more than the full amount actually owed.

It used to be the case that, if the part-payment was made by A by means of a negotiable instrument, such as a cheque, then this was sufficient consideration to discharge the whole debt. The Court of Appeal held in *D & C Builders Ltd v Rees* in 1966[37] that 'no sensible distinction can be taken between payment of a lesser sum by cash and payment of it by cheque ... When honoured, it is actual payment. It is then just the same as cash. If a creditor is not bound when he received a payment by cash, he should not be bound when he received payment by cheque.'[38] Finally at common law, if the part-payment is made by a third party, C, to B, then any action by B against A for the balance will fail.

In equity, there has developed yet another situation in which the rule in *Pinnel's* case may not apply, and this is known as the doctrine of promissory estoppel. In *Hughes v Metropolitan Rly Co* in 1877,[39] it was said by Lord Cairns that:

> It is the first principle upon which all Courts of Equity proceed, that if parties who have entered into definite and distinct terms involving certain legal results ... afterwards by their own acts or with their own consent enter upon a course of negotiations which has the effect of leading one of the parties to suppose that the strict rights arising under the contract will not be enforced or will be kept in suspense or held in abeyance, the person who otherwise might have enforced those rights will not be allowed to enforce them where it would be inequitable, having regard to the dealings which have thus taken place between the parties.[40]

This reasoning was applied in the important case in 1947 of *Central London Property Trust Ltd v High Trees House Ltd*,[41] where the facts were as follows: in 1939, the plaintiffs leased a block of flats to the defendants at an agreed annual rent. In 1940, the plaintiffs agreed to reduce the rent by half because the onset of war had caused many of the flats to become empty, and there was no express time limit set for the duration of this rent reduction. The defendants paid the reduced rent from 1940 until 1945, by which time the flats were again occupied. The plaintiffs then claimed the *full* rent, both for the immediate future and also for the period 1940–45. Now, applying the rule in *Pinnel's* case strictly, the plaintiffs would have been entitled to the full amount, for just as we have seen in other cases, the defendants had provided no new consideration for the second agreement in 1940. But Denning J, as he then was, held that the 1940 agreement was intended as a temporary arrangement, and that from 1945 the originally agreed rent should be payable, though the plaintiffs

---

37 [1966] 2 QB 617.   38 Ibid., at 623, per Lord Denning.   39 (1877) 2 App Cas 439, HL.
40 Ibid., at 448.   41 [1947] KB 130.

were not entitled to claim full back-rent because of the 1940 agreement. The absence of fresh consideration, he thought, did not matter, for the defendants were not seeking to enforce any contract. Applying the doctrine as expounded by Lord Cairns in *Hughes'* case, the court held that the plaintiffs had here made an agreement which led the defendants to rely upon it to the extent of receiving reduced rent from their tenants; the defendants were thus led to suppose that their duties under the original rental agreement were, at least, in abeyance, and it would therefore be inequitable (unfair) to allow the plaintiffs to go back on their agreement of 1940.

The doctrine of promissory estoppel is thus a further exception to the rule in *Pinnel's* case, though there is judicial and academic agreement that the scope of the doctrine is at present unclear. It seems that the defendant must have acted in reliance upon the promise in order for the doctrine to operate, and that the doctrine can be invoked only as a defence to, and not as the basis for,[42] a claim. Apart from this, there are various aspects of the doctrine which are as yet unsettled, and in the light of *Williams v Roffey* and other cases in which the courts have shown a preparedness to decide issues in the light of economic and commercial reality rather than through appeals to strict legal doctrine, it may be that the whole range of cases dealing with these difficult and technical aspects of consideration may soon be reviewed by the courts.

Consideration must move from the promisee

The rule has a twofold significance. First of all, it means that X can only enforce a promise made to him by Y if X can establish that he gave consideration for Y's promise. Thus, in the leading case of *Price v Easton* in 1833[43] A agreed to do some work for B, who in turn promised to pay A's wages over to C. B did not pay C, who attempted to sue for that amount. The attempt failed, because C had provided no consideration for B's promise. Looked at another way – and this is the second aspect of the rule – this case was an attempt by a third party, C, who was not a party to the contract between A and B, to enforce that contract. At common law, an outsider – or 'third party' – who is not a party to the contract cannot bring an action on that contract. This is the doctrine of 'privity of contract' which means, in essence, that 'only a person who is a party to the contract can sue on it'.[44] Thus, at common law, if A and B agree that each shall pay £100 to X, and B fails to pay his share, then X cannot sue B for the money, because X, though the beneficiary of the agreement, is not a party to that agreement, and provides no consideration.[45] The doctrine of

---

42 Though see Lord Scarman's comments in *Crabb v Arun District Council* [1976] Ch 179.
43 (1833) 4 B & Ad 433.
44 Viscount Haldane in *Dunlop Pneumatic Tyre Co Ltd v Selfridge & Co Ltd* [1915] AC 847 at 853.
45 See also *Tweddle v Atkinson* (1861) 1 B & S 393; *Beswick v Beswick* [1968] AC 58. There is some debate among commentators as to whether the two aspects of *Price v Easton* are analytically distinct, or whether they are merely two ways of stating the same idea: see the discussions in, for example, Cheshire, Fifoot and Furmston, op. cit., pp 86–87; J. Poole, *Casebook on Contract Law* (6th edn., Oxford University Press, 2003); J. Poole, *Textbook on Contract Law* (7th edn., Oxford University Press, 2004).

privy of contract has been heavily criticised over the years[46] and the common-law position has been modified by the important Contracts (Rights of Third Parties) Act 1999.

The 1999 Act does not abolish the doctrine of privity of contract, but provides, in essence, that where, by virtue of a contractual agreement between A and B, a benefit[47] is conferred upon C (the third party), then C has the right (subject to certain conditions specified in the Act) to enforce that agreement against the defaulting contracting party. Section 1(1)(a) of the Act provides that a third party may enforce the contract 'if the contract expressly provides that he may'. So if the contract between A and B *expressly provides* that C may sue either of them if they fail to carry out their promise, then, by virtue of this subsection, C may now do so.

However, in the absence of any express provision, s 1(1)(b) states that if a term of the contract '*purports to confer a benefit*' on the third party, then the third party has the right to sue on the contract. According to s 1(2), however, this provision will not apply 'if on a proper construction of the contract it appears that the parties did not intend the term to be enforceable by the third party'. So if A and B expressly provide that the contract shall only be enforceable by themselves, this will override the provision in s 1(1)(b) and C will not be able to sue. It is clear, then, that the provisions of the Act will not apply if the contracting parties expressly so provide. The Act provides that the term 'benefit' can include the payment of money, the transfer of property, or the rendering of a service.

For the Act to apply, the contract must 'purport to confer a benefit' on the third party: it is not enough if third party C receives a benefit, as a result of the contract between A and B, purely coincidentally. For example, if A, a householder, has a faulty house security system which continually malfunctions, and triggers a loud alarm which regularly disturbs A's neighbour C, then if A contracts with B Ltd, who fitted the alarm, to rectify the fault, then C will clearly benefit from the resulting peace and quiet. C would not, however, have any right, by virtue of the Act, to sue B Ltd should the repair prove unsuccessful!

Under the provisions of s 2 of the Act, the contracting parties may not, unless the original contract expressly so provides, subsequently agree to vary or remove the rights of the third party without that party's consent, if the third party has either communicated their assent to, or has relied upon, the relevant term in the contract. The remedies available to third parties affected by the Act include compensation and specific performance (an order compelling the contracting parties to carry out their promises).

Having briefly outlined the legal requirements for a binding contract, we can see that the legal model of the contract, comprising offer, acceptance, consideration and intention to create legal relations, is in essence a conceptual model. Applying the legal idea of the contract to real-life transactions and disputes is thus rather like placing an outline drawing over an original picture, to see how far one corresponds

---

46 See Poole, op. cit.   47 But not a burden: for discussion see texts referred to above.

with the other. In this way, the judges have deciphered the intricacies of business transactions, and recast them in terms of what are in essence fairly simple rules of law. Was there a clear offer made by one party to the other? Was that offer accepted by the other party? Was there consideration? Did the parties intend to create a legal relationship between themselves? If the judges can identify these elements, then there is a contract, breach of which will lead to a remedy for the aggrieved party.

From our discussion so far, it may be appreciated that much of the law of contract is based on judicial responses to the practical needs of business and commerce, and this may be said of the courts' recognition that there are some situations where the ordinary rules of contract should not apply. If one party makes a serious mistake, for example, so that she is not in fact getting what she thought she was getting, the contract may be made void by the court in the absence of true agreement as to the subject-matter of the contract. Again, certain categories of persons, notably the mentally ill, children and those who enter into contracts whilst too drunk to appreciate their actions, are recognised as not having full appreciation of the obligations they may be taking on, and so contracts made by such persons may be set aside. In the case of minors, contracts for 'necessaries' (food, clothing, accommodation and employment) will be enforceable against a minor, whilst other contracts will not. Again, sometimes a contract cannot be fulfilled, not because one party is in breach of the contract, but because of some event outside the control or anticipation of the parties. If I contract to hire a concert-hall for an evening and the hall burns down through no fault of the owner before the night of the performance, there is nothing left to contract about. Here, the law regards the contract as *frustrated*, and the Law Reform (Frustrated Contracts) Act 1943 provides for the court to try to put the parties back in the same financial position they were in before the contract was made.[48]

It must be acknowledged, however, that there are some aspects of the law of contract which have been criticised. One criticism concerns the fundamental notion of the contract as an *agreement*. In its everyday meaning, the term 'agreement' usually connotes the idea of people putting their heads together and willingly and intentionally coming to an explicit arrangement. In law, however, the approach taken to the phenomenon of agreement is said to be an *objective* one: this means that the judges do not enquire into the innermost thoughts of the parties, but look rather at the outward appearance of a transaction. If a disinterested onlooker would infer from the parties' words and/or deeds that an agreement exists, then such an agreement *does*, in law, exist, even though this might not have been the subjective intent of one or both of the parties at the time. We will see more of the problems resulting from this approach, especially in the context of consumer contracts, presently.

Another criticism which some commentators (and indeed judges) have levelled at the law of contract is that the conceptual model of the legally binding contract

---

48   *Taylor v Caldwell* (1863) 3 B & S 826; *Krell v Henry* [1903] 2 KB 740; *Chandler v Webster* [1904] 1 KB 493; the *Fibrosa* case [1943] AC 32.

can often be far removed from real-life situations. Atiyah suggests that in some cases 'it may be very difficult, if not impossible, to find a real offer and acceptance or to decide who is the offeror and who the offeree . . . Such cases show that to insist on the presence of a genuine offer and acceptance in every case is likely to land one in sheer fiction . . .'[49] According to another critic:

> The legal obligation is strictly limited to the promises. These promises are discovered in the unvarying method by which human beings contract with each other, namely by means of 'offers' embodying 'promises' directed by 'offerors' to particular 'offerees' who 'accept' by manifesting assent . . . Case variations were hung on the construct like ornaments on a Christmas tree, glittering but essentially useless.[50]

And the view of one member of the House of Lords is that 'English law, having committed itself to a rather technical and schematic doctrine of contract, in application takes a practical approach, often at the cost of forcing the facts to fit uneasily into the marked slots of offer, acceptance, and consideration'.[51]

How much force is there in the view that the legal contractual model is over-rigid and often unrealistic? Undoubtedly, there are many cases where a good deal of judicial ingenuity has been put into the task of establishing the existence of a contract from a set of given facts; and there are areas within the law (such as the scope of promissory estoppel – see above) which are unclear. There are cases, too, where the courts' conclusions that, on given facts, binding contracts exist, seem to us rather odd: an example is *Thompson v London, Midland and Scottish Rly Co*, decided in 1930,[52] which we will examine presently. But as most modern commentators point out,[53] the ideas of offer, acceptance and consideration are not applied in a wholly inflexible manner, and the rules of contract, it has been suggested, 'from their admittedly rigid and out-dated "base-line" . . . shade off towards a more realistic middle ground more in keeping with the merely approximate certainty of business life'.[54] It might also be suggested that the apparent artificiality and rigidity of the rules of contract owe at least as much to the unrealistic assumptions on which they are based as to the judges' attempts to wrap those rules around real commercial situations.

We have already identified the prevailing social and economic philosophy of the nineteenth century as *laisser-faire* individualism, where the affairs of business, employment, trade and manufacture were thought best left to the individuals concerned, with a minimum of state intervention through government policy or parliamentary legislation. The legal counterparts of *laisser-faire* philosophies underlying the law of contract during the period are the twin assumptions of

49 Op. cit., p 55. See also H. Collins, *The Law of Contract* (4th edn., 2003, Cambridge University Press).
50 Mooney, quoted in J. P. Tillotson, *Contract Law in Perspective* (3rd edn., 1995, Cavendish), pp 51–52.
51 Lord Wilberforce in *New Zealand Shipping Co Ltd v AM Satterthwaite and Co Ltd* [1975] AC 154 at 167.   52 [1930] 1 KB 41.
53 Cheshire, Fifoot and Furmston, op. cit.; Tillotson, op. cit.; Atiyah, op. cit.
54 Tillotson, op. cit., p 52.

freedom and *equality* of contract. In a developing and consolidating capitalist economy, private enterprise and free competition were absolutely basic: in a free market economy, keen competition is crucial, and the attitude of judges and legislators was that it was up to the individuals concerned to strike the best bargains they could negotiate. It was certainly not up to the courts or Parliament to repair bad bargains.

The assumptions of freedom and equality of contract, then, are explicable in terms of the economic philosophies of the day: people were assumed to be free to make whatever bargains they wished on the best terms they could get, and everyone was assumed to enjoy equal positions of bargaining-power. As we saw in chapter 1 in the context of employment contracts, by no means everyone in society *did* have such freedom and equality of bargaining-power. Because the judges never accepted a role as rectifiers of bad bargains, all kinds of possibilities for oppressive contractual terms, dictated by the more powerful of the contracting parties, were opened up. The only thing the judges would look at was the *form* which the agreement took – was it a contract? As long as the agreements before them satisfied the legal tests explained above, the details as to price, interest rates or other matters pertaining to the *content* of the contract did not concern them.

Contract and the consumer: the exclusion clause problem

As far as the ordinary consumer, forced by everyday necessity into contracts with traders and companies of all kinds, was concerned, there was at common law no recognition of unequal bargaining-power, nor any conception of consumer protection through parliamentary legislation. Indeed, the very basis of the common-law model of the contract was a freely negotiated transaction, voluntarily agreed by the parties, with no legal or state intervention or imposition as to the terms of that agreement.

Now, the law of contract differs from other areas of law such as criminal or tort law, in that the obligations imposed through a contract are *self-imposed* obligations, supposedly entered into freely by the parties. Crime and tort do not contain any idea of self-imposed obligation, but rather comprise obligations imposed upon everyone by the state. Because of this feature of contract, and because of the determination of the judges to uphold the principles of contractual freedom, it was, in theory and in practice, possible to write virtually any term into a contract, even to the extent of providing for *the exempting of one party from any legal liability* if certain breaches should take place. These *exclusion clauses* might appear in hotels ('The management accepts no responsibility for loss or damage to guests' property howsoever caused') and in contracts for the hire of machinery ('No liability is accepted in respect of any damage caused to the hirer or his property by this machine'). On bus or train tickets there usually appear such words as 'Issued subject to the terms and conditions of the Blankshire Transport Authority'. If we were to examine those terms and conditions, we would find numerous clauses exempting the authority or company from liability for loss caused by, for example, delayed or cancelled buses or trains, or loss of or damage to passengers' property over a certain financial limit. The effect of such clauses is clear: if we attempt to sue for loss caused by, say, a cancelled train leading to a missed appointment, we would find ourselves unable to recover compensation because the company has explicitly exempted itself from such legal liability.

The courts' attitude to such clauses in contracts has been somewhat ambiguous. In line with the assumptions underlying the law of contract, the judges have, on the whole, accepted that such clauses are perfectly legal and enforceable (the reasoning being that, assuming freedom of contract, consumers disliking such clauses could always take their business elsewhere). At the same time, however, they recognised, through cases coming before them, the possibilities for oppressive and exploitative treatment of consumers by traders in stronger bargaining positions, so that they adopted a strict manner of interpreting such clauses, with ambiguities being resolved in the customer's favour.

There are, nevertheless, many examples of cases where the judges have interpreted exclusion clauses in such a way as to produce what might be thought unfair, and sometimes fantastic, results. In *Thompson v London, Midland and Scottish Rly Co* in 1930,[55] for example, Mrs Thompson bought an excursion railway ticket. On the ticket were printed the words 'for conditions see back', and on the back of the ticket were the words 'Issued subject to the conditions and regulations in the company's timetables and notices and excursion and other bills.' On such notices were words to the effect that excursion tickets were issued subject to the conditions in the timetables, which could be purchased at the station for 6d (2.5 pence). Had Mrs Thompson read these conditions, she would have found, among other 'small print' clauses, the condition: 'Excursion tickets . . . are issued subject to . . . the conditions that neither the holders nor any other person shall have any right of action against the company . . . in respect of . . . injury . . . loss, damage or delay, however caused.' On her return from the excursion, Mrs Thompson fell when getting off the train, because of the negligence of an employee of the railway company, and was injured. She claimed compensation for her injury, but the Court of Appeal dismissed her claim on the ground that she had *agreed* to the clause in the timetable by purchasing the ticket which drew customers' attention to it, and had therefore lost her right to sue. The case is all the more surprising when we consider that, as a matter of fact, Mrs Thompson could not have appreciated the exclusion clause even if she had found it because *she could not read!* (It is now provided, by virtue of the Unfair Contract Terms Act 1977 (discussed below) that any exclusion clause which purports to 'exclude or restrict' liability for 'death or personal injury resulting from negligence' is of no legal effect.)

But in *Thompson*'s case, how could the court maintain, in the circumstances, that the plaintiff had 'agreed' to the condition? The answer is, as we have already

55 [1930] 1 KB 41. And see the earlier case of *Parker v South Eastern Railway* (1877) 2 CPD 416 (CA).

seen, that the courts, though desirous of giving effect to the wishes of the contracting parties, look to the objective, outward appearances of the transaction. In
the court's view, Mrs Thompson had indicated her agreement by accepting the
ticket, and the only relevant additional consideration was whether the railway
company had taken reasonable steps to bring the clause to passengers' attention –
it would clearly be absurd and unjust to hold a person bound by contractual terms,
the existence of which the party had no chance whatsoever of knowing. In
Thomson, the court held that the company *had*, by the various pointers on tickets
and notices, taken reasonable steps to bring their conditions to travellers' attention,
despite the fact that 'the time-table cost nearly a fifth of the fare paid by the claimant
and was evidently a volume of some size, the exemption clause being set out on its
552nd page. The likelihood of its being bought (let alone read) by an excursion passenger was, to say the least, remote . . .'[56]

These days, it is true, the courts have tended to take a somewhat more realistic
view. In *Thornton v Shoe Lane Parking Ltd* in 1971,[57] the plaintiff went to park his
car in the defendants' car-park. Outside the car-park, a sign listed the parking
charges, and stated that cars were parked there 'at owners' risk'. As the plaintiff
drove to the entrance, the automatic barrier rose, a ticket was ejected from a
machine and a light turned from red to green. The plaintiff took the ticket and
drove into the car-park. Upon the ticket was printed, among other things, a statement to the effect that the ticket was issued subject to conditions displayed on the
car-park premises. These conditions were in fact displayed at various places, but
were not visible to drivers as they entered the car-park. Indeed, drivers would have
had to walk around the car-park in order to locate the displays. One of these conditions purported to exclude the defendants' liability for damage to cars and also
for injury to customers. On returning to pick up his car, the plaintiff was injured in
an accident. The defendants subsequently sought to rely on the condition exempting them from liability. In the Court of Appeal, Lord Denning had no doubt that
in this case, given the all-embracing nature of the exclusion clause, there was
insufficient notice given by the defendants to the plaintiff. Indeed, in his Lordship's
opinion, 'in order to give sufficient notice' of so wide a clause, 'it would need to be
printed in red ink with a red hand pointing to it, or something equally startling'.[58]
Megaw LJ pointed out that the first attempt to bring the conditions to the plaintiff's
attention was at a time when:

> as a matter of hard reality it would have been practically impossible for him to with-
> draw from his intended entry on the premises . . . It does not take much imagination
> to picture the indignation of the defendants if their potential customers, having taken
> their tickets and observed the reference therein to contractual conditions . . . were one
> after the other to get out of their cars, leaving the cars blocking the entrances to the
> garage, in order to search for, find and peruse the notices![59]

---

56 G. H. Treitel, *The Law of Contract* (11th edn., 2003, Sweet and Maxwell), p 199.
57 [1971] 1 All ER 686.   58 Ibid., at 690.   59 Ibid., at 693.

The plaintiff's claim succeeded.[60]

The common-law approach is illustrated further by the rule that if a person *signs* a document, then that person is bound by the clauses contained therein, whether he or she has read them or not.[61] The judges, in line with their general views on contractual equality and freedom of choice, have taken the attitude that if someone signs a document without reading it, then he has only himself to blame for the consequences.

The problems raised by these common-law rules for ordinary consumers were clear. First, if consumers wished to travel by rail, to have laundry cleaned by a cleaning company, to buy goods on hire-purchase, to buy a second-hand car or to have a television repaired, they were at the mercy of the traders concerned and their contractual exclusion clauses. As far as the reality of contractual freedom and equality were concerned, the only real choice was to take it or leave it. The consumer was in no position to negotiate with, for instance, a railway clerk or car-dealer over terms. The imbalance of bargaining-power between traders and consumers was a basic fact of commercial life.

The situation for the consumer was worsened by the development of *standard form contracts*: the terms of such contracts 'are set out in printed forms which are used for all contracts of the same kind, and are only varied so far as the circumstances of each contract require. Such terms are often settled by a trade association for use by its members for contracting with each other or with members of the outside public.'[62]

Such contracts may save time, but they may also put the consumer at a disadvantage. There is a huge number of trade associations, ranging from the Association of British Launderers and Cleaners and the British Carpet Manufacturers Association, to the Motor Agents Association and the National Association of Shoe Repair Factories, and it is highly probable that the consumer will be faced with exactly the same terms, *whichever* laundry, car or carpet retailer or shoe repairer is approached. If the supplier is in a monopoly or near-monopoly position, the bargaining position of the consumer is even weaker: once again we see the consumer's real 'freedom of choice' – 'take it or leave it'.

Whilst it is true that the judges have proved incapable, through their conservatism and the inflexibility of their common-law techniques, of providing adequate protection for the consumer, their concern for justice has led them, in cases of clear oppression or exploitation, to adopt interpretative techniques and doctrines of law enabling them to avoid giving effect to the grosser forms of exclusion clause. The narrowness with which judges have interpreted such clauses, for example, has meant that in many

---

60 See also *Interfoto Picture Library Ltd v Stiletto Visual Programmes Ltd* [1988] 1 All ER 348; *Ocean Chemical Transport Inc v Exnor Craggs Ltd* [2000] 1 All ER 519; *O'Brien v MGN Ltd* [2001] EWCA Civ 1279.

61 This is usually known as the 'Rule in *L'Estrange v Graucob*', the case normally cited as authority for this proposition ([1934] 2 KB 394), though in fact there is earlier authority to the same effect.

62 G. H. Treitel, *Law of Contract*, op. cit., p 196.

cases traders were prevented from hiding behind ambiguous escape clauses,[63] especially where the problem concerned *implied* terms – that is, *implied by law* into a contract without any *express* agreement by the parties. The Sale of Goods Act, as originally enacted in 1893, provided for the inclusion into every contract for the sale of goods of certain implied terms (discussed in more detail below), including the *fitness of the goods sold for their purpose* (provided that the purpose was made known to the trader) and the *merchantable* (now *satisfactory*)[64] quality of those goods, and the Act proved to be a useful weapon on the side of the consumer, despite the provision in the Act that these terms could be expressly excluded.[65] Hair dye which made the user's hair fall out would be unfit for its purpose; a new car with a bad scratch would not be of merchantable quality (even though 'fit for its purpose' inasmuch as it was mechanically sound). Compensation would be recoverable in both cases for breach of the implied terms, unless an exclusion clause provided to the contrary.

At common law, the judges' invention of the doctrine of 'fundamental breach' of contract, involving the presumption that the trader could not sensibly be taken to have intended to exclude liability for breach of the fundamental promise in the contract,[66] also proved valuable in the continuing struggle against the imbalance of bargaining-power. But despite such developments, the problem of contractual 'freedom' has remained: and although the courts have developed various devices whereby they may strike down contractual clauses which they feel unduly unfair and oppressive, their insistence on the underlying philosophy of contractual freedom has made that task extremely difficult.

Legislative intervention: the solution to the consumer problem?

This enormous gap between the theory of contractual freedom and equality, and the reality of modern consumer transactions, has been bridged only relatively recently by state intervention through consumer protection legislation and, to an extent, by an increased sense of 'consumer awareness' by many trading concerns.

---

63 See, for example, *Andrews Bros (Bournemouth) Ltd v Singer* [1934] 1 KB 17; *Houghton v Trafalgar Insurance* [1954] 1 QB 247; *Hollier v Rambler Motors (AMC) Ltd* [1972] 1 All ER 399.

64 Sale and Supply of Goods Act 1994, discussed below.   65 *Andrews v Singer*, op. cit.

66 For example, *Karsales (Harrow) Ltd v Wallis* [1956] 1 WLR 936; *Farnworth Finance Facilities Ltd v Attryde* [1970] 2 All ER 774. But despite dicta in *Karsales* to the effect that a fundamental breach operates as a rule of law, so that its effect was to nullify the contract, later cases suggest a different view. In particular, in *Suisse Atlantique Societe d'Armement Maritime SA v NV Rotterdamsche Kolen Centrale* [1967] 1 AC 361 and in *Harbutt's 'Plasticine' Ltd v Wayne Tank and Pump Co Ltd* [1970] 1 QB 447, the approach taken was that the doctrine of fundamental breach was a rule of construction, not of law. This meant that an aggrieved party could elect, despite the breach, to continue with the contract and simply sue for damages, or to terminate the contract altogether. The present position must be gleaned from both the decision in *Photo Production Ltd v Securicor Transport Ltd* [1980] 1 All ER 556 and the Unfair Contract Terms Act 1977; the effect of these being that the aggrieved party who has suffered the other party's fundamental breach retains the right either to terminate or continue the contract, though the exclusion clause itself may be invalidated because it does not pass the test of reasonableness provided for in the 1977 Act.

By the mid-twentieth century, concern over the relative lack of protection afforded to the consumer at common law resulted in the emergence of vociferous consumer protection lobbies. There are various reasons for the emergence of such lobbies at this time. Generally, there had been an economic boom during the 1950s, and the widespread availability of mass-produced expensive consumer goods such as cars, televisions and other domestic items brought the ordinary consumer into contact with hire-purchase, standard-form contracts, and transactions involving 'small print' clauses on an unprecedented scale. There were specific areas of concern, such as high-pressure sales techniques imported largely from the United States, product safety and reliability, and misleading descriptions of goods and services. A notorious example of the latter was the use of 'small print' exclusion clauses in holiday brochures and booking forms which prevented disappointed holiday-makers from obtaining effective legal redress even when the services were not provided.

There were, of course, a number of statutory and common-law provisions which even before these developments *did* constitute protection and/or redress for the consumer in certain cases. Various statutes and regulations governed weights and measures, and standards of hygiene and purity in the sale of food and drugs. The Sale of Goods Act 1893 and the important Hire Purchase Act 1938 provided important, if limited, protection for the consumer; and at common law, the landmark decision of the House of Lords in *Donoghue v Stevenson* in 1932 had paved the way for a series of cases brought in negligence (see chapter 9), where compensation could be recovered by a plaintiff who had suffered loss or damage as a result of negligence on the part of a manufacturer, repairer or supplier of faulty goods.[67] An action in negligence could not be brought, however, unless there had been loss or injury, and so this action was ruled out in cases where goods had proved faulty but no damage had ensued. In the case of goods which were intrinsically dangerous, such as guns, it was settled as early as 1837 in *Langridge v Levy*[68] that the seller could be liable for injuries resulting from defects in those articles.

Apart from these fairly limited cases, however, the private-law framework of contract, involving exclusion clauses and standard-form contracts, prevailed, even though it was increasingly clear that these provisions were inadequate and frequently unfair in their operation in the new affluent consumer society. The impact, then, of campaigning bodies such as the Consumers' Association (publishers of *Which?* magazine) in Britain, and individuals like Ralph Nader in the United States, shows the extent to which matters hitherto left to private law were becoming an important and urgent *public* concern. The major political parties soon pledged their support for measures designed to protect the consumer, and indeed the steady stream of 'consumer protection' statutes, mostly passed since the early 1960s, has been the outcome of various governments' legislative programmes.

---

67 An action in negligence also avoids the problems caused by the doctrine of privity of contract (discussed above). See *Donoghue v Stevenson* [1932] AC 562.   68 (1837) 2 M & W 519.

When considering legislation designed to protect the consumer, it is important to bear in mind that, although the majority of statutes affect the contractual relationship between consumers and traders, some legislation, such as the Trade Descriptions Act 1968 and the Food Safety Act 1990, imposes *criminal liability* on retailers and manufacturers (see chapter 10), whilst other statutory provisions, such as those concerning the liability of producers for injury caused by defective products contained in the Consumer Protection Act 1987 (see chapter 9), affect the pre-existing position in the law of *tort*. In what ways has Parliament provided protections and remedies for the consumer through modern legislation?

Consumer protection legislation: some examples

Hire-purchase and consumer credit

Under a hire-purchase agreement, the customer enters into a contract whereby the goods are *hired* from the trader by the customer, who then pays a series of instalments which are technically payments for this hire. On payment of the final instalment, the customer exercises his or her *option to purchase* the goods, and then – and only then – becomes the legal owner.

Hire-purchase agreements are distinct from other similar types of consumer credit transactions, of which the most noteworthy are credit sale agreements (where the buyer becomes the owner of the goods immediately, though still paying for them by instalments) and conditional sale agreements (where the goods are paid for by instalments, the buyer not becoming the owner until a specified condition, usually the payment of the last instalment, is fulfilled). It must also be noted that although in many such transactions, the credit agreement will be between the customer and the dealer, a very common variation on this theme is for the credit contract to be made between the customer and a *finance company*: on choosing the goods, the customer here enters into a hire-purchase contract with the finance company, and the dealer sells the goods directly to that company for cash. The finance company then becomes the legal owner, and all obligations arising under the hire-purchase contract are between the finance company and the customer. We shall see later that the customer's legal rights against the dealer, in the event of the goods proving to be defective, are unaffected; but for the moment, let us continue to concentrate on the nature of the credit agreement itself, and to address the question of why these agreements have caused so much trouble to many consumers.

The attraction of credit arrangements in a consumer society is that they enable the consumer to enjoy the goods immediately, whilst paying for them over a period of time, and is thus for many people a means of acquiring expensive goods which they could not otherwise afford. The hire-purchase arrangement was not, however, without its drawbacks for the consumer. To begin with, the use by some companies of door-to-door salesmen, trained in high-pressure sales techniques of subtle and not-so-subtle persuasion, led to situations in which the customer could be pressured into signing a contractual document, frequently without reading its small print clauses (which would probably be incomprehensible to all but a trained lawyer anyway) and without realising that substantial legal obligations were being taken on. It was all very well for MacKinnon LJ, faced with a typical hire-purchase contract, to remark in 1938 that 'if anybody is so foolish as to enter into an agreement such as this, I do not know that his case can be considered harsh', but this attitude ignores the realities of modern sales and advertising techniques. By and large, there was no reason at common law why a trader could not impose, through a hire-purchase contract, onerous and oppressive terms on the customer whilst protecting his own interests through exclusion clauses. An example was the notorious 'snatch-back' or repossession clause found in many such contracts, whereby the trader could, on default by the customer in paying an instalment on time, take the goods back immediately, despite the fact that the customer may have defaulted on the twenty-third of 24 payments, all previous instalments having been paid punctually. Here, the customer was left with nothing, and the trader could sell or re-hire the goods to someone else.

To attempt to overcome these problems, at least in so far as they arose from hire-purchase agreements, a number of statutes were enacted, and the Hire Purchase Act 1965 brought together and consolidated previous legislation in this area, providing important protection for the hire-purchase customer. The 1965 Act was, however, superseded by the more wide-ranging Consumer Credit Act 1974, which was itself substantially amended by the Consumer Credit Act 2006, discussed below.

The Act of 1974 was largely based on the recommendations in the report of the Crowther Committee on Consumer Credit in 1971.[69] This report recognised that, in practice, there is little difference between hire-purchase, credit sale and conditional sale transactions, and so the Act regulated *all* 'consumer credit agreements', defined as one where an *individual* (that is, not a corporate body such as a company) enters into an agreement with *any other person* (that is, a dealer, finance company or any other agency dealing in credit), which involves the latter providing the former with credit not exceeding £25,000.[70]

The main protections afforded by the Consumer Credit Act 1974 to the consumer entering into a hire-purchase or other consumer credit transaction are as follows. First, the Act follows the provisions of the Hire Purchase Act 1965 in ending the practice of 'snatching back' the goods, though naturally the 1974 provision extends beyond hire-purchase to cover all consumer credit deals. Essentially, once one-third of the total price has been paid by the customer, the creditor cannot repossess the goods in the event of the customer's default, except through a county court order – and this will be given only after the customer has been allowed more time to pay up (s 90). Second, the problem of the doorstep sales technique is tackled

---

69 1971, Cmnd 4596, HMSO.
70 The amount of credit was originally £15,000. It was increased by the Consumer Credit (Increase of Monetary Limits) Amendment Order 1998, SI 1998/996. Note that the Act fixed the maximum amount of *credit* involved, and not the maximum price of *goods*. As is noted below, recent reforms will have the effect of removing the maximum limit altogether.

by ss 67–73, the effect of which is that if the customer enters into a consumer credit agreement anywhere other than on trade premises (for example, in his or her own home, as opposed to a shop or showroom), then the customer is given a 'cooling off' period of seven days[71] after the final agreement is signed in which to cancel the agreement without incurring any liability whatsoever. The customer must be informed of the right to cancel, otherwise the contract is unenforceable. Once the agreement is thus cancelled (by means of a written notice to the creditor/dealer), the customer is entitled to the return of any money paid, and the creditor is similarly entitled to the return of the goods.

Naturally, the protections provided by the Act are not all one-sided: the creditor/ dealer, it is recognised, may in some circumstances stand to lose on the transaction, and this is especially true if we consider that the customer may terminate the contract at any time during the period of the agreement, in which case the goods taken back by the creditor will, of course, have become second-hand and will probably have depreciated somewhat in value. To try to recompense the creditor in such circumstances, the Consumer Credit Act 1974 provides that, on termination by the customer, all payments due up to the point of termination are payable; and if these sums amount to less than half of the total price of the goods, then the customer must pay additional sums so that 50% of the total price is paid. This section also provides that this rule is variable by the agreement itself specifying a smaller sum; or if the court considers that a smaller sum would adequately compensate the creditor, that court may order that such a smaller sum be paid.

Further, the problem of technical small print coupled with consumer ignorance is tackled (following the provisions of earlier legislation). Sections 60–64 of the Act provide, among other things, that the Secretary of State may, by regulations, specify the form and content of documents embodying regulated agreements 'with a view to ensuring that the debtor or hirer is made aware of' the rights and duties arising under the agreement and the protections and remedies available under the Act. Documents whereby such agreements are executed must contain all pertinent terms, readily legible, and must be signed by both parties to the agreement (s 61). Copies of the agreement must be given to the customer (ss 62, 63); and, by s 64, in the case of a cancellable agreement (see above) the prescribed form must contain notice as to the right to cancel.

The Consumer Credit Act 1974 sets out to regulate not only such consumer credit transactions as hire-purchase, but also virtually all other situations in which credit facilities are made available to the consumer. There are many other ways, apart from hire-purchase, of obtaining credit, such as personal accounts schemes operated by individual stores; credit cards such as Mastercard and Visa; bank loans, and overdraft facilities. Invariably, just as with hire-purchase, the consumer using

---

71 Consumer Protection (Cancellation of Contracts Concluded away from Business Premises) Regulations 1987, SI 1987/2117, as amended in 1998, implementing the European Directive governing doorstep-selling, Council Directive 85/5771/EC. Note that some types of agreement involve different 'cooling off' periods.

such schemes will pay more, in the form of interest charged by the scheme's operators. Although most credit schemes (and certainly all of the well-known ones) are highly scrupulous in their dealings with the public, there are other less prominent and more suspect operators of credit deals. The Consumer Credit Act 1974 provides the opportunity for consumers to challenge, by application to a court, an agreement which imposes 'extortionate' interest rates, and imposes stringent requirements on all traders and others who offer goods or services on credit. The objective behind the Act is 'truth in lending', and all those in the 'credit industry' are required to obtain a licence from the Director General of Fair Trading (who may take away that licence for malpractice: see Part III of the Act). In addition, the Act provides for such matters as the disclosure to customers of true rates of interest (s 20); prohibitions on canvassing for trade by credit brokers and debt counsellors off their trade premises (ss 48, 49); sending to minors any circular inviting them to gain credit (s 50), or giving unsolicited credit cards (s 51); and the general control of all credit transactions such as bank overdrafts, budget accounts, credit cards and so on.

Following a review of the law on consumer credit, the Consumer Credit Act 2006 was designed to reform the structure created by the 1974 Act. The 2006 Act aims, among other things, to increase the extent of consumer protection, strengthen the regulation of the credit industry, and abolish the financial limit on credit transactions.

There were a number of reasons for the review of this area. First of all,

> before the financial deregulation of the 1980s building societies only provided mortgages, banks provided consumer loans and overdrafts and supermarkets sold fruit and vegetables. Now, the market for credit has become highly developed and diversified. The number of licensed lenders, the range and complexity of credit products and the sales strategies used by creditors has developed at an unprecedented rate. This blurring of the boundaries has undoubtedly increased competition but it may also have contributed to some of the less desirable aspects of market behaviour.[72]

The increasing diversity of providers has been accompanied by greater ease of access to credit facilities and a huge increase in the burden of indebtedness, estimated by the Department of Trade and Industry to have increased from an average of £86 per person in 1969 to over £2,700 per person in 2003.[73] This has brought a corresponding increase in the numbers of people with debt problems, a problem compounded by the fact that the less well-off, who find it more difficult to obtain credit, tend to pay far more by way of interest.

The DTI identified unfair and irresponsible selling methods, the lack of effective redress (especially as regards the very low take-up of opportunities for applying to the court for consideration of extortionate agreements), poor customer service and

---

72 House of Commons Research Paper 05/03, *The Consumer Credit Bill*, p 11.
73 Government White Paper, *Fair, Clear and Competitive – The Consumer Credit Market in the 21st Century*, Cm 6040, 2003.

excessively high interest rates as concerns which the 1974 Act was failing to address, along with the need to strengthen the regulatory structure for the consumer credit industry. And one of the most important factors was perceived to be the overriding need for clarity of information provided to customers, both at the time of an application for credit, and later, during the life of the credit agreement itself.

The 2003 White Paper, '*Fair Clear and Competitive – the consumer credit market in the 21st century*', proposed a number of changes, many of which were implemented through delegated legislation.[74] The new primary legislation – the Consumer Credit Act 2006– deals with unfair credit relationships, consumer credit licensing, the abolition of the financial limit (in future, all consumer credit and consumer hire agreements will, unless specifically exempted, be regulated by the 1974 Act regardless of the amount of the credit) and new measures for consumer redress; and also takes into account the European Commission's Consumer Credit Directive of 2002, whose objective is the harmonisation of the laws in member states on consumer credit.

The idea of 'extortionate agreements' is replaced in the Act by a new test of 'unfair relationship'. If the court, after considering all relevant circumstances relating to the relationship between the creditor and the individual debtor, decides that the relationship as a whole is unfair, then the court may make an order to provide redress to the debtor – the Act includes the specification of a range of possible remedies.

A new dispute-resolution service is to be available free of charge, operated through the office of the Financial Services Ombudsman (see chapter 6). Before applying to the Ombudsman, however, the complainant must have attempted to resolve the problem through other avenues, such as the creditor-company's own complaints procedure, but if these have failed, the Ombudsman provides an independent means of resolving the dispute. The Department of Trade and Industry has stated that the aim of these changes is to 'improve the ability of consumers to seek redress, make it easier for borrowers and consumer credit businesses to resolve disputes in a speedy, fair and proportionate manner, and act as an incentive to compliance with the procedural requirements of the [1974] Act and the enhanced licensing regime'.[75]

The Act continues the system of licensing those offering credit through consumer credit companies, and the powers of the Office of Fair Trading in considering applications for licences are enhanced. Similarly, the OFT will have greater powers to monitor companies to ensure that they continue to be fit to hold a consumer credit licence, and to take appropriate action if they are not, such action to include the variation of the terms of the licence, or the revocation of the licence

---

74 These measures comprised the Consumer Credit (Advertisements) Regulations 2004, the Consumer Credit (Agreements) (Amendment) Regulations 2004, the Consumer Credit (Disclosure of Information) Regulations 2004, the Consumer Credit (Early Settlement) Regulations 2004, the Consumer Credit (Miscellaneous Amendments) Regulations 2004 and the Consumer Credit Act 1974 (Electronic Communications) Order 2004.
75 Department of Trade and Industry, *Full Regulatory Impact Assessment – Consumer Credit Bill*, December 2004, p 29.

altogether. In the event of failure to comply with any conditions specified by the OFT, the latter can also impose financial penalties of sums up to £50,000, though there will be a right of appeal against such fines to the Consumer Credit Appeals Tribunal, a new body created by the Act.

By and large, the consumer credit industry welcomed the new government proposals, recognising that the Consumer Credit Act of 1974 had been in operation for some 30 years, during which time the consumer credit industry had undergone radical change, as had consumer behaviour with regard to credit, and weaknesses in the original legislation had become clear.

The consumer credit legislation creates an important regulatory framework, in many ways reflecting the socio-economic realities of modern consumer credit deals. The law cannot, however, prevent the many cases of hardship experienced by people who, having entered into credit agreements, find themselves, by reason of redundancy or other unanticipated change in circumstances, unable to make the payments which the credit agreements require. Moreover, the law is extremely complex, which raises a further major problem: despite the various statutory provisions containing protections and remedies for aggrieved consumers, their efficacy depends ultimately upon consumer awareness of the rights and remedies involved. We shall say more about this problem presently.

Implied terms and exclusion clauses

The common-law position regarding exclusion clauses in consumer contracts for goods and services has been significantly changed by a number of statutes. The original Sale of Goods Act 1893 contained provision, as we saw above, for the inclusion in any contract for sale of goods of a series of *implied terms*, though two important points must be made at this point. First, these implied terms (breach of which usually entitled the aggrieved buyer to repudiate the contract) could be explicitly excluded by the seller; and second, the Act applied to the sale of *goods*, and not the supply of *services*. Thus, if a court held that a contract was for services, and not for the sale of goods, then the consumer was unprotected by any of the implied terms. The provisions as to implied terms in the 1893 Act have been re-enacted in the Sale of Goods Act 1979, but this Act must be read in the light of the important provisions of the Supply of Goods (Implied Terms) Act 1973, the Unfair Contract Terms Act 1977, the Sale and Supply of Goods Act 1994 and the Unfair Terms in Consumer Contracts Regulations 1994.[76]

The main implied terms are, first, as to *title*. The Sale of Goods Act 1979 provides, in s 12(1), that there is an implied term that the seller has the legal right to sell the goods, or, if the agreement is to sell goods at some future point, that the seller will have the right to sell them at that time. Section 13 deals with sales of goods by *description*, and provides that in such cases, there is an implied term that

---

76 SI 1994/3159.

the goods sold will correspond with the description. Thus for example in the case of the sale of a car advertised as being a 1990 Ford, or a store selling a table marked 'pine', then there is an implied term that the goods will in fact correspond to those descriptions. Section 15 similarly provides that where goods are sold on the basis of a *sample* there is an implied term that the bulk of the goods correspond to the sample in terms of quality and freedom from any defect which would not be apparent on reasonable examination of the sample.

Section 14, as amended, deals with what was originally the concept of 'merchantable quality'. This term, used in the 1893 Act, was replaced by the more up-to-date term '*satisfactory quality*' in the Sale and Supply of Goods Act 1994, whose effect is to amend the Sale of Goods Act 1979 so that, by section 14(2), 'where the seller sells goods in the course of a business,[77] there is an implied term that the goods supplied under the contract are of satisfactory quality'. This term is defined as meeting 'the standard that a reasonable person would regard as satisfactory, taking account of any description of the goods, the price (if relevant) and all other relevant circumstances' (s 14(2A)); and s 14(2B) lists a number of factors which may be taken into account – fitness for all the purposes for which goods of the kind in question are commonly supplied, appearance and finish, freedom from minor defects, safety, and durability. Not all of these factors will be relevant in all cases. Undoubtedly there will be difficult cases requiring careful interpretation of these provisions, as indeed there were under the old law,[78] and commentators have suggested that much of the previous case law will still be relevant in deciding the applicability of the new provisions. It should be noted that there are three situations in which the implied term as to satisfactory quality will not apply – where defects are specifically drawn to the buyer's attention prior to the contract being made; where, again prior to the contract, the buyer makes an examination of the goods which ought to reveal the defect, and, in a sale by sample, where reasonable examination of the sample would have revealed the defect, even though no such examination took place.

Section 14(3) makes provision for the situation in which the buyer of goods relies on the judgment of the seller over the purchase of the goods. Where the seller sells goods in the course of a business, and the buyer, expressly or by implication, makes known to the seller the purpose for which the goods are being bought, there is an implied term that the goods sold are reasonably *fit for that purpose*. It makes no difference whether the goods are normally sold for that purpose, though the implied term will not apply where the circumstances show that the buyer is not, in fact, relying on the skill or judgment of the seller, or where it is unreasonable for the buyer so to rely.

---

77 Private sales are thus excluded.
78 See *BS Brown & Sons Ltd v Craiks Ltd* [1970] 1 All ER 823; *Bernstein v Pamson Motors (Golders Green) Ltd* [1987] 2 All ER 220; *Rogers v Parish (Scarborough) Ltd* [1987] 2 All ER 232; *Shine v General Guarantee Corpn Ltd (Reeds Motor Co (a firm), third party)* [1988] 1 All ER 911; *Harlingdon & Leinster Enterprises Ltd v Christopher Hull Fine Art Ltd* [1991] 1 QB 564.

As to the supply of services: the Supply of Goods and Services Act 1982 provides that in contracts for services, there are implied terms[79] that the supplier will use reasonable care and skill in carrying out the service, and that the service will be carried out within a reasonable time and at a reasonable price. Further, where the contract also involves the transfer of property to the customer (as where a garage repairs a car's brakes, and in doing so fits new brake linings) then the implied terms as to fitness for purpose, merchantable quality,[80] title, description and sample, contained in the Sale of Goods Act 1979, apply.

The overall effect of the Supply of Goods (Implied Terms) Act 1973 and the Unfair Contract Terms Act 1977 is that in consumer sales, *none* of the above implied terms in contracts for goods or services can be excluded. A 'consumer sale' is one where (i) the goods are sold in the course of a business, (ii) the goods are not bought in the course of a business, and (iii) the goods are of a type normally bought for private use or consumption. If any of these conditions are not met, the transaction is regarded as a 'non-consumer sale', and exclusion clauses in non-consumer transactions will be valid only if the court holds that they are 'reasonable'. The test of reasonableness laid down in the Act specifies that, in assessing whether the term is reasonable, account should be taken of the guidelines stated in Sch 2 to the Act, which includes the relative strength of the parties' bargaining-power, whether one party could have made a similar contract with another person which did not contain the term, and whether the customer knew or ought reasonably to have known of the existence and extent of the term (having regard to, *inter alia*, trade custom or previous business dealings).

In addition, the 1977 Act provides that no exclusion clause may restrict or exclude liability for death or personal injury arising from negligence, and that any clause excluding liability for other loss arising from negligence may only be valid if, in the opinion of the court, it is reasonable in the circumstances. Furthermore, any insertion by a trader into a consumer contract of any term which purports to exclude liability for breach of the implied terms is now a criminal offence by virtue of subordinate legislation under the authority of the Fair Trading Act 1973.[81] Finally, there is in the 1977 Act a wide power enabling courts to declare invalid any clause in standard form contracts where a trader attempts to exclude liability for a breach of contract, or where a trader tries to provide a different service from that specified in the original contract, thus preventing traders from substituting one

---

79 Note that in the Sale of Goods Act 1979, the implied terms as to title, description, sample and quality are to be treated in England, Wales and Northern Ireland as *conditions*. A contractual term may be either a condition or a warranty, the former being a basic obligation, the latter being a subsidiary obligation. Breach of a condition entitles the aggrieved party to sue for damages, and also to terminate the contract, whilst breach of a warranty entitles the aggrieved party to sue for damages only. Whether a given contractual term is a condition or a warranty is, in the absence of statutory guidance, a matter of interpretation for the courts, and so the effect of this use of words is that the remedy available to an aggrieved party will depend upon the seriousness and circumstances of the breach.   80 See above.

81 Consumer Transaction (Restrictions on Statements) Order 1976, SI 1976/1813, as amended by SI 1978/127.

service or article for that originally contracted for. The extent to which the courts will use this power effectively remains to be seen as and when cases are brought before the courts.

In addition to the above provisions, it is also necessary to consider the Unfair Terms in Consumer Contracts Regulations 1994,[82] introduced to implement the European Directive on unfair terms of 1993.[83] This measure *supplements* existing common-law and statutory provision. It applies only to *standard form* contracts for *goods and services* made by a *consumer*, that is, a 'natural person' (not a corporate body) who is acting for purposes outside his business. The regulations provide that in such contracts 'unfair terms' shall not be binding on the consumer (though the remainder of the contract *will* continue to be binding as long as it is capable of remaining in existence without the unfair terms). An 'unfair term' is defined as 'any term which, contrary to the requirement of good faith, causes a significant imbalance in the parties' rights and obligations arising under the contract to the detriment of the consumer'. However, contractual provisions as to the main subject-matter of the contract and the price are excluded from consideration as to 'unfairness': the consumer cannot complain simply because they have paid too high a price. Factors which may be taken into account by a court when assessing fairness include the strength of the parties' bargaining positions, whether the consumer was induced to agree to the terms, whether the goods or services were sold or supplied to the special order of the consumer, and the extent to which the seller has dealt fairly and equitably with the consumer. Any written terms must be stated in plain intelligible language – a provision which is bound to affect the practices of many businesses; and doubts about the meaning of any term are to be resolved in the consumer's favour.[84]

There is no doubt that these statutes and regulations, taken together, constitute important changes to the common law on exclusion clauses in consumer contracts, although it may still be the case that the general ignorance of what remains a very complex area of law results in the Acts being of limited practical use as a means of protecting the consumer. It is known, for instance, that shop assistants may misrepresent customers' rights when faced with customer complaints; a customer bringing faulty goods back to the shop may be told that the fault must be dealt with through direct communication with the manufacturer, or that the fault is simply 'not the shop's responsibility'. This is, of course, incorrect: the effect of the legislation has been to place the responsibility for defective goods firmly and squarely on the shoulders of the *retailer*. Even where a retailer admits responsibility, the customer may be told that he or she must accept a credit note, rather than a cash refund. This, obviously, is in the trader's interest, as a credit note may be redeemed at that shop only, and no other. In fact, the customer can insist upon a

---

82 SI 1994/3159, now replaced by the Unfair Terms in Consumer Contracts Regulations 1999 (SI 1999/2083).   83 Council Directive 93/13/EEC.
84 This provision is identical to the common-law rule of interpretation concerning exclusion clauses.

cash refund; but here again, consumers' ignorance of their legal rights may serve to neutralise any real benefits conferred upon them by legislation. To take an extreme case: suppose a contractual document such as an order form or guarantee *does* contain clauses purporting to exclude liability for implied terms. Is it realistic to expect the average consumer to appreciate that the clause is invalid by virtue of the Unfair Contract Terms Act 1977? Arguably, the mysteries of consumer protection legislation are largely outside the ordinary person's experience, and it would be naïve to believe that consumers are, in general, aware of the rights and protections conferred upon them by what, after all, are highly technical and complex enactments.

Misrepresentation

A misrepresentation is, in law, a false statement of fact (as opposed to a statement of opinion, belief or law) made by one contracting party which induces the other party to enter into the contract. A misrepresentation is, then, 'pre-contractual': it takes place before the contract is entered into. It may well be that the contents of the statement do not subsequently become incorporated into the terms of the contract, and so the victim will not be able to sue for breach of the contract itself. The Misrepresentation Act 1967 provides remedies for the person who falls victim to such false statements of fact, whether made fraudulently, negligently or innocently. A statement in a holiday brochure that a hotel is 'two minutes from the sea', or a business offered for sale and stated by the seller to be 'worth £25,000 a year', will amount to misrepresentations if they are false, and if the other party is induced by them to make the contract. In cases where misrepresentation is established, the aggrieved party will have private-law remedies of compensation and/or the right to terminate (or 'rescind') the contract, depending on the circumstances of the case and the kind of misrepresentation involved.

Criminal liability

As noted already, various statutes govern such matters as weights and measures, and purity in the preparation and sale of food and drugs. This legislation is administered by local authority departments, and breach of any of the regulations by any trader, or any person involved in the preparation of food and drugs, may result in a criminal prosecution.

Apart from these provisions, the Trade Descriptions Act 1968 makes it a criminal offence to apply a false trade description to any goods or services. A trader who holds out for sale a refrigerator, for example, bearing the sign 'reconditioned', will be guilty of an offence if the article is not, in fact, reconditioned; as will a car-dealer who says that a second-hand car has only covered 30,000 miles when in fact it has been run for 130,000. Note also that the Powers of Criminal Courts (Sentencing) Act 2000 provides that those convicted in a criminal court of criminal offences may be ordered by that court to pay compensation to any person who has suffered loss as a result of that criminal offence.

Is the consumer now adequately protected through legislation?

Various points may be made about the current legal provision for consumer protection. First, it must be remembered that none of the consumer protection measures, whether substantive statutes or regulations made under empowering statutes, makes any changes in the fundamental common-law notion of the contract. The contract remains the 'bridge' between trader and customer; what has happened is that some of the common-law assumptions about contractual agreements, notably equality of bargaining-power and freedom of contract, have been seen to be misconceived, with the result that the most oppressive manifestations of the traditional judicial approach to contract – mainly exclusion clauses which unfairly protect one party at the expense of the other – have been modified or forbidden.

The net result for the consumer, therefore, is that although the opportunities for legal redress have been considerably extended, the precise forms of legal action through which remedies may be obtained have remained the same as they were a hundred years ago. The private-law action appropriate for most consumer grievances is still breach of contract, whether the breach is of an express contractual term, or one of the terms implied by statute.

This must lead us to consider problems such as consumers' ignorance of their legal rights, and the difficulties they face in seeking redress. The aggrieved person must first be aware that he or she *has* a possible remedy in law: legal advice in consumer matters may be difficult to obtain, especially when we consider that a full county court action may be out of the question, although, of course, it may be that an action through the 'small claims' procedure (see chapter 6) will be appropriate in many cases.

Connected with this is a second major problem. Because consumer protection legislation has been grafted onto the foundation-stone of the law of contract, the technicalities in this area of law are considerable. Even now, a contractual document such as a hire-purchase contract or an insurance proposal form, though containing terms which are perfectly lawful, will invariably contain phrases and expressions which have technical legal meaning, and which most consumers will not easily understand. It is not a simple matter for a person with no legal training to appreciate distinctions between express and implied terms, or to grasp the different legal consequences which various kinds of misrepresentation may have. For many consumers, taking action in a dispute may be seen as being more trouble than the goods are worth. However much consumer rights may be publicised, through the media and information published by the Office of Fair Trading or Citizens' Advice Bureaux, the complexities involved in ascertaining the parties' rights in a contractual dispute may deter all but the most dogged consumer from pursuing what may be a good legal case through to its conclusion.

But what other means of redress are available to an aggrieved consumer? Probably the only effective alternative to some form of legal action is the voluntary provision by many trade associations of codes of practice, which are encouraged and approved by the Office of Fair Trading.[85] Such codes, introduced by organisations including the Association of British Travel Agents, the Association of Manufacturers of Domestic Electrical Appliances, the Motor Agents Association and the Association of British Launderers and Cleaners, usually make provision for clear statements by their members of prices and descriptions of goods and services, spare parts to be kept in stock, complaints to be dealt with promptly, and a conciliation and arbitration procedure if the dispute cannot be settled amicably.

Such codes of practice are examples of 'business self-regulation', the businesses involved wishing to foster good consumer relations (most of us would return to a shop which handled our complaint efficiently and fairly) and to exhibit a degree of 'good citizenship':

> Codes of ethics and social responsibility have sprouted in recent years as the business community has sought to demonstrate its sense of social responsibility . . . Contemporary public debates about the social responsibility of the corporation very much emphasise that the making of profit is only one function of the corporation, and responsibility to employees, consumers, the environment and other groups and values can be reflected in the development and application of codes of practice.[86]

Such schemes are not without their critics. Like the Advertising Standards Authority, these codes and standards are operated by the industries themselves, and it may be argued that they are hardly likely to be wholly impartial when their own interests are at stake. Moreover, not every trading concern belongs to a trade association, and these will not be subject to that association's code; it may well be that it is precisely this type of business whose practices are most suspect. Another problem may be that rules contained within codes of practice may be inadequately enforced. Although it is probably true to say that many consumers have benefited from such codes of practice in cases in which they would almost certainly not have taken the problem to a legal agency for solution, it is interesting that the modern tendency has been for codes of practice produced by particular sectors to be approved by independent agencies – notably the Office of Fair Trading – and sometimes it is clear that they have been established as a way of avoiding the threat of controls through law, as happened in the case of the Advertising Standards Authority, created by the industry itself to establish and oversee its own code of practice.[87]

The practical problems facing consumers with disputes which have slipped through the preventive net of consumer protection legislation must lead us back to the statement by the Molony Committee on Consumer Protection in 1962:[88] 'The consumer's first safeguard must always be an alert and questioning attitude.'

85 Provision for such approval is contained in the Fair Trading Act 1973.
86 Cranston's *Consumers and the Law* (3rd edn., by C. Scott and J. Black, 2000, Butterworths), p 42.
87 See Cranston, op. cit., chapter 2.
88 Final Report of the Committee on Consumer Protection (1962, Cmnd 1781, HMSO).

Despite the reforms of the law through statutory provision, this seems still to be the best advice.

Contract and business: the positive role of the contract

If contracts between traders and consumers have been beset by problems such as the imbalance of bargaining-power, such difficulties rarely hinder contractual relations between businesses. It is worth re-emphasising that the law of contract was developed as a response to the needs of business in an expanding capitalist economy, not only as a means of dispute-solving, but also, and very importantly, as a positive aid to rational business planning. The rights and duties taken on by contracting parties need to be clear if promises are to be effectively fulfilled and disputes avoided. In theory, the law of contract fulfils an important business function by providing exactly this clarity, even though in practice neither consumers nor people in business go about their daily lives with a keen conscious awareness of contract law.

Essentially, the legal framework of the contract, with its attendant ramifications of exclusion clauses, limitation clauses and doctrines of frustration and fundamental breach, may be seen as providing the business community with the means whereby rational, calculated risks and transactions might be carried out in the relatively secure knowledge that rights and obligations could, in the final analysis, be enforced through law. This is an important issue for our understanding of contract law in the modern business world, for it is frequently only as a last resort that lawyers and courts are used to compel contractual performance by one party through litigation by the other. Macaulay, in the United States,[89] and Beale and Dugdale in England,[90] have carried out surveys among people in business which suggest that business contracts are not entered into with legal remedies in mind. As Beale and Dugdale put it, 'such factors as low-risk, mutually accepted norms and duties, and various extra-contractual devices may operate to reduce the use of contract law . . . there is not much scope for using contractual remedies'. Furthermore, both studies found that 'lawyers and legal remedies also tend to be avoided as being inflexible; lawyers are thought not to understand the needs of commerce and those firms who had consulted solicitors were not all satisfied. A similar reluctance to use the law was evident on the planning side.'[91]

The picture emerging from these studies is that business relations between contracting parties rest much more firmly on mutual goodwill and the need for co-operation in both present and possible future transactions, and the prospect of bringing actions to obtain legal remedies is thought by many to be highly damaging to these vital factors. It appears that in this context, as with industrial relations,

---

89 S. Macaulay, 'Non-Contractual Relations in Business' (1963) *American Sociological Review* 28.
90 H. Beale and T. Dugdale, 'Contracts between Businessmen: Planning and the Use of Contractual Remedies' (1975) 2 *British Journal of Law and Society* 1 at 45. See also the discussion in Adams and Brownsword, *Key Issues in Contract*, op. cit.   91 Ibid., p 59.

the law is regarded as being too formal and inflexible to serve the needs of the parties efficiently and constructively.

This is not to suggest that no problems arise within business contracts; certainly, there *is* litigation, frequently over international transactions. Such litigation will, however, only take place when negotiation between the parties and perhaps an attempt to resolve the problem through arbitration (see chapter 6) have failed. Tillotson[92] provides us with a number of examples of complex business contracts – almost invariably standard form contracts – and notes that the use by contracting parties of such standard form contracts may cause problems sometimes referred to as the 'battle of the forms'. Here, both parties, intending to do business with each other, use their own standard form documents in the communications and negotiations. The contents of these forms may well differ in material particulars. In such cases it can be very difficult, if not impossible, to identify a contractual agreement as defined by the judicial model of contract for, as will be recalled, any response to an offer which differs from the terms laid out in that offer cannot, according to the rules of contract, constitute an acceptance of that offer, but must be a counter-offer. In the event of such problems being brought before the courts, the outcome seems somewhat 'hit or miss'.[93] The court may find that, despite the fact that the situation does not 'fit' the contractual model, an enforceable agreement none the less exists;[94] on the other hand, the court may hold that no contract exists, but that the plaintiffs may be entitled to payment by the defendants for any losses incurred.[95] At present, where contracting businesses each use their own standard-form documents, each insisting that the transaction is to be based on their terms, the law has no clear answer to the question as to which set of terms prevails, except by the use of highly pragmatic analyses of the facts of each case. It might justifiably be asked whether this area is one where the legal rules of contract need to be changed so as to enable the courts to deal more clearly and consistently with this type of problem, thus diminishing the gap between legal doctrine and the reality of business transactions, and eliminating as far as possible the need for the courts to distort the classical model of the contract to make it 'fit' modern business practices.

In many commercial situations, businesses do not in fact rationally plan their transactions (or consider possible problematic consequences thereof). In the modern commercial world, it is common for the law of contract, theoretically – and in the eyes of the courts – so central to business transactions, to be marginalised, or not even thought of at all. Where more formal contractual arrangements are made (for example, where the transaction involves large amounts of money) then more use may well be made of contract-law mechanisms. For example, consider the extent to which businesses may try to incorporate into their contracts agreed consequences in the event of anticipated contingencies. There will be provision within

---

92 Tillotson, op. cit. See also Atiyah, op. cit; and Collins, op. cit.   93 Tillotson, op. cit., p 68.
94 See *Butler Machine Tool Co Ltd v Ex-Cell-O Corpn* [1979] 1 All ER 965.
95 This is called a quantum meruit payment. For an example see *British Steel Corpn v Cleveland Bridge and Engineering Co Ltd* [1984] 1 All ER 504.

the contract (notwithstanding the possibility of inconsistencies in the forms used by each party) regarding prices and price increases, delivery dates, provision for arbitration and *force majeure* clauses, which attempt to deal in advance, so to speak, with events which may happen and are completely outside the will and control of the parties (such as war, floods, earthquakes or even strikes), and which may seriously affect the performance of the contract.

In summary, it is true to say that, in business contracts, the old legal rules about offer and acceptance, and the established forms of legal remedy for breaches of contract, are today nowhere near as important as the influence on business of modern commercial practices and economic pressures; and if the reader has formed the impression that consumer contracts and business contracts are worlds apart, then that is not far from the truth. The fact is that their respective problems are not, *essentially*, legal problems at all; one has a dispute over goods and services with a supplier or manufacturer – a practical, everyday problem – and the other has a 'business relations' difficulty. Whilst both types of dispute clearly have legal implications – and indeed the law may offer, at least in theory, specific remedies – it is nevertheless true that, whether due to sometimes unintelligible technicality, inaccessibility of adequate legal solutions, suspicion of the law's formality and inflexibility or a fear that litigation may damage good business relationships, consumers and people in business have in common a reluctance to resort to the legal system for solutions – the very legal system whose judges created, back in the last century, the contractual device which underlies such disputes. Today, the classical notion of the contract is, for everyday purposes, frequently an inadequate and even outmoded means of analysing and resolving what may be important and expensive disputes.

The very notion of 'freely negotiated agreements' is, moreover, becoming increasingly eroded both by statutory rules and regulations and by factors such as international agreements and European Community legislation. State and interstate intervention is, in one form or another, replacing 'free agreement' as the cornerstone of financial transactions of all kinds. Whether the law, as it affects the ordinary consumer or business concern, will duly progress to take account of these social and economic changes remains to be seen; but as Friedmann remarked many years ago, the fact remains that 'the evolution of the law of contract in response to fundamental social changes has overwhelmingly occurred outside the court room'.[96]

96 Friedmann, *Law in a Changing Society* (2nd edn., 1972, Penguin), p 124.

12

Law and government

Among the topics and themes discussed so far has been the increase in state intervention in almost all sectors of social and economic life over the past 100 years or so; the growth of the welfare state, with the accompanying expansion of machinery for dispute-prevention and solution through administrative tribunals and other bodies; the vast increase in legal controls over many activities which, in earlier times, were left to the private arrangements of the individuals and groups concerned; and the changing nature of the state itself, which has moved from a relatively non-interventionist stance to much more positive and direct regulation and control. In recent years central government has sought to deregulate, and to return nationalised and public-sector industries and services to the private sector; but, paradoxically, in so far as this has been achieved, it has been done largely by placing considerable directive power in the hands of central government.

Private sector involvement in the provision of public services has blurred the distinction between 'public' and 'private' sector organisations and functions: what were previously regarded as the proper activities of the state have now often become the responsibilities of private companies – examples range from the privatisation of 'public utilities' such as the power and telecommunications industries, to the contracting-out to private companies of various aspects of the management of hospitals, schools and even prisons.

The reasons for this shift in the old notion of 'public service' are easily identified. Apart from ideological justifications based upon the idea of 'empowering the tax-paying citizen' through enhancing the transparency and accountability of the operation of these services, the attempt has been made over the past 20 years or so to improve their efficiency. Usually, 'regulators' have been created to monitor and, to a certain extent, to control, the activities of the private organisations concerned. Thus, the telecommunications industry is overseen by the Offices of Telecommunication (OFTEL), water services by OFWAT, and so on. The privatisation and break-up of the various components of the rail transport industry, in particular, was accompanied by the dispersal of regulatory functions between a bewildering array of no less than four separate bodies (apart from relevant government ministers) – the Rail

Regulator, the Chief Inspector of Railways, the Strategic Rail Authority, and Railtrack.[1]

The expansion of government activity has itself necessitated, of course, an increase in administrators and administrative agencies charged with the various tasks involved in the implementation of state policies and programmes. Much of the organisation of state activity is structured along the lines of bureaucracy which may, as Weber maintained, be a more efficient form of organisation than any other,[2] but which at the same time constitutes a source of irritation for many who define themselves as being on the receiving-end of organisations whose tasks are hindered by excessive red tape. For many people, the expansion of state intervention and regulation has engendered a deep mistrust of agencies – both public and private – charged with the delivery of public services, both at central and at local levels. Critics argue that the degree of decision-making power which Parliament has vested in these agencies is excessive; that the involvement of private organisations, one of whose primary aims must be the maximisation of profit, leads to cost-cutting and the sacrifice of safety standards; and that the use of that power may involve, potentially or actually, unwarranted intrusions into the affairs of private individuals and groups. It is not the purpose of this chapter to provide detailed descriptions of the various organs of government (such as the civil service, the structure of local authorities or the working of Parliament), or the relationships between government and the many agencies entrusted with public-service functions, but rather to explore some important aspects of the relationships between modern government and the law.

First of all, however, it is important to remind ourselves that legal controls are by no means the only way of regulating the actions of an administrative agency. There are complex frameworks of *economic* and/or *political* controls operating at both central and local government levels. One obvious mode of political control is through the ballot box at local and national elections; and there are many rather less obvious and more subtle ways in which political pressure may be put upon one agency by the actions of another. A mixture of political and economic controls can be seen in the following example. Although the deployment of resources within a police force is, by virtue of the provisions of the Police Act 1996,[3] a matter for the discretion of the Chief Constable of that force, it is still the case that a police force is partly dependent for financial resources upon the local police authority.[4] It may sometimes be that the authority may influence the activities of its police force

---

1 Railtrack was responsible for all rail track, stations, level crossings, etc. It was effectively deprived of all its functions after a series of tragic railway accidents culminating in the Paddington disaster of October 1999, responsibility for which was placed by many critics at Railtrack's door.
2 See chapter 1.
3 Consolidating the Police Act 1964, Pt IX of the Police and Criminal Evidence Act 1984 and certain other enactments.
4 Under the provisions of the Local Government Act 1985, those police forces which were, prior to the Act, regulated by committees of the metropolitan districts (abolished under the Act) are now under the regulation of Police Authorities, whose members are drawn from district councillors and magistrates.

indirectly, by means of economic pressures made possible by this partial control of resources.[5] In addition, the Home Secretary has substantial powers under the Police Act 1996[6] and these powers must be exercised 'in such manner and to such extent as appears to him to be best calculated to promote the efficiency and effectiveness of the police'. In 1992, the then Home Secretary refused to issue a certificate of efficiency to the Derbyshire police, after a highly critical report on that police force by the Inspector of Constabulary. The report stated, among other things, that the police in that area were seriously underfunded by the local police authority: this may be seen as a case where clear though indirect pressure is placed on local authorities by central government. The 1996 Act gives further powers to the Home Secretary, among them the power to direct a police authority to take any necessary measures in the light of adverse reports by Inspectors of Constabulary, and to specify to police authorities the amount of their budget requirement for any financial year.

In some cases of dispute between public bodies, we may find that the problem is dealt with by means of a mix of political and legal devices. Consider the matter of local authorities' independence of central government. It is often thought that locally elected authorities such as district and county councils enjoy a high degree of autonomy of central government, to the extent that, apart from the many and varied duties imposed upon them by statute to provide local services and facilities,[7] the policies of local councils can be formulated and implemented without intrusive interference or control by central government. Such autonomy has, however, always been limited; and in recent years government legislation has further diluted local autonomy in a number of ways.

To begin with, a local authority's income is only partly derived from local sources. For many years, local income came from rates levied on domestic and commercial property, plus other forms of revenue such as rents from council houses. In 1990, the local rating system for domestic properties was abolished, and replaced by the community charge (the 'poll tax'), a flat-rate charge payable by every adult person. This highly unpopular tax proved short-lived, and was replaced by the 'council tax', a charge based once again on the value of property. Finance raised locally, however, only accounts for a small proportion of a local authority's income, the remainder coming from central government in the form of a substantial grant.

This financial connection may be a source of friction between local and central government, and is an increasingly important means of control by the latter over the former. This may be particularly marked if the local authority and central government are controlled by opposing political parties. The Conservative govern-

---

5 See *R v Secretary of State for the Home Department, ex p Northumbria Police Authority* [1989] QB 26.

6 These were extended by means of amendments to the 1996 Act in the Police Reform Act 2002.

7 Various statutes impose a variety of duties upon local authority bodies to carry out their functions. See, for further detail, standard texts on local government law.

ments of the 1980s, for example, deeply committed to the reduction of public expenditure, looked critically at those local authorities which they regarded as profligate spenders, and (through the Rates Act 1984 and Local Government Finance Act 1988) introduced the device of 'capping', whereby these local authorities might be penalised for exceeding centrally-determined annual budgets.[8] The tensions which can occur between central and local government are further illustrated by the abolition in 1985 of the Greater London Council and the six metropolitan councils – all, prior to abolition, Labour-controlled. The White Paper preceding the legislation[9] which abolished these bodies argued the case for increased efficiency at local government level, though it also noted that the search by these authorities for a wider role in local government might 'lead them to promote policies which conflict with national policies which are the responsibility of central government'. Many critics saw these developments as a direct attack by central government upon elected local bodies which happened to disagree profoundly with central government policies. There had certainly been several instances of such disagreements. There was, for example, the reluctance of some (Labour-controlled) authorities to implement the provisions of the Housing Act 1980, which put into effect the government's policy of giving council house tenants the right to buy their homes (see chapter 5). Some authorities at first signalled their refusal to carry out these provisions, and even when it became clear that to do so would be unlawful, some councils none the less adopted a policy of deliberately 'going slow' in the implementation of the statutory right to buy.

Some commentators have perceived a general shift in the relationship between central and local government, in the direction of greater concentration of power in the hands of the former at the expense of local democracy.[10] Certainly, central government has in recent years taken on substantial control over local authorities. The introduction in 1999 of the 'best value' concept requires local authorities to 'make arrangements to secure continuous improvement in the way in which (their) functions are exercised, having regard to a combination of economy, efficiency and effectiveness'[11] and local government is to a great extent subject to the overriding scrutiny and controls, both with regard to strategic and operational matters, of central government.

Local authority expenditure is tightly controlled by means of the Audit Commission for Local Authorities, a body created in 1982 and currently subject to the provisions of the consolidating Audit Commission Act 1998. The Act requires

---

8 The system of rate-capping was substantially amended, and made somewhat more flexible, by the Local Government Act 1999.   9 *Streamlining the Cities* (1983, Cmnd 9063, HMSO).

10 The arguments are discussed in A. Cochrane, 'The Attack on Local Government: What it is and What it isn't' (1985) *Critical Social Policy*, Issue 12. See for further discussions C. Turpin, *British Government and the Constitution* (5th edn., 2002, Cambridge University Press); S. Leach and G. Stoker, 'The Transformation of Central-Local Government Relationships' in C. Graham and T. Prosser (eds), *Waiving the Rules: The Constitution under Thatcherism* (1988, Open University Press); I. Leigh, 'The New Local Government' in J. Jowell and D. Oliver (eds), *The Changing Constitution* (5th edn., 2004, Oxford University Press); P. Craig, *Administrative Law* (5th edn., 2003, Sweet and Maxwell).   11 Local Government Act 1999, s 3.

the auditor to be satisfied that a local authority has ensured 'economy, efficiency and effectiveness' in its use of resources,[12] and the elasticity of these terms has facilitated significant control over local authorities. The Audit Commission itself, though ostensibly rigorously independent of central government, may be thought none the less to have critical linkages: its members are appointed by the Secretary of State for Local Government, who may also direct the Commission as to how it carries out its functions.[13]

Many would argue that matters such as these are not for lawyers at all, but are rather matters of *policy*, to be decided by politicians, or by administrators who are entrusted with the task by Parliament. Indeed, as we saw in chapter 6, the doctrine of the separation of powers, though not rigidly adhered to in England, requires at the very least that the courts should adjudicate on questions of *law*, and should not delve into matters which are the rightful constitutional province of the executive or the legislature. The dividing-line between law and policy is, however, by no means always easy to draw, as we shall see.

Remedies in administrative law

Expanding briefly on one or two of the instances mentioned above: the term 'welfare state' often conjures up images of various state benefits (old age pensions and other state payments); it refers to such institutions as the education system, the social services, the health service and many of the various functions of local government. As we have seen, interventionist policies, and legislation which implements these policies, can often intrude upon 'private affairs'. Statutory power, for example, is given to local authorities to purchase privately owned buildings or land compulsorily, for purposes such as clearance or redevelopment programmes – though the authority must compensate the owner for doing so, and must also ensure that the proper procedures laid down in the relevant statutes are complied with. Similarly, planning legislation provides that people must obtain planning permission before altering the structure or use of any land or buildings. If a householder builds, say, a garage without complying with these requirements, then it may mean that the garage has to be taken down again. Here again, the authority must act within its legal powers, and must not step beyond those powers or act in an unreasonable manner. If a public authority can be shown to have acted in one of these ways, then the aggrieved citizen may have a remedy in law. Some of the remedies available, such as that of complaining through the relevant ombudsman have been discussed above (see chapter 6). Here, we are primarily concerned with the legal remedies which may be available through court action.

Consider, for example, the case of *Cooper v Wandsworth Board of Works* in 1863.[14] Here, a statute provided that before any building was commenced, seven

12 Section 5(1).
13 On this see, in particular, M Radford, 'Auditing for Change: Local Government and the Audit Commission' (1991) 54 *MLR* 912.   14 (1863) 14 CBNS 180.

days' notice had to be given to the local Board of Works in order that the Board could inspect the land and give any necessary directions for drainage. The Act also provided that in the event of such notice not being given before building commenced, the Board could lawfully demolish the building. The plaintiff had begun to build a house, and the work was well in hand when the Board of Works, claiming that the required notice had not been given, pulled down the house without giving the plaintiff any notice of their intention to do so, nor any opportunity to explain why notice had not been received. The plaintiff sued the board for trespass, arguing that although the statute clearly gave the Board the power to demolish the building, the Board should have given the plaintiff the opportunity to present his side of the story: in other words, he claimed that he should have been given a fair hearing before the demolition was carried out.

The court decided in the plaintiff's favour, stating that 'although there are no positive words in [the] statute requiring that the party shall be heard, yet the justice of the common law will supply the omission of the legislature'. This case raises a number of important issues which we shall explore later, but at this point it is important to note the dual role of the law in the field of government and administration. On the one hand, the law *facilitates*, through statutory provision, the carrying out of administrative functions; on the other hand, it provides in many cases (though not all) for *controls* on administration. Hence, aggrieved citizens suffering excesses or breaches of statutory powers by administrative agencies may be entitled to some form of legal remedy against the agency concerned.

Cooper's case is a good illustration of the principles of what we might call the 'ordinary liability' of public bodies. Such liability can be contrasted with other forms of liability which can attach to such bodies; the distinction has been explained by Wade thus:

> There is the family of ordinary private law remedies such as damages, injunction, and declaration; and there is a special family of public law remedies, principally certiorari, prohibition and mandamus, collectively known as the prerogative remedies . . . Within the 'ordinary' and 'prerogative' families the various remedies could be sought separately or together or in the alternative. But each family had its own distinct procedure. Damages, injunctions and declarations were sought in an ordinary action, as in private law; but prerogative remedies had to be sought by a procedure of their own, which could not be combined with an ordinary action . . . This anomaly, though it gave rise to little difficulty in practice, was an obvious target for law reform; and in 1977 it was removed by the provision of a comprehensive procedure, 'application for judicial review', under which remedies in both families became interchangeable.[15]

In *Cooper*'s case, the plaintiff brought his action on the basis of trespass, a part of the law of tort, and was awarded damages – a member of the 'family' of ordinary private-law remedies. The Board of Works was held liable, just as if the Board had been a

---

15 H. W. R. Wade and C. F. Forsyth, *Administrative Law* (9th edn., 2004, Oxford University Press), pp 559–60.

private individual. This, of course, is because the Board was a *corporate body*, that is, a body treated in law as if it were a person, as in the case of the limited company. Within the field of administration and government, many agencies and departments enjoy corporate status. Thus, local authorities, many government departments and central government itself (as the *Crown*) are corporate bodies, as are such varied agencies as health authorities, the British Airports Authority, the British Broadcasting Corporation and many more. The status of such bodies, and their relationship with government departments involved with their functions, is established by the statutes (or, as in the case of the BBC, the Royal Charters) which bring them into existence. Their liability for wrongful acts, however, depends upon a variety of factors, such as the precise extent of their powers or duties as laid down in the relevant statutes, or the kind of wrongful act which is the subject of the complaint.

It is crucial, for example, especially when considering private-law remedies of the kind sought in *Cooper*'s case, to identify the appropriate defendant. In *Stanbury v Exeter Corpn* in 1905,[16] the plaintiff brought an action for negligence against a local authority, which was the employer of an inspector of animals. The Diseases of Animals Act 1894 imposed a duty on local authorities to appoint inspectors, and regulations made by the relevant government minister under the Act imposed certain duties on them. In this case, the inspector had seized sheep believed to be infected, at a market, and it was of this action that the plaintiff complained. The action failed, however: the court pointed out that the inspector's duty was imposed directly upon him by ministerial regulation, and *not upon the local authority which employed him*. The authority could thus not be held vicariously liable (see chapter 9) for the alleged wrongful act of the inspector, for in these circumstances it was the inspector, and not the local authority, who should properly have been the defendant.

It is convenient to mention briefly here the liability in private law of the *Crown* (the legal form of central government administration) in general. The main provisions are contained in the Crown Proceedings Act 1947, which puts the Crown in the same position as any other public authority with regard to its liability in tort and contract. Liability will therefore attach to any breach of contract by the government to which it is a party; and to any tortious act, except in so far as an otherwise tortious act might be expressly authorised by statute. This means that if a statute provides that a government department is empowered to do an act which inevitably results in, for example, discomfort to other private individuals, then what would otherwise be actionable private nuisance is rendered lawful by virtue of that statutory authority. (For example, statutory authority may be given to run a railway which will probably cause discomfort to those living near the railway line.)

Two other important private-law remedies should be noted. These are the equitable remedies of the injunction and the declaration. The injunction is an order requiring a defendant to abstain from doing something (or, in the case of a

---

16 [1905] 2 KB 838.

mandatory injunction, to *do* something);[17] a declaration is simply a statement by the court as to the legal position in a given situation. The latter remedy has been criticised as lacking enforceability, though Garner has pointed out that 'administrative agencies are not to be expected to ignore an adverse declaration of a High Court judge'.[18]

Often, specific remedies are provided by statute, as, for example, where special tribunal machinery is created, or where planning legislation provides for public inquiries in the event of objections to proposed actions. It is in matters such as these that allegations may arise that an agency or minister concerned has failed to observe the procedures laid down by statute; or has acted *ultra vires*, that is, exceeding or abusing the statutory powers; or has committed a breach of natural justice. In such cases, it may be possible to invoke the special public-law remedies known as the 'prerogative remedies' of *certiorari*, prohibition and *mandamus*. The first two were explained by Lord Atkin thus:

> Both writs are of great antiquity, forming part of the process by which the King's Courts restrained courts of inferior jurisdiction from exceeding their powers. Prohibition restrains the tribunal[19] from proceeding further in excess of jurisdiction; certiorari requires the record or the order of the court to be sent up to the King's Bench Division, to have its legality inquired into, and, if necessary, to have the order quashed . . . But the operation of the writs has extended to control the proceedings of bodies which do not claim to be, and would not be recognised as, courts of justice. Whenever any body of persons having legal authority to determine questions affecting the rights of subjects, and having the duty to act judicially, act in excess of their legal authority they are subject to the controlling jurisdiction of the King's Bench Division exercised in these writs.[20]

The names of these prerogative orders have recently been changed as part of the reform and modernisation of the judicial review procedure. '*Certiorari*' is now called a 'quashing order', 'prohibition' has been re-named a 'prohibiting order', and '*mandamus*', which has the effect of commanding a person or agency to perform a public duty imposed on it by law, is now a 'mandatory order'. The circumstances in which these writs may be granted will be discussed in more detail presently, but there are one or two general points which can conveniently be explained here.

First, changes in the procedural rules governing the availability of remedies in administrative law have reduced, to some extent, the procedural problems involved in obtaining these remedies.[21] The application procedure – now called, simply,

---

17 This remedy is rarely used, because the prerogative remedy of *mandamus* serves the same function.
18 J. F. Garner and B. L. Jones, *Administrative Law* (8th edn., 1996, Butterworths), p 312.
19 'Tribunal' is used here in the wide, general sense, meaning any panel having jurisdiction to decide cases, including courts.   20 In *R v Electricity Comrs* [1924] 1 KB 171 at 204.
21 Civil Procedure Rules, Pt 54. On the new rules of judicial review procedure, see M. Fordham, 'Judicial Review: The New Rules' (2001) *Public Law* 4; T. Cornford and M. Sunkin, 'The Bowman Report, Access and the Recent Reforms of the Judicial Review Procedure' (2001) *Public Law* 11.

'application for judicial review' – has been simplified, though problems remain. There remain in these procedures 'protections against claims' against public authorities which 'it [is] not in the public interest for courts of justice to entertain': such claims, according to Lord Diplock in *O'Reilly v Mackman*,[22] include 'groundless, unmeritorious or tardy attacks on the validity of decisions made by public authorities in the field of public law'.[23] This case established that applicants cannot evade these safeguards by using private-law procedures where the public-law element in the application should lead to an application for judicial review. This principle of 'exclusivity' whereby public and private law are kept distinct, has been criticised, and there are exceptions, as where cases involve both public and private law issues.[24] However, the principle remains, and its effect is to maintain the protections for public bodies to which Lord Diplock referred.

The applicant must have *locus standi*, or, as it is now expressed, 'a sufficient interest in the matter to which the application relates'.[25] Historically, the precise requirements for *locus standi*, or simply 'standing', varied, depending on which prerogative remedy was being sought, the requirements for *mandamus* being rather stricter than for *certiorari* or prohibition. Standing in cases involving the latter two remedies would be satisfied in the case of:

> any person who is a 'person aggrieved' and that includes any person whose interests may be prejudicially affected by what is taking place. It does not include a mere busybody who is interfering in things which do not concern him: but it does include any person who has a genuine grievance because something has been done or may be done which affects him.[26]

But what of applications for *mandamus*, especially since the streamlining of the procedure and the use of the term 'sufficient interest' with regard to all the remedies? In *R v Lewisham Union Guardians*[27] in 1897, it was held that the applicant must have a recognisable *legal right* in order to satisfy *locus standi* for an application for *mandamus*. This test was diluted somewhat in later cases:[28] in *IRC v National Federation of Self-Employed and Small Businesses Ltd*,[29] another case where *mandamus* was being sought, the House of Lords discussed the matter of *locus standi* in the light of the newer phrase 'sufficient interest'. Though it is clear from this case that the strict test insisted upon in earlier cases no longer applies,[30]

---

22 [1982] 3 All ER 1124.   23 Ibid., at pp 1130–1131.
24 See *Mercury Communications Ltd v Director General of Telecommunications* [1996] 1 All ER 575; *O'Rourke v Camden London Borough Council* [1997] 3 All ER 23; *Trustees of the Dennis Rye Pension Fund v Sheffield City Council* [1997] 4 All ER 747; *Andreou v Institute of Chartered Accountants in England and Wales* [1998] 1 All ER 14.   25 Supreme Court Act 1981, s 31(3).
26 *R v Liverpool Corpn, ex p Liverpool Taxi Fleet Operators' Association* [1972] 2 QB 299 at 309, per Lord Denning MR.   27 [1897] 1 QB 498.
28 See, for example, *R v Customs and Excise Comrs, ex p Cooke and Stevenson* [1970] 1 All ER 1068; and *R v Hereford Corpn, ex p Harrower* [1970] 3 All ER 460. In both these cases, it was recognised that some genuine interest falling short of a specific legal right might be sufficient to satisfy the *locus standi* requirements for *mandamus*.   29 [1982] AC 617.
30 See also *R v Metropolitan Police Comr, ex p Blackburn* [1968] 1 All ER 763.

and that an applicant need no longer have a specific legal right in the matter, no precise or exact requirements were stated in the *IRC* case. Lord Wilberforce explained that:

> There may be simple cases in which it can be seen at the earliest stage that the person applying for judicial review has no interest at all, or no sufficient interest to support the application: then it would be quite correct at the threshold to refuse him leave to apply . . . But in other cases this will not be so. In these it will be necessary to consider the powers and duties in law of those against whom the relief is asked, the position of the applicant in relation to those powers or duties, and to the breach of those said to have been committed. In other words, the question of sufficient interest can not, in such cases, be considered in the abstract, or as an isolated point: it must be taken together with the legal and factual context.[31]

What seems to emerge from the case is that the 'sufficient interest' requirement will hold for all the remedies, although what will actually *amount* to 'sufficient interest' will vary, depending on 'the strength of the applicant's interest, the nature of the statutory power or duty in issue, the subject-matter of the claim and the type of illegality which is being asserted'.[32] Thus in *R v Liverpool Corpn ex p Liverpool Taxi Fleet Operators' Association*,[33] the corporation was under a duty to issue licences for taxis, and to fix the number of licences to be granted. The corporation decided that the number of licences was to be increased, though the Taxi Fleet Operators' Association was not consulted about this. The Association sought leave to apply for judicial review of the corporation's decision. It was held that the Association had sufficient standing. Although the corporation's decision did not affect taxi drivers' legal rights, it certainly affected their financial interests, and that was held to be sufficient.

What about interest-groups, and groups who claim to be acting in the public interest? In the years following the *IRC* case, a number of groups were allowed standing – the names of the cases themselves indicate the nature of the groups concerned, examples being *Covent Garden Community Association Ltd v Greater London Council*;[34] *R v Hammersmith and Fulham London Borough Council, ex p People Before Profit*[35] and *R v Secretary of State for Social Services, ex p Child Poverty Action Group*.[36] But in *R v Secretary of State for the Environment, ex p Rose Theatre Trust Co*[37] in 1990 it was held that groups of concerned individuals will not usually have *locus standi* to challenge a decision if their only interest involves disagreement with the policy decision involved, though in 1994, in *R v HM Inspectorate of Pollution, ex p Greenpeace Ltd (No 2)*[38] in which Greenpeace sought to challenge a decision concerning the nuclear reprocessing plant at Sellafield, it was held that Greenpeace *did* have *locus standi*, since the issues raised by the application were

---

31 [1982] AC 617 at 630. See also *R v HM Treasury, ex p Smedley* [1985] QB 657.
32 P. P. Craig, *Administrative Law* (5th edn., 2003, Sweet and Maxwell), p 730.
33 [1972] 2 QB 299.   34 [1981] JPL 183.   35 (1981) 80 LGR 322.   36 [1990] 2 QB 540.
37 [1990] 1 All ER 754.   38 [1994] 4 All ER 329.

serious, and the organisation included members who lived in the areas affected. And in *R v Secretary of State for Foreign Affairs, ex p World Development Movement*,[39] again involving a pressure-group, the group concerned, a well-established organisation concerned with foreign aid, was held to have sufficient standing for a number of reasons. In this case, Rose LJ listed a number of factors which might affect the outcome, which included the importance of the issue raised, the absence of any other responsible challenger of the decision in question, the nature of the breach of duty against which a remedy is sought, and the prominent role of the particular applicants in this case, with their 'national and international expertise and interest in promoting the protecting aid to underdeveloped nations'. His lordship acknowledged that recent cases had indicated a rather more liberal stance on this issue,[40] though it remains the case that there are substantial ambiguities in the case law, and that it is at present very difficult to state the legal test for standing with any precision.

There are, in addition, time-limits relating to applications for these remedies. The changed Rules of the Supreme Court provide that an application for leave to apply for judicial review must be made promptly and in any event within three months from the date when the grounds for the application first arose. The Supreme Court Act 1981 provides that in the case of 'undue delay', the court may refuse relief if it is of the opinion that the award of a remedy would cause substantial hardship, would substantially prejudice the right of any person or would be detrimental to good administration. These provisions relate not only to the prerogative remedies, but also to cases involving administrative action where private-law remedies such as declarations, injunctions or damages are sought. These provisions were interpreted in *R v Dairy Produce Quotas Tribunal, ex p Caswell* in 1990[41] to mean that if there has been delay, and in any event if the application for leave has not been made within three months, the court may refuse to grant leave to apply unless it considered that there are good reasons for extending the period. However, even if the court feels that there are good reasons for the delay in applying, it may still refuse leave (or, if leave has already been granted, the remedy applied for) if it is of the opinion that the granting of relief would be likely to cause hardship or prejudice or be detrimental to good administration.

An applicant should also note that the prerogative orders, like the equitable remedies of injunction and declaration, are *discretionary*: even if the challenge to the administrative agency is held to be good, the remedy *may* not be granted if an alternative remedy is available, or if the court thinks that the applicant's own conduct has been unreasonable. For example, in *Ex p Fry*[42] a fireman was ordered to clean another officer's uniform. Rather than carrying out the act, and com-

---

39 [1995] 1 All ER 611.
40 But see the warning note sounded by C. Harlow, 'Public Law and Popular Justice' (2002) 64 *Public Law* 1.   41 [1990] 2 AC 738.   42 [1954] 2 All ER 118.

plaining about it afterwards, he refused to clean the uniform on the ground that the order was not lawful. He was subsequently brought before his commanding officer, who cautioned him by way of punishment. The fireman applied for *certiorari* in the attempt to quash this disciplinary sanction. His application was refused. In the Court of Appeal, Singleton LJ spoke of his refusal to obey the order as 'extraordinarily foolish conduct' and continued: 'in these days it behoves everyone to act reasonably. If every fireman or every policeman is to take it upon himself to disobey an order of this kind and to say "I do not think it is lawful", it will become almost impossible to carry on any public service.'[43]

One issue which has been debated by the courts is the difficulty of defining exactly which organisations and agencies will be subject to judicial review, which is, historically, for reviewing *public*, not private-law agency decisions.[44] One view is that any body deriving its powers and duties from statute, as opposed to private (for example, contractual) agreement, will be subject to judicial review. Certainly, some cases suggest that if a private-law remedy such as breach of contract is available to the aggrieved party, then judicial review will not be applicable.[45] Another view is that everything depends upon the nature of the power in question – whether the exercise of that power has consequences for the public, or a substantial section thereof, and whether or not there may be private-law remedies available, in which case judicial review may be held not to be available. The latter approach, which is inherently more flexible, has been adopted in most recent cases – notably the *Datafin* case in 1987[46] – though several other recent decisions have tended to limit the breadth of this very general test.[47] In *R v Disciplinary Committee of the Jockey Club, ex p Aga Khan* in 1993,[48] for example, it was held that a decision of the Jockey Club was not subject to judicial review because that body did not perform a 'governmental' function.

Because of the impact of the Human Rights Act 1998, however, the matter does not end with the somewhat uncertain state of the case-law. As we noted in chapter 4, by virtue of s6 of the Act, it is unlawful for a 'public authority' to act in a way which is incompatible with any Convention right,[49] and such action may be challenged by means of judicial review. Although the same section excludes from its ambit the Houses of Parliament and anyone 'exercising functions in connection with proceedings in Parliament', it is clear that all other public bodies – including central and local government, the police, the prison service, the immigration

43 [1954] 2 All ER 118 at 121.

44 For an excellent critical discussion of the 'public/private' distinction in this area of law, see I. Harden and N. Lewis, *The Noble Lie* (1986, Hutchinson), esp. chapter 3.

45 See *R v Football Association of Wales, ex p Flint Town United Football Club* [1991] COD 44.

46 *R v City Panel on Takeovers and Mergers, ex p Datafin* [1987] 1 All ER 564; *R v Royal Life Saving Society, ex p Howe* [1990] COD 440; *R v Football Association Ltd, ex p Football League Ltd* [1993] 2 All ER 833. See further D. Pannick, 'Who is subject to judicial review and in respect of what?' (1992) *Public Law* 1.

47 *R v Lloyd's of London, ex p Briggs* [1993] 1 Lloyd's Rep 176.

48 [1993] 2 All ER 853. For similar outcomes see *R v Insurance Ombudsman Bureau, ex p Aegon Life Assurance Ltd* [1994] CLC 88.   49 See chapter 4.

authorities, health and education authorities – will be within the definition of 'public authority'. Section 6 also provides that:

(3) in this section 'public authority' includes—
   (a) a court or tribunal, and
   (b) any person certain of whose functions are functions of a public nature . . .

This subsection clearly recognises that an organisation may perform a mixture of public and private functions, for example:

> a university . . . will be a public authority by virtue of s.6(3)(b), since some of its activities (e.g., selecting, teaching, and examining students in relation to publicly funded degree courses) are almost certainly of a public nature. Actions taken in relation to privately-funded research contracts, however, would not fall within the scope of the (Act).[50]

The definition of 'public authority' within s6 of the Human Rights Act 1998 would seem to be wider than the post-*Datafin* 'narrow' judicial approach. Clearly, the law here is in a state of development – will we see the adoption by the judges of the 'section 6' approach across the whole range of judicial review; or will the courts develop a kind of 'twin track' judicial approach to this issue, with challenges to acts of public bodies based on the Human Rights Act 1998 tending to be recognised as falling within the more liberal definitions of s6, and challenges based on 'traditional' judicial review tending to be caught up in the more restrictive judicial categorisations evident in the case law? It is too early to discern any pattern, though most commentators feel that the former is the preferred, and most likely, outcome.

Given these considerations, and the almost infinite variety of statutory bodies exercising a vast array of discretionary powers as well as statutory duties, further fundamental questions arise. What should be the appropriate role of the law *vis-à-vis* administration? On what grounds may the judges intervene in administrative decision-making? In what kind of case is judicial review applied for? How appropriate are the present remedies, and the procedures for obtaining them, in modern society?

The role of law in the administrative process

We described above the dual role played by the law in relation to the administrative process. Regarding its function as a *facilitating* mechanism: all this means is that we invariably find that administrative agencies (such as tribunals or local authorities) and procedures (such as those affecting the granting or refusal of planning permission) are established by means of legal machinery: statutes or statutory instruments.[51] It is with regard to the *controlling* function of the law that debates and controversies arise.

---

50 R Stone, *Textbook on Civil Liberties and Human Rights* (4th edn., 2002, Oxford University Press), p 19.   51 See chapter 7.

Some writers, notably the constitutional lawyer Dicey writing towards the end of the nineteenth century,[52] consider that the role of the law is to guarantee and protect individual freedom against an increasingly powerful and interventionist state. Dicey contrasted the English position, as he saw it, with that of France, and was deeply critical of the French system of administrative law (the *droit administratif*) which he regarded as a 'body of special rights, privileges or prerogatives as against private citizens'.[53] Rather than create a system of law quite separate from private law, Dicey insisted, it was essential that the administration should remain subject to the 'ordinary law', administered by the 'ordinary courts'. This was an essential means of controlling administrative power, of preserving and protecting the rights of the citizen, and of opposing what he regarded as the move towards collectivism: state intervention on behalf of the community at the expense of individual interests and liberties. Dicey's exposition of the relationship between law and administration was, of course, closely related to his ideological commitment to individualism and his dislike of collectivist state action.

In fact, not only did Dicey misrepresent the French administrative law system,[54] but he also failed to take into account the extent to which various specialised administrative agencies and procedures, all subject to 'non-ordinary' legal rules, had developed in England by the end of the nineteenth century. Despite this, Dicey's work has been very influential,[55] not least because of his insistence on the importance of the *rule of law*: the idea that everyone, including government ministers and other administrative agencies and public bodies, must act according to the law and within the powers vested in them by statutory authority.[56] Furthermore, Dicey's exposition of the rule of law embraces the important proposition that the ordinary courts have inherent jurisdiction to scrutinise administrative actions and declare upon their validity or otherwise, and thus operate as defenders of individual interests and liberties. These principles are still seen by many as crucially significant: 'the rule of law remains . . . a vital necessity to fair and proper government. The enormous growth in the powers of government makes it all the more necessary to preserve it.'[57] Many writers and judges, following Dicey, thus look critically on many statutes which confer extensive discretionary powers on administrative bodies or government ministers, or which purport to exclude administrative action from judicial scrutiny in the courts.

Of particular significance here is the rise of specialised regulatory agencies, introduced alongside the move towards the privatisation of various industries

---

52 A. V. Dicey, *The Law of the Constitution* (first published 1885, 10th edn., reprinted 1985, Macmillan).   53 Ibid., p 336.

54 For informative and concise discussions on the French system of administrative law see, for example, Wade and Forsyth, op. cit., pp 24–5; S. A. de Smith and R. Brazier, *Constitutional and Administrative Law* (8th edn., by R. Brazier, 1998, Penguin), pp 504–505.

55 See the excellent critique of Dicey's writings on the rule of law by H. W. Arthurs, 'Rethinking Administrative Law: A Slightly Dicey Business' (1979) *Osgoode Hall Law Journal* 1.

56 For a useful and concise discussion see J. Jowell, 'The Rule of Law Today' in Jowell and Oliver (eds), *The Changing Constitution*, op. cit.   57 Wade and Forsyth, op. cit., p 24.

previously under nationalised (that is, governmental) control (see chapter 3). Examples include OFTEL (regulating telecommunications), OFGEM (regulating the gas and electricity industries) and OFWAT (charged with the regulation of the water services industry). These agencies are of particular interest because

> The drastic powers of the regulators to investigate, to make rules, to impute fault and to impose penalties involve a mixture of legislative, administrative and judicial functions and pose obvious problems of administrative justice ... [A] person aggrieved by the actions of a regulator sometimes has the right of appeal to a tribunal and thereafter to a court. On other occasions that person will have little choice but to seek judicial review of the regulator's decision.[58]

Despite their expertise and efficiency, however, regulatory agencies attracted the criticisms that they may favour certain organisations or interest-groups as against others,[59] and that they are insufficiently accountable for their decisions and actions. In terms of *political* accountability (that is, to ministers) there may well be problems arising from both the relative invisibility of discreet ministerial direction, and the reluctance of ministers to intervene for fear of political repercussions.

In terms of *legal* accountability, clearly regulatory agencies must remain within the terms of their functions as provided by the statutes which set them up: failure to do so will render them liable to legal intervention by means of judicial review. But one problem here is that the courts can intervene only when aggrieved parties take the initiative in challenging an agency's decision, and even in these (relatively rare) instances, any intervention by the courts is on the ground that something has gone wrong in the individual case, rather than on the basis of a continuous monitoring of the agency's work.

There are a number of theories as to what should be the appropriate role of the law in this area. The traditional justification for judicial intervention is essentially that propounded by Dicey: the need to ensure that public bodies with wide powers are subject to control through the law. This approach has been characterised by Harlow and Rawlings as the 'red-light' conception of administrative law:[60] the idea that the law, or more particularly the judges, must intervene to prevent the abuse or excess of governmental power. An alternative approach – the 'green-light' approach[61] – regards the use of administrative power for the benefit of the community as necessary and appropriate, with the law being used to provide the means whereby administrative activity can more effectively and efficiently be carried out. Harlow and Rawlings explain that this is not to suggest that:

> green light theorists favour unrestricted or arbitrary action by the state. What one person sees as control of arbitrary power may, however, be experienced by another as a brake on progress ... Where red light theorists favour judicial control of

58 Ibid., pp 156–7.
59 See *R v National Lottery Commission, ex p Cameolot Group plc* [2001] EMLR 3.
60 C. Harlow and R. Rawlings, *Law and Administration* (2nd edn., 1997, Butterworths), chapter 2.
61 Ibid., chapter 3.

executive power, green light theorists are inclined to pin their hopes on the political process.[62]

In other words, green-light approaches tend to prefer the idea of control and accountability through democratic political processes, rather than through investing the judges with this role: 'to emphasise this crucial point, in green light theory, decision-making by an elite judiciary imbued with a legalistic, rights-based ideology and eccentric vision of the "public interest" . . . was never a plausible counter to authoritarianism',[63] Approaches which stress the beneficial uses of administrative power may, however, include the recognition of the importance of compensation for those whose private interests are adversely affected by administrative action.

The modern view, which has been called the 'rights-based' approach, links judicial review of administrative action with rights, and especially human rights as defined in the European Convention, incorporated into English law by the Human Rights Act 1998. As we have seen, the Human Rights Act 1998 places the courts, and hence the judges, at centre stage, for it is in the courts that challenges to actions by public bodies which allegedly constitute infringements of protected human rights will now take place.

The Act therefore not only embraces the legitimacy of judicial intervention for the protection of fundamental rights, but also acknowledges the judicial role in the interpretation of legislation in such a way as to protect those rights. Before going on to consider these developments in more detail, it is useful none the less to remind ourselves that some critics question the ability of the judges to take on such a role, for all kinds of reasons:

> The whole history of administrative tribunals shows the need for specialist bodies in certain areas of administration and adjudication. Certainly, if such bodies deal with questions which they were not set up to deal with, and . . . so act outside their jurisdiction, they should be reviewable by the courts. Otherwise they should not be interfered with by the judges who are more likely than not to introduce inconsistency and injustice into complex areas of administration.[64]

Griffith is sceptical of the ways in which the judges in England approach the issue of review of administrative action, holding that not only are they for the most part

---

62 Ibid., p 67. Harlow and Rawlings, in their analysis of the various positions taken by commentators and theorists, develop the analogy to take in approaches which draw on elements of both red and green light positions – 'amber light theory' – and recognise the impact of the changes in systems of control introduced, in particular, during the 1980s, which shifted the emphasis away from control through law and the courts, towards reliance on *political* control through regulatory devices such as audit, efficiency-related performance indicators and privatisation, in the quest for 'economy, efficiency and effectiveness'.

63 Ibid., p 68. For some examples of controversial judicial decision-making in the public-law arena, see J. A. G. Griffith, *The Politics of the Judiciary* (5th edn., 1997, Fontana). For further discussion see chapter 14.

64 J. A. G. Griffith, 'Constitutional and Administrative Law' in P. Archer and A. Martin (eds), *More Law Reform Now* (1983, Barry Rose); and see J. A. G. Griffith, 'The Brave New World of Sir John Laws' (2000) 63 *MLR* 2.

ill-equipped with regard to expertise in most areas of administration, but also that they cannot help but make political decisions, disguised as matters of law, because of their social and professional background. We shall consider this proposition in more detail presently.[65] Whether it is wise to place a great deal of faith in the capacity of political institutions (particularly those involving the democratic process) to impose effective curbs on excessive administrative zeal or abuse of power is debatable. We have seen how powerful interest-groups can influence the legislative process, and interest-groups exist, too, within the administration – notably the civil service.[66] Might there not be a danger that administrative policies emanate from misplaced ideas of community or national interest which are really sectional interests in disguise? If the courts had no role in scrutinising administrative decisions, then how exactly would those decisions be challenged and reviewed? Certainly, the courts have always insisted on their jurisdiction to review the decisions of such agencies in certain circumstances. It has been suggested that, with regard to the relationship between the judiciary and government, the judges must be vigilant guardians of the principles of legality and fundamental rights, and be prepared to strike down what they define as abuses of government power. Certainly, the number of applications for leave to apply for judicial review has dramatically increased in recent years, rising from 356 in 1980[67] to 4,207 in 2004,[68] and many of these are challenges to central government departments or government agencies.

If, in considering the instances discussed in this chapter, the impression is gained that at times administrators and judges have been at loggerheads, with the former striving to minimise judicial intervention and the latter struggling to retain a degree of control over administrative action, then that impression is not far from the truth. The judiciary has consistently and jealously guarded what it regards as the legitimate jurisdiction of the courts over administrative action. The judges have purported to ensure that tribunals, public bodies and government ministers remain true to principles of legality, and do not exceed or abuse powers entrusted to them by Parliament. Unfortunately, because administrative law in England has developed in such a sporadic and piecemeal fashion, with very few clear and consistent principles, such 'principles of legality' are not easy to ascertain. Indeed, some argue that the judges have taken advantage of this lack of precision, together with the discretionary nature of public law remedies, to pick and choose the issues in which they are prepared to intervene. We shall return to this matter presently.

65 And see chapter 14.
66 For useful material on the civil service see G. Drewry, 'The Executive: Towards Accountable Government and Effective Governance?' in Jowell and Oliver, *The Changing Constitution*, op.cit.; D. Oliver, *Constitutional Reform in the UK* (2003, Oxford University Press), ch. 12; H Barnett, *Constitutional and Administrative Law* (4th edn., 2002, Cavendish), pp 322–332.
67 Law Commission, *Administrative Law: Judicial Review and Statutory Appeals*, (1994, Law Com No 226, HMSO).   68 *Judicial Statistics* (2004), p 31.

The grounds for judicial intervention in administrative activity

The main doctrinal foundation on which judicial review of administrative action is based is that of *ultra vires*. To understand this doctrine, however, we must clarify the various types of function which an agency may perform, for the readiness of the courts to intervene depends (or so it appears from the cases) on what *kind* of decision is being challenged.

Given the great variety of administrative powers and procedures, is it possible to develop a coherent classification of functions? The Committee on Ministers' Powers thought so, in its report of 1932.[69] The Committee distinguished between 'judicial' and 'administrative' functions on the basis that the former 'disposes of the whole matter by a finding upon the facts in dispute and an application of the law . . . to the facts so found', whilst the latter involves 'administrative action, the character of which is determined by the minister's free choice'. Thus, 'administrative' is characterised by policy considerations and discretionary choice, and not the application of legal rules. A third function, 'quasi-judicial', was explained as referring to a decision involving the finding of facts, and applying administrative policy thereto.

How helpful are these distinctions? Wade and Forsyth consider that some such analysis helps clarity of thought, but warn that 'the courts . . . are addicted to distinctions which are more superficial and more confusing . . . and which by no means always help to clarify. Nor is it very profitable to take concepts out of their particular contexts and analyse them in the abstract'.[70] Griffith, discussing this aspect of the committee's report, was less charitable, perceiving judicial forces at work behind the scenes:

> You will recall that the quasi-judicial decision was distinguished from the judicial by the fact that the Minister who made the . . . quasi-judicial decision acted according to policy whereas the judge in his judicial functions did, of course, nothing of the kind. In a purely administrative decision, there was no obligation to consider and weigh submissions and argument, to collate evidence or to solve issues. Everything was at the discretion of the administrator.
>
> This nonsense, screaming its absurdities to heaven, was received with respectful, even smug, acceptance by His Majesty's judges. Respectful because they agreed with it. Smug because they were largely responsible for it. What pleased the courts was the almost infinitely extensible or contractable nature of these concepts. Previously the opportunity for the courts to intervene had been measured by a piece of string to which they could add bits or from which they could cut bits but only with some difficulty. Now they were presented with . . . a piece of elastic. If they wished to intervene the administrative became the judicial or the quasi-judicial. If they wished not to intervene they put on their music-hall turn which begins with the words 'Parliament has entrusted the Minister . . . with the power to take these decisions. Far be it from us to presume to replace the discretion of the Minister . . . with our own'.[71]

69 1932, Cmnd 4060, HMSO.   70 Wade and Forsyth, op. cit., p 40–1.
71 J. A. G. Griffith, *Administrative Law and the Judges* (1978, Haldane Society), p 10.

Examination of the extremely complex case law in this area seems to support Griffith's somewhat acerbic remarks, especially those cases which have come before the courts in recent years. Let us consider briefly judicial activity through the cases. It is extremely difficult to classify the case law into watertight compartments, but three general areas will be examined: judicial responses to attempts to oust their jurisdiction, disputes raising the question of *ultra vires*, and cases in which the judges have considered the applicability or otherwise of the principles of natural justice.

Can the courts' jurisdiction be excluded?

Statutory provisions may attempt to prevent the courts from intervening in administrative action in a number of ways. It may be, for example, that a statute provides that a decision of an administrative agency 'shall be final', or even 'shall not be questioned in any legal proceedings whatsoever'. What effect have such phrases had on the courts' capacity to question such decisions?

It has been held on a number of occasions[72] that such terms as this are to be interpreted to mean that there is no appeal from the decision, in the sense that there can be no re-hearing of the case, nor consideration of the facts or the merits of the case before any court; but that the possibility of judicial intervention still exists for the purposes of reviewing the *legality* of the decision: did the deciding agency act *ultra vires*? Was there some other jurisdictional defect affecting the legality of the decision? As Lord Denning said in one case, 'Parliament only gives the impress of finality to the decisions of the tribunal on condition that they are reached in accordance with the law',[73] and the courts have consistently reserved to themselves the jurisdiction to enquire into that condition.

In *Anisminic Ltd v Foreign Compensation Commission* in 1969,[74] a case regarded by many commentators as representing a high-water mark of judicial intervention, the issue concerned the payment of compensation by Egypt to companies and individuals who had suffered damage to their property during the Suez crisis of 1956. The compensation was to be distributed by the Foreign Compensation Commission in accordance with the statutory provision that 'the determination by the Commission of any application made to them under this Act shall not be called into question in any court of law' (Foreign Compensation Act 1950, s 4(4)). One of the principles informing the work of the commission was that only British owners of property were to receive compensation. Because Anisminic Ltd, though originally a British company, had been sold to an Egyptian concern, the commission excluded that company from receiving compensation. On application by the company to challenge this decision, the House of Lords held that the commission, by enquiring into the successors in title of the company, had exceeded their

---

72 For example, *R v Medical Appeal Tribunal, ex p Gilmore* [1957] 1 QB 574.
73 [1957] 1 QB 574 p 585.   74 [1969] 2 AC 147.

jurisdiction, that their decision was null and void on the ground that it was *ultra vires*, and that the clause purporting to exclude the court did not protect the commission from judicial intervention on this ground.

What is interesting about the *Anisminic* case is that the court interpreted the decision of the Foreign Compensation Commission to be an error as to their jurisdiction. As a matter of fact, the compensation fund had been established in 1959, and the relevant statutory instrument containing the commission's terms of reference clearly stated that applicants and their successors in title should be British nationals at that date. Anisminic Ltd had, however, ceased to be in British hands *before* 1959; it would seem that they were, therefore, excluded from compensation. Could not the commission have reached this decision whilst remaining within their jurisdiction? The House of Lords thought not, and the effect of such a conclusion would have been to exclude judicial intervention (because the commission's decision would not then have been *ultra vires*) by reason of the ouster clause. Is this an example of the courts' interpreting facts in particular ways *because they wish to intervene*? Wade and Forsyth are of the opinion that 'there is no situation in which these clauses can have any effect. The policy of the courts thus becomes one of total disobedience to Parliament'.[75]

A less dramatic method of restricting judicial review is for a statute to enact that an administrative decision may be challenged as long as the challenge is brought within a specified period, but may not be challenged after that period has expired. In *Smith v East Elloe Rural District Council*[76] the allegation was that a local authority had acted wrongfully in taking land by means of a compulsory purchase order, the making of which had been procedurally defective. The Acquisition of Land (Authorisation Procedure) Act 1946 provided, *inter alia*, that compulsory purchase orders could be challenged on certain grounds within six weeks, after which such an order could 'not be questioned in any legal proceedings whatsoever'. The House of Lords held that this statutory provision served to exclude the jurisdiction of the court after the six-week period had expired, and the action was not permitted to proceed. From an administrative point of view, it seems sensible that a specific period is provided, after which challenge is ruled out, for 'it would clearly be unsatisfactory if the prospect of some future challenge caused public development schemes to be suspended or delayed on a prolonged basis'.[77] The *East Elloe* case has been followed more recently in *R v Secretary of State for the Environment, ex p Ostler* in 1976,[78] where an individual sought unsuccessfully to challenge compulsory purchase orders for a road scheme; the complainant had not brought his application within the six-week period because he had not realised that his property would be affected.

75 Wade and Forsyth, op. cit., p 719.   76 [1956] AC 736.

77 P. Leyland and G. Anthony, *Textbook on Administrative Law* (5th edn., 2005, Oxford University Press) pp 427–8.

78 [1977] QB 122. And see, for other examples, *R v Secretary of State for the Environment, ex p Kent* [1990] COD 78; *R v Cornwall County Council, ex p Huntingdon* [1994] 1 All ER 694.

Ultra vires: unlimited judicial intervention?

As we have seen, the basic ground for judicial intervention in administrative activity is that the agency in question has exceeded or abused its powers. The *ultra vires* doctrine is extremely wide in its ambit, covering both *substantive ultra vires* (where the body has abused or exceeded its powers) and *procedural ultra vires* (where a specified procedure has not been complied with, such as a requirement to observe the rules of natural justice, considered in the next section). Once again, much depends on the way in which judges interpret both the administrative action and the statutory provisions which authorise that action. One crucial distinction which must be made when considering the authority of an administrative agency is that between statutory *duties* and discretionary *powers* entrusted to an administrative body. If the agency is under a duty to do something, the non-performance of that duty will be actionable. If, however, the agency is simply empowered to do something, then this implies discretionary choice in the matter. But none the less 'the court assumes that Parliament cannot have intended to authorise unreasonable action, which is therefore *ultra vires* and void'.[79]

Thus, for instance, in *R v LCC, ex p Corrie* in 1918,[80] the secretary of a branch of the National League of the Blind applied for permission from the London County Council to sell pamphlets, in aid of blind people, in public parks. The Council wrote to her, stating that their policy was not to issue permits for such purposes, and that it was 'not possible to make exception to this rule even in a most deserving case'. The secretary argued that the Council, by implementing a blanket policy of refusal of permits in all cases, were fettering their discretion to give or refuse consent to particular applications; that they were under a duty to consider her application on its merits; and that only after doing so could they exercise their discretion to give or refuse consent. The court agreed with this argument.

But does this mean that if a statutory provision entrusts an agency with discretionary powers, the courts cannot intervene in the exercise of those powers as long as no accompanying duty is breached? What, for example, do the courts make of statutory terms such as 'if it appears to the Minister that . . .' or 'if the Minister is satisfied that . . .'? To what lengths ought a minister to go in his or her enquiries?

---

79 Wade and Forsyth, op.cit., pp 344–5.
80 [1918] 1 KB 68. And see, for example, *R v Torquay Licensing Justices, ex p Brockman* [1951] 2 KB 784; though compare *British Oxygen Co v Board of Trade* [1971] AC 610, where the House of Lords accepted that an authority may validly work with reference to a general rule or policy so long as it is 'always willing to listen to anyone with something new to say' (at 625). And in *R v Secretary of State for the Environment, ex p Brent London Borough Council* [1982] QB 593, the minister had, after consultation with local authorities, obtained statutory power to reduce the rate support grant to authorities who in his opinion were excessive spenders. After the Act was passed, the minister would not hear any further representations from local authorities, and decided on reducing the grant in respect of several local authorities. The Divisional Court held that he had wrongfully fettered his discretion by refusing to 'listen to any objector who shows that he may have something new to say' (ibid., at 733). And see *R v Secretary of State for the Home Department, ex p Dinc* [1998] COD 326.

How must a minister satisfy him or herself as to a particular state of affairs? If a statute provides, for instance, for objections to a proposal to be heard, does it provide that a minister *must* hear objections, or simply that he or she *may* do so? And if he or she does hear them, is he or she obliged to take those objections into account? Often such questions as this are not easily answered, and are certainly very rarely addressed specifically in the statutes themselves. As has been suggested above, the courts do not readily accept that administrators should have unfettered discretion. Consider, for example, the important case of *Padfield v Minister of Agriculture* in 1968.[81]

Here, the Agricultural Marketing Act 1958 provided that complaints about marketing schemes established under the Act could be heard by a committee of investigation 'if the Minister in any case so directs'. The plaintiff complained about prices paid to farmers such as himself in southern England by the Milk Marketing Board. The minister refused to refer the complaint to the committee of investigation, claiming that he had an absolute discretion in deciding whether or not to refer such complaints. He argued that the complaint should have been handled by the Milk Marketing Board rather than the committee, and that if the latter had dealt with the complaint, he would have been expected to give effect to the committee's recommendations. The House of Lords held that these reasons were not good reasons in law, and that, although the minister had considerable discretion in the matter, he was not entitled to act in such a way as to frustrate the intentions of the statute.

In so far as any general principles are discernible in the law as to when courts may or may not hold administrative action to be *ultra vires*, the leading case usually cited is *Associated Provincial Picture Houses Ltd v Wednesbury Corpn* in 1948.[82] In this case, Lord Greene in the Court of Appeal explained that:

> It is true that discretion must be exercised reasonably. Now what does that mean? Lawyers familiar with the phraseology used in relation to exercise of statutory discretions often use the word 'unreasonable' in a rather comprehensive sense. It has frequently been used and is frequently used as a general description of the things that must not be done. For instance, a person entrusted with a discretion must . . . direct himself properly in law. He must call his own attention to the matters which he is bound to consider. He must exclude from his consideration matters which are irrelevant to what he has to consider. If he does not obey those rules, he may truly be said, and often is said, to be acting 'unreasonably'. Similarly, there may be something so absurd that no sensible person could ever dream that it lay within the powers of the authority. [Consider] the example of the red-haired teacher, dismissed because she had red hair. This is unreasonable in one sense. In another it is taking into consideration extraneous matters. It is so unreasonable that it might almost be described as being done in bad faith; and, in fact, all these things run into one another . . . *It is true to say*

81 [1968] AC 997. But see *Nakkuda Ali v Jayaratne* [1951] AC 66; and see also *Congreve v Home Office* [1976] QB 629; *Secretary of State for Education and Science v Tameside Metropolitan Borough Council* [1977] AC 1014.   82 [1948] 1 KB 223.

> *that, if a decision . . . is so unreasonable that no reasonable authority could ever have come to it, then the courts can interfere.*[83]

Although the '*Wednesbury* principle' has been referred to by the courts in many later cases, it hardly provides a clear legal test for deciding whether an administrative agency has or has not acted unreasonably in particular circumstances. In some cases 'unreasonable' has been treated by the courts as doing something which no sensible person or authority would do. In *Secretary of State for Education and Science v Tameside Metropolitan Borough Council* in 1976,[84] a case concerning the implementation of the then Labour government's policy of introducing comprehensive education, a Conservative-controlled borough council informed the Secretary of State that it did not intend to reorganise the grammar schools in its area along comprehensive lines. Plans had, in fact, been drawn up for the reorganisation of the schools by the preceding Labour-controlled administration in the borough, and the Secretary of State directed the council that they must implement those plans. The statutory provision entitling the minister to give such a direction was contained in s 68 of the Education Act 1944, which stated that 'if the Secretary of State is satisfied . . . that any local education authority . . . have acted or are proposing to act unreasonably . . . he may . . . give such directions . . . as appear to him to be expedient'. The House of Lords upheld the decision of the council. The court's interpretation of the statutory provision was that 'unreasonably' meant behaving in a manner in which no reasonable authority would behave; it did not mean behaving in a manner with which the minister simply disagreed, and the facts revealed no evidence on which the Secretary of State could have come to the conclusion that the authority was acting 'unreasonably' in the above sense of the word.

In other cases, however, 'unreasonable' has been treated as denoting a somewhat different standard. For instance, in *Wheeler v Leicester City Council* in 1985,[85] the council banned a rugby club from using playing fields in a public park. The facts of this case occurred some years before the end of apartheid in South Africa, and the council had imposed the ban because three of the club's players had been selected by the English Rugby Football Union to play a tour of matches in that country, and had participated in that tour. The ban was imposed after the tour of South Africa had ended. In response to this challenge to their action, the council, which was firmly committed to racial equality and fairness, argued that it had been motivated by a concern to promote harmonious race relations in the city, in accordance with the Race Relations Act 1976. The court's view was that the imposition of the ban was unlawful: despite the council's motivation, it was unreasonable and unfair to

---

83 At 229–230 (emphasis added). For a useful discussion which attempts to categorise the various ways a public body may act *ultra vires*, but which recognises the fact that, as Lord Greene said, 'all these things run into one another', see H. Barnett, *Constitutional and Administrative Law* (4th edn., 2002, Cavendish), chapter 25. And see Lord Irvine of Lairg QC, 'Judges and Decision-makers: The Theory and Practice of *Wednesbury* Review' (1996) 59 *Public Law*.

84 [1976] 3 All ER 665. And see *Laker Airways Ltd v Department of Trade* [1977] QB 643. For discussion see J. Jowell and A. Lester, 'Beyond Wednesbury: Substantive Principles of Administrative Law' (1987) *Public Law* at 368.   85 [1985] AC 1054.

punish the club for failing to comply with the council's demands. The actions of the three players had not been illegal; most of the judges (except, perhaps for Lord Roskill)[86] however seem to have felt that the council's action, though 'unreasonable', had not been 'absurd' or 'perverse' – it was simply unfair and hence unlawful.

Interestingly, in *Council of Civil Service Unions v Minister for the Civil Service* in 1985[87] – the 'GCHQ case' – the word 'irrational' seems to have been substituted for 'unreasonable' in Lord Diplock's explanation of the grounds for judicial intervention:

> One can conveniently classify under three heads the grounds on which administrative action is subject to control by judicial review. The first ground I would call 'illegality', the second 'irrationality' and the third 'procedural impropriety' . . . By 'illegality' as a ground for judicial review I mean that the decision-maker must understand correctly the law that regulates his decision-making power and must give effect to it . . . By 'irrationality' I mean . . . a decision which is so outrageous in its defiance of logic or of accepted moral standards that no sensible person who had applied his mind to the question to be decided could have arrived at it.[88]

In the *GCHQ* case, the Prime Minister, as minister responsible for the civil service, issued an Order in Council which prohibited civil servants working at the Government Communications Headquarters (GCHQ) from belonging to trade unions. This action had been taken in order to prevent any industrial action which might affect the work of monitoring signals and hence national security. In the House of Lords, the court acknowledged the legitimate expectation of the civil servants to be consulted prior to an executive action such as this, which clearly affected their employment rights, that expectation could be displaced by the more important consideration of national security. In *R v Secretary of State for the Home Department, ex p Brind* in 1991,[89] it was held not to be unreasonable for the Home Secretary to ban the broadcasting of speeches by representatives of Sinn Fein or the Irish Republican Army. It was recognised that such a ban entailed a denial of the freedom of expression, and indeed the European Convention of Human Rights was considered in this case. It was held however that there could be no presumption that the discretionary power exercised in this case by the Home Secretary (by virtue of powers given to him under the Broadcasting Act 1981) *must* be exercised in a manner consistent with the European Convention, whose contents were not, of course, at that time incorporated into English law.

And in *R v Ministry of Defence, ex p Smith*,[90] which concerned the enforced discharge from the armed forces of the applicants in pursuance of a Ministry of Defence policy to the effect that homosexual men and women could not serve in the armed forces, it was argued that the policy was in breach of the European

---

86 See Lord Roskill's judgment at p 1079.   87 [1985] 2 All ER 1106.   88 Ibid., at 950.
89 [1991] 1 All ER 720.   90 [1996] 1 All ER 257.

Convention, as well as a breach of the European Community Directive[91] on equal treatment for men and women in the field of employment. It was held, however, that the policy, which was supported by Parliament, could not be said to be irrational; that the Directive was not concerned with sexual orientation; and that breaches of the European Convention on Human Rights must be dealt with in that court, and not the English courts. Since the enactment of the Human Rights Act 1998, of course, this is no longer the case, and we will return to this issue presently.

We have just seen examples of cases in which the courts have refused to intervene on the basis of 'unreasonableness'. It is clear, on the other hand, that an apparently unlimited discretionary power will not in itself prevent the courts from finding grounds for intervention, nor from declaring, where they think it appropriate, that the exercise of such discretion might be *ultra vires*.

As the *Wednesbury* principle makes clear, another justification for overturning the exercise of administrators' discretionary powers is that the agency in question has taken into account irrelevant considerations,[92] or has acted with improper motives. In *Bromley London Borough Council v Greater London Council* in 1982,[93] the Greater London Council (GLC), following its election promise to cut London Transport fares, had sought to levy a supplementary rate upon the London boroughs in order to finance the reduction. Bromley London Borough Council challenged the validity of this supplementary rate, and both the Court of Appeal and the House of Lords held that the GLC had exceeded its powers. Not only did the GLC have a statutory duty to encourage the 'economic' operation of London Transport and not deliberately (and avoidably) run the system at a considerable loss, but also, said the House of Lords, the GLC in taking these steps was in breach of its 'fiduciary duty' towards ratepayers to maintain a fair balance between the provision of services and the cost to those ratepayers. It is interesting that, in the Court of Appeal, the GLC was expressly criticised for interpreting an election promise as a firm mandate – something which, in the *Tameside* case, the local authority was applauded for doing.

There are many other situations in which the courts have invoked the doctrine of *ultra vires*: where local authority by-laws have been held to be unreasonable,[94] for example, or where a person possessing a statutory power has been held to have wrongly delegated that power to another.[95] The cases mentioned here show how wide the applicability of the *ultra vires* doctrine is, especially in the hands of judges who, it seems, will try to find grounds for intervention if they desire to step in. It is certainly hard to state precisely any set of principles which consistently inform judicial decisions in this area, and some of the grounds for intervention (such as

---

91 Council Directive 76/207/EEC. See chapter 8.
92 For example, *R v Birmingham Licensing Planning Committee, ex p Kennedy* [1972] 2 QB 140.
93 [1983] 1 AC 768; *Prescott v Birmingham Corpn* [1955] Ch 210; *Roberts v Hopwood* [1925] AC 578.
94 *Powell v May* [1946] KB 330; the *Tameside* case, above.
95 Though the courts accept that a minister's powers can properly be delegated to his departmental officials: *Carltona Ltd v Commissioner of Works* [1943] 2 All ER 560.

'unreasonableness') are intrinsically flexible and imprecise. It may be, too, that the extent of judicial intervention depends upon the overall complexion of the judiciary at any particular period.[96] Sometimes, the judges have been somewhat reluctant to interfere with ministerial discretion,[97] and at others, they seem prepared to go so far as to take 'it upon themselves to tell Ministers that they acted wrongly not because they had taken decisions which were *ultra vires* in substance or in procedure but because they had taken policy decisions on grounds which the courts disapproved of'.[98]

The Human Rights Act 1998: 'in law, context is everything'

In the *GCHQ* case, Lord Diplock considered whether there might be a further ground for striking down administrative action: that of 'proportionality'. This concept has its origins in European law, and means that *administrative authorities must use appropriate means to achieve a particular objective, and must not go beyond what is necessary to achieve that objective.* Thus in *EC Commission v United Kingdom* in 1982,[99] the European Court held that the United Kingdom government had acted disproportionately, in the above sense, in restricting the importation of poultry products in order to prevent a particular disease: as the ban affected countries where the disease had not been detected for a number of years, the action was out of proportion to the objective. And in the (English) case of *R v Barnsley Metropolitan Borough Council, ex p Hook*[100] the Court of Appeal held that the revocation of a market-stall holder's licence on the grounds that the holder had urinated in the street was disproportionate to the offence, which it described as an 'isolated and trivial incident'. But in the case of *Brind*, discussed above, the same court took a different view of the concept. One of the grounds on which the Home Secretary's prohibition on broadcasts was challenged was that the prohibition was out of proportion to the stated aims of preventing offence being caused to viewers and listeners, and of ensuring that terrorist organisations were starved of the 'oxygen of publicity'. The court declined to accept the 'proportionality' argument as a distinct and separate ground, preferring to treat the situation within the general test of 'unreasonableness'.

With the enactment of the Human Rights Act 1998, and the consequent incorporation into English law of most of the provisions of the European Convention of Human Rights, the principle of proportionality must be reconsidered by the courts when dealing with applications for judicial review on the grounds of *ultra vires*. This is because proportionality has been adopted by both the European Court of Human Rights and the European Court of Justice[101] as a relevant test for deciding

96 See chapter 14.
97 For example, various cases decided during wartime suggest judicial reluctance to interfere with administrative action of certain types, probably on the basis that such intervention is inappropriate during emergency conditions. The best known such case is probably *Liversidge v Anderson* [1942] AC 206.
98 Griffith, *Administrative Law and the Judges*, op. cit., p 16, discussing the *Padfield* and *Tameside* cases.
99 [1982] 3 CMLR 497.   100 [1976] 1 WLR 1052.   101 See chapter 8.

on the legality of the actions of public bodies. In *Smith and Grady v United Kingdom*,[102] ex-members of the armed forces, dismissed on the grounds of their acknowledged homosexuality, whose claims under judicial review had been rejected in the English courts (see above), claimed before the European Court of Human Rights that their Convention rights had been breached. That court held that there had indeed been a breach of the applicants' rights under Article 8, concerned with the right to privacy.

Article 8(1) states that 'everyone has the right to respect for his private and family life, his home and his correspondence', and there can be interference by a public body with this right only if such interference is 'in accordance with the law and is necessary in a democratic society in the interests of national security, public safety or the economic well being of the country, for the prevention of disorder or crime, for the protection of health or morals, or for the protection of the rights and freedoms of others' (Article 8(2)). The court held that the ban on homosexuals serving in the armed forces could be justified only if it was established that it was 'necessary in a democratic society', that it answered a 'pressing need', and that it was 'proportionate'. In considering the refusal of the English courts to interfere with the Ministry of Defence's ban, the European Court of Human Rights stated that:

> the threshold at which the High Court and Court of Appeal could find the Ministry of Defence policy irrational was placed so high that it effectively excluded any consideration by the domestic courts of the question whether the interference with the applicants' rights answered a pressing social need or was proportionate to the national security and public order aims pursued, principles which lie at the heart of the Court's analysis of complaints under Article 8 of the Convention . . . In such circumstances, the Court finds that the applicants had no effective remedy in relation to the violation of their right to respect for their private lives guaranteed by Article 8. Accordingly, there has been a violation of Article 13[103] of the Convention.

The incompatibility between the criterion of 'proportionality', and the test of 'irrationality'/'*Wednesbury* unreasonableness' arose once again in the House of Lords' decision in *R (Daly) v Secretary of State for the Home Department* in 2001.[104] The facts were that the applicant, who was serving a sentence of imprisonment, had, in his cell, correspondence with his solicitor about his case. He was subject to a policy of cell searching, as instructed by the Home Secretary in pursuance of powers contained in the Prison Act 1952. The policy required that prisoners be excluded during cell searches and provided that officers were to examine, but not to read, any legal correspondence in the cell to check that nothing had been written on it by the prisoner, or stored between its leaves, which was likely to endanger

102 (2000) 29 EHRR 493.
103 Article 13 is concerned with the right to an effective remedy for breaches of other rights contained in the Convention. This Article was not incorporated into English law by the Human Rights Act 1998, the government arguing that provision for adequate remedies was provided within the Act itself, in s 8.   104 [2001] 2 AC 532.

prison security. The applicant applied for judicial review of the decision to require prisoners' absence during the examination of their legally privileged correspondence.

In the House of Lords, the application was successful. It was held that prisoners had the right to confidential privileged communication with their legal adviser, and that the policy of requiring the prisoner's exclusion when such correspondence might be examined during a cell search was a breach of Article 8. The need to maintain security, order and discipline in prisons and to prevent crime, might justify the exclusion of an individual prisoner if particular circumstances justified it, but the blanket exclusion of all prisoners during examination of privileged correspondence amounted to a degree of intrusion greater than was justified by the objectives it was intended to serve. The policy was therefore unlawful under common law, because it undermined the privileged (that is, protected) nature of correspondence with one's legal advisor; and it was a breach of the applicant's right to privacy under Article 8. The interference was not proportionate: it was greater than was necessary for the prevention of disorder and crime.

Lord Steyn explained that there was a material difference between the *Wednesbury* grounds of review, and the approach of proportionality applicable in respect of review where Convention rights are at stake:

> The starting point is that there is an overlap between the traditional grounds of review and the approach of proportionality. Most cases would be decided in the same way whichever approach is adopted. But the intensity of review is somewhat greater under the proportionality approach . . . I would mention three concrete differences without suggesting that my statement is exhaustive. First, the doctrine of proportionality may require the reviewing court to assess the balance which the decision maker has struck, not merely whether it is within the range of rational or reasonable decisions. Secondly, the proportionality test may go further than the traditional grounds of review inasmuch as it may require attention to be directed to the relative weight accorded to interests and considerations. Thirdly, even the heightened scrutiny test developed in *R v Ministry of Defence, ex p Smith* is not necessarily appropriate to the protection of human rights. It will be recalled that in *Smith* the Court of Appeal reluctantly felt compelled to reject a limitation on homosexuals in the army . . . The European Court of Human Rights came to the opposite conclusion . . . [T]he intensity of the review, in similar cases, is guaranteed by the twin requirements that the limitation of the right was necessary in a democratic society, in the sense of meeting a pressing social need, and the question whether the interference was really proportionate to the legitimate aim being pursued.
>
> The differences in approach between the traditional grounds of review and the proportionality approach may therefore sometimes yield different results. It is therefore important that cases involving Convention rights must be analysed in the correct way. This does not mean that there has been a shift to merits review. On the contrary, . . . the respective roles of judges and administrators are fundamentally distinct and will remain so . . . [T]he intensity of review in a public law case will depend on the subject

matter in hand. That is so even in cases involving Convention rights. In law context is everything.[105]

If the adoption – at least for cases involving the Human Rights Act 1998 – of the 'proportionality' test requires the court to 'assess the balance which the decision maker has struck' and requires 'attention to be directed to the relative weight accorded to interests and considerations', it will be interesting to see, as the case law develops, how the courts maintain the proposition that these developments do not involve a 'shift to merits review'.[106] In the important case in 2004 of *A and Others v Home Secretary*[107] the House of Lords had to consider the lawfulness of the indefinite detention without trial of non-British people who were suspected of being involved in terrorism. The Home Secretary had been given the power to authorise such detention by the provisions of the Anti-Terrorism, Crime and Security Act, introduced in 2001 after the terrorist attacks on the USA in September of the same year. Nine people had been detained under these powers and in these proceedings challenged the Home Secretary's power regarding detention.

Clearly, on the face of it, indefinite detention without trial is an infringement of the right to liberty guaranteed by Article 5 of the European Convention on Human Rights, but that ECHR provision contains a number of exceptions, and Article 15 expressly provides that many of the rights (including those under Article 5) may be 'derogated from' (that is, departed from or taken away) in the event of 'war or other public emergency threatening the life of the nation', to the extent 'strictly required by the exigencies of the situation'. Such a derogation was agreed by the government with the Council of Europe.

Among the many issues arising from the case and considered carefully by the House of Lords in this case was the *proportionality* of indefinite detention without trial in these circumstances. Acknowledging that the assessment of any threat to national security was a matter for political, rather than judicial, judgment, it was the task of the courts to protect Convention rights, especially those as important as the right to liberty, by undertaking an 'intensive review' of the measures adopted in the particular circumstances.

In the view of a majority of the House of Lords, the indefinite detention provision was a disproportionate measure. Various reasons were given for this conclusion. In the first place, the 2001 Act was discriminatory (contrary to Article 14 of the European Convention) in that the provisions as to indefinite detention without trial applied to non-British nationals suspected of international terrorism but not to British nationals who might be suspected of the same threat. Second, these provisions were held to be disproportionate – some judges suggested that those suspected might have been dealt with in some less draconian ways than indefinite

---

105 Ibid., at 547–548.
106 See J. Jowell, 'Beyond the Rule of Law: Towards Constitutional Judicial Review' [2000] *Public Law* 671; P. P. Craig, *Administrative Law* op. cit., pp 617–32.   107 [2004] UKHL 56.

imprisonment without trial. The House of Lords therefore declared that the 2001 Act was incompatible with the European Convention on Human Rights.

The increasing importance of the concept of proportionality in this area[108] has led to an exploration of the relationship between proportionality and the traditional notion of 'unreasonableness' (discussed above). Some have questioned whether there is any substantial difference between the two, and indeed whether proportionality is, in fact, more flexible and therefore a more appropriate tool for the assessment of a public body's actions. For example, in the *Alconbury* case,[109] Lord Slynn said

> I consider that even without reference to the Human Rights Act 1998 the time has come to recognise that this principle is part of English administrative law, not only when judges are dealing with Community acts but also when they are dealing with acts subject to domestic law. Trying to keep the Wednesbury principle and proportionality in separate compartments seems to me to be unnecessary and confusing.[110]

At this stage, as the judicial and academic debates on the matter continue, it remains to be seen whether *Wednesbury* unreasonableness will eventually be superseded by the newer but extremely significant concept of proportionality as a distinct ground for judicial review.

Natural justice: the 'duty to act fairly'

Similar patterns of judicial activity can be seen in considering the applicability or otherwise of the principles of natural justice. This term has no mysterious or magical meaning: it simply refers to a duty to act fairly, and this duty is usually defined as comprising two aspects. The first, the *audi alteram partem* principle, is that a body having a duty to observe natural justice shall give each party the opportunity to be heard; the second principle, *nemo judex in causa sua*, means that 'no one shall be judge in his own cause', or in other words, that the decision must not be tainted by bias.

In his explanation of the public-law remedies of *certiorari* and prohibition, Lord Atkin referred to 'any body of persons having legal authority to determine questions affecting the rights of subjects, and having the duty to act judicially'. 'Acting judicially', it will be recalled, has long been regarded as different from 'acting administratively', and in the law relating to natural justice much has depended on this distinction. We have seen some criticisms of this, and there is a strong argument that the distinction between 'judicial' and 'administrative' is fallacious. Even so, the distinction is one to which the courts for many years subscribed; and, at least until *Ridge v Baldwin* in 1964,[111] they held that the duty to observe natural justice

108 See also *R (Farrakhan) v Home Secretary* [2002] EWCA Civ 606; *R (ProLife Aliance) v British Broadcasting Corporation* [2003] 2 All ER 756; *R (Clays Lane Housing Co-operative Ltd) v The Housing Corporation* [2004] EWCA Civ. 1658.

109 *R (on the application of Alconbury Developments Ltd) v Secretary of State for the Environment, Transport and the Regions* [2003] 2 AC 295.

110 At p 321. See also the judgments in *Daly*, op. cit.   111 [1964] AC 40.

existed only where the agency in question was acting *judicially*, and not where the decision was purely *administrative*. Let us consider some of the more important cases.

We have already encountered, in *Cooper v Wandsworth Board of Works* in 1863,[112] circumstances where the courts in the last century were prepared to hold that a public body had acted wrongly in carrying out an action affecting the property of another without giving that other a chance to put his case. If, however, we look more closely at the nature of the power which was vested in the Board of Works, it is plainly administrative: the Board was not engaged in any form of *adjudication* of Cooper's legal rights, but rather had an administrative discretion to take certain action (to pull down the house) if a specific condition was satisfied (failure to give due notice before starting to build). The court none the less interpreted the Board's decision as being 'judicial', Byles J stating categorically that 'they had acted judicially, because they had to determine the offence, and they had to apportion the punishment as well as the remedy'.

For many years thereafter, the courts' approach to the question as to whether natural justice applied was to consider the nature of the function performed by the administrative body: was it judicial or administrative? Even when it was held that the agency was performing a judicial function, however, the matter still remained as to *how* the principles of natural justice should be observed. In *Local Government Board v Arlidge* in 1915,[113] for example, a local authority had made a closing order in respect of Arlidge's house, which the authority thought was unfit for habitation. Arlidge appealed against this decision to the Local Government Board; a public inquiry was duly held before a housing inspector, and the latter sent his report back to the Board, who then confirmed the closing order. Arlidge sought to quash this decision on the grounds, *inter alia*, that he had not been given an oral hearing by the Board, and had not been allowed to see the inspector's report. The House of Lords rejected his complaint, being of the opinion that, *although the Board was acting judicially*, it was not appropriate to expect that it should operate like a court of law, but that as long as it acted fairly it could legitimately follow its own procedures.

In *Errington v Minister of Health* in 1935,[114] a case concerning a slum clearance order, council officials and civil servants had private discussions after a public inquiry had been held, and visited the houses affected by the order without informing the owner. The court here held that the order was made in breach of natural justice, and quashed the clearance order, stating that although the minister's final decision was an administrative one, the public inquiry procedure was judicial or quasi-judicial, and natural justice should have been observed. But in 1948, in *Franklin v Minister of Town and Country Planning*,[115] the minister had made a draft order designating Stevenage as the first 'new town' under the New Towns Act 1946. A public inquiry was held after objections were made to this proposal. Before this,

---

112 Above, note 14.   113 [1915] AC 120. And see *Board of Education v Rice* [1911] AC 179.
114 [1935] 1 KB 249.   115 [1948] AC 87.

the minister had made public statements that Stevenage was to be a new town, and had answered objectors at a meeting by saying, 'It is no good your jeering – it is going to be done.' After the inquiry, the minister confirmed the order. Rejecting the challenge to the legality of the minister's action on the grounds of bias, the House of Lords held that the minister's actions throughout were 'purely administrative', and that therefore there was no obligation to observe natural justice.

It is difficult to reconcile decisions like these, but it was not until 1964 that a different approach began to be adopted. In that year, in *Ridge v Baldwin*,[116] a chief constable who had been acquitted of criminal charges was dismissed by the Watch Committee. Although there was no statutory duty to do so, the House of Lords held that he should have been given a hearing before the dismissal, and that the dismissal was therefore void. After this case, the courts began to decide that natural justice might apply even though the functions called in question might be administrative ones. In *Re HK (An Infant)* in 1967,[117] the court held that natural justice applied to an immigration officer's decision as to whether an immigrant was entitled to enter the country, even though the decision was stated not to be judicial. The Lord Chief Justice said that there was a requirement to act 'fairly', and this line was followed in later cases until in *Council of Civil Service Unions v Minister for the Civil Service*[118] in 1984, it was stated in the House of Lords that the notion of 'natural justice' should be 'replaced by speaking of a duty to act fairly'.

In the same case, the court recognised the significance of the concept of 'legitimate expectation' in the context of judicial review enquiries concerned with natural justice. This concept has been summarised thus:

> Broadly speaking, legitimate expectation has been taken to mean that some advantage, for example, the entitlement to consultation, may be given to a person in a situation where they have no legal right. Essentially, they may have a legitimate expectation of a particular type of treatment. If this expectation is not realised, it will be protected by judicial review proceedings.[119]

So, in *R v North and East Devon Health Authority, ex p Coughlan* in 1999,[120] the health authority had decided to close a home for the severely disabled. The applicant was a resident in the home, and the authority had decided to transfer her to the care of a local authority. The applicant had, however, been promised by Exeter Health Authority (the predecessor to the present health authority) that the home would be her home for life, and the court held that this promise created a legitimate expectation which could not be overridden by any public interest. The case law is inconsistent, however, as regards what the courts will and will not accept as 'legitimate expectation' and there are judicial dicta to the effect that this notion may be no more than one aspect of the duty to act fairly.[121]

116 Op. cit.   117 [1967] 2 QB 617.   118 Op. cit.
119 P. Leyland and G. Anthony, *Textbook on Administrative Law* (5th edn., 2005, Oxford University Press), p 360.   120 [2001] QB 213.
121 See the remarks of Lord Templeman in *Lloyd v McMahan* [1987] AC 625.

If there has been an express undertaking, then the person to whom the undertaking was made may legitimately expect that the undertaking will be honoured. In *R (on the application of A) v Lord Saville of Newdigate (Bloody Sunday Enquiry)* in 1999,[122] the applicants had been soldiers present in Londonderry, Northern Ireland, on 'Bloody Sunday', 30 January 1972. They had been involved in the firing of live ammunition, and when they gave evidence to the Widgery enquiry, set up to look into these events, there had been an express assurance as to their anonymity. A new enquiry into the events of 30 January 1972 was set up in 1998, under Lord Saville, and it was made clear that the previous assurances as to anonymity would not apply – the applicants would have to provide fresh evidence as to why their anonymity should be preserved. The applications to have the original promises of anonymity honoured were successful in the Court of Appeal, where it was held that the original promise created a legitimate expectation that this would be a continuing promise to uphold anonymity, and that the new enquiry had not accorded the original promise sufficient weight when considering its own procedures.

Conclusion

Without a doubt, the numbers of applications for the judicial review have risen dramatically over the past 25 years or so, but despite the increase in applications, this area of law has been heavily criticised by many writers. McAuslan,[123] for example, argued some years ago that developments in administrative law were fundamentally out of step with the aims and objectives of modern administration. He used the notion of 'collective consumption', by which he meant 'those consumption processes whose organisation and management cannot be other than collective given the nature and size of the problems'.[124] Examples include education and health services, environmental, housing and transport facilities, and land use and planning. The point about such services is that they are, and must be, 'organised, planned and managed on a collective public basis – by central and local governments or by quangos – as they are consumed collectively'.[125] And McAuslan pointed out that the development of administrative agencies to make decisions and carry out policies in these, and many other, areas has involved many different types of problems and tensions, often about resources and resource-management, which are rarely if ever addressed by the courts through judicial review.

McAuslan's argument is that tensions within the administrative framework, caused by reductions in public expenditure and consequent struggles over resources, become resolved through judicial review procedures into *legal* disputes, whereas such disputes are often *political* problems about resources and different

---

122 [1999] 4 All ER 860.
123 P. McAuslan, 'Administrative Law, Collective Consumption and Judicial Policy' (1983) 46 *MLR* 1. See also Craig, op. cit.; H. W. Arthurs, 'Rethinking Administrative Law: A Slightly Dicey Business' (1979) 17 *Osgoode Hall Law Journal* 1; C. Harlow and R. Rawlings, *Law and Administration* (2nd edn., 1997, Butterworths).   124 Ibid., at 2.   125 Ibid.

approaches to policy. The law's response to such cases, because of the nature of judicial review proceedings, is to *individualise* and thus *privatise* what are essentially *collective, public* questions. McAuslan, like Griffith, considers that the judges perform a political role, albeit disguised in legalistic terms.

The traditional role of judicial review may be summed up as dispute-resolution in individual cases, but is also about securing of accountability of public bodies and promoting good public administration. Harlow and Rawlings suggest that these functions are brought together into what they term a 'public interest model' of judicial review, 'in which the courtroom is seen as a platform for public discussion and forum for debate of matters of public interests by litigants who are increasingly interest and pressure groups', and in such a context, they suggest, courts are beginning to function as a 'surrogate political process, responsive to the pressure created by generous access to the courtroom'.[126] Such a process would clearly undermine not only the traditional purpose and function of judicial review, but would also further reduce the real extent to which the doctrine of the separation of powers operates in this country, bringing the judges into the open fields of political discourse. Of course, commentators such as Griffith have long argued that judges acted politically *despite* constitutional doctrine to the contrary, and it is certainly difficult to read some of the cases discussed in this chapter without finding a measure of agreement with this point of view.

Whatever the views of the theorists, it is now the Human Rights Act 1998, more than any judicial, political or academic forces, that seems to be shaping the future of judicial review. We saw above, for example, how decisions not only of the European Court of Human Rights, but also – in the *Daly* case – of the House of Lords, seem to be shaking the foundations of the citadel of '*Wednesbury* unreasonableness'. It remains to be seen whether the judges who develop this area of law will simply build an extension to house 'human rights' issues onto the existing structure of judicial review, or whether we will see a completely new jurisprudence built on the new foundations of the Human Rights Act 1998, and the case law and concepts of the European Court of Human Rights.

126 Op. cit, pp 602–603.

13

The legal profession

The law is one of the most powerful carriers of dominant social definitions of acceptable and unacceptable conduct. It is perhaps the most significant social institution for the settlement of disputes, and it contains within its rules and procedures means whereby infringements of the law, from the trivial to the most serious, can be dealt with. Lawyers form an important group of the various personnel involved in these procedures, and it is important to understand the kinds of services which lawyers provide, as well as the occupational, social and educational background of this body of experts whose work is so closely tied up with the maintenance of social norms embodied in the law and the legal system.

Lawyers, it is often said, are a response to a social need. Disputes crop up in all corners of society, among every social class, and such disputes and problems can involve anything from marriage breakdown to criminal charges, contested wills to commercial transactions. The trouble is that in many cases the solution to the dispute is not something which can be determined like a mathematical equation. Most cases involve questions of social values, the most fundamental of which is probably 'justice', and judgments about those cases are based upon evaluation rather than issues of hard fact. Law embodies dominant social norms and values, and lawyers are engaged in their everyday work in maintaining those values through their function of implementing the law.

Over the past 40 years, however, the legal profession and its work have attracted substantial criticism. During the 1970s, critical discussion focused on the alleged failure to respond to the problems created for the ordinary citizen in areas such as housing, social security, consumer advice and employment protection; and the general failure by many lawyers, to put it simply, to 'get through to the community'. In 1976, a Royal Commission on Legal Services (the Benson Commission) was set up to enquire into the profession and its work, although little emerged from that exercise by way of substantial change. Virtually nothing was recommended in the Benson Commission Report[1] in terms of changes to the way in which the profession is organised (that is, the two separate branches of solicitors

---

1 *Report of the Royal Commission on Legal Services* (The Benson Report) (1979, Cmnd 7648, HMSO).

and barristers) and most of the positive proposals in the report seemed to be directed towards increasing lawyers' work (and hence their income) and maintaining their status.

In the 1980s, the profession came under heavy fire from government, the main charge this time being that the ways in which lawyers traditionally carried out their work amounted to 'restrictive practices' and that lawyers' clientele often did not get 'value for money'. One of the ways in which change was introduced to address some of these matters was the abolition of the statutory protection enjoyed by solicitors in their monopoly of conveyancing (the legal procedures involved in the transfer of real property):[2] the Administration of Justice Act 1985 broke that monopoly by creating a new profession of 'licensed conveyancers', though, as we will see later, further proposed changes in that area of work in the early 1990s failed to materialise. Throughout the 1980s, too, the profession had been at the centre of the debate led by the Lord Chancellor's desire to curb the rising cost of legal aid, which we discuss in more detail below; and by the late 1990s and beyond, the legal profession was fundamentally affected both by continuing criticisms of its organisation and operation, and by the government's widespread modernising reforms of the legal system. Before exploring these developments, however, it is instructive to examine some of the characteristics of the profession itself.

Lawyers have traditionally held themselves out as 'professionals', which, sociologically, carries the implication that, as professionals, lawyers occupy key positions within society, respected by lay people as having possession of specialised knowledge and the claimed ability to solve clients' problems. The sociological analyses of professions suggest that professional people are identifiable by reason of their possession of five traits, or characteristics: (i) command of a systematic body of theoretical and specialised knowledge; (ii) professional authority; (iii) the approval and support of the community; (iv) a rigorous code of ethics regulating their activities; and (v) a professional 'culture'.[3] A somewhat similar set of characteristics was listed in the Benson Commission report in 1979,[4] and it has been commented that this approach:

> ensured that, among other things, self-regulation would continue and that the 'altruistic' nature of the lawyer/client relationship would preclude the introduction of the market. The client would continue to be grateful to the lawyer for a service based on trust, confidentiality, and independence rather than upon competition and economic choice. The term 'money' was not to be discussed with or by the client, as the crucial terms were 'service' and 'justice' – and on justice no price can be placed.[5]

2 It is estimated that up to half of solicitors' income came from conveyancing. See G. Chambers and S. Harwood-Richardson, *Solicitors in England and Wales: Practice, Organisation and Perceptions* (1991, Law Society).
3 See, for example, E. Greenwood, 'Attributes of a Profession' (1957) Social Work, July; G. Millerson, *The Qualifying Associations* (1964, Routledge and Kegan Paul).   4 Op. cit.
5 P. Thomas, 'Thatcher's Will' (1992) *Journal of Law and Society*: Special Issue – Tomorrow's Lawyers (ed. P Thomas), p 4.

It is obvious that professionals such as lawyers or doctors claim to have command of specialised, expert knowledge.[6] The difficulty lies in deciding exactly what kind of knowledge it is. Professionals usually claim that their training and skills enable them to diagnose and identify problems, and to solve those problems by the application of objective, scientific knowledge. Some would argue, however, that professionals (especially doctors and lawyers) rarely, if ever, *merely* bring to bear objective scientific knowledge, but rather that they are frequently involved in making value-judgments about clients and their problems. A number of critics, for example, have suggested that 'mental illness' is often not so much a clinically diagnosable condition, susceptible to treatment through applying factual scientific medical skills, but a condition which is *socially* defined, arising from a patient's failure to conform to dominant social norms which then puts the patient out of step with both law and medical expectations.[7] Similarly, the medical treatment of many aspects of women's health is seen by critics as a reflection of *attitudes* towards women and health care, rather than a matter of purely scientific objectivity.[8] This is not to suggest that all medical skill is fundamentally a matter of value-judgment and personal opinion: there can be little room for alternative explanations and diagnoses when a medical practitioner is faced with a broken leg, and clinical expertise is called upon to provide the appropriate treatment for the problem thus identified. The point is that there may be *some* – perhaps many – areas of physical and mental illness where medicine is less dependent on rational scientific knowledge than the profession would publicly concede.

The lawyer's claim is to a body of knowledge which, though rational, is even more rarely based upon scientific principles. Law is, as we have said, a normative discipline, involving judgments about fact-situations which necessarily involve interpretation, definition and values. A client may enter a solicitor's office, for example, and request that the solicitor undertake divorce proceedings on that client's behalf. A broken marriage, however, is not like a broken leg: it may not be easy, to begin with, to ascertain that the marriage *has* broken down. Even when that 'diagnosis' is chosen, the appropriate 'treatment' may be selected from a range of possible ways of dealing with that problem, from persuading the client that conciliation may be more apt than a divorce, to accepting the client's plea that proceedings for ending the marriage through legal formalities be initiated. Whichever solution is offered by the solicitor will not be the outcome of hard-and-fast clinical rules, but rather the lawyer's 'professional judgment' about what the client wants or needs.

It is the body of professional knowledge, and the claim to be able to use it to deal with clients' disputes and problems, that maintains and enhances the lawyer's

---

6 See R. Dingwall and P. Lewis (eds), *The Sociology of the Professions: Lawyers, Doctors, and Others* (1983, Macmillan).

7 See, for example, I. Kennedy, *The Unmasking of Medicine* (1983, Granada).

8 See, for example, the articles on women's health care in B. Hutter and G. Williams, *Controlling Women* (1981, Croom Helm).

professional authority. Lawyers present themselves to clients, and indeed to the community, as having the *authoritative voice* on all legal matters, and this arguably structures to a great extent the relationship between lawyer and client. Some have argued that the professional-client relationship is one based on *power*: the professional has what the client wants or needs; he or she defines the manner in which the service is to be given and, equally importantly, defines the very *nature* of the client's problem. Typically, the client cannot argue that the professional's opinion or advice is wrong, inaccurate or inappropriate, for it is usually acknowledged by the client that the professional knows best what is in the client's interests.

Abel, drawing upon sociological analyses of professions, has produced a substantial analysis of the legal profession in the United Kingdom, and the ways in which it has attempted to respond to both criticism and structural changes in the market for legal services. He notes that:

> Producers of a service who succeed in constructing a marketable commodity only become an occupation. In order to become a profession they must seek social closure. This project has two dimensions: market control and collective social mobility . . . All occupations are compelled by the market to compete . . .[9]
>
> The professional project is directed not only toward controlling the market but also toward enhancing professional status . . . the lengthy training professionals must complete perhaps may better be understood not as the acquisition of technical skills but as a sacrifice necessary to justify future privilege: only this can make sense of the relative poverty endured by students, . . . the tedium of study, the indignities of apprenticeship, the anxiety inflicted by examinations and the lengthy postponement of adulthood.[10]

Abel discusses, among other issues, the question of 'how lawyers constructed their professional commodity (legal services) and sought to assert control over their market and to enhance their collective status',[11] and he shows how in recent years the legal profession has increasingly come under pressure from various quarters, with the result that it can no longer maintain its position of independence, exclusivity and high status so easily.

What has happened is that the legal profession can no longer justify itself simply by reference to the 'professionalism' which in the past served to legitimate its position in the community. The line pursued by government during the 1980s and 1990s was to confront all occupational groups perceived as operating restrictive practices, occupying a monopolistic or near-monopolistic position in the marketplace, or failing to provide services which offer value for the client's money. The legal profession was acutely affected by these policies: among the alleged 'restrictive practices' within the legal profession, identified by – in particular – the three Green Papers published in 1989 which contained the Lord Chancellor's plans for reform,[12]

---

9 R. Abel, *The Legal Profession in England and Wales* (1988, Blackwell), p 10.   10 Ibid., p 17.
11 Ibid., p 31.
12 These were *The Work and Organisation of the Legal Profession* (1989, Cm 570); *Contingency Fees* (1989, Cm 571); and *Conveyancing by Authorized Practitioners* (1989, Cm 572).

included the right to argue the client's case in court (the 'right of audience'), conveyancing, and various other rules and conventions concerning barristers. One effect of the pressures for change has been to undermine seriously the profession's privileged position as a 'professional' group, and to force lawyers to enter and operate within the open competitive marketplace. And apart from these concerns, there was continuing worry within government over the spiralling cost to the public purse of the provision of legal services – especially the cost of legal aid – bringing further confrontation between lawyers and the government (usually in the form of the Lord Chancellor).

Even before these assaults by the government, which we will examine in more detail presently, the legal profession has been undergoing profound change for other reasons. The profession's *control* of the supply of lawyers and legal services has decreased: whereas once the legal profession closely controlled its own intake by means of apprenticeship and instruction by the profession itself, the huge expansion of law courses in higher education has led to the current situation where entry into the profession is at present almost exclusively by graduates with law degrees.[13] This, coupled with a period of growth within the profession during the 1980s, has resulted in a large increase in the numbers of practising lawyers, especially solicitors, whose ranks have risen 12 times as fast as they did in the first half of this century. This expansion has been accompanied, however, by a tendency for the legal profession to lose certain types of work – for example, through people choosing to represent themselves in courts and tribunals, through 'do-it-yourself' divorce procedures, through the loss of conveyancing work, or through other professional groups such as accountants making inroads into tax law – which were once among the lawyer's exclusive specialisms.[14]

The legal profession has always made much of the ideal of equality – that everyone is entitled to receive the same quality of legal services, irrespective of personal circumstances – to support the argument for continued state subsidisation through legal aid, and to support the availability of legal representation not only before courts, but also before tribunals (see chapter 6) in those areas where state intervention through welfare provision or employment protection affects so many people's lives, in order to protect claimants from the denial of rights by state authorities.[15]

Of course, one abiding concern of the legal profession, and an important plank in its edifice of legitimation, has been its *independence*, both of state or other institutions and in terms of its self-image as disinterested and objective in its dealings with clients and with the law. Indeed, the claim to independence has been an

---

13 See Abel, op. cit., Part IV; M. Partington, 'Legal Education in the 1990s' (1992) 19 *Journal of Law and Society*. For an idea of the nature of provision of legal education in the UK, see P. Harris and M. Jones, 'A Survey of Law Schools in the United Kingdom, 1996' (1997) 31 *The Law Teacher* 1; P. Harris and S. Beinart, 'A Survey of Law Schools in the United Kingdom, 2004' (2006) 39 *The Law Teacher* 299.   14 See Abel, op. cit., chapter 12, esp. pp 177–189.

15 Hence the Benson Commission's proposed extension of legal aid to tribunal hearings.

important aspect of the legal profession's maintenance of its monopoly of legal services. The trouble is that when the state is called upon for substantial financial subsidisation from public funds through legal aid, then the state, on behalf of the community, can legitimately claim its own say in the way in which the profession is run. Furthermore, at a time when so many organisations and industries are regulated through new independent agencies, the legal profession remains one of the relatively few professions which still regulates itself – and again, this has been justified through the proclaimed need for 'independence'. In the 1970s, The Benson Commission tried to head off any threats to this independence: 'Legal services are required more and more by private individuals who are in dispute with authority in one of its many forms and to protect the interests of clients in such cases, the independence of the legal profession is of paramount importance'[16] and the Commission's report expressed the fervent hope that 'the profession should have a period of orderly development free, so far as possible, from external interventions'.[17]

Such a period of peace and quiet, however, was not to be; but before we examine recent developments in more detail, we need to gain a general overview of the traditional organisation and work of lawyers.

The divided profession and its work

The legal profession is divided into two branches, solicitors and barristers.[18] Each of the two branches has its own controlling body – the Law Society and the Bar Council respectively – and an intending lawyer must decide, at a relatively early stage in legal training, whether to practise as a solicitor or a barrister, because apart from the initial period of legal education (almost invariably a law degree course) the two branches are mutually exclusive in terms of personnel and training, although rather less so in terms of their work.

The controlling bodies exercise strict codes of professional ethics and standards of practice: this is one of the ways in which the exclusivity of the profession, and its claim to produce high standards of work, are maintained. Both bodies act as disciplinary agencies to deal with any alleged breach of these codes, and for serious breaches a member of either branch of the legal profession may be 'struck off'. This aspect of the independent self-governance of the profession has been strongly criticised over the years, however, and an increasing degree of independent scrutiny of complaints has been introduced. In 1990, the office of the Legal Services Ombudsman was introduced. The LSO supervises the handling of complaints by the professional bodies, and acts as a higher-level means of investigation for those not satisfied with the way in which the professional bodies themselves have dealt

16 Benson Commission Report, op. cit., p 52.
17 Benson Commission Report, op. cit., recommendation 3.2.
18 For a detailed analysis see M. Zander, *Cases and Materials on the English Legal System* (9th edn. 2003, Cambridge University Press), chapter 8.

with their complaints. In subsequent years, the number of bodies who may be involved with the regulation of lawyers has multiplied: Zander has commented that

> [A] report in 1997[19] said that the areas regulated included entry, training, planning, competition, cost and quality of, and access to services and complaints. The bodies and agencies involved include the Lord Chancellor's Department, Parliament, and Master of the Rolls, the Attorney-General, the National Audit Office, the Office of Fair Trading, the courts, the Legal Aid Board (now the Legal Services Commission) and the Legal Services Ombudsman.[20]

The introduction of the Legal Services Ombudsman did little either to diminish the criticisms of the legal profession, or to reduce the increasing number of complaints about legal services. The LSO was, moreover, critical of the ways in which many of these complaints had been handled by the professional bodies. In 2003, a review of the regulation of legal services, chaired by Sir David Clementi, was announced by the government, and the ensuing 'Review of the Regulatory Framework for Legal Services in England and Wales'[21] was published in 2004.

Clementi discussed three main issues - the existing complex regulatory framework for legal services, the complaints systems (based on the principle of lawyers investigating complaints into their own profession) and the restrictive nature of current business structures within the legal profession which have changed little over time. The latter issue includes the vexed question as to the extent to which lawyers continue to operate within an environment which permits restrictive practices in the way they work. In addressing the problems arising from these issues, Clementi made a number of recommendations. First, he proposed a new regulatory framework, which would comprise a new Legal Services Board to provide consistent oversight of the Law Society and Bar Council. The Board itself would have statutorily-defined functions and regulatory powers, which would include the power to delegate some regulatory functions to the professional bodies, subject to their competence and appropriate governance arrangements. A new *complaints system* would be set up, incorporating a new independent, easy-to-access body, the Office for Legal Complaints, which would deal with consumer complaints in respect of all members of the legal profession and which would be under the supervision of the Legal Services Board.

On the question of *business structures* and restrictive practices, Clementi recommended the establishment of a new type of law firm – Legal Disciplinary Practices – which would bring together solicitors, barristers, and possibly non-lawyers, to provide legal services. The latter proposal would continue a trend which began in 1991, when it became possible for members of both branches of the legal profession to come together into partnership. In 2001, the Office of Fair Trading had recommended the broadening out of such organisations to

---

19 R. Baldwin, *Regulating Legal Services* (1997, Lord Chancellor's Department Research Programme No. 5/97)).   20 M. Zander, *Cases and Materials on the English Legal System*, op.cit., p 781.
21 (2004) Department for Constitutional Affairs.

include non-lawyer members, and Clementi proposed the implementation of this proposal.

The Clementi Report was, perhaps not surprisingly, criticised by the legal profession, with the Bar, in particular, stating its anxiety over the possibility of the principle of independence being compromised, and of non-qualified personnel being involved in the running of legal practices. The Government, however, accepted the Clementi proposals, and published a White Paper, 'The Future of Legal Services: Putting Consumers First' in October 2005. This was followed by the draft Legal Services Bill, containing provision for the implementation of the Clementi proposals, in May 2006. It remains to be seen how, if at all, the new framework will improve the accessibility of complaint-handling procedure and the consumer-focus of those responsible for providing legal services.

The Bar's response to Clementi, with its warning about the dangers of non-lawyers entering law firms, reflects what has always been the *exclusivity* of the two branches of the profession. This exclusivity is particularly promoted by the methods of professional of training and socialisation. All lawyers undergo extensive periods of education, both through formal academic learning and through practical training in legal work. In the case of solicitors, this practical training takes the form of a two-year period, after obtaining a law degree and completing the one-year full-time Legal Practice Course, in a training contract with a firm of practitioners. For intending barristers, the period of training is rather more complicated and less financially secure, but possibly more intensive because of the immersion of the novice in the traditions and practices of the Bar. Apart from undertaking various examinations in law, the prospective barrister must also join one of the four Inns of Court, where the life of the barrister is learned. The various rules and institutions of the Bar serve to socialise the novice into the established ways of that branch of the profession, where customs, traditions and etiquette play so great a part. Barristers' professional, and often much of their social, life involves an exclusive and somewhat socially isolated experience, where the company in which they move comprises, very often, other barristers and judges who are members of the same Inn.[22]

For many people, the image of the typical lawyer and his work is that presented in the formal setting of the courtroom. Here, it is traditionally the barrister, in wig and gown, who presents the case and expresses the arguments on the client's behalf; the solicitor's task is to deal directly with the client, to ensure that the barrister chosen is properly and fully instructed, to collect and collate all relevant evidence (such as witnesses' statements, letters, photographs and so on) and to ensure that all relevant persons are present in court on the day of the trial.

This image of lawyers and their work is, however, somewhat misleading: the traditional division of functions in the courtroom is being broken down. Although

---

22 See C. Glasser, 'Civil Procedure and the Lawyers – the Adversary System and the Decline of the Orality Principle' (1993) 56 *MLR* 307 at, esp. 318–324.

traditionally only barristers have full 'rights of audience' (that is, the right to address the judges' bench directly on the client's behalf) in all courts, solicitors have for some time had full rights of audience, too, in magistrates' and county courts, and in some Crown Courts. In the Access to Justice Act 1999 provision is made (in Part III) for full rights of audience in all courts for barristers, solicitors and other lawyers employed by other organisations, such as, principally, the Crown Prosecution Service, subject to satisfying training requirements.

The issue of rights of audience has been highly controversial in recent years. The Courts and Legal Services Act 1990 provides that solicitors (and for that matter anyone else) might apply for additional rights of audience. This provision followed the Lord Chancellor's proposals in the 1989 White Paper *Legal Services: A Framework for the Future* [23] and was designed to enhance both the quality of advocacy, and the freedom of choice as to who should be able to act as an advocate. Applications for additional rights of audience were to be considered by the Lord Chancellor's Advisory Committee on Education and Conduct, and the views of that Committee were then taken into account by the deciding forum, comprising the Lord Chancellor and four senior judges.

As soon as the 1990 Act was passed, the Law Society submitted its application for additional rights for solicitors, which would extend their rights of audience to all Crown Court cases where no jury was used (for instance, guilty plea cases and committals for sentence); and further applications for additional rights were submitted by the Government Legal Service and the Director of Public Prosecutions (for the Crown Prosecution Service). All these applications were opposed by the Bar, for obvious reasons. The latter two applications were rejected; and although the Law Society's application was not found acceptable in its original form, the Advisory Committee felt that solicitors could enjoy additional rights subject to their undertaking training in the skills of advocacy. Although at first, take-up of these opportunities by solicitors was rather slow, but by 2005, around 2,000 solicitors had qualified for rights of audience in the higher courts – a very small proportion of the total number of solicitors, but, it may be thought, a considerable number of advocates, compared with the total number of barristers (see below).

The provisions in the Access to Justice Act 1999 clearly went much further than those in the 1990 Act: there is now no restriction, in principle, on any suitably qualified and trained person acquiring full rights of audience. The Act established a new body – the Legal Services Consultative Panel [24] – to advise the Lord Chancellor in these and any other matters 'relating to any aspect of the provision of legal services'.[25]

A second traditional distinction between the two branches of the legal profession is that the practice has been in the past to recruit judges, at all levels except magistrates (who are not legally qualified), from the ranks of barristers, not

---

23 (1989, Cm 740, HMSO).
24 Replacing the Lord Chancellor's Advisory Committee on Education and Conduct (ACLEC).
25 Section 35(2).

solicitors. Since the Courts Act 1971, however, this picture has been changing. The present position is governed by the Courts and Legal Services Act 1990, which provides that, depending on the level of seniority of judicial appointment in question, solicitors may be appointed to the judiciary as long as they satisfy (among other things) the criteria laid down in the Act relating to the period of time during which they have held rights of audience in particular courts. For example, anyone who has held rights of audience in the Crown Court or county courts for ten years may apply to become a circuit judge or recorder.

Another important qualification to the 'courtroom image' of the legal profession is that nearly all of the profession's work is done *outside* the courtroom. Both solicitors and barristers are often retained for the giving of advice. Such advice may be on taxation or company matters, matrimonial or property affairs, civil or criminal disputes and so on.[26] It must not be supposed that solicitors are ignorant of the law; it is only in certain cases that the advice of a barrister is sought. Indeed, one of the arguments often put forward for retaining the division of the legal profession is that it enables barristers to become highly expert on specialised and technical areas of law which the more down-to-earth and practical nature of solicitors' work is thought not to allow. It may, however, fairly be said that the two branches engage in the same sort of work – that of advice and consultancy – and for solicitors in particular, such work is usually far more rewarding financially than court work.

Conveyancing, together with other property matters, has traditionally accounted for about half of solicitors' work, though this proportion has fallen quite substantially in recent years for the reasons explained above. Conveyancing involves a series of fairly complicated stages, including the completion of forms, negotiations between the buyers and sellers of real property, and the drawing-up and exchange of contracts between them for the transfer of that property. Although in theory anyone can undertake their own conveyancing (riddled with pitfalls though it is) there are legal restrictions as to who can undertake this work for payment. We have already noted that the Administration of Justice Act 1985 removed the solicitors' monopoly on conveyancing by providing for the establishment of a new occupational group of licensed conveyancers; and although the Lord Chancellor's Green Paper on conveyancing had proposed that financial institutions such as banks and building societies should compete with private solicitors for this type of work, those institutions did not show any great interest at the time.

Another major area of solicitors' work taking place outside the courtroom involves *matrimonial disputes*, which may raise issues such as separation or divorce proceedings, the attendant problems concerning children and the disposal between the parties of family property. Since the widening of the grounds for divorce, first introduced in 1969, divorce itself is for many people largely a legal formality, with undefended divorce petitions as the norm. Usually, only if there are difficulties

26 For detailed summaries of the different types of work undertaken by solicitors, see the Law Society's 'Fact Sheet' series – for example 'Categories of Work undertaken by Solicitors 2005', see also R. Woolfson, J. Plotkinoff and D. Wilson, *Solicitors in the Employed Sector* (1994, Law Society).

concerning the fate of the children of the marriage, or questions as to the matrimonial property, or if the divorce petition is defended by one spouse, will there be a full court hearing.

Connected with domestic and family matters is *probate* work, which involves the sorting-out of wills and the estates of deceased persons. Sometimes, such a case can involve court proceedings, as, for example, where a will is contested, but such court cases are relatively infrequent. For the solicitor, however, this type of work, dealt with, so to speak, from the office, constitutes a sizeable proportion of the total workload.

Much of the remainder of the solicitor's business is taken up with company and taxation matters, advising as to business contracts or partnerships – such work usually being non-contentious, involving no disputants – and providing assistance and advice on contentious matters. Commercial legal matters comprise lucrative business for solicitors, and it must be borne in mind that the larger, multi-partner firms, often (but not always) based in London, carry out extremely profitable commercial (often international) work. Although it is still normal for solicitors' firms to comprise three or four partners, some of the largest commercial firms have over eighty partners, and in 2005, the 1.4% of solicitors' firms with 26 or more partners employed over one-third of all solicitors in private practice.[27] At least one such city firm has an annual turnover of more than £1 billion. So significant is legal commercial business for these firms that in 2001, eight leading London firms, working with a handful of established law schools, developed a specialised 'commercial law' version of the Legal Practice Course to assist recruitment to their firms of what they regarded as suitably qualified candidates. In 2006, three of the original eight had gone even further, and had begun to operate their own 'elite' LPC courses.

When studying the considerable spread of types of work undertaken by lawyers, it is important to bear in mind, first, that out of the considerable number of lawyers (there were more than 11,500 barristers[28] in 2004, and 126,142 solicitors, 100,938 of whom held practising certificates,[29] in 2005) a substantial minority[30] – about 20% – are employed not in private practice, but in industry, trade and commerce in both public and private sectors, and in national and local government. Second, it is by no means inevitable that clients bringing their problems to solicitors' offices will always deal directly with qualified solicitors. Much of the day-to-day work in a solicitor's office may be carried out by trainee solicitors, working towards their final qualifications, or else by *legal executives*.[31] Legal executives comprise a sizeable group of law professionals (numbering at present around 22,000) who work in solicitors' offices and who, though not qualified solicitors, are legally trained and will have gained the qualifications awarded by the Institute of Legal Executives

27 Law Society Strategic Research Unit, *Trends in the Solicitors' Profession: Annual Statistical Report 2005* (2006, Law Society).   28 General Council of the Bar, *Annual Report 2005* (2005).
29 Law Society, *Annual Statistical Report 2005* (2006, Law Society).   30 Ibid.
31 On legal executives, see Abel, op. cit., pp 207–210; R. Smith, 'Lawyers Whose Time has Come' (1991) *NLJ*, 11 October.

(ILEX). Technically they work under the supervision of solicitors, though, like solicitors, legal executives are fee-earners for the firm, carrying out a good deal of often specialised legal work. Furthermore, the 'ILEX route' is a recognised avenue for becoming a solicitors: having obtained ILEX qualifications and passed the Legal Practice Course, ILEX Fellows may, by reason of their experience in employment in a solicitors' firm, qualify as solicitors having been exempted from the training contract stage of solicitors' training.

Given the wide range of problems which are brought to solicitors' offices by clients, it will, of course, sometimes be necessary to engage the services of a barrister, either because litigation is envisaged or in order to take specialised advice. For many years it was the case that the services of barristers could only be obtained through a solicitor – it was not possible for people requiring legal services to approach them directly. This usually meant that the fee-paying client had to retain, and duly pay for, the services of two lawyers instead of one; and this has been a very important argument put forward in favour of unifying the two branches of the profession. It was argued before the Benson Commission[32] for example that the divided profession can lead to situations where cases are delayed, or where problems are dealt with inefficiently; some argued that clients' confidence in the legal services provided might be reduced by seeing the case passed over to a barrister whom they have never met, after having developed trust and confidence in the solicitor to whom they brought the case; and last, but not least, it was argued that a fused profession would greatly reduce clients' costs because only one expert who deals with the case from beginning to end would have to be paid, rather than two, or perhaps more.

The Royal Commission considered these arguments, as well as those for retaining the divided profession in its existing form, which can be summarised as follows. First, it was argued that barristers should be kept free from direct access by clients in order to ensure that their specialised skills are efficiently used, and that they are able, as a result of a certain distancing from clients, to provide completely objective advice on clients' problems. It may be that the force of this argument has been lessened in recent years, with many solicitors, especially those working in large firms, becoming highly specialised in particular areas of law.

Second, it was argued that fusion would lead to a decline in the quality of advocacy, and hence to a decline in the quality of the administration of justice itself, by effectively 'diluting the specialist knowledge and standards of the Bar'.[33] Noting an increased need for specialism in legal services, and the need for effective advocacy of a high standard, the Benson Commission rejected the proposals for fusion and recommended that the divided profession continue in its present form.

The government accepted the Benson recommendations on fusion, though developments in the years which followed continued, in practical terms, to blur seriously the dividing-line between solicitors and barristers. One example is the increase

---

32 Op. cit., chapter 17.   33 Ibid., p 199.

in solicitors' rights of audience, discussed above. Another is the opening-up of direct access by clients to barristers, rather than having to go through a solicitor.

Direct access to barristers was proposed in a government Green Paper in 1989, and although highly controversial, the proposal eventually resulted in the Bar permitting certain professional bodies (such as architects, surveyors and accountants) directed access to barristers. Debate and controversy continued, however, with regard to allowing ordinary clients direct access, until in 2004, it became possible for clients to approach barristers directly for legal advice, drafting documents, and certain other services, though there are restrictions on what barristers may do by means of direct access in the fields of immigration law, criminal law, and family law. Detailed guidance for the public, issued by the Bar, explains in full the essential differences between the services of barristers and solicitors, and indeed acknowledges that there are certain types of legal work that barristers are not lawfully permitted to carry out.

Given these developments, it is arguable that, although the debates on 'fusion' of the profession are perhaps not as hotly conducted as they once were, developments *within* each branch is, in effect, gradually bringing fusion, in practical terms if not in organisational terms, closer to becoming a reality.

The social composition of the legal profession

Like all professional groups, as commentators agree, the legal profession is essentially middle-class in outlook and, usually, in origin.[34] The middle- and upper-middle-class background of lawyers is more marked among barristers than among solicitors, though some argue that the class distinctions are gradually being broken down between the branches of the profession. The Benson Commission report showed the predominance in the 1970s of professional and managerial backgrounds, as indicated by fathers' occupations. In 1989, a survey carried out by the Law Society's Research and Policy Planning Unit, of a sample of about 1,000 solicitors,[35] showed that over one-third had attended a fee-paying independent (or public) school (though this proportion has been declining oveer the years); 11% had attended direct-grant grammar schools; 34% had been to state grammar schools, and only 14% had attended secondary modern or comprehensive schools.

The peculiarities of recruitment into the legal profession, coupled with its unique position within the social structure, still tend to favour the middle- and upper-middle-class aspirant lawyer. The cost of undergraduate legal education, even allowing for the deferred payment of university fees from September 2006, is extremely high. Fees for full-time postgraduate training on the Legal Practice Course may be between £5,000 and £9,000, and may be even higher for the full-time Bar Vocational Course. For many potential recruits, these fee-levels may well be

34 Abel, op. cit., chapters 4 and 11.
35 G. Chambers, 'Solicitors in Private Practice: A Survey of Education, Career and Social Background' (1992) *NLJ*, 12 and 19 June.

prohibitive, and it must be remembered that living expenses, too, must be found during the period of training, when novices are not allowed to take on cases for themselves and earn their own fees.

Since 1990 the Bar has operated a scheme whereby barristers' chambers pay their pupils during their pupillage year; initially the amount payable was £6,000 per year (though some barristers' chambers paid pupils rather more than that) and has now been increased to £10,000. Even after qualification, however, a high income is not immediately guaranteed, partly because barristers must build up their reputation before cases begin to arrive regularly, and partly because fees earned for the first few cases may well take months to be paid. In many cases, too, pupil barristers will start their careers with substantial debt incurred as a result of the cost of the initial stages of legal education and training.

For an intending solicitor, the two years spent as a trainee are usually fairly lean financially, as they, too, will in all probability have built up substantial debts and are by no means well-paid – in 2005 the minimum starting salary for trainee solicitors was £16,450 in London and £14,770 elsewhere. Such considerations suggest that an intending lawyer, whichever branch of the profession he or she chooses, would do well to come from a background which is financially secure, and preferably have some form of independent income with which to supplement the leaner times of training and early experience. Not surprisingly, surveys have shown[36] that many lawyers *do* come from middle- and upper-middle-class backgrounds: for example, studies of judges, who are traditionally recruited from the ranks of barristers, clearly show a predominance of public school and Oxford or Cambridge university educational backgrounds.[37]

Not only is the legal profession predominantly middle- and upper-middle class: it is also a profession long dominated by *white male* practitioners. The significantly lower proportion of black and other ethnic minority lawyers to white, and the lower numbers of women in the profession (especially the Bar) has attracted considerable criticism over the years. With regard to solicitors, it was not until 1985 that a Race Relations Committee was established by the Law Society to monitor entry by members of black and other ethnic minority communities. In 1986 only 1% of solicitors with practising certificates came from such backgrounds, though this figure had risen to 9.4% by 2004–5, and in the same year the Law Society reported that 18% of admissions to the Roll were from ethnic minority backgrounds.[38] There is, however, evidence of discrimination against black students upon graduation, and of difficulties due to ethnic background in the working environment even when jobs can be obtained.[39] Law Society statistics relating to the year 2004–5 indicate that almost half of solicitors from minority ethnic groups

36 Abel, op. cit.; and see P. McDonald, ' "The Class of '81" – A Glance at the Social Class Composition of Recruits to the Legal Profession' (1983) 9 *Journal of Law and Society* 2.   37 See chapter 14.
38 Law Society, *Annual Statistical Report 2005* (2005).
39 M. King, M. Israel and S. Goulbourne, *Ethnic Minorities and Recruitment to the Solicitors' Profession* (1990, Law Society); D. Harvie, 'Minorities in a Recession', (1992) *NLJ*, 29 May.

holding practising certificates were employed in private practice firms with four or fewer partners, and that only 22% of minority ethnic solicitors with practising certificates occupied positions as partners within solicitors' firms, as compared with 36% of white European solicitors

With regard to barristers, although the Bar has long attracted – and indeed encouraged – students from overseas, the expectation was that, once qualified, they would return to practice in their home countries. Writing in 1988, Abel reported that:

> in the last ten years, . . . a small but significant racial minority has emerged in the Bar as the black population of Britain has grown, and legal aid has helped them secure representation . . .
>
> Although the Senate . . . has acknowledged the existence of racial discrimination, it rejected affirmative action as a solution. It did amend the Code of Conduct in 1984 to prohibit discrimination . . . and in autumn 1986 it issued guidelines on applications for pupillages and tenancies and on distribution of work in chambers, prohibiting racial discrimination; but it may be equally noteworthy that barristers' clerks objected to these limitations on their discretion and the Senate chose not to make them practice rules in order that they might remain hortatory but unenforceable.[40]

There is little doubt that the Bar's record on this issue is unimpressive. There remains evidence that black barristers experience discrimination and racism both in obtaining places in chambers and in obtaining work. In order to do something to remedy the situation, the Bar announced in 1991 a 5% target for the employment of black barristers and solicitors entering practice: in 2005, the Bar's published statistics indicated that 11% of barristers came from minority ethnic groups, as did (in July 2005) 17% of registered pupils.

The number of women practising lawyers is rather higher for both branches of the profession but, even here, there is no reason to believe that equality has been achieved. Despite a lamentable history within the solicitors' branch[41] that included a ban on women until 1919 (a change forced on the profession by legislation passed in that year), the proportion of women becoming solicitors has risen dramatically in recent years and in 2004–5 was 60% of the total admitted to the Roll, with women also accounting for 41% of all solicitors with practising certificates in that year.[42] But although the situation may have improved over the years this does not mean that there is equality in terms of career progression: Law Society figures for 1999–2000 show that of solicitors with 10–19 years' experience in private practice, 84% of men were partners (or sole practitioners) compared with 58% of women. By 2004–5, the proportions of both men and women who were partners or sole practitioners had decreased, though more markedly for men (68%) than for women (45%). Probably more depressing is a research finding that almost a third of women solicitors have experienced sexual discrimination at work, and one in five

---

40 Abel, op. cit., p 78.   41 Abel, op. cit., pp 172–176.
42 Law Society, *Annual Statistical Report 2005* (2005).

have experienced harassment. A survey of 631 members of the Association of Women Solicitors reported in 2001[43] that 32% said they had experienced sex discrimination at work, compared with 2% and 4% respectively who claimed to have suffered discrimination on grounds of race or disability.

The history of the Bar is similar to that of the Law Society. Abel, reviewing the various surveys carried out over the past 30 years or so, identifies a number of barriers operating to discriminate against women at the Bar:[44] discrimination in obtaining pupillages and tenancies; scholarships awarded by the Inns of Court which were available only to men; the exclusion of women from meetings; the refusal of banks to grant overdraft facilities to women barristers starting out in their careers; the obstacles posed by the profession's 'unconscious acceptance of the traditional division of labour in childrearing'[45] which forced many women to leave the profession for family reasons; and so on. The Benson Commission found that overall, women barristers earn substantially less than their male counterparts. Although the number of women becoming barristers has risen dramatically (women now account for about 33% of all barristers, as compared with about 13% in 1985) there are very few female heads of chambers, and in 2002 women comprised only 8% of QCs.[46]

The cost of legal services

Everyone knows that legal services are not cheap. Solicitors' fees for non-contentious matters are high and, if a case goes to court, there may well be barristers' and court fees to pay as well as the solicitor's own charges. The Civil Justice Review, initiated in 1985 by the Lord Chancellor, whose Report appeared in 1988,[47] found that claimants' costs in London in 1984 were, on average, £6,830, and outside London £1,540; and it was estimated that when both sides' costs were taken into account, costs in the High Court were between 50 and 75% of damages awarded, but in the county court these could be as high as 125% of damages. A survey by Genn carried out for Lord Woolf's Report on Access to Justice (see chapter 6) of 673 High Court cases during 1994–95 showed average costs for clinical negligence cases at £38,252, for commercial cases at £29,418 and for personal injury cases at £20,413.[48]

If a case involves a substantial claim, is complex or is taken on appeal to a higher court, then of course costs escalate dramatically. For many people – and not necessarily the poorest sections of the community – such costs would render legal solutions out of the question were there no state-subsidised system of financial assistance. From 1951, such a system – the legal aid and advice system – was in

43 Law Society's *Gazette*, 13 July 2001.   44 Abel, op. cit., pp 79–85.   45 Ibid., p 82.
46 Reported in Zander, op. cit., p 720. See also C. Barton and C. Farrelly, 'Women in the Legal Profession' (1998) *NLJ*, 24 April.
47 *Report of the Review Body on Civil Justice* (1988, Cm 394, HMSO).
48 The survey appears as Annex III to the Interim Report, 1996.

operation in this country, though there had been financial assistance available before then through the 'Poor Person's Procedure' for High Court actions, and through other limited schemes. The scheme introduced by the Legal Aid and Advice Act 1949 was the first extensive and systematic attempt to provide a generally available, state-subsidised legal aid system. Financial legal aid, available for civil and criminal court cases, was later supplemented by provision for *legal advice and assistance*, whereby solicitors undertook work falling short of court appearances (the Green Form Scheme). Apart from the schemes operated by practising solicitors, the Sex Discrimination Act 1975 and the Race Relations Act 1976 set up the Equal Opportunities Commission and the Commission for Racial Equality respectively, and both these bodies may give legal assistance, including representation, to complainants bringing discrimination cases to courts and tribunals.

The legal aid and advice scheme was based on the idea that the legal profession should provide state-subsidised legal services for individuals with legal problems who qualified for such aid under whichever regulations and conditions were in force; the client's eligibility for legal aid would depend, in civil and criminal cases, upon 'merits' and 'means' tests. Initially the client took a problem, such as a dispute over a defective new car, to a solicitor, where eligibility for legal advice under the Green Form Scheme would be investigated. Under this scheme a solicitor could undertake ordinary legal work (except for most aspects of conveyancing and the making of wills, and court work) up to a limit, normally, of two hours' work. Since 1977, undefended divorce cases were not eligible for legal aid, but the Green Form Scheme was available. And the work which a solicitor could undertake included assistance with certain hearings to which the client may be a party (known as Assistance by way of Representation, or ABWOR): this form of assistance was available for matrimonial cases heard by magistrates' courts, Mental Health Review Tribunal hearings, representation of clients in respect of whom there was a police application under the Police and Criminal Evidence Act 1984 for extended detention in custody, and care proceedings where the parents were to be represented.

Eligibility under the schemes depended upon the client's *disposable income and capital*, that is, income and capital after certain deductions were made for rent, taxes and other necessary outgoings. Depending on the figures thus arrived at, the client was liable to make a contribution towards the total cost – the more the income and capital, the greater the contribution.

If a client's problem involved court work – as might happen, for example, if the car-dealer in the above example refused to repair or replace the defective car; or if a client was facing criminal charges – then the question arose as to the client's eligibility for either civil or criminal *legal aid* – the two involved different tests of eligibility – for representation in court. Civil legal aid, technically available for nearly all civil court hearings (except defamation and, as noted above, undefended divorce cases), was administered by the independent Legal Aid Board, created in 1988, using two sets of criteria - a means test, and the question of the merits of the action to which the client proposed to be a party. The Legal Aid Board had to be satisfied that the applicant 'had reasonable grounds for taking, defending or being a party to the proceedings'.

The financial limits periodically set for civil legal aid were consistently criticised as excluding a large proportion of the community whose financial standing was such that they were outside the means test limit, but not so great as to enable them readily to undertake civil litigation without considerable personal financial strain. During the 1980s and 1990s, however, the Conservative administrations were far more concerned about the cost of legal aid than about extending its applicability.

For *criminal* legal aid, there were means and merits tests similar to those for civil legal aid, though the 'merits' test for criminal cases was such that the application had to show that legal aid was 'in the interests of justice'. In practice, the vast majority of defendants in the Crown Courts received legal aid, though there was much more variability between magistrates' courts as to whether legal aid was granted to defendants appearing before them.[49] The national 'duty solicitor' scheme (whereby a rota of solicitors attending magistrates' courts ensures that a lawyer is always on hand to give help and advice to those appearing before the magistrates) may well have made some difference to the proportion who are represented.

The state subsidisation of legal services was subject to new controls in the 1980s and 1990s, largely driven by the then Lord Chancellor's determination to cut the enormous cost to the public purse of the legal aid scheme. There is no doubt that the number applying for both civil and criminal legal aid had rocketed over the years, with a correspondingly large increase in the cost of financing the system,[50] which cost around £1,500 million in 1997. The reasons for this vast increase in the demand for legal services have been stated to be the problems consequent on unemployment (mortgage difficulties, problems with debts) and the rise in crime, though the advent of the duty solicitor scheme for criminal cases must have contributed to the cost of criminal legal aid, irrespective of any rise in the number of those accused of criminal offences.

Between 1986 and 1997, the Lord Chancellor, in an attempt to control the cost of the legal aid scheme, and the legal profession, in the attempt both to protect and expand the scheme and protect their own interests and those of their clients, remained locked in battle over the future of legal aid, and the skirmishes were, in the main, won by the government. The Courts and Legal Services Act 1990 reflected government policies regarding 'restrictive practices', and in particular the objectives of encouraging more competition in the provision of legal services.[51] This Act made changes with respect to conveyancing and litigation, and put in place new

---

49 See R. Young, T. Moloney and A. Sanders, *In the Interests of Justice?* (1992, Institute of Judicial Administration, University of Birmingham).

50 A. Gray and P. Fenn, 'The Rising Cost of Legally Aided Criminal Cases' (1991) *NLJ*, 29 November; C. Glasser, 'Legal Aid – Decline and Fall', Law Society's *Gazette*, 19 March 1986; Lord Mackay of Clashfern, 'Access to Justice: The Price' (1991) 25 *The Law Teacher* 96; Zander, op. cit., pp 560–64; Abel, op. cit., pp 116–119, 226–234.

51 On this Act see M. Partington, 'Change or no-change? Reflections on the Courts and Legal Services Act 1990' (1991) 54 *MLR* 702.

arrangements for the handling of complaints against solicitors and others who provide legal services. In particular, it created the Legal Services Ombudsman, who was given substantial powers to investigate complaints.[52] Although in practice the 1990 Act may not have radically affected the organisation of the profession, it represented a significant move in the direction of more government intervention in the ways in which legal services were provided.

The New Labour government, elected in May 1997, had vaguely promised in their election manifesto a 'wide-ranging review' and had spoken of 'local, regional and national plans for the development of Legal Aid according to the needs and priorities of regions and areas. The key to success will be to promote a partnership between the voluntary sector, the legal profession and the Legal Aid Board.' What the New Labour government actually delivered was the wholesale replacement of the legal aid and advice scheme with a completely new system for providing help for those needing legal services. In its 1998 White Paper, *Modernising Justice*, the government outlined the main drawbacks with the old legal aid scheme as:

- being too heavily biased towards expensive, court-based solutions to people's problems. Because the scheme is open-ended, it is impossible to target resources on priority areas, or the most efficient and effective way of dealing with a particular problem. Legal aid is spent almost entirely on lawyers' services. In practice, it is lawyers who determine where and how the money is spent;
- sometimes criticised for backing cases of insufficient merit; and for allowing people to pursue cases unreasonably, forcing their opponents to agree to unfair settlements;
- [providing] few effective means or incentives for improving value for money. Because any lawyer can take a legal aid case, there is little control over quality, and no scope for competition to keep prices down;
- [being] not possible to control expenditure effectively. The few means of control available, for example cutting financial eligibility, are crude and inflexible.[53]

The proposals for a new statutory scheme outlined in the White Paper were implemented in the Access to Justice Act 1999. The Act replaced the Legal Aid Board with a new body, the Legal Services Commission, which operates under the direction of, and is responsible to, the Lord Chancellor. The Commission is responsible for the establishment and maintenance of two new systems – the *Community Legal Service*, which replaces legal aid for civil and family cases, and the *Criminal Defence Service*, which replaces legal aid for criminal cases.

The Community Legal Service, according to the White Paper, would have 'two complementary roles. It will improve access to information, advice and assistance services, by working with other funders to identify local needs and co-ordinate funding. It will also manage a new CLS fund that will replace civil legal aid.'[54] The aims were to rationalise and ensure the greater co-ordination of and co-operation

---

52 See Annual Reports of Legal Services Ombudsman (HMSO); Zander, op. cit., pp 782–6.
53 *Modernising Justice: The Government's Plans for Reforming Legal Services and the Courts* (1998, HMSO), para 3.8.   54 Ibid., para 2.3.

between the many and varied providers of legal advice and other services – solicitors in private practice, advisers working in voluntary advice agencies and law centres, Citizens' Advice Bureaux, and so on; to develop a systematic and co-ordinated system of funding these services; and to seek to ensure minimum core standards of quality by means of 'kitemarking' the providers of legal services. Funding is allocated to service providers by means of contracting:

> In future, lawyers and other providers will only be able to work under the scheme when they have a contract with, or a grant from, the LSC . . . Contracting is a flexible way of procuring services, because contracts can take many different forms, tailored to fit different circumstances . . .[55]

Contracting also has the advantages, it is claimed, of enabling better control of budgets; of helping to ensure the quality of service through performance-monitoring; and of promoting better value for money by encouraging competition and (through being able to fix the prices of services to be provided) enabling clients to be aware, at the outset, of the likely costs to them in terms of contributions or legal costs. Once again, we see the centrality of the government's insistence on seeking 'best value'.

Under the new scheme, then, civil disputes may be subsidised by means of legal advisers bidding for funds from the Community Legal Service which may be used for the provision of a range of legal services, from the simple provision of legal advice through to dispute-resolution and legal representation. All providers, whether private solicitors, law centres or any other organisations, and whether acting independently or in 'community legal service partnerships',[56] participate in the new system.

Under the Access to Justice Act 1999, Schedule 2, however, legal services (beyond the provision of general information about the relevant law) relating to certain types of legal problem will not attract funding by means of the Community Legal Service. The principal excluded areas are personal injury cases, conveyancing, making wills, matters concerning trust law, defamation, matters relating to company law or other matters relating to the carrying on of a business. Criminal matters are also excluded, because, it will be recalled, a separate Criminal Defence Service is established by the Act. Most of the excluded matters are self-evidently not appropriate for subsidisation from public funds; but the exclusion of personal injury cases requires further explanation.

The Access to Justice Act 1999 makes provision for conditional fee arrangements, which have, in fact, been part of the legal services landscape since the Courts and Legal Services Act 1990. In essence, a conditional fee arrangement is

55 Ibid., paras 3.17, 3.19.
56 These are partnerships between local authorities, the Legal Services Commission, and other funding bodies, whereby local legal services and advice agencies work together to co-ordinate local provision with local need, taking account of any special priorities or problems which may affect that local area.

an agreement between a solicitor and a client whereby if the client loses the case, he or she pays their solicitor nothing; but if he or she wins, they pay the solicitor's fee, plus an additional 'uplift', or 'success fee', which might even lead to a solicitor doubling his or her normal fee if the claim is successful. This type of arrangement has had a controversial history: originally, such an agreement between lawyer and client was illegal as 'maintenance and champerty' (the offences of financing someone's litigation, and of taking a financial interest in the outcome of such litigation), and although these two criminal offences were abolished in 1967, it was still not permissible, under Law Society rules, for lawyers to make such arrangements with clients. In the late 1980s, the Lord Chancellor issued a Green Paper on 'Contingency Fees' in which views were sought as to whether such arrangements ought to be allowed. There was considerable support for the introduction of such arrangements, and provision for contingency fees was duly made in the Courts and Legal Services Act 1990. The maximum 'uplift' was originally proposed as a relatively small percentage – only 10 or 20% – though following representations from the Law Society that this might be too low a percentage to persuade lawyers to take on risky cases, the Lord Chancellor agreed on a maximum success fee of up to 100%. Clearly, such a possible financial result might make even legally uncertain cases an attractive proposition, although in 1997 a research report on conditional fee arrangements, based on 200 such arrangements and involving 121 solicitors' firms, suggested that the norm for the 'success fee' was 43% of the normal fee chargeable.[57]

The conditional fee is now very much part of the financing of legal services, especially for personal injury cases (except for clinical negligence which remains outside the contingency fee system), though the arguments which have traditionally been put against such arrangements remain to be considered. To begin with, there is, even with the built-in 'success fee' possibility, the likelihood that solicitors will not be interested in taking on those cases which they regard as having only limited or remote chances of success. After all, why should lawyers waste their time for no financial return? And at the other end of the spectrum, there may be unseemly haste amongst solicitors to undertake work which they see as particularly lucrative. Critics point to the unsavoury tendencies of some American lawyers to indulge in 'ambulance-chasing' – that is, to be on the spot quickly after an accident or disaster, and engage the services of victims with 'no-win, no-fee' offers containing terms which, if the case is successful, guarantees the lawyer huge percentages of compensation payments. Against these objections, of course, is the argument that under any scheme, including the previous legal aid system, unscrupulous solicitors might adopt tactics (such as artificially prolonging the length of time a case takes to be concluded) in order to enhance their fee. The Law Society has recognised that a system of conditional fee arrangements needs proper regulation to avoid abuse,

---

57 S. Yarrow, *The Price of Success: Lawyers, Clients and Conditional Fees* (1997, Policy Studies Institute).

and the Access to Justice Act 1999 provides the basic statutory framework for the operation of the system.[58]

Apart from those cases for which conditional fee arrangements will be made, what other legal services may be provided by means of support from the Community Legal Service, and when will these services be available? A person taking their problem to a legal adviser – whether a solicitor, law centre or other provider – may be able to obtain one or more 'levels' of legal services. Apart from the possibility of a free or low-cost initial interview, which some advisers may offer, Community Legal Service funding falling short of full legal representation may cover 'legal help' (advice and assistance), 'help at court' (legal assistance at court hearings, but not full representation) and 'approved family help' (assistance with family disputes through negotiation or mediation). Services beyond these levels are categorised as legal representation (the type of service previously covered by legal aid), and comprise either assistance provided by a lawyer to investigate the strength of the client's claim, or full representation if legal proceedings are taken.

Depending on the level of service required, the adviser must apply on behalf of the client[59] to the regional offices of the Community Legal Service for a decision as to whether funding will be available for that problem, and there is a financial eligibility test. The rules and limits as to financial eligibility are changed from time to time, and the complexities of the system are such that the details are best obtained from the organisations themselves – the Legal Services Commission web-page contained an on-line 'eligibility calculator'.[60] There will be a contribution payable by clients[61] whose disposable income is more than a specified amount per month, the amount of the contribution increasing on a sliding scale as the amount of disposable income increases.

Apart from the financial criteria for eligibility, the system incorporates tests as to the *merits* of particular claims – the criteria on which the merits are tested vary according to types of case and the particular circumstances of the client, but the detailed criteria are those specified in the Legal Services Commission 'Funding Code'.[62]

For criminal cases, the Legal Services Commission is responsible for the operation of the Criminal Defence Service. Again, various levels of service are covered, ranging from 'advice and assistance', involving, for example, the provision of general advice (including legal advice provided at police stations under the duty solicitor scheme – see above), writing letters, or preparing a written case, 'advocacy assistance', covering the cost of preparing the client's case and initial representation in certain cases in

58 For a discussion of the implications of conditional fee arrangements on barristers, see P. Kunzlik, 'Conditional Fees: The Ethical and Organisational Impact on the Bar' (1999) 62 *MLR* 850.
59 Some advisers may be 'fully approved' by the Community Legal Service, in which case they can decide, without applying to the Service, on the availability of many levels of service.
60 www.legalservices.gov.uk/civil/calc/whatis_calculator.asp.
61 Except for immigration cases, in which no contributions are payable.
62 The Funding Code may be found at the Community Legal Service website at www.legalservices.gov.uk.

magistrates' and crown courts, and 'representation', covering the preparation of a person's defence, and representation – if necessary by a barrister – in court.

Only private solicitors' firms who have contracts with the Legal Services Commission, or lawyers who are 'public defence lawyers' employed by the Commission itself, may provide funded services under the Criminal Defence Service, and once again there are financial eligibility criteria which clients must satisfy. For Advocacy Assistance and for Representation, there is no applicable means test,[63] although applicants must satisfy the merits test, which is that it is in the interests of justice that the applicant be legally represented in the criminal case concerned. The Access to Justice Act 1999 provides[64] that:

> in deciding what the interests of justice consist of in relation to any individual, the following factors must be taken into account—
>
> (a) whether the individual would, if any matter arising in the proceedings is decided against him, be likely to lose his liberty or livelihood or suffer serious damage to his reputation,
>
> (b) whether the determination of any matter arising in the proceedings may involve consideration of a substantial question of law,
>
> (c) whether the individual may be unable to understand the proceedings or to state his own case,
>
> (d) whether the proceedings may involve the tracing, interviewing or expert cross-examination of witnesses on behalf of the individual, and
>
> (e) whether it is in the interests of another person that the individual be represented.

Although there are aspects of the new funding system which, at first glance, look similar to the old legal aid system – such as the inclusion of means and merits tests – the new provisions represent a dramatic change in the arrangements for the public funding of legal services. Generally speaking, the new system is much more complex, and is much more tightly controlled by means of the new Legal Services Commission and, in particular, the Community Legal Service, both in terms of the cases – especially civil cases – which successfully attract public funding, and also in terms of the checks on the quality of service which lawyers provide through the contracting system and through the device of 'quality kitemarking' service providers. The reforms also strive to bring new levels of co-ordination between the various types of providers of legal services, though it remains to be seen whether this type of work will continue to attract large numbers of private practitioners.[65]

What *is* likely is that publicly funded legal services will continue to be provided by organisations other than solicitors in private firms. Born out of a general belief among lawyers and others during, in particular, the 1970s, that because of cost,

---

63 After Crown Court trials, the trial judge may require the accused to make a contribution if it is reasonable in all the circumstances of the case, including the accused's financial circumstances.

64 In Sch 3. This list is very similar to the list of factors provided under the previous legal aid scheme, though the 1999 Act also gives the Lord Chancellor power to amend the list.

65 See discussions in Zander, op. cit. See also R Miller, 'What's the Future for Legal Aid?' (2002) *NLJ*, 15 March.

social distance, etc the poorer sections of the community were not obtaining the legal advice and help which they needed from private solicitors, a number of developments have taken place. Law centres have been established in many cities, aiming to provide legal services, including representation, for local communities.[66] Usually the centres are set up in busy shopping areas, so that legal services may be available to ordinary people in the local High Street. The staff operating in such centres invariably include qualified solicitors, and finance, always a serious problem in such cases, is derived from various sources, such as charities and local authorities, as well as from income from publicly funded work.

After a period during which funding problems caused much uncertainty for many Law Centres, since the early 1990s several law centres received funding directly from the Legal Aid Board, which recognised the value of developments which law centres had pioneered. Many are now funded, through contracts, by the Legal Services Commission.

Law centres, in addition to providing free legal advice and assistance for individual clients, frequently provide assistance for local groups and campaigns. This type of work has attracted criticism. Such criticism from the professional establishment is quite consistent with the law's general reluctance to recognise and accommodate *group* or *class* interests within its procedures. The legal system, and especially the legal aid system, normally operates on the principle whereby problems and conflicts are *individualised*, thus making it difficult to use the legal system as means to further the interests of groups who may be affected by a particular problem. Since the early 1980s, the possibility of representative actions has been developed, at least to the extent that a 'class' action may be available where each member of the class, or group, had a common element in their claims; and, in 1991, a guide for group actions was issued by the Supreme Court Procedure Committee, and the most recent reforms to civil justice, introduced after Lord Woolf's report, incorporate specific provision for 'multi-party actions'. Such actions have in recent years been taken in respect of a number of major disasters, including the King's Cross underground station fire, the victims of the Dalkon Shield contraceptive and the Hillsborough football stadium disaster.

Apart from law centres and other legal advice centres, Citizens' Advice Bureaux (CAB) have rapidly expanded in number. They operate from over 3,000 locations, handling over five million new cases a year, and some kind of legal advice is needed in many of these cases. The CAB organisation has an efficient and encyclopaedic information system, which may be used for the purpose of giving advice by any CAB office. Of course, a CAB adviser who is not a lawyer may well define a client's problem as essentially 'non-legal', and a client with an accommodation or a family problem may be referred to local authority departments for help rather than advised to take any formal *legal* action.

---

66 See R. Campbell, 'The Inner Cities: Law Centres and Legal Services' (1992) *Journal of Law and Society*, op. cit.

Conclusion

We have in the legal profession a prestigious and influential group of practitioners, supposedly there to ensure that the law's promises of justice for everyone are satisfied, but whose most lucrative work continues to be the handling of the problems of the rich rather than the trials of the poor; the ways in which the profession has been reorganised and legal services opened up to other providers are having the result that whilst some large City of London firms thrive, others have had to reduce their size, and many smaller provincial solicitors' firms have been under threat. The Law Society has recognised that 'for smaller firms, particularly those doing large amounts of legal aid work, there are likely to be real difficulties arising from the government's reforms in the area of legal services'.

Commentators seem to be agreed that the old image of the solicitor as a 'professional person' has given way to commercial reality: the modern lawyer must be concerned with profitability and remaining competitive in an uncertain market. Changes in the structure, work, outlook and remuneration of the legal profession will not change the fact that lawyers, like every other occupational group, must seek the work which is most rewarding financially. The affairs of business, the transfer of real property and the problems of the wealthy continue to provide *some* lawyers with work and high income, whereas the problems of the poor – dealing with landlords, settling local authority and social security problems, representing defendants in court or at tribunals – will never be the kind of work which brings in large amounts of money.

But in the final analysis, the attraction to the legal profession of business and 'property' types of work is understandable, given the concentration by the legal system in general on the management and protection of property. It is primarily the law, therefore, not lawyers themselves, which highlights the problems of the middle- and upper-middle classes at the expense of the poor, and it is at least arguable that, were social and economic inequality in our society to be attacked through changes in the legal, political and economic structure, then consequent changes in the work and organisation of the legal profession would not be far behind.

14

The judges

Although we often speak of 'the judges' as though they were a homogeneous group within the court and judicial structure, there is in fact a whole variety of judges, operating in different courts and at different levels in the court hierarchy (quite apart from those legally qualified persons who chair tribunals).[1] At the top of the hierarchy of courts of law are members of the House of Lords and the Court of Appeal, appointed from the ranks of Court of Appeal judges and High Court judges respectively; lower down, the judges of the High Court are appointed from among senior and eminent barristers; and at county court level, Circuit Judges and Recorders are appointed from the ranks of the legal profession – at present still mainly from barristers, though in June 2006, around 10% of Recorders were solicitors.[2]

The exception to this general pattern of judicial recruitment from amongst practising barristers is, of course, found in the magistrates' courts, where the bench only exceptionally comprises trained lawyers; usually, laymen and women are appointed as Justices of the Peace on the basis of their experience and general standing in the local community. Although they receive some training in the law, magistrates are to a large extent dependent for legal knowledge upon their clerks, who are legally qualified and whose task it is to advise the court on matters of law in cases heard before them. In certain urban areas, however, district judges (magistrates' courts), who are full-time paid magistrates, are appointed from among barristers and solicitors.

The popular image of the judge is of someone removed socially and, in an important sense, physically from the day-to-day activities and preoccupations of society, though this clearly is hardly accurate in the case of magistrates. The role of the judge in court has been compared with that of an umpire, taking relatively little part in the trial itself, but presiding over the proceedings, seeing fair play between the disputants, ensuring that no misleading or prejudicial evidence is presented, and controlling the trial with the aim of arriving at a decision based upon the facts as elicited through legal argument and examination of witnesses and other evidence by either side. Where there is a jury trial (today, usually only in the Crown Court[3]) the task of the judge is, additionally, to summarise the evidence on both

1 Chapter 6.   2 'Judiciary of England and Wales' Monthly Statistics, June 2006.
3 And even here, only in cases where the accused pleads 'not guilty'. Juries are now virtually absent from civil trials. In defamation (that is, libel and slander) cases, juries had the function of assessing

sides of the case for the jury's benefit, making sure that the jurors are acquainted with the relevant law to apply to the facts, and sending them away to reach a decision based on a full appreciation of the points at issue in the case.

In criminal cases, the presiding judge or magistrate must also pass sentence upon conviction of the accused, and this function has done much to capture the popular imagination. Before the suspension of capital punishment in 1965, and certainly during the days of the eighteenth century when there were over 200 capital offences on the statute-book, the judge had, literally, the powers of life and death over those convicted of such offences:

> In the court room the judges' every action was governed by the importance of spectacle . . . scarlet robes lined with ermine and full-bottomed wigs in the seventeenth-century style, which evoked . . . awe from ordinary men. The powers of light and darkness were summoned into the court with the black cap which was donned to pronounce sentence of death, and the spotless white gloves worn at the end of a 'maiden assize' when no prisoners were to be left for execution.[4]

According to Glanville Williams, the English legal system has produced 'judges of intelligence, alertness, patience, toleration and firmness . . . A very large number have been men of outstanding ability and attainments, who have throughout their judgeships been held in the very highest esteem.'[5] And, more recently, Pannick has stated that 'because judges are men, not machines, we must expect judicial frailties and not judge them too harshly',[6] but concludes that 'English judges have every reason to be proud of the quality of their performance . . .'[7]

Are these rather complacent opinions justified? In this chapter we take up various questions concerning the judges, their functions, their backgrounds and their mode of appointment; in particular, we will examine the charge that in twentieth-century society, where there is continuous change in social values, economic patterns, political institutions and class differences, the judiciary has shown itself to be a highly conservative force, unable or unwilling to bring itself (and the legal system which it administers) up to date and into line with modern social conditions.

The social background of the judiciary

If, as was suggested in chapter 13, the members of the legal profession (especially barristers) tend to come from social and educational backgrounds which are predominantly middle and upper-middle class, then it may fairly be said that members

amounts of compensation for successful plaintiffs, but frequently came under fire for awarding sums thought to be excessive. The Courts and Legal Services Act 1990 provided the power for Appeal Courts to reduce awards to 'proper' levels, and the Defamation Act 1996 provided for cases to be heard without a jury. For an excellent account of the jury, its present status, and the problems which have been associated with it, see C. Elliott and F. Quinn, *English Legal System* (6th edn., 2005, Pearson), ch. 12.

4 D. Hay, 'Property, Authority and the Criminal Law' in D. Hay et al., *Albion's Fatal Tree* (1977, Peregrine), p 27.   5 G. Williams, *Proof of Guilt* (1963, Stevens), p 22.

6 D. Pannick, *Judges* (1987, Oxford University Press), p 18.   7 Ibid., p 205.

of the higher levels of the judiciary represent a distillation of those social class currents within the legal system.

To begin with, senior judges are appointed exclusively from the ranks of experienced and established barristers, whose social background still tends to be at the higher levels of the social class structure. We should not, therefore, be surprised to discover that studies have consistently shown that judges tend to have extremely homogeneous backgrounds and educational patterns. Griffith[8] cites a number of surveys which show a marked pattern of public school education, followed by Oxford or Cambridge University. One such study cited found that of the 34 Law Lords and Lords Justices of Appeal, 29 had attended public schools and Oxford or Cambridge University.[9] Regarding the social background of the higher judiciary, Blom-Cooper and Drewry, in their study of the House of Lords,[10] found that out of 49 of the 63 Law Lords holding office between 1876 and 1972, 34 had fathers who were lawyers or members of other professions; and figures published by the Lord Chancellor's Department in 1995 showed that 80% of judges in the House of Lords, Court of Appeal, and High Court were educated at either Oxford or Cambridge Universities.[11]

The uniform social and educational pattern which such studies consistently reveal raises certain questions about the general social and political outlook of the judiciary as a whole. There are many instances of judicial utterances which some might consider to raise doubts as to the extent to which some judges are fully acquainted with contemporary social reality outside their own social class, sex and age-group. Examples include the judge who asked, in a case in 1985, 'Who is Bruce Springsteen?' and the statement by the judge in a rape trial in 1982 that the victim, who had innocently hitched a lift in the accused's car, had been 'guilty of a great deal of contributory negligence'.[12] More recently, judges have been at pains to emphasise the extent to which they are in touch with social reality. In a speech given in July 2006, for example, the Lord Chief Justice, Lord Phillips, explained that 'we do travel on buses and tubes and bicycles, we push trolleys around supermarkets, we have normal family concerns . . . and day by day our work gives us an insight into what is happening in all sectors of society . . .'[13] And a glimpse of an awareness of an altogether more arcane aspect of modern society was provided in a newspaper interview with a High Court Judge who asked the interviewer

> would you know what I was talking about if I asked for 'an 'Enry' and said 'it's for Percy'?. . .. It means I want an eighth of an ounce of cannabis for personal use. That is part of the world we judges live in and a part with which we are most definitely in touch.[14]

8 J. A. G. Griffith, *The Politics of the Judiciary* (5th edn., 1997, Fontana), pp 18–20.
9 *Labour Research*, January 1987. According to a more recent *Labour Research* survey, 'Judging the Judges' (1999, *Labour Research* No 88) not much has changed.
10 L. Blom-Cooper and G. Drewry, *Final Appeal: A Study of the House of Lords in its Judicial Capacity* (1972, Clarendon Press).   11 Reported in the *Guardian*, 18 May 1995.
12 These and other examples are cited by Pannick: op. cit., chapter 2.
13 Reported in the *Guardian*, 19 July 2006.   14 Interviewed in the *Observer*, June 11 2006.

In more general 'party political' terms, the social class distribution of the judges is exactly that sector which we normally associate with support for the traditional Conservative Party, which generally represents the interests of the higher levels of the social class structure (for example, by protecting business interests, maintaining the institutions of private property and private enterprise, concerning itself with issues such as the preservation of law and public order in the face of arguments for legal, political and social change, but preserving a paternalistic concern for the less privileged). Blom-Cooper and Drewry state that:

> the uniformly middle-class backgrounds of the judges, coupled with a long spell of legal training (in itself, a powerful instrument of socialisation) does much to shift the ideological complexion of the judiciary well to the right of centre, whatever the extent of overt party political affiliation in individual judges.[15]

Indeed, in support of the last point, there is some evidence suggesting that 'overt party political affiliation' on the part of individual Law Lords is of itself no indicator of the way in which such a judge is likely to decide a case.[16] Lee has analysed the various surveys which examine critically judges' educational and social origins, and suggests that little should be read into the mere fact alone that many of them come from upper-middle class, Conservative-oriented backgrounds: he argues that the thesis presented by Griffith and others – that their background invariably inclines them towards Conservative views and hence decisions – seems:

> to assume, mistakenly, that judges have homogeneous views. It does seem to assume, mistakenly, that they always decide for the Conservative government. It does seem to assume, mistakenly, that the interests of the State, its moral welfare, the preservation of law and order and the protection of property rights are all dangerous values to be associated solely with the Conservatives. It does seem to assume, mistakenly, that cases involve one class against another.[17]

Lee is critical of what he regards as 'simplistic, naive and misguided'[18] allegations of class bias within the judiciary, and argues that:

> the legitimate complaints of the Left about occasional judicial decisions will never be taken seriously so long as they are submerged in a welter of rhetoric about the background of the judges. At no point is the connection between background and decisions explained. At no point are alternative explanations canvassed. It is foolhardy to dismiss all judicial decisions because of the judiciary's background.[19]

Though there is much force in this argument in so far as it warns against a crude generalisation which links judicial background with political views which find expression in judicial decisions, it remains true that from time to time judicial utterances are reported in the national press which must raise doubts among some members of the

---

15 Op. cit., p 169.
16 D. Robertson, 'Judicial Ideology in the House of Lords: A Jurimetric Analysis' (1982) 12 *British Journal of Political Science.*   17 S. Lee, *Judging Judges* (1988, Faber and Faber), p 34.
18 Ibid., p 36.   19 Ibid., p 38.

community about the lack of bias within the judiciary. Griffith, whose approach is particularly criticised by Lee, cites several worrying examples of overt racist and sexist comments by individual judges, usually resulting in condemnation by either the Lord Chancellor or other members of the judiciary. The danger is that unacceptable statements by individual judges may well undermine public confidence in the judiciary as a whole, and despite Lee's warning, such a possibility must be taken seriously.

With regard to magistrates, the official policy is to avoid any political influence and to seek to appoint people 'regardless of ethnic origin, gender, marital status, sexual orientation, political affiliation, religion or, subject to the physical requirements of the office, disability' in order to address the 'need to ensure that the composition of each bench broadly reflects the community which it serves'.[20] Though few would argue with this aim, it seems that the reality is that the magistracy may not be as 'broadly balanced' in political terms as it might be. Government figures published in 1992 revealed that there is a strong preponderance of Conservative-voters among magistrates:

> The Government gave information on political affiliations of magistrates in 10 areas at the time of appointment . . . A clear pattern emerges. In the two Oldham constituencies, for instance, Labour polled about 52 per cent of the vote at the general election but only 27 per cent of magistrates support Labour. Tories with 32 per cent of the vote, make up 36 per cent of the Bench. The same is true of Bristol, where Labour won 40 per cent of votes, slightly higher than the Tories. Yet 142 Bristol magistrates say they are Tory, and 85 Labour.[21]

Figures published by the Lord Chancellor's Department in 1995 reveal that in a sample survey of 218 newly appointed magistrates in England and Wales, 91 were Conservative voters, 56 Labour, 41 Liberal Democrat, and 4 Plaid Cymru. Only 24 had no political affiliation.[22]

The attempt to create a magistracy characterised by a genuine cross-section of political views has proved difficult. New approaches to the idea of 'political balance' have been examined, though it was reported in 1999 that:

> Officials will now be examining a new approach which involves looking at occupational categories, to be used alongside factors such as age, sex and regional spread . . . In the meantime, the Lord Chancellor's Advisory Committees (which undertake the initial recruitment of lay magistrates) will continue to be asked to ensure the voting pattern for their area, as shown in the last two general elections, is broadly reflected in the composition of their bench.[23]

The appointment and training of judges

Until recently, 'the most remarkable fact about the appointment of judges [has been] that it is wholly in the hands of politicians'.[24] At the lower levels of judicial

20 Department for Constitutional Affairs.   21 The *Independent*, 5 July 1992.
22 The *Guardian*, 18 May 1995.
23 Lord Chancellor's Department, *Press Notice*, 25 October 1999.   24 Griffith, op. cit., p 20.

appointment (magistrates up to High Court judges), appointments were made by, or on the advice of, the Lord Chancellor (a member of the Cabinet and also a judge in the House of Lords); and in the case of judges of the Court of Appeal and House of Lords, appointments were made, technically, by the Prime Minister, again on the advice of the Lord Chancellor. This system has recently been substantially changed, but before we consider these changes, it is useful to gain an overview of the different types of judges.

There are currently around 30,000 magistrates, who are not legally qualified and who preside over around 700 magistrates' courts. They are appointed by the Lord Chancellor after consultation with local advisory groups, of which there are just over 100. The idea is that magistrates should be appointed from all walks of life, and should reflect the diversity of occupation, background, religion, ethnic group, gender, and so on. From time to time, campaigns are launched in order to attract more people – particularly more people from those sections of the community who hitherto have been under-represented, or unrepresented, in the magistracy. According to the Department for Constitutional Affairs, the following characteristics are required of a magistrate – sound judgment and personal integrity; good knowledge of their local community; the ability to listen to all sides of an argument; the ability to contribute to fair and reasonable decisions; reliability and the ability to make a time commitment.

The appointment of district judges, recorders, and circuit judges is carried out by means of open competition. Posts are advertised nationally in newspapers and other publications, and enquirers receive details of the post, the criteria for appointment and an application form. When considering these procedures, it is vitally important to bear in mind that successful applicants must satisfy, as well as other criteria, the required time-period for which they have had rights of audience (see chapter 13) in specified courts. A Recorder, for example, must have had rights of audience in the Crown Court or county court for ten years; a district judge must have had rights of audience for seven years. The other criteria are contained in a detailed framework specifying the skills and competences required: these include, among other criteria, comprehensive legal knowledge and experience, integrity, independence, skills and analysis and judgment, and management and communication skills.

From April 2006, the recruitment and selection of many judicial office-holders is carried out by the independent Judicial Appointments Commission (JAC) – a body set up by the Constitutional Reform Act 2005. Although the Lord Chancellor either appoints, or (for the highest levels of the judiciary) makes recommendations for appointment by the Queen, recommendations as to the best candidates are made by the new Commission. The year 2006–7 is a transition period, during which the JAC will operate by means of established transitional arrangements, but eventually the JAC will also be responsible for the appointment of magistrates.

The Judicial Appointment Commission replaces the Commissioners for Judicial Appointments, created in 2001 to review judicial appointment procedures to ensure that appointments were made on the basis of merit, and to investigate complaints. The fifth (and final) report of the Commissioners, published in 2006, notes that

> In 2001, although the overall quality of the judiciary was not in doubt, the appearance was that judges, most of whom came from very similar backgrounds, seemed simply to 'emerge' from a process fraught with secrecy and unable to shake off suspicions of patronage and favouritism. The judiciary was seen by many to be a closed shop. There seemed to be little chance of advancement for anyone not from the right school, college and socio-economic background . . .[25]

The CJA reports that although substantial progress has been made to address these issues, there remains a substantial amount of work to be done by the new Judicial Appointments Commission to 'continue the momentum towards achieving a fair, open, transparent and accountable appointments process', to embed the principles of diversity, and, in particular 'to convince women, ethnic minorities and others that there is not a judicial culture that is prejudiced against the appointment of those perceived as not fitting the current mould'.[26]

It remains to be seen whether the new Judicial Appointments Commission will succeed in ensuring that the new system of judicial appointments achieves these objectives. Certainly, one of the most persistent criticisms of the judiciary is that women and members of ethnic minority groups are massively under-represented.

The proportion of women and members of ethnic minority groups appointed by means of the open competition system has been increasing, but it is in this context that the statutory requirement for a specified period 'rights of audience' qualification is most important: judges can only be appointed from among lawyers with the relevant type and amount of experience, and so it is arguable that the proportions of appointments of women and applicants from ethnic minority groups is related to the numbers of female and minority ethnic practitioners (see chapter 13). As the pool of lawyers holding the required qualifications for appointment to the bench expands, the numbers of women lawyers and lawyers from ethnic minority groups will also grow, though clearly this will take time.

At the higher levels of judiciary, there is (as at April 2006) one female member of the House of Lords (out of twelve); three out of a total of 37 Court of Appeal, and eleven out of a total of 108 High Court, judges were women. There were 71 women out of 631 circuit judges, 199 out of 1,401 Recorders, and 99 out of 449 district judges. There were no judges from ethnic minority groups in the House of Lords or the Court of Appeal, and only one in the High Court. Ten circuit judges, 67 recorders, and 14 district judges were from ethnic minority groups.[27] Equality of opportunity still has a long way to go.

Training for judges is provided by the Judicial Studies Board, which runs courses which all newly appointed judges are required to attend before sitting as judges. In addition, new appointees must also spend a period of time sitting in court with an

---

25 Commission for Judicial Appointments, *Annual Report 2006*, p 4.   26 Ibid., p 6.
27 These and other relevant judicial statistics may be found at www.judiciary.gov.uk/keyfacts.

experienced judge and, if their work will involve criminal cases, they must also spend time visiting prisons and meeting with probation officers. The Judicial Studies Board organises updating seminars covering new legislation, and sessions dealing with specialist areas of law. The work of the Judicial Studies Board is carried out by five committees, dealing with criminal, family, magisterial, tribunal and civil work. A sixth committee – the Equal Treatment Advisory Committee – services the other committees, advising them on race and ethnic minority issues, gender and sexual orientation, unrepresented parties and children, and disability. This committee also publishes guidelines to judges on all aspects of equality of treatment in courts and tribunals. Special consideration has been given – with dedicated and substantial government funding – to judicial training on human rights, since the passage of the Human Rights Act 1998.

Judges, politics and the process of decision-making

We have noted the complex issue of the relationship between law and politics in several chapters, and in chapter 12, when we considered aspects of administrative law, we saw some of the difficulties inherent in this interface in the context of both historical and contemporary developments in that part of the law. In this section, we consider further the extent to which the judiciary – especially the senior judiciary – may be thought to stray on occasion beyond the realms of the legal into the territory of politics. Much of that discussion will focus upon analyses of judicial activity within the courtroom, though recently some judges have entered rather more public arenas to debate issues of contemporary significance. It is noteworthy that this type of judicial commentary is a relatively recent phenomenon – in days gone by it was not considered appropriate for judges to comment publicly through newspapers or other media.

We have seen the extent to which Parliament has, through the Human Rights Act 1998, laid the responsibility upon the judges to ensure that respect for and protection of human rights (as defined in the European Convention on Human Rights) are implemented. In chapter 12 we noted the development and impact of notions such as proportionality and legitimate expectation, and saw, through some case-examples, how these concepts are beginning to shape English administrative law. A clear and public tension has, however, emerged in the wake of the terrorist attacks on New York and Washington in 2001 and in London in July 2005. In the context of new UK legislation designed to maintain national security and to combat terrorist activity – and in particular the Anti-Terrorism, Crime and Security Act 2001 and the Prevention of Terrorism Act 2005 – members of the judiciary have seriously and openly questioned the compatibility between certain measures enacted in this legislation and the recognition and protection of human rights. We saw earlier, in the case of *A and Others v Home Secretary* in 2004,[28] how the House of Lords held

---

28 [2004] UKHL 56. See chapter 12.

that the holding without trial of those suspected of terrorism was unlawful. The debate as to the judicial role in maintaining the balance between human rights and national security extended beyond the courtroom during 2005, with statements from some politicians, notably the (then) leader of the Conservative Party Michael Howard, criticising the judges for favouring the human rights of suspected terrorists, and in effect opposing the anti-terrorism laws. In response, Lord Carlisle, the independent reviewer of the anti-terrorism legislation, strongly maintained that national security remains central to judicial concerns, and that it was no part of the role of government to influence the ways in which the judiciary carried out its functions; and Sir John Donaldson and other senior members of the judiciary entered the debate in defence of the judges, calling on politicians not to interfere with the ways in which the judges did their job.

The 2005 legislation, which introduced 'control orders' whereby the movements of persons suspected of terrorist activity could be subject to one or more of a series of restrictions, was heavily criticised as infringing human rights, and the tensions between politicians and the judiciary continued into 2006. In June of that year a High Court decision which quashed control orders against six suspects on the basis that the orders infringed human rights drew the fire of members of government, who accused the judge in the case of 'misunderstandings and errors', and senior judges, including the Lord Chief Justice, warned that persistent ministerial criticism of the judiciary was undermining public confidence in the criminal justice system. Many critics pointed out, moreover, that the judges' insistence on the careful scrutiny of legislative measures in the light of the need for appropriate protection of human rights was simply the outcome of the government's own Human Rights Act which clearly laid that very responsibility upon the judiciary.[29]

It is arguable that these developments, played out under the spotlight of newspapers and television, merely bring to the surface the kind of tensions which have always been inherent in cases having political import: similar tensions lurk beneath many decisions during the 1980s in cases involving challenges to government policy over, for example, cuts in local government public spending. In constitutional terms, these controversies certainly serve to emphasise the fact that the constitutional doctrine of the separation of powers, and in particular the requirements for an independent judiciary, is by no means always easy to maintain in practice.

Such tensions between judges and politicians were, of course, virtually unknown in previous eras. In contrast with modern trends towards appointment on merit alone, there once was a time when judicial appointment was commonly based upon candidates' party political service, loyalty or experience, or upon their political affiliations or known views. Paterson, drawing on the material in Heuston's *Lives of the Lord Chancellors, 1885–1940*, found that it was possible to identify such

---

29 Similar criticisms were made regarding adverse ministerial comments on judicial decisions in the sphere of sentencing: during 2006, a number of sentencing decisions attracted negative publicity, though it was clear that such decisions were made in full compliance with recent government legislation.

appointments;[30] and it is also possible to identify, through decided cases, the effects of such a system of judicial appointments. To take one well-documented example, in the trio of cases at the turn of the century involving trade union activities – *Allen v Flood* (1898),[31] *Quinn v Leathem* (1901)[32] and the *Taff Vale Railway* case (1901)[33] – Lord Halsbury, then Lord Chancellor, and a judge with extremely conservative and anti-union views, attempted in all three cases to 'pack' the bench with colleagues having similar attitudes to his own. He was successful in doing so in all but the first. The net result of these decisions (taken together with the known anti-union attitudes of both judges and politicians over the preceding 200 years[34]) was such that trade unionists were left in no doubt that the judges (and by implication the law itself) were anything but their allies. We shall look at other examples of political attitudes of the judges later, but for the moment we should note that, as Lord Hailsham, himself a House of Lords' judge until his retirement, an active and prominent member of the Conservative Party and a man with considerable experience of life as Lord Chancellor, once said, 'activity in politics is not, and never has been, a bar to appointment to the bench'.[35]

Stevens, in analysing the development since 1800 of the House of Lords as a judicial body,[36] has documented the progress of that institution from being essentially political, where final appeals were heard not by professional judges, but by peers of the realm, to being an institution whose judicial function came to be carried out by professional lawyers. These developments occurred quite late in the history of the House of Lords, from the Reform Act 1832; through the intervention by Peel in the case involving conspiracy charges against the Irish political activist Daniel O'Connell in 1844 when the Lord President of the Privy Seal advised lay peers against intervening in the matter under consideration by the Law Lords;[37] up to the restructuring of the court system in the 1870s and the constitutional crises of 1910 and 1911. The origin of the House of Lords as an essentially political body, then, with its judicial function only gradually becoming distinct from its political function, serves to sharpen the distinction between the former's central concern with law, and the latter's concern with policy.

To say this, however, is merely to acknowledge a particular historical development, which has culminated in the firmly established convention that lay peers take no part in the judicial activities of the House (these being the concern of the Law Lords, the professional judges elevated to the House by reason of their experience as judges). This historical perspective serves to highlight the link between the

---

30 A. Paterson, 'The Judges: A Political Elite?' (1974) 1 *British Journal of Law and Society* 2.
31 [1898] AC 1.   32 [1901] AC 495.
33 *Taff Vale Railway Co. v Amalgamated Society of Railway Servants* [1901] AC 426.
34 See chapter 1.
35 Cited in Paterson (1974), op. cit., p 125. See J. A. G. Griffith, *The Politics of the Judiciary* (5th edn., 1997, Fontana); Smith and Bailey's *The Modern English Legal System* (4th edn. by S. Bailey, M. Gunn, and D. Ormerod, 2002, Sweet and Maxwell); Pannick, op. cit., chapter 3.
36 R. Stevens, *Law and Politics: The House of Lords as a Judicial Body 1800–1976* (1979, Weidenfeld and Nicolson).   37 Ibid., pp 32–34.

judiciary and other political institutions: the judiciary, at all levels of the court structure, is a part of the overall political structure of society, albeit a part which enjoys the reputation for independence of any executive governmental function, as we saw in chapter 6.[38] But as suggested above, this constitutional position of independence does not necessarily mean that political considerations play no part in the process of judicial decision-making.

The delicate balance between being seen to be independent of politics and at the same time a part of the political structure, has been discussed in various ways and with various emphases by many commentators. Hay[39] notes the behind-the-scenes 'stage-managing' of local assizes during the eighteenth century, in which local gentry and visiting judges shared a common concern that the populace should remain faithful to law, state and the established political order, hence posing no threat to the existing social and political arrangements. The death penalty, the formal and symbolic trappings of the courtroom, the presence of an enormous number of capital offences on the statute-book, all combined to make this essentially political task of maintaining the status quo relatively easy, as well as obscuring the instrumental political concerns of the rulers of the period behind the appeal to the neutrality and supremacy of the law. Another historical study, by Glassey,[40] traced the relationship between appointments to the magistracy and political affiliation and patronage between 1675 and 1720, showing the clear connections between such appointments and long-established families of high social status during the period.

The issue of public confidence in the independence of the judiciary crops up in the media from time to time, and in recent years the judiciary has been 'battered and bruised'[41] by a series of cases in which there was a clear and most serious miscarriage of justice. First came the release from prison of the Guildford Four in 1989, followed in 1991 by the quashing of the convictions of the Maguire Seven, followed in the same year by the successful appeals by the Birmingham Six – all of whom had been convicted of terrorist activity, including the bombing of public houses in Guildford and Birmingham. Later, in 1997, came the release of the men convicted of the murder of the newspaper-boy Karl Bridgewater. It eventually transpired that all of the defendants in these cases had served long periods of imprisonment for crimes they did not commit, though all of the cases had previously been re-examined and duly rejected by the Court of Appeal. Not surprisingly, among the questions asked in the media at the time was, simply, why had the court not recognised earlier the weaknesses in the Crown's case against these defendants (and in particular the police and scientific forensic evidence in some cases)? The Birmingham Six case is interesting for, among other things, Lord Denning's

38 On judicial independence see also the article by Lord Bingham in T. Bingham, *The Business of Judging* (2000, Oxford University Press); and R. Stevens, *The Independence of the Judiciary* (1993, Oxford University Press).   39 Op. cit.

40 L. K. J. Glassey, *Politics and the Appointment of Justices of the Peace 1675–1720* (1979, Oxford University Press). And see A. H. Manchester, *Modern Legal History* (1980, Butterworths), chapter 9.

41 M. Tregilgas-Davey, 'Miscarriages of Justice within the English Legal System' (1991) *NLJ*, 17 May.

previous refusal to grant legal aid to the defendants in 1975 to allow them to bring an action against the West Midlands police:

> If the six men win it will mean that the police were guilty of perjury, that they were guilty of violence and threats, that the confessions were involuntary and were improperly admitted in evidence and that the convictions were erroneous. That would mean the Home Secretary would either have to recommend they be pardoned or he would have to remit the case to the Court of Appeal. This is such an appalling vista that every sensible person in the land would say: 'It cannot be right that these actions should go any further'.[42]

In other words, it seemed to his Lordship more important that public confidence in the criminal justice system should not be undermined than that six innocent men should be freed.

This series of events did little to bolster public confidence in the higher judiciary[43] and there are more cases of people in prison in respect of whose convictions there may be serious doubt. In the wake of the release of the Birmingham Six came the establishment of a Royal Commission on Criminal Justice, chaired by Lord Runciman, whose terms of reference included issues arising after trial and, in particular, arrangements for considering allegations of miscarriages of justice. The recommendations of the Commission on this point were implemented in the Criminal Appeal Act 1995, which set up the Criminal Cases Review Commission, which has the power to refer cases of convicted persons to the Court of Appeal if it considers that 'there is a real possibility that the conviction, verdict, finding or sentence would not be upheld . . . [in the Court of Appeal] . . . because of an argument, or evidence, not raised in the proceedings which led to it or on any appeal or application for leave to appeal against it'. It is to be hoped that this new body will play an important part in effectively preventing miscarriages of justice in the future.

In a more general context, and drawing on many cases from various areas of social activity as illustrations, Griffith has catalogued and discussed the extent to which the role of the judiciary (in particular the judges of the higher courts) can be seen to overlap into the sphere of political decision-making.[44] In particular, Griffith discusses the broad areas of industrial relations, personal rights and freedoms, property rights and squatters, judicial control of ministerial discretion, the uses of conspiracy, and cases involving students and trade union members. He argues that 'judges are part of the machinery of authority within the State and as such cannot avoid the making of political decisions';[45] and that the senior judges in particular have, by reason of their legal education and their working life as practising

---

42 Quoted in Griffith, op. cit., pp 307–308.
43 Or in the police, for that matter. The West Midlands Serious Crime Squad had to be disbanded due to corruption, and investigations into the activities of this group of officers continued for some months afterwards. It has been commented that 'Not one police officer accused of malpractice arising from the many miscarriages of justice put right by the Court of Appeal since 1989 has been convicted of a criminal offence': D. Rose, In the Name of the Law (1996), cited in Griffith, op. cit., p 212.   44 Griffith, op. cit.   45 Ibid., pp 292–329.

barristers, 'acquired a strikingly homogeneous collection of attitudes, beliefs, and principles, which to them represents the public interest'.[46] For Griffith, the idea of an impartial and neutral judiciary, especially in cases involving a political element, is mythical:

> judges in the United Kingdom cannot be politically neutral because they are placed in positions where they are required to make political choices which are sometimes presented to them, and often presented by them, as determinations of where the public interest lies; . . . that interpretation of what is in the public interest and therefore politically desirable is determined by the kind of people they are and the position they hold in our society; . . . this position is part of established authority and so is necessarily conservative, not liberal.[47]

When first published, Griffith's book met with considerable criticism, particularly, as one might expect, from members and ex-members of the judiciary. Lord Devlin, once a judge in the House of Lords, responded to some of Griffith's assertions and arguments.[48] To a large extent, Devlin's reply may be summarised as a resounding 'so what?'. To begin with, he explains, there is no denying the homogeneity of political and other outlooks on the part of the judges, but then the same is true of most other institutions in our society, or at least, those of them which 'like the law are not of a nature to attract the crusading or rebellious spirit'.[49]

Further, argues Devlin, the question posed by Griffith, which is, 'do the judges allow their devotion to law and order to distort their application of the law when they apply it to those who do not think as they do?' is beset by the twin difficulties of lack of unanimity among the senior judges whom Griffith, according to Devlin, seeks to present as 'a small group of senior judges who are policy makers':[50] 'The law lords are sometimes divided: more frequently they quarrel with the Court of Appeal.'[51] And the constraints imposed by the length of Griffith's book do not, argues Devlin, allow any rigorous analysis of the cases under discussion. Devlin accepts that Griffith's perspective may be seen as the view from the left, and explains that criticisms of the judiciary might also be made by those taking a different ideological stance: 'Professor Griffith cites cases on the use of police powers which he finds to be "alarming"; someone right of centre could probably produce a list of cases which would alarm him by their tenderness towards crime.'[52] In short, Devlin is inclined to the view that too much is made by Griffith of the 'politics of the judiciary', for 'their politics are hardly more significant than those of the army, the navy and the airforce; they are as predictable as those of any institution where maturity is in command'.[53]

It is hard to resist the comment that the politics of the armed forces may well be significant; there are countless examples of military coups and dictatorships in various parts of the world throughout recent history, and in contemporary Britain we need only look as far as the history of the role of the armed forces in Northern

46 Ibid., p 295.   47 Ibid., p 326.
48 P. Devlin, 'Judges, Government and Politics' (1978) 41 *MLR* 501. See also Lee, op. cit.
49 Ibid., p 506.   50 Ibid., p 508.   51 Ibid., p 506.   52 Ibid., p 507.   53 Ibid., p 510.

Ireland. And Devlin's criticisms do not detract from the general thesis presented by Griffith that the political inclinations of the judiciary can, and sometimes do, influence the outcome of cases coming before them. Devlin may well be correct when he points out that the tendency of the judiciary and of the law itself is to constitute a force for stability, law and order, and we should therefore not be too surprised when the judges, charged with the administration of the law, seek to maintain that stability, sometimes in the face of determined and militant forces for change.

Judicial insistence on the maintenance of 'law and order' may well, however, be inconsistent on occasion with other currents in society, where rapid change has long been the norm in many areas of social life. Present-day society, with its almost daily advances in technology, its socio-economic diversity and inequality and its multiplicity of moral and political divergences, exhibits instability in virtually every aspect of social, economic and political activity. Given the truism that, in the twentieth century, the law in one way or another touches more and more people in an ever-increasing range of activities, it is hardly surprising to find tensions within some parts of the legal system between forces for change and forces for conservatism; such tension must be at its clearest when issues involving policy or politics come before the courts.

To say that there is a danger (which Devlin would not deny) that general political affiliations and attitudes may affect judicial decision-making is not to suggest any kind of 'judicial conspiracy', nor that the antics of Lord Halsbury in the trade union cases of 1898–1902 would be repeated in English courts today. The point is rather that any manifestation of political or ideological stance is a matter neither for surprise nor denial. Judges play a creative role in the legal system, not only by virtue of their development of the common law but also in the manner in which they perceive and interpret 'facts' in cases before them. Cases directly or indirectly involving political considerations (public order, industrial relations, state security, issues of morality or race relations, to mention but a few examples) and cases involving new issues which are without precedent *do* crop up from time to time. It would therefore be quite unrealistic for us to expect judges, given their backgrounds and professional experience, to analyse and interpret the facts of cases in a manner divorced from their personal perceptions and preconceptions of the social and political world. What is interesting is not that political nuances enter judicial pronouncements *per se*, but rather the complex ways in which the reasoning in such decisions is presented. In short, to what extent do the judges operate in a context of unbridled freedom to decide cases as they choose, and to what extent are there institutional constraints which tend to limit the lengths to which they may go?

Several general comments may be made at this point, before we discuss specific aspects of the problem. To begin with, an important constraining factor is the necessity, noted by Weber,[54] Frank[55] and others, for judicial decisions to be

---

54 M. Weber, *Law in Economy and Society* (1979 edn. Harvard University Press), chapter 3.
55 J. Frank, *Courts on Trial* (first published 1949; 1973 edn. Princeton University Press).

presented not as the outcome of subjective, arbitrary or capricious reasoning by the judge, but as the result of the application of *objective* criteria. This is the difference between the statement 'in my opinion, you are guilty' and the statement 'according to the law, you are guilty'. The former statement we would regard as somewhat suspect, as being unfair or biased. The issue of public credibility and confidence in the judiciary is once again relevant here: we would not place much faith in a legal system which allowed judges to decide cases according to their whim or their personal views about the parties to a dispute. We expect judges to decide cases in accordance with existing law, without personal views or prejudices colouring their judgment.

Despite such expectations, however, some writers have argued, from differing standpoints, that there are strong elements of subjectivity in judicial decision-making. Some American legal writers have denied that judicial decision-making is simply a matter of 'rules determining decisions', but maintain that judges often decide cases according to intuition, or 'hunch',[56] and proceed to justify ('rationalise') their decisions by dressing them up in the cloak of legal rules. Others adopt a rather more complex approach, stressing the subtle relationships between legal rules and judicial creativity. Another argument centres on the debates about the 'rule of law', one interpretation of which[57] is that in our society everyone – including government – is subject to the law of the land: we live under 'the government of laws, and not of men'. Some writers, notably Thompson, have argued that there have been many occasions in history where judges have used this proposition to mask decisions which in reality reflect the 'rule of a class'.[58] Against such an argument, it might be said that it is precisely because those in authority, including judges, are subject to existing legal rules that judges can act only within a framework of constraints which those rules impose upon them.

The necessity of deciding cases by means of objective criteria brings us to consider a second and extremely important constraining factor operating upon judicial reasoning and decision-making. This factor is the existence of that set of criteria whereby the judge reaches a decision: the legal rules and principles themselves. There are various schools of thought as to the extent to which judges are constrained by the law itself, and much will depend, in general terms, upon the nature of the legal system under consideration. In England, there once was a time – during the nineteenth century in particular – when the 'declaratory theory' of judging prevailed.

56 J. Hutcheson, 'The Judgement Intuitive: The Function of the "Hunch" in Judicial Decisions' (1928) 14 *Corn LQ* 274.
57 The phrase has been subjected to a number of definitions. For a discussion of the constitutional definition, see H. W. R. Wade and C. F. Forsyth, *Administrative Law* (9th edn., 2004, Oxford University Press), chapter 2; C. Turpin, *British Government and the Constitution: Text, Cases and Materials* (5th edn., 2002, Cambridge University Press), chapter 1; J. Jowell, 'The Rule of Law Today' in J. Jowell and D. Oliver, *The Changing Constitution* (5th edn., 2004, Oxford University Press). And see above, chapter 12.
58 E. P. Thompson, *Whigs and Hunters* (1977, Peregrine), p 259.

This theory holds that judges have no creative, or law-making, function, and little or no discretion in handling rules; their task is the declaration and application of existing rules to cases coming before them. Even the common law, which is the outcome of judicial law-making (see chapter 7), was held to be the result of the judges' merely declaring what the law is, and not the result of law-making activity. Few today would hold to this theory in such a form, although Dworkin, in particular, has argued[59] that judicial discretion in handling rules does not exist in the sense that most modern writers would believe. Dworkin has presented the idea of law as 'integrity', meaning that:

> law's constraints benefit society not just by providing predictability or procedural fairness, or in some other instrumental way, but by securing a kind of equality among citizens that makes their community more genuine and improves its moral justification for exercising the political power it does . . . [Integrity] argues that rights and responsibilities flow from past decisions and so count as legal, not just when they are implicit in these decisions but also when they follow from the principles of personal and political morality the explicit decisions presuppose by way of justification.[60]

Integrity thus seems to constitute some kind of ideal, in the light of which a judge, in determining the solution to a case, constructs his or her decision by interpreting the relevant law. It is linked to the notions of coherence both in terms of the content of laws and the ways in which those laws are interpreted.[61] And, ultimately, integrity, Dworkin argues, enables the judge to ascertain the 'right' answer as between two conflicting rules or principles. Thus, Dworkin's hypothetical judge, when faced with having to decide between two conflicting principles, makes a choice between the two, and declares that he:

> settle[s] on this choice because I believe that though the impulse behind each of the two principles is attractive, the second is more powerful in these circumstances. This requires me to declare a certain number of past judicial decisions mistakes and to overrule these if my jurisdiction permits. But the number of decisions I must count as mistakes is neither so great nor of such fundamental importance, viewed from the perspective of legal practice as a whole, that disregarding them leaves me no solid foundation for the more general interpretation I have just described.[62]

Integrity is thus about continuity and coherence in law and adjudication; Dworkin argues that it enables the judge to arrive at a 'right' answer where there is no clear solution. Space here does not permit anything more than this all-too-brief statement of Dworkin's arguments, but it must be said that in terms of legal theory, those arguments seem to add little to the existing body of legal writings on and about law, in so far as they posit an ideal to which legal officials such as judges 'ought' to subscribe (see chapter 2), and in terms of judicial discretion in decision-making it must be said that the 'right answer' thesis runs against the tide of modern

---

59 R. Dworkin, *Taking Rights Seriously* (1977, Duckworth); *Law's Empire* (1986, Fontana).
60 *Law's Empire*, pp 95–96.   61 Ibid., chapter 6.   62 Ibid., pp 271–272.

academic and even, today, judicial opinion[63] as to the extent to which judges are constrained by the framework of legal rules and principles.

It is interesting to compare Dworkin's picture with other approaches. We have already noted the older 'declaratory theory' of judging which holds that what judges do is not to create but merely to *declare* the law; and it is noteworthy that the sociologist Max Weber, writing in the early twentieth century, presented a classification of various *kinds* of law and legal systems,[64] one of which – the 'logical formal rational' type of law[65] – comprised a set of legal precepts from which the legal answer to every case might be found. Such a legal system in such a 'pure' form has, however, never existed, even within European legal systems (especially the German system) whose highly codified legal rules approximated most closely to this particular theoretical model.

Regarding the English system with its common-law traditions, Weber acknowledged that there were aspects which approximated more to other types of law in his classification. In particular, he perceived elements of 'substantive rationality' within a common-law system, which means that decisions in particular cases may be guided by *criteria other than those of the law itself*, such as an appeal to ethics, religion or political ideology. This type of law, then, is by no means a 'seamless web' which always provides the 'right answer', but is rather a complex framework of legal and *non-legal* rules, standards and principles, any or all of which may operate either to constrain or to free a judge in making a decision in a given case.

The extent to which legal rules and principles constrain judicial choice in decision-making remains, therefore, a matter for some debate. We may agree with Lord Radcliffe who stated that 'there never was a more sterile controversy than that upon the question whether a judge makes law. Of course he does. How can he help it?'[66] But the real issues surely are precisely how, and to what extent, rules and principles serve to limit that discretion and law-making activity.

In addressing these issues, a number of factors must be considered. First, what clues may be found within the judgments of the courts themselves? Second, how do the judges actually perceive and define their role, and what light do those perceptions and definitions throw on the matter of judicial creativity?

As to the first of these factors, a study of the speeches of the Law Lords over a 12-month period by Murphy and Rawlings[67] examines the ways in which the judges' speeches are 'glued together'[68] and what the authors call the 'strategic deployment of discursive techniques'[69] used by the judges in dealing with the cases before them.

---

63 See Lord Devlin, 'The Judge as Lawmaker' in P. Devlin, *The Judge* (1979, Oxford University Press); Lord Reid, 'The Judge as Lawmaker' (1972) 12 *Journal of the Society of Public Teachers of Law* 22; and for discussion of these judges see Stevens, op. cit., chapter 13 and A. Paterson, *The Law Lords* (1982, Macmillan/SSRC).

64 Weber, op. cit.   65 See Weber, op. cit., esp. the Introduction by M. Rheinstein, pp L-LI.

66 Quoted in Stevens, op. cit., p 447.

67 W. T. Murphy and R. W. Rawlings, 'After the *Ancien Regime*: The Writing of Judgments in the House of Lords 1979/1980' (1981) 44 *MLR* and (1982) 45 *MLR*.

68 (1981) 44 *MLR* at 617.   69 Ibid.

Noting some critics' characterisation of some House of Lords' decisions as 'superficial', these authors argue, with reference to a number of cases decided during the period of the study, that there may be detected within Law Lords' speeches a considerable degree of assertiveness – often unsupported by any sustained or developed line of reasoning drawn from detailed discussion of previous cases or legal principles. This is not true of all the cases analysed, however, for in certain cases 'we find lengthy discussions of case law or of historical background, and sometimes extensive "overview" discussions conducted in the manner of a treatise writer. In other words, the Law Lords have some criteria of selection which determine when an elaborate discussion is required.'[70] The specific charge of superficiality, the authors explain, is hard to analyse, partly because it depends largely on what critics themselves consider to be significant or insignificant issues, or superficial or thorough discussions. What must be differentiated, however, are superficiality and *particularisation*; the latter refers to a prominent technique used by the judges on occasion, whereby the issues in a case may be reduced to, say, defining the meaning of a particular word in a statutory provision, on which matter the entire case is deemed to rest. Particularisation may, in some cases, result from the convention that Law Lords' judgments only deal with matters raised before the court by counsel, and it may be that on occasion a particular matter is elevated to pivotal status by counsel in the course of argument.[71] The effect of particularisation, it is argued, is to reduce the issues in a case to 'manageable proportions, a process which thereby generates a fairly common necessity of evading or suppressing "difficulties". Particularisation is not reducible to a "superficial" treatment of conventional legal material.'[72]

Another technique used by the judges – predominantly, according to Murphy and Rawlings, when faced with a problem of statutory interpretation – is to explore the implications and possible consequences of deciding in accordance with the 'literal' as opposed to the 'ordinary' or 'common sense' meaning of a term. It is argued, however, that when a given interpretation is adopted, there is little by way of sustained and careful enunciation of the reasons for that choice of interpretation. In yet other instances, the judges purport to seek the purpose of legislation, or claim to fill 'gaps' in statutes by means of judicial modification, or present complex statements as merely asserting the obvious – again with little explicit reasoning to support the conclusions arrived at. Where there is no 'statutory text' to interpret, examples are given which suggest that judges will explicitly consider matters of 'policy' (that is, factors outside the existing legal rule framework itself); though here again, the authors claim that with regard to at least one of the cases discussed, 'there is no indication in any of the speeches of how [the relevant] matters are to be worked through thoroughly in the writing of a judgment. Rather, assertion suffices.'[73]

70 Ibid., p 621.
71 For example, see the discussion on *Bromley London Borough Council v Greater London Council*, below and see chapter 12. In this case, much was stated to depend on the interpretation of a single word – 'economic' – used in the statute under consideration.   72 (1981) 44 *MLR* at 622.
73 (1982) 45 *MLR* at 41.

When evaluating this kind of study, it is important to remember that it is conducted at a particular level of analysis concerned only with the text of the judgments, and does not in itself address the central question of the structural position of the higher judiciary. Neither does it deal, as the authors acknowledge, with the social implications of the cases discussed, in terms of the *effects* of the decisions; nor with the extent to which judges' decision-making – or even their 'assertions' – were the outcome of the political predilection of particular judges. Although the study illuminates what are often cited as lacunae or weaknesses of reasoning within the Law Lords' judgments, these political dimensions are not discussed, despite the authors' ultimate recognition that 'we are led to questions of power and how power circulates within a society'.[74]

This political dimension is arguably of great significance, especially when we note that the cases under review concerned, among other matters, the legal position of trade unions,[75] the role of the Advisory, Conciliation and Arbitration Service,[76] the law relating to immigration,[77] the status of a tax avoidance scheme,[78] the law relating to contempt of court[79] and the question of the extent to which a government department can withhold documents from inspection by a court in the 'public interest'.[80] All of these are issues on which writers such as Griffith would presumably argue that the political position of the judges was vitally important in analysing the judgments. In assessing the methodology of this study, then, one question we might wish to consider is the nature of the relationship between the position of the judges and the way in which judgments are constructed. Arguably, one does not automatically illuminate the other; and each is in itself inadequate in explaining the connections between what judges *are* and what they *do*, and between what they *do* and what they *say they do*. Such connections are particularly important when the judges choose to adopt a creative role in individual 'hard' cases – cases, that is, where existing legal rules do not apparently cover the facts before the court – or in some of the other kinds of case identified by Paterson, discussed below.

Paterson's study concerns the work of the judges in the House of Lords[81] with a view to discovering the Law Lords' own perceptions of their role and their work. Rather than concentrating upon the judges' structural position in society, Paterson's methodology was that of role analysis: the examination of 'the conduct that is expected of [the judge] in the particular social position which he occupies'.[82]

---

74 Ibid., at 61.
75 *Express Newspapers Ltd v McShane* [1980] 2 WLR 89; *Duport Steels Ltd v Sirs* [1980] 1 WLR 142.
76 *United Kingdom Association of Professional Engineers v Advisory, Conciliation and Arbitration Service* [1981] AC 424; *Engineers' and Managers' Association v Advisory, Conciliation and Arbitration Service* [1980] 1 WLR 302.
77 *Zamir v Secretary of State for the Home Department* [1980] 3 WLR 249.
78 *IRC v Plummer* [1980] AC 896; another case concerning tax liability heard during the relevant period, and discussed by Murphy and Rawlings, was *Vestey v IRC* [1980] AC 1148.
79 *A-G v BBC* [1981] AC 303.
80 *Burmah Oil Co Ltd v Governor and Company of the Bank of England* [1980] AC 1090. See below for further discussion of this point.
81 Paterson, *The Law Lords*, op. cit.   82 Ibid., p 3.

His findings are based on observation of cases, interviews with Law Lords, barristers and others working closely with these most senior judges, and the analysis of (mainly) common-law cases heard by the House of Lords between 1957 and 1973. We learn that the Law Lords are to a large extent both actors and their own audience, in that their judgments seem to be influenced only by their fellow Law Lords. This finding is qualified to the extent that certain conventions tend to constrain this apparent independence – such as the convention, mentioned above, that a judgment should discuss only matters raised by counsel during the case, or raised and considered by the courts below. Although this convention is strongly adhered to, it is acknowledged that the judges can and do structure the course of counsel's argument by means of interventions and questions.

Paterson acknowledges a point made by other observers, which is that much will depend upon individual judges' personalities; the senior, presiding judge in particular can influence or control the course of argument, and some judges are more prepared than others to intervene. Judges' personalities will also affect the final outcome of the case. Whether or not a judge is prepared to dissent from the majority; whether a judge possesses particular persuasive powers, or even obstinacy, leading him or her to try to direct or force the conclusions of his or her colleagues; or whether judges feel they must defer to the opinions of colleagues whose experience or intellect they respect: all are factors which illustrate the *individualistic* aspect of what is commonly thought of as a *group* decision-making process.

Paterson examines the work of the Law Lords from the point of view of the perceived objectives of judicial decision-making, especially in terms of what he calls:

> the tension between the drive for stability and certainty in the common law, which requires that disputes be adjudicated in accordance with previously announced norms and the drive for adjudication on the basis of individuated justice, which in certain cases will require that previously announced norms will be radically altered or departed from.[83]

That the Law Lords acknowledge this tension between justice and certainty emerges clearly from the many quotations from judges. The problem is especially acute in those 'hard' cases where there is no binding or strongly persuasive precedent, where precedents or principles may conflict, where the ratio of an ostensibly relevant precedent is unclear, or where the court is being asked to distinguish or overrule a binding or strongly persuasive precedent.[84]

Continuing to use role analysis, Paterson analyses the various types of judicial response to these problems, by identifying various potentially conflicting expectations of a judge which are raised in reaching a decision. The main expectations are that the judge should justify the decision by reasoned argument, that he ought not to legislate (that being the role of Parliament), that the decision should be consistent with existing law, and that the decision should achieve a just and fair result.

83 Ibid., p 123.   84 See chapter 7.

These expectations may conflict: for instance, where the judge is being asked to overrule a precedent (thus creating new law) in order to reach what he or she feels is a just decision. The responses which judges may make when faced with such conflict are, argues Paterson, threefold. First, the judge may react *positively*, by redefining the judicial role so that the conflict is reduced, or by meeting with colleagues to discuss the problem. Second, the response may be *adaptive*, involving either the ranking or the weighing of the competing expectations, or (perhaps more significantly) evading the issue by means of 'dissimulation' – essentially, obscuring the existence of the conflict: 'The Law Lords imply that compliance with each of the expectations involves no breach of the others, when in truth they actually violate one or more consequent on a ranking according to the criteria (used for such ranking) or according to the comparative ease with which the expectations' violation can be concealed.'[85] The third response may be *withdrawal*, that is, a judge's acknowledgement that a given result may not be to their personal liking, but that their role obliges them to arrive at that result none the less.

Applying these approaches more generally, Paterson emphasises the extent to which the general character of the House of Lords over particular periods may change, largely because of the dominance of presiding Law Lords with entrenched views on the role of that court. Thus, the period 1957–62 was characterised by an adherence to precedent rather than an expansion or rationalisation of the law – this reflecting the views of the then senior Law Lord, Viscount Simonds. From 1962 until 1966, there was a more activist 'judicial law-making' approach, albeit under the cloak of 'dissimulation', which Paterson perceives as characteristic of the dominant member of the court during this period, Lord Reid. In 1966, the House of Lords made its announcement that it would no longer regard itself as necessarily bound by its own decisions, declaring itself free to depart from those decisions 'when it appears right to do so'[86] and in the years following this Practice Direction, Paterson explains, Lord Reid remained a dominant force in enunciating the principles and limitations affecting any proposed break with a previous House of Lords' decision. Essentially, these principles, as presented over a period of time and in a number of cases by Lord Reid, were that the freedom to overrule previous Lords' decisions should be used sparingly; that a case ought not to be overruled if to do so would upset people's expectations of the law, render the consequences of the overruling unforeseeable, engage the judges in piecemeal reform in an area of law which ought to be comprehensively reformed, or involve a change in the way in which statutes or other documents had been interpreted; and that a case ought to be overruled if it caused uncertainty in the law or was not considered to be just or in keeping with contemporary social conditions or conceptions of public policy.

These principles, moreover, had to be related, according to Lord Reid, to the area of law in question. Areas such as property, contract, family and criminal law, where

---

85 Op. cit., p 130. But see Griffith's review, (1982) *Journal of Law and Society*, Winter, p 298, where it is suggested that 'dissimulation' is 'a synonym for dishonesty'.
86 [1966] 3 All ER 77. See chapter 7.

certainty was of vital importance, were not ones in which the freedom to overrule would be used as readily as the areas of tort and public and administrative law, where judicial development of the law has been regarded by the judges as legitimate and appropriate.

Paterson thus explores the relationship between judicial freedom of choice and the constraints (real or apparent) which limit or restrict that choice. He concludes that the Law Lords *do* have considerable discretion in reaching decisions, but that there are real constraints which may curb excessive activism: institutional forces, the perceived need to decide according to law, and the restraint shown by judges themselves, which can shift over periods of years. The overall picture presented is thus at odds not only with that of adherents of the 'declaratory theory' of judging, but also with that of Griffith, in so far as he has argued that there is a lack of 'any clear and consistent relationship between the general pronouncement of judges on [the] matter of creativity and the way they conduct themselves in court'.[87] Paterson counters this view by pointing out that 'we have seen that the perceptions elicited from the Law Lords in interviews, from their publications and speeches, of these norms and guidelines (ie their perceptions of their role) were highly consistent, both *inter se*, and with their performance in actual cases'.[88] This conclusion would certainly seem to be supported by Paterson's analysis of the 29 cases heard by the Lords between 1966 and 1980 in which the court was asked to depart from one of its own precedents. Although some caution must be exercised when evaluating the judges' responses to interview questions, in that Law Lords are hardly likely to admit to any political predilections in deciding cases (and indeed the interviewer is hardly likely to antagonise the subject by asking such questions), Paterson's research provides a useful and interesting insight into the apparent working of the higher judicial minds.

The difficulty involved in making generalised statements remains, however, as is shown by Paterson, and by others such as Devlin[89] and Stevens.[90] Perhaps all that can be said is that the framework of rules, principles and practices operates as a set of constraining influences on judicial decision-making, but that these influences will act upon judges to differing degrees, depending on factors such as the nature or novelty of the case in hand, the attitude of particular judges to the questions of judicial discretion and creativity, the court where the case is heard[91] and so on. Assuming that such a constraining framework *does* affect, to a greater or lesser degree, judicial handling and interpretation of cases coming before them, the next question is that of the manner in which that discretion is, so to speak, wrapped up and delivered in the form of judicial pronouncements. We have already considered

87 Griffith, op. cit., p 284.   88 Paterson, op. cit., p 188.   89 Op. cit.   90 Op. cit.
91 The case of Lord Denning is illustrative here, though by no means typical of the judges as a whole. In 1957, he was appointed to the House of Lords, but returned to the Court of Appeal in 1962. Believing that the Court of Appeal has more significance as an appellate court than the House of Lords, it is there (no doubt in the knowledge that his decisions might be reviewed in the Lords itself) that some of Lord Denning's most controversial and 'creative' judgments have been delivered.

some aspects of this problem as it has been addressed by Murphy and Rawlings, but one important task remaining is to consider some of the criteria used by the judges to justify those 'hard' case decisions which are not clearly dictated by existing rules or precedents; these cases include those areas identified by Griffith and Devlin where the political outlook of the judges may tend to sway their decisions.

We have, in previous chapters, seen examples from the areas of criminal law, administrative law, tort and contract in which judicial conceptions of public policy have played a part in determining the outcome of novel cases. The terms 'public policy' and the 'national interest' are two frequently used bases for such decisions, especially where, as we have suggested, the existing framework of law provides no clear answer. In many such cases, most people would probably find the result of this reasoning and justification process quite unobjectionable, as, for example, in the case of *Donoghue v Stevenson* in 1932[92] where no clear rule existed to decide the liability of a manufacturer whose alleged negligence resulted in injury to the consumer of his product (see chapter 9). In many recent cases involving the tort of negligence (some of which are discussed in chapter 9) and *Williams v Roffey Bros* in 1990,[93] in particular, in contract, judicial conceptions of *public policy* have increasingly been openly admitted by judges as constituting one of the bases on which they reach a particular decision, even though in some cases a particular approach to public policy has failed to attract general judicial approval or acceptance.[94]

Allied to judicial acknowledgment of the importance of policy issues is the technique, frequently employed by judges engaged in statutory interpretation, of appealing to 'reason' or 'common sense'. Murphy and Rawlings provide several examples of this technique: an example is provided by *Bromley London Borough Council v Greater London Council* in 1982 – the 'Fares Fair' case.[95] Here, the Labour majority on the Greater London Council (GLC) attempted to implement its election manifesto promise to reduce fares on London Transport buses and underground trains by imposing a supplementary rate upon the London boroughs, by means of which the fare reduction might be financed. Bromley Council challenged this action on the ground that it was not within the GLC's statutory powers, and applied to the court for an order quashing the supplementary rate.

The case is interesting for several reasons: the public controversy which greeted the Lords' decision in favour of Bromley; the explicit condemnation of the GLC's actions by some of the judges in both the Court of Appeal[96] and the House

---

92 [1932] AC 562.   93 [1990] 1 All ER 512.

94 Again, Lord Denning provided a number of examples. Frequently challenging orthodox legal doctrine in cases where he felt it to be inappropriate in modern society, Denning's decisions in the Court of Appeal have often been overturned in the House of Lords. See, for example, the progress of *Gallie v Lee* [1971] AC 1004; *Morgans v Launchbury* [1973] AC 127; and *Duport Steel Ltd v Sirs* [1980] 1 WLR 142. Lord Denning was also one of a very small number of judges who unsuccessfully argued that in the law of contract, unfair or oppressive exclusion clauses ought to be struck down as 'unreasonable'. Such a view found little support among other judges, though Parliament has now intervened in this area: Unfair Contract Terms Act 1977. See chapter 11.

95 [1982] 1 All ER 129, CA; affd [1982] 1 All ER 129, HL.

96 Notably Watkins LJ ('a hasty, ill-considered, unlawful and arbitrary use of power') at 149.

of Lords;[97] the five judgments of the House of Lords which, though eventually reaching the same conclusions, seem to follow quite different paths to get there;[98] and the way in which all of the judges in the Court of Appeal and the House of Lords made much of the significance of the word 'economic' as it appeared in the relevant legislation, the Transport (London) Act 1969. Section 1 of this Act provided that the GLC[99] had a duty to develop policies to 'promote the provision of integrated, efficient and economic transport facilities and services for Greater London'. All the judges agreed that the word 'economic' must be interpreted in such a way as to give it its 'ordinary business' meaning of being 'cost-effective', despite the fact that, as various observers have pointed out,[100] the provision of public transport by a local authority is a highly complex operation, having due regard to social as well as the financial aspects; it cannot sensibly be reduced to a relatively simple, particularised[101] question of the meaning of ambiguous statutory terminology.

The judges are often to be found engaged in *presuming*: in declaring what Parliament 'must be taken' to have intended. In this, as in other matters, the higher courts tend to justify decisions by means of *assumptions*; and in many areas where the 'public interest' is involved in judicial deliberations, we find that decisions ultimately rest upon the assumption that our society is characterised by a strong uniformity of political, economic and moral values, and by standards of behaviour with which every 'reasonable' person is presumed to concur. It is instructive to consider the deeper assumptions underlying these ideas: first, that there really exists such a uniformity of values, and, second, that the judges have the capacity, and indeed a duty, to ensure that such values are protected and maintained through the law. There are many manifestations of this pattern of judicial activism: we will consider some example areas.

First, the judges have always regarded *national security* as being of paramount importance, even to the extent of displacing individual claims of right. Several instances may be noted. In *Duncan v Cammell Laird* in 1942[102] the defendants had built the submarine *Thetis* which sank during tests with the loss of 99 men. The plaintiffs were the legal representatives of the victims, suing for compensation for the men's deaths. Their case depended upon bringing evidence of the plans and other documents relating to the design of the submarine, but the Admiralty objected to the disclosure of such documents in court because it might prejudice

97 '. . . a thriftless use of moneys obtained by the GLC' at 166, per Lord Diplock.
98 G. Cunningham MP, remarked of the Lords' decision, in a Parliamentary debate, 'Each of the five judgments rambles over the territory in what can only be called a head-scratching way, making it impossible for the consumer of the judgment to know at the end what the law is held to be, except negatively, and then only negatively on a few points. When one puts the five judgments together, the effect is chaos.' Quoted by J. A. G. Griffith, 'The Law Lords and the GLC' (1982) *Marxism Today*, February. See also D. Pannick, 'The Law Lords and the Needs of Contemporary Society' (1982) *Political Quarterly* 318.
99 The GLC, along with the other metropolitan councils, was abolished in 1985. See chapter 12.
100 For example, Pannick, op. cit.
101 See also *R v London Transport Executive, ex p Greater London Council* [1983] QB 484.
102 [1942] AC 624.

national security. In the House of Lords, this objection was upheld, despite the crucial nature of this evidence for the plaintiffs' case. The readiness of the courts to accept the word of ministers of government that certain evidence should not be adduced in court attracted considerable criticism, though it was not until *Conway v Rimmer* in 1967[103] that the House of Lords took back for itself the power, in appropriate cases, to decide whether or not ministerial objection to disclosure was in fact sufficient to displace the interests of the individual party to the dispute.

Similar considerations motivated the judges in *A-G v Jonathan Cape Ltd* and *A-G v Times Newspapers Ltd* in 1975,[104] when the courts held that publication of Cabinet discussions, even though they took place some years previously, might be restrained 'when this is clearly in the public interest'; and in *Home Office v Harman* in 1981,[105] a case in which a solicitor acting for a convicted prisoner in an action against the Home Office showed certain Home Office documents to a journalist, who duly wrote an article criticising the Home Office. The documents had been made public during the court action, but the solicitor was held to have acted in contempt of court in revealing their contents to the journalist. In the Court of Appeal, Lord Denning said that he perceived 'no public interest whatever in having these highly confidential documents made public. Quite the other way. It was in the public interest that these documents should be kept confidential . . . I regard the use made by the journalist in this case of these documents to be highly detrimental to the good ordering of our society . . .'[106]

A second example-area concerns *morality*. The judges have consistently regarded themselves as arbiters of moral standards, defending their ideas of a somewhat conservative and, some would say, out-dated morality in the name of what Lord Devlin referred to in 1959 as the 'public morality', which the law could and should be used to protect and maintain. He argued that 'there are certain standards of behaviour or moral principles which society requires to be observed; and the breach of them is an offence not merely against the person who is injured but against society as a whole'.[107] We saw some examples of the judges' belief in their role as protectors of the 'public morality' in chapter 2; yet the judicial protection of moral standards extends beyond the range of criminal law. Such concerns are the basis of much judicial comment and decisions in family law, and in the law of contract we find cases such as that of *Pearce v Brooks* in 1866,[108] where the judges refused to accept the legality of an agreement between the plaintiffs and the defendant whereby the former had hired out a carriage to the latter, to be used for the purposes of prostitution.[109] In *Glynn v Keele University* in 1971,[110] a student who was excluded from residence on the campus for nude sunbathing failed in his attempt to challenge this disciplinary action. Although the court accepted that, in

103 [1968] AC 910.   104 [1976] QB 752.   105 [1981] QB 534.   106 Ibid.
107 Lord Devlin, *The Enforcement of Morals* (1959, Oxford University Press), p 7. See chapter 2.
108 (1866) LR 1 Exch 213.
109 See also the discussion of the court in *Coral Leisure Group v Barnett* [1981] ICR 503.
110 [1971] 1 WLR 487.

denying him a chance to put his side of the case, the university official had acted in breach of natural justice (see chapter 12), the court none the less felt that the offence was such as to 'merit a severe penalty according to any standards current even today'. And in 1971, in *Ward v Bradford Corpn*,[111] the Court of Appeal denied a remedy to a student-teacher who had broken the rules of her hall of residence by permitting her boy-friend to remain in her room overnight for a period of about two months. She had been expelled by the college and, despite irregularities in the manner in which the disciplinary procedure had been carried out, Lord Denning stated firmly his belief that her behaviour was not suitable for a trainee teacher: 'she would never make a teacher. No parent would knowingly entrust their child to her care.'[112]

In such matters of morality, the tension between judicial conservatism and an increased social tolerance of moral behaviour which is not to everyone's taste, is manifest. It is worth asking the question whether, in today's climate in which sexual and other moral matters are relatively freely discussed and practices once regarded as beyond the pale are fairly openly indulged in, the attitude of the judges may in some cases be too far removed from the 'real social world', so to speak, to protect the interests of all involved. Having said this, however, one outstanding case in which the judges showed themselves well aware of modern public attitudes towards sexual morality was *R v R* in 1991[113] – the case which overturned the common-law rule that a husband could not be criminally liable for committing rape upon his wife. In the Court of Appeal, Lord Lane stated that the old common-law rule had become 'anachronistic and offensive and we consider that it is our duty having reached that conclusion to act upon it' – a view with which the House of Lords unanimously agreed.

Other notable areas where the courts have referred, in the various cases before them, to the 'public interest', or equivalent terms, include the law of property, where the judges have consistently upheld the protection of traditional rights to private property as against, for example, private tenants (through restrictive interpretation of rent legislation) and squatters; the law relating to conspiracy where, until the Criminal Law Act 1977 clarified and somewhat restricted the range of the offence, the judges had been quite prepared to uphold convictions for the offence, even though the activity allegedly planned by the conspirators had not been carried out;[114] and the law relating to public order and industrial disputes.[115]

The problems underlying these assumptions and views on the part of the judiciary revolve around the difficulty of identifying exactly what constitutes the 'public interest' in a given area – even if such a monolithic entity exists at all. By what

---

111 (1971) 70 LGR 27.   112 Ibid.
113 [1992] 1 AC 599. See V. Laird, 'Reflections on *R v R*' (1992) 55 *MLR* 386.
114 Sometimes it is hard to see how the prosecution could establish that the substantive harm *could* be done. In *Shaw v DPP* [1962] 2 All ER 446, for example, by what means could it be shown that the defendant's publication of a 'directory' of prostitutes *had* 'corrupted public morals'?
115 See the cases analysed by Griffith, op. cit., chapter 3.

criteria do the judges, who wield considerable power in such cases, discover which particular body of attitudes or standards in our society constitutes *the* public interest? Perhaps Lord Devlin, once again, expressed the view of most judges:

> English law has evolved and regularly uses a standard which does not depend on the counting of heads. It is that of the reasonable man . . . It is the viewpoint of the man in the street . . . He might also be called the right-minded man. For my purpose I should like to call him the man in the jury-box, for the moral judgment of society must be something about which any twelve men or women drawn at random might after discussion be expected to be unanimous.[116]

But how likely *is* such consensus? Society is by no means homogeneous: it is composed of many groups and individuals differing in terms of sex, age, ethnic and cultural background, social class and political power. Would it be possible to obtain a unanimous judgment from any group of randomly selected people on the issues of industrial relations, prostitution or any of the other areas where the assumptions held by the judges, particularly in the appellate courts, have come to the fore? Surely *any* interest-group might convincingly register a belief that *their* policies, beliefs or attitudes were an accurate reflection of a 'public morality' or a 'public interest'? Unless we are, literally, to embark upon a national referendum on all such matters, there would seem to be no clear way of ascertaining what the majority of people believe to be right or acceptable behaviour, with any degree of accuracy. Moreover, such loose phrases such as 'society believes this' or 'society has decided that' obscure the fact of pluralistic interests and differential access to policy-making channels within the social structure. What is, therefore, presented as being in the 'public interest' may in fact serve limited, sectional interests, as we saw with respect to several example-areas in chapter 2.

Conclusion

On the one hand, we have, especially at the pinnacle of the court structure, a body of judges whose social class and educational background are likely to persuade them towards a conservative outlook on the social world, and a belief that there are traditional and widely-held social values which they, as judges, have to uphold; and on the other, we have the rest of society, comprising groups and individuals with strikingly heterogeneous beliefs, attitudes and principles. How far can the judiciary in its present form contribute to the solution of the many social problems affecting the rest of the community? Few would deny the importance of a judiciary which commands the confidence and respect of those subject to its pronouncements, but the *caveat* must always be put, that the members of that body must be prepared to take on the responsibilities of ensuring that the law keeps in step with

---

116 Devlin, op. cit., p 15. In the light of the jury-vetting procedures which have been used in recent years, one may seriously wonder just how 'random' the selection for jury service may have become.

the changing needs of society. Whether the judiciary, as presently constituted, can modify their attitudes and actions to further these broad social aims may be doubted. It has been suggested that 'it seems improbable that courts will ever be able to accomplish, save by miniscule changes moving with glacial slowness, the sort of revolutionary shifts in power which would be necessary to change the system entirely'.[117]

It is no answer for the judges to argue that such changes in society and in law are the business of Parliament, not the judiciary, for, as we have seen, there is abundant evidence that judges are (and always have been) prepared to engage in deciding issues which have clear and controversial political import. Some have tried – not always successfully – to reform the law in an explicit manner; others, by taking refuge behind ambiguous statutory terminology or appeals to nebulous concepts such as the public interest, have cloaked judicial discretion and activism with the guise of 'mere applications of the law'.

But reform is in the air. The broadening of the socio-economic, ethnic, and occupational bases from which judges are appointed, the establishment of appointment processes which transparently link appointment to merit rather than background, the growth in the proportion of professional lawyers other than barristers appointed to judicial office (see chapter 13), and the recruitment into the legal profession of a wider cross-section of the population, should herald a new era for the composition and outlook of the judiciary.

117 W. Chambliss and R. Seidman, *Law, Order and Power* (2nd edn., 1982, Addison Wesley), p 249.

Index

WITHDRAWN
FROM THE LIBRARY OF
UNIVERSITY OF ULSTER